Teaching for Student Learning

Becoming an Accomplished Teacher

Teaching for Student Learning: Becoming an Accomplished Teacher shows teachers how to move from novice to expert status by integrating both research and the wisdom of practice into their teaching. It emphasizes how accomplished teachers gradually acquire and apply a broad repertoire of evidence-based teaching practices in the support of student learning.

The book's content stems from three major fields of study: 1) theories and research on how people learn, including new insights from the cognitive and neurosciences; 2) research on classroom practices shown to have the greatest effect on student learning; and 3) research on effective schooling, defined as school-level factors that enhance student achievement and success. Although the book's major focus is on teaching, it devotes considerable space to describing how students learn and how the most effective and widely-used models of teaching connect to principles of student learning. Specifically, it describes how research on teaching, cognition, and neuroscience converge to provide an evidence-based "science of learning" which teachers can use to advance their practice. Key features include the following:

- *Evidence-based practice* – This theme is developed through: 1) an ongoing review and synthesis of research on teaching and learning and the resulting guidelines for practice; and 2) boxed research summaries within the chapters.
- *Instructional repertoire theme* – Throughout the book teaching is viewed as an extremely complex activity that requires a repertoire of instructional strategies that, once mastered, can be drawn upon to fit specific classrooms and teaching situations.
- *Synthesis of learning theories* – Throughout the book cognitive, behavioral, and brain-based theories of learning are synthesized and their implications for teaching, curriculum design, assessment, and classroom and school organization described.
- *Standards-based school environments* – Education today is dominated by standards-based school environments. Unlike competing books, this one describes these environments and shows how they impact curriculum design and learning activities. The objective is to show how teachers can make standards-based education work for them.
- *Pedagogical features* – In addition to an end-of-book glossary, each chapter contains research boxes, reflection boxes, itemized end-of-chapter summaries, and end-of-chapter learning activities.
- *Website* – An accompanying website contains a variety of field-oriented and site-based activities that teachers can do alone or with colleagues.

Richard I. Arends is emeritus Professor and Dean of the School of Education at Central Connecticut State University. A former classroom teacher, he has authored or co-authored over a dozen books on education.

Ann Kilcher is President of Paideia Consulting Group, Inc., based in Halifax, Nova Scotia. A former classroom teacher, she has worked as a consultant for the past 20 years in Canada, the United States, England, and Southeast Asia.

Teaching for Student Learning

Becoming an Accomplished Teacher

Richard I. Arends
Ann Kilcher

NEW YORK AND LONDON

Please visit the companion website at:
www.routledge.com/textbooks/9780415965309

First published 2010
by Routledge
711 Third Avenue, New York, NY 10017

Simultaneously published in the UK
by Routledge
2 Park Square, Milton Park, Abingdon, Oxon OX14 4RN

Routledge is an imprint of the Taylor & Francis Group, an informa business

© 2010 Taylor & Francis

Typeset in Minion by
Swales & Willis, Exeter, Devon

Library of Congress Cataloging-in-Publication Data
Arends, Richard.
    Teaching for student learning / Richard I. Arends, Ann Kilcher.
        p. cm.
    Includes bibliographical references and index.
    [etc.]
    1. Effective teaching.   2. Teachers—In-service training.   3. Learning,
    Psychology of.   I. Kilcher, Ann.   II. Title.
    LB1025.3.A755 2009
    371.102—dc22   2009017940

ISBN10: 0-415-99888-3 (hbk)
ISBN10: 0-415-96530-6 (pbk)
ISBN10: 0-203-86677-0 (ebk)

ISBN13: 978-0-415-99888-8 (hbk)
ISBN13: 978-0-415-96530-9 (pbk)
ISBN13: 978-0-203-86677-1 (ebk)

CONTENTS

FIGURES

TABLES

PREFACE

Teaching for Student Learning is a book about what accomplished teachers do to ensure that their students flourish rather than flounder and about how teachers become accomplished through a long and complex journey characterized by desire and commitment to continuous learning. We have written specifically for teachers with some experience, those who have survived the induction period and who are now ready to refine their craft and to begin providing leadership for instructional improvement in their classrooms, in their schools, and in the larger teaching profession.

Our readers will find that we take the perspective that teaching cannot be separated from learning and that we know quite a bit about both. We emphasize the importance of having tight connections among curriculum, instruction, and assessment. We emphasize that we should base our practices on the large knowledge base about teaching and learning rather than stick to traditional ways of doing things. We also take a rather broad view of teaching and learning; learning is more than doing well on standardized tests; teaching is more than being able to perform a few favorite strategies well. Finally, we believe success is never fully realized until teachers join with their colleagues school-wide and take collective responsibility for all students.

We are writing *Teaching for Student Learning* at a time when many are worried and concerned about our schools and about the "state of public education." Parents and family members worry about the quality of education their children are receiving and whether or not they will be adequately prepared to be successful in college or in work. Citizens and policy makers are concerned about the ever-rising costs of education and about whether or not educators are being held accountable. Students worry about the relevancy of much of what they are asked to learn and whether or not their education will make them competitive in a world that is increasingly global and interdependent. Although many of these worries and concerns can be (and are) addressed by policy makers and agencies who govern schools, we believe that the ultimate arbitrators of success in our schools are *classroom teachers, the literally millions of talented individuals who open their classrooms every day, plan lessons, make assignments, and monitor what their students learn.* When decisions about instruction are made wisely and when lessons are executed well, students flourish. Done poorly, these acts of teaching result in a breakdown of learning and students flounder.

As teachers, we become accomplished by attending to our own learning. It is important to learn *about* effective teaching practices by acquiring knowledge normally found in books such as this one or from college courses or in-service workshops. It is equally important, however, to acquire knowledge about one's own practice through dialogue with colleagues in learning communities and through thoughtful reflection. We have strived to provide a number of features in *Teaching for Student Learning* that we believe will help our readers learn about their own practice. For instance, in every chapter you will find *Reflections* aimed at helping you reflect on what you have read and to consider the ideas we describe in relation to your own classroom and school. Similarly, we insert in every chapter *Research Boxes* that summarize important research pertaining to the chapter's topic. Again, these are provided not only to illustrate the range of research that makes up the knowledge base on teaching and learning, but also to allow you to think about the research and what it means to your teaching. Finally, we conclude each chapter with a feature we call *Constructing Your Own Learning* and have written an online *Fieldbook,* both of which recommend specific experiences and learning activities that will allow you to apply and practice the ideas and strategies described in particular chapters. Some of these have been designed for you to do alone; others have been designed to be done with classmates or colleagues.

Finally a bit about the authors. You will note that throughout the book we often use first person and refer to ourselves as teachers. We do this because even though we have held numerous positions in our careers, we still view ourselves primarily as teachers. Together, we have over 80 years of experience teaching elementary, middle, high school and college students and teaching teachers in workshops and seminars across North America, Europe, the South Pacific and several countries in Asia.

ACKNOWLEDGMENTS

We want to acknowledge and extend thanks to our fellow co-teachers and in-service providers who have taught us so much about teaching and learning over the years, as well as the literally thousands and thousands of beginning and experienced teachers who we have come to know through our classes and workshops. As with all acts of teaching, we often learn more from our students than they do from us.

Several reviewers provided invaluable critique of the manuscript as it was being developed. We want to thank specifically the contributions of Dr. Gary Galluzzo, George Mason University, Dr. Traci Koskie, Western Washington University, and Dr. Anthony Normore, California State University, Domingas Hills. We also want to thank our special friends, Lawrence Ryan and Sonja Rich, who provided so much valuable assistance throughout the writing process with research, editing, proofreading, and comments.

Finally, we want to thank our editors, Lane Akers, Alexandra Sharp, Sioned Jones, Caroline Watson and Tamsin Ballard, who assisted with the editing and production process.

RICHARD I. ARENDS

Richard Arends is Professor of Educational Leadership and Dean Emeritus at Central Connecticut State University. Prior to coming to Connecticut, he was on the faculty and served as chair of the Department of Curriculum and Instruction at the University of Maryland, College Park. He received his MA in American intellectual history from the University of Iowa and his Ph.D. in education from the University of Oregon, where he was also on the faculty from 1975 to 1983. Professor Arends taught in elementary, junior high, and high school for over a dozen years and continues to serve as a community volunteer.

Professor Arends' special research interests are teaching, teacher education, and organizational development and school change. He has authored or contributed to over a dozen books on education, including the *Handbook of Organization Development in Schools, System Change Strategies in Education, Exploring Teaching,* and *Learning to*

Teach, the latter of which is now in its eighth edition. He has worked widely with schools and universities throughout North America and around the Pacific Rim, including Australia, Samoa, Palau, and Saipan. The recipient of numerous awards, he was selected in 1989 as the outstanding teacher educator in the state of Maryland, and in 1990 he received the Judith Ruskin award for outstanding research in education given by the Maryland chapter of the Association for Supervision and Curriculum Development (ASCD). Between 1995 and 1997, Professor Arends held the William Allen (Boeing) Endowed Chair in the School of Education at Seattle University.

He currently lives in Seattle, Washington, where he pursues favorite projects and continues to write.

ANN KILCHER

Ann Kilcher is President of Paideia Consulting Group, Inc., based in Halifax, Nova Scotia. She has worked as a consultant for the past 20 years, predominantly in Canada and the United States, but also in Europe and Asia. Prior to consulting she worked with the Saskatchewan Department of Education and taught elementary school. She was Executive Director of Leadership at the Public Education Foundation in Chattanooga, TN from 2000–2005. She has been an adjunct instructor at the University of Regina, the University of Maryland, College Park, and Saint Mary's University. She received her B.Ed. and M.Ed. from the University of Regina and her Ph.D. in education from the University of Maryland, College Park.

Ann's special research interests are teaching, educational change, organizational development, and leadership development. She has authored many articles and publications, including the *Mentoring Resource Book, Writing School Annual Reports, Peer Coaching, School Improvement Planning: Models and Approaches,* and *Establishing School Advisory Councils.* She has worked widely with schools, districts, departments of education, educational foundations, and universities in Canada and the United States. She has also consulted and conducted professional development institutes in Europe (England, Finland, Ireland, and Sweden) and Asia (Hong Kong, Malaysia, and Thailand). She has worked on large scale, long-term change projects with the Bill and Melinda Gates Foundation, the General Electric Foundation, and the National College for School Leadership in England.

1

TEACHING AND LEARNING IN TODAY'S SCHOOLS

At Southside High School teaching is no longer a private activity. Improving instruction is an ongoing goal, and there are many opportunities for teachers to share and help one another. Through the use of peer visitations, examining student work, study groups and reflective dialogue, teachers at Southside work and learn together. Monthly teachers use *peer visitation* to observe two of their colleagues. Over the course of a year, each teacher will participate in 18 classroom visits. A different subject area is featured each month so all teachers open their doors to their colleagues. Teachers also participate in *study groups* that meet once a month. Each group determines the topic they will pursue. One group is participating in a book study, reading Alfie Kohn's *What Does it Mean to Be Well Educated?* Another group is using action research to study the effects of different motivational techniques. A third group is designing the process that will be used for the school's senior project, and a fourth is examining samples of student work.

School-wide, a *new teaching strategy*, identified by various departments, is introduced and discussed at the first faculty meeting of the month. After experimenting with the new strategy, teachers reassemble in small groups to share how they used the strategy and how it worked for them. Finally, Gail Kennedy, the school's principal, leads the faculty in a *reflective dialogue* once a month. An article is distributed a few days in advance, and different protocols are provided to structure the reflective dialogue sessions. Southside High School is a different place than it was a few years ago. A true learning community has been created for teachers and for their students, one that helps them meet the many and varied challenges of teaching in twentieth-first century schools.

Teaching in today's schools is complex and challenging, and it requires developing a learning community that supports **teacher learning** like the one we just observed in Southside High School. Expectations for teachers are high and responsibilities are demanding. Teachers must not only focus on the day-to-day learning of an increasingly diverse student population, but they must also make sure students achieve success on high-stakes **accountability** measures. Additionally, society expects *all* students to acquire complex intellectual skills needed to be successful in today's knowledge society; unequal student outcomes are no longer acceptable.

This book is about what **accomplished teachers** do to meet today's challenges, and ensure that all students are achieving at high levels. On the surface the relationship between teaching and student learning may appear to be obvious and quite simple. In practice, however, effective teaching is not as straightforward as some would like to believe. Instead, helping all students learn turns out to be an undertaking that is difficult and complex. Fortunately, we know much more today than we did a few decades ago about how students learn and what teachers can do to affect their learning. At the same time, some aspects of teaching and learning remain a mystery, and unfortunately, some of what we know remains unused. We invite our readers to join us in an inquiry about what is known about teaching and learning, learn how to use this knowledge and these practices effectively, and become involved in a mutual quest to uncover more. Becoming an accomplished teacher is a life-long journey; providing leadership for improved instruction is every teacher's challenge.

We have written *Teaching for Student Learning* for teachers who have successfully navigated the initial induction period. You have mastered the fundamentals of teaching, and you are quite confident in your interpersonal skills and in classroom management. You are now ready to concentrate on both refining your skills and adding to your **repertoire** of effective teaching practices. You are committed to understanding more deeply the relationship between your teaching and student learning. You are eager to investigate differentiation and to concentrate on engaging each and every student. You are ready and willing to provide leadership by extending your influence beyond the confines of your classroom into the school, community, and the profession.

This book's primary purposes are to help teachers move along the continuum from novice to expert status and to become more confident in their abilities to help *all students make appropriate progress* in social and academic learning. We take the perspective that teaching cannot be separated from learning. Indeed, *teaching is the "art and science" of helping students learn.* We define learning as change in the minds and intellectual character of students. We summarize much that is known about the science of teaching and learning and encourage you to work with your colleagues on refining and continuing to compose the art of helping students learn. We also believe that those who are committed to teacher learning—mentors, coaches, staff developers—will find this book and its companion *Fieldbook* a useful resource in their work.

We want to accomplish several goals in this introductory chapter. First, we will describe our views about what it means to teach today in what we (and others) have labeled a *standards-based environment,* one best characterized by externally imposed standards and accountability. We will provide a short history lesson on how we got to where we are and describe the challenges posed by this environment. We will also discuss the increasing **diversity** of students in classrooms and the press for instructional differentiation to meet varying needs. We acknowledge the geo-economic and technological advances that have flattened the world and created a global community.

Second, we will focus on the importance of **teacher development** and learning. Today's environment requires that teachers keep up with new and ever-changing conditions and challenges and devote a significant portion of their time to learning new and more effective ways of teaching. We will describe what is involved in developing understanding of different kinds of knowledge, attaining expertise, and acquiring an ever-expanding repertoire of effective teaching practices. Our discussion about teacher development and learning in this chapter will serve as an introduction to a much more thorough discussion of this topic in Chapter 15.

Third, we believe that many of the shortcomings in today's schools can only be solved through **teacher leadership**, and that many of our readers are ready to provide this leadership not only for instructional improvement in their own classrooms but also beyond—in the school, community, and the profession.

Finally, the chapter concludes with a brief tour of the book and highlights some of its unique features. You will see that we have written *Teaching for Student Learning* primarily for teachers. We believe that experienced teachers will be reading this book as part of a college class or with colleagues as part of a study or improvement group in particular schools. We believe our readers are teachers who are interested in gaining new knowledge, reflecting on their work, examining the work of their students, and studying the relationships between teaching practices and student outcomes. In both instances we believe that this book, and the *Fieldbook* that accompanies it, can serve as a guide for discussion and experimentation. We also believe these resources can assist teacher and school leaders, particularly those who coach and support teachers as they work toward improving classroom practices.

So, we invite our readers to come with us on a journey aimed at discovering and improving professional practice, to use each chapter to learn individually, but also to see each chapter and corresponding activities as opportunities to learn and to work collectively with colleagues.

> **REFLECTION**
>
> Consider for a moment why you are reading this book—part of a class; workshop; school study group? How might you use this experience to improve your teaching practices? The practices of your colleagues?

TWENTY-FIRST CENTURY TEACHING

The schools in which many of us now teach are not the schools we attended in our youth. New realities exist today that were not present a few years ago. Three of these realities have created the conditions for teaching and learning in the twenty-first century: societal press for standards and accountability, increased **student diversity**, and fundamental changes in technology and globalization. Below, we discuss these realities and suggest how they impact teachers and leaders in today's schools.

Standards-based Education and Accountability

Over the past two decades, a new system of schooling has emerged. Called **standards-based education**, the system rests on several core beliefs: (1) that an agreed upon set of standards can be designed to guide teaching and learning; (2) that every child and youth should be held to high expectations for meeting these standards; (3) that all teachers can achieve high standards by using **evidence-based practices**; and (4) that educators should be held accountable for student learning, currently interpreted to mean acceptable student academic achievement as measured by standardized tests.

How did we get to this conception of schooling? Some aspects of the standards and high-stakes testing movements that characterize today's schools date back to the early part of the twentieth century. Several elements, however, gained new urgency and momentum in the 1980s and 1990s as more and more citizens and policy makers became convinced that the public schools were failing and that the reason for this failure was education's lack of external accountability. In 1983, *A Nation at Risk: The Imperative of Educational Reform* (National Commission on Excellence in Education, 1983) was unveiled. This report, commissioned by the Reagan Administration, offered a myriad of recommendations:

- increase core course requirements for high school graduation;
- set higher and more rigorous standards at all levels of education; and
- implement the use of standardized tests to measure student achievement.

A decade later, under a different administration, Congress passed the *Goals 2000 Act of 1994*. This legislation promised that by the year 2000 several goals for education would be achieved:

- All students in America will start school ready to learn.
- The high school graduation rate will increase to at least 90 percent.
- U.S. students will be first in mathematics and science achievement.

While the recommendations outlined in *A Nation at Risk* and the goals of *Goals 2000* were never realized, they did bring about a fundamental change in the way we thought about education, and they served as preludes for the continuing development in the United States of federal involvement in education and the passage of No Child Left Behind Act (NCLB) in 2002. As our experienced teacher readers know, NCLB required alignment of classroom instruction to state-prescribed standards, yearly testing to hold schools accountable for ensuring that all students meet these standards, and sanctions imposed on schools that failed. Although NCLB is unique to the United States, similar regulations currently exist throughout North America, Europe, and some countries in Asia.

This view of schooling differs in some important ways from the textbook-based and norm-referenced perspectives of the nineteenth and twentieth centuries. Theoretically, it alters what students are expected to learn and the proficiency levels they are expected to achieve. Instead of working "for a grade" or to pass a particular course, students are expected to meet agreed upon standards and these standards are meant for all students rather than only the most capable. This view of schooling requires new and different practices for teachers. As Schalock, Schalock, and Girod (2007) have pointed out, this system of schooling demands "the alignment of instruction with standards; the integration of curriculum, instruction and assessment; and the differentiation of instruction to accommodate the learning histories and needs of individual students . . ." (p. 2). *Alignment, integration,* and *differentiation* become the core work of teachers in a standards-based system of schooling.

Many educators have embraced standards-based education. The major teachers' unions supported the initial conceptions of the No Child Left Behind legislation. Most teachers believe that efforts to raise expectations for all students are a good thing, and they believe in instructional differentiation. At the same time, several worrisome flaws have been identified, particularly in the ways in which standards-based education has been translated into public policy. For instance, the standards movement has produced a huge array of standards that cannot be realistically achieved given the current time constraints of K-12 schooling. Holding high expectations and calling for increased rigor has led governing agencies to require more courses, more Advanced Placement courses, and success on exit exams as prerequisites for high school graduation. These strategies have had some unfortunate and unintended consequences.

Standards-based and high-stakes testing strategies have not produced the results in student learning many envisioned. Scores on the **National Assessment of Educational Progress (NAEP)**, for instance, have been very modest over the past decade and many students who start ninth grade do not graduate from high school. Recently, Landsberg (2008) reported on Oakes' California Dropout Research Project that found declining graduation rates (now below 50 percent) in Los Angeles public schools. According to the study, this decline started when California raised standards and began requiring students to pass an exit exam prior to receiving a diploma.

Other flaws and shortcomings have also been identified. Nichols and Berliner (2007) have observed that the standards movement and high-stakes testing have narrowed the curriculum, demoralized teachers (causing some to cheat), and produced students who can neither think for themselves nor take responsibility for their own learning. It has focused instruction on students just below the acceptable passing levels on standardized tests while ignoring those who are very low performing and very high-performing. Seed (2008) has observed that, as currently practiced, the standards movement has over-invested in testing and moved forward with "ungrounded" theories about what will bring about real improvement.

An increasing number of researchers and educators (Nichols & Berliner, 2007) are beginning to question whether standards-based education and schools *alone* can close the achievement gaps, when the cause of these gaps stems mainly from lack of economic well being and social privilege. Instead, these reformers argue for the need to address first the larger societal issues of social class inequalities and home and community environments. This perspective is perhaps best represented by a group of distinguished educators and policy experts who recently issued *A Broader, Bolder Approach* (Economic Policy Institute, 2008). This group believes that we should reject traditional beliefs that bad schools are the main reason for poor achievement and that school improvement *alone* can raise the "achievement of disadvantaged children." Members associated with a Broader, Bolder Approach do not argue against continued efforts to pursue school improvement or the need for accountability, but instead support strong, new, and sustained investments in pre-school education and improved health services for the poor. Most important, they believe that more attention should be paid to the students' out-of-school experiences that in all too many instances lack the "cultural, organizational, athletic, and academic enrichment" activities provided by middle-class parents.

Regardless of its flaws and new initiatives, the standards-based conception of schooling has become an important part of the policy context that affects teaching and learning, and demands for accountability and high-stakes testing are not likely to go away. As we write, for instance, a new federal administration is starting to outline its goals for public education, and on several occasions President Obama has said that the solution to lower test scores is not lower standards but instead "tougher and cleaner" standards. Further, the larger public is not likely to be sympathetic to problems faced by educators dealing with accountability issues. Most professionals today—nurses, accountants, realtors, attorneys, and so on—work in environments that have institutionalized accountability measures, and as one observer put it, "they find [our] complaints about accountability to be out of touch and whiny" (Seed, 2008, p. 9).

The shifts in the ways we view education present teachers with enormous opportunities and challenges. On the one hand, standards-based education and accountability have widespread support and have elements that hold potential for securing high-level learning for all students. These elements should be maintained. On the other hand, as teachers we know that this approach can also be overly bureaucratic and contains elements that limit the suc-

> **REFLECTION**
>
> How has the standards-movement affected your classroom? Your school? What positive impact has it had? What about negative effects and/or unintended consequences? Check with a classmate or colleague to see if their opinions are the same as yours.

cess of many students. We believe these challenges can be met in the years ahead if teachers provide grass roots leadership and take important collective action in the support of student learning. It is clear we all have a lot of work to do.

Diversity and Differentiation

We do not have to tell our experienced teacher readers about classrooms characterized by diversity. You see it every day and history tells you that the demographics of our society and of our schools in the first part of the twenty-first century are vastly different than when public schools were fashioned a century and a half ago; indeed, they are different than even a few decades ago. An increasing number of students in our schools have non-European ethnic and racial backgrounds, are **English language learners (ELLs)**, and live on the edge of poverty.

Between 1970 and 2005, the proportion of minority students in schools increased from slightly more than 20 percent to almost 45 percent. In the western United States, students from non-European cultures now constitute a majority, reaching over 50 percent (National Center for Educational Statistics, 2007) in states such as California. The number of students who do *not* speak English as a first language has also increased significantly over the past 30 years. In 1980, the number of ELLs in classrooms was approximately 10 percent. By 2005 this number had more than doubled, to 20 percent. Most ELLs speak Spanish as their first language, but many other languages are also represented such as Arabic, Chinese, Russian, and Tagalog. The range of students with different kinds of abilities has also risen dramatically. When the Education for All Handicapped Children Act was passed in 1975, between 5 and 8 percent of students in public schools were identified as having disabilities. In 2005, this statistic had doubled to almost 15 percent. Today, well over half of students identified with disabilities spend 80 percent of their day in regular classrooms, a significant increase from 1975 (National Center for Educational Statistics, 2007).

Perhaps the most important diversity factor is the one associated with children who live in poverty and who live in families and communities that are economically and socially impoverished. The Broader, Bolder Approach Group calculated the following effects of impoverishment on the achievement gap:

- Child health differences explain approximately 25 percent of the black–white achievement gap.
- Residential mobility differences explain approximately 14 percent of the black–white achievement gap.

- Income differences explain as much as 80 percent of the achievement gap between children from low-income families when compared to middle-class families (Economic Policy Institute, 2008).

Increased diversity in classrooms has several important implications for teachers. First, as teachers, we are being asked to address differences by providing differentiated instruction. We are required to provide curriculum and instruction that meet the needs of each and every learner and that ensures them some measure of academic and social success. No longer is it acceptable to simply teach a lesson aimed at the average learner. Rather, we are expected to scaffold our instruction so it will provide challenges and support for struggling as well as able students. Second, the voices of parents and caregivers of students with disabilities and who are ELLs can no longer be ignored. As compared to earlier times, they are more likely to visit schools and to become actively involved in their children's education. Third, diversity matters because, as described in the previous section, it is now recognized that school improvement efforts alone will not close important achievement gaps. Educators must join with many others to expand the concept of education to students' lives outside of school. This requires initiating policies that focus on more than academic and cognitive growth, and developing stronger working relationships among schools, families, and local neighborhoods and communities.

At the same time, diversity is not only a challenge, it is also an opportunity. Diverse learners are a valuable resource. They make our classrooms more interesting, and they provide day-to-day models for helping students learn how to live in a global society.

Teaching in a Flat World

Advances in technology over the past two decades have changed the role of education and the way we teach in some important and significant ways. Computers and information technologies available to today's youth were non-existent when the authors were growing up and were likely only in their infancy stages when our readers were in school. The globe is shrinking and getting more competitive. Thomas Friedman (2005) has described in convincing detail how technology and geo-economics have flattened the world and reshaped our lives. Technological advances have increased global access to information and to jobs, and it has made communication instantaneous. Anyone who is smart and has Internet access can provide services and products to just about anyone else in the world. Events and crises in one place on the globe no longer affect only immediate neighbors, but global neighbors too. Today, our students will leave school and enter a global world and economy even if they never choose to travel or work abroad. The next generation of students will enter a world where many jobs will be outsourced from the developed countries of North America and Europe and where they will be required to compete with large numbers of people in other countries with university degrees who are willing to work for less money.

Learning in a "**flat world**" has become both easier and more difficult. Access to huge quantities of information has expanded opportunities for learning but so too has it provided complex choices. Today's students can find almost anything on the Internet; the problem is how do they sort through the vast array of information and determine its quality, accuracy, and reliability. Similarly, media advances have captured student attention and hold the potential for greater engagement. These same advances, however, have caused many students to become impatient with in-school learning and the more traditional approaches to teaching.

In recent years, international tests and major studies (e.g., Barber & Mourshed, 2007; Darling-Hammond, Wei, Andree, Richardson, & Orphanos, 2009) have identified and compared the world's best performing school systems. These studies highlight the problems and possibilities of educating students in the twenty-first century. Most significant in all of the comparisons is the primacy of teacher effectiveness and leadership and how these are developed through continuous learning—topics we take up in the next sections.

> **REFLECTION**
>
> Think for a moment about Friedman's contention that we are living in a flat world. Do you agree or disagree? If you agree, how has this situation influenced your life; your family; your community; and your teaching?

TEACHER DEVELOPMENT AND LEARNING

Becoming a truly accomplished teacher doesn't happen overnight or with the acquisition of a teaching license. Instead, it requires paying attention to our own learning and it takes purposeful action over a lifetime. College classes and in-service workshops are important venues for learning to teach more effectively; however, they are insufficient. Twenty-first century schools have changed the way we work and learn. New learning opportunities and settings are required, settings where teachers can develop competence and expertise and learn new teaching practices together with colleagues and within schools and classrooms. In this section we provide perspectives about teacher development and learning, and we introduce ideas about how teachers move from novice to expert status. This discussion will be expanded on in Chapter 15, where we describe several strategies that enhance teacher learning and how learning can be integrated into the day-to-day work of teaching. Some may wish to turn to this chapter next.

Progression of Teacher Development

Like child development, as teachers we develop cognitively and affectively over time. A number of models and theories have been proposed to describe these **stages of teacher development**. One model has emphasized the *stage* aspect of development and proposes that teachers progress through a series of stages over the span of their careers. Among the first to propose a stage theory was Francis Fuller (1969). Her research identified three progressive stages. The first stage she labeled the *survival stage*, when beginning teachers focus mainly on themselves and their teaching. At this stage they show concern about interpersonal adequacy, whether students like them, and classroom control. In the second stage, labeled the *teaching situation stage*, teachers begin focusing on the teaching situation itself and show concern about the availability of time and resources and about their own lack of a repertoire of effective teaching practices. Eventually, teachers find ways to cope with survival issues and their teaching situations; the fundamentals of some aspects of teaching and classroom management become routine. It is during a third stage of development, labeled *student results and mastery stage*, that teachers increase their concern for students, and student learning and welfare drive their planning and instructional decisions. The three stages initially identified and observed by Fuller have been the focus of research on teacher development for a good number of years. In the 1980s, Feiman-Nemser (1983) defined the stages more thoroughly but found that, overall, the same ones existed. Research and reviews of research by Richardson and Placier (2001), and more recently by Conway and Clark (2003), confirm that stage theory has withstood the test of time.

Joyce and Showers (2002) provided a slightly different framework for considering teacher development and learning, particularly as it applies to learning new teaching strategies. In their efforts to help teachers learn particular **models of teaching**, they concluded that learning new teaching skills takes time and includes several processes: initial learning of the skills involved; experimenting with the new approach; extended practice; and opportunities for reflection. During initial learning, teachers learn about a new strategy or skill by acquiring knowledge and understandings about the theory behind the strategy and about the student outcomes it is intended to achieve. New knowledge alone, however, is insufficient to use a new approach effectively. Instead, according to Joyce and Showers, it requires multiple opportunities to experiment with the new approach. This means practicing the strategy in collegial settings and with the support of a skilled coach, as well as opportunities for personal dialogue and reflection. We will come back to the concepts of peer observation and coaching in Chapter 15.

Teacher Expertise

Some educators have approached teacher learning and development from the perspective of how teachers think (Berliner, 1994, 2001; Bransford, Brown, & Cocking, 2000; Carter, Cushing, Sabers, Stein, & Berliner, 1988). They have been particularly interested in differences found in the thinking processes of novice and expert teachers. The ultimate goal of developing into an accomplished professional teacher from this perspective is acquiring what has been labeled **teacher expertise**. This becomes a very important goal in a world where change is the norm and where expectations for teachers are constantly expanding. Here are some things that researchers (Berliner, 1987, 1994, 2001; Glaser 1987, 1990) have found about what expert teachers can do as compared to novice teachers.

- *Experts are able to perform a number of tasks automatically without having to stop and think about how to do them.* Expert teachers manage classrooms and classroom routines efficiently and effectively. Novice teachers have to stop and think before taking action.
- *Experts understand problems at a deeper level than novices.* Expert teachers have a breadth of understanding that allows them to apply relevant principles quickly. Novice teachers have only surface understandings that they slowly bring to bear on problems.
- *Expert teachers are more flexible in their teaching than novices.* Expert teachers take advantage of new information and can quickly make instructional adjustments. Novice teachers find making adjustments difficult and are more likely to stick to their initial plans, whether or not these plans are working.
- *Expert teachers have more confidence in their instructional abilities than novices.* Experience and a broader depth of knowledge make expert teachers more certain about the actions they take. Novice teachers often display tentativeness.
- *Experts make substantially more inferences from information than do novices.* Expert

teachers can ignore or influence the flow of classroom events. Novice teachers often allow the flow of events to influence and overwhelm them.

- *Experts are able to recognize patterns of classroom activities and events.* Experts interpret cues and processes accurately, whereas novices are often confused and cannot make sense of what is going on.

The last factor of expertise above was illustrated in a very interesting study, summarized in Research Box 1.1.[1]

REFLECTION

Does the research identifying differences between experts and novices match your own observations and experiences? Can you provide exceptions in your own development? You may wish to discuss these questions with a colleague or classmate.

Inquiry **RESEARCH BOX 1.1**

Sabers, D., Cushing, K., & Berliner, D. (1991). Differences among teachers in a task characterized by simultaneity, multidimensionality, and immediacy. *American Educational Research Journal*, *28* (1), 63–88.

Expert and novice teachers were asked to examine the same videotape segment of a classroom lesson. As illustrated below, teachers identified as experts were able to see patterns about what was happening. Novices, on the other hand, did not see patterns and they were often confused. Here is what some of the subjects said:

Expert 6: On the left monitor, the students' note taking indicates that they have seen sheets like this and have observed presentations like this before. It's fairly efficient at this point because they're used to the format they're using.

Expert 7: I don't understand why the students can't be finding out this information on their own rather than listening to someone tell them . . . if you watch the faces of most of them, they start out for about the first two or three minutes paying attention to what's going on and then just drift off.

Expert 2: I haven't heard a bell, but the students are already at their desks and seem to be doing purposeful activity, and this is about the time that I decide they must be an accelerated group because they came into the room and started something rather than just sitting down and socializing.

Novice 1: I can't tell what they're doing. They're getting ready for class, but I can't tell what they're doing.

Novice 2: She's trying to communicate with them here about something, but I sure couldn't tell what it was.

Novice 3: It's a lot to watch.

(Summarized from Hammerness et al., 2005, p. 361)

Developing Expertise

But more precisely what is expertise and how is it acquired? Hatano and Oura (2003) and Hammerness et al. (2005) point out that teachers develop two different types of expertise: *routine experts* and *adaptive experts.* According to Hammerness et al. (p. 49),

> *routine experts* develop a core set of competencies that they apply throughout their lives with greater and greater efficiency. In contrast, *adaptive experts* are much more likely to change their core competencies and continually expand the breadth and depth of their expertise.

They also report that each type of expertise has two dimensions: efficiency and innovation. The efficiency dimension involves a teacher's ability to retrieve and accurately apply knowledge and skills to specific teaching situations. For example, routine teachers with high efficiency may possess a rich repertoire of teaching practices, know when it is appropriate to use a particular practice such as small group learning to teach spelling, and can enact this practice with a degree of automaticity. At the same time, these highly efficient teachers may not possess the capability to change their existing practices by adopting new and different ways of doing things.

The *innovation* dimension, on the other hand, involves a teacher's ability to move beyond known approaches and routines, to rethink what they are doing, and to be open to the acquisition of new strategies and skills. An example of innovation would be when a teacher adopts a new approach for teaching reading after concluding that previous approaches have failed, or finds a different way to work with a new student from the Ukraine who cannot speak English but who has different learning needs as compared to most Spanish-speaking students in the school.

Accomplished teachers with adaptive expertise have learned how to balance both the efficiency and innovation dimensions (Schartz, Bransford, & Sears (2005). They can perform many routine teaching practices with automaticity and efficiency, but they also have the ability to adopt new practices when olds ways of doing things fail. Hammerness et al. (2005, p. 51) argue that the processes of efficiency and innovation are complimentary "when appropriate levels of efficiency make room for innovation." However, they are "antagonistic when one blocks the other."

As with other aspects of teaching, teachers appear to develop adaptive expertise by progressing through a set of stages or levels ranging from novice to expert. Dreyfus and Dreyfus (1986) identified five levels, as summarized in Figure 1.1.

Berliner (2001) has observed that teachers develop to the competent level over a period of five to seven years, but that only some move on to proficient and expert levels. Obvious goals in the light of our concern about teacher development are to find ways to help *all* teachers become competent and proficient more quickly and to afford more of us to progress beyond this level to the level of expertise. That is

> **REFLECTION**
>
> What do you think about the concept of "adaptive expertise"? Where would you place yourself on the developmental levels of expertise? Do you see yourself as having routine or adaptive expertise? What about a balance between the two?

Stage 1: Novice level
- the novice is deliberate
- the behavior of the novice is usually rational and relatively inflexible
- the novice conforms to a set of rules and procedures
- student teachers and first-year teachers may be considered novices

Stage 2: Advanced beginner level
- the advanced beginner is insightful
- they can recognize similarities across contexts
- they know when to ignore rules and when to follow them
- advance beginners may still have no sense of what is important
- many second- and third-year teachers are likely to be advanced beginners

Stage 3: Competent level
- the competent performer is rational
- they make conscious choices, they set priorities, and decide on plans
- they determine what is and is not important—what to attend to and what to ignore
- competent performers are not quick, fluid, or flexible yet

Stage 4: Proficient level
- the proficient performer is intuitive
- proficient individuals have a holistic way of viewing situations
- they can predict events more precisely
- proficient individuals are still likely to be analytic and deliberative in deciding
- about the fifth year, a modest number of teachers may move into proficient level

Stage 5: Expert level
- experts are arational
- they have an intuitive grasp of situations and non-deliberative ways to respond
- they show fluid performance
- they know where to be and what to do at the right time
- experts act effortlessly and fluidly

Figure 1.1 Developmental stages of expertise
Source: Summarized from Drefyus and Drefyus (1986).

why we have written about this topic here and why we expand on approaches to teacher learning in Chapter 15.

Teacher Knowledge

A final aspect of teacher learning and development in regard to this book addresses the question, "What is the nature of **teacher knowledge?**" Cochran-Smith and Lytle (1993) identified the importance of making distinctions between two kinds of teacher knowledge: (1) knowledge *about* effective practice; and (2) knowledge about *one's own* practice. The first kind consists of information in the form of theory and research that provides knowledge about practice. This includes knowledge about subject matter, about how students learn, and about how and why to use particular instructional strategies. For example, teachers need knowledge about cooperative learning or reciprocal teaching strategies before these practices can be used effectively, or they need to know about formative assessment to differentiate instruction. This type of knowledge is most often acquired from reading books such as this one, attending classes, or going to workshops.

A second kind of knowledge is knowledge of one's own practice. This is knowledge about particular practices individual teachers use in their classrooms and the effects these have on student motivation and learning. The reflection boxes we provide throughout the book and the approaches to teacher learning described in Chapter 15 are particularly valuable for helping to construct knowledge about one's own practice because they provide structures for discussion and reflection on teaching practices. For example, the process of examining student work can help a teacher decide whether or not a particular practice used to produce the work was successful. Observing each other teach and providing coaching can help us obtain knowledge about our practice and take steps to improve it. Discussing an idea with colleagues can sharpen our understanding of the idea and help discover how it might be used in our day-to-day practice.

Teachers can also *create new knowledge* about curriculum implementation and about instructional practices. For example, teachers may choose to use action research to compare the effects of two different instructional strategies, or they may investigate the consequences of using different types of reward systems on homework or student effort. Perhaps they may choose to replicate a study done elsewhere to see if comparable effects can be found in their own particular classroom or school. Teacher-led inquiries help focus specifically on the relationships between instructional practices and student learning, and, when done collaboratively, they can help us take collective as well as individual responsibility for student learning. We will describe this type of knowledge and how it is created through action research in Chapter 15.

TEACHER LEADERSHIP FOR TODAY'S SCHOOLS

We believe today's schools require teachers who will assume leadership in their classrooms for student learning. Leadership, however, should not stop at the classroom door. We believe it should be extended beyond, to the school, the community, and the profession. In this section, we describe our views about teacher leadership, a view not intended to play down the importance of the principal's instructional leadership role but instead one that emphasizes the importance of teacher leadership if classroom and school-wide improvement are to be accomplished.

Why Teacher Leadership Today?

The idea of teacher leadership is not new. Individual teachers have been providing leadership in schools for a long time, and a variety of programs have been devised over the past half-century that put teachers in many different kinds of leadership position. Today, however, the idea of teacher leadership has gained momentum for reasons we discuss below.

School Improvement Imperative As described earlier in the chapter, a changing world has transformed our expectations for education and for student learning. Over the past 30 years the world has become more interconnected, classrooms have become more diverse, and a new system of schooling has evolved that is standards based and rests on the belief that every child and youth can learn and be held to high standards of achievement. This system of schooling differs in important ways from the system of earlier eras, and it has placed new and different demands on educators, particularly teachers.

One of the more important demands is what Danielson (2006) has called the **school improvement imperative**, which places continuous pressure on educators (principals and teachers) to improve the achievement of all students and to close the achievement gap between students who have traditionally done well in school and those who have lagged behind. School improvement pressures come from many sources—federal and state legislators, local school boards, families, and reform-minded educators. And, though as teachers we may disagree with some reform initiatives, most of us agree that improving schools so every child reaches his or her potential is a worthy goal to pursue. To accomplish this goal requires teachers who will assume responsibilities and provide leadership not only for instructional improvement in their own classrooms but also for the school, the community, and the profession.

We believe that teacher leadership is essential for both small- and large-scale changes. Most large-scale reforms cannot achieve success unless teachers implement and help sustain innovative structures and practices. There are many examples of reforms that didn't survive because teachers did not provide support and leadership. Inquiry-based curricula, early team-teaching programs, open-spaced classrooms, differentiated staffing, and merit pay are only a few that quickly come to mind. And, though teacher involvement in large-scale reforms is essential, perhaps the more significant contribution is the leadership provided for innovative practices initiated by teachers themselves in their classrooms and schools.

Principals Can't Do It Alone Traditionally, it has been the school's principal who has been expected to provide leadership for school improvement, and there is a vast literature that emphasizes that the principal's "leadership is second only to classroom instruction among school-related factors that contribute to what students learn" (Leithwood, Louis, Anderson, & Wahlstrom, 2004, p. 3). We know, for example, that successful principals create school-wide environments so teachers can focus on improving instruction. They chart a clear course for the school and help secure a collaborative vision for teaching and learning. They are knowledgeable about what good instruction looks like and they search out models of **best practice** to share with their faculties. They modify schedules and organizational structures to ensure time for teacher learning and effective use of time for student learning. They also build collaborative processes and procedures that enable teachers to have conversations about teaching and learning. Perhaps most important, principals create a professional learning community that fuels teacher creativity and fosters continuous learning and improvement (Fullan, 2008a; Leithwood, Day, Sammons, Harris, & Hopkins, 2007).

However, as important as principal leadership is, there is an increased recognition that the expectations for principal leadership in today's schools are nearly impossible to meet, and a growing consensus exists that principals cannot do it alone. The demands on principals require leadership to be distributed and shared by teachers in the school (Fullan, 2008b; Spillane, 2006). Further, we know that important changes inspired by a particular principal often disappear when the principal moves on to a different school or new administrative position. This supports the argument for an expanded leadership role for teachers whose tenure in schools is longer and who are the custodians of the school's institutional memory and important school improvement accomplishments.

Professionalization of Teaching Finally, our views about teaching and the teaching profession have changed over the past 30 years. Teachers have traditionally been viewed as individuals who existed at the bottom of a bureaucratic and hierarchical system. Real leadership and influence resided with formally designated administrative roles, while teachers were responsible mainly for implementing the plans and designs conceived by others. Teachers worked alone and were governed by norms that not only supported autonomy but also sanctioned efforts to not interfere with other teachers.

Today many of us hold a more professional view of teaching, a view where teaching practices are informed by research and teachers are capable of making complex judgments about how best to achieve student learning in their classrooms and school-wide. This new view requires the recognition that expertise about teaching and learning in particular subjects and particular grade levels rests with teachers more than anyone else and requires that everyone in the school exercise leadership in the support of student learning.

Differing Perspectives and Paths to Teacher Leadership

Those that have written widely on the topic of teacher leadership (Danielson, 2006; Killion & Harrison, 2006; Lieberman & Miller, 2004, 2008; York-Barr & Duke, 2004) agree that teacher leadership consists of teachers extending their influence beyond their own classrooms while continuing to teach students, and that the motivation for assuming leadership varies. Some, for instance, decide to exert leadership after becoming truly accomplished in their own classroom. They are motivated to extend their reach into the school, the community, and the profession. For others it may come after what Danielson (2006) has labeled "professional restlessness," or a readiness to take on tasks for the satisfaction of meeting new challenges. Regardless of the motivation, today many avenues are available for those who want to take on leadership responsibilities.

Formal Leadership Roles Traditionally, the main ways in which teachers could satisfy their desire for greater influence were to become active in their unions or to become administrators, both of which required them to leave the classroom. More recently, in the 1970s and 1980s a range of *formal roles* was designed to encourage teacher leadership. Teachers were often assigned as mentors for a school's student teachers or new teachers, or they became department- or grade-level chairs. Teachers on special assignment (TOSAs) also became popular as teachers were assigned specific responsibilities to help coordinate school or district-wide reforms, most often those associated with curriculum implementation and staff development. Killion and Harrison (2006) have described some of the more formal leadership roles designed for teachers. Many still exist today, as summarized in Table 1.1.

In most instances, the roles described in Table 1.1 take teachers away from their classroom, at least for part of the day. They involve assuming assigned management responsibilities and often are used by teachers as stepping-stones to careers in educational administration. An example of this situation was experienced a few years ago by one of us. A large university employed accomplished classroom teachers as clinical teachers to supervise its interns. Teachers were relieved of classroom teaching responsibilities for a two-year period and maintained offices in both the school and the university. At the end of the two-year period they were expected to return to the classroom. The accomplished teachers, in addition to supervising interns, also used the time and the university setting to acquire advanced degrees and/or administrative certificates. Over a period of a decade only one or two of the clinical teachers returned to teaching; most secured permanent placements at the university or acquired an administrative position in their school district.

Table 1.1 Formal leadership roles for teachers

Resource specialist	Teacher leaders find and secure professional resources for teachers. They share websites, articles, lesson plans, and loan their books to teachers.
Instructional specialist	Teacher leaders coach colleagues as they implement new teaching and learning strategies such as differentiated instruction and formative assessment.
Curriculum specialist	Teacher leaders know standards, curriculum maps, and pacing guides. They help teachers use them to ensure curricular coherence throughout the school.
Demonstration teacher	Teacher leaders work inside classrooms demonstrating lessons, co-teaching, coaching, giving feedback, and helping teachers implement new ideas.
Staff developer	Teacher leaders lead professional development sessions. They facilitate teachers learning from and with one another.
Mentor	Teacher leaders provide critical support for new teachers. They help those new to the profession with procedures, pedagogy, and personal issues.
Grade or department chair	Teacher leaders participate as grade level or department chairs. They also serve on the school leadership team and represent the school externally.
Data coach	Teacher leaders help faculty learn how to analyze and use data to inform and strengthen their instructional decisions.

Source: Summarized and adapted from Killion and Harrison (2006).

Informal Actions and Influence We believe that assuming formal leadership roles is important for schools and for the teaching profession. However, a different view of teacher leadership, and one many teachers prefer, is where teachers exert leadership in more *informal ways*. In these situations teachers do not assume special management responsibilities nor do they gain their authority or influence from assigned formal roles. Instead, they are recognized and gain influence by the work they do (often voluntary) with their students, their colleagues, and members of the community and profession.

These informal teacher leaders focus mainly on improving instruction for student learning in their own classrooms and school-wide. They help create learning communities for the purpose of achieving both small-scale and large-scale instructional improvement. They serve on school and district-level committees where they can influence policies and programs. They are proactive in bringing the community into the school and leading out in the community.

We are prone to promote teacher leadership that is more informal, where influence is gained from deeds rather from assigned roles and where most of the time is spent in the classroom. In our view, this type of leadership represents the highest form of professionalism and provides the best chance for improving schools and student learning. But what do informal teachers do? Following are some examples of teachers who assumed some informal leadership roles and experienced a degree of success:

- *Leadership within a grade level or department.* Roger believed that the middle school where he taught had a very weak English-language arts curriculum. He had noticed that there was little coordination among grade levels, most teachers emphasized teaching literature over composition, and many assumed that all of their students were accomplished readers. Roger expressed his concerns at a department meeting and appealed to his colleagues to look into this situation. At first his concerns were met with opposition, but after several meetings the faculty agreed to take three courses of action: (1) develop curriculum maps for each course and the whole department that would show what was being taught across classrooms and grade levels; (2) collect test scores and analyze reading levels of a sample of students at each grade level; and (3) contact professional associations such as the National Council for Teachers of English and the International Reading Association to identify the latest thinking about the amount of emphasis to put on literature as contrasted to composition.

- *Leadership at the school level.* Gail was very disappointed with the elementary school where she taught. Test scores on the state's mastery tests were consistently below grade level and among the poorest in the district. Even though teachers had been admonished by the principal, scores continued to slide. She decided it was time for her and her colleagues to do something about the situation. She began taking a professional stance about instructional practices at grade-level and school-wide faculty meetings. She persuaded several colleagues to help her collect information about assessment practices and what other schools had done to turn around poor student performance. As they studied and discussed their situation, faculty discovered that though they spent considerable time each year prepping students for mastery tests, they were doing very little to provide ongoing formative assessment. After almost a year of listening to Gail and other teachers, the faculty as a whole accepted a policy that restricted the number of hours that could be devoted to prepping students, and they established a committee to study the effects of their new policy. They also began working in grade-level teams for the purpose of creating a series of formative assessments.

- *Leadership in the community.* Victoria, a teacher at Southside High School, the school we featured in our opening scenario, was concerned about the negative attitudes her ninth graders had toward homework and the lack of family support. She proposed to the faculty that they form a new study group to focus on homework and parent involvement. The faculty agreed that these were important issues and several members signed up to attend agreed-upon monthly meetings. At their first meeting, members discussed how students in their class approached homework and the lack of parental involvement they had observed. There seemed to be some consensus that students had a very negative attitude toward homework and that parents were not very involved in insisting that homework be completed. After several meetings, where articles about homework were read and discussed, the study group agreed to take the following recommendations to the whole faculty: (1) develop a brief (two- or three-page) homework policy statement that would specify the importance of homework and outline expectations for students and parents; and (2) design and conduct a workshop for parents where teachers would go over their homework policy and explain to parents the best ways to help students complete homework assignments.

All three of these examples show different leadership paths teachers can take and actions that lead to improved school practices and student learning. These are also actions that are applauded by colleagues and community members.

Dispositions and Skills for Teacher Leaders

Some people take naturally to leadership, while others find it more problematic. Regardless, those who have studied teacher leadership have found that effective teacher leaders possess a common set of **teacher dispositions** and skills. They have dispositions that allow them to be optimistic in regard to improvement and respectful of and open-minded toward the views of others. They are flexible individuals who are willing to work hard. They also have a set of important skills for working with colleagues and other members of the school community. In Table 1.2 we summarize the dispositions and skills required of effective teacher leaders that were identified by Danielson (2006) and York-Barr and Duke (2004).

Issues and Challenges Facing Teacher Leadership

The ways in which schools have been traditionally organized have created barriers to fully using teacher leadership. York-Barr and Duke (2004), Danielson (2006), and Johnson and Donaldson (2007) have identified several issues and challenges surrounding the effective use of teacher leaders:

- *Role confusion.* Teacher leaders' roles are often ill-defined and teacher leaders are left to define their own roles in the absence of any comprehensive framework or established set of differentiated responsibilities to provide guidance and legitimacy. Too many teacher leaders spend their time as apprentices or assistants in administration.
- *Teacher resistance.* Some colleagues resist teacher leaders because of the traditional norms of teaching—such as autonomy, egalitarianism, and seniority—persist in many schools. Colleagues can view teacher leaders as intruding into their instructional space. The egalitarian nature of teaching hampers teacher leaders' work. Colleagues can question why one teacher should stand out. Others question the "special privileges" they perceive as coming along with the role. Veteran

Table 1.2 Dispositions and skills required of teacher leaders

Dispositions	Skills
• are deeply committed to student learning	• can use evidence and data in decision making
• are open-minded and respectful of the views of others	• can recognize and take initiative
• are optimistic and enthusiastic	• can mobilize people around a common purpose
• hold high expectations for self and others	• can articulate common goals and persuade colleagues to join them
• are creative and flexible	• can search for good ideas, find resources, and take action
• are persistent	• can monitor progress and sustain the commitment of others
• are willing to work hard	• have strong interpersonal and group skills

Source: Summarized from combined works of Danielson (2006) and York-Barr and Duke (2004).

teachers who have seniority can view teacher leaders who are younger or new to the school as too inexperienced to offer advice and suggestions.
- *Lack of principal support.* Principals play an important role in facilitating teacher leadership. They need to be active rather than passive supporters and need to help teacher leaders broker relationships. They must build support by explaining the role, establishing responsibilities, and working with the schedule to incorporate the work of teacher leaders into the structures of the school. This means the principal will have to provide common planning time, substitute coverage for peer observations, use faculty meetings for teacher learning, ensure professional development for teacher leaders, and expect teachers to work on improving instruction.

CONCEPTUAL FRAMEWORK AND QUICK TOUR

We conclude this chapter by providing our readers with a quick tour explaining what guided our writing and what to expect in the rest of the book.

Our Conceptual Framework

Just as it is important for teachers to tell their students what a particular lesson or unit is going to be about, we believe it is important for us to explain to our readers what this book is going to be about, particularly the conceptual framework that has guided our thinking and writing. Further, we believe that providing a set of lenses to view the centrality of teaching to student learning will help to organize the vast amount of information on teaching and learning currently available. The framework we use in *Teaching for Student Learning* and depict in Figure 1.2 highlights four important dimensions:

- The *nature of knowledge* that informs educational goals and curricula.
- The *nature of learners* and how they *learn.*
- The *nature of teaching* and the strategies and models that comprise a teacher's instructional and assessment repertoire.
- The importance of *context* and its influences on curriculum, teaching, and learning.

As portrayed in Figure 1.2, the interaction among curriculum, teaching, and learning does not exist in isolation. Instead, it is heavily influenced by the fourth dimension, *context*, which includes the values held by members of particular communities, their schools, and their goals for education. This framework is not unique to us. Conceptions of the needs of learners and demands of the curriculum and the community date back

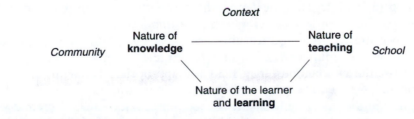

Figure 1.2 Framework for thinking about teaching and student learning

to Dewey (1902, 1916). Further, the interactions among teachers, learners, content, and context have been articulated more recently by Arends (2009), Ball and Cohen, (1999), Bennett and Rolheiser (2001), and Darling-Hammond and Bransford (2005). These ideas have also been embedded fully in the standards developed by the **National Board for Professional Teaching Practices (NBPTP)** as statements about what constitutes effective teaching.

Teaching for Student Learning will employ this framework as we explore how effective teachers use best practices for the purposes of helping students learn enduring understandings and skills. By best practice, we mean a wide range of practices that have been shown to be effective by scientific evidence and/or by the collective wisdom of experienced teachers. Similarly, our perspectives on *student learning* are not confined to those understandings and skills that can be easily measured with standardized tests, but instead go beyond and include learning associated with higher level thinking and problem solving, with dispositions for appreciation of the arts, music, and literature, with being able to work cooperatively in complex work and social environments, and with being effective citizens in our local and global communities. *Knowing* in this context emphasizes deep understanding of enduring ideas and essential questions and the ability to take responsibility for one's own learning.

As with our definitions of learning and knowing, we also do not confine our discussion of *learners*. As experienced teachers know and as we described earlier, students in our classrooms represent great diversity. They speak many languages; they represent many cultures. Some come from homes characterized by status and wealth; others from poverty and neglect. Regardless, all learners are expected to have equitable access to education and schools are expected to help them learn the requisite understandings and skills required for personal, civic, and economic success.

We also cast a rather wide net in our discussion of teaching. We will tend to emphasize the evidence-based aspects and **scientific basis of teaching**. It will be our contention that, though much remains to be learned, we know a great deal today about how students learn and how teachers can affect their learning. We will strive to summarize many aspects of the research that exists on effective teaching and offer practical guidance about what this research means for classroom practice. However, our discussion will not be confined to the scientific perspective alone. We will also explore what Nathaniel Gage (1984), over two decades ago, labeled the **art of teaching**; that side of teaching that departs from method and procedures and embraces, in Gage's terms, processes of "style, and rhythm, and appropriateness." Or, what Tomlinson and Germundson (2007) have labeled the *jazz of teaching* that incorporates "polyrhythm, call-and-response, and improvisation." This is an aspect of teaching that cannot be measured very well because of its complexity and artistry. Nonetheless, it is important. In summary, what we strive for in *Teaching for Student Learning* is a comprehensive view of student learning and an integrated view of teaching as both an art and a science.

Throughout the book we will also emphasize the importance of *context* in teaching and learning, because teaching and learning are social in nature. Students come to school from a variety of families and communities. Families differ in the ways they raise their children, in the expectations they hold for appropriate behavior, and in the amount of encouragement and support they provide. Communities and neighborhoods vary significantly in the safety and nurturing they can provide to children and youth and to the resources they can allocate to childrearing and education. All of these factors have important influences on how teachers teach and what students learn. Further, as discussed earlier in the chapter, teaching and learning today are influenced greatly by larger societal trends and policy environments. For instance, the demographics of our society and of our schools in the first part of the twenty-first century are vastly different than when public schools were fashioned a century and a half ago; indeed, they are different than even a few decades ago. Demographics and technologies have impacted today's youth and our society in large and significant ways.

Finally, we have strived to write this book in a way that helps define effective teaching, a task much easier today than in previous eras. After many years of considerable disagreement about how to define effective teaching, the past two decades have produced a welcome and growing consensus about what accomplished teachers should know and be able to do. Take, for instance, the words used by Linda Darling-Hammond and John Bransford (2005, inside cover) writing for the National Academy of Education:

> in addition to strong subject matter knowledge, all . . . teachers (should) have a basic understanding of how people learn and develop, as well as how children acquire and use language, which is the currency of education. In addition . . . teaching professionals must be able to apply that knowledge in developing curriculum that attends to students' needs, the demands of the content, and the social purposes of education, in specific subject matter to diverse students, in managing the classroom, assessing student performance, and using technology in the classroom.

These statements were written to reflect not only the authors' views but also the vision held by the National Board for Professional Teaching Standards (NBPTS). As many of our readers know, the National Board was created in 1987 following a Carnegie Commission report on *Teaching as a Profession*. Over the years the National Board has strived to define rigorous standards for what teachers should know and be able to do and to provide a mechanism for certifying teachers who can meet these standards. The standards defined by the National Board are expressed in five core propositions that define the accomplished teacher:

- *Proposition 1*: Teachers are committed to students and learning.
- *Proposition 2*: Teachers know the subjects they teach and how to teach those subjects to students.
- *Proposition 3*: Teachers are responsible for managing and monitoring student learning.
- *Proposition 4*: Teachers think systematically about their practice and learn from experience.
- *Proposition 5*: Teachers are members of learning communities.

In the main, we agree and embrace the Darling-Hammond, Bransford, and National Board's definition of accomplished teaching, and our readers will find that we have incorporated many aspects of this vision into both the text and the *Fieldbook* that accompanies it.

Quick Tour of Teaching for Student Learning

We have strived to organize this book in a way that makes transparent our conceptual framework and our perspectives about student learning and accomplished teaching. The beginning chapters of *Teaching for Student Learning* provide foundational knowledge about teaching and learning and pay particular attention to important contextual and environment variables. Chapter 2 provides a primer about how students learn, drawing on research in the neurosciences and the cognitive psychology of school learning. Chapter 3 focuses on motivation and the critical role motivation plays in the teaching–learning process. Chapter 4 includes discussions about the nature of knowledge, particularly how our current perspectives impact the purposes of schools and curriculum design. Chapter 5 describes instructional differentiation as an important feature in contemporary classrooms and provides practical guidance to teachers on ways to attend to individual needs and learning styles. Chapter 6 addresses assessment and strives to summarize the latest differences between assessment *of learning,* assessment *for learning,* and *assessment as learning,* along with important implications for teaching. Throughout these chapters we argue for the need to have careful and clear alignment among the desired outcomes we hold for students and the practices we use to differentiate instruction and to assess learning outcomes.

Throughout Part I we emphasize that teaching and learning are inseparable, and that success in teaching depends on affecting student learning. Some of our discussions in these early chapters will be brief because they are intended only to introduce important ideas and principles. These discussions will serve as advance organizers for more elaborate discussions found in subsequent chapters where the implications of particular principles are applied to specific teaching models and strategies.

A basic part of *Teaching for Student Learning* lies in Part II, Chapters 7 through 14, where we organize the discussion about what teachers do, namely, employ particular strategies and models of instruction to enhance student learning. We describe an array of teaching strategies in some detail. These chapters, however, are not simply descriptions about "how to do it." Instead, for each strategy we provide information about:

- The assumptions made about the nature of knowledge implied in the strategy.
- Principles from particular theories of learning that explain why and how a particular strategy works and how it should be used.
- Evidence that demonstrates the strengths and weaknesses of a particular strategy.
- Classroom learning environments required to implement the strategy effectively.
- Teacher and student behaviors and roles required when using the strategy.
- The most appropriate assessment strategies to measure student learning associated with the learning outcomes the strategy has been designed to accomplish.

We have organized teaching models and strategies around the "goals" they were designed to accomplish, i.e., build declarative knowledge, develop skills, enhance higher-level thinking and problem solving, and promote collaboration. This concept will be developed more fully later. In the chapters in Part II, our readers will find a continued emphasis around the theme that effective teachers are not restricted to a few favorite approaches, but instead have a repertoire of effective practices. We will also take the point of view that debates from earlier eras about the superiority of one practice over another are futile and counterproductive. No single approach is consistently superior to any other. Instead, it is much more profitable to view the potential useful-ness of any practice when considering each particular class of students and each teach-ing–learning situation. Selection of a particular approach or strategy should depend on the learning goals and nature of learning materials to be learned, prior knowledge learners bring to the learning situation, and the expectations for and characteristics of particular groups of students. Given this perspective, it is quite likely that a teaching approach that works well in one situation with a particular group of students may work poorly in another situation or setting.

In Part II of *Teaching for Student Learning* we describe both teacher-centered (i.e., presentations, direct instruction, and concept teaching) and student-centered (i.e., cooperative learning and problem-based learning) approaches to instruction. Accom-plished teachers are those with a diverse repertoire of effective practices from which they can choose, depending upon a complex array of variables associated with any particular teaching–learning situation.

In the final chapter of *Teaching for Student Learning* we will move outside the class-room and focus on the context of teaching. We discuss school level conditions for supporting and promoting teacher learning and change. The perspective we take in this chapter is that, for teachers to be effective, they must work in settings where they can use what they know, and where support and accountability are present. They must be provided with opportunities to demonstrate leadership as they come to know their students and families. Most important they must have an environment where they are encouraged to work and learn with their fellow teachers. Schools where teachers come together and make agreements about what is going to be taught, how students will engage in learning, and how learning will be assessed are schools that make a difference in what students learn in every classroom.

SUMMARY AT A GLANCE

- Teachers today must not only focus on student learning associated with daily and weekly lessons, but must also make sure students find success on high-stakes accountability measures. This makes the job of teaching more complex and more difficult than in earlier eras.
- Three major aspects of today's world have created a different set of demands on teaching and learning: the press for standards and accountability; increased stu-dent diversity; and technological advances and globalization.
- Increased demands on teachers require changes in the ways we work and also put increased demands on the ways we learn. Teachers must not only continue to teach for student success, but also seek out learning situations so new practices and new roles can be acquired.
- There is a progression in teacher development and practicing teachers learn in many ways. Approaches for helping teachers acquire knowledge about their own practice through study and reflection and with colleagues are among the most effective for helping teachers acquire expertise.
- Expert teachers do things differently than novices. Teachers develop both routine expertise and adaptive expertise.
- Today's schools require teachers to exert leadership for improving instruction not

only in their own classrooms but also school-wide, as well as into the community and the profession.

• *Teaching for Student Learning* has been developed around a conceptual framework that emphasizes the interactions among teachers, learners, content, and context. It takes a rather broad view about the nature of knowledge and what constitutes effective teaching and successful learning.

CONSTRUCTING YOUR OWN LEARNING

Working with a classmate(s) or colleague(s) in your school, initiate *dialogue* and *action* that will promote learning about your own teaching practices. Begin by having a dialogue about your own teaching. How has it progressed and matured over the years? What aspect of your practice is supported by research? By the wisdom of experience? By the art of teaching? Identify specific actions you and your partner can take aimed at improving a particular teaching practice. Consider visiting each other's classroom and then engage in discussions about what you saw and pose questions that allow you to explore each other's teaching practices.

RESOURCES

Danielson, C. (2006). *Teacher leadership that strengthens professional practice.* Alexandria, VA: Association for Supervision and Curriculum Development.

Darling-Hammond. L. & Bransford, J. (Eds.). (2005). *Preparing teachers for a changing world.* San Francisco, CA: Jossey-Bass.

Friedman, T. (2005). *The world is flat: A brief history of the twenty-first century.* New York: Farrar, Straus & Giroux.

Senge, P. (1990). *The fifth discipline: The art and practice of the learning organization.* New York: Doubleday.

Part I
FOUNDATIONS FOR STUDENT LEARNING

2

HOW STUDENTS LEARN: A PRIMER

There is nothing more important to a classroom teacher than finding answers to the question, "How do my students learn?" This is true because teaching cannot be separated from learning. Indeed, *teaching is the "art and science" of helping students learn,* and our success as teachers depends on changing the minds and intellectual character of students, unlike the plight described in the scenario below.

Why Didn't They Learn?

It is 6:30 in the evening. Jennifer sits alone in her classroom finishing grading the essay exam she gave over "light and color." She sighs with disappointment as she realizes that most of her students display serious misunderstandings about the principle that seeing is the process of detecting light that has been reflected off some object. Or, as she has explained to them so many times, "When light bounces off things and travels to our eyes, we are able to see."

Jennifer believes that she did a good job of teaching the unit. She was well organized, explained her expectations, and went over the main points several times. A major assignment focused on "the physics of light," and several small group discussions explored the topic in depth. Jennifer thought her explanations were accurate, and she had strived to clear up all of her students' misconceptions. Nonetheless, students simply didn't learn. "Why," she asked herself? Were they not paying attention? Was the topic too difficult? Were my assessments inadequate to accurately measure what they actually learned? Were they not ready? She wished she had someone to talk to about this, but alas in her school, teachers didn't readily seek out advice from one another. Jennifer went home, made herself a Caesar salad, and had a glass of wine. However, the dilemmas of her students' learning continued to bother her all evening.

This is a scenario that most of us have experienced at one time or another. Whether we were teaching K-12 students or college, we believed we had taught well—presented information with clarity, discussed the topic in depth, and assigned meaningful homework. Yet our students did not learn the most important concepts and ideas we were trying to teach. Why? What is at fault? Were we indeed not as good as we thought we were with lesson organization and presentation? Were the students at fault because they didn't pay attention or perhaps they didn't work hard enough? Or, was the topic inappropriate for our students' given their prior knowledge, readiness, and intellectual development? These are all questions about how people learn or fail to learn and are the primary foci of this chapter.

As described in the previous chapter, at the heart of our conceptual framework for *Teaching for Student Learning* are theories and research that help explain learning. A vast amount of information exists on this topic and will be introduced here and then expanded in subsequent chapters. The emphases in this chapter will be on describing what we know about learning, from studies in the **neurosciences** over the past several decades, followed by somewhat parallel insights and perspectives gleamed from **cognitive psychology**, particularly as it is applied to school learning. In both instances, we will strive to provide a framework for thinking about student learning in schools and classrooms, but most important we will spell out the practical implications this research has for classroom practices.

THE SCIENCE OF LEARNING

Over the past century, educators, psychologists, and neuroscientists have developed what has come to be referred to as the **science of learning** (Ashcraft, 2006; Bransford, Brown, & Cocking, 2000). This science of learning has evolved from an emphasis in the early part of the twentieth century on **behaviorism** to newer conceptions resulting from studies in the past few decades in the neurosciences and in cognitive and developmental psychology. This evolution of thought has changed our understandings of learning in some pretty dramatic ways and has serious implications for the classroom practices we employ.

Let's begin with a brief history lesson. Behaviorists, as the name implies, believed that the study of learning should be confined to the study of observable behaviors. This approach was actually a reaction to earlier reliance on more subjective approaches to the study of human thought and learning. Behaviorists strived to find connections between stimuli such as drives and external forces (sensory input) and subsequent behavior (learning). As experienced teachers, you know about the classic experiments in the behavioral tradition. Dogs were trained to salivate (learned behavior) when they heard a bell (sensory input). Cats learned through conditioning to pull strings that allowed them to acquire food. Behavioral perspectives led educators to adopt beliefs that knowledge was somewhat constant, that it could be standardized, and that it could be transmitted to students in rather straightforward ways. These perspectives also led to conceptions about classroom learning environments and management systems, namely that students could be managed (controlled) through selected use of rewards and punishments.

Many of us were prepared as teachers to embrace **behavioral principles of learning and teaching**. We were taught to present (transmit) information to students clearly and precisely. We were encouraged to use motivation and classroom management procedures characterized by clear goals and precise expectations for student behavior, and to employ rather elaborate systems of rewards and punishments to achieve students' compliance. Efforts to achieve school and student success from this perspective led to the development of standardized curriculum (knowledge is constant) and standardized tests (learning is observable) aimed at measuring the degree to which students mastered specified skills and ideas associated with agreed-upon standards, mainly through memory and recall.

Some aspects of teaching and learning are best served by application of behavioral principles. For example, it is important to have clear goals and expectations; it is important to hold students accountable for achieving agreed-upon and well-defined standards. Providing feedback and applying positive reinforcers can sometimes effectively motivate students. However, many aspects of teaching and learning have not been well served by this perspective. A

> **REFLECTION**
>
> Consider the use of behavioral principles in your own teaching. What positive effects has it had on your students' learning? What about negative effects? What about in your own learning? Over coffee or lunch, compare your ideas about learning with a classmate or colleague.

severe weakness of behaviorism in regard to student learning is its reliance on observable behavior as the primary measure of student learning. This makes it difficult to consider several other important aspects of learning such as **emotions**, reasoning, problem solving, and critical thinking, all of which exist in the mind but cannot necessarily be observed directly; although that too has changed, as we will see with newer imaging technologies. Finally, an over-reliance on behaviorism and extrinsic rewards can lead to an unnecessary uniformity in classrooms and can result in negative consequences in regard to student motivation and learning.

During the past several years, new research on the brain, mind, thinking processes, and human cognition has provided important new perspectives about learning. In the years ahead, these perspectives will expand even more and have immense influence on the ways we conceive teaching and learning, the ways we design our curriculum, and the assessments we use to measure student outcomes. Some of the key ideas and concepts from this research are introduced here; they will be described in more detail in later chapters as we strive to show the connections between ideas from learning theory and particular instructional and assessment practices. In the sections below, we will describe ideas that have emerged from the biology of learning, followed by a section describing important perspectives and principles from cognitive psychology about the nature of intelligence, and about how our memory and **information processing** system works. Through all of this you will find that the instructional implications that stem from both the neuro and the **cognitive sciences** have many similarities. You will also find that, in some instances, the theory and research in these fields raise more questions than they provide answers.

BIOLOGICAL PERSPECTIVE OF LEARNING

During the past 20 years there has been a spate of research on the mind and the brain. This research, conducted mainly by neuroscientists, has converged and confirmed the evidence resulting from studies conducted by cognitive psychologists about the processes of learning, thinking, and problem solving. In this section, we provide an introduction to this topic, but do so with a sense of *constraint and modesty*. Much has been made of late about "brain-based education," and many of our readers will be aware of ideas that have appeared in some educational journals and the popular press. Some of this writing is interesting and provocative, but we believe that all too often it oversimplifies a very complex topic. So called brain-based teaching strategies also have been adopted in faddish ways and speculations about the applications of this research have often gone way beyond what neuroscientists actually know. Examples of this would include speculations about right-brain, left-brain learning that were so popular a decade ago and, more recently, claims about **brain growth** spurts and capacity (see Bransford et al., 2000; Bruner, 1999; Woolfolk, 2005). Judy Willis (2007), who practiced neurology for 15 years before becoming an educator, has pointed out that, "the findings from neuroimaging research for education and learning are still largely suggestive; they have not demonstrated a solid empirical link between how the brain learns and how it metabolizes oxygen or glucose" (p. 699). In *Teaching for Student Learning*, we will try to weave our way through the complexity of this topic and to show the implications for education in straightforward ways. We will also strive to be parsimonious in our discussion and describe ideas that have enduring value for classroom teachers and leave out those that have less relevance.

The most important and perhaps most fundamental insight obtained from the biology of learning is that learning changes the *physical structure of the brain* and, in turn, these physical changes alter the functional organization of the brain (see, for example, Willis, 2006; Zull, 2002). According to Bransford et al. (2000), learning "organizes and reorganizes the brain" (p. 115). With this understanding, some theorists, such as Zull (2002, p. xiv), maintain that, stated simply, "teaching becomes the art of changing the brain."

But how does this work? How does the brain change structurally? How does learning affect the brain's functional organization? How do we know? This is not the place to provide extended answers to these questions. However, we can benefit from some basic understandings about how the brain is studied, the anatomy of the brain including the emotional aspects of the brain, and our sensory and motor systems.[1]

How the Brain is Studied

Let's begin with a brief discussion about how the brain is studied. Since the time of the early Greeks, and perhaps earlier, philosophers have recognized the associations that existed among mind and brain, memory and learning. However, it has been only in the past few decades that neuroscience has produced knowledge that provides a clearer picture (literally) about these associations, about how the brain is structured, and about how it functions. This research has been made possible by imaging technologies, of which there are many. Three of the most important technologies are **functional magnetic resonance imaging (fMRI), position emission technology (PET)**, and **quantitative encephalography (qEEG)**. Using these technologies, neuroscientists are able to study and to take pictures of the brain as it works (burning glucose and oxygen or emitting electrical patterns) and thus make direct observations of a variety of brain functions, including those associated with physical, mental, and emotional learning. These technologies can measure changes in the brain's metabolism and create three-dimensional computer images (**tomographs**) of the brain as it does its work. **Brain mapping** techniques are described a bit more thoroughly in Research Box 2.1.

Brain mapping techniques such as those described above have allowed researchers to explore the activation of various regions of the brain and to study how the brain functions as it performs particular tasks or as it reacts to sensory stimuli. Much of "imaging" research has been conducted on animals in laboratory settings or with people who have impairments of one type or another. This research has provided invaluable insights in helping understand learning disabilities and brain disorders associated with

---

Inquiry **RESEARCH BOX 2.1**

Willis, J. (2006). "Brain mapping techniques," in *Research strategies that ignite student learning*. Alexandria, VA: Association of Supervision and Curriculum Development.

Brain-mapping techniques allow scientists to track which parts of the brain are active when a person is processing information. The levels of activation in particular brain regions determine which facts and events will be remembered. . . . fMRI allows scientists a view of brain activity over time. In one study focusing on visual memories, subjects were placed under fMRI and then shown a series of pictures. The researchers found that activity levels in the right prefrontal cortex and a specific area of the hippocampus correlated with how well a particular visual experience was encoded and how well it was remembered (Brewer, Zhao, Desmond, Glover & Gabrieli, 1998).

Another study focused on verbal memory. Subjects were asked to analyze words either by their meaning (whether the concept was abstract or concrete) or by their appearance (whether the word was in uppercase or lowercase letters). Activity levels in the prefrontal cortex . . . and the parahippocampal area . . . predicted which words were remembered in subsequent tests. Furthermore, they discovered that words were much more likely to be remembered when subjects concentrated on the meaning of the words rather than on their appearance (Wagner, Schacter, Rotte, Koutstaal, Manrl & Dale, 1998).

Alzheimer's, Huntington's disease, and Parkinson's. However, this research has also helped clear up misconceptions held in earlier times about the brain and about learning. Today, it is safe (with some caution) to make some generalizations from this research about how learning occurs in normal children and youth and in classroom settings, as we will do in later sections of this chapter.

Neurons and Synapses
Many of you will have attended workshops on "how the brain works" or taken courses in psychology or cognition and you will have familiarity with the topics we discuss next. Others, however, will be less familiar, so before we go on we want to present some basic information about the brain and to explore how the brain is structured and how it functions. The brain is made up of nerve cells called **neurons**. It is estimated that the human brain has more than 100 billion of these cells. These minuscule structures receive information or input from our sensory organs—ears, eyes, nose, mouth, and skin. They can also receive information from other neurons. The center portion of a neuron consists of the cell's body that helps regulate activity. Extending from neurons are short nerve fibers called dendrites. **Dentrites** are the input side of the neuron and receive messages from other neurons and from axons. **Axons** are nerve fibers that transmit messages through chemical and electrical impulses from the neuron to dendrites and to other neurons. Some neurons also send information back to physical parts of our body, such as to our muscles, skin, and some of our internal mechanisms. Neurons send messages by the release of chemicals that cross small gaps between one neuron's dendrite and the axon of another. These gaps are called **synapses.** This

process allows us to interact with our environments. It is important to understand the role nerve cells play, how cells are connected to one another, and how they communicate because this is where some of the *change and learning occurs*. Several terms important to understanding this process are displayed in Figure 2.1 and then described below:

- *Neurons*: The name for nerve cells that store and transmit information. Scientists estimate that the brain in comprised of over 100 billion neurons.
- *Axons*: Long nerve fibers that transmit messages through electrical impulses from the body of the neuron to the dentrites.
- *Dentrites*: Short fibers that extend from nerve cells. This is the input side of the neuron. They receive messages from the axons and relay them to the nucleus of the cell.
- *Synapses*: These are the junctions or small spaces between neurons where information and messages are passed from neuron to neuron. Only a small portion of these exists at birth. Most (two-thirds) are developed later.
- *Neurotransmitters*: **Neurotransmitters** are chemicals between axons and dendrites that send messages in the form of chemical signals from one neuron to another.
- *Myelin*: **Myelin** is a substance that covers axons that protect the nerve fiber and speed nerve impulse transmission.[2]

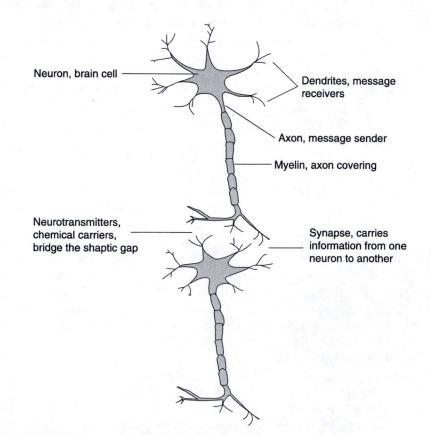

Neuron, brain cell

Dendrites, message receivers

Axon, message sender

Myelin, axon covering

Neurotransmitters, chemical carriers, bridge the shaptic gap

Synapse, carries information from one neuron to another

Figure 2.1 View of a neuron (nerve cell) and how messages are transmitted

Neurons, their networks, and synapse production are significant to teaching and learning. Learning results in physical changes in this aspect of the brain. The process of *synapse production and addition* takes place throughout our lifetimes. Bransford et al. (2000) have written that during early years it is believed that synapses are "overproduced and then selectively lost," and over time some neurons become more "*powerful and efficient*," mainly as a result of experience and through learning (p. 117).

This process influences the overall structure of the brain and highlights the importance of exposing children and youth to high quality information and to rich learning environments. It also emphasizes the importance of the senses for passing on information to neurons in the brain. We will return to both of these topics and address the instructional implications later in this chapter, as well as in later chapters, when we describe approaches to teaching that require rich learning environments and active student involvement. Research Box 2.2 below illustrates how some neuroscience research has demonstrated the effects of rich learning environments.

Inquiry **RESEARCH BOX 2.2**

"*Making* rats smarter," summarized from Bransford et al. (2000) and based on the research of Greenough (1976), Greenough, Juraska, and Volkmar (1979), and Turner and Greenough (1985).

In a series of studies, rats were placed in two types of environments. Rats in one group lived communally and were placed in a "complex" environment where they were provided "rich" opportunities to explore and play. Rats in the other group were placed in an impoverished, barren laboratory environment where they lived alone.

After experiencing the two environments until adolescence, both groups were given a learning experience, with the following results:

- Rats in the complex environment made fewer errors at the beginning of the learning task and they learned more quickly to make no errors at all than did their counterparts raised in the impoverished environment.
- The brains of rats in the complex environment as a result of learning were altered more than impoverished rats. They had 20–25 percent more "synapses per nerve cell in the visual cortex" than rats from the more barren cages.

Regions and Brain Functions

The brain is comprised of several different regions. These regions specialize in particular tasks and are affected by different types of sensory input. For example, some areas of the brain process spoken language, others see words acquired from reading, and still others help us with of our thinking and cognitive processing.

The largest area of the brain is the **cerebral cortex** (also called the neocortex or **cerebrum**). The cerebral cortex is the outer part of the brain that looks like a bunch of wrinkles and folds. This is where most of the neurons that store and transmit information described in the previous section are located. This part of the brain is also the area that develops more slowly but is most influenced by the external environment (Berk, 2002; Meece, 2002; Woolfolk, 2005). The cerebral cortex is divided into left and right hemispheres and consists of four different locations or lobes and the **cerebellum**. Neuroscientists have labeled the lobes with the following names: **frontal lobe, occipital lobe, temporal lobe**, and **parietal lobe**. Each of these locations coordinates different functions, and growth occurs at different times and at different rates in each of the parts. The four lobes and the cerebellum are shown in Figure 2.2. The functions associated with each lobe are described below:

- *Frontal lobe*: Place where some types of thinking, problem solving, and planning occur.
- *Parietal lobe*: Place that deals mainly with orientation and certain kinds of recognition; concerned with reception and processing of sensory information.
- *Temporal lobe*: Place that deals with sound and speech, some aspects of long-term memory, language, and emotion.
- *Occipital lobe*: place where visual processing occurs.
- *Cerebellum*: Helps coordinate balance, posture, repetitive movements, and some aspects of reasoning and thinking.

These parts of the brain plus the brainstem, which connects the brain to the spinal cord and controls such things as heart rate, breathing, sleeping and digestion, and the spinal cord itself, serve as the important components of our central nervous system. All

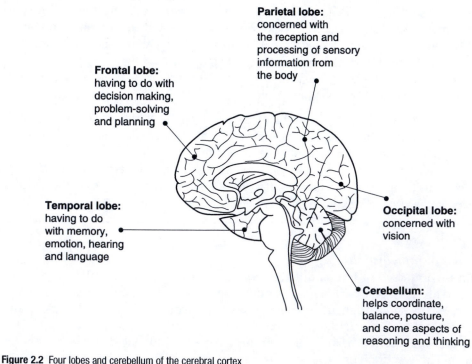

Figure 2.2 Four lobes and cerebellum of the cerebral cortex
Source: Adapted from Dana Alliance for Brain Initiatives (2003).

of these tasks require the coordination of millions of neurons and most take place almost instantly, within a fraction of a second. It is these areas that are studied with the imaging technology described earlier. Particular regions of the brain "light up," so to speak, as the brain goes about performing tasks and doing its work. Although different regions of the brain serve primary functions, these processes do not occur in isolation. There are many instances of overlaps as one area of the brain works to help other areas.

In the center and lower part of the brain are several other areas that are very important for learning and memory. These are displayed in Figure 2.3 and again described below.

- *Thalamus*: The **thalamus** relays, sorts, and directs signals back and forth between the spinal cord and the cerebrum. This is where information from the senses (except smell) enters the brain.
- *Hypothalamus*: The **hypothalamus** is the place in the brain where signals from the brain and the body's hormonal system interact.
- *Amygdala*: Located in the center of the brain, the **amygdala** coordinates emotional reactions such as anger and has important influences on eating, reactions to stress (taking flight or pursuing fight), and sexual interest.
- *Hippocampus*: An important part of the inner brain involved in learning and memory.

The different parts of the brain and their functions have implications for teaching and student learning. First, as we described earlier, it is through learning that physical structures of the brain change and their functions reorganize. Second, it is important to understand that various regions of the brain specialize in particular tasks and require particular kinds of stimulation for learning to occur. Third, it is likely that different parts of the brain are ready to learn at different times, requiring developmentally appropriate learning activities (Ashcraft, 2006; Bransford et al., 2000).

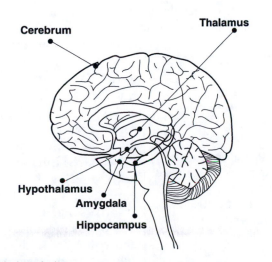

Figure 2.3 Important areas of the lower brain
Source: Adapted from Dana Alliance for Brain Initiatives (2003).

More than Cognition: Emotions and Feelings

Another important insight gleaned from the biology of learning is that *not all learning is cognitive* and that there are strong connections between the cognitive and the emotional. Emotions and feelings are learned, and they in turn play an important role in all types of cognitive learning. Let's begin with definitions of emotion and feeling. According to LeDoux (1997) and Zull (2002), evolution gave humans our fundamental emotional systems. Two that are especially important to learning are our **fear system** and our **pleasure system**. Zull writes, "our fear system makes us want to run, fight, hide or even 'play possum' . . . our pleasure system makes us want to come closer, get more, make ourselves more visible" (p. 50). He explains that we are born with the "capacity for fear and pleasure, but not necessary knowledge of *what* to fear or *what* gives pleasure" (p. 51). We acquire this latter knowledge as we grow up and interact with our environment. For example, most of us learn to fear certain things (an angry, barking dog or a pointed handgun) and we learn to derive pleasure from other things such as the taste of sugar, the sound of music, or our dog's welcoming, wagging tail. In many ways, these emotional systems have great influence on our lives. Some believe that they precede cognition, and there is considerable consensus that they cannot be dismissed in the learning process (Goleman, 1995; LeDoux, 1997; Zull, 2002).

Although emotion is connected to many areas of the brain, certain regions inside the lobes of each hemisphere appear to do most of the work. Flight–fight reactions to stress (emotions of great importance to teaching and learning), for instance, are coordinated primarily in the amygdala but can also be influenced by other areas. According to LeDoux (1997), as humans we are constantly monitoring our external experiences and signals that are gathered from the environment go from our senses directly to the amygdala, often automatically. The important implication for teaching that will be expanded on later is that "fear" or "threat" can be an overwhelming emotion that prevents student involvement in cognitive tasks.

Emotions such as fear or pleasure exist at the subconscious level. Feelings, on the other hand, are in the body and result from our emotional awareness. This happens because the brain releases chemicals into our bodies. Perhaps the best-known example of this is the messages sent to our adrenal glands and subsequent release of adrenalin when we experience danger. Or, getting sweaty palms when we are nervous or flushing when we are embarrassed. Other chemicals exist (perhaps over a dozen) that trigger various kinds of feeling, such as affection and love.

Feelings can help us remember and learn; they can also make us forget. For example, some events in our lives when we experienced intense emotional reactions—such as seeing the Eiffel Tower for the first time, listening to a stirring rendition of our favorite song, or the touch of a first kiss—stay in our memories forever. Others, often those that are frightening and painful, are blocked from memory and may soon be forgotten. If we want our students to learn,

> **REFLECTION**
>
> What have been your experiences in regard to the importance of emotions and feelings in your teaching and your students' learning? Are they similar or different to those we expressed here? What steps do you take to provide your students with a safe environment characterized by positive feeling tones? Have you and your colleagues taken any steps to secure a safe, school-wide psychological environment?

we must understand the role of emotion and feelings, recognize their importance, and plan instruction accordingly. Again, this is an assertion that we will return to in later chapters as we consider the instructional implications of emotions and feelings.

In summary, learning can be defined as changes that occur in the learner's brain. Teaching is what teachers do to affect these changes. It is important for teachers to remember the primacy of experiences and that, while experiences come from outside the brain, it is the brain itself that integrates these experiences and turns them into knowledge and understanding. It is equally important to recognize that different parts of the brain are ready to learn at particular times and that effective instruction ties particular learning goals and learning activities to times that are most appropriate to maximize student growth.

Instructional Implications of the Biological Perspective of Learning

So, what implications does knowing about how the brain learns have for our teaching? Although, as we said before, many of the findings from the neurosciences have not been empirically linked directly to classroom practices, they are nonetheless very suggestive and well worth paying attention to. Findings and their implications are discussed below.

Brain Growth It is clear that learning causes growth of neurons (brain cells where information is stored) and that it alters the physical structure and functional organization of the brain. In response to learning, dendrites increase in size and number, neural networks change, and synapse production is increased. Every time a learner participates in an instructional activity or segment, neurons are activated. Some teaching practices facilitate brain growth while other act to deter it. Obviously, as teachers we want to employ practices that stimulate growth. Following Willis (2006), we offer the following:

- For any instructional segment *use multiple modalities* and *multiple sensory pathways*. Enrich all lessons with multisensory input. These actions stimulate the various senses and help students grow more brain connections. For instance, verbal information causes interaction with the temporal lobes, whereas visual information influences connections in the occipital lobes. We will come back to this many times in later chapters when we emphasize the importance of using graphic organizers, mind maps, and conceptual webs. Experiential and "hands-on" activities are similarly useful for stimulating multiple senses.
- Create and maintain **rich learning environments**. Earlier we described how experiments with animals have shown that enriched learning environments increase dendrite production and synapse connections. This is also true for classroom learning environments. It is important to create environments that are rich in resources, both those acquired by the teacher and those that result from student work. Classrooms should also contain a variety of elements aimed at stimulating the various senses: visual, auditory, taste, and olfactory.

Differentiated Development It is equally clear that different parts of the brain are ready to learn at different times, that cognitive functions are differentiated, and that learners have different modes and capabilities for using these different modes. We recommend the following:

- *Recognize that brain development may be incomplete* in some areas and for some students. The best example is the incomplete development in the prefrontal cortex, the region for emotional stability and reasoning, and resulting cause of the poor judgment and unpredictability often observed in teenage behavior.
- *Differentiate instructional goals and learning activities* so different levels of development are considered and different learning modes of processing such as visual and verbal can be used. We devote a whole chapter to this topic later in the book.

Prior Knowledge and Personal Meaning Knowledge is stored in the brain and new information enters the brain through one of the senses and goes through the limbic system. New information that can be connected to **prior knowledge** and that has personal meaning moves more efficiently through the limbic system. Too often lessons are designed from the perspective of where we are as teachers instead of where our students are. Storage and subsequent retrieval is also more efficient when new learning allows students to build and expand on what they already know and when the subject of the lesson is something they care about. We recommend the following:

- Plan lessons and use strategies so students can make *connections between prior knowledge and new learning materials.* Use scaffolds and advance organizers, metaphors and analogies, and specially designed graphic devices and visual imagery aimed at helping students recognize patterns, see relationships, and build bridges between prior and new knowledge. We will return to these practices and describe them in more detail in several subsequent chapters.
- Plan lessons and use strategies that help students *personalize new learning materials.* Help them see relationships between the new materials and their current interests, hobbies, and pursuits.

Role of Emotions and Feelings Emotions and feelings are learned and, in turn, influence greatly all types of cognitive learning. Feelings of fear and of joy stimulate the amygdala in different ways. Fear and anxiety blocks learning; positive feelings facilitate it. We recommend the following:

- Create classroom environments that are *free from threat* and that have positive feeling tones.
- Plan lessons and use strategies that provide an *appropriate amount of challenge* to students and avoid those that they will not understand or can't keep up with.
- Avoid strategies or *actions that cause too much stress.* Do not tell students that some of them are going to fail or teach a lesson where only a few are ready to learn. Don't teach lessons in a language that students barely understand. Avoid making poor test scores or performances public.

Brain Filtering As experienced teachers, we know that before students can learn something we must capture their attention. This is true and important because the brain filters all incoming stimuli and makes decisions about what to attend to and what to ignore. Below are strategies for getting students' attention:

- Make effective use of *surprise, drama,* and *humor.*
- Use *advance organizers* and other lesson capturing strategies.

- Use *stories or music* to help students get in a positive emotional state prior to a lesson.
- Attend to "*teachable moments*" when they happen. All experienced teachers know what these are.

These findings are summarized in Table 2.1.

We believe the topic of gaining attention is so important that we will return to it later in the chapter and then again throughout the book, particularly in regard to the instructional strategies described in Part II.

COGNITIVE VIEWS OF LEARNING

For the past several decades, cognitive psychologists have been developing theories and an impressive knowledge base about how people learn. Their theories and research provide us with a pretty clear picture about how learning occurs in classrooms, including growth in the cognitive, social, and emotional domains. As you will see, the results from research in the cognitive sciences are consistent and converge with many of those in the neurosciences described in the previous section. However,

Table 2.1 Summary of findings from the neurosciences about learning and their implications for teaching

Brain growth and changes in neural networks: Learning changes the physical structure and functional organization of the brain.	Make use of multiple modalities and stimulate multiple senses and sensory pathways.
	Create and maintain rich learning environments.
	Make effective use of surprise and drama.
Differentiated development: Different regions and lobes of the brain support different functions and develop differently; cognitive functions seem to be differentiated.	Recognize that brain development may be incomplete in particular students or groups of students.
	Differentiate instructional goals and learning activities.
Knowledge storage and meaning: New information enters the brain more efficiently when it is connected to what students already know and when it has personal meaning.	Help students connect new learning materials to what they already know.
	Help students personalize new learning materials.
Role of emotion and feelings: Emotion and feelings are connected in several ways and greatly influence both learning and cognition	Create classrooms free from threat and with positive feeling tones.
	Plan lessons and use strategies with appropriate amount of challenge.
	Avoid actions that cause stress or promote fear.
Brain filtering: The brain filters what to attend to and what to ignore.	Make effective use of surprise, drama, and humor.
	Use advance organizers and other lesson-capturing strategies.
	Use stories or music to help students get in a positive emotional state
	Attend to "teachable moments."

unlike research in the neurosciences, many of the studies in the cognitive sciences have been conducted with normal student populations and in actual classroom settings. Therefore, the findings are often easier to grasp and have clearer and more straightforward implications for classroom practices than those that stem from the neurosciences.

In this section we will describe briefly the cognitive view of learning and several key ideas associated with this perspective. We will also discuss the implications the cognitive perspective has for teaching practices. As with the previous section, we view our discussion here as a primer for getting started with the promise that specifics will follow in later chapters where we will apply specific **cognitive principles of learning** to particular instructional practices.

The Cognitive Perspective

Although there are multiple branches and traditions that make up the cognitive view of learning, there is nonetheless an agreed-upon general set of beliefs. Ashcraft (2006) has written that cognitive science is the "scientific study of the mind," and, more specifically, the "study of learning, human memory, and cognitive processes." Even though we can't actually see memory and cognitive processes, cognitive psychologists agree that they exist, that they can be studied, and that humans are active participants in their own learning and cognition. This view has led to several ideas that are important for teachers and for our teaching practices. Four of the most important include: (1) human intelligence is not a unitary ability but instead has multiple dimensions; (2) the human memory system structures learners' abilities to gather information from the environment, process it, and store it for later use and transfer; (3) what learners already know is the most important and critical element in what they will learn; and (4) when learners develop **metacognitive knowledge** they become aware of their cognitive processes, can monitor progress toward particular learning goals, and can employ appropriate learning strategies to enhance learning.

Broader Conceptions of Human Intelligence

As teachers, we know that an important element in learning is the *abilities* learners bring to learning situations, particularly abilities to acquire and use knowledge, to solve problems, and to master a variety of other cognitive tasks. Think for a moment about students in your class. What kinds of abilities do they have? How do they differ? How do their abilities affect their learning?

Traditionally, psychologists and educators held the view that human beings had specific mental abilities associated mainly with memory and reasoning. We labeled these abilities "intelligence." At the beginning of the twentieth century, psychologists in Europe and the United States developed tests aimed at measuring intelligence and deriving a standard score that came to be known as the **intelligence quotient (IQ)**. These IQ tests were developed for multiple reasons. France's Alfred Binet wanted to have a means to identify children who needed extra help. In the United States, Lewis Terman and others wanted an objective way to determine which individuals could benefit from higher education or who would have "best fit" in the army or other life pursuits.

Over time, these initial IQ tests have fallen out of favor. They have been replaced, however, by tests that tend to measure more general or content-specific knowledge, such as the standardized mastery tests given by state departments of education or college admission tests such as the well-known SATs and ACTs aimed at predicting academic success in college. Critics have pointed out several shortcomings in all of these tests. Concern has been expressed because the tests measure a rather narrow range of abilities, mainly those associated with memory, recall, and abstract reasoning, or because they are confined to a rather narrow band of the curriculum, mainly knowledge and skills associated with literacy and numeracy. Others (Gay, 1997; Oakes & Lipton, 2006) have argued that these tests may have little to do with inherent ability or actual achievement, but instead reflect the social and cultural backgrounds of the test creators and the test takers. In other words, these tests are culturally biased. They favor individuals who come from middle-class families and with European backgrounds. They do not measure abilities and perspectives held by students of working-class families or those who are raised in non-English speaking homes or families that represent African, Asian, or Middle Eastern cultures. Obviously, this situation poses problems if we proclaim to desire an inclusive educational system that is concerned about the success of all students.

> **REFLECTION**
>
> Think about the experiences you have had with standardized tests, as a student or as a teacher. Have these tests been useful; fair? Why; why not? Have you seen any change over time? Compare your experiences and views with a classmate or colleague.

Today, many psychologists and educators have challenged the unitary nature of intelligence and have argued instead for a **multiple intelligences** perspective. Among the best known is Howard Gardner (1983, 1993). He conceived of intelligence as consisting of three abilities:

- the ability to solve problems that one encounters in real life,
- the ability to generate new problems to solve, and
- the ability to make something or offer a service that is valued within one's culture.

In addition, he theorized that intelligence is much more than a single dimension and instead consists of eight different intelligences: *logical mathematical, linguistic/verbal, musical, spatial, bodily-kinesthetic, interpersonal, intrapersonal,* and *naturalistic.* Gardner (1998) also has speculated that learners may possess other abilities or intelligences, such as spiritual intelligence. He contends that all people possess all of these intelligences and that we use them as needed in different situations and contexts of learning. Most important, students possess each of the intelligences to some degree or other and they can be more fully developed through instruction and experience.

Robert Sternberg (1985, 2002) has likewise conceived of intelligence as more than a general or unitary dimension. His **triarchic theory of intelligence** consists of three different cognitive processes or abilities: analytical, creative, and practical. People with **analytical intelligence** like to reason and they have good organizational abilities. They have ability to complete academic, problem-solving tasks and excel in being "book smart", doing well in school exams and assignments. People with **creative intelligence** have the ability to successfully deal with new and unusual situations by drawing on existing knowledge and skills. They use their imagination and enjoy open-ended tasks with many possible answers. People with **practical intelligence** deal well with everyday personal and practical problems. They are "street smart" and have the ability to make adjustments in different situations effectively. They can do things (take things apart and put them together) and have great procedural abilities (Sternberg, 1985).

A non-cognitive ability has also been recognized as another type of intelligence (Goleman, 1995). Goleman (p. 317) defined this type as **emotional intelligence** and wrote that it is the "capacity for recognizing our own feelings and those of others, for motivating ourselves, and for managing emotions well in ourselves and in our relationships." Four major domains are of most importance: two domains that focus on the personal competence—knowing and managing ourselves, such as *self-awareness* and *self-management*; and two domains that focus on knowing and managing relationships—*social awareness* and *relationship management*. Emotional states and abilities, as described previously, have received support from neuroscience as attempts have been made to study the interaction between the cognitive and the emotional in learning situations. Part of our responsibility as teachers is to develop and nurture our students' multiple and emotional intelligences. We will return to these theories and ideas in Chapter 5 on differentiation and describe their instructional implications.

The theories of multiple intelligences have *not* been free from criticism. Klein (2002), for instance, has argued the categories are too broad to be useful. Gardner (1998) has expressed concern about the misuses educators have made of his multiple intelligence theories. Overall, however, the idea that intelligence is more than a unitary ability provides us, as teachers, with a broader lense from which to view the abilities and potential of our students. And, as we will describe later in this chapter and then again in some detail in Chapters 5 and 6, multiple intelligence perspectives provide an important conceptual framework for differentiating instruction, as well as for thinking about the assessment of students' learning.

Learning Styles and Preferences As will be described in the next section, individuals differ in how they perceive the world and in how they process information in their memory systems. We also differ in the ways we approach learning situations. Many models have been proposed that describe differences in learning styles (sometimes referred to as cognitive styles) and **learning preferences**. Here, we provide only highlights of these topics and how they may affect how people learn.

Learning styles refer to the way individuals perceive and process information, and in general styles can vary in a number of ways. Some individuals appear to perceive situations as a whole or they see the big picture. Others tend to perceive the separate parts. These two styles have been labeled **field dependent** and **field independent**. Distinctions have also been made between **in-context learning** and **out-of-context learning**. In-context learning is learning that takes place in the setting where it is needed. For example, learning to cook at home for one's family, or learning to drive a car on a neighborhood street instead of a driving simulator. Out-of-context learning, on the other hand, takes place in settings not connected to real or practical needs to learn. Most school learning is out-of-context learning, a situation that often leaves students from cultures where in-context learning is emphasized confused.

Visual and verbal distinctions among learning styles have also been observed. Mayer and Massa (2003) say that some individuals are visual learners. They have good spatial abilities, tend to think in images and visual information, and prefer instruction that contains pictures and graphic images. Others, however, are verbal learners. They may have poor spatial abilities but high verbal abilities. They think in words and verbal information and prefer instruction that uses words such as verbal explanations or expository text.

Additional learning style models have been developed by Gregorc (1982), Kolb (1984), McCarthy, (1996), and Silver, Strong, and Perini (2000). In general, they describe cognitive and personality dimensions that influence how individuals learn and the type of learning situation or environment they prefer.

A good example is Gregorc's model developed in the 1980s. Gregorc (1982) developed a two-dimensional model that translates into four styles of thinking and learning. The first dimension consists of ways individuals see the world (concrete or abstract), and the second how they order their work (sequential or random). He identified four styles of thinking that stem from the two dimensions: concrete sequential, concrete random, abstract sequential, and abstract random. *Concrete sequential thinkers* like order and details. They require structures, timelines, and organization; they learn from lectures, presentations, and reading. *Concrete random thinkers* (also known as divergent thinkers) like alternative ways of doing things; they enjoy experimentation and creating. They like to make choices about how they learn and how they demonstrate their learning. *Abstract sequential thinkers* love theories and abstract thought; their thinking processes are rational, logical, and intellectual. They like learning through investigation and by analyzing new ideas, concepts, and theory; they need time so the learning makes sense to them. *Abstract random thinkers* live in a world of feelings and emotions; they like to discuss and interact with others. They learn best when they can personalize information, so cooperative learning, centers, stations, and partner work appeal to them.

The *learning preference* model developed by Rita and Kenneth Dunn (1978) is another popular approach. This model describes learners as visual, auditory, tactile, or kinesthetic. **Visual learners** like illustrations, charts, pictures, and diagrams. They need to be able to "see" or "read" information. They construct meaning visually. **Auditory learners** like to learn from lectures, stories, and songs and from participating in discussions. Their sense of hearing and their aural pathways in the brain are strong. *Tactile learners* like hands-on learning such as drawing and writing. They need to be able to touch and manipulate to learn. *Kinesthetic learners* like role playing, simulations, drama, and sports. They need movement, freedom, and to be physically involved in the learning process. The Dunns also highlight other factors (noise, temperature, persistence, responsibility, structures) that teachers need to take into consideration when planning and organizing learning.

We will return to the topic of learning styles and preferences and their instructional implications in Chapter 5. Before we leave the topic here, however, we want to express some concerns about learning styles and preferences. There is a lack of consensus about which of the various styles and preferences are of most importance and many psychologists, such as Stall (2002) and Woolfolk (2005), are skeptical about their overall value. This skepticism exists mainly because research has not supported the claims made by many of the developers. Coffield, Moseley, Hall, & Ecclestone (2004), after careful examination of the Dunn and Dunn and the Gregorc inventories used to assess learning styles, concluded that they were not valid or reliable and "should not be used in education or business" (p. 127, as cited in Woolfork, 2005, p. 126). Stall (2002) went even further and argued that no evidence existed that "assessing children's learning styles and matching to instructional methods has any effect on learning" (p. 99, as cited in Woolfork, 2005). This does not mean, however, that learning styles and preferences should be ignored. Of course, it is important to pay attention and to recognize differences in our students and plan instruction that will accommodate these differences. It is also important for us to teach our students about *how they learn and think* and their preferences for learning environments. We will come back to these topics in the next section and in chapters that follow.

Memory and Information Processing

Developed over the past several decades, there are several variations and models of information processing and of memory, some of them you may already know about. We cannot provide a detailed discussion here about all the variations, but instead will provide brief descriptions from a cognitive perspective of important concepts and processes that help humans gather, process, store, and retrieve different types of knowledge. Figure 2.4 illustrates the basic components and interaction of the information processing model. Each of these components will be described below.

Sensory Memory for Gathering and Processing New Information

New information and knowledge enter our brains from the environment through one of the senses—sight, hearing, touch, smell, and feel into **sensory memory**. In humans, these senses are highly developed and capable of monitoring the environment continuously for input and transforming stimuli into information that makes sense. For our purposes here, learners (students) play an active role as they interact with their environment and make decisions about what to pay attention to, what to learn, and what to remember for later use and transfer. Sometimes the interpretation of sensory stimuli is called **perception** and our initial perceptions are influenced greatly by what we already know. Principles associated with how we acquire and initially process information have important implications for teaching and learning. They help explain why students often do not learn what we teach and bring into focus the need to gain attention and provide multiple stimuli if we are to affect student learning.

Storing Information in Short-term Working Memory

As soon as new information is noted and transformed it is stored temporarily in **short-term working memory**. Some have referred to short-term working memory as the "workbench" of the memory sys-

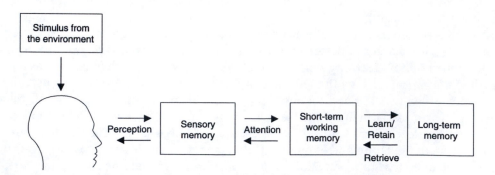

Figure 2.4 Components and interactions of the information processing system
Source: Based on Ashcraft's conceptualization.

tem. It contains what we are thinking about at a particular moment (new information) and also begins to make connections to what we already know (prior knowledge). For instance, if you are solving the problem 25 × 12, mentally you hold the intermediate products of 50 and 25 in short-term working memory and then add them together there.

The capacity of short-term working memory is rather limited and lasts for only a short time. The critical reality of this limited capacity will be explored in more detail later when we describe instructional activities associated with delivering a good lecture or using direct instruction to teach a new skill.

Retaining Information in Long-term Memory Information in short-term working memory will soon be forgotten unless it is integrated and retained in **long-term memory**. Long-term memory is often likened to a computer. Information must be coded before it can be stored and cannot be retrieved unless provided with appropriate cues. Today, it is generally accepted (see Ashcraft, 2006) that information is stored in long-term memory as visual images or as verbal codes or units. This is a feature that we will return to when we explain why it is important to describe ideas and concepts not only with words, but also to illustrate them visually with graphics and pictures. Finally, learners are conscious of some things stored in memory (**explicit memory**) and remain unconscious of others (**implicit memory**). For instance, we are conscious of many of our own experiences and declarative knowledge that we can recall or communicate to others. We are unconscious, however, of many of our emotional reactions and some procedural knowledge and skills that have been learned so thoroughly they have become habits, such as walking, riding a bicycle, or greeting a friend. We have a saying to explain the automaticity of implicit memory, "though I haven't done this for years, I have never forgotten how." (See Ashcraft, 2006.)

Figure 2.5 provides an example that shows how short-term working memory and long-term memory work and interact in an instructional situation.

Organizing Knowledge in the Memory System Knowledge is organized in the memory system in a variety of ways. Theorists in the cognitive sciences (Ashcraft, 2006;

Suppose that a second-grade teacher wants Joe to learn the fact that the capital of Texas is Austin. The teacher asks Joe, "What is the capital of Texas?" and Joe says, "I don't know." At the same time, Joe may set up an expectancy that he is about to learn the capital of Texas, which will cause him to pay attention. The teacher then says, "The capital of Texas is Austin." Joe's ears receive this message along with other sounds, such as the other pupils' speech and traffic outside the school.

All of the sounds that Joe hears are translated . . . and sent to the sensory register. The pattern that the capital of Texas is Austin is selected for entry into short term working memory; other sounds are not entered.

Joe may then code the fact that the capital of Texas is Austin by associating it with the fact that he once visited Austin. This coding process causes the new fact to be entered into long-term memory.

The next day, Joe's teacher asks him, "What is the capital of Texas?" This question is received and selected for entry into short-term memory. There it provides cues for retrieving the answer from long-term memory. A copy of the answer is used by the response generator to organize the speech acts that produce the sounds, "Austin is the capital of Texas."

Figure 2.5 Short-term working and long-term memory
Source: After Gagné et al. (1997), p. 78.

Table 2.2 Types of knowledge and examples of each

Types of knowledge	Definition	Examples
Declarative knowledge	Knowing about something	
Factual	Knowing the basic elements	Rules of a game; definition of germ theory
Conceptual	Knowing relationships among elements	Relationships among germ theory and human illness
Procedural knowledge	Knowing how to do something	Being able to hit a golf ball; view bacteria under a microscope
Conditional knowledge	Knowing when to use particular declarative or procedural knowledge	When to use a microscope; which formula to use for figuring square feet; when to pass

Bransford, Brown & Cocking, 2000; Gagne, Yekovich, & Yekovich, 1997) make distinctions among several types of knowledge. Normally they identify three major categories: declarative knowledge, procedural knowledge, and conditional knowledge. Most of our readers know that **declarative knowledge** is knowledge we have about something. Declarative knowledge can be further divided into factual and conceptual. Factual knowledge consists of the basic elements of something, whereas *conceptual knowledge* is knowing the relationship among the basic elements. **Procedural knowledge**, on the other hand, is knowing how to do something, such as how to view bacteria in a microscope, hit a golf ball, or ride a bicycle. **Conditional knowledge** is knowledge we have about when to apply our declarative or procedural knowledge. Conditional knowledge is closely associated with metacognition, a topic we will discuss later. Table 2.2 summarizes the various types of knowledge and provides examples of each.

Knowing about the types of knowledge is important because, as we will see later, it helps determine the type of teaching strategy for particular lessons.

Schema Theory Information in the form of facts, concepts, and relationships is also stored in memory as propositions, productions, images, and schema. **Propositions** are "units" of declarative knowledge, whereas **productions** are basic units of procedural knowledge. Both are stored and connected in long-term memory through propositional networks. Although some debate exists as to the exact nature of **schema theory** and of *propositional networks*, there is consensus that they exist (see McVee, Dunsmore, & Gavelek, 2005). Images are representations or visual pictures we have of things. For example, we carry around visual images of the people we know and many aspects of our environment. These images are often much stronger than our ability to verbalize them. Take, for instance, the often-cited saying, "I can't remember names, but I never forget a face." The term *schema* is the more abstract and complex knowledge structures that we have. They consist of a vast array of information stored in long-term memory. Ashcraft (2006) and Cooper (1993), as well as many others, have compared a person's schemata (plural for schema) to office filing systems, where information is stored in various files and as new information is acquired the mind creates new files. Over a period of time the whole system grows and expands and becomes what Ashcraft (2006) has called our "stored framework or body of knowledge about some topic" (p. 314). Notice the similarity between this idea and those ideas described earlier in the discussion of brain growth.

Role of Prior Knowledge and Readiness Students, even at very young ages, come to classrooms with unique experiences and have varying readiness to learn particular things. They also hold a variety of conceptions as well as misconceptions about the world and how it works. They also differ widely in the amount of information and understanding they bring to each learning situation. What they know has been labeled **prior knowledge**. Prior knowledge is one of the most important factors in determining what students will learn. For instance, paying attention to particular stimuli while ignoring others is to a large extent influenced by what we already know. Prior knowledge also greatly influences the process of transforming stimuli into information in working memory and for integrating and retaining it in long-term memory. The concept of prior knowledge is illustrated in an interesting fashion in Research Box 2.3.

Inquiry **RESEARCH BOX 2.3**

Lionni, L. (1970). *Fish is fish*. New York: Scholastic Press.

Lionni (1970) describes a fish who is keenly interested in learning about what happens on land, but the fish cannot explore land because it can only breathe in water. It befriends a tadpole who grows into a frog and eventually goes out onto the land. The frog returns to the pond a few weeks later and reports on what he has seen. The frog describes all kinds of things, such as birds, cows, and people. The book (written by the fish) shows pictures of the fish's representations of each of the descriptions: each is a fish-like form that is slightly adapted to accommodate the frog's descriptions—people are imagined to be fish who walk on their tailfins, birds are fish with wings, cows are fish with udders. The tale illustrates both the creative opportunities and dangers inherent in the fact that *people construct new knowledge based on their current knowledge*.

(Adapted from Bransford, Brown & Cocking, 2000, p. 11)

Student readiness to learn is an idea closely related to the concept of prior knowledge. According to Russian psychologist Lev Vygotsky (1978), readiness to learn is governed by a learner's two different levels of development: the level of actual development, and the level of potential development. Level of actual development defines a student's ability to learn something on their own. The level of potential development, on the other hand, defines what an individual can learn with the assistance of another person. The level between the learner's actual level of development and the level of potential development Vygotsky called the **zone of proximal development**, which we have illustrated in Figure 2.6.

The implication of this idea for teaching is quite clear. For some knowledge, the learners' lack of current knowledge makes it impossible to learn more. On the other

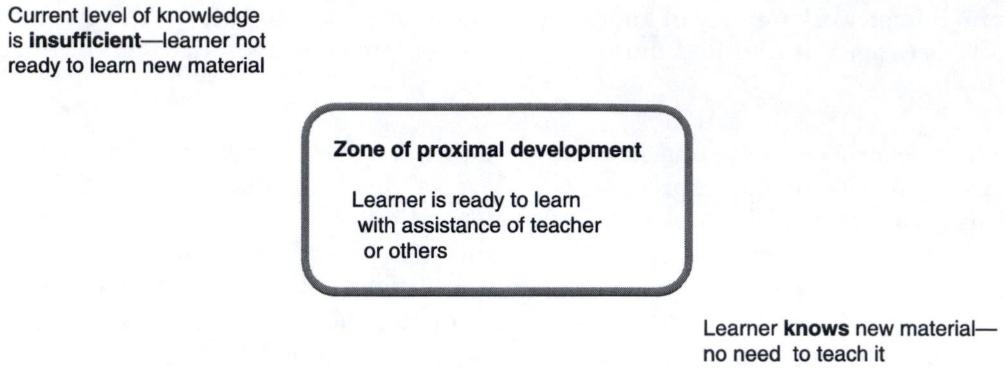

Current level of knowledge
is **insufficient**—learner not
ready to learn new material

Zone of proximal development

Learner is ready to learn
with assistance of teacher
or others

Learner **knows** new material—
no need to teach it

Figure 2.6 Learner readiness and zone of proximal development

hand, teaching what the learner already knows is a waste of valuable instructional time. It is within the zone of proximal development that the learner is ready to learn, particularly when provided assistance by the teacher or other knowledgeable person.

Transfer Some say, and we agree, that the ultimate goal of all learning is **transfer**. This is the ability to take what has been learned in one setting or context, in our instance the classroom, and use it in another setting, such as work or leisure. The principles behind transfer are used to support the need of a well-rounded or liberal college education or for inclusion of more general academic curricula in high schools. We believe that transfer from the more general and abstract can occur and that this is more effective than "training" people for specific jobs or to perform particular tasks.

Transfer, however, does not come easy or automatically. For instance, using such teaching strategies as presentation and direct instruction can help students learn specific skills and help them acquire specific information. For example, we can help students memorize the "law of supply and demand" so they can describe this principle accurately on an essay test. We can get them to discuss the merits of "environmentally friendly" social policies. However, getting students to apply the supply and demand principle when considering policies for dealing with rising gasoline prices or for supporting particular recycling practices in their own lives and communities doesn't happen easily. There are several steps teachers can take to promote transfer that we will describe later in the implications section.

Metacognition A final aspect of the cognitive perspective of learning is metacognition, something that has gained heightened importance as our society's perspectives on knowing have shifted from those valuing information acquisition and memorization to perspectives where abilities to find information, to use it in problem-solving situations, and to *know how to learn* are those most highly prized. **Metacognition** is generally defined as learners' awareness of their own cognitive processes and their abilities to employ particular learning strategies to reach desired learning goals. A number of years ago John Flavell (1985, p. 232) provided one of the initial definitions of metacognition:

[It is] one's knowledge concerning one's own cognitive processes. . . . Meta-cognition refers, among other things, to the active monitoring and consequent regulation and orchestration of these processes in relation to the cognitive objective on which they bear, usually in the service of some concrete goal or objective.

Most theorists and researchers (Brown, 1987; Bruning, Schraw, Norby, & Ronning, 2004; Gagné, Yekovich, & Yekovich, 1997) who study metacognition agree that it also consists of the three types of knowledge discussed in the previous sections: (1) *declarative knowledge* about oneself, about how memory and learning occur, and about various learning strategies that can be employed to realize learning; (2) *procedural knowledge* consisting of having the skills for employing particular learning strategies effectively; and (3) *conditional knowledge* that helps one decide which particular learning strategy to use and why. An example of a student using these three types of knowledge would be when a visually oriented student knows *about* conceptual mapping, *can* make a conceptual map, and knows when to use conceptual maps as a way to understand and remember important information that is going to be on a test.

Ideas about metacognition also help us understand how learners use their knowledge to regulate thinking and to perform cognitive monitoring. **Cognitive monitoring** refers to the learners' abilities to select, use, and monitor the use of particular learning strategies for the purpose of accomplishing the learning task at hand. Again, an example of effective cognitive monitoring would be a student's ability to select and use an appropriate learning strategy (say the link-word strategy) to master a new foreign language word and then to check and assess the effectiveness of using this strategy by asking: "Is this working for me?" "How am I doing?" "Should I use a different strategy?"

REFLECTION

With a colleague or classmate, reflect on your own learning. How aware are you of your own cognitive processes? What about your abilities to employ particular learning strategies? How have your awareness and abilities changed over time?

Often the difference between highly successful learners and those who are having trouble in school is their understandings of metacognition and their skills for employing particular learning strategies. Much is known about how to teach students to predict their own performance, to monitor progress toward understanding or skill acquisition, and to take responsibility for and control of their own learning.

Instructional Implications of Cognitive Views of Learning
As with the neurosciences, theory and research from the cognitive sciences have important implications for teaching in several areas: teaching with multiple intelligence perspectives in mind, recognizing the importance of prior knowledge, knowing how to gain students' attention and teach for transfer, and having strategies to help students become efficient in their own learning. Each of these is discussed below.

Use Multiple Intelligences We will provide a more detailed discussion of the theory of multiple intelligences and its implications in Chapter 5 on instructional differentiation. Here, however, we want to highlight briefly the instructional implications and use of this theory. We recommend the following:

- Use the multiple intelligences lens to think about students' abilities. It provides a wider and more accurate picture than does the unitary view.
- Plan lessons and strategies with multiple goals and objectives and beyond those associated with the logical-mathematic and linguistic.
- Expose students to a range of materials designed to stimulate various types of intelligence.
- Provide students with activities that develop skills associated with each type of intelligence.
- Personalize and differentiate instruction.

Attend to Prior Knowledge and Readiness The fact that student readiness to learn and what they already know are the most important factors in what they learn has enormous implications for teaching and classroom practices. These include:

- Recognize that the learners' prior knowledge will vary widely and this variation increases as students proceed through the grades.
- Develop formal and informal ways to assess students' knowledge and skills. Strive to determine their zones of proximal development. We will provide rather detailed ways to do this in Chapter 5.
- Take time to remind students what they already know.
- Begin every lesson with actions that activate prior knowledge. Make appropriate use of advance organizers, personal anecdotes, analogies, metaphors, stories that relate to students' lives, and outlines or graphics that visually illustrate how new information will relate to what students already know.
- Have a wide range of print and visual materials designed for a broad spectrum of prior knowledge.

Attend to Attention Focusing and attending to particular stimuli are critical for learning to occur and, as all experienced teachers know, gaining students' attention is among the first tasks of any lesson. Students cannot integrate and store information they have not attended to or perceived. Gaining **attention** to particular stimuli or messages is difficult because, as teachers, we face stiff competition from many forces in today's information-rich environments. Further, extended attention is limited. Teachers use a variety of strategies to get their students' attention, a few of which are summarized below:

- Make sure students understand the purposes of a particular lesson by giving them brief, clear overviews and providing them with reasons why the lesson is important.
- Arouse student curiosity with humor and the dramatic.
- Make creative use of voice, movement, and gesture.
- Use strategies that require students to use a variety of senses. For example, give a lesson that requires the use of taste and smell.

Teach for Transfer Transfer can be facilitated by numerous actions taken by teachers aimed at helping students process and store information in long-term memory.

Bransford et al. (2000) have described four characteristics and conditions for learning that promote transfer; these are paraphrased below.

- Strive for mastery of **initial learning**. Topics that are covered lightly or skills only partially mastered are unlikely to be transferred or used in new situations or in different settings. We are sure that you can think of many instances where this has happened in your own learning.
- Know the effects of *context* on transfer. Knowledge that is overly contextualized can reduce transfer, whereas abstract representations of knowledge can help promote transfer. Transfer is also more successful when students are asked to solve specific cases and then provided with additional similar cases. It also helps to ask students to provide solutions that apply to multiple problems.
- View transfer as an *active process* rather than a passive end product of a particular set of learning experiences.
- Remember new learning involves transfer based on *previous learning or prior knowledge*, a fact that has important implications for the design of instruction (summarized from Bransford et al., 2000, pp. 53–77).

Teach Students How to Learn Providing students with metacognitive skills helps them become aware of their own cognitive processes so they can monitor their progress and take responsibility for their own learning. Here is a brief list of strategies teachers can use for this purpose (many more follow in later chapters):

- At all levels and in a variety of types of lesson, include direct instruction to help students learn metacognitive skills, particularly those that help them predict their performance and monitor progress.
- Use and model learning strategies to provide practice opportunities, and help students consider when to use particular strategies.
- Emphasize the importance of *learning how to learn* and admonish and motivate students to take responsibility for their own learning.

Table 2.3 summarizes instructional implications of cognitive view of learning.

Table 2.3 Summary of findings from cognitive science and their implications for teaching

Findings from cognitive psychology	Implications for teaching
Multiple intelligence. Instead of a single dimension, learners have been found to have multiple abilities and intelligences.	• Recognize wide variation among students in regard to their abilities in several domains. • Plan lessons and strategies that help develop and use learners' multiple intelligences.
Prior knowledge and readiness. The most important element in what learners learn is what they already know. Prior knowledge of learners varies widely and this variation increases as students proceed through the grades.	• Develop formal and informal ways to assess and recognize students' prior knowledge. • Plan and execute every lesson so students' prior knowledge is activated • Have a wide range of print and visual materials available for student use.

Continued overleaf

Table 2.3 *Continued*

Findings from cognitive psychology	Implications for teaching
Attention. Learning begins when learners gather information from their environments and then store it for later recall and use. Learners play an active role in what they attend to, what they learn initially, and what they remember.	• Make the purpose and rationale of all lessons clear. • Gain students' attention at the beginning of every lesson by arousing curiosity, stimulating multiple senses, and making active use of the dramatic.
Transfer. Transfer is the ultimate goal of education and is affected by the ways students are helped to process and store new learning materials.	• Work for transfer by making sure initial learning is mastered. • Provide opportunities to see situation or problem in a variety of settings or contexts. • View transfer as an active process rather than a passive end product.
Metacognition. Metacognitive skills make students aware of their cognitive processes, and help them regulate and monitor their learning.	• At all levels and in every lesson, integrate strategies that help students learn metacognitive strategies. • Provide ample opportunities to practice strategies and to consider their appropriate use. • Encourage and motivate students to learn how to learn, take control, and be responsible for their own learning

SUMMARY AT A GLANCE

• The evolution of thought and the science of learning have changed our understanding about how students learn and about how we should teach in fundamental ways.

• Biological perspectives, based on theory and research in the neurosciences, provide new insights about the brain and its functions. This theory and research, although sometimes overstated, has important implications for classroom practice in such areas as how the brain grows and filters stimuli from the environment, how it stores knowledge and makes meaning, and the important role emotions and feelings play in cognitive learning.

• Discoveries in cognitive psychology provide important understandings about how learning occurs in classrooms. We have a pretty firm grasp on how the memory and information processing systems work to gather, interpret, store, and retain information.

• Together, biological and cognitive perspectives help us understand the importance of multiple intelligences, learning styles, readiness and prior knowledge, and metacognition. These perspectives highlight the importance of paying attention to attention, teaching for transfer, and helping student learn how to learn.

CONSTRUCTING YOUR OWN LEARNING

Working alone or with colleagues or classmates, describe two or three students in your class(es) who believe that memorization of what you say, as the teacher, and what they read in their textbooks is what learning is all about. Do brief biographies of them—include their expectations of education, why they think memorization is so important, and so on. Using information from this chapter, develop a set of strategies that could help students expand their views of learning and that might motivate them to take responsibility for learning beyond rote memory. Consider how you might use their current attitudes and prior knowledge to help them.

RESOURCES

Bransford, J., Brown, A., & Cocking, R. (2000). *How people learn: Brain, mind, experience, and school.* Washington, DC: National Academy Press.

Bruning, R., Schraw, G., Norby, M., & Ronning, R. (2004). *Cognitive psychology and instruction* (4th ed.). Columbus, OH: Merrill.

Pressley, M., & Woloshyn, V. (1999). *Cognitive strategy instruction that really improves children's academic performance* (2nd ed.). Cambridge, MA: Brookline Books.

Willis, J. (2006). *Research-based strategies that ignite student learning.* Alexandria, VA: Association for Supervision and Curriculum Development.

3

MOTIVATION AND STUDENT LEARNING

INTRODUCTION AND PERSPECTIVE

Many people are concerned about why some students are fully engaged and acquire the goals deemed important in schools while others remain unmotivated and uninvolved. These are important concerns and several explanations exist regarding the lack of **motivation** on the part of children and youth. Some believe the problem rests with students. They are *not* interested in what schools teach, and they are unwilling to expend very much effort. Others place the blame squarely on schools and teachers. The curriculum is out-of-date and irrelevant; school structures keep students in passive roles; and teachers' methods remain rigid and non-interactive. Still others see the problem as the result of contemporary society and our values. There is a lack of commitment by adults to children. Youth spend too much time watching TV, playing computer games, and idolizing celebrities who model anti-intellectual attitudes and values.

There is no one more concerned about the lack of student motivation than those of us who are classroom teachers. In many elementary schools and in secondary classrooms, observers find students who aren't listening, who aren't participating in group activities, and who fail to complete their homework assignments. All of this leads to the common teacher lament: "They could do it, if only they would try." As experienced teachers we know that if we do not motivate our students, then the rest of teaching can be given away. Motivating students, however, is no easy task, and acquiring and sustaining high levels of student engagement remains one of teaching's most important challenges. To consider this complexity, reflect on the examples of the unmotivated learners described below and consider what you might do to move them to a higher level of engagement:

- *Gifted Gina.* Gina has been identified as gifted and talented, but she shows little interest in her schoolwork. She spends much of her classroom time with her head down; she turns in less than half of her homework. Over the years teachers have admonished Gina, telling her that she is smart, that she can do better, and that she should work harder. None of these admonitions has resulted in much change.
- *Athletic Alan.* Alan is very athletic and excels in several sports. He is also smart. However, he is a source of frustration to his teachers and his coaches. His teachers are frustrated because he doesn't pay attention in class, extends little effort when involved in group activities, doesn't complete homework, and never studies for tests. His teachers get disgusted with him because he is not living up to

his academic potential; his coaches worry because his low grades threaten his eligibility.

- *Withdrawn Wilma.* Wilma is a fairly bright student. However, she is withdrawn. She has a low opinion of herself and doesn't seem to care about anything. She seldom participates in activities, acts shy during classroom discussions, and resists group work altogether. Her teachers have observed that she often completes her homework but seldom turns it in.
- *Careful Carrie.* Carrie does fairly good work. However she is overly concerned about not doing everything perfectly and works only for external rewards. If it is not going to be graded or on the test, she ignores it. If she perceives a learning task to be one that she might not get the highest grade, and if she has a choice, she will choose one that she perceives to be less challenging.
- *Entrepreneurial Ed.* Ed is a bright young man who has no time for school or schoolwork. Since the age of 12, he has held a variety of jobs and has been involved in numerous money-making schemes. His goal is to be a millionaire by the age of 30. Ed does not believe attending school or doing homework will help him meet this goal. He skips classes regularly and never turns in assignments. He is smart enough to do quite well on most tests, so he maintains a minimal, but passing, grade point average. Efforts by teachers to get him to pay more attention to his school work fall on deaf ears.
- *Penny Pawn.* Penny is an attractive student with slightly above average abilities. However, she has little confidence in herself, and she doesn't believe that she has much influence over what she does or what she accomplishes. She has a sense of obligation to do what her teachers want her to do, but she seldom tackles challenging tasks on her own. Her favorite excuse is, "this is too hard."

You recognize these students. You have had them in your class, and you know that each of them presents unique challenges that require special interventions. In this chapter we will address the meaning of student motivation and how it is closely connected to student learning. We begin with brief descriptions of three major theories of motivation: **reinforcement theory, needs disposition theory**, and perspectives about motivation stemming from **cognitive theory**. This will be followed by descriptions of an array of motivational strategies that stem from these theories and that can be used in classrooms and schools. The chapter concludes with some final thoughts about how schools may change in the future and how these changes may bring about more student engagement and learning. For now, however, teachers seem to be the front line of defense against student apathy.

THEORIES OF MOTIVATION

What is it that energizes our behavior? Why did you choose to get out of bed this morning? Go to school? Go to work or go shopping? Why are you reading this chapter on motivation? Why are you reading it now rather than later? What activities will engage you next? More broadly stated, "Why do we do what we do?" The answer to all of these questions has to do with human motivation and what causes individuals to take action. Pintrich (2003) has observed that the word "motivation" itself comes from a Latin verb *movere*, referring to "what gets an individual moving." Several theories have been developed to explain why people behave the way they do and why students expend effort in school. It is beyond the scope of this chapter to describe in detail all that is known about human motivation. Instead, we will strive to provide a brief overview of three major theories that are most applicable to teaching and learning and from which effective motivational strategies have been developed.

Reinforcement Theory

Most psychologists make distinctions between internal factors such as needs and curiosity that propel individuals to act and external factors such as rewards or punishments. Behavior sparked by one's own interests or pure enjoyment is called **intrinsic motivation**. In contrast, **extrinsic motivation** is at play when individuals take action to capture a desired **reward** or to avoid **punishments** or social embarrassment. You can think of examples of intrinsic and extrinsic motivation in your own life. When you read a textbook so you can get an "A" on a test, you are being motivated by an external reward. However, when you read and reread a poem because you love the poet's use of words to describe a lovely scene, you are being influenced by internal factors.

Behavioral perspectives, particularly reinforcement theory, rest mainly on extrinsic motivation and have had significant influence on how we approach human behavior in all aspects of life and definitely how, traditionally, we thought about student motivation and learning in schools. You remember from Chapter 2 that reinforcement theory rests on the centrality of external events for directing behavior and the importance of positive and negative reinforcers to get individuals to behave in desired ways. **Positive reinforcers**, normally in the form of rewards, are intended to get individuals to repeat desired behaviors. **Negative reinforers**, on the other hand, are used to cause individuals to avoid certain behaviors. Many practices to get people to behave in desirable ways in adult life stem from reinforcement theory. We give rewards in the form of medals for acts of good citizenship or bravery. We punish drivers who break traffic rules with hefty fines. Sales persons work for fees and commissions. Workers in general expect high levels of performance to be rewarded with raises and bonuses; they expect poor performance to result in demotions or layoffs.

Historically, educators have embraced reinforcement theory. Practices stemming from this perspective about motivation still dominate many aspects of teaching, sometimes by design, sometimes as a result of unconsciously sticking to traditional ways of doing things. For example, we use praise, good grades, gold stars, and privileges as incentives to get students to develop desirable habits and to engage in desired

> **REFLECTION**
>
> Consider for a moment what motivates you. Do you respond mostly to extrinsic factors or are you motivated by internal goals? How does this influence the way you motivate your students? Compare your thoughts and patterns about motivation with a classmate or colleague.

academic and social behaviors. Low grades, reprimands, and various forms of punishment are used to discourage undesirable student behaviors. Classroom management programs, such as the "assertive discipline," use behavioral principles to get students to behave in appropriate ways. "Direct instruction" and "scripted reading programs" likewise aim at getting students to learn basic skills and processes by applying reinforcement principles. However, as we will describe later in the chapter, many of these practices are currently disputed. Some reform educators (Kohn, 1995, 1996; Noddings, 2001, 2006; Oakes & Lipton, 2006) believe that practices based on reinforcement theory do not enhance student motivation and learning, but instead produce the opposite effects and lead to conformity and compliance. We will return to this assertion in more detail later in the chapter and provide a perspective that encourages a balanced use of extrinsic and intrinsic motivational strategies.

Needs Theory

Needs, or *needs disposition,* theory is a second perspective about motivation that has important implications for education and for teaching practices. There are several variations of needs theory; however, the major premise behind each variation is that humans are roused to take action to satisfy innate physical and psychological needs or intrinsic desires. The classic statement of needs theory, and one many of our readers are familiar with, stems from the work of Abraham Maslow, who, in the middle of the twentieth century, posited that humans have a hierarchy of needs ranging from those at lower levels, such as physiological needs for food, shelter, and safety, to those at higher levels, such as needs for belonging, love, knowing, and self-actualization. Maslow's hierarchy of needs is illustrated in Figure 3.1.

According to Maslow (1970) needs drive behavior, and only when needs at the lower levels are satisfied will individuals be motivated to satisfy higher-level needs. The classroom implications of Maslow's work are quite obvious and have influenced educational practices for some time. For example, we provide breakfast and hot lunches to help students satisfy needs for food and nourishment. Similarly, we strive to establish safe environments so students' needs for security are met. We take these actions because we

Figure 3.1 Maslow's hierarchy of needs

believe that children who are hungry or feel threatened are unlikely to pursue higher-level needs for knowing and understanding and for appreciating aesthetics.

Educators and psychologists, such as McClelland (1958), Atkinson and Feather (1966), and Alschuler, Tabor, and McIntyre (1970), took Maslow's more general ideas about human needs and applied them directly to needs most relevant to teaching and in-school learning. For our purposes, we will consolidate their work by asserting that students are motivated to invest energy in schools and to take action in the pursuit of three outcomes: achievement, affiliation, and influence. The desire for *achievement* is satisfied when students strive to learn particular subjects or acquire difficult skills and are successful in their quest. **Affiliation needs** are satisfied when students gain friendship and emotional support from their teachers and peers. **Influence needs** are accomplished when students believe they have some say and control over their learning and are provided a degree of choice and **self-determination**. When teachers plan lessons that allow achievement, affiliative, and influence needs to be satisfied, students will exert an incredible amount of effort. On the other hand, when classroom or school practices frustrate these needs, students escape to other activities. Achievement motivation, sometimes called "intent to learn," is the most important aspect of needs theory, and, as we will describe later, the one that has been the most carefully studied and that has very important implication for teaching (see Wigfield & Eccles, 2002).

Another set of ideas associated with needs theory stems from the work of deCharms (1976), Deci and Ryan (1985), and Csikszentmihalyi (1990, 1998). In general, these theorists believe that individuals take action to satisfy needs for choice and self-determination and that these internal pressures are more important than the influence of external events. You will note the similarities between the needs for choice and self-determination and the previously described need for influence. DeCharms (1976) used the concept of pawns and origins in his research and analysis. **Pawns**, like Penny and Wilma in our opening student profiles, are individuals who believe they have little influence or control over what happens in their lives, whereas **origins** believe they are in charge of their behavior. DeCharms believed that over-emphasis on extrinsic rewards and external pressures by teachers lead students to feel like pawns and this in turn dampens their motivation to learn. On the other hand, teachers can take steps to play down external rewards and encourage students to see that they can be origins in life and in learning.

Csikszentmilhalyi (1990) viewed the need for choice and self-determination somewhat differently. For several years he studied the events in people's lives when they reported to be totally involved, times when "it felt like being carried away by a current, like being in a flow" (p. 127). Csikszentmihalyi labeled these times "**flow experiences**," and he maintained that they occur as a result of individuals having choice to pursue their own goals and to gain satisfaction from intrinsic needs. Again, ideas associated with these theories have important implications for schools, classrooms, and teaching practices. Csikszentmilhalyi has expressed particular concern about the way many classrooms and schools are structured, and that the extensive use of external rules and rewards deters teachers from setting up learning experiences that allow students to experience flow.

Cognitive Perspectives

Cognitive theorists provide a third perspective about motivation. Similar to need theorists, cognitive theorists believe that involvement and engagement in classrooms result not from external pressures but instead from the cognitive beliefs and interpretations students hold about learning activities and events. Perhaps the most fully developed cognitive theory is Bernard Weiner's **attribution theory** (1986, 1992). This theory is based on the premise that individuals come to perceive the causes of their success and failure in different ways. According to Weiner, students can attribute their successes and failures to four causes: ability, effort, luck, and difficulty of the learning task. These attributions can also be classified as either internal or external. **Internal attributions** occur when individuals attribute successes and failures to themselves (ability and effort); **external attributions** occur when they blame external causes or circumstances (luck or difficulty).

Cognitive theorists also have examined the *expectations* students hold for success in learning tasks and how much they value the rewards associated with task accomplishment. Feather (1969), Pintrich and DeGroot (1990), and Tollefson (2000), for example, have theorized that students will expend effort: (1) if they have an expectation they can perform a particular learning task successfully; and (2) if they place fairly high *value* on the rewards associated with completing the task. Students who do not value rewards associated with particular tasks or who believe they cannot be successful—i.e., **expectancy of failure**—will expend little effort. Our profile student, Entrepreneurial Ed, is an example of a student who is not motivated because he does not value particular learning tasks and their associated rewards. Experienced teachers can all report many examples of students who do sloppy homework and then simply "shrug off" an assigned failing grade.

Bandura's (1977, 1986) **social learning theory** can also be viewed as a cognitive perspective of motivation and one that is very similar to the **expectancy of success** described above. Bandura's research led him to believe that students make personal interpretations about past accomplishments and failures and then set goals based on these interpretations. Students tend to avoid learning tasks they believe they will fail at, while selecting tasks for which success seems probable. Bandura also believed that individuals set goals that will bring internal satisfaction when attained and that this internal satisfaction affects effort more than external rewards such as gold stars or grades. Bandura labeled students' beliefs about their abilities their **self-efficacy**. Beliefs about efficacy to accomplish learning tasks develop as a result of success or lack of success in school. If students expend considerable effort and do not experience success, they will modify their expectations for their own performance and begin expending less effort. On the other hand, success enhances self-efficacy, leads to higher levels of effort, and results in more success. As we will see later, there are several strategies teachers can employ to help change students' beliefs about their abilities and about their chances for success.

Another perspective about student self-efficacy is what some have labeled **agency** (Bandura, 1996; Bruner, 1986; Johnston, 2004). The essence of this idea is that students with agency believe that they can successfully accomplish their goals and that the environment, in our case the classroom and school, is responsive to their actions. On the other hand, students lacking agency believe that there is not a relationship between what they do and what happens to them. Subsequently, they set low goals and become depressed and helpless. Those who have studied and written about agency, such as Johnston (2004), believe the language teachers use and their interactions with students are important elements in developing a sense of agency in students, a topic we will come back to in the next section on strategies for increasing student motivation.[1]

<table>
<tr><td>

REFLECTION

From your own experiences, how valid are the cognitive theories of motivation? Do they accurately describe what motivates students in your classroom? What about your own motivation? You may want to compare your views with those of a classmate or colleague.

</td></tr>
</table>

Finally, the type of goals set by teachers for students or by students themselves has important effects on motivation. Goals interact with students' self-efficacy and the amount of effort they are willing to exert on learning tasks. Goals for our purposes here can be classified into two types: learning goals and performance goals (Dweck, 1986, 2002; Tollefson, 2000). **Learning goals** (sometimes called mastery goals) are set to focus on improvement. Individuals strive to learn and improve their abilities regardless of how their overall performance may measure up in comparison to others or to some absolute standard. An example of a learning goal would be when a physically challenged student who can run a mile in 12 minutes sets a goal for herself to run it in ten minutes, knowing full well that many people have performed the same run in less than four minutes.

Performance goals, on the other hand, focus on comparing one's abilities with those of others or to some predetermined standard, e.g., having the highest class GPA or meeting all the state standards in mathematics. Often individuals who set performance goals believe that external rewards, such as grades or "looking good," are more important then the learning itself. An over-reliance on performance goals is often detrimental to learning, and students with learning goals, as contrasted to performance goals, can be expected to expend more effort to attain them (Pintrich & Schunk, 2002). It is important to point out, however, that some use of performance goals most certainly is desirable, particularly if used in tandem with learning goals, a topic we will return to in later sections. Table 3.1 summarizes the three theories of motivation and shows the implication of each for teaching and learning.

INCREASING STUDENT MOTIVATION

At the beginning of this chapter, we made the assertion that lack of student engagement in schools constitutes a major contemporary problem. We also wrote that student disengagement has been attributed to three major factors: the characteristics students bring with them to school, the schools' inability to offer meaningful curriculum and learning experiences, and larger societal values. We take the position that lack of student engagement can be partially attributed to all of these factors. Our readers, however, will find that we offer no "silver bullets" or "tried-and-true recipes" that will guarantee success. Instead, motivating students, like many other aspects of teaching, requires doing lots of little things well and choosing wisely from a repertoire of practices known to support rather than undermine motivation.

The practices we describe stem from both cognitive and behavioral theories, because in real life we choose to take action for both intrinsic and extrinsic reasons. When

Table 3.1 Theories of motivation and their educational implications

Theories of motivation	Educational implications
Reinforcement theory: Individuals are motivated to take action and behave in certain ways in order to obtain valued rewards or to escape negative sanctions and punishments.	Many traditional school and classroom practices stem from reinforcement theory. Some of these can enhance student motivation. However, others tend to suppress rather than support student engagement and learning.
Needs theory: Individuals are motivated to take action because of their desire to satisfy a variety of needs. The most basic of these needs are for food and safety. Others stem from needs for understanding, to experience friendship, and to have control and choice over environments and events.	It is important for schools to have conditions where students satisfy basic needs for food and safety if these are missing in their lives. It is also important for teachers to teach in ways that help students satisfy needs such as self-fulfilment, self-determination, to have influence, and to experience achievement and affiliation.
Cognitive theories: Motivation for action results from an individual's beliefs and the way they interpret the events around them, particularly attributions about success and failure. Students' actions are also influenced by the way they value particular types of goal and their expectations for success in accomplishing them.	Teachers in classrooms can work toward helping students attribute their successes and failures to internal causes (ability and effort) rather than external causes and circumstances (luck and difficulty). It is important in classrooms for teachers to provide learning experiences that challenge students, that they value, and for which they have a high probability of success. They can also help students focus on learning goals rather than performance goals.

internal factors fail, external ones may kick in and vice versa. We study hard because we want good grades and gold stars, but we also do it because it gives us satisfaction. We may choose a career that requires working with others because it will help satisfy our need for affiliation, but we are also pleased when it provides us with external rewards such as a paycheck and a month-long vacation. In the sections that follow, we organize our recommended motivational strategies into two major categories: (1) helping students change their attitudes and perceptions about learning, and (2) modifying classroom procedures and teaching methods.

Changing Attitudes and Perceptions about Learning

Ultimately, learners control motivation. Each individual decides as the day unfolds to engage or disengage in activities based on interest, relevancy, difficulty, energy, choice, and consequences. Helping students to understand motivation and to make good choices is key to empowering them in the classroom. We offer several strategies that can influence students' attitudes and perceptions and their motivation for learning.

Focus on Alterable Factors There are many things students bring with them to school that teachers can do little about. For example, there is not much teachers can do (except to understand them) to alter factors such as students' home lives, some aspects of their personality, or their early childhood experiences. It is true that these factors have shaped students' lives and will have some influence on how much energy they will expend on their schoolwork. However, there is not much teachers can do to change these factors in significant ways. Instead, teachers can be more effective if they concentrate on **alterable factors**. For instance, teachers can alter their own attitudes about children who come from different backgrounds and develop understandings about how these students view school and learning through their own cultural lens. As teachers, we can adopt beliefs that all students have capabilities and that *each can learn*. We can also learn to recognize neglected strengths in students and help students set realistic learning goals based on these strengths. Perhaps most important, teachers can help alter the way students interpret their successes and failures and the expectations and goals they hold for themselves.

Alter Views about Success and Failure It is likely that most students enter school for the first time holding some beliefs about success and failure. They also prefer certain activities over others, and they place value on rewards (internal and external) associated with accomplishing particular tasks. Some, at a rather young age, expect to do well; others do not. We described earlier how some students attribute their successes and failures to internal factors such as effort, whereas others attribute them to luck or external circumstances. However, these views are not necessarily fixed, and they can be altered. Butler (1989) and Tollefson (2000), for instance, have found that most very young children attribute success to effort rather than ability. However, by the age of seven or eight, and later in middle school, they start understanding normative comparisons and how effort interacts with ability. Teachers can strive to understand the views their students have about their successes and failures, analyze their own interactions with these students, and employ a variety of specific interventions to change these views, such as:

- Make direct statements about a student's work. Stress the importance of effort to success. Attribute failure or poor work to low effort; attribute success to high effort.
- Explain to students that different levels of ability may require different levels of effort. However, resist the general admonition, "if only you would try harder. . . ."
- Evaluate student work in ways that demonstrate relationships between success and effort or failure and lack of effort.
- Plan lessons and structure classrooms to maximize task involvement.
- Design and assign learning tasks with high value, e.g., for which successful completion will bring desired internal and external rewards. Remember these rewards will vary from student to student.
- Do not excuse failure and do not respond to poor work with pity, sympathetic feedback, or false praise such as "good try." These actions can have unintended consequences, e.g., students and peers view the receiver as lacking in ability.

Use Language to Develop Self-efficacy and Agency Johnston (2004) has written that we can maximize children's agency (and self-efficacy) by developing their belief that they can affect their environment and that they have "what it takes" to affect it. Language, according to Johnston, plays a significant role in this development. Below are some examples of the type of teacher comments that can influence a sense of agency in literacy instruction (ibid., p. 31):

- How did you figure that out?
- What problem did you come across today?
- How are you planning to go about this?
- Where are you going with this piece of writing?
- Which part are you sure about and which parts are you not sure about?
- Why would an author do something like that?

Notice how all these comments encourage students to figure things out for themselves, which in turn develops a sense of agency and well-being.

Pay Attention to Goals and Goal Orientations Just as students hold beliefs about why they fail or succeed, so too do they have views about their goals and goal orientations. As described earlier, some students have performance goal orientations; they strive to reach performance standards, often set by others, or they try to better their own performance as compared to the performance of others. There is nothing wrong with performance goals. We want students to work towards excellence and to excel. However, there is a downside to putting too much emphasis on performance-oriented goals. This situation can lead to excessive competition and a reliance on evaluations by others—praise from peers or grades from teachers. Other students hold learning goal orientations; these students compete with themselves and are motivated by internal factors such as the satisfaction of learning something new. According to Tollefson (2000), goal orientation interacts with students' attributions of success and failure. She writes, "Students with performance goals are most likely to interpret failure as a sign of low ability and (in turn) withdraw effort. Students with learning goals see failure as a cue to change their strategy for completing a task and to increase their effort" (p. 70).

The level of difficulty and challenge are other aspects of students' goal orientations. Setting goals that are impossible to achieve will lead to frustration and withdrawal. On the other end of the continuum, boredom and apathy result if goals are set too low. Students are more likely to become engaged and to persevere longer when pursuing goals that are challenging yet realistic and achievable. Teachers who are effective motivators help students adjust the level of difficulty of their learning goals to match their abilities. We will return to this topic in Chapter 5 on instructional differentiation.

Two final features of students' goal orientations need to be considered: **goal clarity** and the *length of time* it takes to achieve a goal (see Tollefson, 2000). When students set their own goals they need to be taught the importance of specificity. For example, a goal such as "learning about civil wars," although laudable, is not as measurable as "learning the causes of the civil war in Palestine." How far in the future a goal can be completed is also important. Students are likely to persist in the pursuit of a goal if it can be accomplished in the near term as compared to goals that will be realized only in the far distant future. This often requires breaking long-term goals into proximal goals that can be accomplished in the short term. Writing a term paper is an example of a goal that is rather long term. However, a series of short-term goals such as collecting relevant resources, specifying major sections of the report, and writing one section of the report at a time are shorter in duration and help motivate the writer to remain engaged. We know this to be true in our own motivation to keep working on this book. Books, like many other writing tasks, are written page-by-page and chapter-by-chapter. Below are some specific actions teachers can take to help alter the goals and goal orientations of their students.

- Teach students the difference between performance and learning goals and encourage them to set learning goals where they compete with themselves rather than others.
- Resist focusing too heavily on performance goals, because this type of goal can undermine learning for intrinsic purposes. At the same time, encourage students to reach for high standards.
- Focus evaluation on "improvement," not just performance.
- Help students set goals that have an appropriate level of specificity and difficulty.
- Help students set "short-term" or proximal goals that can be accomplished in the near future.

Modifying Classrooms and Teaching Practices

Many educational reformers, Kuhn (2007a) and Ritchhart (2002) for example, believe that we focus on the "wrong side of education" and devote too much attention to student characteristics and what they bring to school (as we did in the previous section) to explain their lack of motivation. They argue that, instead of attempting to blame or change students, we should focus on the ways we have structured schools and classrooms and the ways we teach. According to Ritchhart (p. 10):

The root of the problem is that we are teaching the wrong thing. We don't have our sights set on providing students with an education that develops their intelligence. We've misplaced precisely the kind of ideal that can *lead* and *motivate* us.

Traditional structures, such as the curriculum fragmentation found in most secondary schools and the age-graded classroom that still dominates elementary education, prohibit the flexibility for differentiating instruction and for using practices that can make learning relevant and meaningful to students. Similarly, the "standards movement" we described in Chapter 1 may be working at cross-purposes with efforts to develop self-efficacy and learning goal orientations in students and to implement curriculum designed around students' interests and intrinsic values. Tollefson (2000, p. 80) has described the current situation accurately:

Teachers whose students fail to achieve standards are placed in the position of attributing student failure to variables over which they have no control (e.g., student ability, . . . nonsupportive families, school district policies that are difficult to alter, and/or lack of community support) in order not to attribute student failure to inadequate teaching skills. If failure to achieve standards is attributed to stable, external factors, there is little motivation for teachers to change their teaching strategies or to expend additional effort in working individually with students.

However, she offers hope as she goes on to write (ibid.):

If standards can reflect improvement and if building administrators recognize teachers' efforts to implement interactive, individualized teaching strategies, teachers may adopt teaching strategies that increase the likelihood of improved student [motivation and] achievement.

In Chapter 15 we describe a variety of actions teachers can take collectively to change their schools. Here, however, we will focus on specific classroom practices that can increase student motivation and that can also be put into practice almost immediately.

Balance the Use of Extrinsic and Intrinsic Rewards The use of extrinsic rewards is widespread in our society, and many economic and commonsense ideas about human behavior rest on reinforcement principles. In schools there has been a long tradition of using extrinsic rewards (positive reinforcers) such as praise, grades, and recognition to get desired behavior and of using negative reinforcers (such as extra homework, detention or other forms of punishment) to deter undesirable behavior. As we were writing this chapter, New York City decided to offer cash rewards to students in the fourth and seventh grades who have good attendance records and who do well on standardized achievement tests. Washington DC has proposed a similar program. It is reported (Schwartz, 2007, p. 1) that "high achieving seventh graders will be able to earn up to $500 in a year."

On the surface reinforcement theory seems to make sense; it is rather straightforward and intuitive. It conforms to our beliefs that people work for external incentives and that the more incentives, the better. However, accomplished teachers know that there are unintended and negative consequences associated with a heavy reliance on external motivators. John Dewey warned of this situation a long time ago. He wrote that all too often schools:

> put a premium on physical quietude, on silence, on rigid uniformity of posture and movement; upon a machine-like simulation of the attitudes of intelligent interest. The teachers' business is to hold the pupils up to these requirements and to punish the inevitable deviation that occurs.
>
> (Dewey, cited in Kohn, 1996, p. 7)

There is also a substantial body of research that shows that extrinsic incentives can sometimes compete with intrinsic incentives and produce negative consequences. Schwartz (2007), for example, described a study where nursery school children were asked to draw with special markers. Later, some of them were given "good player" awards while others were given nothing. Researchers observed the children over time and discovered that students given the awards were "less likely to draw at all, and drew worse pictures, than those who were not given awards" (p. 1). The conclusion reached from this study was that "children draw because drawing is fun . . . it leads to a result: a picture. The rewards of drawing are intrinsic to the activity itself. The 'good player' award gives children another reason to draw: to earn a reward . . . *this recognition undermines the fun . . .*" (ibid.). It appears that providing extrinsic rewards for learning tasks that are already intrinsically interesting can actually decrease motivation. An obvious question to ponder, however, is why so many students fail to get intrinsic satisfaction from the activities offered by their schools.

It is likely that the use of external rewards in schools will continue, at least in the near future. Spaulding (1992), however, provided a set of guidelines that can help teachers minimize the more negative effects of extrinsic motivation and strike a balance between extrinsic and intrinsic motivation:

- Use extrinsic rewards when there is no intrinsic reward to undermine, e.g., when no person is likely to experience intrinsic satisfaction in the learning task.
- Use extrinsic rewards when the likelihood is minimal that they will undermine self-determination, e.g., make the extrinsic reward an opportunity to make choices.
- Emphasize the informative, not the controlling, nature of extrinsic rewards. e.g., provide detailed descriptive comments about the quality of the work before assigning a grade.

Design Lessons around Students' Interests Bennett and Rolheiser (2001, p. 82) remind us that, "when we say students are not interested, it is not that they are not interested—rather, they are simply not interested in what we want them to be interested in." Accomplished teachers know this and Bennett and Rolheiser's comments highlight how important it is to design lessons around student interests and provide learning activities known to provide intrinsic satisfaction. This is not an easy task in today's educational environment. However, below are some ideas that have worked for us:

- *Personalize learning.* When lessons and teaching are personalized motivation is enhanced. Examples of ways to personalize learning include: treating students' mistakes with dignity, using students' names, listening to and accepting students' ideas, and remaining nonjudgmental and inquiry oriented, e.g., "That is a very interesting idea, can you tell me more?" One of the most important ways of personalizing learning, however, is differentiating instruction so that particular lessons match particular students' motivations and their capabilities.
- *Relate lessons to students' lives.* Finding out what students are interested in and then connecting lessons to their lives is another way to build on students' interests and intrinsic values. The example in Research Box 3.1 shows how one teacher made Shakespeare relevant to a class of second language learners.
- *Make lessons novel and capture students' curiosity.* Asking novel questions, such as "Suppose you believed in reincarnation. In your next life, what would you accomplish that you didn't accomplish in this life?" Or, "What do you think would happen if the automobile suddenly disappeared?" Similarly, getting students involved in all kinds of activities such as field trips, simulations, and listening to guest speakers carry their own intrinsic value and keep students engaged.

> **REFLECTION**
>
> What have been your experiences in using student interest as a motivator? Has it worked? If yes, why? If no, why not? Think about other teachers in your school. Are there some known for making good use of things their students are interested in? Are there others who say, "student interests are not important"? Consider bringing two teachers together to discuss their views.

Two cautions need to be mentioned in regard to using students' interests as a motivational strategy. First, attempts to make lessons interesting, novel, or vivid may turn into "pure entertainment," a

---

Inquiry

RESEARCH BOX 3.1 Personalizing Shakespeare

Banks, J., Cochran-Smith, M., Moll, L., Richert, A., Zeichner, K., Lepage, P., Darling-Hammond, L., Duffy, H., & McDonald, M. (2005). Teaching diverse learners. In L. Darling-Hammond & J. Bransford (Eds.), *Preparing teachers for a changing world: What teachers should learn and be able to do.* San Francisco: Jossey-Bass, pp. 235–236.

Ms. Carrington is a . . . teacher at John Burroughs Middle School in San Leandro, California. Her English class has 28 students, who speak five different languages other than English. . . . The children are African American, Samoan, European American, Chinese, Filipino, Cambodian, and Latino. Some students walk to school, whereas others take public transit . . . most qualify for free or reduced lunch.

Ms. Carrington's choice about what and how to teach are tightly constrained by district-wide curriculum frameworks and state-mandated proficiency tests in every major subject area. . . . She is required to teach a unit on Shakespeare's sonnets, although her students have shown little interest in any kind of poetry, let alone Elizabethan sonnets.

In previous lessons, Ms. Carrington has used modern music to spark the children's interest in poetry, which worked well to capture their attention. At this point, she doesn't want the children to lose interest. She wonders whether she should stray from the required curriculum and teach modern poetry in order to maintain their interest, or continue with the required curriculum and try to connect to their experiences to keep them engaged in the required texts. If yes, what strategies should she use to bridge the gap between her children and Shakespeare? Some of her colleagues have suggested using technology, which seems like a good idea because many of her students excel at the computer and have already responded well to audio. But, what type of activity would be most effective?

Ms. Carrington ended up having students do a web quest and then set up a class-generated Shakespeare website. Sonnets selected by students were posted on the website, along with interactive sound and video. Students were engaged because Ms. Carrington used technology and the Internet, something students were already interested in, to teach a part of the required curriculum that was quite foreign to them. (Summarized from pp. 235–237)

---

situation that can distract from important educational goals. Second, relying too heavily on current interests of particular students such as rap music, computer games, or pop culture may deter students from developing new interests, which, after all, is one of the most important purposes of education.

In Chapter 5, we will describe in some detail how to identify student interests and needs.

Create Safe Classrooms with Positive Feeling Tones Experienced teachers know that classrooms are complex social systems where group norms exist and where individuals' needs are ever present. And, anyone who has been a frequent visitor to classrooms knows that the environments found in them vary significantly. Some are characterized by warmth and cohesion and find students working in cooperative ways; others are cool, fragmented, and impersonal and students compete fiercely with one another. Remember also from Chapter 2, the important role emotions, particularly stress and fear, play in cognitive learning. Effective teachers are those who can develop classroom environments that attend to the social and emotional needs of students while at the same time securing a high level of academic engagement. In these classrooms students feel safe, and they believe that they will have a say in what is going on. Those who study classroom environments, such as Richard and Patricia Schmuck (2001) and Kohn (1996, 2000), have found that positive classroom environments are characterized by several key elements. Developing each of these elements is important if we want to have students who are highly engaged and who consistently persist in learning tasks. We recommend the following:

- *Positive feeling tones and caring relationships.* Students put forth more effort in environments that have **positive feeling tones** and where relationships are caring and supportive. These classrooms are simply pleasant places to be, and for some students they may be the single most safe, secure and supportive place in their otherwise tumultuous lives. Positive feeling tones and **caring relationship**s do not develop automatically. Instead, they result from many things teachers do on a day-to-day basis, ranging from establishing structures and norms so students can work together in caring and cooperative ways to simple verbal pronouncements such as, "You are such an interesting group of students. I love each and every one of you dearly."
- *Open and participatory communication.* A critical feature of all social settings is the way participants communicate with one another. In classrooms, this process is especially critical because most student learning takes place through teacher–student and/or student–student verbal interactions. Positive classroom environments are characterized by **open communication**, where teacher and students have trust in one another, where they can speak freely, and where everyone shares valuable airtime. This is contrasted to situations where individuals do not feel free to express their views or where communication is dominated by the teacher or perhaps a few outspoken students. Specific strategies to broaden classroom participation will be described in more detail in later chapters.
- *High expectations and norms for shared goals.* Positive learning environments are incomplete unless high expectations for student learning exist. In these classrooms, students believe that the teacher expects them always to do "their best." Students in these classrooms also have high expectations for each other and expect everyone to extend effort and strive to work up to their individual capabilities.
- *Friendship patterns free from cliques.* Friendships are important to all of us and particularly to children and youth. It is primarily through friendship that our need for affiliation is met. Students without friends normally show high levels of emotional distress and low levels of motivation and academic achievement. It is important to develop classroom environments that have peer groups relatively free from cliques and where no student feels left out or friendless.

Plan Lessons to Satisfy Students' Needs As we have seen, needs theory tells us that students will invest energy in activities that allow them to experience satisfaction in the pursuit of achievement, affiliation, and influence. Students' needs for achievement are satisfied when learning tasks are challenging yet doable. Group work and social activities help satisfy affiliative needs. Needs for influence and self-determination are satisfied when students have a say over their classroom environment and a choice of learning tasks. There are numerous things teachers can do to design lessons and learning activities to satisfy students' **achievement, affiliative**, and **influence needs**. These are described below:

- *Ways to satisfy achievement needs*:
  - Encourage students to work towards challenging learning goals and help them understand that individual growth is often more important than achieving some absolute standard.
  - Design lessons where learning tasks allow students to maximize the use of their particular types of intelligence and learning styles.
  - Differentiate learning activities so each student is presented with tasks that have an appropriate level of difficulty and challenge.
  - Provide students with timely and specific feedback on how they are doing. Feedback on poor performance gives students information on how to improve; feedback on good performance provides intrinsic motivation.
  - Encourage self-evaluation and teach students how to evaluate their own work.

- *Ways to satisfy affiliative needs*:
  - Use icebreakers early in the school year to ensure that students know each other's names and have the opportunity to share out-of-classroom personal information.
  - In some group activities and assignments, pair isolates with students who are socially able.
  - During class meetings, encourage students to discuss how they feel about their classroom and its friendship patterns.
  - Don't be afraid to use some instructional time for social activities such as recesses, holiday parties, or parent visits. Properly conducted, these activities help students satisfy their need for affiliation.

- *Ways to satisfy influence needs*:
  - Use cooperative learning and problem-based instructional strategies, as described in Chapters 13 and 14. These approaches allow students considerable choice in the topics they study and in the type of learning strategies they employ.
  - Develop lessons that help students feel like "origins" rather than "pawns."
  - Hold regular planning sessions or class meetings with students so they can help decide next steps to take with particular lessons, as well as assess the type of progress they have made so far. This process allows students to influence the direction of instruction and can also provide important feedback to teachers.

Teach to Students' Strengths and Recognize Neglected Strengths Another important key to motivation is to discover and teach to student strengths. Sometimes this means taking what may be perceived as a weakness and reframing it in a new or more positive light. It may also mean discovering hidden talents and helping students view their talents positively.

Students' strengths can be used for motivational purposes; however, they often go unrecognized. Recently, the eminent American psychologist Robert Sternberg and his colleagues reported on research they conducted that demonstrated how students from under-represented minority groups have culturally relevant knowledge and cognitive abilities that schools should use to motivate and promote learning. They studied children from non-mainstream cultures in Alaska and Kenya to find out what kind of knowledge and skills these children possessed that were relevant to their everyday lives. These studies are summarized in Research Box 3.2.

Sternberg and his colleagues concluded from these studies, and several more like them, that students often have knowledge and skills neglected by traditional schooling. They argue that teachers who become aware of this knowledge can use it to provide the motivation and scaffolding students from non-mainstream cultures need to be successful in learning the knowledge and skills emphasized in mainstream schools.

Structure Learning Experiences to Accomplish Flow You read earlier Csikszentmihaly's concept of "flow." Flow learning experiences are when individuals become totally involved, sometimes to the point of being unconscious of other things going on around them. In Csikszentmihaly's words, "actor and action become one," and motivation stems from internal rather than external causes. Flow experiences require building on student interests and finding the appropriate level of challenge, topics described in the previous section. Learning experiences that are too easy and do not require the level of skills possessed by students are not very interesting to them. On the other hand, experiences that are too difficult and beyond the skills students possess produce frustration and stress *not* flow. Learning experiences that encourage "flow" build on students' interests and intrinsic values and they provide the appropriate level of challenge.

Csikszentmihaly (1990, 1998) has written that the way many schools and classrooms are organized makes accomplishing flow experiences difficult. For instance, classrooms that are inclusive and diverse often have learning activities that may be interesting and challenging to some students but have little meaning for others. Rigid schedules in many middle and secondary schools prevent teachers from initiating flow experiences, as does emphasis on external rules, grades, and teaching strategies that keep students in passive roles. All of these factors inhibit the type of involvement and enjoyment that could come from flow experiences.

Stress Cooperative Goal and Reward Structures Learning goals can be structured in three ways: competitive, individualistic, or cooperative. Competitive goals exist when students perceive they can reach their goal only if other students do not reach theirs. Grading on a curve and winning in a competitive sport are examples of activities with competitive goal structures. Individualistic goals are those where the achievement of a goal by one person is unrelated to achievement of the goal by others. Working toward predefined standards or toward one's own learning goals are examples of individualistic goal structures. Cooperative goals, on the other hand, exist when students perceive that they can reach their goals only when other students also reach theirs. Rowing together or completing a joint project would be examples of activities with cooperative goal

---

(Inquiry) **RESEARCH BOX 3.2** Culturally-relevant Knowledge

The Alaska study: Grigororenko, E.L., Meier, E., Lipka, J., Mohatt, G., Yanez, E., & Sternbert, R.J. (2004). Academic and practical intelligence: A case study of the Yup'ik in Alaska. *Learning and Individual Differences*, *14*, 183–207.

Researchers assessed the practical knowledge and skills of 261 secondary students from seven different Inuit communities in southwestern Alaska. Assessment instruments measured student knowledge about herbs, fishing, folklore, and survival. Here is an example:

> When Eddie runs to collect the ptarmigan that he has just shot, he notices that its front pouch (balloon) is full of food. This is a sign that: (a) There's a storm on the way; (b) Winter is almost over; (c) It's hard to find food this season; (d) It hasn't snowed in a long time. (A is the correct answer.)

Eskimo students scored very well on this test, particularly those from the more rural areas. The same students didn't do very well on the schools' standard achievement measures. This information about students' background knowledge was subsequently used to build a mathematics curriculum based on Alaskan cultural knowledge, e.g., use of fish racks as the basis for lessons on area, perimeter and the relationship between the two.

The Kenya study: Sternberg, et al. (2001). The relationship between academic and practical intelligence: A case study in Kenya. *Intelligence*, *29*, 401–418.

A study similar to the Alaska study was conducted with rural students in Kenya. The focus of the assessment was students' knowledge of natural herbal medicines used to combat parasitic illnesses. Here is an example of a test question:

> A small child in your family has homa. She has a sore throat, headache, and fever. She has been sick for three days. Which of the following five yadh nyaluo [Luo herbal medicines] can treat homo? (a) Chamama. Take the leaves and fito [sniff medicine up the nose to sneeze out illness]; (b) Kaladali. Take the leaves, drink, and fito; (c) Obuo. Take the leaves and fito; (d) Ogaka. Take the roots, pound, and drink; (e) Ahundo. Take the leaves and fito. (A, B, and C are correct.)

As with the Alaskan students, Kenyan students did well on this test as compared to their performance on standardized tests. The researchers also observed that they did better on the test than the Western researchers could do. Again, these data were used to develop culturally-relevant curriculum for Kenyan students.

---

structures. A heavy reliance on competitive goal structures in classrooms leads to unhealthy comparisons and makes students' "ability" rather than their "effort" the principal ingredient for success. Cooperative goal structures, on the other hand, lead to interdependence and most often to more student motivation and engagement.

Teach with Authenticity and Passion Some observers contend that motivating students cannot be translated into a set of best practices, that it is not about using particular motivational strategies to secure student cooperation and engagement, but instead it is the way we *are* as teachers that makes the difference. It is the "teacher as person," our internal commitments, and our deeply held beliefs about learning that are most important. This includes abilities to develop **authentic relationships** with students that are free of power and control. It also includes holding beliefs that each child can learn and that one's efficacy can make learning happen. Carol Ann Tomlinson and Amy Germundson (2007, p. 27) have compared this aspect of teaching to creating jazz:

> Teaching well . . . is like creating jazz. Jazz blends musical sounds from one tradition with theories from another. . . . It incorporates polyrhythm. It uses call-and-response, in which one person comments on the expression of another. And, it invites improvisation. . . .
>
> Teaching, too, makes music with the elements at a teacher's disposal, merging them just so to ensure a compelling and memorable sound. Like jazz, great teaching calls for blending different cultural styles with educational techniques and theories. It requires recognizing that there are independent rhythms in the classroom. Most of all great teaching demands improvisation in how teachers invite an array of young lives into the music with us. Different teachers create jazz in different ways in the classroom. *But excellent teachers always create it.*

Classrooms with jazz-like fusion, according to Tomlinson and Germundson, have curricula that "gets under the skin of young learners," directs them toward big ideas and helps them to make connections to their personal lives. These classrooms have teachers who show keen interest in their students' lives and who know how to connect in ways that will "contribute to the students' well being." Assessment in these classrooms is not about judging learning but about giving feedback; 'assessment as learning' informs process. It sounds a lot like jazz" (ibid., pp. 29–31).

Using the jazz metaphor may make particular teaching behaviors appear to be mysterious and perhaps elusive. However, what Tomlinson and Germundson describe is not too different than the behaviors identified by Gloria Ladson-Billings (1994) in her now classic study about why some teachers are highly successful in motivating African American students. Ladson-Billings found four things that successful teachers did. First, they *saw and valued their students' racial ethnic differences* and believed strongly that all students can succeed. Second, the successful teachers held a *passion for knowledge* and they displayed this passion to their students in many different ways. Knowledge to these teachers was not something static but instead was always evolving; it was something which both students and teachers should be striving to acquire. Students were encouraged to strive for excellence, but they were also taught that standards are complex and that individual student's backgrounds and abilities have to be taken into account. Third, the successful teachers studied by Ladson-Billings developed strong **communities of learners** in their classrooms. Students in these classrooms learned and were encouraged to make meaningful connections and to build deep relationships with each other and with their teachers. They were encouraged to learn cooperatively, to take responsibility for each other's learning, and to extend this cooperation and responsibility beyond the classroom walls. Finally, successful teachers had *strong*

Table 3.2 Summary of strategies to increase student motivation

Helping students change their attitudes and perceptions	Modifying classrooms and teaching methods
Focus on controllable and alterable factors.	Use a balance of extrinsic and intrinsic rewards.
Help students alter their views about success and failure.	Design lessons built on students' interests and intrinsic values.
Pay attention to students' goals and goal orientations.	Create safe classrooms with positive feeling tones.
	Plan lessons to satisfy student needs. Teach to students' strengths.
	Structure learning experiences to accomplish flow.
	Stress cooperative goal and reward structures.
	Teach with authenticity and passion.

academic programs; in this particular instance, programs in math and language arts. However, they rejected more traditional methods and instead emphasized *communal activities* that were consistent with the African American culture, and helped students stay connected to their community through apprenticeships where real-life experiences became part of the official curriculum.

Abilities associated with passion and authenticity seem to come naturally for some individuals, e.g., "the born teacher." Others seem never to develop these abilities no matter how long they teach. Most of us, however, if we have desire and persistence can learn how to be authentic with students, to recognize and appreciate their unique strengths, and to act toward them in ways that are socially just—all behaviors that result in motivation and learning.

In Table 3.2 we provide a summary of the strategies teachers can use to help change student attitudes and perception about learning and ways classrooms and teaching practices can be modified to increase motivation and learning.

SOME FINAL THOUGHTS ABOUT MOTIVATION AND THE RELEVANCY OF CONTEMPORARY EDUCATION

We conclude this chapter with two questions we posed at the beginning: "Why do so many of our students lack motivation to do well in school?" and "Why do so many fail to acquire the goals we deem important?" There are no simple answers to these questions and the causes, as we have described, are multiple. It is our belief that schools in the long term need to change in pretty drastic ways if they are to become relevant and engaging for all youth. These changes will require a radically different curriculum to achieve redesigned twenty-first century goals. Steven Wolk (2007) wrote recently that the prevailing curriculum in our schools is adequate if our goal is to prepare drones and if we don't care how many students tune out or drop out. He argued that if we want to help all students to become creative, caring, and thoughtful citizens, then a new curriculum is required. Instead of organizing curricula around traditional subjects, such as English, math, and history, Wolk offers some of the following organizers for our consideration: environmental literacy, caring and empathy, multicultural community, social responsibility, peace and nonviolence, media literacy, love of learning, gobal awareness, money, family, food, and happiness. These are the subjects he believes will provide relevancy because they connect directly to students' lives.

Ritchhart (2002) goes even further. He believes that we are "teaching the wrong things" and in the "wrong way." For education to be relevant to today's students, he argues for a total redesign of education with a set of goals that help students acquire intellectual character, abilities for creative and reflective thinking, and dispositions to be curious, open-minded, and truth seeking.

Rinne (2007), however, has a slightly different perspective on motivation and relevancy. He says that the secret to motivation "lies within each lesson itself" (p. 1) and is up to teachers. Accomplished teachers are able to reveal to their students the intrinsic appeal of particular subjects and they can challenge them with authentic, real-life problems that exist beyond the classroom walls. In Chapter 14 we describe an approach to teaching called "problem-based learning" (PBL). Teachers who use PBL present students with authentic and meaningful problems that serve as springboards for inquiry and action both within and outside the classroom. This type of learning experience aims at helping students develop higher-level thinking skills and also provides them with opportunities to observe and learn adult role behaviors.

If educational change comes as slowly in the future as it has in the past, new goals and new curricula will not arrive quickly. In the meantime, the burden for motivation will rest on those of us who are teachers and what we can do independently in our own classrooms and with the colleagues in our schools. We conclude with a quote from Leon Botstein that provides hope for what can be accomplished:

> Every parent knows that a child wants to know things about the natural world. They're not worried about who Thomas Jefferson was. They're worried about why the sun rises, why it snows, why the stars glitter in the sky. *Every child wants to know.*
>
> (Epstein, 2007, p. 661; italics ours)

SUMMARY AT A GLANCE

- Student motivation is one of the most important factors for getting students engaged in school and to help them acquire important educational goals.
- Three major theories help explain why students are motivated to take action and to expend effort in schools: reinforcement theories, needs theories, and cognitive theories.
- Reinforcement theories rest mainly on the centrality of external events and how positive and negative reinforcers influence behavior.
- Needs theories take the perspective that humans are roused to take action to satisfy innate physical and psychological needs.
- Cognitive theories of motivation take the perspective that student involvement and engagement result not from external events, but from the cognitive beliefs students hold and the interpretations they place on learning activities.
- Securing greater student engagement requires doing many things well and employing strategies known to support rather than undermine motivation.

- Major motivational strategies can be divided into two major categories: those that aim at helping students change their attitudes and perceptions about learning, and those aimed at modifying classroom practices.
- Today, many students lack motivation to do well in school. Some believe that major redesign of schools and of curricula are required to change this situation. In the meantime, teachers must do much of the heavy duty motivation lifting.

CONSTRUCTING YOUR OWN LEARNING

Working with a classmate or colleague, construct conceptual webs that inventory your current motivational practices. If you haven't used webs before, you may wish to look at the explanations and examples we provide in Chapters 5 and 11. Compare your webs. How are they the same? How do they differ? Now select two or three of the student profiles we provided at the beginning of this chapter. Develop a set of goals you could set for each student and identify possible intervention strategies you might employ to increase each student's motivation to learn.

RESOURCES

Ferguson, D., Gwen, R., Meyer, G., et al. (2001). *Designing personalized learning experiences for every student.* Alexandria, VA: Association for Supervision and Curriculum Development.

Kottler, J., Zehm, S., & Kottler, E. (2006). *On being a teacher: The human dimension* (3rd ed.). Thousand Oaks, CA: Corwin Press.

Noddings, N. (2006). *Critical lessons: What our schools should teach.* Cambriedge: Cambridge University Press.

Sullo, B. (2007). *Activating the desire to learn.* Alexandria, VA: Association for Supervision and Curriculum Development.

Watkins, C. (2005) *Classrooms as learning communities: What's in it for schools?* New York: Routledge.

4

CURRICULUM DESIGN FOR STUDENT LEARNING

INTRODUCTION

Deciding what to teach is fundamental to effective teaching. It defines the purposes of our instruction, and it has a major influence on what our students learn. Making decisions about what to teach, however, is no simple task. Knowledge continues to grow exponentially, and important educational stakeholders hold very different views about what is important for children and youth to learn. Classrooms have limited instructional time; competition for curriculum space is fierce. Ultimately, it is classroom teachers who must negotiate between curriculum expectations and scarce time resources. When decisions are made wisely and curriculum design is done skillfully, our students develop a sense of where they are going and what they are expected to learn. Decisions made poorly lead to confusion and a breakdown in student learning.

In this chapter we turn to a discussion about what is taught and why, and most importantly, how the design of curriculum affects student learning. Let's begin by considering two curriculum design situations:

- *Vignette 1*: It is mid-May and eighth-grade history teacher, Kathy Rawlings, realizes that she has just finished her unit on nineteenth-century westward expansion. This leaves a mere three weeks to get through the Civil War, considered the midpoint in American history and the place eighth-grade teachers should get to by the end of the school year. She decides she needs to speed up, a decision that will make it impossible for her to spend time on a project-based assignment comparing the social life of youth in the mid-nineteenth century to the social life of youth today nor to devote time to the popular mock student debate on slavery. She will also have to give the Mexican–American War short shrift. Instead, she decides to march chapter by chapter through the remainder of the textbook. If she can cover 20 to 30 pages a day, she can make it.
- *Vignette 2*: Every spring, fifth-grade teacher, Bill Richardson, teaches a unit on the "life cycle." Although this unit is part of the fifth-grade science and social studies curriculum, Mr. Richardson likes to integrate the unit with a variety of activities associated with art, music, and language arts. His goals for the integrated unit, however, have never been very clearly defined. In language arts, students write and illustrate stories about important events in their families' lives—births, weddings, deaths, and so on. They watch a video on the "Life cycle of the Pacific salmon," and make drawings of salmon swimming upstream to spawn. They visit websites

and collect information about dams on the Columbia River, and listen to Native American music. One of the student's fathers fishes commercially for a living. Bill invites him to visit the class and to talk to students about how salmon are an endangered species. The father brings some smoked salmon for students to sample.

Both of these vignettes reveal common curriculum design flaws. The first shows pressure to cover curriculum content by marching headlong through selected topics and the textbook. The second illustrates a familiar curriculum unit that affords student participation in a series of hands-on activities, some of which are likely highly motivational, but without clear goals or measurable outcomes. Both approaches leave little chance for students to gain much understanding. Both also lead to considerations about the nature of knowledge and how our perspectives about curriculum influence what we choose to teach and how.

This chapter is about the important role teachers play in translating formal curriculum frameworks into meaningful learning experiences for students. First, we will describe some enduring curriculum debates that have persisted in education over a considerable length of time that influence directly and indirectly what we teach. We will then provide our perspective on what we mean by curriculum, taking the view that there are really two curricula. One is the **formal curriculum** influenced by subject matter associations and planned and adopted by state departments of education and school districts. The second is the **enacted curriculum**, the one designed by classroom teachers and experienced by their students. The chapter concludes with a somewhat detailed discussion of processes and strategies available to assist with planning and execution of curriculum decisions in classrooms.

CURRICULUM IN PERSPECTIVE

Some Personal Tensions

This has been a difficult chapter for us to write, and before we get started we want to share personal tensions we experience about what is happening to curriculum in schools today. On the one hand, we support all kinds of efforts to develop standards that help clarify what students need to know and be able to do. We believe that standards should be communicated clearly to citizens who support the schools, to families, and, most importantly, to students themselves. We also believe that it is crucial to set **high expectations** for all students. As a society, we can no longer afford a curriculum that holds different expectations and content for students depending upon their race, gender, or socio-economic status. This type of discrimination is unfair to students and a waste of valuable human resources.

On the other hand, we (along with others) have been disappointed in the way the standards movement at state and national policy levels has evolved and influenced curriculum decisions. The No Child Left Behind legislation has tended to narrow the curriculum for many students and has produced, at the time of this writing, only modest gains in student achievement. Efforts by states and local educational agencies to set higher standards and to achieve alignment between what is taught and what is assessed have created unintended consequences that too often detract from rather than support effective teaching. Simply put, too many content standards have been identified—a situation that has led teachers, more than ever, to rush quickly and lightly through the curriculum so everything can be covered. We report these tensions at the beginning of the chapter because we suspect many of our readers will be experiencing similar ones. The challenge for all of us is to find ways to embrace high expectations and a common curriculum while maintaining a commitment to help each student progress according to his or her individual readiness and capacities.

Toward a Definition of Curriculum

Over the years the curriculum has been variously defined. Traditionally, curriculum theorists, such Ralph Tyler (1949), viewed the curriculum as a set of purposes, body of knowledge, and a scope and sequence written by knowledgeable individuals for the purpose of providing guidance to teachers about what and how to teach. Others (Apple, 1990; Chomsky, 2002) have viewed curriculum as attempts by particular political and economic interests to shape what goes on in schools consistent with their particular visions about the world and the purposes of education. We believe both of these definitions are more or less accurate. However, as you will read in later sections, we are more interested in the ways teachers and their students experience the more formal curriculum on a day-to-day basis. In this respect, we embrace a definition provided by Darling-Hammond and Bransford (2005, p. 170):

> Curriculum . . . is the learning experiences and goals the teacher develops for particular classes—both in planning and while teaching—in light of the characteristics of students and teaching context.

This definition expands our perspective beyond formal curriculum documents that prescribe goals, purposes, and topics to be taught to what actually happens in classrooms as individual teachers adapt and carry out instruction within a particular context and with a particular group of students. This definition places teachers at the center of the curriculum design process, where we believe they should be. This does not mean, however, that as teachers we are free to ignore the larger social purposes of education or externally designed curriculum frameworks and standards because these too, as we will see, have important influence on the goals we adopt and the learning experiences we choose.

Enduring Curriculum Debates

Deciding on an appropriate curriculum for schools has always been a contentious topic, particularly in democratic societies. Important differences have resulted in several enduring, somewhat philosophical, debates. Understanding these debates is important because they serve as a backdrop for the day-to-day decisions we make as we strive to make sense of the formal curriculum and plan particular learning experiences for students.

Beliefs about the larger **social purposes of education** have historically been a source of considerable debate about what to teach. You are familiar with some of the more classic historical statements about the social purposes and processes of education. During the colonial period, Benjamin Franklin articulated the importance of making education practical. In the early years of the Republic, Thomas Jefferson expressed the necessity of strong civic education for the survival of democratic government. Horace

Mann believed in the universality of education. In the early part of the twentieth century, the National Education Association challenged the academic curriculum of that era and adopted a set of principles for secondary education that helped establish universal high school education and that emphasized both academic and **vocational preparation**. More recently, John Goodlad (1984, 2004) described how curriculum in a democracy should be designed that would enable schools to achieve four major purposes: academic, vocational, social and civic, and personal. Although all of Goodlad's purposes are embraced in general by our larger society, their enactment in particular communities can be the source of considerable controversy. Community members decide on the relative emphasis to put on developing intellectual skills in preparation for college (the **academic preparation curriculum**) as contrasted to the vocational skills needed for work, or the important social skills required for citizenship as compared to those that lead to personal development and understanding. This debate also often encompasses questions about who should have access to education, who should go to college or enter non-college jobs, or who should be allowed to learn in their native languages.

Who should *control* the curriculum and whether these controls should rest at the national or local levels has been another enduring debate. Traditionally, **curriculum control** was left mainly to the states and local school districts. For the past half century, however, there have been increasing efforts to expand the role of the federal government and allow it to exert more influence over what is taught and how. The best examples of recent influences have been federal regulations requiring racial integration, legislation requiring equal educational opportunities for students with disabilities, and required performance standards such as those legislated in the No Child Left Behind Act. Recently, Deborah Meier and Diane Ravitch (2006) highlighted differences between those who want to see more national influence on curriculum as compared to those who favor maintaining local control. Ravitch has argued for a core curriculum built around the academic disciplines of history, literature, mathematics, science, art, music, and foreign language. She wants this curriculum to be prescribed and to be made the basis for a required national exam. Meier, on the other hand, prefers a more local approach to curriculum. She "doubts that anyone can ensure what children will really understand and makes sense of . . . [if the curriculum] is designed by people who are far away from the actual school communities and classrooms" (p. 1).

It is likely that you have experienced this debate in your own school and community. For example, some members of your community may have argued that education is best served when the curriculum is standardized and prescribed, while others may have raised serious concerns about the right of any government to impose standardized tests on local schools. Also likely, are instances when local teacher and parent groups have challenged the right of the state to impose a statewide **standards-based curriculum** instead of encouraging those developed locally.

A third enduring debate has been the relative importance of *curriculum content* (what is taught) versus *process* or *habits of mind* (how students come to know what is taught). This debate was particularly evident during the 1960s and 1970s, when discipline-centered curricula in the sciences, social sciences, and mathematics were developed with an emphasis on the "processes of science" and the ways scientists and mathematicians think (the **process curriculum**) instead of an emphasis on the actual subject matter content. More recently, it has been reflected in curricula such as those developed by

Costa and Kallick (2000) and Ritchhart (2002) that focus on habits of the mind and learning how to think instead of more traditional content. On the other side of this debate are those who support the development of standards in every academic subject and at every grade level and who argue for policies that require all students to meet the same content standards.

Perhaps the most enduring debate concerns the long-standing differences regarding what should be the major *source* of the school's core curriculum. On one side of this issue have been those who believe that the academic disciplines should be the principal source for a common curriculum. Much of the curriculum reforms in the past half-century have been influenced by this position, including the development of curriculum frameworks and content standards in today's standards-based environment. On the other side have been those who have argued for a more student-centered curriculum, designed around interests and key experiences of children and youth. Progressive education in the early part of the twentieth century embraced this perspective. Today, it forms a plank in the constructivist platform on curriculum and student learning.

> **REFLECTION**
>
> Take a moment to consider the larger social purposes of education and some of the enduring debates about these purposes. Where do you come down on these issues? How do your personal beliefs about purposes influence the curriculum in your classroom? How do your views compare to those of other teachers in your school?

As teachers, we may not explicitly consider on a day-to-day basis the larger social purposes of education or the enduring debates about who should control the curriculum. At the same time, these issues affect the ways schools and classrooms are structured and governed, the courses we are asked to teach, and the curriculum frameworks and resources available for our use. It is important that we understand these larger forces and how decisions made at various at levels will affect the learning and day-by-day educational opportunities of our students.

BRINGING THE CURRICULUM INTO SCHOOLS AND CLASSROOMS

The larger social purposes of education are often defined at policy level and by curriculum theorists. Before classroom teachers become involved, however, these more abstract and philosophical statements are turned into standards and curriculum frameworks, most often under the leadership of professional subject matter associations and by districts or state departments of education. This process leads to two different curricula: the formal curriculum and the enacted curriculum.

The Formal Curriculum

The formal curriculum grows out of conceptions held about the larger social purposes of education. We have already seen how traditional curriculum theorists viewed the curriculum as a set of purposes and a scope and sequence of topics assembled in the form of curriculum guides. Some of our more experienced readers may remember these guides. They were written at a rather high level of abstraction, were *not* highly prescriptive, and were intended to be used as the name implied—curriculum *guides*. Today, however, the formal curriculum is much more prescriptive than in earlier times. In most instances, it provides detailed descriptions about what *students are expected to know and be able to do*. As teachers, we experience the formal curriculum from three important sources. One, members of national subject matter and professional associations make available content standards that define appropriate curriculum for their subject and grade level areas. Often, classroom teachers serve on the committees that define these standards. As teachers, however, we are not obligated to follow our professional association's standards very closely. Subject matter standards, however, get incorporated into state content standards, which are a second important source for determining the formal curriculum. Standards developed by state departments of education are usually published in formal documents and on websites. They are intended to serve as the basis for the curriculum in our classrooms and we are expected to pay attention to them. A third source that influences classroom curricula is **high-stakes tests**. Today, these tests have been developed in every state and are aligned (more or less) to particular content standards. As teachers, we know that both our school's and our own reputation rests on how well students do on these tests. Figure 4.1 illustrates the multiple influences that national subject matter organizations, state department of education, and mastery tests have on the curriculum of local schools and classrooms.

In our current standards-based environment, it is the state departments of education that have the most influence on the formal curriculum. Let's look briefly at how the formal curriculum is designed and presented.

State departments of education develop documents that outline the knowledge and skills students are expected to acquire. Normally, these are described in **curriculum frameworks** and have three primary components: (1) lists of **content standards** organized under specific categories or themes and by grade level and subject area; (2) **benchmarks** or checkpoints linked to each standard that designate the degree of student mastery of a particular standard at a particular point in time; and (3) **performance indicators**—assessment items that measure student mastery. To illustrate how this is done, we have drawn on specific examples of curriculum frameworks and content standards from two states—Ohio and Connecticut. We choose these two for illustrative purposes because we think both states have done a reasonably good job, and the approaches they use are representative of those used in most other states.

The Ohio State Department of Education uses the following approach for designing its curriculum frameworks and content standards. For each subject area, Ohio identifies a limited number of categories of standards deemed important. For example, the ten

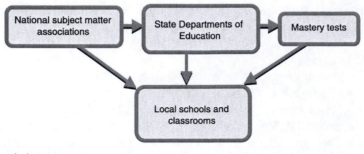

Figure 4.1 Three curriculum sources

- Phonemic Awareness, Word Recognition and Fluency Standard
- Acquisition of Vocabulary Standard
- Reading Process: Concepts of Print, Comprehension Strategies and Self-monitoring Strategies Standard
- Reading Applications: Informational, Technical and Persuasive Text Standard
- Reading Applications: Literary Text Standard
- Writing Process Standard
- Writing Applications Standard
- Writing Conventions Standard
- Research Standard
- Communication: Oral and Visual Standard

Figure 4.2 Ohio's K-12 English Language Arts standards
Source: Information summarized from Ohio State Department of Education website, 2008.

standards listed in Figure 4.2 have been identified for K-12 English Language Art Curriculum.

In addition to these more global standards, the Ohio model also provides more detailed standards and benchmarks. Standards describe precisely what students should know and be able to do; benchmarks serve as checkpoints for student progress toward meeting a particular standard and are divided into grade-level clusters. Performance indicators have also been developed to measure student progress at each grade level. The Ohio overall structure is illustrated in Figure 4.3.

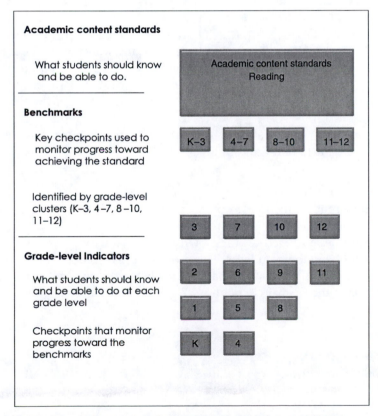

Figure 4.3 Ohio's structure for organizing content standards, benchmarks, and performance indicators
Source: Illustration based on information on the Ohio Department of Education website, 2008.

This model is similar to ones used in other states. Analysis of the Ohio K-12 English Language Arts framework shows that the ten standards have been defined by 215 benchmarks and 1,171 grade-level indicators, a situation we will discuss in more detail later.

The state of Connecticut takes a slightly different approach and stresses the importance of **curriculum alignment** among three aspects of instruction: (1) standards organized around major themes that define what students should know and be able to do; (2) curriculum as described in state and local frameworks; and (3) formative and summative assessments that show student progress toward achieving mastery. The three components of the Connecticut model are illustrated in Figure 4.4.

Like Ohio, Connecticut defines its standards and assessments and organizes them under core **curriculum themes**, grade-by-grade and subject-by-subject. Table 4.1 shows how this is done for two sixth-grade science standards.

Notice how the Connecticut approach shows content standards as statements of major science concepts organized under major themes and referred to as the "big, essential questions." In the right-hand column in Table 4.1 are the expected performances associated with each standard. Teachers are told that these performances will be included on the state's science mastery tests. This approach has been reported to be quite successful. One of the authors lived and taught in Connecticut as the state's frameworks were being developed and knows from first-hand reports that, for the most part, they have been well received by K-12 teachers. Teachers reported that the Connecticut mastery tests are aligned to the state standards, and that they accurately assess what teachers believe to be important for students to know and be able to do.

> **REFLECTION**
>
> With a classmate or colleague, discuss the way **curriculum standards** and frameworks are designed in your state. How do they compare to the examples we have provided? Do you think they are better or worse? Why? Do frameworks facilitate or deter your teaching? What about student learning?

The Enacted Curriculum

Regardless of how much direction (or prescription) is provided by state departments of education or school districts, it is classroom teachers who make the ultimate decisions about curriculum design based on their own teaching situations and what they know about their content and their students. The choices we, as teachers, make about content and learning experiences for students have been labeled the *enacted* curriculum. This is the one that brings the formal curriculum to life for our students and provides them

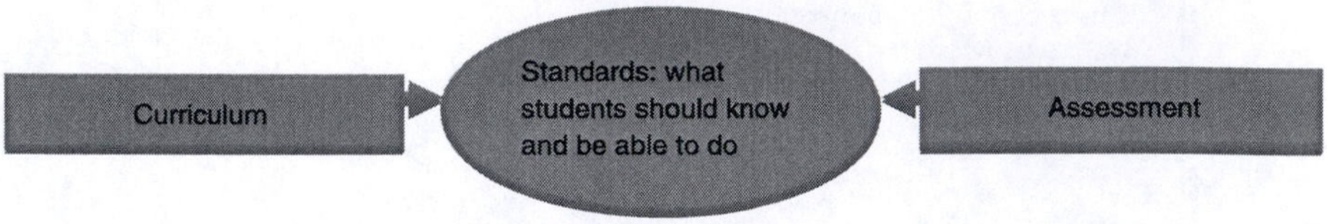

Figure 4.4 Connecticut alignment between curriculum and assessment
Source: Illustration based on information on the Connecticut Department of Education website, 2008.

Table 4.1 Sixth grade core themes, content standards, and expected performances

Content standards	Expected performances
Theme: Properties of Matter—How does the structure of matter affect the properties and uses of materials?	**C1.** Describe the properties of common elements, such as oxygen, hydrogen, carbon, iron, and aluminum.
6.1 Materials can be classified as pure substances or mixtures, depending on their chemical and physical properties.	**C2.** Describe how the properties of simple compounds, such as water and table salt, are different from the properties of the elements of which they are made.
• Mixtures are made of combinations of elements and/or compounds, and they can be separated by using a variety of physical means. • Pure substances can be either elements or compounds, and they cannot be broken down by physical means.	**C3.** Explain how mixtures can be separated by using the properties of the substances from which they are made, such as particle size, density, solubility, and boiling point.
Theme: Matter and Energy in Ecosystems—How do matter and energy flow through ecosystems?	**C4.** Describe how biotic factors, such as temperature, water, and sunlight, affect the ability of plants to create their own food through photosynthesis.
6.2 An ecosystem is composed of all the populations that are living in a certain space and the physical factors with which they interact.	**C5.** Explain how populations are affected by predator–prey relationships.
• Populations in ecosystems are affected by biotic factors, such as other populations, and biotic factors, such as soil and water supply. • Populations in ecosystems can be categorized as producers, consumer, and decomposers of organic matter.	**C6.** Describe common food webs in different Connecticut ecosystems.

Source: Information summarized from the Connecticut Department of Education website, 2008.

with a sense of "where they are going" and "what they are expected to learn." Several aspects of the enacted curriculum are important to consider.

First, evidence has shown that, regardless of how good and creative curriculum materials are or how precisely standards have been stated, these factors do not replace the teacher who makes day-to-day decisions about how to use the materials and standards. Karen Zumwalt (1989) summarized this point quite accurately a number of years ago:

> Decisions, made explicitly and implicitly during the planning and interactive phases of teaching, influence and are influenced by one's vision of what one hopes students to learn. When one makes instructional decisions (e.g., use whole group instruction in math; use reading workbooks for practicing separate component skills; use the tests which accompany the social studies textbook), the nature of the curriculum for students . . . is affected. Choices of "how" are more than instrumental; they influence the curriculum, often in profound ways . . . teachers need to understand this interrelationship if they are to be thoughtful and reflective about their practice.
>
> (p. 175; as cited in Darling-Hammond and Bransford, 2005, pp. 183–184)

Researchers who have studied teachers who work effectively in urban schools have also highlighted the importance of the teachers' curriculum design skills. A good example stems from the work of Gloria Ladson-Billings (1994), who studied elementary teachers who had been nominated by principals and parents for their abilities to work successfully with African American students. After observing selected teachers weekly for over a year, one of Ladson-Billings' major conclusions was that effective teachers had a passion for knowledge and, to a person, had designed a relevant, **coherent curriculum** that focused on literacy and numeracy and emphasized ways of learning meaningful to African American students.

How teachers choose to allocate instructional time is another important aspect of the enacted curriculum. Research dating back a good number of years has demonstrated consistently that curriculum choices made by teachers have significant impact on what students learn. The **time-to-learn** studies conducted in the 1970s and 1980s (Fisher, Berliner, Filby, Marliave, Cahen, and Dishaw, 1980; National Education Commission on Time and Learning, 1994) produced three important findings:

1. The way instructional time was allocated and used was strongly related to student academic achievement.
2. Teachers varied considerably in the amount of time they planned for and allocated to particular subjects. For instance, in some elementary classrooms as few as 60 minutes were allocated to reading and language arts; others spent as many as 150 minutes on these subjects.
3. In many classrooms, a large proportion of time was allocated to non-instructional activities.

Overall, effective teachers were those that provided "learning opportunities" for students to experience activities aimed at acquiring important academic skills.

More recently, the importance of "time to learn" has again been demonstrated (Gewertz, 2008; Viadero, 2008). Schools across the country have been expanding school hours so teachers can help students master important academic skills. They have also experimented with ways to make students' out-of-school experiences, such as after-school and community programs, become part of the curriculum and exist as another set of learning opportunities. Although it is inconclusive as to which of various strategies for extending learning time works best, it is quite clear that, when more time is provided, it leads to more student success (Viadero, 2008).

Finally, studies of curriculum reforms and school effectiveness (Edmonds, 1981; Joyce, Hersh, & McKibbon, 1993; Marzano, 2003) have likewise demonstrated how individual teachers implement particular curricula and how the decisions they make impact student learning. Most important have been findings that, when teachers in particular schools agree and collaborate on educational goals and curriculum design, these actions have strong effects on student learning (Fullan, 2001, 2007; Lee & Smith, 1996; Levine & Lezotte, 1990). An example of research about the importance of teachers taking collective responsibility for curriculum is highlighted in Research Box 4.1.

We will return to the idea of teachers taking collective responsibility in Chapter 15.

Inquiry **RESEARCH BOX 4.1**

Lee, V., & Smith, J. (1996). Collective responsibility for learning and its effects on gains in achievement of early secondary school students. *American Journal of Education, 104,* 103–146.

Lee and Smith wanted to find out the effects on student learning when teachers took collective rather than individual responsibility for learning. To study this question, they used data from a large study sponsored by the National Center for Education Statistics that surveyed over 22,000 students and their teachers when students were in eighth grade and again in eleventh grade. Lee and Smith measured learning gains made by students in four subjects: mathematics, reading, history, and science. They also acquired measures of how much teachers in particular schools took collective responsibility for student learning on a scale from high collective responsibility to low collective responsibility. The data they collected are displayed in Table 4.2.

Table 4.2 Mean gains in student achievement between eighth- and eleventh-grade students attending schools with high, medium, and low levels of teacher responsibility for student learning

Subject	Level of collective responsibility for learning		
	High ($n = 1,226$)	Medium ($n = 8,801$)	Low ($n = 1,665$)
Math gain	6.57	5.39	4.95
Readinig gain	3.70	2.51	1.61
History gain	2.95	1.51	1.26
Science gain	3.43	1.54	1.33

Source: Lee and Smith (1996). Reprinted with permission.

Many findings resulted from this overall study, but for our purposes here one finding stands out: *Students gained most in all subject areas in schools where teachers enacted a curriculum that displayed a high level of collective responsibility for student learning and least in schools where a low level of collective responsibility was displayed.*

In summary, the big idea we want to leave with you is that, on the one hand, there is a formal curriculum developed by state and local education agencies and by subject matter associations. This curriculum specifies content standards and topics to be taught and it prescribes what students are to learn and do. The formal curriculum is important and, as teachers, we must pay attention to it. On the other hand, the curriculum comes into the classroom through the enacted curriculum, meaning the way the curriculum is actually experienced by students as a result of the teachers' choices about what to teach, how to structure learning time, and the learning activities and assignments to use on a particular day. We believe that it is this enacted curriculum that has the most profound effect on what students ultimately learn.

STRATEGIES AND TOOLS FOR CURRICULUM ENACTMENT

To design a viable, coherent curriculum requires avoiding several design flaws while making effective use of tools and strategies that are available for curriculum decision making. Common design flaws to avoid consist of selecting inappropriate content for students, failing to prioritize important ideas, and lacking clear performance indicators. Those to embrace and use are described below and organized into four categories of design strategy: (1) design curriculum with the larger purposes of education in mind; (2) design curriculum that is consistent with your own personal capabilities and beliefs; (3) design curriculum so it connects with students' lives; and (4) design curriculum so the current standards-based environment works for teaching and learning not against it.

Connecting Curriculum to the Larger Social Purposes of Education

The enduring debates we described in the previous section are efforts by various stakeholders to define the larger purposes of education. Differences are played out as formal curriculum is being developed. However, they are also played out as members of local communities and particular stakeholders strive to make their voices heard about what is important. This is simply the way it is with public education in a democratic society. Wise curriculum design, then, requires teachers to be aware of the larger social purposes of education and to understand the differences expressed by community and stakeholder groups. For instance, it is important to recognize that academicians and subject matter groups, such as the National Council for Mathematics Teachers or the National Council for Teachers of English, in most instances, will advocate for a curriculum that covers the major ideas and processes of inquiry in their subject fields. Others may strive to influence the curriculum to accomplish religious or political purposes, such as efforts by religious groups in several states to ban the teaching of evolution and replace it with ideas associated with intelligent design. Individuals in state departments of education who write curriculum frameworks and standards strive to find compromise among competing voices, but they too may have particular curricula preferences. In general, they reflect a set of values that curriculum should be centrally imposed and prescribed. In local communities, we also find groups who differ about the purposes of education. Community business leaders may want schools to pursue a curriculum that prepares youth for work. Some parents may want schools to emphasize basic skills. Others, such as a recent protesting parent group in an upper middle-class New York suburb, want schools to spend less time prepping students for standardized tests and to spend more time teaching them how to think, solve problems, and develop appreciation for the visual and performing arts.

Teachers, individually and in concert with their colleagues, must find ways to meet the demands of the state and district's formal curriculum, listen to the desires family and community members express for their children, while simultaneously considering foremost the needs of students. As with many aspects of teaching, this is no simple task. Being aware of the larger social purposes of education and some of the enduring debates, however, can assist in curriculum decision making. Joining with other teachers for curriculum discussions and reflection can likewise ensure wise decisions that are philosophically grounded.

Connecting Curriculum to One's Own Personal Beliefs

Attending to larger societal demands is only one facet for making knowledgeable and judicious curriculum decisions. A second is to attend thoughtfully to our own capabilities and beliefs, including our understandings about the nature of knowledge, the subjects we are expected to teach, and our beliefs about how people learn. Attending to these beliefs helps develop our own *personal sense* of where we and our students are going and the best route to get there.

Let's look at some examples of how our personal capabilities and beliefs might influence curriculum design, along with questions we may need to consider. Our personal understandings of the subject matter influence what we decide to teach. We are more likely to treat topics lightly if we don't know very much about them, while proceeding with more confidence and clarity with those subjects we know well. Our knowledge of curriculum frameworks and content standards also helps us develop a sense of direction, as do the textbooks and learning resources available for our use. This is not to imply that we should teach only those subjects we know well while ignoring others. Instead, it means we should be aware of our strengths and weaknesses and design curricula accordingly.

Curriculum design is also influenced by the beliefs we hold about the nature of knowledge and what is most worth knowing, who should have access to knowledge, and how students learn. Take, for instance, our views on the nature of knowledge and what is most worth knowing. Some people believe that knowledge is known, somewhat constant, and relatively fixed. If we hold similar views, it is likely we will enact a curriculum that identifies knowledge deemed most important and then transmits this knowledge to students in the form of facts, concepts, and principles. Others believe that knowledge is rather flexible, somewhat personal, and formed and constructed by learners as they interact with their environments and with each other. A curriculum design from this perspective is no longer viewed wholly as a document that contains sets of topics to be covered and transmitted, but instead as sets of learning events and activities connected to standards where students and teachers negotiate meaning jointly. Here are questions to consider about the nature of knowledge and what is most worth knowing:

- What does it mean to be an educated person? How does my curriculum help or hinder my students becoming educated?
- Should the needs and interests of individual students in my classroom prevail or should the knowledge identified by the larger society come first?
- What is the appropriate emphasis for western ideas, literature, and culture as contrasted to ideas, literature, and culture of others?
- If I am an elementary teacher, what are the proper priorities for literacy and numeracy; for the fine arts and physical education?
- If I am a secondary teacher, what is the appropriate balance between the academic and vocational; between core and the extra curricula; between required courses and electives?
- What are the relationships between and priorities of knowledge associated with formal, in-school learning in my classroom as contrasted to less formal and out-of-school learning of my students in their families and communities?

These are rather complex questions with no definitive answers. The important thing is to keep them in mind as we enact curriculum in our classrooms each day and over the course of the school year.

Another set of important questions to think about in the process of curriculum design are those associated with who should have access to different kinds of knowledge:

- Should my goals address the needs of all students or focus on identifiable segments of students in my class?
- I want all my students to meet high standards, but many lack prior knowledge or have limited abilities. How differentiated should I make my curriculum?
- How do I make my curriculum available to students who are not interested?
- Should I differentiate my curriculum based on predicted students' career and higher education aspirations?
- If my classroom is composed of diverse learners, how much should I use ability grouping? How do I give diverse learners equal opportunities to learn and reach high expectations?

Finally, our curriculum design is influence by our personal beliefs about how students learn. Important questions described more thoroughly in Chapter 2 included:

- Is learning facilitated when teachers identify specific types of knowledge and focus in units of work and daily lessons? Or, is learning enhanced when teachers provide experiences for students that allow them to construct their own unique understandings? Or, is it a combination of both that is important?
- Do my students learn more when I take great care to cover all the learning materials designated for my grade level or subject area? Or do they learn more if I make sure they fully understand a topic before moving on?

> **REFLECTION**
>
> With a classmate or colleague, pick two or three questions from the lists above and compare the beliefs you each hold. Are your beliefs mainly the same or are they quite different? If different, in what ways do they differ? Identify particular instances where the beliefs you hold influenced what you taught and how.

We don't pretend that every teacher can or needs to develop definitive answers to these questions; however, we encourage all to recognize the perplexing situations they pose and to be aware and make explicit the choices we make.

Connecting Curriculum to the Lives and Needs of Students

We believe that the best curriculum is designed from the learner's point of view and does two things. It connects particular content and learning activities to students' lives and it provides them with appropriate challenges. In later chapters we will discuss in some detail the importance of instructional differentiation. Here, however, we will confine our discussion to two perspectives about how to determine what a particular group of students needs to know and be able to do.

In a standards-based, high-stakes testing environment, elementary teachers must ensure that their students are taught (and taught well) the knowledge and skills that will be on their state's (and/or district's) standardized tests. As you know, these tests vary from state to state, but primarily they cover core academic subjects: reading, writing, mathematics, science, and social studies. In secondary schools, teachers must ensure that their students are prepared to do well on subject matter exams required for graduation and on tests of academic skills used to make college admission decisions, such as the SATs and ACTs. To ignore the important roles that state mastery and college admission tests play in our students' lives or fail to prepare them properly is a serious disservice to students.

Obviously, the curriculum must also be tailored to the particular abilities, readiness, and prior knowledge of students and to their particular needs and interests. This is a difficult challenge for teachers for a number of reasons. For example, in most schools, the model of education we employ requires teachers to teach in age-graded or subject area classrooms. The students in these classrooms, however, have various abilities, needs, and interests. We also require teachers to focus on essential standards and goals, many of which may not match up very well to the capabilities of many of our students. This calls for teachers to modify instruction so they can attend to student differences, find ways to have all students achieve some measure of success, and to balance group and individual norms and needs. Fortunately, we know quite a bit about how to do this; we will not go into it here, however, because it is the major subject of the next chapter, on instructional differentiation.

Determining and responding to students' needs is one of the most complex and difficult tasks faced by teachers. Recently, Nel Noddings (2005) discussed and provided an important perspective on how to identify and respond to what children and youth need. She begins by making a distinction between inferred needs and expressed needs. **Inferred needs**, as the name implies, infer what others such as parents, curriculum developers, or teachers believe students need to know. The formal curriculum we described previously is based on inferred needs and based on the assumption that we know what students need. Many goals parents have for their children, such as going to college or preparing for a particular career, are also based on inferred needs.

Expressed needs, on the other hand, are needs identified by students themselves. Noddings says that often teachers, curriculum developers and parents infer one set of needs, while students express "quite another." She provides some examples. Curriculum developers may infer that students need to add fractions, a need not openly expressed by many students. Teachers may infer the need for students to learn particular academic subjects; children and youth may express the need to learn how to live. Parents may infer the need for their teenage son to be prepared in academic mathematics so he can get into college while the son may express the need to learn a craft that does not require a college education.

How can teachers respond to the gaps or conflicts between inferred and expressed needs? According to Noddings, a response used by some teachers is to discard inferred needs when students challenge them. She argues that this isn't a very good or practical solution. On the other hand, holding tightly to the view that every inferred need must be addressed is perceived as authoritarian and can be easily dismissed by students. Noddings recommends the following criteria for deciding when a student's expressed needs should be recognized:

1. The expressed need is fairly stable over a considerable period of time and/or it is intense.
2. The expressed need is demonstrably connected to some desirable end or, at least, to one that is not harmful; further, the end is impossible or difficult to reach without the object wanted.
3. The expressed need is in the power (within the means) of those addressed to grant it.
4. The person expressing the need is willing and able to contribute to the satisfaction of the need (paraphrased from p. 61).

Nodding also provides a strategy for dealing with the inevitable conflict between inferred and expressed needs. She believes that teachers can manage the standard curriculum in sensitive ways, remaining aware that what they want students to learn may not coincide with what students want to learn. This requires negotiating needs and modifying curriculum based on students' readiness and interests. It also means entering into dialogue with students about the inferred curriculum. Rather than responding to a student's challenge such as, "Why do we have to study this?" with a response such as, "The powers to be told me I have to," respond instead with serious discussions with students about some of the larger purposes of education described earlier: What are the aims of education in our culture? What does it mean to be educated? She also suggests that, as teachers and educators, we should not force all students into academic courses in the name of equity, but instead fight to develop a "relevant curriculum around interests other than the academic."

> **REFLECTION**
>
> With a colleague or classmate, discuss the idea of inferred and expressed needs. Consider how far you think teachers should go in discarding the formal curriculum to meet the expressed needs of students? Discuss how the two of you agree or disagree on this topic.

Making Standards Work for You

The standards movement has produced an array of curriculum frameworks and content standards. This may change in the future, but today, standards, benchmarks, and high-stakes testing are a fact of the social context of teaching. And, regardless of one's personal philosophy, we really do not have a choice about whether or not to pay attention to the standards-based educational environment. We can, however, find ways to make standards work for us by using them to facilitate rather than detract from teaching.

The main problem to solve is one that Nichols and Berliner (2007) and Marzano and Haystead (2008) have described as far *too much content*, a situation that detracts from effective teaching in serious ways. For example, Marzano and Haystead reported that a decade ago over 200 standards and 3,093 benchmarks had been identified in national and state-level documents across 14 subject areas. When researchers asked teachers how long it would take to teach the knowledge and skills found in these standards and benchmarks, they reported that instructional time would have to be increased by 71 percent and require extending schooling to grades 21 or 22. In the process of writing this chapter, we discovered the same phenomena. In state after state and subject after subject, we found many more standards, benchmarks, and performance indicators than could possibly be achieved in the instructional time available. We found in our earlier example of Ohio's K-12 English Language Arts Standards that the ten overall standards were expanded to include 215 benchmarks and 1,171 grade-level performance indicators. The number of indicators varied from a low of 57 in kindergarten to a high of 99 in eighth grade. The grade-level average was slightly over 90. This number would require teachers to meet one indicator every two days in a normal 180-day school year.

Not only is there too much content, but many standards have more than one dimension or element, as Marzano and Haystead (2008) found when they analyzed the benchmarks from the National Council of Teachers of Mathematics' fifth-grade standards. They provide a simple illustration of what we mean by a standard having more than one element. The benchmark reads:

- Student will develop fluency in adding, subtracting, multiplying, and dividing whole numbers.

Though the knowledge and skills described in this benchmark are related, the "underlying processes are not the same." This benchmark actually encompasses four different processes:

- The process of adding whole numbers.
- The process of subtracting whole numbers.
- The process of multiplying whole numbers.
- The process of dividing whole numbers.

Further analysis of the mathematic standards by Marzano and Haystead found a total of 241 benchmarks for grade K-12. However, each benchmark addressed more than a single dimension, and "741 unique elements were revealed" (p. 9). The fact that so many standards and benchmarks exist, and that so many contain more than one element, requires teachers to reconstitute and revise them. Ainsworth (2003) and Ainswsorth and Viegut (2006) call this process "unwrapping" the standards; Marzano and Haystead (2008) call it "unpacking" the standards. It requires choosing among standards and reconstituting important standards so they contain a single dimension.

Before describing how to winnow and **reconstitute standards**, let's first note some unproductive paths to avoid. One, as teachers, we could race through all the standards and benchmarks to make sure all content is covered. Two, we could pick among the standards and choose to teach those we like best. Or three, we could simply ignore standards and benchmarks and allow our own preferences to determine curriculum design. We believe that none of these paths will lead to the type of student learning deemed important. Treating a lot of content lightly will *not* result in student understanding and in-depth learning; picking or ignoring particular content is no longer educationally responsible. On the other hand, there are several strategies teachers have devised for winnowing out the least important standards and for reconstituting standards found to be multidimensional.

Making Less More Let's tackle the *winnowing* problem first. A long time ago, Jerome Bruner (1960, p. 121) warned, "one cannot cover any subject in full, not even in a lifetime, if coverage means visiting all the facts and events and morsels." Think about how much more knowledge and content exists 50 years after Bruner made this observation. Theodore Sizer (1992) and his colleagues encouraged teachers in their high school reform projects to follow two important principles: "less is more" and "learning can't be rushed." More recently, a report of a study of high school science curricula (Cavanagh, 2009) concluded that students who had been required to focus intensely on a few core topics in their high school science courses did better in their first-year college science classes than did students who covered many topics sparsely.

Strategies exist to help eliminate the nonessential and to identify knowledge and skills deemed most important.

Economy and Power Jerome Bruner (1960) recommended use of the concepts of economy and power as a means to limit the number of topics and ideas in a teacher's curriculum. Using the **economy principle** means being very careful about the amount of information and the number of concepts or skills presented in a single lesson, a unit of work, or over a whole course of study. It means helping students examine a few critical ideas in depth rather a cursory introduction of many. Using the **power principle** means designing lessons around big ideas, those central to a subject's structure, and ones that can be taught so students gain understanding and discover relationships among a few salient specific facts and essential concepts. In most instances (but not all), teachers can rely on the major themes used to organize standards and benchmarks to represent the big or powerful ideas. Using economy, however, calls for decisions about exactly what and how to teach on a particular day.

Let's take an example of how the idea of economy might be used to teach one of the core themes in the Connecticut science curriculum described earlier: "*Matter and energy in ecosystems: How do matter and energy flow through the ecosystem?*" We think most science educators would agree that this is an essential question addressing a big and important idea. Referring back to Table 4.1 shows that one of the content standards under this theme is "*populations in ecosystems are affected by biotic factors, such as population . . ..*" One of the performance expectations prescribed that students should be able to "*explain how populations are affected by predator–prey relationships.*"

How might lessons be designed so students will understand and can explain this important idea and demonstrate mastery of the performance indicators? One approach might be to present students with a series of lessons where various predator–prey relationships are explained and discussed. Examples might include: wolves–mountain lions–domestic cattle; hawks–field mice; man–whales–sharks, and so on. Employing the concept of economy, however, might lead the teacher to design instruction around a single example of a predator–prey relationship, perhaps wolves. Wolves have an intrinsic interest to students in upper elementary and middle schools and the relationship between wolves and humans sparks considerable controversy among several groups, such as environmentalists, hunters, and ranchers. Students could be asked to do research on the history of wolves, including myths about them, how they almost became extinct in the twentieth century, and how contemporary efforts to support wolf populations have led to concern by farmers and ranchers whose livestock fall prey to them. We believe the in-depth exploration represented in the second approach would likely lead to greater understanding of the standard and more success on its performance indicators.

Enduring Understandings With the same purposes in mind, Wiggins and McTighe (1998, 2005) have provided a slightly different set of words to describe the economy and power principles. Their framework for setting curricular priorities is adapted and illustrated in the nested rings shown in Figure 4.5.

The background in Figure 4.5 can be viewed as all of the content in any particular field or topic. Since everything cannot be taught, Wiggins and McTighe maintain that teachers can approach reducing the entire field by asking three important questions. The largest of the rings in the figure symbolizes the first question: "What is worth a student being familiar with?" This would be the content that could be skimmed quickly or covered lightly. The middle ring illustrates the second question: "What is important for a student to know and be able to do?" A student's education would be incomplete if these essentials have not been mastered either because they are needed in life or they will be found on mastery exams. Finally, the inside ring in the framework represents the third question: What are the big and enduring ideas that should remain with students after they have forgotten most of the details?"

But, you may be asking, how does one go about determining what is important to know and what are the **enduring understandings**? Again, Wiggins and McTighe offer four criteria for teachers to use in selecting ideas and topics to teach:

1. To what extent does the idea, topic, or process represent a "big idea" having enduring value beyond the classroom?
2. To what extent does the idea, topic, or process reside at the heart (or central structure) of the discipline?
3. To what extent does the idea, topic, or process require coverage? (For instance, will it be included on important state or district standardized tests?)
4. To what extent does the idea, topic, or process offer potential for engaging students?

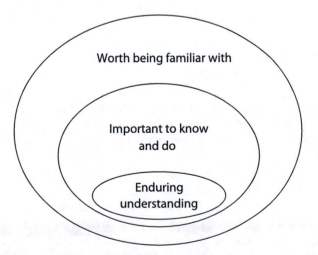

Figure 4.5 The Wiggin–McTighe framework for establishing curricular priorities
Source: Adapted from Wiggins and McTighe (1998), p. 10.

If an idea or topic does not meet any of the criteria, then it is probably safe to discard it from the curriculum.

Getting to point where we embrace the power, economy, and enduring understanding principles is difficult for most of us. As teachers, we always know more than we can teach; we are also always tempted to cover everything and fill lessons with too many ideas and topics. Teachers face the same problem as the authors of this textbook face. We want to share with you all that we know, and all too often forget that you have limited time and motivation to learn everything that may interest us. Film editors face the same problem. However, good ones know that leaving many feet of film on the editing floor results in more interesting and pleasing movies, just as leaving some topics untaught leads to more student motivation and learning.

Getting to Single Dimensions Now let's turn to the lack of **unidimensionality** and begin by asking why this situation is important. It is important for benchmarks and performance indicators to have a single element so measurements can be designed to assess student progress toward mastery of the targeted knowledge or skill. The process of identifying single elements can also lead to more clarity, reduce redundancy, and pare the number of standards or benchmarks deemed important to address. Below are examples of how benchmarks can be unpacked and how corresponding measurements can be designed to assess student mastery.

In addition to providing a model for thinking about enduring understandings, Wiggins and McTighe (1998, 2005) have also provided us with a curriculum design process that calls for first identifying the assessment component of a single element performance indicator. They observed that, though teachers have been instructed to start the planning process with goals and objectives, in reality they most often start with the textbook and favored teaching activities. To catch teachers' attention, Wiggins and McTighe argue for **backward curriculum design**, a process that puts the development of particular assessments and the identification of evidence that will be acceptable to demonstrate that students have attained desired understandings or skills at the beginning of the planning process. Clarifying desired outcomes leads, then, to more effective use of teaching resources and planned learning experiences. Stages of the backward design process are illustrated in Figure 4.6.

An application exercise using the backward design process is included in our *Fieldbook*, and Research Box 4.2 illustrates how a particular high school teacher used backward design in his day-to-day teaching.

Steps for Reconstituting Finally, we have found the five steps described below to be a helpful process for identifying standards, benchmarks, and performance indicators deemed essential, and analyzing each for multidimensionality.

Step 1: Identifying and Understanding Essential Standards. The process of reconstituting standards consists of identifying those deemed essential and thoroughly understanding each. A particular standard is essential if it addresses an important question or enduring idea or if it is included prominently on mastery tests students are required to pass. A thorough understanding of the standard can help translate it into a language students can understand. Thorough understanding is accomplished by studying the standard carefully, considering what students would know and be able to do if they

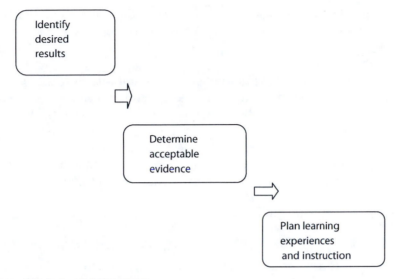

Figure 4.6 Stages of the backward design process
Source: Illustration based on information from Wiggins and McTighe (1998), p. 9.

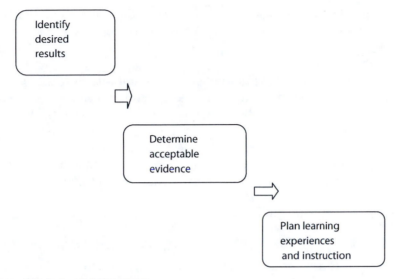

RESEARCH BOX 4.2

McCutcheon, G., & Milner, H. (2002). A contemporary study of teacher planning in a high school English class. *Teachers and Teaching: Theory and Practice, 8* (1), 81–94.

Researchers, McCutcheon and Milner, observed and interviewed Bill, a 25-year veteran English teacher, about his approach to planning. They found that while "many teachers seem to plan on a day-to-day or weekly basis, Bill planned each course (long) before he teaches it . . . a form [labeled by the researchers] as 'long-range pre-active planning'" (p. 84). For example, in preparation for a new course on "Major British Writers," Bill would read through his school's course of study and state standards, and he would research how other teachers had taught the course. They found that Bill avoided too much detail in his plan, because he wanted to have an improvisatory nature to instruction and discussions and be able to take advantage of students' prior knowledge. Too much planning restricts the flow of exploration and discussion. Bill says, "as we are having a discussion, maybe something in the literature strikes me, but they (students) may not have had the experience to draw on it. So sometimes I have to be able to go out in left field, and I don't always know ahead of time where I'm going to go or exactly where the discussion will take us. That preempts too much short-term planning" (p. 86).

McCutcheon and Milner (2002) found from their study of Bill that he did not plan by objectives but through a form of mental imaging and rehearsal, explained as "*backward building,*" similar to the Wiggins–McTighe backward planning approach. Bill said that teachers should "envision where we want the students to end up and then make plans backwards from there" (summarized from pp. 91–92).

mastered it and/or providing analysis of what a knowledgeable person does when he or she has a thorough knowledge of an idea or can perform a particular skill with expertise.

Step 2: Analyzing Standards for Declarative and Procedural Knowledge. In Chapter 2, we made distinctions between *declarative* knowledge and *procedural* knowledge. Most standards communicate two important outcomes: what students should know (declarative knowledge) and what they should be able to do (procedural knowledge). Both kinds of knowledge are obviously important. However, a critical aspect of reconstituting standards is to separate the two kinds of knowledge. We recommend a simple process of reading through a standard and underlining key ideas or concepts (declarative knowledge) and perhaps circling skills (procedural knowledge). Most often, key concepts will be nouns; skills will be verbs. For example:

- *Declarative knowledge to be underlined*: Populations in ecosystems can be divided into three categories: producers, consumers, and decomposers of organic matter.
- *Procedural knowledge to be circled*: Develop a category scheme and categorize the following ecosystem populations.

Step 3: Identifying Precursory Subskills and/or Bodies of Enabling Knowledge. As described previously, many standards contain numerous subskills and/or understandings tucked into the overall standard. This situation makes it difficult to communicate an outcome clearly to students and to assess whether or not it has been achieved. Popham (2008) has provided us with a tool he labels the **learning progression**. This tool helps communicate learning outcomes to students, and it assists teachers to enhance student learning. He defined a learning progression as a:

sequenced set of subskills and bodies of enabling knowledge that . . . students must master enroute to mastering a more remote curriculum aim [or standard] (p. 24).

You might also want to think of learning progressions as the "building blocks" that need to be put in place in order to get to the overall standard or instructional outcome. Here are some examples of familiar learning progressions. In mathematics, before students can calculate the area of a rectangle they must be able to measure the rectangle and know how to multiply. Subskills and **enabling knowledge** for writing a good essay are numerous: knowing the structure of an essay, being able to write a capturing introduction, mastering accepted practices of sentence and paragraph construction, and the like. To understand the nature and causes of a particular civil war requires some understanding about what motivates civil wars in the first place, such as the need for land, disputes over ideology or theology, or just plain desire to have power and control. Figure 4.7 provides a visual representation adapted from Popham (2008) to help understand learning progressions.

Note that the hypothetical instructional outcome targeted in Figure 4.7 has two enabling knowledge objectives and four subskill objectives, and it is anticipated that, to teach these enabling knowledge and precursory objectives, will require a total of seven lessons.

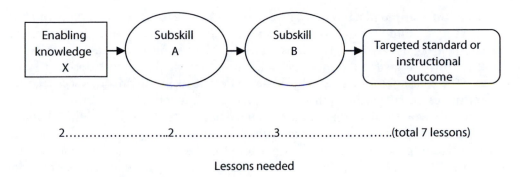

2.....................2.........................3...........................(total 7 lessons)

Lessons needed

Figure 4.7 A visual representation of a learning progression
Source: Illustration based on information from Popham (2008).

Step 4: Determining Assessments. This step consists of determining assessments needed for each enabling knowledge and subskill and for the overall standard or instructional outcome. This is an important step because if there are no ways to measure formally or informally, then there is no way to collect evidence whether or not students have reached the desired learning outcomes associated with the standard. We will provide much more information about designing performance assessments in Chapter 6.

Step 5: Building an Instructional Sequence. A final step in this reconstituting process is to design an instructional sequence to teach in some logical order the enabling knowledge and precursory skills. In most instances, this sequence will be influenced by the teacher's understanding of the standard, the building blocks required for getting there, and students' abilities and prior knowledge.

Figure 4.8 summarizes the steps to follow in unwrapping and reconstituting essential content standards.

Curriculum Mapping

We believe strongly that, as individual teachers, it is in our students' best interest if we listen to and work with our colleagues when deciding what to teach. This is true for several reasons. There is simply not enough time for us to teach what another teacher has already taught. Similarly, the stakes are too high to choose not to teach a particular piece of knowledge or skill because we assumed that someone else has covered it, only to find out later that this assumption was wrong. Most important, however, a coherent curriculum and the synergy it produces can only be achieved if teachers at grade and department levels and school-wide know what each other are doing and have adopted common approaches that make it clear to students what is expected of them.

Step 1: Identify and develop a thorough understanding of standards deemed most essential.

Step 2: Analyze each standard for both declarative (concepts and ideas) and procedural (skills) knowledge.

Step 3: Identify precursory(enabling) knowledge and subskills required to master the standard or instructional outcome.

Step 4: Determine assessments required for each enabling knowledge and subskill and for the overall standard or instructional outcome.

Step 5: Build an instructional sequence that teaches the enabling knowledge and precursory skills in the most "sensible order."

Figure 4.8 Summary of process for identifying and unwrapping essential content standards

Curriculum mapping is a final tool we describe that teachers can use to help limit "what is taught," and one that is particularly useful for teams of teachers to analyze what is being taught across classrooms and grade levels. Although there are several curriculum mapping strategies, we prefer the one that has been developed by Heidi Jacobs (1997, 2003). Jacobs agrees with what we described in the previous section, that big ideas and essential questions should comprise the heart of the curriculum and, with us, she too has worried that demand for coverage has led to superficial rather than in-depth student understanding. Her curriculum-mapping process provides a tool for teachers to accomplish several things. It is a tool for teachers to analyze what they are doing individually and to find out what other teachers in a particular school or school district, or across departments and grade levels, are doing. It also can help teachers examine how well their curriculum is aligned to standards so it can be inspected for gaps and redundancies.

The process of curriculum mapping begins with individual teachers using a template to outline the ideas, knowledge, and skills emphasized in their classroom, the essential questions they address, and intended learner outcomes. We provide an example of a curriculum map designed by an eleventh-grade social studies teacher in Table 4.3.

Depending upon the situation, these outlines are shared with other teachers in the grade level, departments, or within an entire school or school district. Together, teachers then construct maps of their curricula. The important thing about these maps is that they show the planned curriculum, including areas of overlap and gaps that may exist.

Today, worldwide networks exist that encourage teachers to share their curriculum maps with colleagues around the country and the world. Software programs also exist to support curriculum mapping. We list mapping networks and available software in the resource section of this chapter. The *Fieldbook* that accompanies this book also provides more detailed explanations about how to construct curriculum maps.

SOME FINAL THOUGHTS

As we expressed at the beginning, this has been a difficult chapter for us to write because we have mixed feeling about the ways the standards movement and high-stakes testing have evolved. On the one hand, we support efforts to develop standards that help clarify what students need to know and be able to do and that hold high expectations for all students. At the same time, we have been disappointed with the effects the standards movement has had on curriculum. Too often it has narrowed the curriculum and set an impossible number of standards for teachers to achieve.

If we had written a chapter on curriculum design two decades ago, we would have highlighted how important teachers' curriculum decisions are, and we would have emphasized the importance of individualizing curriculum and learning activities for particular students. We would *not* have devoted much space to explaining how to revise and reconstitute state and district standards so as to make them workable for teachers and students, nor would we have spent so many words advising teachers to slow down. We hope that things will change in the years ahead and believe several reforms are needed. Curriculum writers (many of whom are classroom teachers) need to show restraint and provide teachers with a limited number of topics and content standards and encourage them to add to these depending upon their students' interests and abilities. The larger teaching profession, who advocated initially for NCLB, needs to speak out to state and federal agencies and to policy makers at every level. We need to encourage setting standards and requirements that match the time and resources society is willing to provide for their children's education. Teachers and administrators in local schools need to join with the many parents and citizens who believe the curriculum has

Table 4.3 Curriculum map for high school economics

	January	February	March	April	May
Essential questions	• What constitutes the study of economics? • What is microeconomics? • How do supply and demand affect our everyday lives? • How do different businesses operate?	• What is macroeconomics? • What distinctions do economists make between micro- and microeconomics? • How is competition created and maintained? • What determines the health of our economy?	• What roles do consumers play in the American economic system?	• What are the basics of buying, saving, and budgeting. • What are the pitfalls to avoid?	• How does the American economic system differ from other economic systems?
Content	Microeconomics • Supply and demand – Demand – Elasticity – Supply – Combined supply and demand • Business organizations – Proprietorships and partnerships – Corporations • Competition and monopolies – Perfect competition – Monopoly/ oligopoly	Macroeconomics • Measuring the economy's performance – National income accounting – Inflation – Fluctuation • Government monetary and fiscal policies – National budget – Taxation • Money and banking – Fluctuations – History • Federal Reserve – Money supply – Federal organization	Consumer Economics I • Introduction – Basic problem – Trade-offs • You as a consumer – Income/ consumption – Buying principles • Debt – Sources of credit – Applying for credit	Consumer Economics II • Buying Necessities I – Food – Clothing – Advertising appeals – Marketing • Buying Necessities II – Housing – Automobile • Saving and investing – Why save? – How the stock market works	Comparative Economic Systems • Economic systems • American economic system • European economic systems • Controlled economic systems, as in Russia and China • Examples of economic systems in developing countries • International economic institutions – World Bank – UN agencies – NGOs *(Continued)*

Table 4.3—*continued*

	January	February	March	April	May
Understanding	• Can explain and graph the law of supply and demand • Can explain elasticity • Can explain how supply and demand affect our economy • Can compare and contrast different business organization types	• Can identify the measures used to study the economy • Can explain how inflation works and analyze its effects • Can explain how the Federal Reserve affects the money supply • Can list the duties of the Federal Reserve chairman • Can summarize the role of banks and money • Can define employment and inflation	• Can explain and apply the role of a consumer • Can describe sources of credit • Can analyze advertising from the point of view of consumers and producers • Can create a mock ad campaign	• Can list and describe steps for buying a house or car • Can create a personal budget • Can read a stock market quote page • Can identify components of a stock portfolio • Can demonstrate knowledge of the process of buying stock	• Can compares/contrast the different economic systems • Can explain issues relating to global economics • Can explain economic problems faced by developing countries • Can explain the role of the World Bank, NGOs and how each function
Assessments	• Formative quiz • Supply and demand performance assessment	• Formative quiz • Analysis of macroeconomic problem situations	• Formative quiz • Ad campaign exercise • Personal budget simulation	• Formative quiz • Stock market simulation	• Formative quiz • Comparative economics project • Final essay exam

Source: Table has been revised from original idea found on the website of the Ankeny Community School District that no longer exists and for which district personnel report that the initial author is unknown. Printed with permission.

become too narrow and inflexible, and that we need a curriculum that gets us back to some of the broader purposes of education.

SUMMARY AT A GLANCE

- Making wise curriculum decisions is among the most important aspects of a teacher's work. When done skillfully, students develop a sense of where they are going and what they are expected to learn. Done poorly, they lead to confusion and breakdowns in student learning.
- Curriculum is influenced by the larger social purposes of education (academic, vocational, social and civic, and personal), and there have been several enduring debates that have influenced how the formal and enacted curriculums have been designed and implemented. These include: who controls curriculum, the importance of content versus process, and whether the source of curriculum content should be the academic disciplines or the expressed interests and needs of students.
- There are two curriculums found in classrooms: the formal curriculum adopted

by subject matter associations, state departments of education, and school districts; and the enacted curriculum, the one designed by classroom teachers for a particular group of students.

- The formal curriculum today is very prescriptive and is characterized by state- and school district-designed curriculum frameworks, content standards, and by high-stakes, standardized tests.
- The teacher's enacted curriculum is the one actually experienced by students and has profound effects on what students actually learn.
- When designing their enacted curriculum, teachers pay attention to the larger purposes of schooling, their own beliefs about the nature of knowledge, and their beliefs about how students learn.
- In the current standards-based educational environment, teachers must find ways to make the standards work for them. This requires winnowing down the large number of identified standards and teaching toward only those deemed most essential. It also often means reconstituting standards so each can be successfully accessed.
- Backward design, learning progressions, reconstituting processes, and curriculum mapping are tools teachers can use to make standards work for them and to ensure that curricula in classrooms and across classrooms address essential questions and big ideas.

CONSTRUCTING YOUR OWN LEARNING

Working alone or with colleagues, use one of the tools we have described for personalizing curriculum or unwrapping standards. For instance a third to fourth grade-level team might use "mapping" to inspect their curricula for gaps or redundancies, or a high school department might analyze the standards that define what their students should know and/or standards that lack unidimensionality, and then rewrite these standards and develop measurement devices that can be used to assess student progress.

RESOURCES

Ainsworth, L., & Viegut, D. (2006). *Common formative assessments.* Thousand Oaks, CA: Corwin.

Curriculum Mapping websites: http://currmap.learningpt.org/default.htm.

Jacobs, H. H. (ed.), (2003). *Getting results with curriculum mapping.* Alexandria, VA: Association for Supervision and Curriculum Development.

Marzano, R., & Haystead, M. (2008). *Making standards useful in the classroom.* Alexandria, VA: Association of Supervision and Curriculum Development.

Popham, J. (2008). *Transformative assessment.* Alexandria, VA: Association for Supervision and Curriculum Development.

5

INSTRUCTIONAL DIFFERENTIATION

Jack has come to teaching as a third career. First, he spent time in the army. Then, he was a medical technologist and in medical sales for three decades. Finally, in his fifties, he turned to teaching, a love that he had wanted to pursue as a young man. After completing an alternative teacher certification program, he accepted his first teaching job as a middle school physical sciences teacher. He was very excited, but his excitement was quickly tempered with the realities of the classroom and life in schools. One of the biggest surprises was the wide range of talents and the diversity of the learners present in his classes. He had kids who couldn't read, students new to the United States who were struggling to learn English, students who were very smart, kids not interested in school or learning, poor kids and rich kids, and there were twice as many boys than girls.

Jack knew his science content, and he was pretty confident in his teaching abilities. He planned great lessons, but was frustrated that his students were performing poorly on assignments and tests. After talking with other teachers, his principal, and a consultant, he decided he needed to learn about differentiated instruction (a topic that was new to him and one that he had not heard much about in his teacher education program). Jack went to workshops, observed other teachers, and read about differentiation. Then he began experimenting. He started with collecting materials in different formats and at different reading levels. Then, he turned to planning lessons differently and moved from mostly whole group instruction to using flexible grouping part of the time. He also designed varied learning activities and gave students more choices in their assignments. In addition, he invested more time in getting to know students as individuals and finding out about their interests, the ways they liked to learn, and their special abilities and talents. He prepared a learning profile for each student. It took time and Jack is still learning, but today he is teaching differently, and his students are indeed learning more. He continues to offer more choices and each year adds new strategies to his repertoire.

We address **instructional differentiation** earlier in this book, rather than later, because we see it as an important way of thinking about teaching and learning in the twenty-first century. Differentiation is not an addition to teaching. Instead, it is a perspective and a philosophy that shapes curriculum, planning, instruction, assessment, and classroom management. Today, all teachers are expected to be responsive to the needs of the diverse learners in their classrooms. Providing the same learning opportunities for all students, at the same time and at the same pace, no longer provides the quality of learning opportunities required for the range of students in our classrooms.

In this chapter, we start by giving a definition of instructional differentiation and by providing frameworks for understanding its use. We describe some of the research that supports instructional differentiation and then look at effective teaching in the **differentiated classroom** and the implications for planning, implementing, and assessing instruction. We describe the differentiated learning environment and how it differs from the more traditional, **teacher-centered classroom**. Next, we describe a number of strategies for our experienced teacher readers to consider as they implement differentiation. Finally, we highlight some challenges and tensions created by instructional differentiation.

DEFINITION AND RATIONALE FOR DIFFERENTIATION

Differentiation is the practice of adjusting the curriculum, teaching strategies, assessment strategies, and the classroom environment to meet the needs of all students. A differentiated classroom provides different pathways for students to acquire content, to process information and ideas, and to develop products that demonstrate understanding (Tomlinson, 2001, p. 7). Differentiated instruction is student-centered rather than teacher-centered; it is the recognition of and commitment to planning for student differences. On a simple level, differentiated instruction is starting where students are rather than adopting a standardized approach to whole class teaching. It is teaching that is "responsive and proactive" rather than "prescriptive and reactive." Differentiation is a commitment to starting where each child is and using multiple approaches to take them as far as possible.

Diversity—this one word describes the typical classroom that can be found almost everywhere in North America. It speaks to the richness, the challenges, and the possibilities of learning and teaching in the twenty-first century. As you know, our classrooms are full of differences: in gender, in culture, in cognitive levels, in abilities, in intelligences, in learning styles, in languages, and in interests. Increasingly, society holds the expectation that all students will be provided unique and personalized opportunities to learn. The challenge for those of us who are teachers is to provide learning experiences to accommodate the range of diversity in students that arrive each and every day.

REFLECTION

What is the composition of your class(es)? What is the most challenging aspect of diversity for you as a teacher? What are its positive aspects? Are you already differentiating your instruction and looking for more ideas or is this a new concept to you? With a colleague or classmate, discuss how pervasive instructional differentiation is in your school(s).

While some have observed that the origins of differentiated instruction find their roots in the one-room schoolhouse and that Dewey (1938) wrote about this approach to education in the early twentieth century, differentiated instruction, as we know it today, was more widely introduced in the 1980s in response to the new theories about human intelligence and the growing work on learning styles. In 1985, Guild and Garger wrote one of the first books on differentiated instruction, titled *What is Differentiated Instruction?*

Marching to Different Drummers. In it, they focused specifically on how to differentiate instruction to account for different learning styles. At the same time, educators who were concerned with special categories of learners, such as struggling or gifted students, began recommending the use of differentiated instructional strategies and challenged the idea that different categories of learners should be separated to address their special needs. Today, few schools have special classes, and most classrooms are comprised of learners with a diverse range of abilities and needs, a situation that again calls for instructional differentiation.

DIFFERENTIATED INSTRUCTION FRAMEWORKS

A variety of frameworks exist for thinking about and organizing the differentiated classroom. We will highlight two of them here. Perhaps the best-known framework is the one provided by Carol Ann Tomlinson, who has been writing about this topic since the 1990s (Tomlinson, 1995, 1999, 2001, 2004; Tomlinson & Eidson, 2003a, 2003b; Tomlinson & Strickland, 2005). Dodge (2005) has also developed a framework that helps us understand instructional differentiation. As you will see, these two frameworks provide alternative ways for thinking about and implementing differentiated strategies in your classroom.[1]

Tomlinson's Framework

Tomlinson (2001) described a six-part framework for differentiation. Her framework begins with the student and proposes that students' **academic readiness**, their *interests*, and their **learner profiles** should guide the planning of learning activities. She also illustrates how *content, processes,* and *products* can be varied to meet different student needs. Differentiation by *readiness* means extending student knowledge, understanding, and skills a bit beyond what they can do independently. Teachers, Tomlinson argues, should move individual students beyond their comfort zones and provide support to bridge the gap between what is known and what is unknown. Remember Vygotsky's zone of proximal development described in Chapter 2.

Tomlinson also maintains that student readiness can vary along continuums by subject areas and by knowledge dimensions. This requires application of differentiated learning experiences for students. These continuums and recommended applications are shown in Table 5.1.

Differentiation by *interest* means connecting school work to what students are interested in. This requires identifying the interests students bring with them to the classroom, as well as helping them create new ones by exposing them to different ideas, topics, and opening up new windows on the world for them. Differentiating by **learning preference** means providing optional learning tasks and activities so students can learn in ways that capitalize on their strengths and can identify and understand how they learn best (learning styles). In Research Box 5.1 we highlight a summary of two studies conducted by Sternberg and his colleagues that provide support for differentiating instruction.

Finally Tomlinson's (2001) framework calls for teachers to provide multiple strategies for organizing and differentiating content (curriculum), processes (instruction), and products (assessment) to accommodate students' levels of readiness, varied interests, and different learning preferences. We discuss several strategies she recommends later in the chapter

Table 5.1 Tomlinson's readiness continuums

Dimension	Continuum—From → To	Application
Level of knowledge	Foundational to transformational	Moving from basic knowledge and understandings to intricacies and extensions
Level of abstraction	Concrete to abstract	Moving from basic information to meanings and implications
Level of complexity	Simple to complex	Moving from the big picture skeleton to detailed descriptions
Number of variables or options	Single options to multiple options	Moving from a few steps or solutions to complicated directions (or a variety of options)
Knowing to doing	Small leaps to big leaps	Moving from reading or talking to applying and doing
Level of structure	More structure to less structure	Moving from well-laid out activities to advanced and open-ended tasks
Level of independence	Dependence to independence	Moving from skill building to structured independence, to shared independence, to self-guided independence
Pace	Slow to quick	Speeding up or slowing down based on student progress

Source: Information summarized and adapted from Tomlinson (2001).

Dodge's Differentiation in Action

Dodge (2005) provided teachers another framework to think about differentiation, and she contends that there are both simple and complex ways to respond to diversity. As with Tomlinson's framework, Dodge starts with understanding learners. She recommends that teachers think about the three phases of learning—pre-learning, during learning, and post-learning—and consider how choice and options for students can be provided at each stage. Dodge's framework involves five categories of strategies: providing choice, building instruction around Bloom's taxonomy, using multiple intelligences, flexible grouping, and **tiered lessons**. She believes that providing choice is the *easiest* way to begin differentiation, while providing tiered lessons is the most *difficult*. She encourages teachers to start slowly and add differentiated strategies associated with each of her five categories to their repertoire over time. Some of the strategies recommended by Dodge will be described later in the chapter.

REFLECTION

Which of these two frameworks (Tomlinson versus Dodge) do you like best? What makes most sense to you in thinking about addressing diversity and making changes in your classroom?

Inquiry **RESEARCH BOX 5.1**

Sternberg, R.J., Torf, B., & Grigorenko, E. (1998). Teaching for successful intelligence raises student achievement. *Phi Delta Kappan, 79*(9), 667–779.

In two studies, researchers tested the theory of successful intelligence in practice. Successful intelligence was defined as: (1) triarchic instruction where teaching materials were taught in ways that enabled student to use not only their memory ability but also their analytical, creative, and practical abilities; and (2) teaching materials in a way that enabled students to use their intellectual strength. The first study (a social studies investigation) involved 225 ethnically diverse third-graders (ages seven to eight), generally of low socio-economic status, in two different schools. The second study (a psychology investigation) involved 142 eighth graders (ages 12 to 13) attending summer programs at two different universities.

In both studies, students were divided into three groups. Students in the experimental group received triarchic instruction to promote their intellectual understanding of the material. The material was taught for memory but also analytically, creatively, and practically. Students in the control group received analytical and critical-thinking instruction only. This group was the "strong" control, because it represented the kind of instruction that is often provided when teachers are trying to promote "critical thinking." Students in the third group—also a control group—received conventional (memory-based) instruction. They were taught the material mainly through presentation and explanation.

Memory instruction and assessment involved questions that asked what, where, when, and how. Analytical instruction and assessment involved activities where students were required to compare and contrast, and to analyze, evaluate, and judge. Creative instruction and assessment involved activities that required students to create, invent, discover, and imagine. Practical instruction and assessment involved activities that allowed students to use, utilize, implement, and apply. In all of the groups, the assessments used were the same and included multiple-choice questions for assessing memory, as well as performance assessments measuring analytical, creative, and practical achievements.

The results of both studies indicated that, on average, on the analytical, creative, and practical performance assessments, students in the triarchic-instruction group out-performed students in the other two conditions. And, the students in the analytical-instruction group outperformed the memory-based instruction group. The students in the triarchic-instruction group were also superior to the other two groups on the multiple-choice memory assessments, although the other two conditions did not differ from each other. The results were somewhat stronger—but in the same direction—in the secondary school study as compared to the primary school study. The researchers concluded that teaching in multiple and differentiated ways facilitates student under-standing, and it allows students to capitalize on their strengths and compensate for their weaknesses.

EFFECTIVE TEACHING AND LEARNING IN THE DIFFERENTIATED CLASSROOM

Historically, most teachers taught to the whole class; all students learned the subject in the same way, at the same time, and at the same pace. The classroom was teacher-centered and teacher-organized. The differentiated classroom, on the other hand, is student-centered and student-organized. Instruction is based on student interests, learning preferences, and academic readiness. In this section, we describe ways to plan, manage, and assess student learning in the differentiated classroom. We will also compare the differentiated classroom to the traditional classroom and describe how the roles for students and teachers differ.

Planning for Differentiation

Three aspects of planning for differentiation are important: clarifying content, diagnosing student readiness, and designing varied learning experiences. First, key concepts, essential questions, and curriculum standards to guide student learning need to be identified. This step is very similar to planning for a traditional classroom. Second, students' readiness, interests, and learning profiles need to be assessed to gain information about students' strengths and weaknesses and about the best ways for matching and grouping. Third, a range of learning tasks, activities, experiences, and assessments should be designed that can provide the necessary variety to lead and manage **student-centered classrooms**. These two latter steps distinguish planning for a differentiated classroom from more traditional ones.

Assessing and understanding individual learners is key to accommodating differences. Many teachers who differentiate instruction develop a learning profile for each student and record a range of specific characteristics about the individual, such as their academic readiness (below grade level, at grade level, above grade level), their different intellectual strengths (Gardner's [1993] multiple intelligences or Sternberg's [1985] **analytic intelligence** versus **creative intelligence** versus **practical intelligence**), their interests, and their thinking styles or preferred learning styles (**field dependent** versus **field independent** and impulsive versus reflective). Many of these concepts were discussed in Chapter 2. Guidelines and a template for learner profiles are provided later in the chapter.

In traditional classrooms, teachers typically present material and then provide a common learning task or assignment for all students. In a differentiated classroom, teachers design a range of learning tasks, assignments, and alternative assessments, and they purposefully plan different pathways for students to access content and to understand new information. Initially, when teachers venture into differentiation they offer limited options; as they get more sophisticated, they learn to manage multiple learning activities to support each student's learning. In the strategies section of this chapter, we present a variety of ways to design learning options for students. When planning for differentiation we need to ensure that:

- Lessons include critical and creative thinking for *all* students.
- Lessons engage and challenge *all* students.
- There are varied learning opportunities and choices for *all* students.
- There is a balance between student-selected and teacher-assigned tasks and working arrangements.

1. **Clarify key ideas, concepts, generalizations, or principles**. The first step to consider is the curricular content, standards, and outcomes. It is important to be crystal clear about the content that all students will be expected to master.
2. **Assess students**. Students' academic readiness levels, interests, and learning preferences provide a roadmap for thinking and planning—at the beginning and along the way. Assessment (before, during, and at the end of learning) is key to differentiation.
3. **Design alternative ways to access content**. Think about the different ways students will be able to access content and the alternative formats that can be used to learn the identified key ideas and concepts. Consider materials that will be needed to accommodate different approaches to curriculum and different levels of student readiness, interests, and learning styles.
4. **Organize alternative ways for learning**. Design and organize a variety of student learning activities and teaching strategies to provide students with choices about how they learn and how they can engage with content.
5. **Identify alternative ways for student assessment**. Consider options that can be provided for students to demonstrate their learning. Think about the various ways they can show what they know and can do.
6. **Think about grouping and classroom arrangements**. Identify ways students can be grouped. What are the implications for classroom organization? Will students work independently, with partners, in small groups, or participate in whole-class activities?
7. **Develop systems for monitoring student work and record keeping**. Consider templates, checklists, charts, organizers, rubrics, and systems that can be used to manage students and their work.

Figure 5.1 Planning guidelines for differentiating instruction

As described in Chapter 3, challenge and choice are two important factors influencing student motivation. These two concepts are especially important when planning for a differentiated classroom. Challenging work means creating assignments or tasks that are slightly beyond a student's comfort zone. The goal in the differentiated classroom is to stretch all students and get them to "work up." Because choice is key to motivation, providing opportunities for choice is fundamental to addressing diverse needs.

Guidelines for planning are described in Figure 5.1, followed by a template for a differentiated lesson plan in Figure 5.2.

Managing the Differentiated Classroom

Managing the differentiated classroom requires a complex set of skills and strategies. It also requires a mindset of flexibility and tolerance for activity, movement, and higher noise levels. With students working on different tasks in different **learning configurations** (independently, in pairs, and in small groups), the classroom becomes a very busy place, and students need to be taught both independent and cooperative work skills. It will also be necessary to establish routines for starting work, ending work, and making transitions. Expectations for talking and listening need to be clarified. In addition, differentiating requires record-keeping routines so multiple assignments, projects, and varying completion dates can be monitored.

Several experts on differentiation recommend that teachers develop a variety of templates for managing student work. Dodge (2005), for example, proposed that teachers develop task cards, student opinion journals, **learning logs**, note taking formats, and student portfolios. Task cards provide directions for different learning activities and assessments (i.e., Jigsaw, partner talks, **artifact boxes**, multiple intelligence product lists), and can be used over and over; this facilitates student independence and reduces time required to repeat multiple sets of instructions. **Student opinion journals** (statements of belief and evidence to support beliefs and opinions) and learning

Essential question or topic			
Standard(s)		Outcomes/Objectives	
Pre-assessment			
Introduction			
Learning assignment options			
Grouping: **Whole group** **Small group** **Pairs** **Independently**			
Summary strategies			
Assessment options			

Figure 5.2 Differentiated instruction lesson planning template

logs (where students record reflections) provide structured formats for students to record their thoughts and what they are learning. They can also provide ways for teachers to communicate with students who are working on different kinds of assignment. All of these techniques provide guidance to students as they pursue independent study or mutual work with peers. A **portfolio** (collection) of student work can also provide a communication tool for conversations with students about their learning and progress.

Carolyn Coil (2004, 2007) has also developed a set of tools for teachers: **product criteria cards**, a tic-tac-toe student choice activities organizer, and a tiered lesson plan format. Product criteria cards define expectations for assessing student-produced work and artifacts; they outline the four or five criteria that will be used for specific

Table 5.2 Product criteria card samples

Diagram or chart	Presentation
1. Organizes items in sequence	1. Voice clarity and projection
2. Shows relationships between items	2. Eye contact
3. Labels parts clearly	3. Content organization
4. Provides a short explanation for each component	4. Clear, strong beginning and ending
	5. Visual supports

Source: Information summarized and adapted from Coil (2004).

assessments. Product criteria cards can be used over time and across subject areas. Two sample product criteria cards are displayed in Table 5.2.

The **tic-tac-toe organizer** and the tiered lesson plan format are described in the strategies section of this chapter. All these templates and organizers are essential to manage student work and to keep track of progress for teachers who are making full use of differentiation.

In every classroom there will always be "early finishers" and "late finishers." Tiered assignments (described later in the chapter) require students to work on assignments of varying levels of difficulty and their use helps with overall pacing. Having optional activities for "early finishers," to help them remain focused, however, is also important. Enrichment or stretch activities can include web quests, games, problem-

> **REFLECTION**
>
> What is your tolerance for movement, noise, and flexibility? How do you manage to keep track of all your students and their different styles, needs, and levels? Will criteria cards, journals, templates, and portfolios work for you?

solving activities, thinking skills practice activities, and reading and arts projects. Late finishers also need special consideration. Consider having late finishers keep project journals that list short-term goals and due dates or set up situations where learning pairs can meet to provide pressure and support for finishing assignments and projects on time.

Assessment in the Differentiated Classroom

Assessment is ongoing and an integral part of instruction in the differentiated classroom. Collecting diagnostic information is the starting point for developing student learning profiles and for establishing what students know and are able to do in specific content areas. Two different ways of assessing readiness have been used by many teachers. One way is to determine if the student is working below grade level, at grade level, or above grade level. A second way is to determine if the student is novice, developing, proficient, or advanced in a particular area. As you know, asking and watching students are perhaps the easiest ways to discern interests and capabilities. What books do they choose? What do they talk about? What captures their attention? Alternatively, an interest inventory can also be used to learn about what students know and what motivates them. Determining learning preferences can also be done through discussions, surveys, or inventories.

Close monitoring during learning and formative assessment (daily, weekly, quarterly) allows teachers to use flexible grouping to address individual needs over time. There are quick and easy ways to monitor student understanding, including checklists, individual white boards, self-assessments, peer assessments, quizzes, one-minute papers, exit slips, green–yellow–red cones, fist-of-five, rubrics, and thumb voting.

Assessing after learning or summative assessment involves determining mastery, making evaluations, assigning grades, and determining placements. Portfolios, performance products, student-led conferences, interviews, culminating projects, mind maps, research papers, and exams are examples of strategies for final assessment. Evaluation and grading must respect student differences and emphasize the individual growth of each student. We describe many formative and summative assessment strategies in Chapter 6.

Teacher and Student Roles

Differentiated classrooms require changes in teacher and student roles. Responsibility for learning shifts from the teacher to the student. Rather than being the primary expert in the room who transmits knowledge, teachers become facilitators and coaches while students become active participants in their own learning. Students make choices based on their interests and learning preferences; they learn alone, tutor each other in pairs, and work in small groups. Over time, students become increasingly self-directed and independent.

The goal for each student is to maximize growth from their current learning position. The goal for us, as teachers, is to understand more and more about each student so that learning activities can be designed to match learner needs. Goals for both students and teachers are to increase skills for independent work. Tomlinson (1993) provided a four-stage framework for understanding student independence: stage one is skill building; stage two is **structured independence**, stage three is **shared independence**, and stage four is **self-guided independence**. In Table 5.3, the respective roles for students and for teachers at the four different stages are described.

The Differentiated Learning Environment

The differentiated classroom is a busy place, with actively engaged students working in different patterns. An observer might see a combination of interest and **learning centers**, study areas, computer stations, and work areas for artistic and scientific discoveries. If the topic being investigated requires additional resources, some students may be using other school learning areas (e.g., library, gym, auditorium, computer lab). Others may require the resources offered on the Internet. While this description is more typical of an elementary classroom, we know of a variety of work places and groupings of students in middle and high school classrooms that are differentiated as well. Take, for instance, the following example:

> Jasbir teaches middle school social studies and has her room divided into four learning zones. One group of students works in the computer zone while another group is engaged in a small group discussion activity in the second zone. A third group works in pairs editing a paper, and in zone four several students work independently doing journal reflections and taking turns meeting individually with the teacher on their research projects. Jasbir has developed a weekly framework where students participate in each of the four learning zones; this allows her

Table 5.3 Stages of student independence

Stage	Student role	Teacher role
One: Skill building	• developing ability to make simple choices • following through on short-term tasks • using directions appropriately	• providing specific choices, directions, and timelines • monitoring follow through
Two: Structured independence	• choosing from teacher-generated options • following through on longer-term and more complex tasks • engaging in self-evaluation	• determining choices • defining timelines • establishing evaluation criteria
Three: Shared independence	• generating problems to be solved • designing tasks and setting timelines • establishing criteria for evaluation	• reviewing student plans • focusing or "tightening" plans • monitoring production process
Four: Self-guided independence	• planning, executing, and evaluating own tasks • seeking assistance or feedback when necessary	• providing assistance and feedback on request

Source: Information summarized and adapted from Tomlinson (1993).

to have individual meetings with each student every week and to be sure they received sufficient peer support.

> **REFLECTION**
>
> Where are you on the continuum between a traditional classroom and a differentiated classroom? How long have you been experimenting with ideas related to differentiated instruction? What ideas interest you most or seem most doable?

In summary, the differentiated classroom environment has pockets of all kinds of learning activities and a variety of grouping situations. This environment is substantially different than the ones found in the more traditional classroom, as we illustrate in Table 5.4.

INSTRUCTIONAL STRATEGIES THAT SUPPORT DIFFERENTIATION

As described previously, we can differentiate instruction in three major ways: by content (curriculum), by process (instruction), and by product (assessment). In Figure 5.3, we show a variety of strategies that support differentiation across these three areas. Some are relatively straightforward and can be implemented easily; others are more complex and require more commitment and investment of time. Each of these strategies will be discussed in more detail in the remainder of the chapter.

Develop Learner Profiles

An effective and relatively simple way to get started with differentiation is to create a learner profile for each student. Start a file for each student and staple the learner profile

Table 5.4 A comparison of traditional and differentiated classrooms

Traditional classroom	Differentiated classroom
Teacher centered and teacher organized.	Student centered and student organized.
Planning involves choosing content, designing assignments, and constructing an assessment.	Planning involves identifying standards, diagnosing student readiness, interests, and preferences, and designing multiple pathways for learning and assessment.
Linguistic and logical-mathematical intelligences are most important.	Multiple forms of intelligence are recognized and respected.
Student interest is rarely used.	Student interest is frequently employed.
Curriculum guides and textbooks drive instruction.	Student readiness, interests, and learning profiles shape instruction.
Whole-class instruction dominates.	Varied instructional formats are used: whole group, small groups, pairs, and independent study.
Common assignments are the norm.	Assignment choices are the norm.
Limited instructional strategies are used.	A variety of teaching and learning strategies are employed.
Textbooks are the primary resources with some supplementary materials available.	A variety of resources in different formats at different levels are available.
Choices are limited.	Students are encouraged to make learning and assessment choices regularly.
Teacher directs student behavior most of the time.	Teacher facilitates development of student independence and decision making.
Common standards of excellence are established.	Excellence is defined by individual growth and progress.
Common assessments are used for the whole class.	Student assessment takes many forms.
Assessment is the final stage of the lesson or unit.	Assessment is ongoing (diagnostic, formative, and summative).

to the left-hand side of the folder. Be sure to add notes and artifacts to the files as students' readiness, interests, and abilities change over the course of the year. Remember that each student will be at different levels for different subject areas. Learner profiles are normally prepared by teachers in the lower grades and prepared in collaboration with students in the higher grades. As described earlier, interviews, observations, checklists, and surveys are useful tools for collecting learner profile information. We provide some samples of these tools in the *Fieldbook* and a template for designing a learner profile in Figure 5.4.

Provide Content in Varied Formats and at Different Levels of Difficulty
Another starting point for differentiation is to collect resource materials at different levels of difficulty on particular curricular topics. Teams of teachers can work together to accomplish this task and thus reduce the amount of time required. It is recommended that at least four levels of material be available on a given topic:

Simple strategies <---> Complex strategies		
· Learner profiles · Materials in varied formats and at different levels of difficulty · Different levels of questions/thinking · Choice activities and assessments	· Flexible grouping and working arrangements · Learning contracts · Curriculum compacting · Peer tutoring, mentors, and experts · Multiple intelligences · Learning styles and preferences	· Cubing · Learning centers or stations · Problem-based learning and cooperative learning · Tiered assignments

Figure 5.3 Strategies supporting differentiation

- *Level 1*: simple (below grade level).
- *Level 2*: average (at grade level).
- *Level 3*: complex (above grade level).
- *Level 4*: professional (expert level).

It is wise to have available both fiction and nonfiction resources and materials in both visual and auditory formats. Varying research materials (artifacts, visuals, print materials, interviews, technology, original documents) that are available will increase options for students. Providing students with choices of level and choices of format is a great starting point for differentiation and will immediately address differences in readiness, interest, and capability. Below are two examples of teachers who have used this strategy:

Amanda, a third grade teacher in Tennessee, has collected over 2,500 books for her differentiated approach to literacy. This diverse library provides her with a rich set of resources to address the varied needs and interests of her urban learners.

Elaine, a high school chemistry teacher in Wisconsin, uses a range of resources, including newspaper stories, magazine articles, National Public Radio program transcripts or podcasts, and local resource people, to introduce chemistry elements to her students. She starts with a real-life event or story from popular media to ease her students into the textbook material. She uses materials from industry, the library, and the Internet to extend students' understandings.

Attend to Different Cognitive Processes
Providing learning activities that require the use of different kinds of cognitive processes can help challenge students and move them increasingly into more rigorous work. In 1956, Bloom proposed a taxonomy with three domains of objectives: cognitive, affective, and kinesthetic. Many of you are aware of his cognitive domain, in which he identified six levels of thinking ranging from the simple to the more complex: knowledge, comprehension, application, analysis, synthesis, and evaluation. Students of Bloom (Anderson & Krathwohl, 2001) revised his taxonomy and developed a new

Name: _____   Date: _____

Multiple intelligence strengths	_____ linguistic _____ visual spatial _____ intrapersonal _____ musical		_____ logical-mathematical _____ kinesthetic _____ interpersonal _____ naturalistic	
Sternberg	_____ analytical	_____ practical	_____ creative	
Learning style	Visual	Auditory	Kinesthetic	Tactile
Learning style	Concrete sequential	Concrete random	Abstract sequential	Abstract random
Working preference	Independent	Pairs	Small group (triad or quad)	Large group
Environmental factors	a. _____ quiet b. _____ bright light c. _____ morning d. _____ orderly		_____ background noise _____ subdued light _____ night _____ random	
Activity/task characteristics	a. _____ structured b. _____ needs the big picture c. _____ likes to conceptualize/create d. _____ final deadline		_____ open-ended _____ needs to know the details _____ likes to get it done _____ staged timelines	
Readiness Literacy	Below level/ Beginner	On level/ Novice	Above level/ Proficient	Expert level/ Advanced
Readiness Math	Below level/ Beginner	On level/ Novice	Above level/ Proficient	Expert level/ Advanced
Readiness Science	Below level/ Beginner	On level/ Novice	Above level/ Proficient	Expert level/ Advanced
Interests				

Figure 5.4 Template for a learner profile

taxonomy with two dimensions. A **knowledge dimension** that identified four kinds of knowledge—factual, conceptual, procedural, and metacognitive—and a **cognitive processing dimension** that included the categories of: remembering, understanding, applying, analyzing, evaluating, and creating. As with Bloom's original levels of thinking, the cognitive processes in the revised taxonomy range from the simple to the more complex. We believe it is important to provide multiple and differentiated learning experiences for students that require them to use the full range of cognitive processes. We will return to Bloom's revised taxonomy in later chapters and describe how it can be used to plan and to teach students how to think.

Provide Choice in Learning Activities and Assessments

Providing choice in learning activities and assessments allows students to learn based on their interests and capabilities. **Choice opportunities** include having different reading selections, research topics, homework options, class activities, note-taking strategies, research methods, reporting formats, and assessment strategies. Dodge (2005) recommends that teachers use Bloom's cognitive processes, Gardner's multiple intelligences, and learning styles as three ways to organize and offer choice. She has also developed a tool called **choice boards**, which can be used to display options for learning activities or assessment strategies. A choice board consists of four, six, or nine boxes. Each box in the choice board contains a different kind of learning activity, assignment, or assessment strategy. A similar chart can be used for homework and provides students with different ways to review material by outlining options using learning styles or multiple intelligences. An example of a choice learning activities board is displayed in Table 5.5 and a sample of a choice homework board is presented in Figure 5.5.

Table 5.5 Sample choice board for learning about global warming

Standard: Students will be able to describe characteristics, causes, consequences of, and solutions for global warming.	
Consult two websites and prepare a graphic organizer highlighting key points on global warming.	Prepare a photo essay displaying evidence of global warming in the local area.
Interview a local environmentalist about ten ways we can individually contribute to preserving the earth.	Write a two-page research paper on global warming identifying causes and solutions.

Coil (2004) described the tic-tac-toe strategy as another way to provide for student choice. Nine options to master a common standard are listed in what she labeled the tic-tac-toe activity chart. Students choose three learning activities going across, going down, or going diagonally. The tic-tac-toe format allows teachers to provide choices while ensuring that students complete a variety of activities that will help them learn about a particular topic. An assessment tic-tac-toe can also be developed to correspond to the learning activity choices. A student activity tic-tac-toe for learning about Malaysia is displayed in Table 5.6.

It is important to build a tic-tac-toe around common standards and to plan an assessment strategy to ensure that, while students study different aspects of a subject, all students are accountable for learning the facts and concepts associated with the overall standard. Having students who investigated different rows or columns form a group will facilitate sharing of all ideas.

Standard: Students will understand the essential tenets and application of the trade agreements the U.S. has with trading partners.

In addition to reading the article on the North American Free Trade Agreement (NAFTA) distributed in class today, choose one of the following:
- create a chart identifying the different agreements between Canada and Mexico and the US
- choose two visa types and write a paragraph for each
- investigate the cost of a trip (flight and hotel) to Canada or Mexico
- develop a 25-word vocabulary list related to NAFTA
- create a top-ten list of guidelines about NAFTA

Figure 5.5 Sample choice homework chart

Table 5.6 Learning activities on Malaysia using tic-tac-toe format

Standard: Students will describe the historical, cultural, geographic, and political perspectives of an Asian country.

Find out the history of Malaysia. Create a timeline indicating ten key historical events.	Research Malaysia-specific clothing. Prepare a collage or picture collection from magazines or the Internet.	Create Jeopardy questions about Malaysia. Include four categories of questions and four questions for each category. Write questions and answers on 3×5 index cards.
Find pictures of 15 different animals that are native and specific to Malaysia. Prepare a set of cards with pictures on one side and explanations on the other.	Find out about the major cultures in Malaysia. Write a paragraph on at least four different groups. Be sure you have an aboriginal group and the largest group.	Find a world map and locate Malaysia indicating major areas, cities, and neighboring countries.
Develop three menus that reflect different ethnic groups in Malaysia. Provide explanatory notes of dietary restrictions and delicacies.	Create a brochure to highlight three distinct holiday options in Malaysia.	Research a Malaysian actor, musician, or writer. Find a film clip, song, or written artifact. Prepare a five- minute presentation.

Practice Flexible Grouping and Small Group Arrangements

Students need opportunities to work alone, with a partner, in small groups, and also with the whole class. These different arrangements allow them to work in their preferred learning style and also to be exposed to new ways of learning. It helps them learn how to work both independently and cooperatively. Different students need varying amounts of direction and structure to work, learn, and be productive in groups. Since student performance will vary over time and by subject area, it is important to permit movement between groups. **Flexible groups** can be structured randomly using some criteria or can be purposefully structured based on personal talents, interests, and readiness. The importance of group work is highlighted in Research Box 5.2.

Dodge (2005) described what she labeled "the **half-class strategy**." The class is divided into two halves. Teachers work with half the class for 10–15 minutes, while the second group works independently on activities such as reading, working with a graphic organizer on the lesson, or writing a reflective piece. Teachers then switch groups and work with the other half of the class, teaching a mini-lesson at their level. Because this strategy requires planning for only two groups of students, it is an effective way to get started with differentiation.

Teaming students with learning partners encourages individuals to explain or describe to a peer in their own words what they are learning. Partners can also do "accuracy checks" of each other's work (proofread or edit), and learn from each other. Learning partners can be determined by the teacher or chosen by students. Students can work with someone else at the same level who has a common interest or a similar learning style. In general, it is a good idea for students to have different learning partners for different subjects.

Inquiry **RESEARCH BOX 5.2**

Lou, Y., Abrami, P., Spence, J., Poulsen, C., Chambers, B., & d'Apollonia, S. (1996). Within-class grouping: A meta-analysis. *Review of Educational Research*, *66*(4), 423–458.

Researchers from three different universities conducted a meta-analysis in two parts using 165 studies on the effects of within-class grouping on student achievement and other outcomes. The first set included 145 studies and explored the effects of grouping versus no grouping. The average achievement effect size was +0.17 favoring small-group learning. The second set included 20 studies that directly compared the achievement effects of homogeneous versus heterogeneous ability of within-class grouping on student achievement. The results favored homogeneous grouping. Overall, the researchers found that students in small within-classroom learning groups achieved significantly more than students who were not placed in learning groups.

In addition, students placed in within-class learning groups had more positive attitudes about learning and stronger self-concept measures. The meta-analysis reported that low-ability students tended to learn better in heterogeneous groups, medium-ability students tended to learn better in homogeneous groups, and high-ability students fared well equally in either group setting. Researchers concluded that, to be maximally effective, within-class grouping practices required the adaptation of instructional methods and materials for small-group learning.

Tomlinson (2001) proposed another quite easy way to differentiate instruction on a daily basis. She recommended organizing students into three groups for the independent practice phase of a particular lesson. Teachers can provide a follow-up mini-lesson to students in the group that is struggling with the lesson's topic, while a second group works on an assignment with independent practice, and the third group works independently to enhance member understandings of the topic.

Gregory and Chapman (2001) described a **wagon wheel teaming strategy** for forming groups with four concentric circles with a fastener that allows for spinning. The inner circle has a student at the expert level (E), the two middle circles have the names of average-level students (A), and the outer circle has the names of beginning-level students (B). Once the wagon wheel is constructed, teachers rotate the circles to form new groups. Students will often be in different groups depending on the subject; they may be below grade level in one subject, at grade level in several subjects, and above grade level in yet another subject.

It is important to point out that flexible grouping means just that. Students work in different groups based on achievement, interest, and learning preference. These

> **REFLECTION**
>
> Grouping students can be challenging and controversial. How do you handle grouping in your classroom? What is the balance of individual, small group, and whole group learning? What about grouping policies in your school? Discuss with a classmate or colleague ways you might consider using flexible grouping.

groups do not remain static for an extended period of time. Instead, they are flexible and movement is fluid as students change groups as progress is made in particular subject areas.

Use Learning Contracts

A **learning contract** is a written agreement between the teacher and a student that guides independent work. The contract identifies daily and weekly goals, activities, timelines, resources, and products the student will produce as they engage in their independent work. The content, learning strategies, and products vary by student interest and ability. Conferences (weekly or bi-weekly) are set up to provide feedback and to discuss student progress. We provide a sample learning contract in Figure 5.6.

Implement Curriculum Compacting

Reis and Renzulli (1992) developed a strategy labeled **curriculum compacting**, designed to help advanced learners maximize their learning time. It allows them to engage in more rigorous and independent work. There are three phases to the curriculum compacting strategy:

- Phase one involves *assessment of students* and identification of candidates for compacting. During this phase, teachers use pre-tests, student work samples, and conferences to assess which students have attained 70–75 percent mastery of the content. Students who are identified for compacting are exempt from whole-class instruction in the content areas they have mastered and thus "gain time" for learning more challenging and, for them, perhaps more interesting material.
- Phase two involves *developing a plan* for teaching the skills and understandings the student has not mastered (joining whole-class activities, homework, demonstrating mastery with a product).
- Phase three involves *the teacher and the student in designing an independent, challenging project,* such as an investigation, a service learning opportunity, a web quest, job shadowing, or an online search. Project parameters, goals, timelines, strategies, and criteria for evaluation are jointly established to guide the student's independent work.

Arrange Peer Tutoring and Use Mentors and Experts

At times, all students require one-on-one instruction and guidance. One student may be struggling to understand a basic concept, another may have specific questions, and a third may be working at an advanced level. Sometimes a peer tutor can help a struggling student gain needed background knowledge, or a pair of students can work together to prepare for a test or to give each other feedback on an assignment. Highly talented students also benefit from working with others. They benefit from working with intellectual peers, but also from being a member of a mixed group where they can experience being a leader. In either case, **peer tutoring** is a valuable strategy for promoting student learning. Teachers who use peer tutoring strategies, however, should proceed with caution. It can be viewed by some as a form of student exploitation.

Name:	Date:

Topic: _____

Goals: _____

_____

Activities and resources

Assessment: I will show what I have learned by:

Checkpoints:

Completion date: _____

Student: _____   Teacher: _____

Other agreements

Figure 5.6 Sample learning contract

Mentors are generally older students or other adults who provide coaching and guidance to a younger or less experienced student. Organizing mentors provides individual support for students. Perhaps you have established on-going mentor relationships by partnering with another teacher who teaches at a different grade level; some teachers only use mentoring as a strategy for a selected group of students.

Experts are individuals who have content expertise and experience in a particular subject or area. They interact with advanced students and provide challenge and support. For example, a high school student interested in pursuing engineering might participate in an expert seminar with engineers from a local business or a student interested in a career in journalism might attend a weekend writers' workshop taught by several local journalists.

Attend to Multiple Intelligences

As described in Chapter 2, all students are smart, albeit in different ways, and they possess multiple intelligences. Attending to different intelligences is another strategy that can support instructional differentiation. Gardner (1993), you remember, maintained that there are at least eight different types of intelligence: *logical mathematical, linguistic/verbal, musical, spatial, bodily-kinesthetic, interpersonal, intrapersonal,* and *naturalistic.* He contended that all people possess all of these intelligences, but that some are more developed (perhaps more natural) than are others. All can be developed more fully, and also used to guide lesson adaptation that will play to students' strengths.

Whole-school curricula have been designed around Gardner's theory of multiple intelligences, but here we are interested in what teachers can do in their own classrooms to ensure that students are involved in the full range of their abilities. One way to begin using ideas from multiple intelligence theory is to design learning activities and assignments that focus on the different intelligences and have students choose those that play to their particular strengths. We describe a variety of learning activities in Table 5.7. We propose that teachers start with offering choices in a few different intelligences.

The same idea can be applied to the *analytical, creative,* and *practical* cognitive processes identified by Sternberg (1985), in his **triarchic theory of intelligence**. Recently, Sternberg (2009) recommended the following as ways to tailor instruction for teaching analytically, creatively, and practically:

- *Teaching analytically*: Encourage students to analyze, critique, judge, compare and contrast, and to evaluate and assess. Students could analyze a political argument, critique a poem, or judge the quality of a work of art.
- *Teaching creatively*: Encourage students to create, invent, discover, and predict. Students could create a work of art, invent a machine, predict what would happen if the national debt keeps increasing or if global warming is not slowed down.
- *Teaching practically*: Encourage students to apply, use, put into practice, or implement what they have learned. Students could balance a checkbook, figure out compound interest on a home mortgage, implement a constitution for their classroom, or use a language they are learning by conversing with a native speaker.

As we did in Chapter 2, we leave this section with a word of warning about possible misuses of multiple intelligence theory. Gardner (1998) wrote that he had observed situations where teachers tried to include every intelligence in every lesson or used an activity associated with a particular intelligence as background for other lessons that emphasized a different intelligence, such as playing music while students work on their math problems. He said these were misapplications of his theory. He also warned against setting criteria and grading the various intelligences.

Consider Learning Styles and Preferences

Students also have different learning styles and *preferences*. These were also introduced in Chapter 2 and they can be used to help differentiate instruction. Again, you will

Table 5.7 Learning activities to match various intelligences

Intelligence	Learning activities
Linguistic	• develop a vocabulary list of key terms related to racism • write a haiku poem on a topic of your choice • choose an author—read four pieces—write a critique of the collection of works • find two reliable Internet sites on the civil war
Logical-mathematical	• complete two problem-solving/brain teaser activities • show three different ways to solve a math problem • participate in a CSI exploratory activity • visit a science museum
Visual-spatial	• select a piece of art—describe the artistic features • create a mind map explaining ecosystems • create a graphic organizer • choose a city or country—find a map—explore—introduce us to six interesting places
Musical	• compose a rap • select a concept—find five musical selections to illustrate • go to a musical or watch a musical movie—identify three of your favorite scenes • choose a song of the month using at least four different genres
Bodily kinesthetic	• select and perform a dance with a partner • design and implement an exercise program • compile a hands-on set of materials to learn a topic • identify and lead three teambuilding activities
Interpersonal	• interview a new citizen about the citizenship process • design a problem-based learning project with a small group • join a club • design a learning contract which includes a service component
Intrapersonal	• keep a reflective journal • complete a personality instrument • write a two-page essay on friendship • create a scrapbook with pictures and captions
Naturalistic	• compile a photo essay on global warming using a local example • interview a local scientist about their work • visit a natural refuge or go on a virtual tour—make field notes • design an artifact box on a topic of your choice

remember the big idea about learning styles and preferences was that individual students differ in the way they perceive the world, the way they process information, and the environments in which they prefer to learn. Some students see the whole and the big ideas first, while others tend to focus on the separate parts. Similarly, some students tend to focus on the more abstract aspects of a problem or situation, whereas others tend to focus on the more specific and concrete details. Students also vary in their learning preferences or modalities. Some prefer learning verbally and through their auditory senses, while others may construct meaning visually. Students may also prefer one type of learning environment to others. Elements of the environment that have been considered to be important include: overall structure, amount of support, degree of independence, and availability of peer interaction.

As with designing instruction to account for different intelligences, the same can be done for different learning styles and preferences. For example, teachers can accommodate students who vary in regard to how concrete or abstract they see the world by making some learning activities more structured and detailed, while providing others that are more discovery oriented. In the same way, some lessons can be designed to take into account students who prefer verbal and auditory learning, while others can be designed to support those who learn best visually. There have been several inventories created by learning style developers (Gregorc, 1982; Kolb, 1984; McCarthy, 1996; Silver Strong, & Perini, 2000) that can be used to assess learning styles in a more formal way. However, most teachers make these determinations by observing and watching their students in learning situations and talking to them about how they think they learn best and what kind of learning activities and environments they prefer.

We issue the same warning for learning styles and preferences that we commented on about different kinds of intelligence. There is not a consensus about which learning styles and preferences are the most important (Stall, 2002; Woolfolk, 2007), nor has much evidence been collected about how their use affects instruction. That does not mean, however, that the ideas of learning styles and preferences should be ignored. Their popularity with teachers over the years provides experiential support for the use of ideas associated with learning styles, and certainly it is important to explore all aspects of how best to help students learn.

Explore Cubing

Cubing is a strategy developed by Cowan and Cowan (1980) to expose students to different perspectives and ways of thinking about a topic. It consists of devising a six-sided cube, with each side outlining different tasks, assignments, or kinds of question. Different sides of the cube could feature the six cognitive tasks outlined in Bloom's revised taxonomy. So, the sides would challenge students with tasks requiring remembering, understanding, applying, analyzing, evaluating, or creating. Different colored cubes could also be used to designate Sternberg's different kinds of intelligence: analytical, creative, and practical. For example, blue cubes could contain analytical tasks, green cubes creative tasks, and red cubes practical tasks. Students choose to do a series of tasks in one form (intelligence) or they could be assigned to complete two tasks in each color (or intelligence). A third variation for using cubes might be related to learning preferences or styles.

Students sit in groups at a table and work with the cube. Sometimes students roll the cube and tackle the task that rolls up. Everyone rolls until they have a task related to the topic. Students can work alone or help one another. Once tasks are completed, the students at the table share their work so all perspectives on a topic are covered. This allows all students to work in their preferred learning mode some of the time, but also to work with and understand different modalities of learning. Cubing encourages differentiation and stretches students' thinking, extends ideas, and helps them make meaningful connections.

Organize Classroom Learning and Interest Centers
Organizing learning and interest centers is another way of providing different pathways for learning. Interest centers can be developed around different topics or subjects. They can also be organized around different aspects of a specific topic or unit of study. Alternatively, learning centers can be arranged by learning strengths or preferences—students can participate in analytical, creative, and practical activities, or complete visual, auditory, and kinesthetic assignments. Centers can also be thought of as sets of activities rather than places. Boxes or crates of materials and activities can be brought to tables rather than students going to stations or centers. Below are two examples of how teachers have used learning centers:

> One elementary school in Georgia differentiates math instruction at each grade level. Math is taught at the same time using a common format during the one-hour block. Half of the time is devoted to learning centers. When the learning center time arrives, students move between classrooms to work at different centers to reinforce, practice, or extend learning. Groups of students play different math games in each of the rooms. Several pairs work with multiplication flash cards, while others work on multiplication story problems. Still others may be involved in estimating and measuring using manipulatives. Teachers have worked in teams to develop multiple learning activities.
>
> Gilda, a high school biology teacher, organizes her class into learning stations for each unit. She has a computer station, a laboratory station, a small group station, a teaching station, and an assessment station. At the start of the unit, students receive a nine- or 12-box worksheet with assignment choices indicating which tasks all students complete, which tasks designated groups complete, and which tasks are optional. Different tasks or assignments are completed at different stations. This approach to unit planning and varied assignments allows Gilda to consult with individual students on their learning path throughout the unit since the stations are set up for the duration of the unit. The stations and the unit organizer accommodate individual, pair, and small group learning opportunities.

Use Cooperative and Problem-based Learning
Cooperative learning strategies can be used to provide differentiated learning opportunities for students. Jigsaw involves students dividing up a topic, learning about different aspects of it, and then teaching other group members what they have learned. Group investigation allows even greater diversity as groups of students identify topics and questions to investigate, and decide on learning strategies to use for their joint study. **Problem-based learning (PBL)** also allows students to pursue their own investigations as individuals, with learning partners, or in small groups. Chapters 13 and 14 provide fuller descriptions and examples of cooperative learning and PBL.

Design Tiered Assignments[2]
Tiered assignments provide yet another way for teachers to differentiate learning activities and provide alternative ways for students to reach the same goal. Tiered assignments consist of a series of related tasks or learning activities designed at varying levels of complexity but related to the same essential question or standard. Teachers assign different activities to different students or groups of students. Dodge (2005) maintains

that developing tiered assignments is one of the more complex differentiation strategies to implement. While choice of assignments can cater to student interests and learning preferences, tiered assignments can also involve developing assignments at different levels of complexity. Dodge proposes a three-step method for doing this:

- *Step 1*: Develop an activity for the on-level learners.
- *Step 2*: Develop an activity for your struggling learners that provides them with additional support, materials, and instruction.
- *Step 3*: Develop a more complex activity that will stretch your advanced learners. She cautions to be sure the activity is more complex not just more work.

Tiered activities and assignments should be built around the essential understandings and skills that all students must learn. Another way of thinking about tiered lessons is developing basic, intermediate, and advanced learning tasks. A basic task focuses on ensuring understandings and provides reinforcement and practice. An intermediate task involves the use of application and analysis skills. An advanced activity requires more complex research, greater independence, and creation of new ideas.

> **REFLECTION**
>
> Learning centers and tiered assignments provide for differentiation. Which strategy fits best with your style? Does one seem easier than the other? Consider ways you might work with a colleague to implement a strategy you have not used before.

Coil (2004) encourages teachers to introduce and conclude particular lessons with the whole class. After the introduction, have students begin tiered activities that have been designed to challenge them at an appropriate level. Like Dodge (2005), Coil recommends three levels of activity, ranging from the basic to the more complex. She also proposes three ways for identifying appropriate levels for particular students: assign each student to a level based on the teacher's best judgment, allow students to choose between two of the three levels, or provide complete choice among the levels.

CHALLENGES AND TENSIONS OF DIFFERENTIATED INSTRUCTION

While differentiation has many advantages for students, it can be challenging for teachers, at least initially. Although we advocate differentiated instruction, we also acknowledge that switching from teacher-centered to student-centered instruction is not easy. To fully implement a differentiated classroom requires fundamental changes in the way we think about learning and about our teaching practices. Three challenges can be particularly difficult: how to deal with state and national standards, how to deal with the scarce resource of time, and how to access varied resources.

Responding to student diversity while simultaneously meeting state and national standards poses a challenge and a dilemma. On the one hand, advocates of differentiated instruction argue for the need to recognize student differences and to provide instruction appropriate to each student's needs. On the other hand, state and national standards push for standardization and common outcomes. We believe success requires finding mutual ground in the two positions. Differentiation is about varying the process of instruction (how students learn), while standards are about common content and learning outcomes. As discussed throughout this chapter, the first step in planning a differentiated classroom is to identify required standards and outcomes, followed by designing different learning opportunities that match individual student's interests and abilities. At first, this seems like a dilemma in fact, it can be seen as a two-stage process in ensuring common expectations yet providing diverse opportunities for all learners. A second problem related to standards and common outcomes is the overwhelming number of standards identified for each grade level. As described in Chapter 4, Marzano (2003), in reviewing the huge number of standards, estimated that students would have to stay in schools until grades 21 or 22 to accomplish the current expectations. In Chapter 4, we provided a variety of ways to cluster standards and focus on those most essential to partially resolve this dilemma.

Time and access to resources can also be problematic. To shift from whole-class teaching to differentiated instruction requires additional investments. We propose two actions teachers can take. One is to work in teacher teams. When teachers collaborate with colleagues, the load is lightened. Different teachers can take responsibility for accessing resources for different subject areas or different topics. This will require strategic and systematic planning over a number of years. A second action is to engage family and community partners in acquiring resources and helping manage the differentiated classroom. For example, Deborah, a high school business teacher, has cultivated several community partners through her social network. Yearly, she assesses her school's needs and writes short proposals requesting purchase of specific resources. Other teachers have become masters at scanning the environment for resources, for example capitalizing on book sales and industry technology upgrades. Still others invite parents and caregivers into the classroom to help monitor student work and manage files and resources.

SUMMARY AT A GLANCE

- Differentiation is the practice of adjusting the curriculum, teaching strategies, assessment strategies, and the classroom environment to meet the needs of all students.
- A differentiated classroom provides different pathways for students to acquire content, to process new information and ideas, and to develop products that demonstrate understanding and mastery.
- Differentiated instruction is student-centered and student-organized rather than teacher-centered; it is the recognition of and commitment to planning for student differences. Understanding student diversity, interests, and preferences, as well as strengths and weaknesses, is the starting point.
- There are fundamental differences between a traditional classroom and a differentiated classroom. Moving to differentiation affects planning, instruction, assessment, management, and organization of the learning environment.
- There are a range of strategies (from simple to complex) that teachers can implement to begin or extend differentiation in their classrooms. Simple strategies include: developing learner profiles, providing varied materials, providing choices, and using flexible grouping.

- More complex strategies involve: attending to multiple intelligences, using learning centers, developing tiered assignments, and incorporating cooperative learning and problem-based learning strategies.
- Three challenges teachers face as they strive to achieve differentiated instruction are: negotiating the dilemma of differentiation versus standardization, managing time, and accessing varied resources.

CONSTRUCTING YOUR OWN LEARNING

If you are only starting to differentiate or if you are well on the way, consider forming a study group of classmates or colleagues to continue learning new strategies. First, you will want to consider what approach to take. Do you want to follow a specific framework or to simply begin experimenting with different strategies? Your group will most likely want to learn about and discuss the range of possible ways for introducing choice and variety in your classroom. We suggest you map out a yearly plan of three or four ways to change your instruction. Everyone could try the same strategy or individuals could try different strategies. The study group provides both the pressure and the support needed to make changes, work through challenges, and celebrate successes.

RESOURCES

Benjamin, A. (2002). *Differentiated instruction: A guide for middle and high school teachers.* Larchmont, NY: Eye On Education.

Dodge, J. (2005). *Differentiation in action.* New York: Scholastic.

Fogarty, R. (2001). *Different learners: Different strokes for different folks.* Chicago, IL: Fogarty and Associates.

Forsten, C., Goodman, G., Grant, J., Hollas, B., & Whyte, D. (2006). *The more ways you TEACH, the more students you REACH: 86 strategies for differentiated instruction.* Peterborough, NH: Crystal Springs Books.

Gregory, G.H., & Chapman, C. (2001). *Differentiated instructional strategies: One size doesn't fit all.* Thousand Oaks, CA: Corwin.

Tomlinson, C. (2001). *How to differentiate instruction in mixed-ability classrooms* (2nd ed.) Alexandria, VA: Association for Supervision and Curriculum Development.

Wormeli, R. (2007). *Differentiation: From planning to practice, Grades 6–12.* Portland, ME: Stenhouse Publishing.

6

CLASSROOM ASSESSMENT

INTRODUCTION

This chapter is about classroom **assessment**. It is more, however, than a presentation of the more traditional topics associated with administering tests and giving grades. Instead, we will focus primarily on the relationship between assessment and instruction and show how the interplay between these impacts in very important ways on how teachers teach and what students learn.

Let's begin by considering Corinne, an eighth-year teacher in Humbolt Middle School, and some of her concerns about her assessment practices:

After six years of teaching, Corinne feels quite confident about her understanding of the subject she teaches to her eighth-grade social studies students. She also is pleased with her classroom management skills and her ever-expanding repertoire of teaching strategies. She has grown dissatisfied, however, with her rather traditional classroom assessment practices. Corrine worries that she is relying too much on tests and quizzes to assess her students' learning. And, though she has heard about alternative ways of assessing student learning such as performance assessments and the use of portfolios, she knows very little about these methods.

Corrine has decided to look more closely at her assessment and grading practices with the aim of transforming them into something quite different. Forming study groups and learning communities is one of the professional development opportunities at Corrine's school. To her delight, three of her colleagues agree to join her in reading about and discussing alternative methods for assessing student learning. They decide to meet twice a month to share ideas, develop joint plans, and report the results of their work to each other.

Assessing and evaluating students is a significant aspect of every teacher's work. Over the past two decades it is has taken on increased importance. According to Stiggins (2004), teachers spend as much as 30 percent of their time in "assessment-related" activities, and in some schools assessment of student learning is tied to promotion and tenure. Assessment and grading are also important to students. The strategies teachers employ influence greatly what students learn, and have long-term consequences for the type of college they attend, and help determine their future careers and life styles.

Many teachers, even those with considerable experience, worry about how to approach assessment and student evaluation. Like Corrine and her colleagues, teachers are concerned that their current practices may be unfair to students, and they want to explore alternative and more effective assessment and grading procedures. Our aims for this chapter are to provide information that will help you understand assessment and evaluation and describe strategies you can use in your classrooms and schools.

We begin by outlining our perspective on classroom assessment and student evaluation and review for our readers some key ideas associated with these topics. We then provide a brief synthesis of the knowledge base on assessment and try to answer the question, "Do assessment practices matter and if so, how?" This is followed by rather detailed explanations of effective assessment practices, with major emphasis on what we define as formative assessment, that is, assessment that can be used: (1) by teachers to guide and adjust instruction, and (2) by students to assess their own learning and adjust their learning strategies and tactics. The chapter concludes with discussions of effective grading practices and strategies for reporting and communicating assessment results to parents and other stakeholders.

ASSESSMENT LITERACY: A PRIMER OF KEY IDEAS AND PERSPECTIVES

The world of assessment has its own language and definitions and the writing on this topic is voluminous. In this section we highlight several key ideas, with which some of our readers may be familiar, and provide a perspective on how we will approach assessment in the discussions that follow.

Key Ideas

Although assessment and evaluation are sometimes used interchangeably, we make important distinctions between them. We define *assessment* as a continuous process of gathering formal and informal information about student learning and about teachers' instructional processes. **Evaluation**, on the other hand, consists of making judgments about the level of students' achievement for purposes of grading and accountability and for making decisions about promotion and graduation.

We also make distinctions between two types of assessment—formative and summative. Briefly, **formative assessment** involves collecting information *prior to or during* instruction, that can be used by teachers to make instructional decisions and in-flight adjustments. Students can also use this information to adjust the learning strategies they are using to learn particular content and to solve problems. **Summative assessment**, on the other hand, involves collecting information *after* an instructional segment has occurred, such as a unit, a semester, or a year's work. Most often, summative assessments are used to make judgments and to evaluate student accomplishments. A teacher's unit or quarter exams are examples of summative assessments, as is the current use of high-stakes tests administered by school districts and state departments of education.

Finally, we use particular language to describe the quality of assessment information. Three terms are important: validity, reliability, and fairness. **Validity** is a term

> **REFLECTION**
>
> Take an assessment you have used recently and analyze it. Was it a formative or summative assessment? Were you assessing to give feedback or for grading? Did you consider validity, reliability, and fairness?

used in measurement to determine the degree to which an assessment measures what it claims to measure. For example, an instrument that claims to measure how well students like history is invalid if it is actually measuring how well they like their history teacher. **Reliability** of an assessment addresses the issue of whether or not a particular formal or informal practice will produce dependable results consistently and over time. **Fairness** addresses the issue of possible bias in an assessment toward any individual or group. An assessment is fair if it offers all individuals the same chance of doing well and if it does not discriminate against any group because of race, gender, or ethnicity. We will come back to these issues later in the chapter when we discuss effective grading and evaluation practices.

Table 6.1 provides brief definitions of key assessment terms, some described above and others we discuss later in the chapter, as a quick reference for Corinne's study group as well as for you.

Perspectives and Purposes

Today, educators must not only focus on student learning in the classroom but also make sure students are successful on high-stakes accountability measures. Assessments serve different purposes, namely, assessment *for* learning, assessment *of* learning, and assessment *as* learning. We illustrate these purposes in Figure 6.1 and then provide a brief description of what we mean by each purpose. We will also use these three purposes as our major organizational scheme for presenting assessment strategies later in the chapter.

Assessment for learning, also called formative assessment, is designed to provide diagnostic information to teachers about students' prior knowledge and formative information about the effects of their instruction on student learning. This form of

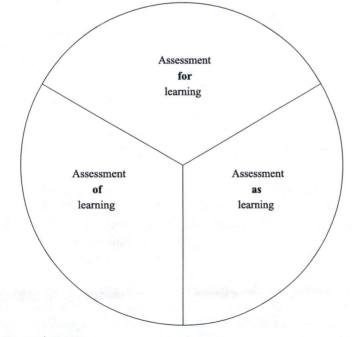

Figure 6.1 Three assessment purposes

Table 6.1 Assessment terms and definitions

Terms	Definitions
Assessment	the process of gathering information, both formally and informally, about students' understandings and skills
Authentic assessment	demonstration or application of a skill or ability within a real-life context
Criterion referenced	criterion-referenced tests measure student performance against a set of standards with determined levels (advanced, proficient, basic)
Diagnostic assessment	information collected *before* learning that is used to assess prior knowledge and identify misconceptions
Evaluation	the process of making judgments about the level of students' achievement for accountability, promotion, and certification
Fairness	addresses the issue of possible bias or discrimination of an assessment toward any individual or group (race, gender, ethnicity)
Formative assessment	information collected *during* learning that is used to make instructional decisions
Grade equivalent	uses a scale based on grade levels and months to establish students' level of performance
Norm referenced	norm-referenced tests compare student performance to a national population of students who served as the "norming" group
Performance assessment	students demonstrate that they can perform or demonstrate specific behaviors and abilities
Percentile	a statistical device that shows how a student compares with students in the "norming" group who had the same or a lower score
Portfolio	a collection of student work with reflections
Reliability	the degree to which an assessment will produce dependable results consistently and over time
Rubrics	a scoring strategy that defines criteria and describes levels of quality (basic, developing, proficient, exemplary)
Standardized tests	standardized, summative assessments designed to provide information on the performance of schools and districts
Summative assessment	information collected *after* instruction that is used to summarize student performance and determine grades
Validity	the degree to which an assessment measures what it claims to measure

assessment also provides students with important information about their learning and the effectiveness of the learning strategies they are using. Although assessment *for* learning does not often get the attention of policy makers or local newspapers, it is the most important form of assessment in regard to student learning. *Our emphasis in this chapter will be on the development and use of effective classroom formative assessment practices.*

Assessment of learning, or summative assessment, summarizes what students have learned at the end of an instructional segment such as a unit of work, a course of study, or a year in school. Assessment *of* learning is designed to serve the functions of accountability, determining class rankings, deciding who should graduate, and making judgments about placements or promotions. End of course exams, senior projects, performance assessments, and high-stakes standardized testing programs that compare students with each other or to a defined set of standards are the most obvious summative assessment examples. Results of assessment *of* learning appear on report cards, transcripts, and in reports to government agencies and local newspapers. As we will describe later, this form of assessment, in an era when accountability and high-stakes testing is widespread, is very important and influences greatly what goes on in schools.

Finally, we consider a third purpose of assessment, **assessment as learning** (Earl, 2003). This form of assessment makes assessment part of, not separate from, the instructional process. Assessment *as* learning involves students in their own continuous self-assessment and is designed to help students become more self-directed learners. Assessment *as* learning also takes the form of peer assessment, with peer interaction and feedback. Although strategies for self- and peer assessment are less well developed as compared to the other two forms of assessment, they are nonetheless very important for two reasons. One, these assessments help achieve what some see as the ultimate goal of education—developing independent learners. And two, students are often more receptive to feedback from peers than feedback from authority figures.

> **REFLECTION**
>
> Think for a moment about the assessment strategies you use in your classroom. Which aspect of classroom assessment (diagnostic and formative, self- and peer, or summative) do you feel most confident about? What aspect do you want to improve? You may find it helpful to compare your responses to these questions with those of a classmate or colleague.

We summarize and provide examples of the different purposes of assessment in Table 6.2. Understanding and using the right assessment strategies for the right reasons assists with instructional planning, enhances student learning, and can facilitate communicating growth and progress to students and their parents. We acknowledge that some assessment strategies can be used for more than one purpose.

WHAT DOES RESEARCH SAY ABOUT ASSESSMENT?

Clearly, it is important to look at the evidence about assessment. "What does the research say about assessment?" "What forms of assessment have the best chance of impacting student learning?" These are important questions today because considerable misinformation exists. Fortunately, there is a growing body of research evidence, including several meta-analyses, that has demonstrated quite clearly assessment effects, particularly the effects of formative assessment on student motivation and learning. The effects of summative assessment and high-stakes standardized testing have also been quite thoroughly studied. Here, however, the results are mixed. In this section, we briefly summarize several important lines of inquiry and highlight conclusions and issues we believe teachers should consider as they develop or revise their own classroom assessment programs.

Table 6.2 Purposes and uses of assessments with examples

Purpose	Uses of assessment information	Examples
Assessment *for* learning	*Diagnostic assessment* To assess prior knowledge, interests, preferences, and misconceptions *Formative assessment* To monitor learning, provide feedback to students, and guide teacher planning	• inventories • surveys • observations • interviews • questioning • teacher-made tests • summarization strategies
Assessment *as* learning	*Self-assessment* To facilitate student self-direction and self-monitoring *Peer assessment* To facilitate students learning from and with one another	• traffic lights • learning journals • peer review • two stars and a wish • rubrics • pre-flight checklist • summarization strategies
Assessment *of* learning	*Summative assessment* To make judgments and report on student learning and progress	• unit exams • mid-term exams • end-of-course exams • performance assessments • standardized tests

Effects of Formative Assessment

There is overwhelming evidence that formative assessment (assessment *for* learning) yields substantial gains in student learning, particularly when assessment is conceived by teachers and closely linked to instruction. In the 1980s, Natriello (1987) and Crooks (1988) completed two solid reviews of the literature on formative assessment and on teachers' practices. Both of these reviews covered a range of topics and processes associated with assessment and student evaluation. These reviews pointed toward the significance of classroom formative assessment and provided important clues about which aspects of assessment were most important. These studies also revealed that many teacher assessment practices, at that time, were weak, encouraged superficial and rote learning, and emphasized grading over learning. Research on formative assessment intensified in the 1990s, as did the reviews of this research (Kluger & DeNisi, 1996; Nyquist, 2003). Black and Wiliam (1998), however, conducted the landmark review, the results of which were published in *Assessment of Education* and summarized that same year in *Phi Delta Kappan*. We have chosen this study and a follow-up study (Black, Harrison, Lee, Marshall, & Wiliam, 2004) to highlight in Research Box 6.1.

It seems clear, at this point in time, that regular use of formative assessment improves student learning, especially for those students who are struggling. Also, there is a growing body of evidence that supports the positive influence of self-assessment and peer assessment (Andrade & Du, 2007; Boud & Falchikov, 1989). Self-assessment has been shown to be effective in math (Ross, Hogaboam-Gray, & Rolheiser, 2002), social studies (Lewbel & Hibbard, 2001), science (White & Frederiksen, 1998), and writing (Andrade & Boulay, 2003; Ross, Rolhesier, & Hogaboam-Gray, 1999). After learning how to use rubric-referenced self-assessments, students reported that they could self-assess more

---

Inquiry **RESEARCH BOX 6.1**

Black, P. & Wiliam, D. (1998). Assessment and classroom learning. *Assessment in Education*, *5*(1), 7–73.
Black, P., Harrison, C., Lee, C., Marshal, B., & Wiliam, D. (2004). Working inside the black box: Assessment for learning in the classroom. *Phi Delta Kappa*, *86*(1), 8–21.

In 1998, Black and Wiliam reported the results of a **meta-analysis** of research and earlier meta-analyses that had focused on formative classroom assessment. You remember from our description in Chapter 3, meta-analysis is a research methodology that allows the results of studies to be combined and for overall "effect size" to be computed. You also remember that effect size is a statistic that compares average improvement in the test scores of students involved in a particular innovative method or practice to the range of scores found for typical students on the same measure.

Black and Wiliam were able to identify 580 relevant research reports or studies and used 250 of these in their meta-analysis. They found that the typical effect sizes of the formative assessment experiments in their review were between 0.4 and 0.7, much "larger than most of those found for [other] education interventions" (p. 141). This caused them to conclude that formative assessment has direct positive impact on *how students study* and *what they learn*. Used properly, formative assessment can lead to "significant learning gains." Interestingly, the reviews also concluded that "formative assessment helps low achievers more than other students."

In a follow-up study, Black et al. (2004) studied teachers' specific assessment practices. Their findings agreed with earlier conclusions that many practices encouraged rote learning, overemphasized grading, and compared pupils with one another instead of measuring growth and improvement. However, they also found effective use of four formative assessment strategies that have a significant impact on student learning: providing feedback to students, questioning, assisting students with self and peer assessment, and using summative assessment information to make adjustments about their own teaching. Recently, Wiliam (2007) concluded that, when implemented well, formative assessment can "*double the speed of learning.*"

---

effectively, that they were more likely to self-assess when they knew what teachers expected, and that their self-assessments were typically followed by serious attempts to revise and improve their work (Andrade & Du, 2007).

Effects of Summative Assessment

While the effects of formative assessment on student learning are overwhelmingly positive, the results of studies on summative assessments, particularly the use of high-stakes standardized tests, are mixed. We described in previous chapters several features of the standards-based approach to education, such as: agreeing on a set of student standards, believing that every child can meet these standards, and assessing student learning with standardized tests for purposes of holding teachers and schools accountable. Currently, there is an ongoing debate concerning the short- and long-term effects of NCLB and high-stakes standardized assessments, which we will return to later.

Some aspects of this approach have had positive effects. It has altered what we expect of *all* students. There is also some evidence that current practices have had positive and long-term effects on student learning. Haycock (1998) and Schmoker and Marzano (1999), for instance, have argued that the standards and standardized testing movement have led to higher teacher and school quality and this has had positive effects on student achievement. Many states report that achievement scores, as measured on their standardized tests, have improved over the past several years.

Standard-based education and high-stakes testing, however, have not produced as much in the way of results as some envisioned, and may have produced some unintended negative consequences. Recently, researchers Nichols and Berliner (2007) reported the negative consequences of the time and energy devoted to annual testing. Earlier, Amrein and Berliner (2003) surveyed state graduation examinations in 18 states. They examined student achievement as measured by the **SAT**, the **ACT**, advanced placement tests, and the **National Assessment of Educational Progress (NAEP)**. They found no evidence that student achievement had increased significantly and that state testing had actually had a negative effect for struggling students. They also reported a number of unintended outcomes, including increased dropout rates, decreased retention rates, teachers and schools cheating on exams, and increased alternative high school diplomas. They concluded that high-stakes testing was pushing low-achieving students out of school rather than helping them succeed.

Similarly, analyses of results on the National Assessment of Educational Progress (NAEP) have shown only modest achievement gains over the past decade and confirm earlier studies that many students who start ninth grade do not graduate from high school. A recent study (McNeil, Coppola, Radigan, & Vasquez Heilig, 2008) reported that high-stakes testing in Texas resulted in a decrease in the number of students completing high school. A similar situation was reported by Landsburg (2008) in regard to the effects of testing high school students in Los Angeles. Long time assessment experts such as Popham (2006) and Nichols and Berliner (2007), among others, have concluded that, although common standardized assessments, benchmark assessments, and interim assessments can play an important role in monitoring student progress and providing system-level information for policy makers, there is still little evidence that such assessments increase student achievement.

REFLECTION

What surprised you most about the research on assessment? What research-based practices are you already using? What thoughts has this review sparked for you?

ASSESSMENT FOR LEARNING

Even though today a great deal of attention is paid to high-stakes testing as a means to fix schools, the fact of the matter is that formative assessments used every day by teachers have the most impact on student learning. What, however, constitute effective formative assessment practices, and how can assessment practices be fully integrated into teachers' instructional programs? Fortunately, these questions have been studied quite thoroughly and the results provide us with clear definitions, criteria, and guidelines. Similarly, experienced teachers have developed an array of formative assessment strategies that provide information for adjusting their instruction and for helping students modify the learning strategies that we describe in the sections that follow.

Recently, noted assessment expert, James Popham (2008, p. 6), provided us with a workable definition, which we paraphrase below:

> *Formative assessment* is a planned process in which assessment evidence and information about student learning is collected and used by teachers to adjust their ongoing instructional programs and by students to adjust their current learning strategies or tactics.[1]

Note some of the key features in Popham's definition:

- Formative assessment is conceived as a planned process, not a test.
- Teachers use assessment evidence to inform instructional decisions and to make needed adjustments.
- Students use assessment evidence to make adjustments in their learning strategies.

Black et al. (2004, p. 10) have used slightly different words to define formative assessment for learning but the meaning they convey is essentially the same:

> *Assessment for learning* is any assessment for which the first priority in its design and practice is to serve the purpose of promoting students' learning.

The features listed by Popham and by Black are important. The fact that the process is *planned* demonstrates that, as teachers, we have integrated assessment processes into our instructional programs in careful and thoughtful ways. *Evidence-based* means that we are basing our instructional decisions on evidence rather than on whim or intuition, and it means students are using evidence to analyze and make decisions about their own learning.

Effective Formative Assessment Practices

We now discuss four effective formative assessment practices that can be implemented in all subject areas at all levels: ensure clarity about learning outcomes, provide effective feedback, assess frequently, and use traditional assessments to inform teaching and learning.

Ensure Clarity about Learning Outcomes Stiggins, Arter, Chappius, and Chappius (2006) contend that students can hit any target if it is clear and constant. Ensuring clarity about learning outcomes is very important in student learning and achievement. Stiggins and Chappius (2005) have provided us with guidelines and overall steps to follow as we consider best formative assessment practices. They recommend the following:

- *Step 1*: Start by identifying learning outcomes (standards) and translate these into student-friendly language.
- *Step 2*: Develop assessments for each learning outcome.
- *Step 3*: Make sure students understand criteria that define success.

- *Step 4*: Provide students with frequent, descriptive, constructive, and immediate feedback on their progress.
- *Step 5*: Create opportunities for students to participate in self-assessment and to receive peer assessments.
- *Step 6*: Involve students actively in assessment and keep careful records so progress can be tracked.

Perhaps the most important aspects of the Stiggins–Chappius recommendations are those aimed at clear communication of learning outcomes and curriculum expectations. Clear targets and specific criteria for success help focus student work. Effective teachers have a variety of techniques to communicate learning goals and expectations to students, such as posting goals and outcomes in language students can understand and providing students with examples of good work at the beginning of a learning segment. Here is an example:

Mary Turbo is a twelfth-grade teacher who supervises the school's required senior project. She starts her first advisory sessions for seniors by distributing two rubrics: one used to assess the research paper; the other used to assess a required presentation. Next, she asks students to work in pairs and review a successful research paper completed the previous year. She then shows video clips of successful senior project presentations from the previous year. These actions communicate clearly to students her expectations and provide them with illustrations of success from previous years.

Provide Effective Feedback Providing effective feedback is the single most important (and effective) way to improve student learning and to inform them about the effectiveness of the learning strategies they are using (Black et al., 2004; Hattie, 1992; Shute, 2008). Sometimes referred to as **knowledge of results**, feedback can be provided in a variety of ways—verbally, in written form, or by using video and/or audio recordings. Regardless of the form, feedback must be handled with care because it can also have a negative effect on student motivation and learning. For instance, learning is negatively influenced when students receive more general feedback, such as "that is correct" or "that is wrong." Similarly, simply assigning a "mark" or "grade" to an assignment or piece of work provides no information to students about what they know, the mistakes they made, or how to improve. According to Black et al. (2004), this kind of feedback is particularly damaging to struggling and low-performing students.

For feedback to be most effective, it must be timely, specific, descriptive and developmentally appropriate (Hattie & Timperley, 2007; Shute, 2008). Feedback should be provided as soon as possible after students have attempted to demonstrate their understanding of particular knowledge or to perform a targeted skill. This means returning **homework** and providing verbal written feedback without delay. Feedback should also be specific and corrective. For example, instead of saying an essay had too many misspelled words, the exact words that were misspelled should be identified and in some instances corrected. Feedback is also more effective if it is descriptive rather than evaluative. Descriptive feedback improves learning; evaluative feedback interferes with learning. Sutton (1997) and Davies (2007) have described the differences between these two types of feedback. We summarize their comparisons in Table 6.3. Note the differences,

Table 6.3 Descriptive versus evaluative feedback

Descriptive feedback	Evaluative feedback
• comes during the learning • uses descriptive language • focuses directly on the learning task • is specific and easily understood • confirms what is correct • identifies mistakes and misconceptions • tells the learner how to improve • provides specific strategies and suggestions for next steps • is immediately usable • is part of an ongoing conversation about learning	• comes after learning • uses evaluative language • tells the learner how they compare to others (norm-referenced assessment) or to what was to be learned (criterion-referenced assessment) • is general and provides praise or blame and non-specific advice • is reported in letters, numbers, or other symbols • is summative and comes at the end of learning

Source: Information summarized from combined works of Sutton (1997) and Davies (2007).

particularly the emphasis on providing correctives such as identifying mistakes and showing steps to make improvements.

Finally, effective feedback is developmentally appropriate. Too much feedback or too sophisticated feedback, particularly for younger or struggling students, can be overpowering. It is important to be selective and to provide appropriate feedback that can be immediately usable.

> **REFLECTION**
>
> In what ways do you provide feedback to your students? Has it mostly been descriptive or evaluative? With a classmate or colleague, discuss what changes you might want to make in your classroom assessment system.

Assess Frequently In many instances, assessments are simply too far apart. This is particularly true of summative assessments given at the end of instructional units or marking periods. Although these assessments may be valuable for determining grades, they are not very useful for informing teachers or students about what has and has not been learned. Two important meta-analyses (Bangert, Kulik, Kulik, & Morgan 1991; Fuchs & Fuchs, 1986) demonstrated rather dramatically the effects of frequent assessments. The Banger analysis of 29 different studies reported that five assessments during a unit of study could result in a 20-percentile point gain in student achievement as compared to only a 13.5 percentile gain with a single assessment. Gains taper off with additional assessments—25 assessments resulted in a gain of 28.5 percentile points. The Fuch and Fuch analysis of 21 studies concluded that two assessments per week resulted in a percentile gain of 30 points.

Use of Traditional Assessments to Inform Teaching and Learning **Traditional assessments**, although they have been designed mainly for summative purposes, can nonetheless provide valuable formative information for teachers and students, and we don't want to downplay their use. Many standardized tests provide valuable information to help teachers diagnose students' prior knowledge and in turn guide planning. Similarly, teacher-made, **paper-and-pencil tests** administered at the end of instructional units or at the end of a grading period can provide relevant information to guide future planning and to make instructional adjustments.

It is important to point out, however, the limitations of traditional assessments. They too often constitute the only assessment information available, and the information they provide may not be timely or valid. Most state or district standardized tests are given yearly; unit and end-of-grading period tests are set every few weeks. Often the results are not available for months. This lack of frequency (and timeliness) does not provide the continuous information about student learning required for making instructional adjustments or allow students to monitor their learning. Further, some of the information provided by summative assessments, particularly standardized tests, may not be valid. This is particularly true when items on a standardized test are not aligned to the curricula aims and to instructional goals deemed important by particular schools or teachers.

In the next section, we describe specific formative assessment strategies that can be used by teachers to diagnose student readiness and prior knowledge and by students to select the most effective learning strategies to use. As we proceed, we want to repeat once more that formative assessment is not an occasional test, but instead a process that is an integral and ongoing aspect of instruction.

Diagnostic Assessment

On several occasions in previous chapters we emphasized what many of our experienced teacher readers know—that what students already know is the most important factor in determining what they will learn. Sometimes however, as teachers, we may pursue instructional outcomes that some students are not ready to consider because they lack sufficient background knowledge. At other times, we may teach what students already know. Getting into the habit of assessing prior to teaching is an effective assessment practice. Information gathered from **diagnostic assessments** can save time, and provide insights about how to differentiate instruction. For some topics, these before-learning assessments can be simple and done informally; others require more extensive and formal strategies. For instance, many of the strategies described later, such as questioning and listening to students, are rather simple to carry out, and they provide important informal cues about students' prior knowledge. Diagnosing more complex reading and mathematics skills or kindergarten readiness, on the other hand, often requires more formal methods.

Inventories Inventories are effective tools for diagnosing students' prior knowledge, interests, and learning preferences. They document areas of strength and areas for development. They help students understand themselves as learners and provide teachers with information for planning instruction and grouping. A number of inventories are commercially available. Many teachers, however, prefer to construct their own. Inventories can also be used to identify group skills, study habits, or interests. Similarly, there are many diagnostic inventories, particularly in the areas of literacy and mathematics, which can provide teachers with rather detailed information about their students and their prior knowledge.

Observations Observations provide another source of information for teachers about what students know and can do. Watching and listening to students working in groups or independently and observing how they interact inside and outside the classroom can reveal their understandings, interests, values, and preferences. Many experienced teachers have found that it is useful to document observations with anecdotal notes or checklists. A key to using observation effectively is to employ this strategy systematically and regularly.

Interviews Finally, interviews can provide information about students' prior knowledge as well as their interests and misconceptions. Interviews have an advantage over inventories in that they allow students to express themselves verbally rather than in writing. They also allow teachers to probe more deeply in search of reliable information. The disadvantage of using interviews is that they take considerable time, a commodity that is always in scarce supply.

Specific Formative Assessment Strategies

There are dozens of strategies and techniques that can be used to assess student learning on a day-to-day basis. We focus on two key ones here: questioning and informal-response techniques.

Questioning Every day teachers engage in discourse with their students and, over the space of an instructional unit, they ask literally hundreds of questions. Planning classroom questioning strategies carefully can be a high-yield formative assessment strategy that results in enhanced student learning. In other chapters, we discuss classroom **discourse patterns** in some detail. Here, however, we focus on two aspects of these topics: ways to frame questions that are worthwhile and that move beyond the factual, and ways to slow down the pace of classroom discourse.

Ask Worthwhile Questions. Often, teachers want to ask very specific, factual questions to elicit whether or not students have grasped some of the basic ideas of a lesson. However, Black et al. (2004) say that teachers should not stop with these factual questions. They should also ask big questions, those that are somewhat open-ended. Big questions allow students to explore critical issues and provide teachers with more in-depth insights into their understanding of particular curricula aims and instructional goals. As described in Chapter 4, Wiggins and McTighe (1998, 2005) use the concept of *essential questions* to emphasize the importance of overarching ideas that reflect the heart of the curriculum. Most of our experienced teacher readers know how to categorize different types of questions according to some taxonomy. We prefer using Bloom's revised taxonomy (Anderson & Krathwohl, 2001), which allows us to categorize questions along six cognitive dimensions on a continuum from the more factual to the higher levels. These are:

- Questions to assess what is *remembered.*
- Questions to assess what is *understood.*
- Questions that require *application.*
- Questions to assess abilities to *analyze.*
- Questions that require *evaluation.*
- Questions that assess *creative* abilities.

Effective use of questioning to collect formative information requires the use of questions at several levels of the taxonomy. We discuss the revised Bloom's taxonomy in more detail for other purposes in later chapters.

REFLECTION

How would you rate your questioning skills? Do you plan for and write questions in advance? Do you use essential questions? Have you ever had someone script your questions? Arrange with a colleague or classmate to visit each other's classroom and observe each other's use of questions and wait time.

Slow Down Classroom Discourse. Studies spread over several decades (Rowe, 1974, 1986; Walsh & Sattles, 2005) have demonstrated that the pace of discourse in most classrooms is much too fast. Instead of waiting for students to respond after a question is asked, teachers too often ask another question, or they answer their own question. It seems that periods of silence in the classroom, as in most social settings, cause nervousness and anxiety. Rowe recommends that teachers employ the three-second **wait-time** rule. Give students three seconds to respond after a question is asked. Wait another three seconds after a student's response before saying anything or asking another question (this is called "wait-time two"). Waiting provides students with more time to think and results in higher quality answers that, in turn, are more useful in assessing what *they really know*. In later chapters we will return to this subject and provide a variety of strategies, such as "Think–Pair–Share," "reciprocal teaching," and "Socratic dialogue," that can be used to slow down discussion and to change the pattern of classroom dialogue.

Informal Student-response Techniques In addition to more complex and formal assessment strategies, teachers also need informal techniques that can help them collect valid information quickly so in-flight adjustments can be made. Leahy, Lyon, Thompson, and Wiliam (2005) described three such techniques: letter cards, whiteboards, and traffic lights.

Letter Cards. This technique has been designed to provide teachers with formative assessment information quickly. Instead of giving the students a quiz with multiple-choice or true-and-false items, students are asked to respond to verbal questions with **letter cards**. Here is how it works. Each student is given a set of seven index cards. Each card contains a letter—A, B, C, D, E to be used to answer multiple-choice questions, and T and F to answer true-and-false questions. The teacher asks (or displays on a projection device) two or three questions pertaining to the lesson and encourages students to respond with one of their cards. Large numbers of students holding a card with the "wrong" response shows clearly that they are not getting it and that more instruction is required. On the other hand, if most of the students respond correctly, the teacher knows they understand the lesson and that it is time to move on.

Whiteboards. The **whiteboard** response technique is similar to the letter card response except it allows students to construct their own responses. Each student is provided a small (8″ × 12″) erasable whiteboard (or chalkboard) and is asked to respond to short-answer type questions—those that can be answered in a few words or a phrase. By scanning student responses, teachers can determine quickly if students understand the concept or if they are confused. The former calls for moving on, while the latter suggests more instruction is required.

Traffic Lights. The **traffic lights** technique is an informal way for students to show teachers their level of understanding of a particular idea or skill as the lesson is being taught. Each student is given three colored cones or plastic cups. One cone is green, one is yellow, and one is red. At the beginning of a lesson the cones or cups are stacked on the student's desk, with the green on top. During an instructional segment, such as a lecture, demonstration, or discussion, students can report their level of understanding of the lesson by ordering the cones. A green cone indicates good understanding of the topic. Yellow indicates partial understanding or unsure. The red cone or cup indicates that the student is lost and confused. Students are taught to independently change their cones as a lesson proceeds. Teachers can also stop in the middle of a lesson and call for a cone assessment. Observing many yellow or red cups alerts teachers that students are not following along and are having trouble understanding what is being taught, a condition that requires additional explanation or asking student with greens cones to help their yellow peers while the teacher works with red ones.

ASSESSMENT AS LEARNING

Black et al. (2004) identified self- and peer assessment as one of four powerful and effective classroom assessment strategies. Earl (2003) also elaborated on strategies that promote assessment *as* learning. In this section, we highlight a number of assessment strategies for engaging students in monitoring their own learning and in contributing to the learning of their peers.

Self-assessment

Helping students become self-directed learners is one of the primary goals of education. One way to achieve this goal is to shift some of the responsibility for assessment from the teacher to the learner. **Self-assessment** involves helping students set their own learning goals, monitor progress toward achieving these goals, and make adjustments in learning strategies as required. Students can be involved in assessment in a variety of ways, including helping establish criteria for success, developing rubrics to measure learning, examining and rating work samples, using learning logs, letter writing, and other strategies described below (Gregory, Cameron, & Davis, 2000; Stiggins, 2005).

Learning Logs Teachers can use learning logs to help students set their own learning goals, to identify learning strategies, and to chart progress and reflect on learning outcomes. Students are encouraged to make entries in their learning logs on a regular basis. Cross (1998, p. 9) asked her students to respond to four questions once a week:

1. Briefly describe the assignment or learning activity you just completed. What do you think was its purpose(s)?
2. Give an example of one or two of your most successful responses. What made them successful?
3. Provide an example of where you made an error or where your responses were incomplete. Why were these items incorrect or incomplete?
4. What can you do differently when preparing for next week's assignment?

To be successful, teachers must show students how to organize their learning logs. One popular method we have observed is to have students divide each page of the learning log into two sections. On the left-hand side of the page students document the topic or activity of the lesson and/or outline main points to remember. They are also encouraged to illustrate their learning in diagrams or charts. On the other side of the page, students record what they have learned and their reflections on this learning.

Using learning logs as a self-assessment strategy affords students opportunities to measure and reflect on their progress and the learning strategies they are employing. Learning logs can also help teachers identify individual misconceptions and misunderstandings, as well as determine group patterns that can provide important information for planning future lessons.

Letter Writing Writing letters to an individual or to an identified audience can also serve as an important self-assessment strategy. **Letter writing** helps students become aware of their understanding of particular topics, as well as the learning strategies they are using. Costa and Kallick (2004) suggest using thought starters such as those listed below to focus students' letter writing:

- Here is my work . . . this is how I approached it . . .
- These are the thoughts I have . . .
- These are the skills and strategies I used . . .
- I am good at these things . . .
- I don't fully understand . . .
- I am confused about . . .
- I agree with . . . I disagree with . . .
- This is how I have changed . . . this what I need to work on next . . .
- The kind of support that is helpful to me . . . unhelpful . . .

This strategy can be extended by having students write different kinds of letter such as: a letter of appreciation, a recommendation letter, a cover letter for a job application, or an advocacy letter. Student letters can also facilitate peer assessment and teacher interaction. Students can critique each other's letters for clarity and content. Teachers can write back to students to provide constructive feedback and to recommend steps to take for improvement.

KWL and RAN The **KWL strategy** (Ogle, 1986) engages students in accessing prior knowledge and framing learning questions and goals prior to an instructional segment, and then reflecting on what has been learned following instruction. The strategy consists of getting students to ask two questions and record notes as they begin to study or read about a topic:

- What do I **K**now?
- What do I **W**ant to know?

The third question is addressed after study or instruction:

- What have I **L**earned?

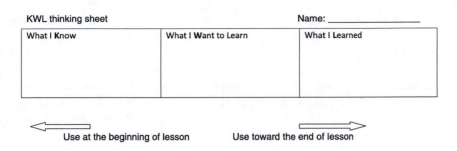

Figure 6.2 Self-assessment using KWL

Often, teachers use a "handout," as illustrated in Figure 6.2, as an aid that assists students with the KWL strategy.

KWL can be used with individual students or with pairs and small groups. It can help students and teachers uncover misconceptions and connect to prior learning. We will return to the KWL strategy in Chapter 10, in the context of teaching thinking skills.

Tony Stead (2005) provided the **RAN strategy** (**R**ead and **A**nalyze **N**on-fiction), similar to KWL but more complex. During a reading assignment students provide information and evidence at different steps, as displayed in Figure 6.3. Students initially record what they think (their predictions). Then, as reading proceeds, they provide evidence about whether or not their predictions are confirmed, identify misconceptions if they existed, and record new information and questions (wonderings) the reading has generated. Thoughts are recorded on sticky notes so they can be moved around as students discover new concepts or ideas.

Peer Assessment

As teachers, we all know that students learn a great deal from each other, and, though we know quite a bit about the use of cooperative learning, we are less knowledgeable about the use of peer assessment. Some are also uncomfortable with using **peer assessment** because sometimes it has been confused with peer evaluation. We view peer assessment as a formative assessment and feedback strategy *not* as an evaluation strategy. It is valuable because its use can increase significantly the amount of feedback students receive and the form in which it is received. Feedback provided in the student's own language is, in many instances, more readily accepted than if it is provided by the teacher.

The effective use of peer assessment, however, requires instruction about how to participate in peer assessment and how to give feedback effectively. It also requires

What I think	Where my thinking is confirmed (page number)	Misconceptions	New information	Wonderings

Figure 6.3 RAN worksheet

teachers to be precise about their instructional goals and the criteria used to determine student success. There are many and various peer assessment strategies. Below we describe four of them.

Find-it-and-fix-it Following either a formative or summative assessment, the teacher reviews test items or assigned work. Instead of marking items or work as correct or incorrect, the teacher identifies the number of errors, and tells students something like the following, "There are five errors in this piece of work. Your job is to work with a partner to 'find and fix' the errors." Students then work together to correct errors and in the process teach each other. This type of peer assessment and interaction results in deeper understanding of the material and helps students clarify misconceptions they may have had.

Pre-flight Checklist This is a peer assessment strategy described by Wiliam (2007). Students trade papers and review each other's work before it is submitted to the teacher. Each student completes a pre-flight checklist by comparing the peer's work against a list of required components and criteria. If components are missing, the work is returned to its owner for revision and then returned again to the peer. Peers must sign off on the "**pre-flight checklist**" before the product is passed on to the teacher.

Two Stars and a Wish The **two stars and a wish** strategy provides peers with opportunities to give each other feedback. Two students exchange their work. They read and review the respective pieces and identify two strengths (two stars) and one area for improvement (a wish). Next, they discuss the stars and the wish with each other. An extension of this strategy is using triads or quads. On the first round, when this approach is used, each student passes their work to the left. Everyone reads their respective piece and provides feedback using two stars and a wish. The group discusses each piece, and each student revises their work. The peer-editing group reconvenes and a second round of reviews proceeds.

Peer assessment is a potentially powerful way to provide students with important information and feedback about their learning. We encourage our experienced teacher readers to experiment with these strategies and to extend our understanding of their use.

Summarizing Strategies Summarizing is a very powerful strategy for enhancing student learning (Marzano, Pickering, & Pollock, 2001). It is important, however, that students do the summarizing and not the teacher. Summarizing helps both teachers and students monitor progress and consolidate learning. Routinely including **summarizing strategies** as part of your classroom assessment strategies helps students show their understanding and consider relationships. Summary strategies can be used as a self- or peer assessment strategy, although they are more powerful when students work together. Dozens of summary strategies have been created and compiled by different writers.[2] We display ten examples of summary strategies in Table 6.4.

Table 6.4 Ten examples of summary strategies

1	**A–B–C summary**	Provide students with an alphabet template. Independently or in pairs students record a word or phase beside each letter of the alphabet related to a specific topic.
2	**Card sort**	Facts, concepts, and attributes are written on index cards or post-it notes. Categories are written on the board. Pairs or triads sort the cards into the correct categories.
3	**Circle check**	Students stand and form a circle. Each person makes a summary statement or comment about the topic being studied. In a more complicated version, each successive comment must be connected to the one before it.
4	**Concept summary**	Students draw a picture or visual symbol, list key terms or concepts, and write a brief summary paragraph to demonstrate their learning.
5	**Exit cards**	Stop instruction and activity five minutes before the end of the lesson and give students a blank index card. Pose a question and each student writes a response. The cards are signed and returned to you as they leave the classroom.
6	**Luck of the Draw**	A series of questions or concepts are written on index cards. Students draw a card and respond to the question or explain the concept. Alternatively, each student writes a summary card, then you draw a name and the "lucky" student reads their summary.
7	**Mind Map**	Students draw a circle or box in the middle of paper and write the topic. Symbols, words, and pictures are drawn around the main topic identifying key concepts and ideas summarizing and illustrating relationships.
8	**One Minute Paper**	Students respond to two questions in a one-minute paper and turn it in as they leave the room. 1. What was your most significant learning today? 2. What question is upper most on your mind?
9	**Quick Writes**	Students write for 90 seconds to two minutes on a concept identified by the teacher. They summarize their thoughts by drawing a picture and writing a short paragraph.
10	**Three-Two-One**	Provide students with a 3–2–1 template and question prompts. For example: three things that interested you, two questions you have, and one surprise.

ASSESSMENT OF LEARNING

We conclude this chapter with a discussion of *assessment of student learning*, the third purpose of assessment we described earlier. We explain how summative assessment and student evaluation can be used not only to determine grades and promotions but also to inform instruction and enhance student learning. Space does not allow for an in-depth discussion of these topics; however, there are many excellent resources available elsewhere, some of which we list in the resource section at the end of this chapter. This lack of detailed coverage does not mean that we believe summative assessment and making judgments about student learning are not important. After highlighting the importance of summative assessment and student evaluation, we briefly describe teachers' summative assessment practices and the use of standardized tests in today's schools. Then, we discuss effective evaluation and grading strategies that can be used in today's classrooms.

Teachers' Summative Assessments

Perhaps someday it will be different, but currently schools and teachers carry immense responsibilities for assessing and evaluating student achievement. Teachers' judgments, represented by the grades they give, have significant long-term consequences on students' lives. They help determine if they will go to college and the type of college they can attend, which in turn will influence their life styles and careers. Similarly, the use of high-stakes standardized tests has important and lasting consequences for what goes on in classrooms and what students learn.

Some observers, including us and likely many of our readers, have been critical of the current uses of standardized testing and some of the processes used by schools and teachers to evaluate students. Observers, such as Amrein and Berliner (2003), Nichols and Berliner (2007), Noddings (2006), and Popham (2008), have argued quite accurately that the standards movement and standardized testing, as we described in Chapter 1, have narrowed the curriculum and constricted what teachers teach. Others, such as Marzano (2006), believe that grading systems that compare students to each other result in unnecessary competition and cause many students, particularly the strugglers, to drop out of school. Others have pointed out that, though teachers strive to be fair in their grading, too often the measurements and marks they use are invalid and unreliable.

On the other hand, most students and their parents accept the schools' role in evaluating students and support the use of standardized tests. Students, according to Doyle (1986), perform schoolwork in exchange for grades, a situation not too much different than adults who work in exchange for a paycheck. Parents show great concern for their children's grades. They know from their experiences as students the consequences that teachers' judgments have had on their own lives. Parents as a whole, however, tend to protect the current grading system, as many school faculties have found if they have attempted to replace it with an alternative. Finally, parents, as well as many other citizens and policy makers, believe that schools should be held accountable for student learning and support the use of district and state-wide testing programs for this purpose.

This leads us to conclude that, even though we may disagree with some aspects of current summative assessment and grading procedures, as teachers, we must take both into account and use them to our advantage in support of student learning. To do differently is to provide a great disservice to our students and to our schools. So what can classroom teachers do?

REFLECTION

Think for a moment about how you grade and evaluate student work. What principles guide your actions? Does your school have consistent and common guidelines for grading and evaluation or do individual teachers make independent decisions? With a classmate or colleague, compare how your grading practices differ.

Teachers' Summative Assessment Systems Traditionally, teachers have relied on teacher-made, paper-and-pencil tests or homework assignments such as book reports and terms papers to measure what students know and to determine their grades. These types of assessment remain popular and are widely used. Today, however, several alternative measurement tools exist that can be used in summative assessment situations. In this section, we review briefly more traditional approaches and then describe some newer alternatives that we believe hold promise.

Paper-and-pencil tests. Teacher-made tests can be divided into two broad categories: those with test items that allow students to *select* a response from alternatives provided, and those with items that require students to *construct* a response. Multiple-choice, matching, and true and false are the most common examples of tests that employ **selected-response items**. Essay and short-answer tests are examples that allow students to *construct their own response*s.

Tests with selected-response items have several advantages. They allow assessment of a broader range of outcomes and curricular aims, and they can be scored objectively and quickly. These tests also have some disadvantages. Constructing good selected-response items, particularly multiple-choice questions, takes considerably more time as compared to writing an essay test item. And, although some test experts might disagree, it is difficult to write selected-response items that measure many cognitive skills associated with higher-level thinking and problem solving. The guessing factor also serves as a disadvantage for tests with selected-response items.

The traditional use of essay and short-answer questions also has advantages and disadvantages. Good essay tests, for example, can tap students' in-depth understanding of a topic and the ways they are thinking about it. They also take less time to construct. On the other hand, scoring essay tests is open to teacher bias and answers can be influenced by students' handwriting instead of what they actually know. They also take considerable time to read and score, and it is also difficult to measure a broad range of topics with essay questions. Short-answer questions are seen as a compromise between an essay test and one that uses selected-response items. A test with short-answer items can sample a rather broad range of topics, can be scored somewhat objectively, and does not take much time to prepare. Short-answer test items, however, are often criticized because they cannot assess more complex understandings, cognitive skills, or processes.

Alternative Assessments Many teachers, educators, and assessment experts have become dissatisfied with the traditional, pencil-and-paper assessments. It is believed these assessments put too much emphasis on assessing basic skills while ignoring higher-level thinking and problem-solving skills. Led by such authorities as Wiggins (1998, 2005) and Stiggins et al. (2006), today it is believed that this situation can be corrected with the use of newer approaches, namely, performance and authentic assessments.

Performance assessments require students to demonstrate by performing what they know or can do, as contrasted to responding to items on a paper-and-pencil test. Examples of performance assessment include writing an essay, completing an experiment, or performing a song. Some performance assessments are done in testing or simulated situations. Other performance assessments, called **authentic assessments**, require students to demonstrate particular skills or knowledge within the context of

Table 6.5 Examples of performance and authentic assessments

• competing in a musical competition	• organizing a conference
• compiling a portfolio	• participating in model United Nations
• conducting an interview	• performing a dance
• constructing a flower arrangement	• planning a trip
• exhibiting at a science fair	• playing a match of tennis
• designing an orienteering course	• preparing a meal
• drawing a map	• displaying work at an art show
• facilitating a meeting	• working with a team building a model
• giving a speech	• writing a letter or recommendation

real-life situations. Examples of authentic assessment include showing a portfolio of one's artwork, performing at a real music recital, participating in a debate, or exhibiting a project at a science fair. Table 6.5 provides additional examples of performance and authentic assessments.

Proponents of performance and authentic assessments (Burke, 1999; Newmann, Secado, & Wehlage, 1995; Oaks and Lipton, 2006; Stiggins, 2006) believe that these types of assessment have several advantages over the more traditional paper-and-pencil tests:

• They allow students to construct, organize, and synthesize their own knowledge.
• They help students learn to consider alternative solutions and points of view.
• They involve students in important inquiry processes.
• They afford students opportunities to address real-world issues and problems.
• For many students, they can generate more motivation and engagement.

The drawbacks of using performance assessments are that developing good ones takes a great deal of time and requires considerable technical knowledge. However, authorities such Gronlund, Linn, and Davis (2000) and Wiggins, (1998, 2005) have developed valuable guidelines that can assist teachers who choose to move in the direction of using performance assessments. They recommend the following:

1. Focusing on learning objectives/standards that require complex cognitive skills and performance.
2. Selecting or developing performance tasks that represent both knowledge and skills central to the learning objective/standard.
3. Writing clear directions for how to complete the performance task.
4. Developing a scoring rubric with a detailed description of what expected performance looks like.
5. Communicating performance expectations clearly to students by sharing rubric with them.
6. Providing necessary support so students are able to understand the performance task and expectations for success

A variety of strategies have been developed by teachers as a means to help organize and evaluate student performance. Student portfolios and artifact boxes are two of the most common ones.

Student Portfolios. Most individuals are aware of the **portfolio** process used in visual arts whereby painters, graphic designers, or ceramists select illustrative pieces of their work and organize them in portfolios that can be used to demonstrate their accomplishments and skills. Musicians, models, and actors use video to do the same thing. In education, portfolios consist of collections of student work that can be used to assess their learning over time. Belgrad, Burke, and Fogarty (2008) outlined four phases of developing a portfolio for assessment purposes: collection, selection, reflection, and projection.

The first phase involves *collecting* numerous examples of student work, such as homework assignments, projects, mind maps, tests, and/or written papers. In some instances, students decide what to collect for their portfolio; in others, the teacher decides. Often, portfolio entries are the result of shared decisions.

The second phase involves the student in *selecting* samples from their collection that provide evidence of learning. Often, teachers provide criteria to guide selection, such as the best pieces, most difficult pieces, work in progress, or work that demonstrates growth over time. During the selection phase, students also delete or remove pieces that do not meet the criteria or that do not provide evidence of learning.

In the third phase, students are asked to *reflect* on their learning by writing an essay that examines why particular pieces were selected and the criteria they satisfy. Costa and Kallick (2004) provided suggestions for guiding students' reflective essays:

- The process I went through to create this portfolio entry was . . .
- . . . influenced me to create this portfolio.
- The risks I took in the creation of this entry were . . .
- New insights I gained about myself as I created this entry were . . .
- This piece was an experiment for me because . . .
- I have discovered that I am good at . . . because of this entry.
- What continues to intrigue me is . . .
- The evidence that shows my growth is . . .

In the fourth phase, the student and the teacher schedule a conference to discuss the portfolio and to *project* future learning goals. Some portfolio conferences are designed so students can engage their parents in a conversation about their learning. Others can be structured to facilitate discussions among peers, older students, and community members.

Artifact Boxes. These are similar to portfolios, but they are more targeted and have a more limited timeframe. They consist of collections of such items as photos, quotes, pictures, graphs, drawings, charts, symbols, or objects, which represent a particular concept or key idea (Dodge, 2005). For example, a student studying a unit on "Our Heritage" in a ninth-grade history class might research and prepare an artifact box that illustrated her grandmother's life. Her box could contain photos, letters, jewelry, newspaper clippings, sheet music, a family tree, and various mementos from Ireland, along with a written description highlighting important dates in her grandmother's life. Another student, in a fifth-grade science class, might prepare an artifact box on ways to "go green" for a unit on the environment. His box might have a recycling guide, photos, special light bulbs, a computerized thermostat, "green" garbage bags, a newspaper article on energy efficient appliances, a formula for calculating one's personal carbon footprint, and an index card listing ten environmentally-friendly actions readily available to everyone.

Scoring Rubrics. **Rubrics** have become a common tool for assessing performance tasks. Everyone is aware of well-known rubrics used in athletic competitions to score performances in gymnastics or diving. We are also aware of "checklists" used to score driving abilities in tests given to acquire a driver's license. In education, rubrics communicate a teacher's expectations and describe clearly the criteria used to judge a performance or piece of student work. They also describe levels of quality. They are particularly useful for scoring writing samples, projects, presentations, and group activities, as well as other portfolio entries.

Measurement experts (Andrade, 2000; Brookhart, 1999) make distinctions between analytic and holistic rubrics. Analytic rubrics provide criteria that allow for the separate assessment of each component of a performance. Holistic rubrics, on the other hand, make a judgment about the performance as a whole, independent of component parts. An example of an analytic rubric for assessing cooperation is described in Chapter 13.

Designing good **scoring rubrics** is an important aspect of performance assessment. Following are guidelines adapted from Airasian (2006) and Mertler (2001):

- *Step 1*: Determine learning objectives/standards that are to be measured by the performance assessment. Align these with the scoring rubric.
- *Step 2*: Identify specific observable attributes of the performance you want to see (specific skills, procedures, processes).
- *Step 3*: Describe characteristics of each attribute you expect to see in the performance, ranging from exemplary to below average.
- *Step 4*: Write narrative quality descriptions for excellent (highest) and poor (lowest) performance.
- *Step 5*: Complete the rubric by describing other quality levels on the continuum.
- *Step 6*: Collect samples of student work as examples at each level; revise rubric as necessary.

High-stakes Standardized Tests

Today, citizens expect schools and teachers to be accountable for student learning. This has led to the use of **standardized tests** administered by states, the national government, and, in some instances, international agencies, to provide evidence about student learning and school success.

Nature of Standardized Tests Standardized tests are either norm referenced or criterion referenced. **Norm-referenced tests** measure an individual student's achievement and compare it to a representative group of students from the same district, state, or country. Norms are established for norm-referenced tests from a random sample (**norming group**) of students from the specific age group for which the test has been designed. Norms for different tests are set at different times. For example, norms for the National Assessment of Educational Progress (NAEP) are set in the spring and revised every seven years. Scores from norm-referenced tests are reported as **percentile ranks** or as **grade equivalent scores**.

Criterion-referenced tests, on the other hand, measure student achievement against a set of standards and indicate to what degree students have achieved mastery of a particular standard. Scores of criterion-referenced tests are most often reported as the percentage of students who have demonstrated basic, proficient, or advanced levels of mastery, as well as those who have failed to reach mastery.

State legislators have legitimized current testing and accountability processes. However, these processes have also been heavily influenced over the past 15 years by major pieces of legislation at the federal level. The *Goals 2000 Act 1994* specified that high standards should be set for all students and that means should be developed to assess student learning. The **No Child Left Behind (NCLB)** legislation of 2002 paved the way to make further use of standardized tests to evaluate students and their schools. The NCLB Act required schools to test students every year in third through to eighth grade. It also required schools with high failure rates to provide tutors for low-achieving students and to provide parents with the opportunity to transfer their children to other schools.

The standardized tests used in most states have focused on four core subjects: literacy, mathematics, science, and social studies. Many states have also adopted high school exams in specific subjects, such as algebra, geometry, biology, chemistry, and civics. In addition, most states have an overall graduation test that students must pass for matriculation. For example, in Ohio students must pass the Ohio Graduation Test (OGT). Results of state standardized tests are turned into "report cards" that compare school districts and individual schools. These comparisons influence greatly what teachers teach and what students learn.

The Classroom Teacher's Role Even though individual teachers do not have much direct influence on the type of standardized tests used in their district or state, they do have an important role to play in how tests are administered and how the results are communicated to parents and other stakeholders.

Test Preparation. Students' test-taking skills and attitudes greatly influence how well they do on standardized tests. Teachers can help students improve their skills by familiarizing them with the type of test-item format to expect and by providing them with practice opportunities. Communicating a positive attitude toward the test and encouraging students to do well is also important. An obvious dilemma for teachers, particularly when test results are used to evaluate their teaching or their school's performance, is whether to "teach to the test." Most believe that teachers should *not* teach directly to the test, but at the same time they should make sure that their students understand the importance of the test and what is going to be on it and ensure that they are given appropriate practice opportunities.

Curriculum Alignment. Often, students do poorly on standardized tests because they have not been taught the knowledge and skills covered by it. For example, if a test assesses students' understanding of algebra prior to being exposed to algebra, it is unlikely they will perform very well. Or, if the rubric used to score the state's writing exam is much different than the one used by teachers in a particular school, it is likely that students will do poorly. As teachers, we need to join with our colleagues to align portions of the curriculum to topics and skills to be covered on required tests. This curriculum alignment, too, may pose a dilemma for teachers. On the one hand, if they do *not* align their curriculum to the test, their students will perform poorly. On the other hand, aligning curriculum too closely to the test may cause important curricular aims and instructional goals to be ignored.

Using and Communicating Test Results. Perhaps the most important roles for classroom teachers in regard to standardized tests are using and explaining test results. Care should be taken to go over test results with students and with their parents. Both need information about what a particular test score means and its limitations. In most instances, standardized test results will show the degree of mastery students have achieved, particularly in the areas of literacy and numeracy. On the other hand, students and parents need to understand that scores on a particular test do not measure all aspects of a student's abilities and that there are always possibilities that a particular score may be invalid or unreliable.

Community members and policy makers also need to be taught about the strengths and limitations of standardized tests, something that newspapers seldom do very well when they report test results. Stakeholders need to be taught the differences between criterion- and norm-referenced tests and the strengths and limitations of each. They also need to understand that students' prior knowledge and abilities have significant influence on how well students do. And, even though everyone attests to the belief that every child can learn, in reality a school or classroom of highly talented and well-motivated students will almost always do better on standardized tests than will a school or classroom of struggling students and a high mobility rate.

Effective Grading and Evaluation

For a long time there has been considerable debate about student evaluation and grading. Many assessment experts believe that grading practices currently used in many schools and classrooms inhibit student motivation and learning (Brookhart, 2004; Guskey, 2000; Guskey & Bailey, 2001; McTighe & O'Connor, 2005; Marzano, 2006; O'Connor, 2007; Reeves, 2008; Stiggins & Chappius, 2005). On the other side, and as many of our experienced teacher readers will attest, many citizens and parents value and support traditional grading practices. These are practices they experienced when they were students. They are cautious and often opposed to changes to grading systems.

Part of the reason that views vary about grading is that grades serve different purposes. Some, O'Conner (2007) for instance, believe that the primary purpose for grades is to summarize student achievement of particular curricular aims and learning goals. Others see the primary purpose of grades as providing a way to sort and to compare students with one another so promotions, class rankings, and college admissions can be determined. Beliefs about purposes influence the kind of grading system schools and teachers develop and the kind that citizens and parents will support.

In an earlier section, we described the differences between norm-referenced and criterion-referenced tests. The same logic can be applied to grading. Traditionally, **grading on a curve** guided many grading practices. When this approach is used, students compete with each other for placement along a predetermined curve. Teachers using this approach assign points to various assignments and exams and count up the total number of points at the end of a grading period. They then give approximately 10 percent of students As, 20 percent Bs, 40 percent Cs, 20 percent Ds, and 10 percent Fs. Grading on a curve and accumulating points has several shortcomings. This approach does not take into account important student differences, does not factor in growth, and often makes unfair use of non-academic factors such as participation and citizenship.

Grading to criterion is an alternative approach for determining grades. This approach requires teachers to define their curricula aims and standards very precisely, measure student performance against criteria associated with the standards, and then tie grades to the degree to which students achieve mastery. Assessment experts offer several guidelines to make grading to criterion effective:

- *Tie grades to specified curricula aims and standards and make the grading system transparent.* Grades should identify the degree to which particular students have achieved mastery of agreed upon curricula aims and standards. These should be communicated clearly to students, as well as the metrics that will be used to translate achievement into a grade.
- *Assess and grade academic and non-academic work separately.* Grades that are used to determine promotion, graduation, or university admission need to accurately reflect academic understandings and skills. Non-academic factors such as behavior, attitude, or participation should not be included in this type of grade. Marzano (2006) and O'Connor (2002) recommend that schools develop a grading system with two separate grades—one that reflects achievement; the other effort, disposition, and work habits.
- *Provide multiple and varied opportunities for students to demonstrate mastery of what they know and can do. Base grades on students' best performances rather than averaging many.* Grading systems need to provide students with second chances and, in McTighe and O'Connor's (2005) terms, "allow new evidence to replace old evidence," particularly when the new evidence provides a fairer and more accurate picture of achievement.

Grading to criterion, however, does not solve all the grading problems and can present teachers with a different set of issues to resolve. For example, if criterion levels are set, should they be set the same for all students? Or, should able students be expected to do more work and perform at a higher level? What level should be expected for less-capable students? What about growth and progress? Should student growth be communicated through a grade? If so, how much weight should be given to growth as compared to overall achievement? Should separate grades be given for achievement and growth?

Finally, regardless of whether grading on a curve or grading to criterion, an effective grading system contains several important features:

- *Have grades (and grading systems) that support student learning and that are accurate, meaningful, and consistent.* Even though summative assessment and grading have high-stakes consequences, they should nonetheless be designed so they encourage rather than discourage student learning. They should accurately reflect student achievement at a particular point in time. Students and parents should find grades a meaningful summary of what students know and are able to do (Guskey, 1996; Wiggins, 1998, 2005). Perhaps most importantly, grades need to be consistent over time and across classrooms and not be characterized by situations, still found in some schools, where each teacher establishes their procedures and policies and where final grades and marks can vary dramatically.

- *Use zeros and averaging sparingly.* Sometimes zeros are used to punish students for missing, late, or incomplete work. Although this practice may result in higher completion rates, when zeros are averaged into final grades they do not reflect a true representation of what students know and can do. This does not mean that teachers and schools should not acknowledge, report, and deal with work that is not completed (Guskey, 2004; Reeves, 2004).

- *Use homework grades as part of final grades only if they demonstrate mastery, such as those given for an essay or project. Do not include grades assigned to homework that was intended to provide practice.* Much homework is assigned to provide practice opportunities for students and becomes part of the learning process. In most instances, it is inappropriate to include homework grades meant as formative assessment as part of the final grade (summative assessment) that appears on report cards.

- *Remember the emotional dynamics associated with evaluation and grading.* Students know at a very early age that a teacher's evaluation of their work and grades has serious long-term consequences. It is normal for them to experience a great deal of anxiety, a condition described in previous chapters, that can seriously affect learning. Stiggins (2006) describes in Table 6.6 the patterns and characteristics of students who are on a *winning streak* versus those who are on a *losing streak.*

DESIGNING A BALANCED ASSESSMENT SYSTEM

It is likely that we will never develop a perfect system for assessing and evaluating student learning. However, we think the use of alternative and performance assessment practices and grading to criterion procedures represent some important breakthroughs in this traditionally thorny problem. We encourage our experienced teacher readers to look carefully at their classroom assessment systems and strive to develop a balanced assessment system that reflects their values and beliefs, that is fair to all students, and that can be communicated clearly to parents and stakeholders.

Finally, many assessment and grading practices are *not* under the control of

Table 6.6 Winning and losing streaks: The emotional impact of assessment

Winning streaks	Losing streaks
• right from the start, students score high on assessments	• right from the start, students score very low on tests and assessments
• they come to believe themselves capable learners	• this causes them to doubt their capabilities as learners
• they become increasingly confident in school	• they begin to lose confidence about learning and school
• they gain emotional strength to risk striving for more success	• they are deprived of emotional reserves to continue risk trying
• they believe success is within their reach if they try	• they believe success is not within reach even if they try

Source: Winning and losing streaks concept from Stiggins (2006).

classroom teachers. Instead, they are governed by school- and district-wide policies. The way high-stakes standardized tests are given and used is an example of something outside the confines of the classroom, as are the way report cards are designed and the type of marks assigned. We encourage teachers to provide leadership for school- and district-wide discussions about assessment and grading practices.

SUMMARY AT A GLANCE

- Assessment is an important part of instruction and serves three purposes: assessment *for* learning, assessment *as* learning, and assessment *of* learning.
- Assessment and student evaluation matter because they have important effects on learning and lasting life consequences.
- Formative assessment (assessment *for* learning) is a planned and continuous process, with the purpose of promoting student learning by providing information for teachers to make instructional adjustments and for students so they can make changes in their learning strategies.
- Effective formative assessments include self- and peer-assessment strategies (assessment *as* learning).
- Teachers need to prepare students for summative assessment (assessment *of* learning) and use the results to inform their teaching and student learning.
- There are dozens of assessment strategies that promote student learning. Teachers should continue to learn about and add new strategies to their repertoire to increase feedback to students to guide their learning.
- Teachers' own summative assessment systems should be balanced and use both traditional measures and alternative measures associated with performance and authentic assessments.
- Many traditional grading practices are perceived by some to be harmful to students. Teachers are encouraged to examine their grading practices, investigate effective practices, and work toward finding grading systems that are valid, reliable, and fair.

CONSTRUCTING YOUR OWN LEARNING

Working alone or with a classmate or colleague, make an inventory of your assessment practices and the beliefs you hold about assessment and student evaluation. You might want to compare your practices with the following criteria: has positive influence on student motivation and learning, is integrated with your instructional practices, is feasible, is reliable, is valid, and is fair. Now develop a set of goals for changes you would like to make in your classroom, in your school, and perhaps in your school district related to assessment.

RESOURCES

Costa, A.L., & Kallick, B. (2004). *Assessment strategies for self-directed learning.* Thousand Oaks, CA: Corwin Press.

Davies, A. (2007). *Making classroom assessment work* (2nd ed.). Courtney, BC: Classroom Connections International Inc.

O'Connor, K. (2002). *How to grade for learning.* Thousand Oaks, CA: Corwin Press.

Stiggins, R.J. (2005). *Student-involved assessment for learning* (4th ed.). Upper Saddle River, NJ: Merrill/Prentice Hall.

Stiggins, R.J., Arter, J., Chappius, J., & Chappius, S. (2006). *Classroom assessment for student learning: Doing it right—using it well.* Portland, OR: Educational Testing Service.

Part II
METHODS AND MODELS OF TEACHING

PRESENTATION AND EXPLANATION

Seventh-grade history and language arts teachers, Maria Romero and Randy Jackson, are preparing to launch a unit on race relations in the United States from the 1930's depression through the 1960's Civil Rights Movement. To kick off their unit they have assigned Mildred Taylor's *Roll of Thunder, Hear My Cry*, a book that has won numerous awards and has become a perennial favorite among middle school teachers and students. The novel is set in Mississippi in the 1930s and is told through the voice of heroine Cassie Logan as she experienced her African American family's struggle against poverty and racism.

This is an absorbing story, but it will be difficult to teach to the diverse group of students found in Ms. Romero and Mr. Jackson's classes. Their inner-suburb classroom has students from a variety of racial and ethnic groups. Some students come from middle-class professional families. Others are Latino and African American from working-class homes. Wide ranges of abilities exist within the classroom. Some students will find the language in the novel confusing; others will have a hard time relating to some of its disturbing scenes.

Today, we find Ms. Romero and Mr. Jackson planning their overall approach. They know their instruction must be tailored to their students' background knowledge for this type of unit and their values and beliefs about race and poverty. From earlier experiences they know that their students will have little information about the depression in the South or about race relationships during the 1930s. They decide that success of the unit will require a series of presentations aimed at providing students with background knowledge about race relations, and about economic conditions in Mississippi at that time.

OVERVIEW AND PERSPECTIVE

Explaining things to students is the instructional strategy used most often by teachers at all levels, except perhaps for those who teach the very young. Evidence collected over several decades shows that, as teachers, we talk a lot. Many have argued that too much time is spent telling and explaining, leading to the admonishment that we should adopt approaches that are "less transmittal and more participatory" (Sfard, 1998). Regardless of this criticism, the presentation–explanation model of instruction remains popular. Experienced teachers know that many educational goals aim at the acquisition of information in the form of declarative knowledge. They know that students are required to learn this information and to understand concepts about an array of topics found in textbooks and curriculum frameworks, and on standardized tests. They know that acquiring basic information about the unfamiliar constitutes the foundation for learning and thinking about more advanced ideas and concepts and for critical thinking.

Presentations and explanations are effective in helping students acquire and process new declarative knowledge. However, the approach we describe in this chapter also aims at achieving two other types of learner outcomes: helping students expand their conceptual structures, and developing habits of listening and thinking. These outcomes are illustrated in Figure 7.1.

Presentations and explanations are not very effective for teaching procedural knowledge, higher-level thinking, or problem-solving skills. Other models described in subsequent chapters have been developed to accomplish these instructional outcomes.

Many observers view explaining and presenting as a passive form of learning. We believe that this does not have to be the case. Students can be actively involved and engaged in presentations and explanations, particularly when these types of lessons are combined with discourse and discussion. Instructional explanations are also often associated with actions performed only by teachers. In reality, however, they are not confined to what teachers say. They are also contained in the explanations found in textbooks, videos and film, Internet text, and the explanations provided by students themselves. Perhaps most important for our consideration here is that ample evidence exists demonstrating clearly that *explaining things well* enhances student learning, while doing it poorly interferes with learning and leads to misunderstanding and confusion (Leinhardt, 2001).

Many explanations take the form of what we normally label as "**lecture.**" We, however, are going to cast our net more widely and include not only more formal lectures but also how instructional explanations occur in many other instructional situations. For instance, instructional explanation occurs when a teacher stops in the middle of a group discussion to explain an idea that appears to be confusing to students or during seatwork when the teacher chooses to clarify a point raised by a student's question. Regardless of the particular instructional situation, presentations and explanations are characterized by several phases. The flow proceeds from: (1) a teacher's initial attempts to gain attention and get students ready to listen; (2) presentation of an advance organizer or scaffold aimed at tapping students' prior knowledge; (3) delivery of new information and ideas associated with a particular topic; and (4) interactions with students aimed at checking for understanding and the use of elaborations that extend students'

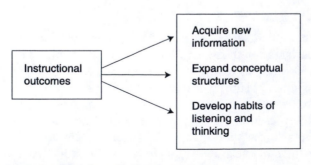

Figure 7.1 Instructional outcomes for presentation and explanation teaching

conceptual frameworks and thinking skills. We expand on each of these phases later in the chapter.

CONNECTING PRESENTATION TEACHING TO THE CONTEXT AND SCIENCE OF LEARNING

The knowledge bases about how students learn from presentation and explanation are quite well developed, and fortunately we know a great deal about the most effective ways to present and explain. Some of you will already be familiar with this information from your own teaching or from experiences in other settings where you were required to give speeches and/or explain things to people. Previously, we introduced several ideas about the context of teaching and about student learning that have direct application for explaining and presenting. Several of these ideas and their implications for teaching are highlighted below. We referenced these ideas previously and will not repeat them here.

- *Learning takes place in human settings.* Rich learning environments help add new connections to the wiring of the brain, while sterile environments retard development. The emotions and feelings experienced by learners greatly influence cognition. These two ideas elicited from the science of learning have important implications. Even though presenting and explaining are mainly teacher-centered acts, rich learning environments can be created—those that appeal not only to the auditory and visual but also to the other senses. Environments can also be created that have positive feeling tones and where students are free from threat.
- *The primary goal of presenting and providing explanation is to build declarative knowledge.* The way explanations are structured, however, also allows students to observe their teacher's thinking processes and in turn build habits of listening and thinking. Also, explanations can sometimes be useful for developing procedural knowledge (how to do something); most often, however, they take a back seat to demonstration and practice, methods described in a later chapter.
- *The importance of prior knowledge is key: what learners already know is the most important factor for determining what they will learn.* This principle is critical when considering what makes a presentation or explanation effective. It provides the theoretical and empirical base for the use of advance organizers and intellectual **scaffolding** we emphasize below.

PLANNING FOR PRESENTATIONS AND EXPLANATIONS

Now we turn to decisions that are required as explanations and presentations are planned. As with many aspects of teaching, a large part of success begins during the planning phase of instruction. It is during planning that teachers take the opportunity to estimate the range of prior knowledge students will bring with them to a particular topic, to choose and limit content based on this diagnosis, to plan ways to design an environment free of threat, and to select the best advance organizers, examples, illustrations, metaphors, and representations. The first three of these actions are discussed below; the latter will be covered in the subsequent section that describes delivering effective presentations and explanations.

Attending to Prior Knowledge, Readiness, and Intellectual Development
It is critical that information provided in a presentation be based on a teacher's estimate of their students' prior knowledge and understandings. Take, for instance, what can happen if a presenter does not take prior knowledge into account. James Zull, a professor of biology, relates a story about what he calls the "lecture of my life."

Professor Zull had been asked by a colleague to fill in for him as a guest presenter and to lecture on *mitochondria*—power plants of the cell. This was a subject that he knew so well that he was "totally relaxed when he walked into the class." During the next 50 minutes Zull gave a brilliant lecture on how cells get their energy from sugar and fats. Without notes, he covered the topic thoroughly and highlighted the main ideas across the chalkboard. He reported that, during the lecture, "nuances were crystal clear. The underlying concepts were powerful . . . yet obvious. I was hot!" (Zull, 2002, p. 135). At the end of the class, he dusted the chalk off his hands and asked for questions. There were none. He attributed the silence to the great clarity of his lecture. He left the lecture hall patting himself on the back.

Zull's colleague invited him to come back during the next class session to check out what students had learned from the "lecture of his life." As he probed for their understanding, he was again met with silence. Finally, one brave student raised his hand and asked, "Professor Zull, could you explain mitochondria again?" It didn't take Zull long to conclude that his lecture had been a complete dud, and the reason for his failure was because he proceeded with faulty estimates of the students' prior knowledge. Students in the class did not have the necessary background information and conceptual understandings to grasp his new ideas about the subject. In turn, they learned nothing about mitochondria. This example is not an extreme case; it has been repeated over and over by all of us who have taught.

As with most other aspects of teaching, there are no proven recipes for collecting information about students' prior knowledge or intellectual development. However, there are some general ideas and methods to consider. The age of a student allows us to have some general understanding about their level of intellectual development (Flavell, Miller, & Miller, 2001; Goswami, 2008; Hunt, 1974; Piaget, 1954). Remember, from Chapter 2, that people go through developmental stages, having quite concrete **cognitive structures** at earlier ages and becoming more abstract later on. Teachers rely mainly on informal diagnostic assessments for determining their students' developmental levels. They do this by asking questions and by watching for verbal and nonverbal cues. It is important to point out that, attending to intellectual development provides no magic wand for selecting the most appropriate content for a presentation or explanation, because within any classroom teachers will find wide variability in their students' intellectual development. They will find some students who can think at a fairly high level of abstraction in some subjects and yet be at a very concrete level for others. Being able to figure all this out and accurately diagnose students' readiness to learn is perhaps what signifies the major difference between the expert and novice teachers we described in Chapter 1.

REFLECTION

With a classmate or colleague, explore the various methods you use to diagnose students' intellectual development and prior knowledge. Which ones work best? Which ones have not worked so well? Perhaps you have stories similar to Mr. Zull's that you will want to share.

Knowing the topics and ideas taught in previous grades, units, or lessons can also assist in understanding what students already know. This knowledge, however, can be misleading. Teachers in previous grades may have run out of time and not taught all the topics recommended in the school's curriculum framework. Many students may also have attended different schools in previous years. Others may not have learned the subjects taught to them.

The use of diagnostic assessments described in Chapters 5 and 6 can be extremely useful for assessing prior knowledge. You remember these were assessments given at the beginning of a unit or lesson or anytime when students seem confused about a topic. These assessments may consist, in some instances, of standardized tests, but most often they are questions or checklists teachers develop themselves. For example, to find out about students' prior knowledge teachers can ask two or three questions about a forthcoming topic and have students provide their answers in writing. Here are some examples of questions that Ms. Romero and Mr. Jackson asked their students prior to their unit on race relations:

- What ideas or impressions do you have about the 1930s?
- How well off were people in Mississippi in the 1930s compared to people today?
- After the Civil War the slaves were set free. By the 1930s, how were African Americans being treated in the United States? In Mississippi? Were they still considered to be slaves?

As we saw in Professor Zull's lecture, knowing background knowledge prior to a presentation is critical, but so is spotting students' **misconceptions**. Inaccurate knowledge about a topic is persistent, enduring, and cannot be purged easily. Teachers need to anticipate and deal directly with misconceptions. Saphier and Gower (1997) observed that accomplished teachers know from their own past experiences that there will be common student misconceptions and/or areas of confusion on a variety of topics. Examples in science and geography abound:

- "Rivers flow from north to south."
- "Wherever you are, it is warmer to the south."
- "Soil is food for plants."
- "Scientific method consists of seven fixed steps and is universal."
- "Air only pushes down."

Teachers also can often predict in advance the subjects their students will find difficult. For example, Saphier and Gower (p. 195) illustrated how a teacher might deal with the concept of "density," always a difficult one for students (and adults for that matter):

After a demonstration of the concept of density with two cups of cornflakes, one crushed and one not, the teacher sketches on the board and says, "Raise your left hand if diagram 1 is more dense and right hand if diagram 2 is more dense. Tina, tell why you chose this one. OK, everyone, in your notebooks, in three lines or less, define density and give one everyday example of something which is more dense than something else.

Sometimes we do not anticipate misconceptions or difficulties in the planning stage of a lesson, but instead spot them in the process of teaching it. When this happens, a misconception must be confronted explicitly by calling students' attention to it, providing ample explanation about the correct idea, and then checking for students' understandings before moving on. All of these instances require teachers to get inside their students' heads so the source of misconceptions can be revealed and actions taken to clear them up.

Choosing Content
Teachers must choose carefully the content for any explanation or presentation. Whether the explanation takes the form of a formal lecture or an informal response to a student's query, several principles should guide the choice of what and how much to explain. In Chapter 4, we introduced the principles of *economy* and *power*. Economy, you remember, encouraged teachers to be very careful about the amount of information and number of ideas chosen to present or explain at any one time. Helping students examine a few critical ideas or a single idea in depth is better than bombarding them with many disparate facts. The power principle encouraged teachers to select the most central ideas and concepts that form the structure of a subject.

We also introduced in Chapter 4 the framework proposed by Wiggins and McTighe (1998, 2005), who argued that content should be chosen to reflect the big ideas and essential questions of a particular subject. These are the ideas that are deemed to have enduring value and are important for students to know about and understand. Following Bruner's and/or Wiggins and McTighe's principles is important because they provide sound guidance for selecting "what to teach" about topics and subjects that can never be totally covered even if we had a lifetime to do it in. We conclude this section with an admonition provided in previous chapters—when deciding what to teach, remember "less is often more!"

REFLECTION

Limiting what we teach is difficult for most of us. With a classmate or colleague, discuss what you have found helpful for defining and organizing your content.

Attending to Classroom Environment and Feeling Tone[1]
In Chapter 2, we spent considerable space describing how emotions affect cognition and how learning situations characterized by fear and threat inhibit cognitive learning, whereas situations characterized by pleasurable and positive feeling tones facilitate learning. There are several instructional implications that stem from these ideas.

Whether a formal lecture or more informal interchange, several aspects of the overall environment are important. Obviously, the physical environment in both elementary and secondary classrooms should be filled with interesting and provocative learning materials, as well as student work. Care should be taken to have ample technology for visual display. For more formal presentations, this means accessible chalkboards, flip charts and technologies for electronic displays. In more and more classrooms, it also means available technologies that allow students to pose questions, give input, or signal understanding during a presentation. Visual display for informal explanations can be accomplished by carrying a clipboard to illustrate ideas and concepts.

The overall learning environment and feeling tone of classrooms are the most important variables. Students simply put forth more effort and learn more in environ-ments that are pleasant, safe, and secure. In the process of providing explanations, several actions by teachers can produce either positive or negative feeling tones. Refer-ring to students' names throughout a presentation helps personalize the subject and enhance student learning, as does striving to relate concepts to their lives and to things they are naturally curious about. Obviously, this requires careful planning on the part of the teachers because any classroom of diverse students will find an array of interests and curiosities.

The attitudes of teachers, particularly how they say things and deal with errors, also are very important in establishing positive feeling tones during an explanation or pre-sentation. A recent discussion we had with a friend highlights this idea. Our friend, a fifties something woman who has a Ph.D. and a very successful career as a therapist, began yoga classes. Although a beginner, she was a highly motivated learner. She believed that yoga would improve her concentration and enhance her physical flexibil-ity. Over a period of four months, she changed classes three times before finding one she really liked. We asked her, "What is it about your most recent class that you like better than the first two?" She replied, "The instructor is so nice." She has a wide range of individuals in the class, with varying degrees of yoga knowledge and experience. How-ever, she never criticizes anyone. When others or I make mistakes with a particular movement, she explains how to do it correctly and then gently tells us, "I am sure you can do it the same way." The yoga instructor in this example establishes a positive feeling tone as she encourages and challenges her students to learn and understand yoga movements and positions.

DELIVERING PRESENTATIONS AND EXPLANATIONS

In this section, we provide step-by-step advice about how to give effective presentations and clear explanations. As described at the beginning of the chapter, **presentation teaching** has some common phases. These phases are summarized in Figure 7.2 and then described in more detail below.

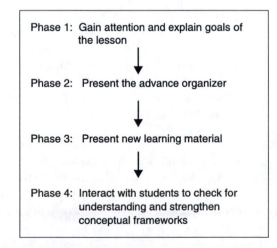

Figure 7.2 Phases of a presentation lesson

Gaining Attention

"They weren't paying attention," is a common teacher complaint, as is the admonition, "if you had been paying attention, you would know what I just said." Remember, in Chapter 2, we spent considerable space describing how our memory and information processing system works and the important role *attention* plays in this process. We defined attention as the process of focusing on selected environmental stimuli, a prerequisite if messages are to end up in sensory and short-term working memory.

Classrooms are cluttered with stimuli; students decide to pay attention to some stimuli while ignoring others. Given this clutter, gaining attention is not easy. It takes skill on the part of the teacher and motivation on the part of students. And, regardless of what kids say about being able to study, listen to music, and watch TV at the same time, it is not true. Most individuals can pay attention to only one demanding topic or task at a time, particularly when the topic or task is brand new and complicated. Therefore, the first job when we decide to present or explain is to gain our students' attention. Below are specific principles and strategies for gaining attention:

- *Attention is influenced by what we already know.* Reminding students what they already know is a good attention-getting device.
- *Attention is influenced by surprise and the dramatic.* Using eye-catching displays, dressing in special costumes, or singing a song will tend to catch students' attention.
- *Attention is influenced by curiosity.* Use of uncommon or unique words, pictures, smells, or tastes can arouse curiosity and in turn capture attention.

Here is an example showing how Ms. Romero and Mr. Jackson captured their students' attention as they were about to provide them with background information about race relations in Mississippi as a prelude to reading *Roll of Thunder, Hear My Cry*.

Dressed in 1930's working-class clothing (overalls and blue shirts), they moved to the front of the room and began the following dialogue:

Mr. Jackson: "Cassie, what's the matter with you girl?"
Ms. Romero [playing Cassie]: "I'm churnin' butter."
Mr. Jackson: "You still takin' a sorrowful long time. You mopin. You feel sick, Cassie?"
Ms. Romero: "I'm scared. Do you know what them men on the bus said to me?"

They continue with this dialogue taken directly from the novel to gain students' attention prior to their presentation on race relations.

Presenting Advance Organizers

After gaining attention, effective presentations and explanations require us to use particular tools to help students connect new learning to what they already know. The **advance organizer** is one such device. Sometimes referred to as intellectual scaffolds, advance organizers are hooks or anchors that help activate prior knowledge and help students prepare to consider the learning materials to follow. Advance organizers have been the subject of research for a good many years and we summarize the research briefly in Research Box 7.1.

Inquiry **RESEARCH BOX 7.1**

Summary of Advance Organizer Research

David Ausebel (1960) carried out the initial research on using advance organizers in the 1960s. He designed a 2,500-word learning passage on the topic of "metallurgical properties of steel." Subjects, in this case college students, were divided into two groups matched on their ability to learn unfamiliar material. The experimental group received a 500-word "advance organizer" at a higher level of abstraction than the content in the learning material prior to being exposed to the 2,500-word passage. The control group just received some general background information. Both groups studied the material for 35 minutes. Students then took a test on the material three days later. Students who had been given the advance organizer before they read the passage retained substantially more information three days later as compared to students who were in the control group.

This research sparked a debate about the effectiveness of presentations using advance organizers. Many studies have been done since that time and several syntheses of this research have been compiled. The research has *not* in every instance produced consistent results. Overall, however, most studies and several syntheses of research on this topic between the 1980s and the present (Luiten, Ames, & Aerson, 1980; Marzano, 2007; Mayer, 2003; Walberg, 1986, 1999) have demonstrated pretty convincingly the positive effects of using advance organizers when presenting or explaining things to students.

Ausubel suggested that advance organizers should be slightly more abstract than the content to be presented. Others (Mayer, 2003) have suggested that concrete examples from the lesson work better. Joyce, Weil, and Calhoun (2000) categorized advance organizers into two types: (1) an *expository advance organizer*, where basic ideas or concepts are presented at a higher level of abstraction and serve as an intellectual scaffold on which to hang new information; and (2) a *comparative advance organizer* used to show students that the new idea or concept is familiar to ideas or concepts they already know. Following are examples of advance organizers used by Ms. Romero and Mr. Jackson as they provided background knowledge about social and economic conditions in Mississippi in the 1930s. Notice how we have set off the advance organizer from more general other introductory comments and from the new learning materials to be presented.

Example 1: Expository Advance Organizer *Introductory comments and establishing set.* Yesterday, we distributed *Roll of Thunder, Hear My Cry* and we asked you to read a few pages in the book to get an idea of what it is about. Today, I am going to give a short talk that will provide you with some background information about life in the South during the 1930s. My goal is for this information to help you understand the book and the historical era it represents. Before I do that, however, I want to give you a big idea that will help you understand something about *time* and *setting* as they relate to historical fiction.

Advance organizer. The big idea I want you to understand is that historical fiction writers, such as Mildred Taylor, strive to make their novels historically accurate in regard to place and time. However, historical novels also will reflect the era in which they were written and the talents and point of view of the author.

Beginning of presentation of new learning materials. Mildred Taylor's historical novel, *Roll of Thunder, Here My Cry*, is set in Mississippi in the 1930s. However, the author grew up in Ohio, went to college in Colorado, and wrote the book in the 1970s. Here are some facts and ideas about Mississippi in the 1930s and about Mildred Taylor . . .

Example 2: Comparative Advance Organizer *Introductory comments and establishing set.* Yesterday, we distributed *Roll of Thunder, Hear My Cry* and we asked you to read a few pages in the book just to get an idea of what it is about. Today, I am going to give a short talk that will provide you with some background information about life in the South in the 1930s. My goal is for this information to help you understand the book and the historical era it represents. Before I do that, I want to give you a big idea that will help you understand the endurance of racism and poverty.

Advance organizer. The big idea I want you to consider is that the ways we treat people have historical roots and that issues such as eliminating poverty and attaining social justice take a long time. Many of the incidents of racism described in *Roll of Thunder, Hear My Cry*, are similar to those held in the South prior to the Civil War; some can still be observed throughout the United States and in our communities today.

Beginning presentation of the new learning materials: We will read about how Cassie Logan and her African American family struggled with poverty and racism in Mississippi during the Great Depression. As we view life through Cassie's eyes, I want you to consider if any of the things she experienced are still with us today in our community. Here are some examples of how African Americans were treated in the South in the 1930s . . .

As illustrated above, the advance organizer or intellectual scaffold is not the same as other techniques teachers may use to gain attention or introduce a lesson. Providing novel activities to arouse curiosity, reviewing the previous day's lesson, or giving an overview of today's lesson are all important, but they are not advance organizers aimed at connecting students' prior knowledge to the new learning material. It is important for the advance organizer to be set off from other introductory comments, as well as from subsequent learning materials. It is important for students to

REFLECTION

Consider your experiences with using advance organizers. Are you already familiar with this device? If so, how successful have you found it to be? What difficulties has its use presented you? Strive to compare your experiences with a classmate or colleague.

understand the advance organizer and what it is designed to accomplish. It is more readily understood when accompanied by visual aides such as a newsprint chart, an overhead transparency, or an electronic image.

Presenting New Learning Materials

The actual act of presenting or explaining new learning materials has the most effect on what students learn. Explaining things well facilitates student learning, while doing it poorly leads to confusion.

Strive for Clarity and Teach in Small Chunks Teachers' abilities to be clear and specific have consistently shown to affect student understanding in significant ways (Hiller, Fisher, and Kaess, 1969; Marzano, 2007; Rosenshine & Stevens, 1986). Nonetheless, the same research that demonstrates the positive effects of **teacher clarity** also shows that many presentations lack clarity. Instead, they are often characterized by vagueness or generalities. Lack of clarity is caused primarily by presenters not having a thorough understanding of their subject, shoddy preparation, or insufficient use of examples and other important explanatory devices. Figure 7.3 provides guidelines for making presentations clearer.

Clarity is not achieved easily. It requires careful attention to planning, organization, and sometimes rehearsal and practice. It also requires reducing a topic or steps to a manageable size and separating the essential from the nonessential. Rosenshine (2002) has referred to this practice as teaching in small steps or chunks and reported what effective teachers do:

> When the most effective teachers in these studies taught new materials, they taught it in *small steps*. They only presented small parts of new materials at a single time. . . . The importance of teaching in small steps fits well with the findings from

---

Be clear about aims and main points

- state the goals of the presentation
- focus on one point at a time
- avoid digressions
- avoid ambiguous phrases

Go through the presentation step by step

- present materials in small chunks
- provide students with an outline when material is complex

Be specific and provide several examples

- give detailed explanations of difficult points
- provide students with concrete and varied examples
- model or illustrate the idea whenever possible—use pictures and visuals

Check for student understanding

- make sure students understand one point or idea before moving on to the next
- ask questions to monitor student comprehension
- ask students to summarize or paraphrase main points
- reteach whenever students appear confused

Figure 7.3 Aspects of clear presentation
Source: Summarized from combined works of Rosenshine and Stevens (1986) and Marzano (2007).

cognitive psychology on the limitations of [short-term] working memory. [Short-term] working memory is small . . . and can only handle a few bits of information at once (p. 7).

Many teachers recognize the value of teaching in small chunks and presenting for no more than ten to 15 minutes before pausing to provide some type of processing opportunity. Processing opportunities may consist of asking students if they have any questions or having a brief discussion. "**Think–Pair–Share**" and other thinking routines we describe in Chapters 10 and 13 are effective ways to help students process what they have just heard before moving on.

Use Examples Examples are one of the best devices for making new material meaningful to students. However, the task of coming up with "good" examples can be difficult. Here are guidelines for developing effective examples, adapted from Hunter (1994):

- *Effective examples highlight the critical attributes of an idea or concept* that distinguish it from other ideas or concepts. Sometimes effective examples come to us as we present a lesson. Most often, however, these spontaneous examples are unclear and can result in confusion. The late Madeline Hunter used to advise teachers that, "thinking on your seat is easier than thinking on your feet."
- Examples *should be clear and unambiguous.*
- Examples *should be connected to students' lives, prior knowledge, and experiences.*
- Good examples limit *distracters from the critical attributes.*
- Good examples sometimes *avoid controversial issues.* In other places, we stress the importance of arousing emotion in learning. However, in some instances too much emotion can divert attention from an important cognitive idea or concept. After an idea is understood, then time can be provided to debate its pros and cons.

Here is an example of an example:

Say Ms. Romero and Mr. Jackson want their students to understand the concepts of prejudice and racism. They might explain that *prejudice* is a preformed opinion about a person or group, most often an unfavorable one and based on insufficient knowledge or inaccurate stereotypes. Examples might include: Chicanos are dirty; poor people are lazy; Muslims can't be trusted. They might go on to explain that *racism*, on the other hand, refers to animosity confined specifically toward people of other races and to beliefs that some races are inherently inferior or superior to others. For example, many people today still inaccurately believe that African American students get lower scores on standardized tests because they have lower intelligence, or that being Asian means you are smarter and will score higher on tests as compared to others. Now compare the two concepts. In the 1930s, deep-seated *racism* existed in the South. Many white people believed that African Americans were intellectually and socially inferior. At the same time, African Americans in *Roll of Thunder, Here My Cry* were also *prejudiced* toward all whites in the community even those who were trying to help.

When providing examples, as teachers we often make reference to ideas, places, events, or famous people. These references are only effective as examples if students know about the reference. A reference to the "monsoon season" will not help clarify the concept if students have never heard the word monsoon. Referring to the "First Gulf War" will be recognized by most people over 25; however, it is likely to be meaningless to a 12 year old who was yet to be conceived when that war was fought.

Use the Rule–example–rule Device The **rule–example–rule device** can be used effectively when presenters are explaining an important generalization or principle. Essentially, this device is performed in three steps:

- *Step 1*: State the rule, principle, or generalization, e.g., "Most wars are fought over influence, ideas, or land."
- *Step 2*: Provide examples of the generalization. The American Revolution was fought over influence. Colonists did not want to be controlled by the British. The American Civil War was fought mainly over ideas. People in the North and the South had different ideas about whether it was morally right to have slaves. The Mexican–American War was fought mainly over land. The United States wanted land in the Southwest United States originally settled by Spain and Mexico.
- *Step 3*: Summarize and then restate the rule or generalization. People's desire to have influence or power over others, to pursue their own beliefs and ideologies, or to have more land can lead to war

Use Explaining Links An **explaining link** is a phrase used to describe prepositions and conjunctions that specify a cause, result, or purpose of an idea or event. Examples of explaining links include: because, if . . . then, therefore, consequently. When presenting or providing explanations, the use of explaining links helps students see the logic and the relationships the teacher is trying to get across. It also provides students an opportunity to observe the thinking processes of their teacher.

Use Verbal Signposts and Transitions Many presentations or explanations contain several important ideas. **Verbal signposts** and **transitions** help students move from one idea to another. For example, the teacher might say, "Up to this point I have been explaining what all of you already know, that light reflects off mirrors. Now I want to turn and help you understand how this process is governed by the law of reflection."

Sometimes, transitional statements summarize important points just made; at others times, they telegraph what is to follow. Here is an example: "Now that we have covered the societal conditions in Mississippi in the 1930s, let's look at how these conditions affected poor African Americans who lived in the state at that time." Transitional statements help students see the organizational structure of a presentation and serve as signposts that show the direction the teacher is going. Writers also use transitional statements. For example, in the preceding sections we described how examples and transitions could be used as powerful explanatory devices that lead students to meaningful understanding.

Use Analogies, Metaphors, and Similes An important aspect of providing explanations is to make comparisons, particularly comparisons of new ideas to those students already have. Analogies, metaphors, and similes are explanatory devices used by writers and presenters to make meaningful connections and comparisons. Let's begin by relating the examples in Table 7.1 (provided by Grothe, 2008) about differences between regular prose or speech intended to merely transmit information to prose or speech enhanced by analogies, metaphors, or similes.

Analogies point out similarities or like features between two things or ideas so comparisons can be made or relationships explored. Most people are familiar with "analogy tests," such as Miller's Analogy or the multiple-choice **analogy** questions found on intelligence and scholastic aptitude tests. These questions, you recall, pose questions such as EYE : SIGHT :: EAR:_____. The answer, of course, is "eye is to sight, as ear is to sound." Again drawing from Grothe's valuable book, here are two other examples of this type of analogy:

- Reading is to the mind, what exercise is to the body (Joseph Addison).
- As soap is to the body, tears are to the soul (Yiddish proverb).

Here we are more interested in the use of analogies as explanatory devices used to help students compare something they already know to new ideas or concepts. Many examples exist:

- Explaining the game of British cricket by making comparisons to American baseball.
- Comparing computer images to information processing in the human memory system.
- Explaining the war in Iraq by comparing it to the war in Vietnam.
- Explaining Columbus' sailors' fear of falling off the edge of the earth with driving across a high bridge with no brakes and no protective railing.

The dictionary defines **metaphor** as an "application of a word or phrase to an object or concept it does not literally denote, in order to suggest a comparison to another object or concept"—as in, "A mighty fortress is our God." We most often associate metaphors as they are used in literature and poetry—"All the world's a stage and all the men and women merely players . . . they have their exits and their entrances. . . ." With this metaphor, Shakespeare constructs the world as a stage and then uses the theater

Table 7.1 Regular prose and speech compared to prose or speech enhanced with analogy, metaphor, or simile

Regular prose or speech used to transmit information	Prose or speech enhanced with analogy, metaphor, or simile
Prose and poetry are two methods people can use to express ideas.	Prose is to poetry as walking is to dancing (Paul Valery).
A committee is a questionable mechanism for making decisions and solving problems.	A committee is a cul-de-sac down which ideas are lured and then quietly strangled (Barnett Cocks).
Adolescence is a time of great turmoil.	Adolescence is a kind of emotional seasickness (Arthur Koestler).

Source: Examples taken from Grothe (2008), pp. 1–3.

metaphor to elaborate on humans who occupy it and the parts they play in a lifetime. If Shakespeare had made the same comparisons using an analogy, he might have written, "people are to the world as actors are to the stage."

Metaphors and metaphorical thinking, however, are not just language devices used by authors and poets. Lakoff and Johnson (1980, 1999), for example, argue that metaphors help us structure our perceptions and understandings of reality. They help shape our lives and they can help students attend to and connect with new learning materials.

Finally, the **simile** is a comparative speech device where one thing is likened to another, usually using words such as "like" or "as." Grothe (2008, p. 12) writes that similes,

> share with analogies and metaphors the goal of relating one thing to another, but they do it in a slightly different way. Look at these quotations [that help us see books in a different way]:
>
> - Books are like imprisoned souls, till someone takes them down from the shelf and frees them (Samuel Butler).
> - Books . . . are like lobster shells; we surround ourselves with 'em, then we grow out of 'em and leave 'em behind, as evidence of our earlier stage of development (Dorothy L. Sayers).
> - No furniture is so charming as a book (Sydney Smith).

Analogies, metaphors, and similes are invaluable devices that can be used by teachers to help students learn. They help "spice up" our explanations and provide important hooks for students to hang new ideas on what they already know.

Use Visual Images and Nonlinguistic Representations The old saying that a "picture is worth a thousand words" has never been more true than when a teacher is explaining a complex idea to students. In what is now considered a classic study, Anderson and Smith (1997) studied the effects of a visual image on children's understanding of light and color. They had children in five classrooms study the following passage:

> Bouncing Light
>
> Have you ever thrown a rubber ball at something? If you have, you know that when the ball hits most things, it bounces off them. Like a rubber ball, light bounces off most things it hits.
>
> When light travels to something opaque, all the light does not stop. Some of this light bounces off. When light travels to something translucent or transparent, all the light does not pass through. Some of this light bounces off. When light bounces off things and travels to your eyes, you are able to see (p. 327).

With this explanation, only 20 percent of the students understood that seeing is the process of detecting light that has been reflected off of some object. In a follow-up experiment, Anderson and Smith provided students with the visual shown in Figure 7.4. In this second experiment, researchers provided students with a picture of the sun, a tree, and a young boy. Arrows illustrate how sunlight strikes the tree and then bounces

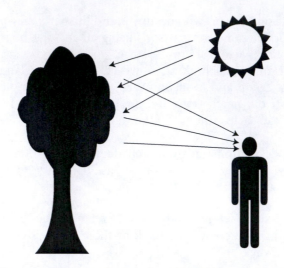

We see when light is reflected off an object and goes to our eyes

Figure 7.4 Role of light in determining what we see
Source: The research was reported in Anderson and Smith (1987).

off it, going to the boy's eyes. This time, almost 80 percent of the students understood the light reflection concept.

In general, if an idea can be converted into a visual image, it should be. Obviously, some subjects and ideas are easier to convert than others. Many ideas and concepts in science, for example, can be illustrated with a visual image of some sort. Some literary ideas may be more difficult. Figure 7.5, however, is an example provided by Zull (2002) on how a music teacher converted Strauss' *Also sprach Zarathustra* into a visual image.

Graphic organizers and **conceptual maps** introduced in Chapters 6 are other favorite forms of providing nonlinguistic representations. These devices highlight the critical attributes of an idea or concept and sometimes the relationships among ideas or concepts. These devices help to make ideas more concrete for students and also can serve as an aide for activating prior knowledge. We will not go into detail here about how to make and use graphic organizers and conceptual maps because these are major topics in Chapter 9.

Keep a Positive Feeling Tone and Display Enthusiasm Earlier, we described the importance of designing learning environments free from threat and that have positive

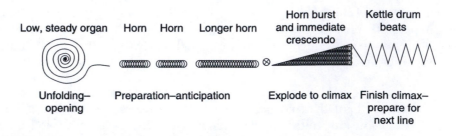

Figure 7.5 Visual map of Strauss' *Also sprach Zarathustra*
Source: Zull (2002), p. 146.

feeling tones. The following are positive and negative verbal actions used by teachers in the process of providing explanations that can affect the tone of the learning environment:

- During an explanation, a student asks a question, the answer for which the teacher believes she has covered quite thoroughly:
  - (positive response) "That is a very interesting question; tell me a little more about why you are asking it?" or,
  - (negative response) "If you had been listening, you would know the answer to that question."

- During a presentation, the teacher is coming to an important but difficult idea:
  - (negative alert) "Listen up, because most of you will not understand what I am about to say." or,
  - (positive alert) "I know the following idea is somewhat difficult, but I am sure you are going to understand it magnificently."

- Toward the end of a lecture or explanation, the teacher says:
  - (negative alert) "I only have time to say this once, so listen carefully." or,
  - (positive alert) "I am going to explain this idea in the time that remains; however, if everyone doesn't get it, I will come back to it tomorrow."

Presenter enthusiasm is also an interesting element in regard to teacher presentations and explanations. Specific behaviors associated with enthusiasm were identified and reported by Collins (1978) as:

- Rapid, uplifting, varied local delivery
- Dancing, wide-open eyes
- Frequent, demonstrative questions
- Varied, dramatic body movement
- Varied emotive facial expressions
- Ready, animated acceptance of ideas and feeling
- Exuberant energy.

The effectiveness of **teacher enthusiasm**, however, has remained unclear. On the one hand, several studies (Rosenshine, 1970; Williams & Ceci, 1997) have shown enthusiasm's positive effects, whereas others (Borg & Gall, 1993) have reported that enthusiasm seems to have little, if any, effect on what students learn. Sometimes we think about enthusiasm similar to the ways we think about acting and the dramatic. Dramatic presentations have been shown to produce positive evaluation

REFLECTION

Some teachers believe that a little "threat" is a good thing to encourage students to pay attention, work harder, and learn more. What opinions do you hold on this issue? What evidence do you have from your own experiences to support your opinions? Consider comparing your opinions and experiences with a classmate or colleague.

from student audiences; however, they do not necessarily lead to the acquisition of important information (Naftulin, Ware, & Donnelly, 1973). It may be that too much enthusiasm and theatrics detract from key ideas teachers are trying to convey. This does not, however, argue against being enthusiastic. It merely warns us that the use of enthusiasm has the potential of being received in one of two ways—as a motivation to learn or as pure entertainment.

Expressing enthusiasm, creating positive feeling tones, and being accepting of students' ideas may come more naturally to some teachers than others. However, we believe that with a little practice all of us can learn to respect differences and to communicate in positive ways with our students.

Table 7.2 below summarizes guidelines for presenting and explaining new learning materials.

Checking for Understanding and Extending Student Thinking

The final phase of a presentation lesson consists of teachers **checking for understanding** and helping students extend their thinking about the new learning material. Mainly, this is accomplished through **questioning** and **discussion**, topics we introduced briefly in Chapter 6. We could have inserted our extended *discussion about discussion* in almost

Table 7.2 Summary guidelines for presenting new learning materials

Teacher actions	Rationale
Strive for clarity	Being clear and specific affects student understanding significantly.
Teach in small steps	Short-term working memory has limited capacity and can only handles a few bits of information at a time.
Use examples	The use of strong examples that highlight the main points or critical attributes of an idea or concept makes new learning material meaningful to learners.
Use rule–example–rule device	Rule–example–rule device helps students understand relationships among important generalizations or principles.
Use explaining links	Explaining links help students see the logic and various relationships among concepts and ideas.
Use verbal signposts and transitions	Verbal signposts and transitions help listeners know where the teacher is going and help them move from one idea to another.
Use analogies, metaphors, and similes	Analogies, metaphors, and similes are devices that help students compare new ideas to what they already know.
Use visual images and nonlinguistic representation	"A picture (or illustration) is worth a thousand words."
Keep a positive feeling tone and display enthusiasm	Expressing positive feeling tones and respecting students' ideas removes "threat" from the learning environment and enhances student learning. Using an appropriate amount of enthusiasm can spark student motivation to learn.

any of the chapters found in this part of the book, because question asking and discourse are strategies accomplished teachers use in all aspects of their teaching. Discussion can be used as a stand-alone lesson when teachers want students to explore an important topic in a whole-class setting. It can be employed in small groups during cooperative or problem-based learning. And, as we will see in later chapters, concept and inquiry-based teaching and jurisprudential inquiry require sustained questioning and discourse among teachers and students.

We have chosen to begin the first part of our discussion about discussion here for several reasons. One, this is the first chapter in the strategies part of the book and information on discussion and questioning will provide foundation information that we can refer to when the topics come up in later chapters. Two, discussion is most often used in conjunction with or following a presentation or some type of explanation. In some instances, it is used to check for understanding of the new learning materials. In others, it is used to extend student understanding and thinking about the topic. Finally, we believe that use of discussion and discourse is one of the major ways to promote active student involvement and engagement in an otherwise teacher-centered activity.

In this chapter, we will provide information on four important aspects of discussion: how to use it to check for student understanding; how to extend student thinking through discussion; how to use questions effectively; and how to respond to students' answers and errors. In later chapters, we will consider some alternatives to the more traditional discussion patterns found in most classrooms and describe how discourse can be slowed down for the purpose of promoting a different kind of student thinking. Later, we will also provide recommendations for how to listen and respond to student ideas, particularly when controversial issues are being discussed.

Checking for Student Understanding As teachers, we check to see if our students understand what has been taught in a variety of ways. Informally, we can monitor and look for puzzled frowns, closed eyes, or deadly silence (like in the Professor Zull example). When we see these facial expressions, we know our students "didn't get it." When students ask questions that are disconnected to the subject of the presentation, that too provides another clue that they may be confused. Hunter (1994) and Bozeman (1995) recommend using group signals with younger students to check for understanding, such as: "raising hands," "thumbs up; thumbs down," or "making plus or minus signs." Another way is the traffic light strategy we described in Chapter 6, where students signal teachers if they are getting it or if they are lost. Today, some schools have technological devices placed on students' desks that allow them to ask questions and to signal their degree of understanding as the presentation moves along. On a more formal level, teachers can give quick oral or written quizzes following a presentation to see how much students have understood and retained. In Chapter 6, we described the "traffic light" technique, where students display different color cones or lights to represent their understanding: Green—I got it; Yellow—I have some questions; Red—stop, I am lost.

Recitation in the form of question asking is probably the favorite and most straightforward means to check for understanding. In this situation, teachers ask students a series of lower-level factual or conceptual questions aimed at revealing understanding and retention of important declarative knowledge. Here are some examples from Ms. Romero and Mr. Jackson's lesson on race relations:

- Can you tell me the average income of individuals living in Mississippi in the 1930s?
- How many African Americans lived in Mississippi in the 1930s? What was their average income?
- How many white people lived in Mississippi? What was their average income?
- How do the incomes of whites and blacks compare?
- What ideas do you now have about the lives of people in Mississippi during the depression?

Note how some of these questions ask for recall of very specific factual information, whereas others ask for slightly deeper understanding of ideas and concepts associated with the lesson. Both can provide teachers with valuable information about how much their students have learned.

Extending Student Thinking Other types of classroom discussion can be designed to probe more deeply into student understanding and to extend their thinking about particular topics. These kinds of discussion are valuable for a variety of reasons. They provide a public setting for students to practice and test their thinking skills. They also provide teachers with a window into the students' minds for viewing the way they are thinking about a topic. To make this type of discussion successful, however, requires attending to several important aspects of classroom questions.

Questioning Patterns and Strategies. Questions help students process the content they are learning. The ways teachers ask questions and the types of questions they ask influence learning and the **discourse patterns** in classrooms and have been the subject of considerable research and debate. Much of this debate has revolved around the cognitive levels of questions (narrow, lower-level questions versus higher-order questions) and how different types of question affect student thinking and understanding. Today, a consensus seems to have emerged that the type of question that should be asked depends on the students we are working with and the type of learning outcomes we are trying to achieve. Gall and Gall (1990) concluded that:

- Emphasis on fact questions is more effective for promoting young children's achievement, when the goal is primarily mastery of basic understandings or skills.
- Emphasis on higher cognitive questions is more effective for students when more independent thinking is required and where the goal of instruction is to promote higher-level thinking.

Most important is the observation by Good and Brophy (2008, p. 316) that, "varying combinations of lower-order and **higher-order questions** will be needed, depending upon the goal you are pursuing. Certain types of questions are useful for arousing interest in a discussion topic, whereas other types are needed to stimulate critical thinking . . . or to see whether students have attained the intended understandings."

One way to determine the type of question to ask is to consider the kind of cognitive process it requires students to use to answer it. You remember, from earlier discussions, that Bloom and his revisionists have identified six different kinds of cognitive processes: remember, understand, apply, analyze, evaluate, and create. These processes are assumed to lie along a continuum of cognitive complexity from the more basic or concrete processes (remembering) to those that are more abstract and at a higher level (analyzing and creating). In Table 7.3, we provide examples of different types of question categorized according to **Bloom's revised taxonomy** (Anderson & Krathwhol, 2001) and the type of cognition each type of question requires.

Other distinctions among question types have been made, such as the difference between convergent and divergent questions. **Convergent questions** require students to focus on a single or best answer, such as one that requires definition or explanation:

> Why did gasoline prices rise when OPEC restricted the amount of oil each member country could export?

Divergent questions, on the other hand, allow multiple answers normally associated with evaluation and creation of new ideas:

> What do you suppose would happen if suddenly all cars were fueled by non-fossil fuels?

Pressley, Wood, Woloshyn, Martin, King, and Menke (1992) and Marzano (2007) describe another type of question, which they label the "**elaborative-interrogation**" question. These are follow-up questions after a student has answered particular inferential questions. Below are some examples:

Table 7.3 Different types of questions according to Bloom's revised taxonomy

Cognitive process	Example of question	Type of cognition required
Remember	How many African Americans lived in Mississippi in the 1930s? What is the definition of racism? Of prejudice?	Retrieval of factual and conceptual knowledge
Understand	What is the difference between racism and prejudice?	Constructing meaning
Apply	If individuals in your community expressed prejudice, what steps might you take to understand their point of view?	Applying or using principles
Analyze	Why do some people have prejudices while others appear to be free of prejudice?	Explaining relationships and overall purposes
Evaluate	Assume two political candidates: One expresses views that you believe are based on prejudice but has an economic policy you like. The other does not appear to be prejudiced but has a flawed economic policy. Which person would you support?	Making judgments based on criteria
Create	What do you think the world would be like if racism and prejudice didn't exist? Do you think this will ever happen?	Generating hypotheses and making predictions

- Why do you believe what you said is true?
- Tell me why you believe that is so.
- What information do you have to support that statement?

We have found elaborative-interrogation questions to be particularly useful for enhancing students' understanding and for helping them extend their thinking about more complex ideas and topics. Their use can also provide teachers with a window for observing the thinking and reasoning processes of their students.

The appropriate difficulty of questions has also been the subject of debate and research. Questions that are too easy lead to boredom; students give up if questions are too difficult. After review of the research, Brophy and Good (1986) offered teachers three guidelines that we believe are still applicable today:

- A large proportion (perhaps as high as three-quarters) of a teacher's questions should be at a level that will stretch students but also elicit correct answers from students in the class.
- The remaining quarter of the questions should be at a level of difficulty that will elicit some response from students, even if the response is incomplete.
- No question should be so difficult that students will not be able to respond at all.

The pacing of question asking is also important. Sometimes a fast pace is desirable, particularly when a teacher is checking for understanding or reviewing specific facts. In most instances, however, students need time to think about the learning materials under consideration. In Chapters 6 and 10, we describe how the pace of discourse in most classrooms is too rapid and how teachers need to slow down and provide longer wait-time during question and answer sessions if they want to stimulate students to think and to provide thoughtful responses.

Responding to Student Ideas and Questions. A final aspect of effective discussion is the overall tone teachers establish and the way they listen and respond to student answers or contributions. Listening is particularly important. Teachers need to listen carefully and strive to understand each student's contribution. Adopting an active listening style and using communication skills, such as paraphrasing, are two ways to show students we are listening and value what they say. Remaining nonjudgmental and inquiry-oriented is another. We will come back to this topic in later chapters.

A dilemma we have all faced as teachers is how to respond to student answers. Effective discussion leaders respond to correct answers with short affirmations not gushy praise. Responding to incorrect or impartial responses, however, is a bit trickier. We like the three-step process recommended by the late Madelene Hunter (1994):

- Step 1: *Dignify* a student's incorrect response or performance by giving a question for which the response would have been correct. For example, "George Washington would have been the right answer if I had asked you who was the first president of the United States."
- *Step 2*: Provide the student with an *assist*, or prompt. For example, Remember, the president in 1828 was also a hero in the War of 1812."
- *Step 3*: Hold the student *accountable*. For example, "You didn't know President Jackson today, but I bet you will tomorrow when I ask you again."

Checking for student understanding and extending their thinking about new information are critical features if our presentations are to be effective. Asking questions and responding appropriately to student opinions are critical features of this phase of instruction and serve as important ways to make a mainly teacher-centered instructional strategy more interactive and student-centered.

SUMMARY AT A GLANCE

- Explaining things to students is perhaps the most used instructional strategy. It is particularly effective for helping students acquire and process new declarative knowledge, strengthen their conceptual structures, and develop listening and thinking skills.
- The flow of presentation lessons and explanations consists of: (1) a teacher's initial attempts to gain attention and get students ready to listen; (2) presentation of an advance organizer or scaffold aimed at tapping students' prior knowledge; (3) delivery of information and ideas associated with a particular topic; and (4) interactions with students aimed at checking for understanding.
- Important planning steps include: diagnosing students' prior knowledge and misconceptions, choosing appropriate content, and deciding how to create a positive learning environment.
- The use of advance organizers is important for effective presentations and explanations. These serve as hooks or intellectual scaffolds to connect what students already know to new learning materials.
- Effective explanations and presentations are characterized by clarity, enthusiasm, the use of a variety of explanatory devices, and actions by teachers to keep the learning environment positive and free from threat.
- Teachers conclude presentations and explanations with actions aimed at checking for understanding and strengthening student thinking.
- Discussion and questioning are favored strategies to strengthen and expand student thinking. Good discussions require using appropriate questioning strategies, asking questions that generate different kinds of thinking, and making sure that questions are at the appropriate level of difficulty.
- Encouraging and responding appropriately to students' ideas and questions establishes the overall tone required for effective student–teacher interaction.

CONSTRUCTING YOUR OWN LEARNING

Pick one or two ideas you love to teach. Develop two examples, two analogies, and two metaphors you have used (or might use) to make the topic clearer to your students. How much difficulty did you have with this task? Why? If possible, compare your work with that of a colleague or classmate.

RESOURCES

Fischer, D., & Frey, N. (2007). *Checking for understanding: Formative assessment techniques for your classroom.* Alexandria, VA: Association for Supervision and Curriculum Development.

Grothe, M. (2008). *I never met a metaphor I didn't like: A comprehensive compilation of history's greatest analogies, metaphors, and similes.* New York: Harper-Collins.

Grothe's website: www.MetaphorAmor.com.

Race, P. (2006). *A lecturer's toolkit: A practical guide to learning, teaching, and assessment* (3rd ed.). New York: Routledge.

8

DIRECT INSTRUCTION

In the previous chapter we described an approach to teaching aimed at helping students acquire factual and conceptual declarative knowledge. We observed two members of a seventh-grade social studies–language arts team use presentation and explanation to help their students acquire background knowledge about race relations in the United States between the 1930s and the 1960's Civil Rights Movement. Now let's look in on another classroom in a neighboring school, where Shelley King, a high school health teacher, is conducting a lesson on cardiopulmonary resuscitation:[1]

Ms. King: "Now class, I want you to observe very closely as I demonstrate the third or C step of cardiopulmonary resuscitation, CHEST COMPRESSION to restore blood circulation."

She returns to the body simulator lying in a prone position.

"Note how I place the heel of one hand over the center of the person's chest between the nipples and place the other hand on top of the first hand."

She demonstrates this action.

"Now note how I use my upper body (not just my arms) to push straight down to compress the chest and then push hard and push fast."

Again, she demonstrates this action.

"In few moments I am going to provide you with time to practice CPR. Some aspects of the practice will be with one of your classmates; other aspects will be with the body simulators. Before we begin, however, I want to review and see how well you understand the CPR process.

"Who can tell me about the ABCs of cardiopulmonary resuscitation? Think for a moment before you respond."

"What does the A stand for?"

Jacob: "It stands for Airway. The first step is to clear the airway."

Ms. King: "Does everyone agree with Jacob's answer? Thumbs up if you do."

"All right, now what about B?"

Carmen: "I think it stands for Breathing. You should check to see if the person's mouth has been injured and if they are breathing."

Ms. King continues by asking about C and then begins explaining what she want her students to do as they begin a guided practice session.

You have just observed Ms. King use direct instruction to demonstrate CPR for her students and then to prepare them to practice this rather complex first aid procedure.

OVERVIEW AND PERSPECTIVE

As our experienced teacher readers know, skill mastery is often the prerequisite to more advanced learning. Before students can perform certain inquiry-oriented experiments in science, they must be able to view specimens in a microscope. To solve algebraic equations requires skills to add, subtract, divide, and multiply. Higher-level thinking proceeds after competencies have been developed in the use of logic, drawing inferences from data, and recognizing bias in argumentation. Successfully completing a problem-based learning project requires research skills and skills for working in groups. Many aspects of reading and writing depend on an array of very specific literacy skills. In Chapter 2, we labeled this type of knowledge *procedural knowledge*—being able to do something. We contrasted this to *declarative knowledge*—being able to understand something or knowing that something is the case. As a general rule, helping students acquire procedural knowledge requires a different approach than helping them acquire declarative knowledge and that is why we have devoted this chapter to direct instruction.

As with the previous chapter, it is our intent to have this chapter not only build on your prior knowledge but also to introduce ideas and strategies that you may not have considered before. We begin by providing our perspective on direct instruction and tie the topic back to the context and science of learning introduced in Chapters 2 to 4. Next, we provide rather detailed descriptions about how to plan for and deliver direct instruction lessons. We conclude the chapter with some ideas about how to assess the instructional outcomes associated with this type of lesson.

Direct instruction was designed specifically to help students master academic and social skills and to acquire clearly structured factual knowledge. These instructional outcomes are highlighted in Figure 8.1.

Before we proceed with descriptions of direct instruction in more detail, we want to place it in context of similar methods that have slightly different labels. Some of you may know this model as **active teaching**—a label used in the 1980s to connote the active, as compared to more student-centered, approaches taken by teachers when they were teaching basic literacy and numeracy skills. Others may know the model as *mastery teaching*—the label used by the late Madeline Hunter (1982) to describe her approach to lesson design and academic instruction. Some say Flanders (1970) coined the term direct instruction; others attribute it to Rosenshine (1979). The label **direct instruction**

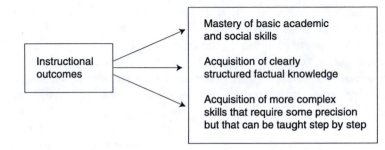

Figure 8.1 Instructional outcomes for direct instruction

has also been used to describe a particular approach to reading instruction (Carnine, Silbert, Kame'enui, & Tarver, 2004). The *direct instruction reading program* rests on some of the same theoretical principles as the approach we describe in this chapter. Because it is confined mainly to reading, we will not describe this approach here. Bloom's (1971) idea of *mastery learning* also is a close relative of direct instruction.

The model we describe here is somewhat generic and can be used for instruction across the curriculum at all levels, in both major and limited ways. Table 8.1 provides examples of the skills across the curriculum that can be taught using direct instruction.

Direct instruction can be used in many different settings and for a variety of purposes. However, the overall flow or syntax of a lesson is characterized by several phases. The flow consists of: (1) teachers gaining students' attention and providing rationale and purpose for the lesson; (2) careful demonstration of the structured knowledge or skill that is the focus of the lesson; (3) structured opportunities for students to practice the skill under the teacher's supervision; (4) checking to see if students are performing accurately and providing feedback; (5) providing independent practice; and (6) seeking closure to the lesson and attending to transfer.

As with presentation and explanation, many view direct instruction as a passive form of learning. As you will see, this does not have to be the case. In an effective direct instruction lesson, students are actively involved in an environment that is brisk-paced and challenging. Also, direct instruction has been in and out of favor over the past century. Early in the twentieth century, progressive educators were critical of methods

Table 8.1 Selected skill components of school subjects

Subject	Skill component
Art	brush strokes; drawing
Foreign Language	pronunciation; grammar
Language Arts	sentence construction; spelling
Mathematics	basic functions and operations
Music	finger placement; note recognition
Physical Education	correct stances; jumping procedures
Science	use of lab equipment; graph construction
Social Studies	map reading; timeline construction

that were too teacher-directed and that provided too much structure to classroom activities. Curriculum reformers of the 1950s and 1960s emphasized the importance of inquiry-based and discovery learning. In the 1970s and 1980s, however, more structured approaches came back into favor, supported by **process–product research** that identified teacher behaviors that seemed to promote a particular type of student learning. Cognitive theorists and educators who viewed student learning from constructivist perspectives almost immediately challenged these approaches.

> **REFLECTION**
>
> Think for a moment about the subject(s) you teach and make a quick list of factual, structured knowledge and basic skills that students must acquire. Do you have a particular approach you use to develop this type of learning? What approaches do colleagues in your school use?

Contemporary critics of direct instruction, such as Kuhn (2007b), point out that the model is based on "wrong" behavioral theories of learning and that the model is overused in many classrooms. We agree with some of what the critics say. Behavioral theories of learning alone are not adequate to teach many aspects of what we want twenty-first century students to learn, and it is true that some teachers rely upon direct instruction exclusively. On the other hand, we take the view that direct instruction is a valuable approach to teaching and one that should be in every teacher's repertoire. If we want students to learn knowledge and skills for which agreed-upon procedures exist, we will be most effective by teaching them in an explicit and direct manner. We also take a balanced view about the "direct instruction–discovery learning" debate. In our view, it depends on what teachers are trying to accomplish. For some content (procedural knowledge) and with some students (particularly beginners), strong instructional guidance is required. For other content (inquiry processes) and with some students (those with relevant prior knowledge), more discovery and problem-centered approaches work best.

CONNECTING DIRECT INSTRUCTION TO THE CONTEXT AND SCIENCE OF LEARNING

The theoretical bases for direct instruction stem from behavioral and social learning theory, as well as some aspects of the perspectives we hold about human cognition. These perspectives and their implications were described in Chapter 2. The ones that have straightforward implications for direct instruction are summarized and highlighted below:

- *Behaviorism* rests on principles of operant conditioning and the use of reinforcement to strengthen desired behaviors while eliminating others. These principles lead to the kinds of teaching strategy observed in direct instruction, such as: carefully observing targeted behaviors, providing for practice opportunities, and *using feedback to reinforce accurate performance.*
- *Social learning theory,* you remember, emphasized that much of learning occurs as learners observe modeled behavior. For classroom teachers, this leads to the importance of demonstrating and modeling required behaviors accurately and in ways that students can understand.

- *Information processing theory* contributes to the overall flow of direct instruction lessons. Again, you will recall from Chapter 2 that new information is received through the senses and stored initially in short-term working memory. Short-term working memory has limited capacity, so complex skills must be divided into sub-skills and explanation and demonstration about them presented in small, meaningful chunks.
- As with the teaching of declarative knowledge, students' **background knowledge** and prior skill levels are important factors for determining what they will learn. Students cannot master skills for which they lack sufficient enabling knowledge and/or skills.

Our understanding of direct instruction also stems from particular research traditions and the practical applications of this research over the past 40 years. During the 1970s and 1980s, educational researchers became disenchanted with earlier attempts to find relationships among the personal characteristics of teachers and student learning. A new research paradigm, called process–product research, emerged. The name implied that what teachers do (process) had important effects on what students learn (product). The emphasis of research on teaching thus turned away from studying teacher traits and toward observing what teachers were doing in their classrooms. Achievement was measured mainly in math and reading, and defined as the acquisition of basic skills and knowledge that could be measured on standardized tests. Literally hundreds of studies in the process–product tradition were conducted between 1970 and 1990, and this research has been summarized on several occasions (Brophy & Good, 1986; Rosenshine & Stevens, 1986; Stronge, 2002; Marzano, 2007). In general, process–product research has demonstrated quite clearly that students learned more in classrooms that were well organized, where teachers held high expectations, and where teachers were actively involved in whole-class instruction characterized by a brisk-paced environment. It is important to point out, however, that the student learning that was studied consisted mainly of mathematics and literacy skills that could be measured by standardized tests. One of the early and now considered classic pieces of research in the process–product tradition is summarized in Research Box 8.1.

REFLECTION

Some critics have argued that teachers have been too dependent on direct instruction and that our continued overuse of the model distracts from accomplishing higher-level learning outcomes. With a classmate or colleague, compare your views on this issue.

Based on the results of process–product research, Rosenshine and Stevens (1986) identified six teaching functions for teachers to follow. These functions were consistent with those recommended by instructional designers of that era (Gagné, 1977; Gagné & Briggs, 1980), who applied information-processing theory to explain how students acquire and store information and the conditions and phases that facilitate student learning. The late Madeline Hunter (1994) also developed a master learning approach to instruction that was widely used across the country in the 1980s and 1990s, based mainly on the process–product research. In fact, you may be teaching in schools where Hunter's seven-step lesson plan is still being used. Summaries of this work are provided in Table 8.2. Note the similarities among all three approaches.

Inquiry **RESEARCH BOX 8.1**

Good, T.L., & Grouws, D.A. (1977). Teaching effect: A process–product study in fourth-grade mathematics classrooms. *Journal of Teacher Education, 28*, 49–54.
Good, T.L., & Grouws, D.A. (1979). The Missouri mathematics effectiveness project: An experimental study in fourth-grade classrooms. *Journal of Educational Psychology, 71*, 355–362.

The research in this box summarizes a series of studies conducted by Good, Grouws and their colleagues during the 1970s. This work is a fine illustration of the process–product research we just described and of how relationships between teacher behavior and student achievement were studied. It also provides the type of evidence that supports the effectiveness of direct instruction.

Between 1972 and 1973, Good and Grouws studied over 100 third- and fourth-grade mathematics teachers in a school district that skirted the core of a large urban school district in the Midwest. The Iowa Test of Basic Skills was administered to students in their classrooms in the fall and spring for two consecutive years. From analyses of achievement gains made by students, the researchers were able to identify nine teachers who were relatively effective in obtaining student achievement in mathematics and nine teachers who had relatively low effectiveness. This led the researchers to plan and carry out an observational study to find out how the effective and ineffective teachers differed. They observed the identified teachers six or seven times during October, November, and December of 1974. *Process* data were collected on many variables, including how instructional time was used, teacher–student interaction patterns, classroom management, types of materials used, and frequency of homework assignments. Student achievement was measured with the Iowa Test of Basic Skills in October 1974 and April 1975. The process data were analyzed to see if there were variables on which the nine high-effective and nine low-effective teachers differed in regard to student achievement. From these comparisons, Good and Grouws concluded that teacher effectiveness was strongly associated with the following clusters of behaviors:

- *Whole-class instruction.* In general, whole-class (as contrasted to small-group) instruction was supported by this study, particularly if the teacher possessed certain capabilities, such as an ability to keep things moving along.
- *Clarity of instructions and presentations.* Effective teachers introduced lessons more directly and explained materials more clearly than did ineffective teachers.
- *High performance expectations.* Effective teachers communicated higher performance expectations to students, assigned more work, and moved through the curriculum at a brisker pace than did ineffective teachers.
- *Task-focused but productive learning environment.* Effective teachers had fewer managerial problems than ineffective teachers. Their classrooms were task-focused and characterized by smoothly-paced instruction.
- *Student-initiated behavior.* Students in effective teachers' classrooms initiated more interactions with teachers than did students in the classrooms of ineffective teachers.

- *Feedback*. Effective teachers let their students know how they were doing. They provided students with process or developmental feedback, especially during seatwork.
- *Praise*. Effective teachers consistently provided less and a different kind of praise than ineffective teachers. This reflected the non-evaluative stance of the effective teachers and demonstrated that praise was effective only when used under certain conditions.

In sum, process–product researchers found that teachers who had well-organized classrooms in which structured learning experiences prevailed produced certain kinds of student achievement better than teachers who did not use these practices.

PLANNING DIRECT INSTRUCTION LESSONS

As described in the previous section, direct instruction can be used across the curriculum and works best with topics that can be broken down into particular procedures or steps. These topics may include how to use particular equipment (microscope), to hit a tennis ball, or read a map, but can also include more complex cognitive processes, such as predicting or summarizing skills used to increase reading comprehension. The major planning tasks associated with direct instruction are associated with deciding which skills or topics are most appropriate for a direct instruction lesson, analyzing the elements of the targeted skill, determining how best to demonstrate these skills, finding the most effective ways to provide students with practice opportunities, and considering the most appropriate learning environment for the type of lesson.

Table 8.2 Three similar approaches to direct instruction

Gagne's eight instructional phases of learning	Rosenshine and Stephen's six teaching functions	Hunter's seven-step mastery learning lesson
Gain attention	Review and check previous day's work	State objectives
State objectives	Present new material	
		Relate standards of performance
Help recall prior knowledge	Provide for guided practice	
		Provide anticipatory set
Present stimulus (new knowledge or skill)	Give feedback and correctives	
Provide learning guidance (modeling)	Provide independent practice	Input, modeling, and checking for understanding
Provide feedback		Provide for guided practice
	Review weekly and monthly	
Elicit performance		Provide for closure
Assess performance		Provide for independent practice

Choosing Appropriate Skills and Topics
As with any approach to teaching, choosing what to teach is an important planning task. Earlier, we provided examples of skills from a variety of curriculum areas to illustrate the skill components found in various subjects. Below we provide additional examples drawn specifically from curriculum frameworks for the states of California and Connecticut:

- Gather historical data from multiple sources.
- Locate the events, people, and places they have studied in time and place (e.g., on time lines and maps) relative to their own location.
- Sort types of living things into groups and show how classification schemes vary with purpose.
- Use properties of numbers to demonstrate whether assertions are true or false.
- Solve multistep problems, including word problems, by using these techniques.
- Establish coherence within and among paragraphs through effective transitions, parallel structures, and similar writing techniques.
- Distinguish initial, medial, and final sounds in single-syllable words.
- Distinguish long- and short-vowel sounds in orally stated single-syllable words (e.g., bit/bite).

When selecting skills to teach using direct instruction, the principles described in Chapter 4 for determining curriculum priorities are important to consider. You remember there were Bruner's (1960) ideas of *economy* and *power* that help limit what is taught and Wiggins and McTighe's (1998, 2005) backward design as a mean for setting curriculum priorities.

Analyzing Skills and Their Elements
Popham's (2008) idea of the progression analysis, also described in Chapter 4, has particular relevance when planning a direct instruction lesson. Again, you will remember that learning progression analysis consists of several actions in regard to a targeted skill-based instructional outcome:

- Determine what an accomplished person is doing when the skill is performed well. This becomes the targeted instructional outcome.
- Divide the skill into sub-skills and identify those that are building blocks or prerequisites to other sub-skills and the overall targeted skill.
- Design lessons for teaching each of the sub-skills and how they are combined for performing the overall skill.

Figure 8.2 provides a visual representation of a skill that has more than one subskill attached to it.

As particular skills are being analyzed, it is important to remember that knowing how to do all the parts or sub-skills may not automatically result in putting all the parts together so the larger, more complex skill can be performed appropriately. For instance, knowing that sentences require a noun and a verb and being able to identify adjectives from adverbs does not necessarily lead to the skill of writing clear, well-constructed sentences. Knowing how to dribble a basketball and how to do a bounce pass may or

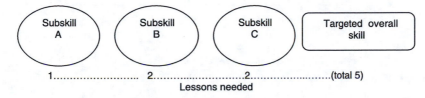

Figure 8.2 A visual representation of a learning progression for a skill with more than one dimension or subskill
Source: Based on the concept of learning progression (Popham, 2008).

may not lead to providing an effective "assist" to a teammate. How sub-skills come together to facilitate a larger, more complex skill needs to be considered in the planning phase of instruction.

Deciding on Demonstration Procedures and Practice Opportunities

Because students learn new skills by observing them being performed by others and by practicing them, designing the demonstration and practice phases of a direct instruction lesson are major planning tasks. Ensuring accurate demonstrations requires that the critical elements of the skill being taught be thought through carefully and steps for performing the skill rehearsed thoroughly. Failure to accomplish this planning task can lead to faulty demonstrations and mistaken student learning. Both guided and independent practice opportunities must be considered prior to the lesson. Procedures for providing effective practice opportunities will be described in the next section.

Planning for Rich, Active Learning Environments

The learning environment for direct instruction lessons is very similar to those used for explanations or presentation teaching. Teachers structure the environment very tightly, maintain an academic focus, and keep things moving along at a fairly brisk pace. It is important to keep disruptions contained to a minimum. Misbehavior that does occur needs to be dealt with quickly. Structured learning environments do not, however, have to be passive, sterile, or authoritarian. It is important for skills to be taught in a rich learning context, where students develop understanding about why they are learning particular skills and where learning time is maximized. Successful direct instruction lessons are those where students are actively engaged, where they are achieving a high degree of success, and where teachers show respect for students as they struggle to master the challenges of the lesson.

DELIVERING DIRECT INSTRUCTION LESSONS

A direct instruction lesson begins with teachers gaining students' attention and explaining the purposes of the lesson, followed by careful demonstration and/or explanation of the skill or sub-skill that is the focus of the lesson. Students are then provided opportunities for structured and **guided practice** of the skill, while the teacher checks to see if they are "doing it correctly." Direct instruction lessons conclude with independent practice, often seatwork or homework, and with activities to bring closure and promote transfer. We have chosen to divide the direct instruction lesson into six phases, listed in Figure 8.3. You will note that these phases are very similar to the steps or phases listed in

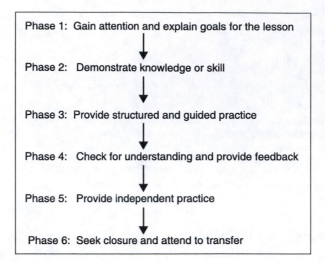

Figure 8.3 Phases of a direct instruction lesson

Table 8.2. You will also note that the overall flow of a direct instruction lesson has several similarities to presentation and explanation lessons.

Gain Attention and Explain Goals

Though gaining attention and getting students ready to learn are important for every lesson, these actions take on increased importance for direct instruction lessons because this type of lesson often focuses on rather discrete skills that may or may not be perceived as important or relevant to students. Every experienced teacher, for instance, has heard the mournful student lament, "Why do we have to learn this?" Student resistance or lack of interest require careful explanation about why a discrete skill or series of discrete sub-skills need to be mastered so more complex, and perhaps more interesting, subjects or skills can be considered. In Chapter 7 we emphasized attention-getting actions, such as: reminding students what they already know, employing surprise and the dramatic, and making use of uncommon or unique words, pictures, smells, or tastes that can arouse curiosity and capture attention. Reviewing the previous day's work, discussing the purposes of the current lesson, and alerting students to the flow of the lesson are additional helpful actions teachers can take to provide a framework for the lesson and to make clear to students what is expected of them.

Demonstrate Knowledge or Skill

In direct instruction, much of what students learn results from observing the teacher. The purpose of the demonstration is to provide behaviors that students can imitate and later perform. The demonstration must be done accurately and in a way that is meaningful to students. This requires that we have thorough mastery of the skill being taught and have made appropriate rehearsal prior to the actual demonstration. An inaccurate presentation or demonstration can cause students to learn to perform the skill incorrectly, a condition that takes considerable instructional time later to correct. Also, the demonstration must be appropriate in regard to students' prior knowledge and skill level. As in the case of helping students to learn new declarative knowledge, if they do not have the prerequisite skill level it becomes nearly impossible to master the new skill. Two common examples can help reinforce the readiness principle:

- Teaching a two year old how to tie their shoestrings as compared to teaching the same skill to a three or four year old.
- Teaching fractions to first graders as compared to teaching them to students in fourth or fifth grade.

Several guidelines can guide the preparation and execution of an effective demonstration:

- Break the skill into small chunks or steps and demonstrate each separately.
- Provide varied examples and contextual information.
- Highlight and get students to focus on the critical attributes of the skill.
- When possible, provide visual representations of the skill.

Let's return to Ms. King's classroom and her lesson on CPR and observe how she gained her students' attention and then demonstrated the proper use of CPR:

Ms. King: "I want each of you to think for a moment about this situation. . . . You and a friend are swimming in your family's swimming pool. Suddenly, your friend disappears. You search the pool frantically and finally spot her lying at the bottom of the pool in the deep end. You dive down, pull her to the surface, and get her onto the deck. You notice immediately that she is gasping but not really breathing. What should you do?"

Ms. King pauses to allow time for students to think. Then she proceeds.

"Over the next several days we are going to learn a first aid procedure called cardiopulmonary resuscitation (CPR). This is a lifesaving technique that can be used in many emergencies, such as heart attack or near drowning. One way to remember what to do when performing this procedure is to consider three steps that are labeled *the ABCs of CPR* and those illustrated on this chart [see Figure 8.4]."

Ms. King points to a chart showing the ABCs of CPR that she has fastened to the chalkboard.

"I am going to demonstrate each step for you and then provide you with opportunities to practice. Let's start with the A step: *Clearing the airways.*"

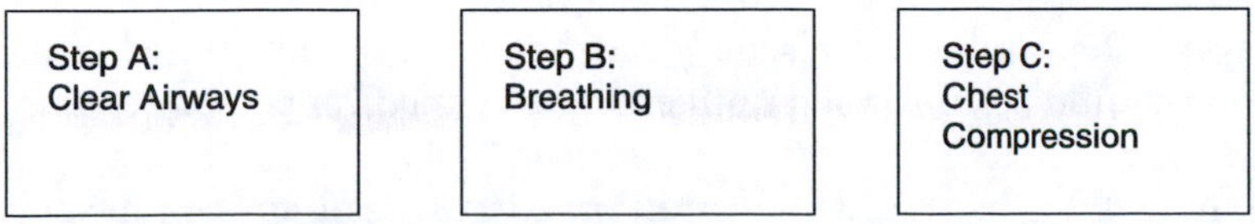

Step A: Clear Airways	Step B: Breathing	Step C: Chest Compression

Figure 8.4 Ms. King's chart: ABCs of cardiopulmonary resuscitation

Ms. King takes a body simulator and places it on its back on the floor; she kneels next to the simulator and says:

"The first thing you want to do is clear the airways and check for breath sounds. Gasping is not considered breathing. Notice how I am looking into the mouth and tipping the head back slightly to open the airway."

Now she progresses to the B step: *Breathing:*

"If you are trained in CPR, begin mouth-to-mouth breathing; if not, proceed to chest compression which I will demonstrate in a minute. In the practice sessions that will follow, I want you to practice the breathing step of the process as I am doing now. Note particularly how I pinch the nostrils shut and cover the person's mouth with mine. Some people are squeamish about doing this with a real person. If you become squeamish in a real-life situation you should not give up. You should skip this step and move to Step C."

Ms. King places her mouth tightly over the simulator's mouth and gives one quick (one-second) rescue breath.

"Notice I am watching to see if the chest rises. If it rises, give the second breath; if it doesn't, tilt the head again and then give the second quick breath."

Now Ms. King progresses to the C step: *Chest compression.*

"You place the heel of one hand over the center of the person's chest between the nipples. Place the other hand on top of the first hand as I am doing now and, while keeping your elbows straight, position your shoulders directly above your hands."

Ms. King demonstrates this action.

"Next, use your upper body (not just your arms) and press down (compress) on the chest approximately two inches."

Ms. King demonstrates this action.

"Notice how I am pushing rather hard and fast. You want to give about two compressions per second."

Ms. King continues her demonstration. Then she says:

"After about 30 compressions, tilt the head back and lift up the chin to clear the airways again. Repeat the two-rescue breath routine I demonstrated in the B step. The process should be continued until emergency medical personnel take over."

You will note that, in this demonstration, Ms. King followed the guidelines we provided previously. She provided context for using the procedure, broke the overall procedure into small chunks or steps, and demonstrated each separately. She signaled when she wanted students to focus on specific attributes of the skill, and she provided a visual representation that had been prepared ahead of time.

Provide Structured, Guided Practice

After demonstrating a particular skill, students must be given opportunities to practice. In fact, practice is the *heart* of direct instruction and the element of the model that makes it so effective for teaching specific kinds of procedural knowledge. The initial practice session should be structured and guided by the teacher. These beginning practice opportunities lead to retention and later transfer to new situations. At the initial stage, student actions must be monitored carefully because, as with a faulty demonstration, incorrect or careless practice will lead to permanent incorrect use of the targeted skill. Remember the old adage, "Practice doesn't make perfect; it only makes permanent."

Here is the way Ms. King chose to provide structured and guided CPR practice for her students:

- First, she had students work in same-sex pairs and practice the A step (airways) on each other. She walked around the room and monitored this action carefully.
- Now using the six body simulators, Ms. King divided students into groups of four or five and asked them to take turns practicing the B step (breathing). Before they started, Ms. King demonstrated the process again. She continued this practice session until it appeared that everyone could perform the B step correctly.
- Now returning to same-sex pairs, Ms. King asked students to practice the C step (chest compression). Again, Ms. King circulated among the pairs, providing feedback and making sure the step was being performed correctly.

In a subsequent class session, Ms. King continued structured, guided practice, this time having students perform all three steps in succession. She, again, was careful to monitor each student's performance, provide feedback as required, and insist on correct behavior.

During guided in-class practice, it is important for teachers to display an active presence. They need to circulate and monitor each and every student. Waiting for quizzical looks on students' faces or for them to ask questions is not sufficient.

As with her demonstration, Ms. King's structured practice conformed to the guidelines supported by research on effective practice described below:

- *Attend carefully to the initial stages of practice.* Many teachers like to have students in a whole group work initially in a rather structured way, so few errors occur and those that do can be spotted and corrected. In most instances, the initial stages of practice should also consist of a simplified version of the skill but as close to the real context as possible.
- *Provide and monitor guided practice with students working alone.* Once it appears that students have a pretty good idea about the skill, opportunities should be provided for them to work alone on the skill. As with the more structured practice, these practice opportunities also should be carefully monitored. Correct use of the

skill should be reinforced, and corrective feedback provided when errors are spotted.

- *Assign short, meaningful amounts of practice.* In general, short and intense practice sessions result in more learning than longer practice sessions. However, the student's age is a factor here. Ten- to 15-minute practice periods are more effective for younger students, whereas older students are capable of practicing for longer periods of time.

- *Aim practice to achieve over learning.* Most skills, even those that are rather simple, take quite some time to master. This is particularly true for skills associated with the performing arts where the goal is to get students to perform required behaviors automatically and under conditions of stress. Joyce et al. (2008) have argued that particular attention should be paid to accuracy and that students should acquire 85 to 90 percent accuracy before going on to the next level of practice.

- *Use massed and distributed practice appropriately.* **Massed practice** is normally defined as practice that is continuous, while **distributed practice** is segmented over time. Although the specific skills involved will determine the exact nature of practice sessions, in general massed practice is preferred for learning new skills and distributed practice is more effective for refining skills already acquired. Two cautions in regard to this guideline, however, should be noted. Using massed practice may lead to boredom and fatigue, particularly with younger learners. Too much time between practice sessions may cause students to regress from what they have learned previously. Most importantly, without multiple practice sessions most skills will be forgotten, leading us to advise that regular review and practice are required.

- *Provide practice in context.* Attempts should be made to have students practice in different situations or contexts. Sometimes this can be done through simulations or virtual environments. Other times, such as in reading, it can be provided by having students read newspapers, instructional manuals and the like, in addition to books and magazines. Our CPR example is one where it is difficult to have students practice in a real-life situation, thus requiring the use of simulated practice settings. Today, an array of computer software programs are available that can provide rather realistic guided practice opportunities for students, particularly in fields such as mathematics, language arts, and the sciences.

Check for Understanding and Provide Feedback

Gaining accuracy with a skill requires feedback. Thus, checking for student understanding and providing feedback is an important phase of direct instruction lessons. Sometime this aspect of the lesson consists of question–answer recitation or discussion, as described in Chapters 6 and 7. In this situation, teachers pose very specific questions to students about the topic or skill and expect them to respond. Most often, however, this aspect of the lesson consists of teachers observing and providing feedback on student performance either directly or from behaviors captured on audio- or video-recording devices. Regardless of the method, effective teachers in every subject, just like coaches in athletics or directors in the performing arts, draw attention to incorrect performance, provide feedback, and demonstrate how to perform the skill accurately. In Chapter 6, we described the work of Brophy and Good (1986), Hattie and Timperley (2007), and

Shute (2008) and their observations that effective feedback should be timely, specific, descriptive, and developmentally appropriate. Further guidelines for providing feedback, including those summarized from Arends (2009), are provided in Table 8.3.

Provide Independent Practice
Once a degree of accuracy has been achieved, students should be provided opportunities to practice independently. The purpose of **independent practice** is to reinforce newly acquired skills and to learn how to perform them without direct teacher guidance. Independent practice should occur, however, only after a degree of accuracy has been achieved, because it is important for students to experience success and not to reinforce errors by practicing a skill incorrectly. It is also important for independent practice to be an *extension of guided practice* rather than an *extension of instruction*. What this means is that independent practice should not be used to introduce additional information or more advanced use of the skill. Instead, it should provide students with opportunities to practice independently, the practice they have already been doing under the teacher's guidance.

Table 8.3 Guidelines for providing feedback during guided practice

Guideline	Example or rationale
1. Provide feedback as soon as possible after the practice.	Should be close enough to actual practice that student can remember performance.
2. Make feedback specific.	Example: "These three words [. . .] were spelled incorrectly" instead of "too many misspelled words."
3. Concentrate on behaviors and not intent.	Example: "I cannot read your handwriting" instead of "you don't work on making your handwriting legible."
4. Keep feedback appropriate for developmental stage of the learner.	Care should be taken not to provide too much feedback or feedback beyond the student's skill level or abilities.
5. Emphasize praise and feedback on correct performance	Although incorrect performance must be corrected, teachers should strive to provide positive feedback on correct performance when students are learning a new skill.
6. When giving negative feedback, follow-up by showing correct performance.	If an essay is full of errors, teachers should point out the errors but also pencil in words or sentences that correct them.
7. Help students focus on process as well as outcomes.	At early stages of learning a skill, students should focus their attention on the process or technique. Focus on getting more proficient can come later.
8. Teach students how to provide self-feedback.	Special care and instruction must be provided so students can judge their own progress and performance.

Source: Summarized from Arends (2009).

The most common settings for independent practice are seatwork and homework. The use of homework for independent practice, however, is not as clear-cut as some believe. Beliefs about homework have changed over time and are often influenced by tradition as much as research. For instance, during the early part of the twentieth century progressive educators believed that homework was too structured and was harmful to students and their families. Today, there are many (Cooper, Robinson, & Patall, 2006; Marzano & Pickering, 2007a, 2007b) who are strong advocates of the use of homework, whereas others (Bennett & Kalish, 2006; Kohn 2006, 2007) believe that it is a waste of time and harmful to student learning. We highlight some of the research on this topic in Research Box 8.2. In Table 8.4 we have provide a more detailed set of guidelines for seatwork and homework based on the research. You will note that the guidelines for seatwork and homework are very similar.

Obviously, the type of skill being learned and the students in a particular class will influence whether teachers use seatwork or homework and how to structure these independent practice sessions. Seatwork works best for skills that need to be carefully monitored and/or for students who are unlikely to complete homework assignments. In-class practice (seatwork) would likely work best with our CPR example, because in real-life situations it is very important that the skill be performed accurately so even independent practice sessions need some type of teacher monitoring. The lack of access to body simulators is another reason that a homework assignment would not be very appropriate for independent practice of CPR.

Inquiry **RESEARCH BOX 8.2**

What We Know about Homework

Homework has been of interest to researchers because it is widely used in schools and also because beliefs about its use and effectiveness have varied greatly. Of most interest have been questions about the positive and negative effects of homework on academic learning for various ages and types of students, as well as possible non-academic impact.

The researchers who have studied this topic most thoroughly are Harris Cooper and his colleagues (Cooper, 1989; Cooper & Valentine, 2001; Cooper, Jackson, Nye, & Lindsey, 2001; Cooper, Robinson, & Patell, 2006). In the recent past, Cooper et al., as well as others, have uncovered several aspects about the effects of homework that we believe are instructive. These have been summarized below:

- *Homework has little effect on student learning in the elementary grades.* It still, however, might be used because it can develop good study habits.
- *Homework does appear to have some effect on student learning in sixth grade and higher.* It is most effective, however, when students find it meaningful and when they can complete it with a high degree of success.
- *Amount of homework matters.* In general, researchers recommend that five to ten minutes per night per grade level is a good rule of thumb to follow.
- *Homework has nonacademic effects.* It provides a means for social communication among students and a source of interaction between students and their parents.

Table 8.4 Guidelines for seatwork and homework

Seatwork	Homework
• Assign seatwork that students will find interesting and enjoyable. Restrict the use of standard worksheets.	• As with seatwork, assign homework that is interesting and potentially enjoyable.
• Assign seatwork that students will have a high probability of experiencing success.	• Give homework that is appropriately challenging but at a level of difficulty where students working alone can perform successfully.
• Make length of seatwork assignment appropriate to the age of the students.	• Use frequent and smaller homework assignments rather than less frequent and larger assignments. This will be influenced by the nature of the skill and the age of the students.

• In general, make seatwork a continuation of the guided practice not an extension or continuation of the instruction.	• Limit the amount of homework assigned:
	  • 10–20 minutes per night for lower grades
	  • 30–60 minutes for high school

• Have clear procedures about what students should do if they get stuck and procedures to follow for students who finish early or lag behind.	• Like seatwork, make homework a continuation of practice not an extension of instruction.
• Monitor students' progress with seatwork, provide assistance as needed, and provide feedback promptly.	• Make homework rules clear and inform parents of level of involvement expected of them. • Return homework with feedback and grades promptly.

Source: Summarized mainly from the work of Cooper et al. (2006).

Homework also has effects beyond just academic learning. Lyn Corno (2001) observed that, "homework involves important social, cultural, and educative issues . . . it is not just an academic task. It is one that infiltrates family and peer dynamics and the nature of teaching in community organizations as well as the school" (p. 529). Homework provides a means for social communication among students and a source of interaction between students and their parents.

Finally, homework, as described previously, is not without its critics. Kohn (2006, 2007) and Bennett and Kalish (2006) challenge the effects of homework and point out several negative unintended consequences. Kohn, for example, has argued that the correlation between homework and test scores is actually quite small and that non-academic benefits such as good work habits and positive character traits could best be described as "urban myths." Critics have also argued that homework is overused and that it leads to "stress, frustration, family conflict, lost time for other activities, and a possible diminution of interest in learning . . ." (Kohn, 2006, p, 2). It persists, according to critics, because of tradition and

REFLECTION

With a classmate or colleague, discuss your views about homework. Do you agree mostly with those who support the use of homework? Or those who challenge its use? Are your views pretty much the same or do they differ?

because of misconceptions held by parents and by educators about the way people learn. We believe different views about the value of homework should not, however, be confused about the value of independent practice as an important step in helping students acquire important skills and procedural knowledge.

Seek Closure and Attend to Transfer

Too often, we run out of time and cut off this final phase of a direct instruction lesson. As with any learning experience, it is important to bring closure to direct instruction lessons. Most experienced teachers do this by summarizing or reviewing the lesson. Encouraging student participation and having them provide brief demonstrations for the whole class can also be effective. A third approach is to provide opportunities for reflection and discussion about when a particular skill should be used and pitfalls to avoid. Special independent practice sessions in a variety of contexts are ways to help students transfer the skills they learned in the classroom to new or real-life situations. These situations are often difficult to provide in many schools; however, they are important and efforts should be made to work toward transfer.

ASSESSMENT OF DIRECT INSTRUCTION LEARNING

Throughout *Teaching for Student Learning* we have emphasized the importance of matching assessment procedures to the learning outcomes teachers are striving to achieve. Because most direct instruction lessons aim at helping students acquire procedural knowledge and abilities to perform particular skills, assessment should obviously focus on performance. For our CPR illustration, observing students perform the procedure would be the best way to assess their abilities. At times, however, teachers may also want to assess students' conceptual understandings of particular processes and will use pencil-and-paper tests to measure these understandings. Again using our CPR example, it may be important for students to memorize and understand the ABC process. This understanding could be assessed with a simple question on a pencil-and-paper test. Likewise, student understanding about when to use CPR and pitfalls to avoid could be assessed with a rather straightforward essay question. It is important to point out, however, that having knowledge about a process or procedure does not mean it can be performed well. Knowing that a sentence requires a noun and a verb does not mean one can write a good sentence. Knowing the letters on the keyboard does not mean that one can type. Knowing the ABCs of CPR does not mean that one can perform this procedure effectively in a real-life emergency situation.

We began this chapter pointing out some of the criticisms of direct instruction and the over-reliance on its use by some teachers. Regardless of the debates, over time many accomplished teachers continue to use the model because they know the importance of teaching skills and teaching them well. Direct instruction will continue to play an important, if perhaps limited, role in a teacher's overall instructional program. The mark of an accomplished teacher is the ability to call on a repertoire of effective instructional practices that will allow choosing an approach to achieve particular learning outcomes appropriate for a particular group of students.

SUMMARY AT A GLANCE

- Direct instruction is an effective instructional model for helping students master basic academic and social skills and for acquiring structured, factual knowledge.
- It is not effective for teaching huge amounts of declarative knowledge or for helping students acquire conceptual understandings or higher-order thinking skills.
- The syntax of direct instruction calls for teachers to take an active stance, to demonstrate specific skills accurately and precisely, and to provide appropriate opportunities for guided and independent practice.
- Practice lies at the heart of direct instruction. The way practice opportunities are structured will determine how well targeted skills will be mastered and retained.
- As with any approach to teaching, success depends somewhat on a rather strict adherence to the model's syntax and on having an appropriate classroom environment. In this instance, the model works best in a well-organized and structured environment. This structure, however, does not mean that the environment should not be rich, democratic, supportive, and caring.
- Varied approaches to performance assessment are required to measure many of the instruction outcomes associated with direct instruction. Paper-and-pencil tests are insufficient.
- Debates about the appropriate use of direct instruction have existed for years. Critics believe that the model is overused and that it is based on inadequate theories about how students learn. On the other hand, it has also been shown to be very effective for achieving particular kinds of instructional outcomes.
- We have taken the view that direct instruction is a valuable model for accomplished teachers to have in their repertoire, but that its use should be confined to achieving goals for which it was designed.

CONSTRUCTING YOUR OWN LEARNING

With a classmate or colleague, design a direct instruction lesson that each of you can teach. Arrange to visit each other's classrooms and critique the lesson as to its appropriateness in regard to the desired instructional outcomes that were identified and its overall effectiveness. Improve the lesson based on feedback and critique.

Or, with a classmate or colleague, examine homework policies in your classroom and in your school. Look at the school's formal policy statements and get examples of assigned homework from several teachers. Summarize what you have found and compare what you are doing in your school with the guidelines provided in Table 8.4. Consider sharing your results with the total faculty.

RESOURCES

Fisher, D., & Frey, N. (2007). *Checking for understanding: Formative assessment techniques for your classroom.* Alexandria, VA: Association for Supervision and Curriculum Development.

Kohn, A. (2007). *The homework myth: Why our kids get too much of a bad thing.* Cambridge, MA: Capo Lifelong Books.

Marchand-Martella, N., Slocum, T., & Martella, R. (2004) *Introduction to direct instruction.* Boston: Allyn & Bacon.

9

USING TEXT, THE INTERNET, AND VISUAL MEDIA TO BUILD BACKGROUND KNOWLEDGE

In Chapter 7, we observed Ms. Romero and Mr. Jackson employ presentation and explanation to provide students with background knowledge for a unit on "Race Relations" and the study of the historical novel, *Roll of Thunder, Hear My Cry*. In this chapter, we will use this classroom situation again to describe how these two teachers now turn to text, multimedia, and the Internet to provide students with background knowledge on a variety of topics associated with their unit.

OVERVIEW AND PERSPECTIVE

In Chapters 2 and 7, we described how our memory system works and how teachers use verbal explanations to help students acquire, process, and interact with new declarative knowledge. Verbal explanation, however, is not the only way that students acquire background knowledge. Reading from text, viewing video or television, and using the Internet are other important sources of information. These sources differ from verbal presentations, explanations, or demonstrations because the latter are primarily structured and controlled by teachers, whereas students are in charge of many of their reading, viewing, and Internet experiences.

In addition to using the Internet and new forms of media as sources of background knowledge, these mediums can also be used to promote visual literacy, perhaps a more important goal. Recently, Susan Metros (2008, p. 102) observed that, "contemporary culture has become increasingly dependent on the visual, especially for its capacity to communicate instantly and universally . . . [and] that students must learn to cope with and intelligently contribute to a culture rife with easy access to the visually rich Web, photo dependent social networks, video saturated media, and graphically sophisticated entertainment and gaming." This shift from the dominance of text to visual images requires us to prepare our students to be visually literate. Students need to learn how to compose visual images and messages, how to be effective consumers of visual messages, and how to make critical judgments about their accuracy and worth.

This chapter focuses on how classroom teachers can assist students to use text, multimedia, and the Internet more effectively and how these resources can be more seamlessly incorporated into our instructional programs. We first explore ways to help students become more effective readers of print materials, mainly expository text. This discussion is followed by explanations about how to help students become more effective online readers and how to critically evaluate information found online. The chapter concludes with a discussion of visual literacy and ways to help students become visually literate and to use visual media more effectively. As you will read, achieving these goals will require adopting an expanded view of literacy and balance our current emphases on reading and writing of text with understandings and use of the visual. It will also require us, as teachers, to learn to teach using new forms of media.

Three caveats are offered before we begin. First, some view television and the Internet as enemies that distract from real, **in-school learning**. We hope we can make a convincing argument that this does not have to be the case and show how these information sources can become valued educational resources rather than distracting rivals. Second, we are fully aware of all the excellent books and other resources that have been published over the past decade about the use of literacy strategies across the curriculum. We suspect that our discussion about "Using Text" will appear to many experienced teachers as a very light treatment in contrast. We recognize this situation. However, we include it here because many of the strategies that have been developed to help students acquire background knowledge from text can serve as a *backdrop* or *foundation* for helping them use the Internet and media sources for the same purpose. Finally, it is not the intent of this chapter to provide information about how to teach reading to young children or to English language learners. Nor is our purpose to have definitive discussions about computers and communication technologies. Instead, the focus will be on how text, the Internet, and the visual media can be used to enhance student learning and how teachers can use these resources across the curriculum.

REFLECTION

What have been your experiences with student use of the Internet and visual media? Has it been mainly a distraction? If not, what have you done to incorporate knowledge gained from these sources into your instructional program? You may want to compare what you have done with approaches used by a colleague or by a classmate.

CONNECTING TO THE CONTEXT AND SCIENCE OF LEARNING

The theoretical and conceptual frameworks about how students learn from reading, viewing, or using the Internet are very similar to the frameworks provided in previous chapters and will not be repeated in any detail here. Key principles and features associated with providing verbal explanations, such as activating prior knowledge, striving for clarity, and attending to metacognitive processes, are equally important when teachers are helping students learn from text, visual media, or the Internet. It is also equally important to keep in mind how students' memory systems work, particularly in regard to attending to new information and processing it from short-term working to long-term memory.

USING TEXT

Teachers in every subject area rely on textbooks, handouts, and other kinds of expository text as input experiences for students. Some of these input experiences lead to the acquisition and retention of new knowledge; others do not. Fortunately, there is a substantial knowledge base on how text can be used more effectively across the curriculum in both elementary and secondary subjects. In general, this research has demonstrated that the ways teachers introduce and structure reading experiences and assignments are critical factors that lead to student learning. In the discussion that follows, we will strive to describe "good reader" strategies as summarized by Pearson, Roehler, Dole, and Duffy (1992), the National Reading Panel (2000), and Marzano (2004, 2007).

Literacy Strategies to Help Students Learn from Expository Text

Distinctions are normally made about the differences between "narrative" and "expository" text. Burke (2000) has written that, "**narrative text** includes such elements as theme, plot, conflict(s), resolution, characters, and a setting. **Expository text**, on the other hand, explains something by definition, sequence, categorization, comparison, contrast, enumeration . . . description, or cause–effect" (p. 142). Our emphasis here will be on expository text and how it can be used effectively to enhance background knowledge. In addition to the narrative–expository distinctions, most reading experts (Ivey & Fisher, 2005; Monti, personal communication, 2007) categorize actions teachers can take to help students interact with and learn from expository text into three phases: prior to reading, during reading, and after reading. We have organized this section in this manner, although we recognize that there are other ways to think about reading and alternative methods to support students during reading activities.

Prior to Reading Effective teachers take a series of actions prior to assigning students to read a particular piece of text. Let's eavesdrop on Mr. Jackson and Ms. Romero's classroom as Mr. Jackson prepares his students for a reading assignment.

> Mr. Jackson: "Class, yesterday you remember Ms. Romero gave a brief presentation on how African Americans were treated in the South in the 1930s, and we considered whether or not this treatment existed in our community today. Now I want you to learn a bit more about this topic. We have a short, three-page article on social conditions in the United States between World War I and World War II. Before you read this, however, I want you to preview it:
>
> - Look at the headings of the four major sections of the article.
> - From these headings, what do you predict the article is going to be about?
> - As you look at the headings ask yourself, "What do I already know about this topic?"

Mr. Jackson is using text to help his students acquire additional declarative knowledge and he is having them engage in *previewing* and *predicting* activities to help them get ready to learn.

Assigning Small Chunks and Differentiating. In Chapter 3, we described how students will remain motivated if learning goals are structured so they can be achieved in the near future as compared to those that take a long time to accomplish. We returned to this principle in Chapter 7, when we described the importance of teachers presenting new information to their students in small chunks. This same principle holds true for reading assignments, particularly for struggling readers. Remember, our short-term working memory has a limited capacity, and there is only so much new information that students (anyone for that matter) can attend to at any one time. **Chunking** involves dividing assignments of larger books or chapters into smaller sections and attending to appropriate preparation strategies for each. Obviously, there are no specific recipes about the size of a particular chunk. Teachers' knowledge about and prior experiences with particular students are important sources of information about chunk size, as is information about how much students already know about a particular topic. In general, students who know more about a topic can handle larger chunks, while those who know less can benefit from smaller chunks.

Previewing and Predicting. In Chapter 7, we described the importance of advance organizers and scaffolds for activating students' prior knowledge and getting them ready to learn. These devices are equally important for getting students ready to learn from text. This can be done in a variety of ways. We can provide students with a purpose for the reading and offer advance organizers similar to those used for explanations. We can also preview by highlighting the main points of a forthcoming reading assignment, either verbally or perhaps with a specially prepared handout. The intent of **previewing text** is to provide linkage between the new information contained in the text and what students already know. Another approach is one used in our Mr. Jackson example. He asked students directly what they think they already knew about the textual content. Getting students to "skim" the material and instructing them to look at the main headings and subheadings and make predictions about what they will find and helping them think in advance how they might approach the reading are additional **prediction reading strategies**. Addressing key vocabulary can also be beneficial, particularly for readers who have limited vocabularies. Previewing activities do not take up much instructional time, but they have been shown to produce large payoffs in student learning.

During Reading There are a variety of strategies that can be taught to students for the purpose of providing support during reading.

Metacognitive Learning Strategies. In Chapter 2 and elsewhere, we discussed the importance of **metacognitive learning strategies**. Here, we are interested in specific learning strategies that help learners encode new information, make new knowledge meaningful, and help them retain it for a longer period of time.

Highlighting a passage helps students locate key ideas and assists them in connecting new information to prior knowledge. Having students make marginal notes is another helpful strategy because it requires them to pay attention to what they are reading and to translate it into their own words. Note particularly the idea of matrix note taking illustrated in Figure 9.1. This is a brief example of elaborating on a particu-

---

Topic: Social Conditions in the South in the 1930s and today

In the 1930s	Today
Mainly rural	Some rural but also urban
Segregated schools	Integrated schools
Segregated neighborhoods	Still mainly segregated neighborhoods
Segregated facilities	Integrated facilities
Great income disparity	Still income disparity

Figure 9.1 Example of matrix note taking

lar aspect of new information in *Roll of Thunder, Hear My Cry* and the handout on "social conditions" assigned by Ms. Romero and Mr. Jackson.

Many students, younger and older, are not very effective highlighters or note-takers. Often, they underline information that is irrelevant or commit a very common error of underlining almost everything. These are skills that require instruction just like any other skill.

Another set of learning strategies is sometimes referred to as *organization strategies*. These consist mainly of regrouping or clustering ideas found in text by dividing them into smaller subsets. They also consist of identifying key ideas or facts from a larger array of information in a passage. Outlining, summarizing, and mnemonics are common organizational strategies.

In *outlining*, students strive to relate a variety of subtopics to some main idea and/or to show the relationship of one topic to another. The table of content of this book is an example of an outline that gives readers a preview of key ideas and topics found in the book and their relationship to each other.

Summarizing, similar to note taking, requires students to develop a brief account in their own words of what they have read. This can be done in writing or verbally. It is a process where readers identify the most important or salient information in a passage and structure it for meaning. It is similar to the use of the paraphrase used to capture the essence of verbal interactions.

Mnemonics form a special category of learning strategies and consist of techniques to assist memory by making associations that do not naturally exist. They work because they help organize new information that reaches short-term working memory in patterns that fit an individual's prior knowledge or schema in long-term memory. Chunking and the use of acronyms are examples of mnemonics that most have used at one time or another to help remember what we have read. Chunking consists of breaking information into smaller parts so it can be more easily remembered. For instance, most of us cannot remember ten numbers randomly strung together. Yet, we can remember a ten-digit telephone number because it has been divided into three chunks: the area code (201), the neighborhood code (247), and the individual number (5488). Automobile license plate numbers are assigned using the same principle and often use letter and number combinations to make the independent chunks easier to remember.

The use of **acronyms** is another common mnemonic and consists of using the first letter of a series of words. Acronyms assist memory by making associations between new and prior knowledge. Every Good Boy Does Fine (EGBDF) is a mnemonic used to help students remember the letters of the scale in music. HOMES is another familiar acronym to help remember the names of the great lakes (Huron, Ontario, Michigan, Erie, Superior). Students do not automatically use acronyms and other good reading strategies as they read. These strategies and how to use them must be taught by providing examples.

Group Learning. Often, we think of reading as something that students do alone. However, over the past two decades teachers and researchers have developed a number of group-based instructional strategies to help students acquire and process new information from text (Biancarosa, 2005; Guzzetti, 2000). For example, teachers can use Jigsaw, Think–Pair–Share, or other cooperative learning strategies described in Chapter 13, to help students work in pairs or small groups to clarify, summarize, and elaborate on ideas found in particular reading assignments.

Perhaps the most widely used group strategy is **reciprocal teaching** developed by Annemarie Palincsar and Ann Brown (1984) and extended by Ash (2005). Using reciprocal teaching, students are taught four specific comprehension strategies: summarizing, asking questions, clarifying, and predicting. To learn these strategies, students are assigned passages in small groups and the teacher models the four strategies by summarizing the passage, asking a question, clarifying a difficult phrase, and predicting what the next section of the passage might be about. As the lesson proceeds, students take turns assuming the teacher's role and serving as discussion leaders. Below is an example of how teachers can help students learn the "summarizing" and "asking questions" elements of reciprocal teaching.

Teacher Introduction
"Today we're going to learn a new way to check whether we understand what we're reading. There are several steps in this process and the first is *summarizing*. After every paragraph we read, we need to make a statement that summarizes the main ideas in it. Then we'll ask a *question* about the material in the paragraph. Our passage today is about snakes. I'll read the first paragraph out loud and then try to summarize it. . . ."

Below are examples of teacher–student dialogue in regard to summarizing and questioning

Summarizing
T: That was a fine job, Ken, but I think there might be something to add to our summary. There is more information that I think we need to include. This paragraph is mostly about what?
S: The third method of artificial evaporation.

Questioning
T: That's good. Keep going. Can you ask a question?
S: How do snakes mate . . .? How am I going to say that?
T: Take your time with it. You want to ask a question about snakes mating and what they do, beginning with the word "how."
S: How do snakes spend most of their time?
T: You're very close. The question would be "How do snakes mate most of the time?" Now you ask it.
S: How does a snake mate most of the time?
(Adapted from Palincsar and Brown, 1984.)

Ash (2005) has added a fifth strategy to the reciprocal teaching approach. This strategy requires students to evaluate a passage critically and identify the author's perspective or point of view. For example:

- What perspective does the author take?
- Whose voice is left out?

• Do you agree or disagree with what the author is saying?"

Reciprocal teaching and other group-based comprehension strategies have consistently been found to help students learn new declarative knowledge and help them become more effective and self-regulated readers.

After Reading Getting students to question and to reflect on what they have read are the primary after-reading strategies, similar to the checking for understanding phase of presentation or direct instruction lessons. These consist of student questioning and reviewing the information found in the reading and perhaps comparing back to the predictions they made prior to reading. They may ask themselves if their initial conceptions and predictions have been confirmed or if their initial ideas have changed. Some teachers like to get students to write short reflective essays, where they put ideas about what they have read into their own words and/or tell what the passage means to them personally. Strategies of questioning and reflecting, whether done through dialogue or in writing, work because they help move new information from short-term working memory into long-term memory.

Independent Reading for Developing Background Knowledge

Teachers use the strategies described above to assist students with teacher-directed reading experiences. Another means for students to acquire declarative background knowledge is through independent (or what has been labeled) **sustained silent reading (SSR)**, a strategy whereby students are provided time, normally 15 minutes or so, to read whatever they like. Most often, SSR programs are designed school-wide and have particular structures. However, individual teachers can set up their own independent reading programs in both elementary and secondary classrooms and across a variety of subject areas.

Janice Pilgrim (2000) has identified several factors that must be present if SSR is to be successful. These include: access to books, book appeal, conducive environment, encouragement to read, non-accountability, and distributed time to read. Marzano (2004) has taken Pilgrim's factors and converted them into a five-step process that can be used at both the elementary and secondary level. For our purposes here, we have shortened the process to four steps and described their use school-wide or independently:

• *Step 1: Students identify topics of interest to them and identify reading materials.* In Chapter 3, we emphasized the importance of interest and appropriate level of difficulty in sustaining student engagement in academic tasks. These factors are important if independent reading programs are to be successful. This means that teachers must gather and make available a rather wide range of materials on a variety of relevant topics and provide students with opportunities to identify topics that interest them. These reading materials will, in most instances, consist of books, magazines, comics, or newspapers that cover the band of reading levels found in a particular class or school. Students may choose to bring something with them from home to read, but Pilgrim (2000) says this should not be a requirement.
• *Step 2: Students are provided uninterrupted time to read in a conducive environment.*

For school-wide programs, Pilgrim recommends 15 to 30 minutes of reading time, at least twice a week. For teachers using independent reading for only their own classroom, 30 minutes is possible in most elementary classrooms, whereas 15 minutes twice a week is probably more realistic given the confined schedules in most secondary schools.

- *Step 3: Students write about or represent the information they read about in their notebooks.* Knowledge obtained through independent reading will be retained in long-term memory if students summarize what they have read in some type of notebook. These may be free responses totally controlled by the student or, in some instances, they may result from prompts from the teacher, such as: "How is the information you read about useful to you? What did you find most interesting? Least interesting? What meaning did it have for you?" Students can also be encouraged to summarize or represent knowledge in some nonlinguistic way, such as using graphic organizers, pictographs, or mind maps described in a later section.
- *Step 4: Students interact with the information.* Finally, it is important for students to have opportunities to interact with the new knowledge they have acquired. This interaction may come as a result of discussion with the teacher but, more realistically, with planned interaction and discussion in small groups. Obviously, the teachers must ensure that these small groups are working effectively and that all students have opportunity to participate. We provide rather detailed information on how to work in groups in later chapters, particularly Chapter 13.

Vocabulary Instruction for Developing Background Knowledge

Over the years there have been heated debates about vocabulary instruction. On one side of the debate are skeptics (Adams, 1990; Nagy & Anderson, 1984), who have argued that, because students encounter and learn so many new words, the ten or so words taught per week in formal vocabulary programs do not impact significantly the volume of words students learn over a year's time. Time spent reading, they believe, will enhance vocabulary development much more than learning a few new words. On the other side of the debate are arguments that reading by itself does not necessarily increase vocabulary and that direct vocabulary instruction is more effective than once thought (Marzano, 2004; Monti, 2007). Some go so far as to assert that vocabulary instruction is a most critical component for developing effective readers (Monti, 2007).

Beck, McKeown, and Kucan (2002a, 2002b) have proposed an idea labeled "**tier words**" that serves as a middle ground in regard to vocabulary instruction. They divide words into three tiers. *Tier 1 words* are basic words that show up regularly in what students read or talk about. They often have physical referents such as those associated with the words table, blue, or canine. These types of word can be easily taught without formal vocabulary instruction. *Tier 2 words* also show up frequently across a number of domains or subjects. They are words used by knowledgeable language users but are unknown or misunderstood by many students. Examples might include words such as exaggerate, ponder, or temperament. *Tier 3 words* are words used less frequently and are often subject specific. Multivariate analysis, chemotherapy, or memory system are examples of Tier 3 words. These words are taught best in context. Beck and her colleagues say that Tier 2 words are those most important to teach in formal vocabulary instruction. These words are used in a variety of subjects and settings and their understanding and use are required for effective learning and communication. Teachers are encouraged to identify Tier 2 words for vocabulary instruction by asking: "Is this word important and useful for what I am teaching and expecting students to learn? Does this word have connections to other words and concepts we are dealing with? Do my students have the relevant background knowledge to make learning about this word possible?"

We tend to agree that direct vocabulary instruction is important and have adapted and summarized the characteristics of successful programs that were identified by Marzano (2004):

- *Effective vocabulary instruction does not rely on definitions.* Instead, use word meanings presented in everyday language.
- *Students must represent their knowledge of words in linguistic and nonlinguistic ways.* Student learning is enhanced significantly when they are taught to represent words using pictures, pictographs, and graphic representations.
- *Effective vocabulary instruction involves the gradual shaping of word meanings through multiple exposures.* Get students to interact with vocabulary in a variety of ways—identifying similarities and differences, comparing and contrasting, and creating analogies and metaphors.
- *Teaching word parts enhances students' understanding of terms.* Teach roots and affixes to help students figure out the meaning of unknown words.
- *Different types of words require different types of instruction.* Different words have different semantic features which students' need to understand.

> **REFLECTION**
>
> With a colleague or classmate, make a list of the reading strategies you have used to help your students become more effective readers of expository text. Are some more difficult to use than others? If you are a subject matter teacher, compare views about your responsibilities for helping students become better readers? Do the same for formal vocabulary instruction.

- *Students should discuss the terms they are learning.* Dialogue and interaction help students develop meaning and deeper understanding.
- *Students should play with words.* Games and word puzzles help stimulate student thinking about words and develop greater understanding.
- *Instruction should focus on terms that have a high probability of enhancing academic success.* Teaching subject-specific terms are most important for enhancing students' background (summarized from Marzano, 2004, pp. 70–90).

USING THE INTERNET

A very few years ago we would not have included "using the Internet" as a source for helping students acquire declarative background knowledge. As short a time as a decade ago, most classrooms didn't have computers, few schools had Internet access, and most students were not connected to the Internet at home. Today, computers are found in almost every classroom, and 95 percent of schools have Internet access. Many schools provide students with laptop computers and according to Trotter (2007), two-thirds of households have computers, and 93 percent of these homes have Internet access. Cohen (2007) reported that over a third of children age five and younger who have computers in their homes also go online, and 75 percent of six-to-eight-year olds make use of the Internet. In addition, the past decade has seen an explosion in all kinds of new digital technologies. Many students have their own MP3 players, cell or iPhones, and many participate regularly in blogs, podcasts, and social networks such as "MySpace," "YouTube," "Facebook", and "Twitter," where they interact with virtual friends and acquaintances.

There are many tech-savvy teachers who have fully integrated the Internet and other technologies into their classrooms. Many others, according to Trotter (2007), have made limited use of these potential resources. Similarly, student use of the Internet is somewhat spotty and is not always well informed. Many have limited skills for reading and using **online text** effectively. We believe that, as teachers, we have a responsibility to help students use the Internet and "read" and critically "evaluate" online text just as we help them read and evaluate expository text.

> **REFLECTION**
>
> Find a classmate or colleague who is ten to 15 years younger or older than you. Discuss how the use of the Internet and communication technologies has changed over the past 15 years. Consider both the positive and negative effects of these changes.

Helping Students Make Sense of Online Text

Studies have shown that students vary significantly in their ability to locate and understand information contained on the Internet. Some students understand search engines and how information is organized. These students can confidently navigate the Web, move from home pages to related pages, and locate the information they are seeking. Many other students, however, have few skills or strategies to make sense of Internet information or to evaluate the information they find (Coiro, 2005; Coiro & Dobler, 2004). One recent study conducted by the Educational Testing Service (ETS) and reported by Trotter (2007), found that only 52 percent of college and high school students could correctly judge the objectivity of a website, and only 40 percent could use multiple terms to conduct a Web search. Not surprisingly, it was the less skilled readers of print text who had the most difficulty reading online text.

Clearly, new skills are required to help students read and make sense of online text. Skills are required to understand how search engines work and how online information is organized within websites. Students need to know how to apply the "good reading" skills described in previous sections to online text. Effective teachers incorporate these new literacy skills in their content instruction just as they incorporate skills for reading text in print. Coiro (2005) and Greenfield and Yan (2006) have suggested four clusters of skills that are critical for reading online text effectively:

- Understanding search results.
- Previewing a website.
- Checking for website accuracy.
- Summarizing and synthesizing online information.

Below we provide more detail about each of these skill clusters and how to use them to help students improve their Internet use.

Understanding Search Results Even the simplest Google search normally results in thousands and thousands of websites. Knowing which ones to read and which ones to ignore is difficult, even for experienced Internet users. It can be overwhelming for many students. It is important to teach students (particularly younger ones) how information is organized on a website and the meaning of such terms as search engine, URL, hyperlink, etc. Coiro (2005) has designed a lesson that helps students critically examine websites and information found in a website address. We have adapted the questions she uses in Table 9.1.

Previewing a Website Earlier we described how "previewing" is a valuable pre-reading activity, where readers skim chapter headings, diagrams, and bold print to get an idea about what a passage concerns. Although it may be a bit more difficult to skim a website than it is to skim pages in a book, the same strategy can be applied to help website readers see the structure and possible topics in the site. Below are steps adapted from those proposed by multiple sources (Coiro, 2005; Evaluating Web Pages, 2007) for previewing and evaluating a website. Note the similarities of these "previewing" strategies to those used to preview text in print:

1. *Read the title of the page* and the title of the website in the margin at the top of the window.
2. *Scan menu choices.* Study the navigational menus that appear at the top or down the left frame. Get the big picture of what is going on.

Table 9.1 Reading and evaluating search results

Overall direction: Do a Google search on a topic such as "Race relations in the United States today." Then, using the handout below (without the answers), have students work in pairs to answer the questions posed.

Question/Answer	How do you know?	Why is it important to know?
How many websites were found using this search? *When we did this search in 2008, we came up with 867,000 sites.*	By looking at the top of the search results page.	I should change my search terms to get a more manageable list.
Of the first ten sites, which site(s) contained empirical data? *In October 2008, we found 3.*	I read it in the description after the hyperlink. I opened the site and previewed the information	The description after the link gives clues to what the site contains.
Of the first 20 sites, which ones would most likely not be available in three months' time? *We found an individual teacher's history page that would likely not be available for very long.*	The URL tells me it's an AOL site, and they change a lot.	Interpreting terms in the URL can suggest whether or not the source is reliable.

Source: Summarized and adapted from Coiro (2005).

3. *Make predictions* about where each of the major links may lead.
4. *Explore interactive features of images* that change as a viewer holds a mouse over them. Look for pop-up menus and scroll bars that reveal additional information about the site.
5. *Identify the creator* of the website and when the site was last updated. Consider what this information indicates about the site.
6. Notice and *try out any electronic support* the site offers, e.g., internal search engine.
7. *Make a judgment* about whether to explore the site further.

These questions could be incorporated into the lesson plan we illustrated in Table 9.1. "Reading and Evaluating Search Results".

Checking for Website Accuracy Making judgments about the accuracy or validity of website information is another important online reading skill and one that teachers need to be more concerned about than they are regarding the information found in printed text. Textbooks, pamphlets, and other print materials provided to students have, for the most part, been carefully edited and verbal and visual images have been vetted for accuracy. Online information and images, on the other hand, are not necessarily reviewed, edited, or vetted. Many assertions stand alone without footnoted references to other knowledge or sources of information. In fact, many websites are designed to persuade and/or to deceive viewers. Students must be taught how to be informed readers and how to evaluate the information they find. Drawing on the work done at Cornell and Johns Hopkins Universities, we provide a series of questions in Table 9.2 that online readers can use to evaluate a website's accuracy, currency, and objectivity.

Summarizing and Synthesizing Information from Online Sources Students find summarizing and synthesizing information from multiple sources difficult regardless of whether the sources are print text or online information. They must be taught how to do more than merely copy or string together a long list of quotes. Synthesizing and summarizing information from the Internet is perhaps more complicated as

> **REFLECTION**
>
> With a classmate or colleague, explore each other's use of the Internet in your respective instructional programs. Are you a heavy or light user? What kinds of problem have you encountered? Successes? What goals do each of you have for future Internet use?

compared to printed text because the information may consist of print, video clips, and discussions on blogs and social networks. Figure 9.2 was designed to provide a template for helping students organize and synthesize information from a website in their own words.

It is doubtful that text in print will disappear, at least in the immediate future. Information contained on the Internet likewise will not diminish in the years ahead. It will only increase and expand as a valuable resource for acquiring background knowledge and for enriching students' learning. Helping students preview, read, evaluate, and summarize online text becomes one of the major challenges for twenty-first century teachers.

Table 9.2 Evaluating website information

Criteria	Questions to ask	What does it mean?
Authorship/Accuracy	What are the website author's credentials? Is any information (email address, biographical information) listed about the author and how to reach them?	It is important to know something about the author and to be able to investigate the author's background and credentials. This allows decisions to be made about accuracy.
Sponsorship/Authority	Who is sponsoring the website? Is a name provided? What domain does the website use? (commercial, com; government, gov; nonprofit, org; educational, edu) Has the sponsor evaluated or vetted the information on the website? Does the sponsor have a political or philosophical agenda? What is the relationship of the author to the sponsor?	Knowing about the sponsor or publisher of a website helps evaluate the information and whether it has been screened. It helps readers determine the amount of authority to attribute to the website.
Currency	It the information current or dated? What is the date of the website? When was it last updated?	Much information on the web is outdated. Currency can be somewhat ensured on websites that are updated regularly.
Point of view/Objectivity	Why was the website created? Does the information reflect a bias? Was the website intended to inform, persuade, deceive? Is there anything about the website that makes the information suspect: propaganda, misinformation?	Just as with any information found in print or other sources, such as television, it is important to know why it was written and for whom.
References/Referral	Where did the website's author(s) get the information? Is information on the website referenced with footnotes or links to other websites? Can the links be accessed? Does the website include a bibliography?	For information on a website to be credible, readers need to know the context in which it is situated. As with print documents, it is important for information to be referenced with footnotes, web links, and bibliographic information.

Source: Criteria and implications came from multiple sources: see www.library.cornell.edu/olinuris/ref/research/webeval; www.library.jhu.edu/researchhelp/general/evaluating. Retrieved April 26, 2009.

USING VISUAL MEDIA

Importance of Visual Literacy

Today, technology and media play a *huge* role in people's lives and particularly the lives of children and youth. Much of the information they receive comes from visual

---

Paste into this organizer segments of text relevant to your research question, then record your summary and your reactions to the text.

My research question is: _____

Source(s): Copy and paste text or image sources here. Make sure to provide the URL for each source.

Summary: The most salient points of the text are:

Personal connection: This information connects to other information I have found in the following ways:

Change: This information changes my thinking in the following ways:

Synthesis: The information from my sources allows me to make the following synthesis.

Final: My supporting statements, informed by at least two of my summaries and at least two of my personal statements, are:

Figure 9.2 How to summarize and synthesize online information
Source: Adapted after Coiro (2005), p. 35. Printed with permission.

resources. This requires that the acquisition of **visual literacy** understandings and skills be major foci of a good education.

Although the exact hours vary from study to study, it is generally accepted that students spend three and a half to five hours viewing television per day and that they confront visual images daily on their MP3s, cell phones, and other technological devices. Many young people (perhaps most) participate regularly on blogs, podcasts, and social networks, all of which have strong visual components. Educators such as Burmark (2002) and Riesland (2007) have recognized the importance of helping students become visually literate and define this type of literacy as having *abilities to understand visual messages and to communicate through visual means.*

Visual literacy helps students learn from media such as television, film, and video, and the non-print features of the online world. It also helps them acquire relevant background knowledge that is visually represented in expository text. Riesland (2007) has observed that more and more textbooks have moved away from using visuals to support text information toward, instead, using text to support visual explanations. Similarly, he reported a significant increase in books for young children that contain visual images and interactive text. And, finally, the old saying that "seeing is believing" is no longer as accurate as it may once have been as more and more instances are found of photos and videos that have been digitally altered.

Today, accomplished teachers recognize the importance of helping students develop visual literacy skills across the curriculum. In Figure 9.3, we have synthesized a list of skills recommended by various visual literacy experts and/or organizations. Space does not allow a full explication of each of these skills. However, we will provide a brief primer about actions teachers can take across the curriculum to promote visual literacy among their students.

Visual literacy consists of abilities to:

- interpret, understand, and appreciate the meaning of visual messages
- distinguish fact from fiction in visual representations
- understand the mechanisms for creating and producing TV programs, CD-ROM, games, films, interactive software, and websites
- recognize news reporting from advocacy broadcasting
- evaluate visual messages for accuracy and objectivity
- use visual thinking to provide solutions to problems
- communicate through visual means

Figure 9.3 Important visual literacy skills
Source: List summarized from combined works of Burmark (2002) and Center for Media Literacy (2008).

Developing Visual Literacy Skills

Most students have a high degree of readiness for becoming visually literate. They are motivated to understand and communicate more effectively through visual means. Some schools offer special classes on filmmaking, Web construction, multimedia, and hypermedia design. However, many do not and the responsibility for developing "basic" visual literacy, similar to teaching reading in the content areas, falls on classroom teachers. In this discussion, we will confine our attention to actions teachers can take to embed visual and image education into their existing curricula and classroom programs.

Attending to Visual Messages Visual imagery is routinely used to communicate across a variety of mediums and fields including the Web, streaming video, digital pictures, and graphic packages. It is important for students to have a working knowledge of basic elements of visual design and the meaning found in visual images. Burmark (2002) has shown how teachers can draw students' attention to the different elements of **visual messages** (typeface, font, and color) and to show them what these elements are communicating to viewers. Similarly, teachers can get students to be more aware of an array of visual images and messages found in their own classrooms. For example, what messages are being sent by the most recent bulletin board displays? What about tabletop projects? Or, posted student art?

Using and Creating Visual Tools A variety of visual tools, such as **graphic organizers, conceptual webs**, and thinking or **mind maps**, exist to help students grasp new knowledge and to make thinking visible. Essentially, these visual tools or graphic organizers, as we will refer to them, are "diagrams with words." They can be used to help students manage and organize information and to display ideas and patterns of thinking. They are particularly helpful for visual learners who like to *see* their thinking on paper. Table 9.3 provides examples of ways that information and knowledge can be visually displayed.

Graphic organizers can be used to visually display a variety of ideas and relationships. They can be designed to show cause and effect, and part–whole relationships; they can be useful for comparing and contrasting particular concepts or ideas. Teachers use graphic organizers during presentations and explanations to assist student

Table 9.3 Ways to visually display information and knowledge

Type	Description
Chart/graph	Representation of tabular numeric data
Table	Matrix for organizing large quantities of information
Flowchart	Hierarchical, branching structure that indicates steps in a process
Diagram	Visual representation of concepts and relationships
Mind or concept map	Nonlinear diagram depicting relationship of ideas and concepts
Storyboard	Graphic organizing device that depicts a sequence of illustrations or images for planning interactive media
Schematic	Technical drawing illustrating parts of an object and their relationships
Map	Simplified depiction of space
Signage/label	Graphic displaying way of finding or identifying information
Photograph/video	Actual object or scene captured with a camera or imaging device
Drawing/painting	Two-dimensional artistic representation created using artists' tools
Immersive environment	Artificial, interactive, computer-created scene or world

Source: Summarized and adapted from Metros (2008), p. 104.

understanding of complex ideas or a set of relationships. They use them to help students understand more clearly some of their thinking processes and metacognitive skills.

Different types of graphic organizer can be used with different groups of students. Simple graphic organizers—like attribute webs, Venn diagrams, or two-column note-charts—help students who are struggling to understand a particular concept. Flow charts, cause and effect organizers, and spectrums help learners to see more complex cause and effect relationships. Other graphic organizers—such as matrixes, proposition charts, and concept maps—can be helpful to promote and clarify more advanced understandings and arguments.

Students can be taught to use graphic organizers as a form of note taking and to summarize and represent visually the knowledge and understanding they have acquired from a presentation or from reading a passage. Saphier, Haley-Speca, & Gower (2006) have designed four different graphic organizer templates that can be taught to students for the purpose of note taking and helping them visually represent their ideas or patterns of thinking. These are shown in Figure 9.4.

Students can use these templates to take notes on a reading or viewing assignment. Saphier and colleagues also suggest that students can be taught how to use them by teachers who first demonstrate their use and then assign independent practice using the following steps:

- *Step 1*: Teacher makes presentation or leads a discussion and records some information into one of the graphic organizer templates.
- *Step 2*: Teacher identifies the template being used and names the kind of thinking it represents.
- *Step 3*: Teacher now assists students to fill in the remaining portion of the template.

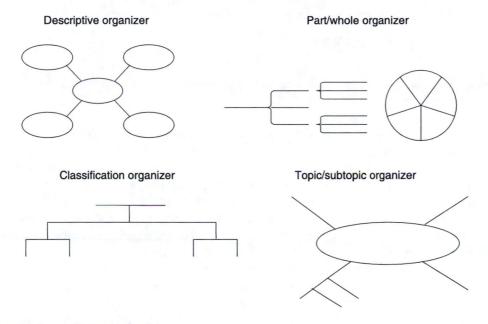

Descriptive organizer

Part/whole organizer

Classification organizer

Topic/subtopic organizer

Figure 9.4 Four graphic organizer templates
Source: From Saphier, Haley-Speca, and Gower (2006), p. 203. Reprinted with permission.

- *Step 4*: Teacher contrives an assignment that will require students to make all the template entries (pp. 203–204).

Dodge (2005) provided another way to help students learn about and use graphic organizers, called "making connections." Teachers instruct students to work with a partner to summarize a topic by creating a graphic organizer. First, each student lists ten important terms about a topic on sticky notes. Partners share their notes. Then they group ideas that go together. On a large piece of construction paper, they write the topic and place the groups of terms together. A circle or box is drawn around each group and labeled. Arrows, bullets, color, and pictures are added to make the graphic. The student pairs then share their graphic organizer with another pair and add new ideas to their final draft. All graphic organizers are displayed, and sometimes a class organizer is generated based on the best ideas from those created.

We will conclude this section with Research Box 9.1. We have chosen to summarize the chronicles of a second-grade classroom teacher and her efforts to promote visual literacy in her classroom.

Teaching with Television, Film, and Video

As teachers, we often consider the impact that out-of-school experiences have on children and youth. We recognize, for example, the importance that family, community, and personal friendship have on student learning. Sometimes we try to incorporate these

RESEARCH BOX 9.1

Inquiry

Williams, T. (2007). "Reading" the painting: Exploring visual literacy in primary grades. *The Reading Teacher, 60*(7), 636–642.

T.L. Williams is a second-grade teacher who, after visiting the National Gallery while vacationing in London, decided to adopt an expanded view of reading, one that goes beyond recognizing vocabulary and decoding printed text to include a wide range of technological and visual elements. After several assignments to provide students with relevant background knowledge about works of art and illustrations, she described her visit to the National Gallery to her students and showed them Munch's painting *Winter Night* and modeled a "think aloud" about what might be going on in the picture. Next, she gave pairs of students postcard prints of paintings from the National Gallery exhibit. She had covered up all information on the back of the postcard and asked students to "read and write" about what they saw taking place in the paintings.

Williams reported that students had a difficult time with this task. Most simply described what they saw: "There is a man." "It is night." "There are lots of stars." Next, she modeled how to transform observable facts to answer other questions such as: "What do we want to know about the painting?" "What is the man doing? What is going on overall in the painting?" After a discussion of these questions, she asked students to write personal stories about two paintings. Slowly students started to "read" the paintings without relying on the words of others, and they began providing more personal, visual, and interpretative readings of a painting's meaning such as the one recorded below: The passage is *exactly* (errors included) as written by one student, basing a story on *A Winter Scene with Skaters near a Castle* by Hendrick Avercamp:

> Once it was snowing in Oslo. A lot of people came out of their houses to go to church. Before the children went to church they had a snow ball fight. Some people rode in the carridge. two people in he carridge met. The next day they saw each other again and fell in love. They made a time to see each other that night. When they saw each other that night they told each other their names, the man said, "My name is Andrew." And, the girl said "My name is Megan." The next day Andrew saw Megan. Andrew went up to Megan and said, "Will you marry me?" Megan said "Yes." And they married. The End.

Williams reported that after this type of activity students:

- gave more attention to visuals in both fiction and nonfiction books; and
- would question the connections between the subject and the images.

The important message Williams leaves with us is that there are ways to get students to do more than simply read text. Instead, we can help them "read visual images." Stripping images, such as a painting, of written contextual clues moves students beyond literacy comprehension and helps develop new visual understandings and skills.

out-of-school experiences into our instructional programs. However, many of us do not consider television and film as resources holding much educational potential. This is interesting because television is among the first cultural experiences children have. Many start viewing as early as 18 months old (perhaps earlier). And, by most accounts (Bransford et al., 2000; Thompson, 2007), students spend more time, if accumulated over a seven-day period, watching television than they spend in school.

Similarly, going to movies is a favorite activity of youth, particularly once they reach their teens. Much has been written about the impact of television and film and the negative effects of violence, sexual portrayal, and vulgar language on the socialization of children and youth. Also, a spate of studies has been done over the last 30 years attempting to gage the effects of television on academic achievement. Thompson (2007) and Thompson and Austin (2003) reviewed this research and concluded that the effects of television remain mixed, with studies showing both negative and positive effects. Our purpose here is not to enter into this debate. Instead, we will argue that the proper use of video, television, and film can promote visual literacy and become important resources for helping students acquire new information and background knowledge on a wide variety of topics.

Video and Film Like textbooks, most educational videos have been carefully prepared and edited for objectivity and accuracy. As a result, teachers can proceed with their use with some confidence. Educational videos are primarily assigned and viewed under the teacher's supervision. Films, however, are often viewed as a result of choices made by students. Guidelines apply for the effective use of video or film similar to those provided earlier in regard to the use of expository and Internet text. These guidelines include:

- *Previewing and predicting* prior to viewing, perhaps providing an advance organizer.
- Teaching students how *to view and take notes* with words as well as with non-linguistic representations.
- *Summarizing* and discussing after viewing the video or film.

Some caution is required when teachers use commercially produced films, whether they are playing in the local theater or being viewed in class on DVDs. Mainly, we need to be aware of community values that will judge some films to be inappropriate for children and youth. These values will vary widely from one community to another. The use of the film *Schindler's List* is a good example. History teachers, in their study of World War II and the Holocaust, have used this Academy Award film widely. In many communities, parents and community members praise teachers' use of this film. This film, however, contains graphic violence and overall themes that families in other communities find objectionable. Many school districts have developed policies and procedures for the use of commercially produced films.

> **REFLECTION**
>
> Think about instances in your community when the viewing of a film or television show has sparked controversy. What issues seemed to be expressed by various groups? Also, consider district policies for getting a film approved for viewing. Do you agree or disagree with your district's policy?

Television Teachers can help students with television viewing in three important ways: fostering critical **viewing skills**, assigning programs for acquiring background knowledge, and teaching them to evaluate media messages for accuracy and objectivity. The first two ways are described here; the third will be discussed in the final section of this chapter.

Judicious television assignments can help students develop critical viewing skills and acquire background knowledge in designated subject areas. Below are examples of possible activities and/or assignments:

- *For developing critical viewing skills:*

  - Have students compare coverage of the same event by two different local television stations and/or by two national news programs.
  - Have students provide written analysis of television's treatment of violence or sexual portrayal.
  - Have students evaluate talk shows for accuracy and objectivity; compare coverage of the same issue on two Sunday morning talk shows.
  - Have students provide analysis of hidden messages in selected television commercials; in selected political campaign ads.

- *For acquiring background knowledge:*

  - Assign and discuss television documentaries on subject matter normally covered in class or in text. Here are some examples at the time we are writing this module: Burns' documentaries on World War II, the Civil War, and National Parks; documentaries on global warming, on Islam, on religious fanaticism, and on Russia under Putin.
  - Assign television programs in which works of literature have been made into films, e.g., Shakespeare plays; films that use Shakespeare plots such as *West Side Story*.
  - Assign and have students write reports on television history programs, e.g., Vietnam; Civil War; World War II; Great Depression.

Analyzing and Evaluating Media Messages

In a previous section, we described a set of questions students can use to evaluate information and images found on the Internet. A similar set of questions can be applied to information portrayed on television, video, or elsewhere. The Center for Media Literacy (2007) has identified several core concepts and questions to guide viewing and evaluating media messages. We have adapted and added to these concepts and questions and display them in Table 9.4. As with most aspects of visual literacy, teachers will find that students are a motivated audience for this type of analysis.

Visual literacy skills are important for effective participation in the twenty-first century. Curricula, content standards, and programs to define and teach these skills to students are starting to emerge and will surely expand in the years ahead.

Table 9.4 Key concepts and questions for understanding and evaluating media messages

Keyword	Core concepts	Key questions
Authorship	All media messages are "constructed" by someone.	Who created this message?
Format	Media messages are constructed using a creative language with its own rules.	What creative techniques are used to attract my attention?
Audience	Media messages are aimed at particular audiences, but different people experience the same message differently.	How might different people understand this message differently?
Content	Media messages have embedded values and points of view.	What values and points of view are represented in this message?
Purpose	Most media messages are created to inform and gain profit and/or power.	Why is this message being sent?
Accuracy and objectivity	Media messages have varying degrees of accuracy and/or objectivity.	How accurate is the message? How do I know? How objective is the message? How do I know?

Source: Summarized and adapted from Center for Media Literacy (2007).

SUMMARY AT A GLANCE

- Print text is an important source for building students' background knowledge, but so is text found on the Internet and visual images portrayed on television and in video and film.
- A rather rich research base exists on best strategies to use for helping students learn from text. Most reading experts organize these strategies into three categories: those used in preparation for reading, during reading, and after reading.
- Vocabulary development and independent reading are two important programs for helping students acquire important background knowledge and for developing literacy skills.
- Today, the Internet has become an important resource for acquiring information and background knowledge. Many students, however, are not very adept at using this resource. Helping students preview, read, evaluate, and summarize online text have become important goals for teaching.
- Technology and visual media play a large role in students' lives. It is important to provide them with the abilities to understand visual messages and to communicate through visual means.
- Television and film, rather than viewed as a distraction from student learning, can be seen as a valuable teaching resource and can be incorporated fully into a teacher's instructional program.

CONSTRUCTING YOUR OWN LEARNING

Working alone or with a classmate or colleague, make an inventory of the beliefs you hold about the Internet and about visual literacy. Also identify practices in your respective classrooms you each use to promote literacy skills and how to use the Internet more effectively. How well have these practices been integrated into your overall instructional programs? You may also want to consider the positive influences the Internet and visual media use have had on student motivation and learning, as well as the negative influences. Now develop a set of goals for changes you would like to make in your classroom, in your school, and perhaps in your school district in regard to Internet use and visual literacy.

RESOURCES

Beck, I., McKeown, M., &Kucan, L. (2002). *Bringing words to life.* New York: Guilford Press.

Eagleton, M., Dobler, E. & Leu, D.J. (2007). *Reading the web: Strategies for Internet inquiry.* New York: Guilford Press.

Fisher, D., & Frey, N. (2008). *Word wise and content rich: Five essential steps to teaching academic vocabulary.* Portsmouth, NH: Heinemann.

Riddle, J. (2009). *Engaging the eye generation: Visual literacy strategies for K-5 classrooms.* Portland, ME: Stenhouse Publishers.

Sprenger, M. (2005). *How to teach so students remember.* Alexandria, VA: Association of Supervision and Curriculum Development.

Wormeli, R. (2005). *Summarization in any subject: 50 techniques to improve student learning.* Alexandria, VA: Association of Supervision and Curriculum Development.

10

TEACHING THINKING

As students enter Chris Elnicki's classroom on the first day of class, he informs them that they have a task to do.

On the front board, under the heading "First Things" is an assignment: "Look around the room and try to figure out what you can tell about *me*." While students glance about, Chris quickly takes roll and then asks, "OK, what did you figure out about me or what questions do you have about me based on the room?"

Students raise their hands and begin to call out their findings. As they do, Chris presses them to explain the basis for their conclusions, to provide evidence and explanations for their thinking. One student offers the observation, "You are patriotic." "What make you think I'm patriotic? What is the evidence?" Chris asks. Pointing around the room, the student responds, "The flag, those posters." Chris gently pushes the student's thinking by offering an alternative explanation, "OK, so I might be patriotic, or this may be a course that tries to teach patriotism. You can probably bet that an American studies course wouldn't be anti-American."

Another student, picking up on the expectation to provide evidence, points to a quote about the ship in the port hanging above the window—"A ship in port is safe, but that's not what ships are built for"—and observes, "You want us to be determined."

(Adapted from Ritchhart, 2002, pp. 72–73)

Students continue to provide ideas about Chris and supply evidence from observations ranging from his wedding band to the cartoons on his bulletin boards. Chris acknowledges their contributions and the conversation continues. Through this opening activity, Chris is setting norms for how dialogues will proceed in his classroom and his expectations for how he wants his students to think and talk about history throughout the year. He is setting the stage for teaching his *students how to think*.

OVERVIEW

Most people agree that one of the primary purposes of schooling is to teach students how to think, and *thinking* as a topic is of interest to many, not just those of us who are teachers. To illustrate the enormity of the interest in thinking, we conducted an Amazon and Google search on the topic of "critical thinking" when we were writing this chapter. The Amazon search produced a list of 28,835 books. Over eight million "critical thinking" hits were registered on Google. Obviously, there has been much written about thinking and thinking skills. It cannot all be covered in this chapter but, instead, we will strive to describe a few topics well and those we believe to be of most concern to our experienced teacher audience. First, we provide several overarching perspectives about thinking and teaching thinking and highlight some of the historical debates that have surrounded this topic. This is followed by descriptions of three "stand-alone" thinking programs and the strategies that have been developed for the purpose of helping students acquire an array of thinking skills and dispositions. Our discussion about how to teach students how to think will be extended into the chapter that follows, where we consider two specific teaching models—concept teaching and inquiry-based teaching. These models have been created for use in particular subject areas (mainly the sciences, the social sciences, history, and literature) for the purpose of helping students develop important conceptual understandings, as well as thinking skills associated with inquiry and discovery.

CONNECTING TO THE CONTEXT AND SCIENCE OF LEARNING

Teaching thinking skills and dispositions rests mainly on cognitive and constructivist perspectives about how people learn. These perspectives were described earlier, in Chapter 2. Learning activities developed from a constructivist perspective recognize the wide variation among students in regard to abilities and the need to provide students developmentally appropriate opportunities to construct their own meaning as they and their teachers jointly engage in learning experiences. For our purposes in this chapter, teaching thinking from a constructivist perspective requires:

- Organizing learning situations that allow students to think, inquire, solve problems, and restructure their own knowledge through these processes.
- Modeling effective thinking and making both the teacher's and their students' thinking processes explicit.
- Encouraging students to engage in **reflective thought** and to become self-regulated, autonomous learners.
- Creating and maintaining learning environments that are rich in resources, that have an appropriate amount of challenge, and that are free from fear and threat.

PERSPECTIVES ABOUT THINKING AND TEACHING THINKING

Contemporary perspectives about the nature of thinking and teaching thinking make important distinctions absent in earlier views on these topics. For example, most theorists today (Nickerson, 1987; Sternberg & Williams, 2002) believe in the universality of the human capacity to think. They point out that, just as we breathe, move, or blink our eyes, we think whether or not we have received any formal instruction. Sternberg and Williams (2002, p. 309) go on to observe that, though everyone thinks, most do it poorly and what is required in schools is to teach students "to think more effectively— more critically, more coherently, more creatively, more deeply—than . . . [they] typically do." Costa (2008) has likewise argued that, "thinking effectively, just as moving with precision . . . takes time and coaching." In sum, no one has to teach anyone how to think, but at the same time, all of us can be taught to think more effectively, critically, and creatively. Learning this type of thinking is difficult work. Good teaching, like that observed in Chris's classroom, is required.

Most theorists and practitioners today also view thinking as having two distinct dimensions. The first dimension consists of a set of *skills or abilities*, such as being able to recognize bias in an argument or to reach conclusions based on sound evidence. These skills are activated in problem-solving situations and make thinking more effective. The second dimension consists of broad **dispositions**, or *habits of mind*, such as curiosity and open-mindedness. These dispositions, according to Ritchhart (2002) and Perkins, Jay, and Tishman (1993a, 1993b), determine how disposed individuals are to think in the first place and how they choose to use their thinking skills and abilities. This view is firmly embedded in some of the programs and strategies described later in this chapter.

> **REFLECTION**
>
> Think for a moment about your own teaching in regard to teaching specific thinking skills as contrasted to developing dispositions. Do you approach the two objectives differently or the same? Some believe it is more difficult to develop positive dispositions toward thinking than it is to teach specific teaching skills. What has been your experience?

Dimensions and Types of Thinking

An important question asked by teachers who want to teach their students how to think is, "What exactly is meant by thinking?" Though there has been general consensus over the years that thinking consists of using particular skills and **cognitive processes**, current efforts to identify these skills and processes have produced different and multiple listings, and the exact nature of particular thinking processes remains somewhat undefined. This problem is further complicated when psychologists and educators conclude that there are different types of thinking and that individuals use different approaches in the ways they think. In the chapters on how students learn and on instructional differentiation, we described how students possess different kinds of intelligences and learning styles and how particular styles influence how they approach problem situations, how they perform intellectually, and what they are likely to take away from a learning experience. We also described, in Chapter 2, how the acquisition of different kinds of knowledge and skills requires different kinds of thinking. We return and expand on these topics here.

Basic and Higher-level Thinking
Current perspectives consider differences between [basic thinking skills] and **higher-order thinking skills** and abilities (Anderson & Krathwohl, 2001; Beyer, 2001a, 2001b). Most taxonomies, including the revised Bloom's which we introduced in earlier chapters and will expand on in the next section, define cognitive processes associated with the more routine patterns of thinking behavior such as remembering and recalling as basic thinking skills, whereas higher-order thinking consists of understanding, comparing, evaluating, explaining, and creating. Some also point out that **higher-level thinking** is a rather complex activity, as Resnick (1987) did when she defined the characteristics of higher-order thinking. We include her definitions in Figure 10.1. Note the words Resnick uses—nuanced judgment, self-regulation, and imposing meaning—to communicate her view about the complexity

---

Higher-order thinking:

- is *nonalgorithmic*. That is, the path of action is not fully specified in advance.
- tends to be *complex*. The total path is not "visible" (mentally speaking) from any single vantage point.
- often yields *multiple solutions*, each with costs and benefits, rather than unique solutions.
- involves *nuanced judgment* and interpretation.
- involves the application of *multiple criteria*, which sometimes conflict with one another.
- often involves *uncertainty*. Not everything that bears on the task at hand is known.
- involves *self-regulation* of the thinking process. We do not recognize higher-order thinking in an individual when someone else "calls the plays" at every step.
- involves *imposing meaning* and finding structure in apparent disorder.
- is *effortful*. There is considerable mental work involved in the kinds of elaboration and judgment required.

Figure 10.1 Characteristics of higher-order thinking
Source: Summarized from Resnick (1987), pp. 2–4.

and *contextual nature of higher-order thinking* and to make distinctions between this type of thinking and that which employs only basic thinking skills.

Divergent and Convergent Thinking Guilford (1967), who explored the nature of human intelligence and the structure of the intellect, described two types of thinking involved as individuals strive to solve problems and make decisions. He labeled these divergent thinking and convergent thinking. **Divergent thinking** is the kind of thinking that proposes many different ideas or solutions. In classrooms, this type of thinking is prompted by questions that are open-ended or start with: "What would happen if. . . ." **Convergent thinking**, on the other hand, moves toward producing single answers or solutions and often starts with "why?" type questions, such as, "Why does water freeze at 32 degrees?" or "Why did the United States go to war in 1941?" Convergent thinking often begins by considering a number of facts and possible solutions and then, through the process of experimentation and testing, narrowing the possibilities to one. Figure 10.2 illustrates the differences between divergent and convergent thinking.

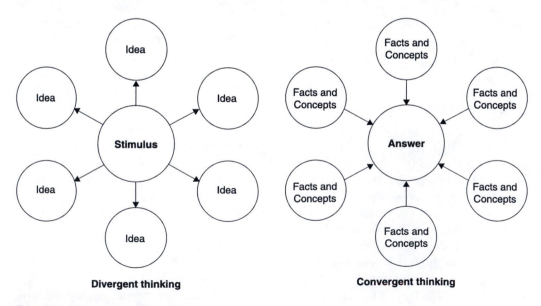

Divergent thinking   Convergent thinking

Figure 10.2 Divergent and convergent thinking

Concept and inquiry-based approaches to teaching that are rooted in the methods of scientific inquiry described in Chapter 11 tend to rely on convergent thinking. Some of the questions and problems used in problem-based learning described in Chapter 14, and in the *Visible Thinking Program* described later, call for students to use both convergent and divergent thinking skills.

Critical Thinking Critical thinking is another type of thinking that gains the attention of theorists and educators alike. As many of our readers know, *critical thinking* focuses on thinking that is reflective and that is directed toward analyzing particular arguments, recognizing fallacies and bias, and reaching conclusions based on evidence and sound judgment. Beyer (1997) has written that critical thinking is the process of determining the "authenticity, accuracy and worth" of particular pieces of information or knowledge. This is somewhat similar to Bloom's cognitive process of *evaluate*. Both focus on making judgments based on criteria and standards. As with other types of thinking, critical thinking has a skill and dispositional dimension. For instance, it requires certain skills to determine if an argument is accurate and worthwhile. But it also requires an inquiry-oriented disposition to want to determine accuracy or worthiness in the first place. As teachers, we are particularly interested in critical thinking. It is this type of thinking that is emphasized in some of the thinking routines described later in this chapter, as well as in chapters on case-based teaching, jurisprudential inquiry, and problem-based learning.

Creative Thinking Creative thinking is another type of thinking of interest to educators. This type of thinking is normally associated with cognitive skills and abilities for coming up with novel solutions to problem situations. In everyday language, we often refer to these as abilities to "think outside the box." Anderson and Krathwhol (2001, p. 68) defined this kind of thinking as abilities to "put elements together to form a coherent or functional whole and to reorganize elements into a new pattern or structure."

Creative thinking skills are highly valued in the workplace, as well as in most other aspects of life where original work is important. In general, it is agreed that there is no all-purpose creativity or creative thinking, but instead creative processes are tied to a particular area, such as music, writing, mathematics, foreign policy, and so on. Most observers (Amaile, 1996; Eisner, 1991; Simonton, 1999) agree personality traits, work habits, particular talents, and competencies, as well as motivation and a conducive social environment, influence effective creativity and creative thinking.

Schools and teachers are often accused of stifling creativity as a result of efforts to cover the curriculum, and to get students to meet predetermined content standards. Teachers who want to support creative thinking, however, are encouraged to promote divergent thinking in their students and to provide time for creative activities and projects in their classrooms. The Visible Thinking Program described in the next section identifies "encouraging creative thinking" as one of its major goals and developers have designed teaching strategies and thinking routines aimed specifically at promoting curiosity and open-mindedness.

Scientific Thinking and Reasoning **Scientific thinking** and **reasoning** also requires special definition and consideration. Essentially, this kind of thinking is reflected in the kinds of processes and methods associated with scientific inquiry and the well-known steps outlined in most scientific investigations that include: (1) problem identification; (2) hypotheses generation; (3) collecting evidence through observation and experimentation; and (4) drawing inferences and conclusions based on evidence. We define this type of thinking in much more detail in Chapter 11.

Gardner's Five Minds Howard Gardner (2007, 2009) recently provided another framework for considering the dimensions of thinking. He maintained that several trends in the contemporary world—the increasing power of science and technology; the interconnectedness of the economic and cultural aspects of the world; and the incessant intermingling of human beings of diverse backgrounds—require that we cultivate five kinds of *minds*. Below, we paraphrase his ideas about the five minds.

The Disciplined Mind. This is the first mind Gardner describes. Traditionally, possessing the **disciplined mind** meant that an individual had mastered a particular body of knowledge well enough to be considered an expert. Complete mastery for most people, however, is impossible. Instead, a disciplined mind applies to individuals who can see the world in a "disciplined way." Schools can assist students to acquire a disciplined mind by helping them grasp what it means to think in a disciplined way in science, history, or the arts. Gardner also tells us that mastery of one discipline is no longer sufficient. Today's world demands minds that are multidisciplinary and transdisciplinary because they allow us to use multiple perspectives for viewing the world.

The Synthesizing Mind. Gardner (2009, p. 1) asserts that perhaps the most valued mind in the twenty-first century is the **synthesizing mind**, "the mind that can survey a wide range of sources, decide what is important and worth paying attention to, and put this information together in ways that make sense to oneself and, ultimately, to others." Note that, for synthesis to be important, it must be understandable and relevant to others. Gardner says skills for this type of mind have never been taught "explicitly" in schools and that we have not determined standards for what a good synthesis is. Finding ways to teach and assess synthesis may be one of the most important contemporary challenges.

The Creating Mind. This is a mind that can forge new ground, something very important as more and more aspects of the world become automated. Gardner believes that developing the **creative mind** goes beyond helping students acquire requisite cognitive processes. Creativity also has a temperament component, a willingness to "venture into the unknown" and take chances. The job of schools, according to Gardner is, "not so much the inculcation of creativity, but rather its protection." Educators promote creativity by encouraging multiple approaches and rewarding "those who make mistakes, but learn from them." Gardner also makes another important observation. Creation is unlikely unless individuals have disciplinary mastery and capacity to synthesize. "You can't think outside the box unless you have a box" (2009, p. 2)

The Respectful Mind. Gardner points out that, as individuals, we are wired from birth to make distinctions among individuals and groups of individuals. Our experiences determine whether we will like and respect others who differ from us or shun and fear them. We live in a time, however, when respect for others cannot be left to chance. We come into contact in our communities, through travel, or the virtual world with literally millions and millions of people. Individuals who have **respectful minds** welcome "exposure to diverse persons and groups," respect them and give them the "benefit of the doubt . . . and avoid prejudicial judgments." The environment of schools and the way we set the tone as educators for dealing with diversity is critical for developing students with respectful minds.

The Ethical Mind. This could be viewed as an extension of the respectful mind, but focuses on several questions about self: "What kind of person do I want to be?" "What kind of work do I want to do?" "What kind of citizen do I want to become?" According to Gardner (2009), answers to these questions recognize the "rights and responsibilities" attendant on each role and the ethical behavior associated with the actions we take in particular roles (p. 3). To develop the **ethical mind** requires an ethical environment— school systems, schools, and classrooms that set an "ethical tone."

Gardner concludes his thoughts about the five minds by observing that nurturing them is not easy. It requires educators, teachers, and others who themselves have acquired the skills and dispositions associated with these minds and who can model discipline, synthesis, creation, respect, and ethics on a regular basis. Ways of teaching thinking and developing minds are the topics of the next section.

Ways of Teaching Thinking

Before you read the following section, think about the questions posed in the reflection box below.

Over time, experienced teachers and curriculum theorists have debated the best way to teach students how to think. One of the oldest debates has been whether or not certain subjects by themselves develop thinking skills. In earlier times, believing that the answer to this question was "yes," led to policies requiring students to study Latin and Greek long after these languages were no longer used in everyday speech. Today, this argument is used to justify the study of algebra, geometry, and calculus. Competing views on ways to teach thinking were highlighted recently in an issue on

> **REFLECTION**
>
> Given all the demands on curriculum space, what proportion of your instructional time do you spend on teaching thinking? What do you believe is the best way to teach students how to think? Do you plan special lessons on thinking skills? Do you use opportunities in content lessons to point out cognitive and metacognitive processes? Or, do you do some of both?

"Teaching Students to Think" in the Association of Supervision and Curriculum Development's professional journal, *Educational Leadership* (2008).

One set of authors, Veronica Mansilla and Howard Gardner (2008), argued that the academic disciplines "embody distinct ways of thinking about the world" and that "disciplines and disciplinary thinking" should be emphasized in schools. The goal of this approach, according to Mansilla and Gardner, is to "instill in the young the disposition to interpret the world in the distinctive ways that characterize the *thinking* of experienced disciplinarians—historians, scientists, mathematicians, and artists. This view entrusts educational institutions with the responsibility of *disciplining* the young mind." (pp. 14–15). Notice the emphasis Mansilla and Gardner put on learning to think like academicians in particular academic subjects.

In the same issue, Nel Noddings (2008) took a different stand. She cited Dewey (1971) and wrote, "it is desirable to expel . . . the notion that some subjects are inherently *intellectual* and hence possessed with an almost magical power to train the faculty of thought. . . . Instead . . . any subject, from Greek to cooking, and from drawing to mathematics, is intellectual . . . in its power to start and direct significant inquiry and **reflection** (pp. 46–47). Noddings goes on to argue that we do our students a disservice when we propose:

> that there is no intellectual worth in such subjects as homemaking, parenting, getting along with others, living with plants and animals, and understanding advertising and propaganda. . . . The point is to appreciate the topics that matter in real life and encourage *thinking* in each area. This is *not* accomplished by first teaching everyone algebra—and thus developing mental muscle—and then applying that muscle to everyday matters (p. 10).

She also argues against the positions taken by Mansilla and Gardner that math courses should teach students how to think like mathematicians or history courses should teach students how to think like historians. Instead, she points out that:

> [There] is the possibility that there may be more than one way to think as a mathematician . . . [and] educational efforts might better be aimed at showing students how to use mathematics to think about their own purposes. For example, carpenters don't need to think like mathematicians, but they do need to think about and use mathematics in their work (p. 12).

It is likely that this debate will be with us for some time because some truth exists on both sides. Learning to think like historians or mathematicians helps students grasp the structures and inquiry processes of these important disciplines that influence greatly how we perceive and understand our social and physical worlds. On the other hand, we agree with Noddings that we do our students a disservice if we don't respect the intellectual worth of subjects important in everyday life.

REFLECTION

With a colleague or classmate, discuss where each of you stands on the matter of requiring certain school subjects over others because they have the unique power to develop thinking skills and dispositions. Also, consider where you stand in regard to Nodding's point of view.

Another historical argument about teaching thinking has centered on which of two approaches, **infusion strategies** or **stand-alone thinking programs**, are most effective. On the one side are those, such as Berman (2001), who believe that it is more effective to teach thinking skills infused into regular curricula subjects such as science, mathematics, social science, humanities, and the like, because *context* is particularly important in regard to thinking skills and dispositions. For instance, thinking about how sound waves travel or how light is reflected off objects in the environment calls for one type of thinking and the use of particular cognitive processes. This type of thinking is different than the thinking involved in analyzing a poem, a novel, or an impressionistic painting. Similarly, thinking about a mathematical problem is different than thinking about the causes of civil wars or the historical era that influenced Darwin's *The Origin of Species*. Concept and inquiry-based teaching, described in Chapter 11, employ infusion strategies.

On the other side of this debate are those, such as de Bono (1983) and Ritchhart (2002), who believe that teaching thinking skills separately from subject matter instruction is more effective because it allows students to focus directly on thinking skills and processes. Proponents of this stand-alone approach believe that what students learn will transfer and can be applied later to specific subject areas.

Finally, employing student-centered, inferential approaches versus using direct instruction for teaching students how to think has also been the topic of historical disagreement. Most inquiry-based models require students to participate in an inquiry process and figure things out on their own. The aim is to help students acquire important thinking skills as they explore interesting questions and puzzling situations. Others, however, favor the use of direct instruction (Beyer, 2001c). When using direct instruction, teachers demonstrate a particular thinking process, skill, or disposition, and then provide opportunities for students to practice.

Several years ago, Cotton (1995) reviewed the research on the relative effectiveness of the infused versus stand-alone approaches and the inferential versus direct instruction approaches. She concluded that no single approach was more or less effective, but instead the critical variable seemed to be how well teachers implemented a particular approach and how appropriate it was for a particular group of students. Her conclusions are consistent with our point of view. We believe that, as teachers, we need a rich repertoire of strategies for teaching students how to think that can be employed effectively depending upon the learning goals we are trying to achieve and the characteristics of the students in our classrooms.

THINKING PROCESSES AND METACOGNITION

What does it mean to think? What is going on in our minds when we are thinking? Most theorists and researchers believe there are different kinds of knowledge and each requires us to use different cognitive processes.

Cognitive Processes in Bloom's Revised Taxonomy

Bloom (1956) and his contemporary revisionists (Anderson & Krathwohl, 2001) have developed a model for defining and considering the role of cognitive processes in our thinking. We have already used this taxonomy in previous chapters to help you think about curriculum development, test and assessment design, and questioning strategies. Here, however, we are interested in the taxonomy and the way it classifies the cognitive processes associated with different kinds of thinking. In their revision of Bloom's work, Anderson et al. constructed a two-dimensional model and renamed the taxonomy as the *taxonomy for learning, teaching, and assessing*. One dimension of the model is the knowledge dimension, consisting of four different types of knowledge arranged along a continuum from the very concrete to the more abstract. We previously described these four types of knowledge in Chapter 2 as: (1) factual knowledge, (2) conceptual knowledge, (3) procedural knowledge, and (4) metacognitive knowledge.

Table 10.1 Bloom's revised taxonomy

Knowledge Dimension	Cognitive process dimension					
	Remember	Understand	Apply	Analyze	Evaluate	Create
Factual knowledge						
Conceptual knowledge						
Procedural knowledge						
Metacognitive knowledge						

Source: Based on concepts from Anderson and Krahwohl (2001).

The second dimension in the taxonomy is the cognitive dimension (ways of thinking) and it contains six categories: remember, understand, apply, analyze, evaluate, and create. These too are assumed to lie along a continuum of cognitive complexity from the more basic or concrete processes (remember and understand) to those that are more abstract and at a higher level (analyze and create). Table 10.1 illustrates the revised taxonomy and relationships between the knowledge and cognitive process dimensions. The cognitive dimension and the cognitive processes, the ones we are most interested in here, are further defined in Table 10.2.

Using Bloom's Cognitive Processes as a Teaching Tool Bloom's taxonomy can be used to teach students about cognition and their thinking processes. For example, charts can be made similar to the one we depict in Figure 10.3 for the purpose of illustrating to

Table 10.2 Cognitive processes in Bloom's taxonomy

Remember: Retrieve relevant information from long-term memory. • recognizing • recalling	**Understand:** Construct meaning from instructional messages, including oral, written, and graphic communication. • interpreting • exemplifying • classifying • summarizing • inferring • comparing • explaining	**Apply:** Carry out or use a procedure in a given situation. • executing • implementing
Analyze: Break material into constituent parts and determine how parts relate to one another and to an overall structure or purpose. • differentiating • organizing • attributing	**Evaluate:** Make judgments based on criteria and standards. • checking • critiquing	**Create:** Put elements together to form a coherent or functional whole; reorganize elements into a new pattern or structure. • generating • planning • producing

Source: Based on concepts from Anderson and Krahwohl (2001).

REMEMBERING Recalling Information	
UNDERSTANDING Explaining ideas or concepts	
APPLYING Using information in another familiar situation	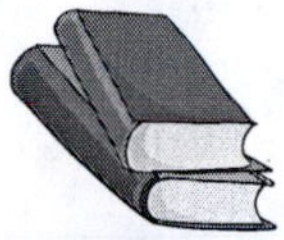
ANALYSING Breaking information into parts to explore understandings and relationships	
EVALUATING Justifying a decision or course of action	
CREATING Generating new ideas, products, or ways of viewing things	

Figure 10.3 Chart to illustrate cognitive processes
Source: Based on concepts from Bennett and Rolheiser (2001).

students the different cognitive processes and how these ideas can be applied to their thinking.

Teachers can use this type of illustration to explain differences among the different cognitive processes or it could be used as the focal point for a small or whole-class discussion where students are asked to provide examples of each process.

Metacognition

Finally, thinking about one's own thinking, or **metacognition**, is another important consideration for teaching students how to think. As described in earlier chapters, metacognition, in more specific terms, refers to learners' abilities to have control over their cognitive processes as they work to accomplish particular learning tasks. It consists of abilities to stand back and examine one's thoughts and to monitor what's going on. John Flavell (1985), one of the originators of metacognition, provided a more formal definition:

[Metacognition] is one's knowledge concerning one's cognitive processes. . . . Metacognition refers, among other things, to the active monitoring and consequent regulation and orchestration of these processes in relation to cognitive objectives on which they bear, usually in the service of some concrete goal or objective (p. 232).

As with other aspects of thinking, metacognition has knowledge, skill, and disposition components. The knowledge component consists of students' understanding of how people learn and about their own cognitive and metacognitive processes. The skill component consists of abilities students have to identify, use, and evaluate cognitive and **metacognitive learning strategies**. The disposition aspect of metacognition is the willingness to work toward self-regulation and employ particular strategies when the learning situation requires it.

The aims of metacognitive instruction are to teach students to learn on their own to become **self-regulated learners**. Dunlosky and Metcalfe (2008) and Pressley, Roehrig, Raphael, Dolezal, Bohn, and Mohan (2003), among others, believe that self-regulated learners have the knowledge and skills to perform three important activities:

1. Accurately *diagnose* a particular learning task and *plan* how to proceed and use particular learning strategies.
2. *Monitor* progress toward accomplishing the learning task.
3. Make changes and *adaptations* as required.

Throughout *Teaching for Student Learning*, we have described a variety of ways to help students become aware of their thinking and we have provided an array of learning strategies that assist in a variety of learning situations. These have included previewing, questioning, and summarizing strategies used in reciprocal teaching and other programs to enhance reading comprehension. They have included study and learning strategies, such as outlining, note-taking, and look-back reflection techniques. In Table 10.3, we include a number of other cognitive and metacognitive strategies and connect these to the three metacognitive activities described above.

As teachers, we know that some students, almost from the start, are self-regulated learners. They are aware of their own cognitive processes, and they can employ thinking and learning strategies effectively to accomplish learning tasks. They can set learning goals efficiently. They know when to go back and read a passage again or to make corrections when errors or misunderstandings occur. On the other hand, many students do not have this knowledge or these skills, particularly students who are struggling. They often have unclear understandings of the goals of a learning task, and they do not consciously choose the best learning strategy to use. Even if they realize they don't understand an idea or concept, they may choose to move forward anyway. They simply fail to monitor their own learning and consequently cannot make midstream adaptations.

Some learning theorists, Sternberg (1985) for example, have speculated that individuals' metacognitive abilities and self-regulation may be determined to some degree by intelligence. Whether or not this speculation is accurate, is not as important as the almost universal agreement that teaching students about metacognitve strategies and how to use them effectively can improve greatly their academic performance. The same

Table 10.3 Metacognitive strategies to assist with diagnosing and monitoring learning situations and for making adjustments

Diagnosing and planning	Monitoring progress	Making adjustments
Define nature and proximity of learning goals	Monitor own learning by consciously thinking about it	Go back and reread or restudy
Identify prior knowledge	Use self-questioning to check comprehension	Make correction of errors or misunderstandings
Consider what final task requires, e.g., term paper, essay test, project	Use self-talk and self-testing	Choose a more appropriate learning strategy
Estimate time required to complete learning	Summarize what has been learned	
Decide which learning strategies will work best	Detect failure, such as an error or misunderstanding	
Determine level of motivation		

debate exists about teaching metacognitive skills as learning skills in general. On the one side are those (Pressley & Woloshyn, 1999) who believe that metacognitive knowledge and skills should be taught explicitly using steps very similar to those we describe in Chapter 8 on direct instruction. The Pressley and Woloshyn guidelines include: emphasizing the importance of metacognitive strategies, teaching a few strategies at a time, providing accurate explanation and modeling, providing practice opportunities with feedback, and encouraging students to monitor how they are doing as they use particular strategies.

Others, such as Bransford et al. (2000), believe that instruction for metacognitive understandings and skills should be an important aspect of schools' curricula. However, they argue that instruction should be infused into subject areas and across the curriculum because the type of cognitive processes and monitoring required are *contextual* and will vary from one subject to another. We take the position we take elsewhere, that both approaches are required. Some metacognitive skills are best learned through direct instruction. However, infusing them across the curriculum is the best way to ensure transfer and appropriate use in academic learning situations.

STAND-ALONE THINKING PROGRAMS AND STRATEGIES

As we described earlier, some contend that infusion strategies have had limited impact on helping students acquire "good" thinking skills. They take this position because too often they have observed that the content objectives of instruction overwhelm efforts to teach students how to think. In response they have developed *stand-alone thinking programs* aimed specifically at teaching thinking skills and dispositions. Here, we describe three of the more widely-known and used programs: Harvard's Project Zero **Visible Thinking Program**, the **Artful Thinking Program**, and the **Six Thinking Hats Program**. We provide more space to the Visible Thinking Program as contrasted to the others for two reasons. One, the rationale and principles behind its development are very similar to those behind the development of the Artful Thinking Program. In fact, many of the same individuals worked on both programs. Two, the Project Zero Program has been more thoroughly studied than the Thinking Hats Program and its uses and effects have been more widely documented and reported in the educational literature.

David Perkins, Ron Ritchhart, Shari Tishman, and a number of their colleagues associated with Harvard's Project Zero, have provided us with a *new* set of lenses for considering why teaching thinking is important and how best to teach students how to think. Ritchhart (2002) has taken the position that teaching students "rigorous high-end thinking" and "dispositions to think" should be the priority goals for education. He uses the term "intellectual character" to refer to individuals who have an "overarching conglomeration of habits of mind, patterns of thought, and general dispositions toward thinking that not only direct but also motivate one's thinking-oriented pursuits" (p. xxii). Ritchhart and his colleagues believe that productive thinking cannot be achieved by merely emphasizing explicit standards or objectives, but instead requires teachers who have high expectations for problem solving and inquiry. Further, they believe classrooms must be structured to encourage and use the language of thinking and to support student thinking every day, all year long.

Project Zero's Visible Thinking Program
The Visible Thinking Program, under development for a number of years by Project Zero personnel at Harvard University, was informed by studies of classroom teachers who were consistently successful in promoting high-end thinking. Also, its development was guided by several overarching beliefs. The first belief, as described above, is that effective thinking is more than having a set of specific skills and abilities. It also consists of a set of dispositions that evokes thinking in the first place. To support this contention, Ritchhart and Perkins (2008, p. 1) have written that thinking "may suffer more from just plain missing opportunities than from poor [thinking] skills." A second belief is that thinking is invisible and happens "under the hoods of our mind." Unlike many other skills, we cannot readily observe our own or each other's thought and cognitive processes. This situation is one of the reasons teaching students to think is so difficult. Third, developers of the Visible Thinking Program believe that we have been teaching the wrong thing in schools. "We don't have our sights set on providing students with an education that develops their intellect. We've misplaced . . . the kind [of education] that can lead and motivate . . . the ideal of intellectual character [and thinking]" (Ritchhart, 2002, p. 10).

Ritchhart's research provided valuable insights into what is required to teach students how to think. We summarize his important study in Research Box 10.1 and then describe how the results have influenced the development and implementation of the Visible and Artful Thinking Programs.

Ritchhart and his colleagues concluded that four specific innovations were required to promote thinking and develop intellectual character. We summarize these four innovations in Figure 10.4 and describe each in more detail below.

Adopt a Dispositional View of Thinking and Intellectual Traits Ritchhart (2002) takes the position that teaching students "dispositions to think" should be the priority goal

---

RESEARCH BOX 10.1

Ritchhart, R. (2002). *Intellectual character: What it is, why it matters, and how to get it.* San Francisco: Jossey-Bass.

In the late 1990s, Ron Ritchhart began a study of classrooms with thoughtful environments and those that had teachers who cultivated and promoted "rigorous, high-end thinking." Using ethnographic and interpretative methods, Ritchhart produced over a year's time case studies of six teachers and their classrooms.

Teachers were selected through an informal nomination process. Teachers, researchers, and other knowledgeable educators were asked for names of "good" teachers in middle school math, social studies, and language arts who really cared about getting students to think. The nomination process produced 45 teachers, from which six were selected.

Ritchhart made 20 visits to each classroom: two weeks at the beginning of the school year; one week in October and November; and one week in the winter term. Ritchhart's observations were conducted from the back of the classroom, where he remained a non-participant as he took notes and videotaped lessons. In addition, each teacher was interviewed six times early on, in the middle, and at the end of the study. In the interviews, teachers were asked to describe how they teach "thinking" and to review and critique the videotapes Ritchhart had made of their class.

Observation and interview data were analyzed during and at the conclusion of the study, using formal ethnographic methods as well as more interpretative and reflective critiques and approaches.

Ritchhart found that it takes a particular type of classroom and teaching if we are to teach students how to think effectively. The classrooms in his study had developed what he labeled a *culture of thinking*, and they had teachers who used specific teaching routines that helped scaffold student thinking. They made thinking visible and nurtured thinking dispositions over time. The implication derived from Ritchhart's study served the basis for what is discussed below.

---

for education. **Dispositions** are not thinking skills, but instead attitudes and habits of mind about thinking that motivate and direct us to engage in thinking pursuits in the first place. After synthesizing the work of several researchers (Costa and Kallick, 2000; Facione, Facioine, & Sanchez, 1992; Paul, 1993; Perkins et al., 1993a, 1993b; Tishman, Perkins, & Jay, 1995), Project Zero staff were able to identify six broad dispositions, grouped into three overarching categories. These categories and dispositions are described in Figure 10.5.

Create Classroom Environments that Focus on Thinking Visible Thinking Program personnel believe that one of the main reasons that many thinking programs do not reach their desired goals is because classroom learning environments lack key features that will help students achieve thinking skills and dispositions. Success depends on developing and sustaining **classroom environments** that enhance students' inclination

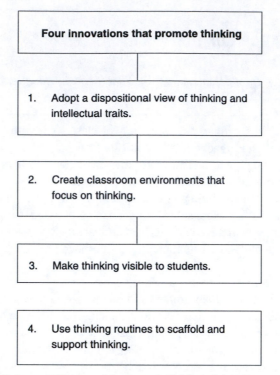

Four innovations that promote thinking

1. Adopt a dispositional view of thinking and intellectual traits.

2. Create classroom environments that focus on thinking.

3. Make thinking visible to students.

4. Use thinking routines to scaffold and support thinking.

Figure 10.4 Four innovations that promote thinking and development of intellectual character

toward thinking and support learning thinking dispositions and skills. Ritchhart (2002, 2005) has identified eight forces that shape this type of classroom environment:

- *Expectations and attitudes*: Holding high expectations and optimistic attitudes for student thinking.

Creative thinking: looking out, up, around, and about
  1. Disposition to be *open-minded*: Thinking that works against narrowness and rigidity and ability to look at things from a different perspective or point of view.
  2. Disposition to be *curious*: Thinking that propels one to explore our world and of finding the interesting and puzzling in all aspects of our intellectual and everyday lives.

Reflective thinking: looking within
  3. Disposition to be *metacognitive:* Thinking that is thinking about one's own thinking and the particular disposition to actively monitor, regulate, and evaluate one's thinking.

Critical thinking: looking at, through, and in between
  4. Disposition to be *seeking truth and understanding*: Thinking that takes a person deeper into the topic at hand and involves weighing evidence, testing hypotheses, and exploring applications and consequences.
  5. Disposition to be *strategic*: Thinking that is organized, methodical, and planned to meet particular goals or solve particular problems.
  6. Disposition to be *skeptical*: Thinking that is probing and that looks beneath the surface of things, ideas, and arguments.

Figure 10.5 Thinking dispositions synthesized by the Visible Thinking Program
Source: Summarized from Ritchhart (2002), pp. 27–30.

- *Time*: Allocating time for thinking. This means providing both time for exploring topics in more depth, as well as time to formulate thoughtful responses to questions.
- *Opportunities*: Providing a rich array of purposeful activities that require students to engage in thinking and the development of understanding as part of their classroom work.
- *Routines and structures*: Scaffolding students' thinking and learning in the moment and providing tools and patterns of thinking that can be used when working independently.
- *Language and conversations*: Using a language of thinking that provides students with the vocabulary for describing and reflecting on thinking.
- *Modeling*: Demonstrating what thinking looks like and showing that the teacher is a thoughtful, inquisitive learner.
- *Interactions and relationships*: Showing respect for and interest in students' ideas and thinking.
- *Physical environment*: Making thinking and the products of thinking visible in the classroom (summarized from Richhart, 2002, pp. 146–147; 2005).

These forces, according to Ritchhart, do not appear in full bloom. Instead, a culture of thinking begins during the first day of class and continues to develop over time. Although the first days of class are often characterized by establishing management and housekeeping routines, Ritchhart (2002) argues that attention should also be given to establishing a culture of thinking and teaching routines. Teachers in Ritchhart's study:

- Conveyed a sense of history of thought and the power of ideas.
- Jumped immediately into big-subject matter issues.
- Established a foundation for ongoing dialogue.
- Set a firm agenda of understanding.

We illustrated how one teacher in Ritchhart's study did this in the scenario at the beginning of this chapter. You remember that when students first stepped into his classroom, Mr. Elnicki conveyed to them the importance of inquiry and how to use evidence to draw conclusions based on what they observed on the walls and bulletin boards, on the questions their teacher asked, and on the way the teacher expressed his own attitudes toward thinking and learning.

Make Thinking Visible to Students Unlike some behaviors, such as dancing, shooting baskets, or writing an essay, cognitive behaviors are pretty much invisible, or, as Ritchhart and Perkins (2008) have written: "thinking happens under the hood, within the marvelous engine of our mindbrain" (p. 1). The Visible Thinking Program has developed several strategies to make thinking in classrooms more visible. One strategy is for teachers to model thoughtfulness and to probe using the types of questions that promote thinking, many of which we described previously and include:

- What if . . .?
- If I told you . . . X . . . what would that do to your theory?
- Have you considered another way to view this problem?
- What is going on in your mind when you say that?

Another strategy to make thinking visible is for teachers to make conscious efforts to use the **language of thinking** and to teach students the meaning of important terms that describe thinking and thinking processes, such as hypothesis, evidence, generalization, perspective, validity, and so on. Being precise about thinking is also important. Table 10.4 illustrates the differences between precise and imprecise in the use of language about thinking.

Finally, Ritchhart (2002) found that effective teachers of thinking used the physical environment to make thinking visible. The products of student thinking such as pictures, portfolios, and essays were displayed throughout the room, as were drafts of reports and reading-response and writing journals. Thinking-rich classrooms also had numerous pictures prominently displayed of students engaged in a variety of thinking endeavors.

Use Thinking Routines to Scaffold and Support Thinking The use of **thinking routines** is at the heart of the Visible Thinking Program. To help understand a thinking routine, consider other types of routine we use in our classrooms. Two that come to mind immediately are housekeeping and management routines. Effective teachers establish housekeeping routines for keeping the environment clean and uncluttered and for collecting and distributing homework. Management routines, such as lining up for recess or procedures for moving from one type of learning activity to another, help maintain order. Teachers also create what researchers (Leinhardt & Greeno, 1986; Perkins, 2003) have labeled learning and discourse routines. Learning routines guide learning and include such actions as previewing prior to a reading assignment or posing questions to review what has been read. Discourse routines structure the way dialogue and conversations occur in classrooms between teachers and students and among students themselves. Raising hands and taking turns are examples of simple discourse routines that have been around classrooms for a long time.

Ritchhart, Palmer, Church, and Tishman (2006) have written that they consider "thinking routines . . . a subset of discourse and learning routines . . . [that provide

Table 10.4 Imprecise and precise language about thinking

Instead of saying (imprecise language)	Say (more precise language)
Let's look at these two pictures.	Let's *compare* these two pictures.
What do you think will happen when . . .?	What do you *predict* will happen when . . .?
How can you put these into groups . . .?	How can you *classify* . . .?
Let's work on this problem.	Let's *analyze* this problem.
What do you think would happen if . . .?	What do you *speculate* would happen if . . .?
What did you think of this story?	What *conclusions* can you draw about the story?
How can you explain . . .?	What *hypotheses* do you have that might explain . . .?
How do you know this is true?	What *evidence* do you have to support . . .?
How else could you use this . . .?	How could you *apply* this . . .?

Source: Adapted from Costa and Marzano (2001), p. 380. Reprinted with permission.

opportunities] for the exploration of ideas, and the rehearsal of one's thoughts prior to sharing." Let's look at two of these thinking routines that have influenced other routine development: the Think–Pair–Share and See–Think–Wonder routines.

Think–Pair–Share (TPS). We describe Think–Pair–Share again in Chapter 13 as a cooperative learning strategy, but here we want to emphasize how it can be used to promote student thinking. Frank Lyman (1981), a clinical professor at the University of Maryland, invented TPS because he believed that the pace of discourse in most class-rooms moved too rapidly. He also had observed that the typical discourse pattern was dominated by the teacher and a handful of students. The routine he created, which was later adopted by the Visible Thinking Program, challenged the assumptions behind whole-group teaching and built in procedures that provided all students *time to think* and *opportunity to respond.* TPS consists of three steps:

- *Step 1, **Thinking**:* The teacher poses a question or issue and asks students to spend a few minutes thinking by themselves.
- *Step 2, **Pairing**:* Next, students are asked to pair with another student and discuss what they have been thinking about. Four or five minutes are normally allocated for this step.
- *Step 3, **Sharing**:* Pairs of students are then asked to share what they have been discussing with the whole class. They are asked to report not only the content of the discussion but also about the way they have been thinking.

See–Think–Wonder. This routine is also comprised of three steps and each step requires a different type of cognitive behavior as students respond to particular questions:

- *Step 1: What Do You See?* This step requires students to observe the phenomena under investigation, to identify parts and dimensions, and to look for connections.
- *Step 2: What Do You Think About That?* This step asks students to construct evidence-based interpretations and to synthesize and draw conclusions.
- *Step 3: What Do You Wonder About?* This step requires students to ask questions, reflect on their learning, and perhaps create novel ideas and metaphors.

An array of similar routines (over 30) has been developed or adapted for the Visible Thinking Program. Some of these we have summarized and listed in Figure 10.6.

Each step in a thinking routine calls for students to perform certain cognitive behaviors. The developers of the Visible Thinking Program have done analyses of all the routines they have created. Table 10.5 provides examples of cognitive behaviors result-ing from using the See–Think–Wonder routine.

Ritchhart et al. (2006, p. 10) pointed out that, "taken together, these epistemic moves characterize a process-oriented conception of thinking that emphasizes critical think-ing, creative elaboration, and reflection." When used over time, thinking routines help students develop patterns of thinking that become, as the name implies, *routine.*

Artful Thinking Program
An adaptation of the Visible Thinking Program has been developed under the auspices of Project Zero in collaboration with the Traverse City and the Michigan Area Public

CLAIM–SUPPORT–QUESTION
1. Make a claim about a topic
2. Identify support for your claim
3. Ask a question related to your claim

CONNECT–EXTEND–CHALLENGE
1. How are the ideas and information connected to what you already know?
2. What new ideas did you get that extend your thinking in a new direction?
3. What is still challenging or confusing for you? What questions or puzzles do you now have?

LOOKING: 10 × 2
1. Look at an image or artifact quietly for at least 30 seconds. Let your eyes wander.
2. List ten words or phrases about any aspect of it.
3. Repeat Steps 1 and 2: Look at the image or artifact again and try to add *ten* more words or phrases to your list.

PERCEIVE–KNOW–CARE ABOUT
1. What can the person or thing perceive?
2. What might the person or thing know about?
3. What might the person or thing care about?

THINK–PUZZLE–EXPLORE
1. What do you think you know about this topic?
2. What questions or puzzles do you have?
3. What does the topic make you want to explore?

HEADLINES
1. If you were to write a headline for this topic or issue that captures the most important aspect to keep in mind, what would that headline be?

WHAT MAKES YOU SAY THAT?
1. What's going on here?
2. What do you see that makes you say that?

Figure 10.6 Sample thinking routines from the Visible Thinking Program
Source: Summarized from Ritchhart et al. (2006).

Table 10.5 Examples of cognitive behaviors used in the See–Think–Wonder routine

Steps in the routine	Broad types of cognitive behaviour
What do you see?	• Generates lots of ideas • Gives evidence and explanations
What do you think about that?	• Looks for comparisons and connections • Constructs reason-based syntheses, summaries, and conclusions • Constructs evidence-based interpretations and explanations • Makes discernments and evaluations • Identifies parts, components, dimensions
What do you wonder about?	• Asks questions • Identifies and explores multiple perspectives • Creates metaphors • Reflects on and consolidates learning

Source: Information based on Ritchhart et al. (2006), p. 10.

Schools. The Artful Thinking Program helps teachers use works from the visual arts and music in ways that will enhance student thinking. According to Tishman and Palmer (2006), the program starts with the premise that "works of art are good things to think about," and then focuses on five thinking dispositions relevant to the arts:

- questioning and investigating,
- observing and describing,
- reasoning and exploring viewpoints,
- comparing and connecting,
- finding complexity.

The Artful Thinking Program has also developed a number of thinking routines, some adapted from the Visible Thinking Program, such as "What do you see?", "What do you think about this?" and "What does it make you wonder?" Other routines have been created specifically for the arts, such as the *Claim/Support/Question* routine:

- Make a claim about the artwork or topic.
- Identify support for your claim.
- Ask a question related to your claim.

Or, the *Perspective Taking-centered* routine:

- Perceive/know/care about.
- Circle viewpoints.

Thinking routines, as used in the Visible Thinking Program and the Artful Thinking Program, are straightforward and for the most part quite easy for teachers to use and for students to understand. Sometimes, however, particular routines can at first be confusing. For instance, Think–Pair–Share requires a new set of discourse behaviors as contrasted to those found in more traditional whole-class recitation discussions. These new behaviors may be discrepant at the beginning, but they are important for students to learn. In summary, thinking routines help make thinking visible and are important tools for teaching students how to think.

de Bono's Six Thinking Hats Program

The final stand-alone program we have chosen to describe is de Bono's Six Thinking Hats Program. Compared to the Visible Thinking Program, the approaches and tools developed by de Bono put more emphasis on thinking styles as contrasted to thinking skills or dispositions, and on the creative aspect of thinking as compared to the more rational, analytical aspects of thinking. He also was one of the first to suggest the use of direct instruction to teach thinking (de Bono, 1983).

De Bono makes distinctions between two major types of thinking—**vertical thinking** and lateral thinking. Vertical thinking (also called linear thinking) is the approach based mainly on logic and reasoning. **Lateral thinking**, on the other hand, is thinking that calls for the use of imagination, creativity, and "thinking outside the box." De Bono, as well as others (Lozano, 2001), believes that people are prone to think in different ways and has identified six ways (or states) of thinking and incorporated them into his Six

> **REFLECTION**
>
> With a classmate or colleague, discuss the idea of thinking styles. In your teaching have you found some students who lean more toward the logical? The emotional? How are the two styles different? Do some students possess both styles of thinking? What factors do you think determine thinking styles? How does all of this influence the ways you approach teaching students how to think?

Thinking Hats Program (1986). This program has been used quite widely in schools as well, as in training programs aimed at helping adults solve problems and make more effective decisions. Each of de Bono's six hats is depicted with a color. The color is a symbol or metaphor that represents each style of thinking: information, logic, emotion, caution, creativity, optimism, and metacognition. Figure 10.7 illustrates the six hats and describes the kind of thinking each represents in a simplified fashion. We encourage readers to go directly to de Bono's work for a more thorough explanation.

Students in the Thinking Hats Program are taught that we all approach problem situations in different ways. Some of us are more logical in our approach, whereas others may rely more on intuition or emotion. Some of us are prone to bringing negative judgments to a problem situation; others may be more positive. The aim of the Six Thinking Hats Program is for students to identify the thinking style they are using, experiment with different styles, and in some instances seek a better balance between various approaches, such as the logical and the emotional or the positive and the negative. This is accomplished by providing students with a problem situation and having them analyze it and then discuss which kinds of thinking they were employing.

ASSESSING THINKING DISPOSITIONS AND SKILLS

For thinking skills programs to be successful requires different types of assessment and evaluation procedures than those normally used. Assessments must go beyond testing students for factual or conceptual knowledge, beyond the cognitive process of remembering and understanding, and include the higher-order processes of analyzing, evaluating, and creating. They must be focused on assessing complex understandings and, most importantly, on assessing thinking skills and dispositions themselves.

Student projects, portfolio artifacts, and on-demand performance tasks (described in Chapter 6) to assess performance are those methods most appropriate for measuring important thinking skills and cognitive processes. Students can be asked to demonstrate their abilities to think through a wide range of authentic performances. Similarly, the conceptual webs and mind maps, students create can also be used to provide insight into their thinking processes and for assessment purposes.

To find out how well students can apply the thinking skills we have taught them requires that we ask them to perform the skills or processes and to explain what they are doing. Beyer (2001a) has suggested an assessment format consisting of three basic elements:

- Assess basic knowledge of the skill—its meaning and what it looks like when someone is doing it.
- Assess expertise in performing the skill.

Type of hat	Thinking the hat represents
White hat represents information	Thinking that attends to information such as sharing ideas or using statistics.
Red hat represents feelings	Thinking that is based on feelings and emotions —thoughts based on intuition.
Black hat represents caution	Thinking that explains why something might not work and assesses and shows up weaknesses.
Green hat represents creativity	Thinking that explores alternatives and looks "outside the box."
Blue hat represents metacognition	Thinking about one's own thinking and alerts one to one's own confusion.
Yellow hat represents logic	Thinking that helps determine the value, accuracy and/or benefits of an idea or action.

Figure 10.7 de Bono's Six Thinking Hats
Source: Initial idea came from Bennett and Rolheiser (2001), p. 330 and their interpretation of de Bono's work.

- Assess metacognitive understanding about how and why a skill is performed.

Finally, students need to be taught and encouraged to assess their own thinking by responding to questions such as: "What strategy did I use in the problem solving situation?", "In completing this project, how did the plan I developed help?" and "What went wrong and why?"

SUMMARY AT A GLANCE

- Teaching students how to think is among the most important goals in education. However, considerable differences of opinion exist concerning exactly what kinds of thinking should be taught and the best ways to teach thinking skills and dispositions.

- A variety of types of thinking have been identified. Among the most important are: basic- and higher-level thinking, convergent and divergent thinking, critical thinking, creative thinking, and scientific reasoning.

- An important aspect of thinking consists of the cognitive processes used in thinking. Bloom and his colleagues have provided a model for classifying thinking processes and for showing their relationships to various kinds of knowledge.

- Perhaps the highest level of thinking is "thinking about thinking" or metacognition. Students must be taught metacognitive skills and dispositions, just as they are taught other kinds of thinking skills and dispositions.

- Some believe that students can best be taught how to think with programs and tools that aim directly at the development of specific skills and dispositions. Others believe that thinking needs to be taught in the context of specific subject areas and disciplines.

- The Visible Thinking and Artful Thinking Programs rest on a set of beliefs that the teaching of thinking must be made more visible and that educators should pay attention not only to the students' abilities to think but also, more importantly, to the dispositions they hold about thinking.

- The strategy of using "thinking routines" helps make thinking visible and provides scaffolds for supporting thinking. Thinking routines can be used across the curriculum and work best in classrooms that focus on thinking and that have discourse and dialogue patterns that demonstrate to students the importance of thinking.

- De Bono's Six Thinking Hats Program emphasizes lateral thinking and provides practice opportunities for students to reflect on how they solve problems and make decisions.

CONSTRUCTING YOUR OWN LEARNING

Working alone or with a colleague, make an inventory of the various kinds of practice you each use in your classroom to teach students how to think. How similar or different are your practices? Do you use mainly practices that aim specifically at teaching particular skills or dispositions? Or, do you rely mainly on infusing the teaching of thinking into content-oriented lessons? Now select one of the strategies for teaching thinking described in this chapter and, with your partner, plan a lesson that you both agree to teach. If possible, observe each other and critique the lesson afterwards.

RESOURCES

Association or Supervision and Curriculum Development (2008). Teaching students to think. *Educational Leadership, 65*(5). A whole issue devoted to teaching students how to think.

Chapman, C. (2008). *Using graphic organizers to develop thinking skills, K-12.* New York: Sage.

Costa, A. (Ed.). (2001). *Developing minds: A resource book for developing teaching thinking* (3rd ed.). Alexandria, VA: Association for Supervision and Curriculum Development.

Ritchhart, R. (2002). *Intellectual character: What it is, why it matters, and how to get it.* San Francisco: Jossey-Bass.

Sternberg, R., Jarvin, L., & Grigorenko, E. (2009). *Teaching for wisdom: Intelligence, creativity and success.* Thousand Oaks, CA: Corwin Press.

Visible Thinking: www.pz.harvard.edu/vt/VisibleThinking_html_files/VisibleThinking1.html.

11

CONCEPT AND INQUIRY-BASED TEACHING

Patricia Seymour is an eighth-grade teacher in an inner suburb of a large East-coast city. Her classroom consists of a diverse student body, with a pretty balanced mix of African American, Puerto Rican, and students whose parents came to the United States from Europe in the late nineteenth century. She teaches in a self-contained classroom that is in a newly designed K-8 elementary school. Today, she is beginning a history lesson that will focus on the "industrial period" of American history. She wants her students to understand this critical period in American history, but she also holds another important goal. She wants them to develop an understanding and appreciation of the role of *primary sources* for interpreting and understanding history.

Ms. Seymour begins her lesson by telling her students that she wants them to be good detectives and figure out (discover) an important concept. She then displays a newsprint chart with two columns and says:

"Class, today I am going to ask you to discover a concept by exploring examples and non-examples of the concept. We will first consider a sequence of examples and non-examples. Then I want you to form tentative hypotheses about what you think the concept might be. Toward the end of the lesson, I will ask you to name and label the concept, check to see how well you understand it, and have you discuss what was going on in your head as you were thinking about the concept as the lesson evolved. Now, focus on the chart I have taped to the chalkboard. In the first column I am writing three examples of the concept. They are _____."

Examples of the concept	
1986 editorial in the *Chicago Times*	
Recording of an interview with Andrew Carnegie	
Teddy Roosevelt's hotel bill	

"Now I am going to provide you with three non-examples of the concept."

Examples of the concept	Non-examples of the concept
	History textbook
	Irish stew
	Chicago, Illinois

"I don't want you to respond yet. Instead *think* for a moment. [Pause] Do you have any ideas or hypotheses about what the concept might be? Are there any attributes or characteristics in the examples that might be important? Is there anything in the non-examples that give you a clue? Now, I am going to add two more examples of the concept and two more non-examples."
[She adds the following examples and non-examples to the chart]
Examples:

- Transcripts of the Rochester town council meeting in 1882.
- Interview with 95-year-old Jessica Bradley, who grew up in upstate New York in the late nineteenth century.

Non-examples:

- Chapter in book about the industrial revolution.
- A contemporary biography of Grover Cleveland.

"Now, I want you to start sharing the ideas and hypotheses you have about the concept. I will record all contributions on the chalkboard."

Ms. Seymour is beginning a concept attainment lesson, a type of lesson with which some of you will be familiar. We included this scenario at the beginning of this chapter because it illustrates nicely the type of lesson that can be used to help students learn not only important content in a subject area, but also to help them learn how to think. We will return to Ms. Seymour's lesson later in the chapter.[1]

This chapter is divided into five major sections. First, we extend the discussion, begun in Chapter 10, about contemporary ideas that guide our perspectives about thinking and teaching about thinking. This is followed by two sections where we explain in some detail how to plan for and execute two specific teaching approaches: concept teaching and inquiry-based teaching. We also extend previous discussions about the kinds of discourse pattern and learning environment that are required in inquiry-oriented classrooms. The chapter concludes with a brief discussion of the difficulties teachers have had over the years in implementing concept and inquiry-based teaching strategies and barriers that must be overcome to achieve success.

PERSPECTIVES AND CONNECTING TO THE CONTEXT AND SCIENCE OF LEARNING

As we described in Chapter 10, most people agree that one of the primary purposes of schooling is to teach students how to think. However, there is considerable disagreement about what is the best way to accomplish this purpose. In this chapter, we extend our discussion about teaching thinking by looking at two specific teaching models—**concept teaching** and **inquiry-based teaching**. Unlike the stand-alone programs described in Chapter 10, both of these models have been developed to be used in particular subject areas (mainly the sciences, the social sciences, history, and literature) for the purpose of helping students develop important conceptual understandings, as well as learning inquiry and higher-level thinking skills. This *infusion* approach is believed to be effective because thinking is contextual and the cognitive processes used to think vary from subject to subject and from problem situation to problem situation.

Today, the dominant perspective on teaching how to inquire and think conceptually stems from cognitive psychology (described in Chapter 2), and, although this perspective has provided the modern rationale for problem solving and inquiry, it actually has a rather long and prestigious history. The Socratic method, still used by many teachers today, dates back to the early Greeks and emphasizes dialogue and inductive reasoning. In the early part of the twentieth century, John Dewey (1916, 1938) described an inquiry, problem-solving approach to teaching using methods not too different from the inquiry methods employed today.

Most contemporary perspectives, however, were influenced by mid-twentieth century educational reformers who wanted to shift the emphasis in classrooms away from knowledge transmission to a renewed priority on inquiry, inductive thinking processes, and conceptual understanding. New curricula were developed first in the sciences (Schwab, 1966), but soon in several other fields. These curricula required students to engage directly in the methods of inquiry, such as observation, data gathering, and hypotheses testing. They gave birth to the inquiry-based teaching model described later in this chapter.

Jerome Bruner (1960, 1961, 1966) and Hilda Taba (1967) developed another model at about the same time that helped students understand the structure and key ideas in particular academic disciplines and provided rich opportunities for invention and discovery. The concept teaching model described in the section that follows owes its intellectual roots mainly to the work of Bruner and Taba.

Concept and inquiry-based teaching consists of *reasoning* and drawing conclusions based on observation and other kinds of evidence and is typically classified into two categories—deductive reasoning and inductive reasoning. **Deductive reasoning** is the process of drawing logical conclusions based on two or more general premises, and goes from the general to the more specific. For example, when you teach your students the law of supply and demand they learn that prices will vary according to the supply of or demand for a particular commodity. An increase in supply or a decrease in demand will produce a price decrease, whereas a decrease in supply or an increase in demand will cause prices to rise. Given these more general premises, students can logically deduce what will happen (if everything else remains the same) to the price of gasoline if suddenly a supplier is eliminated or if refineries cannot produce enough gasoline to satisfy consumer demand.

Inductive reasoning, on the other hand, turns this process upside down, and is defined as a process of drawing conclusions from facts or observations of specific phenomena. This type of reasoning goes from the specific to the more general. Inductive reasoning serves as the foundation for scientific inquiry and research, and includes important processes such as classification, hypothesis testing, making inferences, and drawing conclusions based on valid and reliable evidence. Ms. Seymour's concept attainment lesson we observed at the beginning of the chapter requires students to use inductive reasoning. They are provided specific facts (examples and non-examples) of a particular concept in history (primary source) from which they are expected to make inferences and draw conclusions about the concept, its definition, and its attributes.

Like thinking in general, everyone engages in reasoning. We do not necessarily, however, reason effectively. Students need to be taught to reason not only in the more formal aspects of academic science, but also in all aspects of everyday life. They must be taught to avoid making hasty or fallacious generalizations. They must be taught to remain open and aware of context in inquiry and problem situations because inferences and generalizations made at one time may be disconfirmed later. Concept attainment and inquiry-based teaching emphasize teaching reasoning skills and dispositions, particularly those associated with inquiry in a number of school subjects as well as out-of-school situations.

> **REFLECTION**
>
> With a classmate or colleague, discuss the types of fallacious reasoning you observe most often in your students. How do you explain this? How do you combat fallacious reasoning? How are the approaches each of you use to teach reasoning the same? How do they differ?

CONCEPT TEACHING

At the beginning of this chapter we asked you to observe Ms Seymour's eighth-grade U.S. history class as she and her students began a concept attainment lesson on *primary sources*. Concept teaching strategies were developed to assist students to attain and form conceptual understandings and to practice particular kinds of thinking and reasoning. They were not designed to transmit large amounts of declarative knowledge, but instead to help students construct conceptual knowledge on their own and to engage in cognitive processes associated with higher-level thinking. There are several approaches to teaching concepts. We have selected two approaches to highlight here: the **concept attainment approach** and the **direct presentation approach**. Before we get into the specifics of these two approaches and continue our observation of Ms. Seymour's lesson, we need to consider first some ideas about the nature and characteristics of concepts.

Nature of Concepts

Most learning theorists consider **concepts** as the basic building blocks for higher-level thinking and the foundation on which human communication and understanding rests. Concepts are *mental abstractions or categories* we hold about objects, people, and ideas. A key aspect of teaching concepts is to help students understand the nature of particular concepts. Common examples of concepts include latitude and longitude, relativity, mass, even numbers, widows, mammals, expository text, and so on.

Concepts have *definitions*. For example, a widow is a woman who has been married but her husband has died. A *widow* differs from a woman who has been married but is now divorced. *Latitude* is the angular distance of a location north and south of the equator and it differs from the concept of *longitude*, which identifies the east or west location of the meridian at Greenwich, England. *Expository text* explains something by definition, sequence, categorization, comparison, or contrast and it differs from *narrative text* that contains themes, plot, setting, and character. Definitions and labels for concepts are important for teaching them; however, they are human inventions. Knowing a definition of a concept does not necessarily mean that students have a real understanding of the concept.

Concepts also vary in their nature, or what some have labeled their *rule structure*. For example, some concepts can be described precisely; they have constant rule structures. The concepts of island (a land mass surrounded by water) and triangle (closed figure with three sides and three angles) are example of concepts with constant rule structures. Other concepts, however, have more flexible rule structures where context and relationships influence the definition. For instance, the concepts of poverty, literacy, or a car's boot differ from one social context to another. Poverty means something quite different in Cambodia or Laos as compared to poverty in the United States or Italy. What Americans refer to as a car's trunk is called a boot in England. Endless examples could be given of concepts that have flexible rule structures influenced by context.

Concepts have attributes that help define them. **Concept attributes** are important to highlight for students because these are what lead students to understand or misunderstand them. Some of the attributes are critical and necessary; others are non-critical. A bird as a concept is a good example to illustrate the differences between critical and non-critical attributes. Two critical attributes of birds include having feathers and being warm-blooded. If either of these attributes is missing you don't have a bird. The colors of a bird's feathers or being able to fly are non-critical attributes. One of the difficulties in teaching many concepts, according to Ashcraft (2006), is that students carry around in their minds "prototypes" or "characteristic features" about them. For instance, many students associate birds with flying because most birds fly. They may not know or have forgotten about penguins, birds that cannot fly. Other concepts, however, do not have clear prototypes. For example, what prototype do you have for dogs, cats, cars? It is likely that individuals will differ significantly, and no one kind of dog, cat, or car will be typical for all of us.

Finally, concepts are learned through *examples* and *non-examples*. These elements, in essence, help define the concept and clarify its boundaries. We began the chapter by considering the way examples and non-examples were used in Ms. Seymour's history lesson that aimed at defining and understanding the concept of primary sources.

> **REFLECTION**
>
> What difficulties have you experienced when teaching concepts to students? What have you found to be effective strategies to get students to focus on critical attributes? Do you have a particular strategy to help them move beyond treating a concept simply as a vocabulary word to be defined?

Planning for Concept Teaching

The three goals for concept teaching are listed in Figure 11.1, and below we describe how to go about planning for a concept lesson.

Identifying particular concepts to teach is a critical first step in planning for a concept lesson. Accomplished teachers know that there are literally thousands of concepts that might be the focus of a lesson. However, as we described in Chapter 4, it is important to establish priorities that focus on concepts that are important to know and those that lead to "enduring understandings." Obviously, the students' developmental level of understanding is also an important factor in concept selection. Teaching the concept of *relativity* to second graders would be beyond their grasp, while teaching the

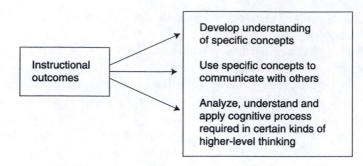

Figure 11.1 Instructional outcomes for concept teaching

concept of triangles to most eleventh graders would be insulting. Strategies previously described for listening to students and checking for understanding are the best means to make sure a particular concept will be appropriate. The key to a successful lesson is helping students link the new concept with concepts they already know.

Curriculum standards and frameworks are good sources for selecting concepts to teach; however, remember our discussion in Chapter 4 about the unrealistic number of concepts that are included in many frameworks. Be careful also because, sometimes, key concepts associated with a topic will be listed as vocabulary words to learn. Getting students to define a new word, however, is not the same as helping them understand it conceptually. Teachers need to decide which concepts to select and which can be viewed as vocabulary words.

The next planning steps consist of analyzing concepts and choosing appropriate examples and non-examples. Concept analysis consists of writing a precise definition of the concept and of identifying the concept's critical attributes. Paying attention to the critical attributes is of particular importance, as is considering the non-critical attributes. As described earlier, pointing out that penguins can't fly but many insects can, illustrates that the attribute of flight present in most birds is not sufficient to define a bird.

Graphic organizers and conceptual webs, described in previous chapters, can be helpful tools for analyzing concepts. When using a **conceptual web**, the concept's name can be placed in the center of the web and then have strands branching out showing the concept's critical attributes. Strands that tie the branches together are also useful for showing relationships among the attributes. Figure 11.2 is a graphic organizer of the concept of primary sources. The graphic organizer is not intended as something to give students. Its aim is to help us develop our own understanding of the concept and its attributes.

Third, examples and non-examples of the concept need to be selected and decisions must be made about how the examples are to be sequenced and used in the lesson. Below are three rules for doing this, paraphrased from Tennyson and Park (1980) and Sternberg and Williams (2002):

- *Rule 1*: Select examples that are as different from one another as possible. For instance, a science teacher teaching *stars* as a concept might include examples of both new and old stars. Or, if teaching the concept of *insect*, the teacher might choose water bugs and ants; both are insects, but they live in very different environments.

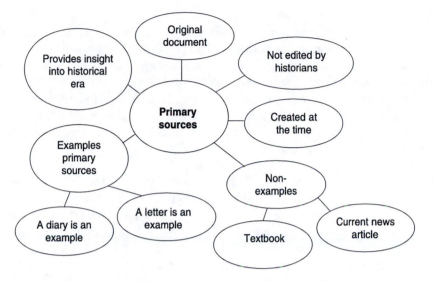

Figure 11.2 Conceptual web for primary sources

- *Rule 2*: Compare and contrast examples and non-examples. Examples of objects in space that are not stars include planets, our moon, and meteors. Examples of states in the United States that are not bordered by oceans include Iowa, Tennessee, and Montana.
- *Rule 3*: Present the easiest and most familiar examples first, in order from the easiest and most familiar to the most difficult and least familiar. Typical examples are likely to be the easiest for students to understand. For example, a science teacher presenting examples of stars might discuss the North Star before mentioning that our sun is also a star. Or, in Ms. Seymour's lesson on primary sources a newspaper article might be presented first because it is commonly known as a primary history source.

Concept analysis and selecting examples and non-examples may be the most important, and often the most difficult, planning task associated with concept teaching.

The final decision in the planning phase for a concept lesson is choosing a particular approach to use. Two approaches are described here. The *direct presentation* approach (Tennyson & Cocchiarella, 1986) consists of the teacher defining and demonstrating a particular concept, providing students with examples and non-examples of the concept, and then providing opportunities to practice. The *concept attainment* approach (Bruner, Goodnow, & Austin, 1956; Taba, 1967) turns this process around and begins with providing students with examples and non-examples of the concept and then, through the process of inductive reasoning, helps students discover and define the concept themselves. Decisions about which approach to use depend on the goals teachers hold for the lesson, the nature of the concept to be taught, and their students. Direct presentation is normally best for concepts of which students have very little or no understanding. Concept attainment, on the other hand, works best if students have relevant prior knowledge related to the concept and/or when the teaching of reasoning and thinking processes take precedent over the concept itself. Both of these approaches are described in more detail in the next section.

Executing Concept Lessons

In this section, we describe actions teachers take at each phase of a concept teaching lesson. We provide the phases for both the concept attainment and the direct presentation approach. The overall flow of the two approaches is essentially the same, although they also vary in some important ways, as illustrated in Figure 11.3.

As can be observed, the two approaches, though similar, differ significantly in phases two and three. Concept attainment has students discover and name the concept through inductive reasoning; direct presentation provides students with the name and definition of the concept at the beginning.

Gain Attention, Explain Goals, and Outline Overall Flow of the Lesson As with most lessons, the teacher begins by gaining students' attention and explaining clearly the purposes of the lesson and how it will proceed. Teachers strive to connect the current lesson to what students already know. If students have had little experience with the concept teaching model, the overall flow of the lesson will need to be explained in some detail, as well as what will be expected of them during each phase of the lesson. A brief explanation will be sufficient for students who have previously experienced this approach. The next two phases vary depending on whether the teacher is using the concept attainment or direct presentation approach. We will provide an example of a concept attainment approach and then compare it to the direct presentation approach.

Provide Examples and Non-examples and Name the Concept The *way* examples and non-examples are provided and sequenced and *when* the concept is named are the defining features of a concept attainment lesson, as contrasted to a direct presentation lesson. In the opening scenario, you saw how Ms. Seymour gained students' attention and provided and sequenced examples and non-examples for her concept attainment lesson. She chose this approach because her students had some knowledge about the industrial revolution and about the use of primary sources in history.

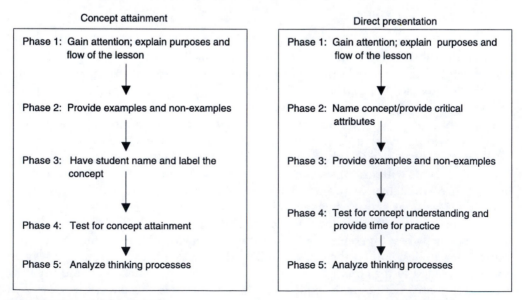

Concept attainment

Phase 1: Gain attention; explain purposes and flow of the lesson

Phase 2: Provide examples and non-examples

Phase 3: Have student name and label the concept

Phase 4: Test for concept attainment

Phase 5: Analyze thinking processes

Direct presentation

Phase 1: Gain attention; explain purposes and flow of the lesson

Phase 2: Name concept/provide critical attributes

Phase 3: Provide examples and non-examples

Phase 4: Test for concept understanding and provide time for practice

Phase 5: Analyze thinking processes

Figure 11.3 Phases of concept teaching

Test for Concept Attainment After students have attained and labeled the concept, the fourth phase of the lesson tests their understanding by providing more examples and non-examples and by asking students themselves to provide their own examples of the concept.

Now let's observe how Ms. Seymour executes these three phases of her lesson on primary sources. Unlike in previous chapters, we have put our sample lesson here in a table format, so the dialogue of both the teacher and the students can be observed along with our commentary.

Phases 2–3 of the concept attainment lesson

Ms. Seymour's directions, dialogue, and questions	Students' responses	Our comments
Phase 2: Examples and non-examples (continued from opening scenario). Ms. Seymour urges students to hypothesize about the concept and its attributes.		
"Now that you have had an opportunity to think about the examples and non-examples, what hypotheses do you have about the concept?"	Students provide the following ideas: • Written things • Human events • Important clues	Teachers need to be patient during this phase. It may take some time.
"What characteristics seem to be important about the ideas you are giving me?"		When some students come up with the concept, the teachers should *not* stop and say, "that's right." Instead, record it and continue accepting other ideas.
Ultimately a student comes up with the concept of primary sources.	I think all of the "yes" examples have to do with sources we use to write history.	
Phase 3: Name the concept. Ms. Seymour now asks students to label the concept, e.g., "What kind of name might we use to describe the concept?"		
If someone comes up with primary sources, then Ms. Seymour may say, "Yes, that is the concept I had in mind." If they have the idea, but the incorrect label, Ms. Seymour may say, "All of your ideas are correct; however, the label historians provide is primary sources."	Students may say: • history sources • oral sources • written sources, etc.	Students should be provided with ample time to think about naming the concept. On the other hand, this phase should not become a *guessing game* that goes on and on.

Phase 4 of the concept attainment lesson

Ms. Seymour's directions, dialogue, and questions	Students' responses	Our comments
Phase 4: Test for concept attainment. "To see how well you understand the concept, I am going to provide you with additional examples and non-examples and you tell me yes or no."		
• 1870 and 1890 map of New York City	That is an example.	
• A history of New York 1870–1890	That is a non-example.	
"OK, now I want you to provide me some examples of the concept that we haven't yet considered."	Students provide additional examples. • Letters from Grover Cleveland to his wife • William Jennings' diary	Teachers should try to get as many students as possible to participate during this phase of the lesson and not rely on the answers of a few to test for understanding.
Ms. Seymour concludes this phase by asking, "If someone comes into this classroom 200 years from now, what examples of primary sources might they find?	Some examples might include: notes left on the chalkboard; the teacher's grade book; a student's journal.	

Now let's turn and observe how Ms. Seymour might teach the same concept using the direct presentation approach. You will note that she begins the lesson the same way, but the way examples and non-examples are provided and the ways the concept is defined and labeled are quite different.

Phases 1–4 of the direct presentation lesson

Ms. Seymour's directions, dialogue, and questions	Students' responses	Our comments
Phase 1: Gain attention and explain flow. "Today, we are going to learn a new concept in history called primary sources." Ms Seymour writes the phrase "primary source" on the chalkboard.		

Ms. Seymour's directions, dialogue, and questions	Students' responses	Our comments
Phase 2: Name the concept and provide critical attributes. "Most people define a primary source as a document, recording, or other information source such as a diary that was created during the historical period under investigation." "The critical attributes of a primary source are: • It provides unmediated information about some historical object of study. • It is a source created at the time period under investigation or by someone who has first-hand information of the time period. "Primary sources can be contrasted to secondary sources that are historical conclusions or interpretations based on primary sources."	Students are listening to Ms. Seymour.	Note that using this approach the teacher is presenting information about the concept using strategies described in Chapter 7.
Phase 3: Provide examples and non-examples. "Here are some examples and non-examples of primary sources. If you want additional information, feel free to ask questions as I go along." Ms. Seymour: • Shows students an old newspaper and says this is an example of a primary source. • Holds up an old history textbook and says, "This is a non-example." • Shows students Teddy Roosevelt's hotel bill and, says, "Here is another example of a primary source." • Shows a third example, perhaps a diary written by an industrialist.	Students listen, but can ask questions I don't understand the differences between a textbook and a diary. They are both books, aren't they? What could historians learn from a hotel bill? I'm confused.	The lesson remains teacher-directed, although students are encouraged to ask questions.

Ms. Seymour's directions, dialogue, and questions	Students' responses	Our comments
Phase 4: Test for concept understanding and provide practice. Ms. Seymour now shows examples and non-examples of the concept and gets students to make judgments about whether they are examples or non-examples. She asks students to say why or why not. She also has students come up with their own examples and non-examples.	Students make yes or no responses and defend their decisions.	This phase is very similar to the "test for attainment phase" used in the concept attainment approach.

Analyzing Thinking Processes The final phase of a concept lesson, regardless of the approach, provides opportunities for students to analyze their thinking processes and to integrate their newly acquired conceptual information. Teachers ask students to think back over the different phases of the lesson and to consider what they were thinking. Questions to pose during this final phase might include: How did you focus on the concept? When did you first understand the critical attributes associated with the concept? When did you first figure out (for concept attainment) the concept? How? Why? How did the non-critical attributes help you understand (discover) the concept? How does the concept relate to other concepts you know about. For developing thinking skills and dispositions, this phase of a concept lesson is critical; it not only helps students integrate new ideas into their existing conceptual frameworks, but also expands their metacognitive abilities.

Both concept and inquiry-based teaching methods rest on constructivist principles of learning. These principles contend that meaningful learning occurs when learners are provided opportunities to select relevant incoming knowledge, to construct it in a way that makes sense to them, and to integrate new knowledge with knowledge they already have. A persistent question relating to using constructivist approaches such as concept and inquiry-based teaching concerns how much guidance or structure teachers should provide. As you just observed in the concept teaching lessons, the concept attainment approach provided much less structure than did the direct presentation approach. Within either approach the teacher could decide to provide more or less guidance by encouraging students to speculate or by asking more focused guiding questions. Fortunately, we have some research evi-

REFLECTION

What has been your experience with how much structure and guidance to provide students when you are attempting to get them to inquire and discover on their own? How do you come down on the issues raised by Mayer and by Kirschner et al.? Compare your opinions to those of a classmate or colleague.

dence that can provide guidance for teachers on this matter, as summarized in Research Box 11.1.

Although Meyer in Research Box 11.1 takes a somewhat balanced approach in regard to the amount of guidance to provide, others are more negative. Kirschner, Sweller, and Clark (2006), for instance, argue that controlled studies "almost uniformly support direct, strong instructional guidance than constructivist-based minimal guidance

---

(Inquiry) **RESEARCH BOX 11.1**

Meyer, R. (2004). Should there be a three-strike rule against discovery learning? A case for guided methods of instruction. *American Psychologist, 59*, 14–19.

In 2004, Richard Meyer summarized the results of over 30 years of research on discovery learning and guided instruction. He reviewed the literatures in three different areas: problem solving, discovery, and forms of discovery associated with computer programming. These literatures covered the decades beginning in the 1950s and extending through the 1990s. Meyer, although he agreed with constructivist instructional methods, was prompted to conduct this review because he believed advocates were putting too much emphasis on discovery and hands-on learning in which "student are free to work in a learning environment with little or no guidance." (p. 14). He focused on studies that compared what he labeled "pure discovery," in which students were given maximum freedom to explore, to those that used "guided discovery," characterized by more structure provided by teachers and systematic guidance toward specific learning objectives.

According to Meyer, two important and consistent findings emerged from these studies. We paraphrase these below:

- Some students do not learn the "rule," "concept," or "principle" involved under pure discovery methods. An appropriate amount of guidance appears to be required.
- Students learn better when they are active but their activity requires guidance in a productive direction.

Meyer makes the point that studies do not negate the importance of constructivist principles, active learning, and freedom to explore and inquire. However, too much freedom fails to help students select relevant incoming information. It is possible that, "they may fail to come into contact with the to-be-learned material" (p. 17). Too much freedom can also prevent the kind of cognitive processing needed for discovery and integration of learning. Of course, a critical question for teachers is to know when and how much guidance to provide. Meyer's answer to that question is, "*Students need enough freedom to become cognitively active in the process of sense making, and students need enough guidance so that their cognitive activity results in the construction of useful knowledge*" (p. 16; italic ours).

during the instruction of novice to intermediate learners" (p. 84) and that unguided instruction may lead to student misconceptions. We suspect that the truth lies somewhere in the middle as to the amount of guidance required, and that the prior knowledge and abilities of students are critical variables to consider as teachers plan concept or inquiry-based lessons.

INQUIRY-BASED TEACHING

Whereas concept teaching helps students understand specific concepts and explore particular thinking and reasoning processes, inquiry-based teaching is more broadly conceived to help students develop understanding about the ways the physical and social world works and the processes used to investigate it. As described earlier, the model owes much of its intellectual roots initially to John Dewey (1916, 1938) and, more recently, to the designers of the curriculum reform movements of the 1950s and 1960s. First in mathematics and the sciences (Schwab, 1966), but later in the social sciences and humanities (Beyer, 1979; Fenton, 1966), these designers developed curricula aimed at accomplishing two goals. One, curriculum that would be built around the basic ideas and structures of knowledge in particular academic disciplines, and two, a curriculum that would provide students with opportunities to practice the *methods of inquiry* used to discover new knowledge in these disciplines.

Goals aimed at developing thinking skills associated with scientific inquiry, particularly the use of data to test hypotheses and to make sound inferences and generalizations, are at the heart of inquiry-based teaching. Bruner's (1960, 1961) discovery learning emphasized inquiry and active student involvement that would lead to personal discovery and understanding. Suchman (1962) provided a slightly different approach, one that emphasized the tentativeness of knowledge in all scientific investigation. He introduced the "discrepant event" or "puzzling situation" that he believed motivated students to inquire. Many current curricula have been designed to incorporate inquiry-based teaching. Some aspects of problem-based learning described in Chapter 14 have also grown out of this tradition.

Planning for an Inquiry-based Lesson

The major planning tasks associated with an inquiry lesson consist of deciding on the primary goals of the lesson and identifying important and motivational problems for inquiry. Grounded in cognitive theories of learning, inquiry-based teaching aims to accomplish both content and process goals. In most inquiry lessons there is new knowledge to be acquired. Mastery of new knowledge, however, is not the primary learner outcome. Instead, students are expected to construct their own understandings, to test their own knowledge, and to learn inquiry strategies. In Figure 11.4 we provide a list of instructional outcomes most often associated with inquiry-based teaching.

A second major planning task consists of identifying a problem or question for inquiry. Richards Suchman (1962) argued that the problem should be presented in the form of a **discrepant event** or puzzling situation because discrepancy and puzzlement spark our curiosity and motivate us to inquire. A "**mystery spot**" is another label that has been used to describe these puzzling situations. A classic example of one of Suchman's inquiry lessons with a discrepant event is described below:

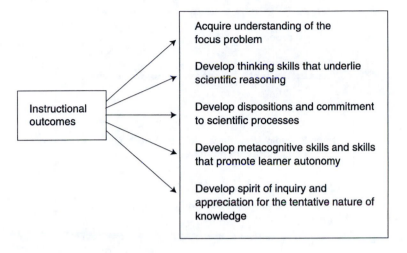

Figure 11.4 Instructional outcomes for inquiry lessons

The teacher holds up a pulse glass. The pulse glass consists of two small globes connected by a glass tube. It is partially filled with a red liquid. When the teacher holds one hand over the right bulb, the red liquid begins to bubble and move to the other side. If the teacher holds one hand over the left bulb, the red liquid continues to bubble but moves to the other side.

The teacher asks students, "Why does the red liquid move?"

As students seek answers to this question, the teacher encourages them to ask for data about the pulse glass and the moving liquid, to generate hypotheses or theories that help explain the red liquid's movement, and to think of ways they can test their ideas.

Magnusson and Palincsar (1995) provide slightly different criteria to guide selection of an inquiry problem. They say it should be:

1. Conceptually rich with regard to opportunities it provides for meaningful inquiry [that will] yield understanding of enduring value.
2. Flexible with regard to developmental issues.
3. Relevant to the lives of children so that it [is] both accessible and interesting . . ." (p. 45).

Their inquiry problems are not necessarily discrepant events, but they are puzzling enough to motivate inquiry. They provide examples such as: How do animals communicate? How do whales communicate? How do gorillas communicate?

Curriculum guides, textbooks, websites and state frameworks are all good sources for finding inquiry problems and topics. Our own understanding of the subject we teach and the lives of our students, however, are perhaps the best sources for finding problem situations to use to focus an inquiry lesson.

Executing an Inquiry-based Lesson

There are numerous variations of inquiry-based teaching. However, most have a syntax that can be divided into six phases, beginning with an explanation of the inquiry

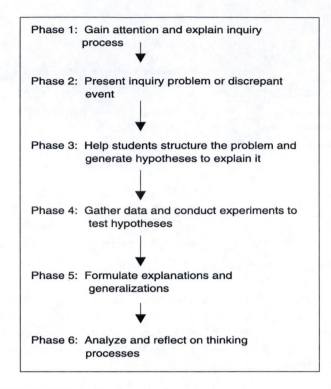

Phase 1: Gain attention and explain inquiry process

Phase 2: Present inquiry problem or discrepant event

Phase 3: Help students structure the problem and generate hypotheses to explain it

Phase 4: Gather data and conduct experiments to test hypotheses

Phase 5: Formulate explanations and generalizations

Phase 6: Analyze and reflect on thinking processes

Figure 11.5 Phases of an inquiry lesson

process and presentation of the problem for investigation. The process concludes with steps that help students generate and test hypotheses and draw valid conclusions. These phases are listed in Figure 11.5.

There are other syntaxes for inquiry lessons that are slightly different than the one we propose in Figure 11.5. We have provided two of these for comparison purposes in Table 11.1. The *BSCS 5E Instructional Model* (BSCS Center, 2009), in the first column, consists of five phases, beginning with engagement and ending with student evaluation of their explanations and elaborations. The Magnusson and Palincsar (1995) **guided inquiry** approach, in the second column, consists of six phases and includes in the final phase opportunities for students to re-engage.

Table 11.1 Two other examples of phases of inquiry lessons

BSCS 5E Instructional Model	Magnusson and Palincsar's Guided Inquiry
Phase 1: Engagement	Phase 1: Engagement
Phase 2: Exploration	Phase 2: Investigation
Phase 3: Explanation	Phase 3: Describe relationships
Phase 4: Elaboration	Phase 4: Construct/review explanations
Phase 5: Evaluation	Phase 5: Report findings
	Phase 6: Evaluate explanation and re-engage

We find the sixth phase of the Magnusson and Palincsar approach particularly interesting because, in contrast to our more linear view, it recognizes the cyclical nature of the inquiry process. Some of the phases have more than one path, requiring inquirers to re-engage and pursue further inquiry. Below are more detailed descriptions of the six phases of our approach.

Gain Attention and Explain Inquiry Process As with any lesson, students' attention must be acquired at the beginning. When teachers are using inquiry-based methods for the first time, students need to be told that one important goal of the lesson is to learn skills associated with the processes of inquiry. They also need to understand the overall flow of the lesson.

Present Inquiry Problem or Discrepant Event Regardless of the particular approach, all inquiry lessons present students with a problem to explore and explain. As described earlier, good inquiry problems are: conceptually rich, puzzling, developmentally appropriate, and relevant to the lives of students.

Now let's turn to Mr. Foreman, who teaches down the hall from Ms. Seymour. This time we will observe a science lesson rather than history, and we will find students involved in a unit on motion, direction, and speed. Mr. Foreman has decided to focus his inquiry lesson on "pendulums," a topic normally taught in upper elementary science classes and one that has quite high interest among students.[2] Here is how he introduced and presented the inquiry problem to his students.

Phases 1–2 of the inquiry lesson

Mr. Foreman's directions, dialogue, and questions	Students' responses	Our comments
Phase 1: Gain attention and explain inquiry process. Mr. Foreman begins the lesson by saying, "For the past several days we have been studying motion. Today, we are going to conduct an experiment using a pendulum. Your job is to participate in the experiment and come up with ideas about why pendulums swing as they do."		Mr. Foreman begins this lesson by drawing students' attention to what they have been studying over the past few days. This is in an effort to connect to prior knowledge and to set the stage for the upcoming inquiry.
Phase 2: *Present inquiry problem or discrepant event.* "I want you to get into your learning groups. After the materials manager gets your supplies, I want each group to: (1) construct a washer pendulum, (2) hang the pendulum so that it swings freely from a pencil taped to the surface		For science lessons, Mr. Foreman has students organized into semi-permanent learning groups with assigned roles.

Mr. Foreman's directions, dialogue, and questions	Students' responses	Our comments
of the desk, and (3) count the number of swings of the pendulum in 15 seconds. I want the note-taker in each group to record the results in the chart I have placed in the front of the room."		For science lessons, Mr. Foreman has students organized into semi-permanent learning groups with assigned roles. In this lesson, Mr. Foreman is presenting the inquiry focus in the form of an activity. Students are asked to conduct an experiment that will produce discrepant data.

Help Students Structure the Problem and Generate Hypotheses to Explain It During the third phase of an inquiry lesson students are encouraged to ask questions, generate hypotheses, seek information, and begin formulating explanations.

Gather Data and Conduct Experiments to Test Hypotheses At some point in an inquiry lesson, the teacher asks students for ways to gather data to test their ideas and hypotheses.

Formulate Explanations and Generalizations After students have had sufficient time to gather information, and to plan and conduct experiments, it is time to bring tentative closure to the lesson by encouraging them to formulate explanations and generalizations. As with previous phases, free exchange of ideas should be supported and rival conclusions considered carefully. Questions to guide this aspect of the inquiry might include:

- "What additional information might be required to make you more confident in your conclusion?"
- "What if I said ... how would that influence your thinking about your conclusion?"
- "Even though you like your explanation, what others might you propose?"

Now let's observe how Mr. Foreman handled these three phases of his inquiry lesson on pendulums.

Phases 3–5 of the inquiry lesson

Mr. Foreman's dialogue and questions	Students' responses	Our comments
Phase 3: Help students structure the problem and generate hypotheses to explain it. "I notice from the data you have put in the class chart that the number of swings recorded by each group is different. Think about that for a moment."	Students observe that the number of swings recorded by each group is different.	See Table 11.2 (p. 275) for types of question teachers might ask during this phase of the lesson.
Mr. Foreman then asks, "Why do you think this occurred? What hypotheses can you come up with that might explain these data?"	A lively discussion begins about why this happened. Several hypotheses are suggested: length of the string, weight of the washer, diameter of the washer, and so on.	
Phase 4: Gather data and conduct experiments to test hypotheses. Mr. Foreman asks, "What might we do to test some of your hypotheses?"	Students respond that perhaps they should repeat the initial experiment to check if they have counted the seconds and swings correctly. They are working on the "error" hypothesis.

When the second set of data is recorded, it is clear that *error* does not explain the differences. | This is the heart of Mr. Foreman's inquiry lesson. Here, students complete their experiment a second time, get the same results, and conclude that they have to isolate particular variables to reach a sound conclusion. |
| "So what do you think? How can the differences be explained?" | Again, students discuss why the results are different and speculate about the length of the string, the weight of the washer, and how high the pendulum was held prior to starting the washer's swing. | |
| As each statement or hypothesis is made, Mr. Foreman writes it on the chalkboard. | Students suggest that they conduct several experiments to test the various hypotheses:
• Vary string length
• Vary washer weight
• Vary starting place
Each group then conducts a new experiment to test one of the hypotheses that has been generated. | |

Ms. Seymour's directions, dialogue, and questions	Students' responses	Our comments
Phase 5: Formulate explanations and generalizations (the following day). Mr. Foreman continues to probe and ask questions.	Each group shares results of their experiments with the whole class.	
Mr. Foreman concludes this aspect of the lesson by asking students to present their data in the form of a graph.	Students conclude that the difference in the number of swings is due to the different lengths of string.	Mr. Foreman uses this phase of the lesson to teach students how to present data from a scientific experiment.

Analyze and Reflect on Thinking Processes The final phase of an inquiry-based lesson requires students to reflect on the lesson and to analyze their own thinking processes. Again, questioning on the part of the teacher is important:

- "When did you first start getting a clear understanding of the question or problem?"
- "Why did you accept some explanations more than others?"
- "Did you have previous experiences or prior knowledge that influenced how you saw the problem? Your final conclusions?"
- "Did your thinking change in the process of the inquiry?"

Below is how Mr. Foreman handled this final phase.

Phase 6 of the inquiry lesson

Mr. Foreman's directions, dialogue, and questions	Students' responses	Our comments
Phase 6: Analyze and reflect on thinking processes. "Okay, now that we have finished our experiments and concluded that the number of swings in a fixed time period increases in a regular manner as the length of the string gets shorter, let's think for a few minutes about our *own thinking* during the process. Think about what your brain was doing: • When did you first get an inkling that the length of the string was important?		Note how this final phase of an inquiry lesson is almost identical to the final phase of a concept teaching lesson.

Ms. Seymour's directions, dialogue, and questions	Students' responses	Our comments
• What doubts did you have? • What makes you sure of your conclusions? • Could your conclusions be wrong? Why? Why not?		

During the inquiry and reflective phases of an inquiry lesson, teachers should encourage free exchange of ideas, be accepting of all ideas, and model behaviors that display the tentativeness of knowledge. Integral to these phases of inquiry lessons is question asking, by both students and teacher. Costa (2001b) has provided some questioning dos and don'ts, summarized in Table 11.2.

Table 11.2 Questioning "dos" and "don'ts" for inquiry lessons

Some questioning "dos"	Questioning patterns to avoid
Use an approachable voice:	*Avoid verification questions or those already known:*
Voice has lilt and melody rather than flat.	What is the name of . . .? How many times did you?
Use plurals to invite multiple answers:	*Avoid closed questions that can be answered "yes" or "no":*
What are some of your goals? What alternatives are you considering?	Can you recite that poem? Can you state the formula for . . .?
Use words that express tentativeness:	*Avoid rhetorical questions in which the answer is given in the question:*
What conclusion might you draw? What hunches do you have to explain this situation?	In what year was the War of 1812 fought? How long is the l00-yard dash?
Use invitational stems:	*Avoid defensive questions:*
As you reflect on . . . As you plan for . . .	Why didn't you complete your idea? Are you confused again?
Use questions that engage specific cognitive operations:	*Avoid agreement questions:*
How would you categorize? What hypothesis do you have? What inference can you make from these data?	This is really the best solution, isn't it? Who can name the three basic parts of a plant? Root, stems, and leaves, right?
Use questions that address external and internal content that is relevant to the student:	
What experiences allow you to make that conclusion? What is going on in your mind when you stated that conclusion?	

Source: Adapted from Costa (2001b), pp. 360–361.

A careful study of the questions in the "do" column reveals that they are constructed to evoke student inquiry, while the "don't" questions will likely close down thinking.

ATTENDING TO CLASSROOM DISCOURSE PATTERNS AND ENVIRONMENTS

The learning goals of concept teaching, particularly the concept attainment approach, and of inquiry teaching are achieved mainly through dialogue and discussion. Teachers assume the role of question askers and discussion moderators. As such, the classroom environment and the language used are of critical importance.

The language used in the classroom affects our abilities to analyze complex problems, reason, and make sound evidence-based judgments. The teacher's verbal questioning and responding behavior affect how students think and respond. In addition, students' verbal contributions provide an opportunity for them to practice their thinking skills and to hear their own thinking. They also provide us, as teachers, with a window for viewing their thinking processes so coaching can be provided. The classroom and its discourse pattern is where this all comes together. Rowe (1986, p. 43) made this important observation:

> To "grow," a complex thought system requires a great deal of shared experience and conversation. It is in talking about what we have done and observed, and in arguing about what we make of our experiences, that ideas [. . .] multiply, become refined, and finally produce questions for further explorations.

For this to occur requires some pretty substantial changes in the discourse pattern found in most classrooms.

Question Asking

We only discuss question asking briefly here, because most of our readers will be well informed on questioning strategies and we have already described this aspect of discussion in earlier chapters. However, in way of review, remember that different types of questions require students to use different kinds of cognitive process. For example, factual questions require students to recall specific information, whereas other kinds of question require them to be analytical and evaluative. Although lower-level questions that seek to diagnose and clarify student understanding of factual and conceptual information are important in any type of discourse environment, concept and inquiry-based teaching focus more on questions that require students to analyze complex problem situations and to arrive at conclusions based on valid evidence.

Traditional Discourse Patterns

Observers over a number of years (Cazden, 1986, 1988; Cuban, 1993; Burbules & Bruce, 2001; Rowe, 1974, 1976) have identified a traditional discourse pattern that is found in most classrooms. They labeled it the **initiation–response–evaluation** (IRE) pattern. This **pattern** normally takes place in whole-class settings and has three phases:

1. *Initiation*: Teacher asks a question about the lesson.
2. *Response*: Students raise their hands, are called upon, and either reply or say nothing.

3. *Evaluation*: Teacher evaluates the response with praise, corrects the response, or answers their own question.

This overall pattern has been with us for a very long time; emerging in the early years of formal schooling, it has persisted to the present. This pattern proceeds at a rapid rate and, according to most observers, has harmful effects on student effort to engage in inquiry (Burbules & Bruce, 2001; Cuban, 1993; Goodlad, 1984). Correct use of **wait-time** and changing the overall pattern of questioning are required to change the IRE pattern and to secure wider and different kinds of participation.

Slowing the Pace

During the 1970s, a science educator, Mary Budd Rowe, was studying how teachers were implementing a new inquiry-based science curriculum. Her study of "wait-time," which we mentioned briefly in Chapter 6, has become a classic and is summarized in Research Box 11.2.

 **RESEARCH BOX 11.2**

Rowe, M. (1974). Wait-time and rewards as instructional variables: Their influence on language, logic, and fate control. Part-one: Wait time. *Journal of Research in Science Teaching, 11*, 81–94.

Rowe studied and observed 96 teachers in two locations who were teaching a new science curriculum. She found that teachers were using the IRE pattern described above and that discussion was proceeding at a very rapid pace. Teachers were:

- Asking students questions.
- Giving students less than one second to answer after the question was asked.
- Repeating the question or asking a different one immediately if students did not respond.
- Reacting or asking another question within an average time of 0.09 seconds if students did respond.

Rowe concluded that this rapid pace prevented students from engaging in inquiry or sustained conversation, one of the important aims of the new curriculum. She decided to conduct an experiment to study the effects on student responses if wait-times were increased. She taught a group of teachers to wait at least three seconds for students to respond after a question was asked and three seconds between a students response and the teacher's reaction. When trained teachers started to use longer wait-times the following occurred:

- The length of student responses increased from eight words per response under the fast pace to 27 words under the three-second wait-time. This signifies considerably longer statements by students after teachers are trained to use wait-time.
- The number of unsolicited but appropriate responses increased from a mean of five to a mean of 17.

- Failures to respond ("I don't know" or silence) decreased. In classrooms prior to training, the "no response" occurred as high as 30 percent of the time. This changed dramatically once teachers started to wait at least three seconds for students to think.
- When wait-time was lengthened, students provided more "evidence-type" statements to support the inferences they were making. They also asked more questions.

Today, the three-second wait-time rule is rather well known; however, many instances can be found where it is *not* followed and where teachers are not giving their students sufficient time to think and to respond. Part of the reason for the persistence of the rapid instructional pace may be that in our culture silence, in almost all social settings, makes us nervous, so we jump in to keep a conversation moving. Waiting in classrooms can also allow unmotivated students to slow down the pace and momentum of a lesson. As teachers, we can take several actions to correct this situation. We can practice waiting at least three seconds until this behavior becomes almost automatic. We can also use the small group techniques, such as Think–Pair–Share and other thinking routines described in Chapters 10 and 13, for purposes of increasing participation and enhancing student thinking.

Creating and Managing the Learning Environment

An overarching concern expressed by developers of the Visible Thinking Program described in Chapter 10, as well as those who advocate concept and inquiry-based teaching, is that it is *not* the details around specific strategies that is significant but the shift of teachers' attention to a different aspect of teaching and learning. This requires in turn a different type of classroom culture and environment. We described earlier the eight forces identified by Ritchhart (2002) that shape classroom culture and how success in teaching students how to think depends on developing and sustaining particular classroom environments. A classroom culture that enhances students' inclination toward thinking and supports the acquisition of thinking dispositions and skills is required.

Others have identified similar features. Magnusson and Palincsar (1995), for instance, emphasize the importance of using "strategies to elicit students' ideas, recognize and refine their emerging understandings, and scaffold students' learning" (p. 49). Schmuck and Schmuck (2001) and Arends (2009) believe that inquiry and thinking thrive best in classroom environments characterized by open communication and discourse, where students show respect for each other and feel included, where students feel they can influence what is going on, and where conflict and differences in ideas can be resolved in productive ways. This type of classroom environment is often difficult to achieve. Without it, however, goals to promote "thinking and inquiry" can be given away.

BARRIERS TO TEACHING STUDENTS HOW TO THINK

Finally, serious efforts have been made to teach students how to think since Dewey (1916) advocated this goal for education almost 100 years ago. And, over the past 50 years, a spate of new programs has been developed to be used alone and across the curriculum. These programs aim at helping students form and attain conceptual understandings and to inquire and develop thinking skills and dispositions. Yet, many of these efforts have come up short. The reason for our lack of progress can be attributed to several barriers that exist, either real or imagined.

Certainly, standardized tests that focus on recall of factual and conceptual knowledge, rather than reasoning and the use of our cognitive processes, make it difficult for teachers to emphasize thinking processes in their classrooms. Some have gone so far as to argue that current testing programs have pushed efforts to teach thinking to the margins. Although newer versions of some tests, such as the SATs, have included problem-solving questions and components, these have not been as dominant as the more traditional "remember" and "comprehension" questions.

Some students and their parents can also be critical of more open-ended and inquiry-oriented approaches. This is particularly true for students who have been highly successful in their abilities to acquire large amounts of information and to recall it successfully on paper-and-pen tests. One of the authors experienced a great deal of student resistance when he attempted to use inquiry strategies in an advanced placement U.S. history class. Students simply believed that they were wasting class time that could be better spent taking notes from lectures that covered the content they believed would be on the AP test. Some parents also hold perceptions (most often inaccurate) that the path to college is developing skills for acquiring and recalling information, as contrasted to acquiring thinking dispositions and skills.

Finally, many of us who are teachers still conceive of an effective education as one that teaches students how to commit to memory large amounts of factual and conceptual knowledge. Or, we may believe that we are *not* as strong in our disciplines or subject areas as we should be and subsequently become nervous about the open nature of inquiry lessons. The result is that we continue to teach as we were taught and newer constructivist conceptions about learning have yet to be internalized to the point of shifting our inner perspectives about what teaching is all about. Also, some teachers may believe that inquiry-based and thinking-skills approaches are not effective pedagogies for teaching students at either the lower or the more advanced levels. As a result, many remedial classes are characterized by the use of direct instruction to achieve acquisitions of basic skills, while more advanced classes find presentation of huge amounts of new information to be the norm. Neither focuses much on teaching students how to inquire and reason.

We have no crystal ball about what the future may hold for teaching students how to think. However, we are optimistic that more and more teachers, as well as more and more parents, will demand a new kind of education where thinking and intellectual character are foremost in defining a good education for today's youth.

SUMMARY AT A GLANCE

- Most people, including teachers, believe that teaching students how to think is one of the primary purposes of education. Concept and inquiry-based teaching are approaches that aim at helping students learn content knowledge while also learning to think and reason.
- Concept teaching is a powerful model for helping students learn new concepts, expand their understanding of concepts they already know about, and develop thinking skills. This model is not effective for teaching huge amounts of subject

matter content, but instead aims at building conceptual understanding that serves as a foundation for higher-level thinking.

- The phases of concept lessons calls for teachers to take an active role in guiding students in discovery and keeping them focused on the inquiry process. At the same time, there are numerous occasions, particularly in the concept attainment approach, where teachers adopt a supportive role, listening to students' ideas, encouraging participation, and giving students ample opportunity to explore their own thinking processes.

- Inquiry-based teaching is a model developed to infuse the teaching of thinking and reasoning skills with teaching content. It can be used across the curriculum; however, it is most suited to subjects that use scientific inquiry, such as the sciences, social sciences, and some aspects of history and the humanities.

- Success of inquiry lessons depends somewhat on a rather strict adherence to the model's syntax that includes phases for stating and testing hypotheses, investigating and experimenting, and constructing and revising explanations.

- Both concept and inquiry-based teaching require classroom discourse patterns and environments that provide students time to think and that are characterized by trust and freedom of inquiry.

CONSTRUCTING YOUR OWN LEARNING

With a colleague or classmate, discuss your approaches to teaching thinking in your respective classrooms. Do you use the concept and inquiry-based methods described in this chapter? If so, what type of successes have you had? What hasn't worked so well? What other approaches do you each know about and use?

Now, plan a concept or inquiry-based lesson together and make arrangements to observe each other teach the lesson. Meet afterwards to provide critique and feedback.

RESOURCES

Audet, R., & Jordon, L. (2005). *Integrating inquiry across the curriculum*. Thousand Hills, CA: Corwin Press.

Chapman, C. (2008). *Using graphic organizers to develop thinking skills, K-12*. Thousand Oaks, CA: Sage Publications.

Costa, A. (Ed.). (2001a). *Developing minds: A resource book for teaching thinking* (3rd ed.). Alexandria, VA: Association for Supervision and Curriculum Development.

Erickson, H. (2002). *Concept-based curriculum and instruction: Teaching beyond the facts*. Thousand Hills, CA: Corwin Press.

National Center for Teaching Thinking: www.nctt.net.

12

CASE-BASED TEACHING AND JURISPRUDENTIAL INQUIRY

Mr. Beaudet is teaching his American Studies class in Akron, Ohio. Let's observe his students, who are in the middle of a discussion about government eavesdropping:

Mr. Beaudet: So, what do you think about the case we have been studying . . . should a government agency be permitted to listen in on individuals' cell phone conversations, particularly in a situation like this when one of the individuals being monitored is a suspected terrorist?

Louise: Definitely, this is a situation where welfare and security overrides all other concerns. We must stop terrorists who are threatening our country, regardless of the costs.

Mr. Beaudet: Whose welfare are you talking about, Louise? How is it to be preserved?

Louise: Well, the welfare of our community of course. The agency's actions are consistent with long-standing traditions guaranteed by the Constitution that the government should protect citizens from external threats.

Mr. Beaudet: "OK, I think I understand your position. Does anyone have another position to express?

Kaleb: Yes, although Louise has made a good point, I don't agree with her. The overarching value is not welfare and security; it is personal freedom and individual privacy. These have been guaranteed in our Constitution and the Bill of Rights. How do we know a particular individual is a terrorist unless he or she has been found guilty in court? If you give a government agency permission to eavesdrop on a terrorist, what's to prevent them from listening to you or me?

Students in Mr. Beaudet's classroom are considering a case where the government has arrested an individual based on monitored telephone conversations. Students are expressing their opinions with each other about the conflicting values that shape this particular public policy. On the one side are those who believe the primary responsibility of government is to provide security and to protect individuals from external threat—in this case, a terrorist organization. Others, however, see things differently and argue for the importance of maintaining freedom and privacy. The teacher is using jurisprudential inquiry, a model of teaching designed specifically for this type of inquiry situation.

This chapter is organized into five sections. We first consider the rationale for **case-based teaching** and **jurisprudential inquiry** and connect these models to the context and science of learning. We then describe case-based teaching, including the goals it is intended to achieve and how to plan for and execute a case-based lesson. This is followed by a similar discussion of jurisprudential inquiry, which we treat as a special class of case-based teaching. The chapter concludes with an extension of previous explanations about discussion and discourse patterns, particularly those required if case-based teaching and jurisprudential inquiry are to be effective, and brief comments about the assessment strategies that are most appropriate for this type of teaching.

PERSPECTIVES

As we described in several previous chapters, the content, goals, and methods used in particular lessons determine the modes of inquiry students employ and the cognitive processes they are required to use. The teaching models described in Chapters 10 and 11 were designed primarily to teach students how to use scientific reasoning and to inquire into physical and social phenomena associated with academic and real-world problems. Case method and jurisprudential inquiry, the foci of this chapter, pursue different purposes. These models have been designed to help students think about social and ethical issues, and about public policy issues that normally are laden with value conflict. As you will see, studying these types of issue requires different forms of inquiry as compared to those we previously described.

Rationale for Studying Complex Social Issues

We all know that the contemporary world confronts us with a spate of complex problems and an array of moral and ethical dilemmas. We are faced with global warming and fuel shortages yet our lives are highly dependent on fossil fuels. Farmers, city dwellers, and fishers lay competing claims for scarce water resources. Hardly a day goes by without news that an elected official or business leader some place in the world is being charged with corruption or misconduct. In the United States, Canada, and countries of Western Europe, we are caught in highly complex dilemmas about what to do with people who want to enter our country, particularly those who enter illegally. On the one hand, we need their labor; on the other, they are breaking the law, they make demands on our educational and health-care systems, and perhaps they are taking jobs from those already here. Racial and ethnic conflict still exists in many parts of the world, and in recent years, it appears that religious and ideological differences are taking on new importance in regard to conflict and public policy.

Concrete or straightforward solutions are not clearly evident in any of these situations. Instead, solutions remain complex, sometimes counter-intuitive, and almost always rest on conflicting social values that are legitimately in competition with one another. Solving multifaceted, value-laden issues calls for citizens who can identify the complexity of issues, who can recognize the ethical and moral dimensions involved,

---

REFLECTION

Today's world presents citizens with an array of complex problems to solve and requires special kinds of analytical skills and dispositions. Based on your experiences, how well do you think schools in general are doing to help students learn these skills and dispositions? What about your own school? Compare your views and opinions with a classmate or colleague.

and who have the analytical tools to seek rational decisions while tolerating ambiguity and disagreement. Desire for individuals who have these abilities is not new. Jefferson argued that an effective democracy required educated citizens who could engage in dialogue about public issues. Over a century ago, Dewey (1916) promoted problem solving and group learning in schools so students could grapple with problems they would later confront as citizens. More recently, Postman (1995) wrote, "You cannot have a democratic—indeed, civilized—community life unless people have learned how to participate in a disciplined way as part of a group" (p. 45; cited in McNergney, Ducharme, & Ducharme, 1999, p. 5).

Connecting to the Context and Science of Learning

Like concept and inquiry-based teaching, case-based teaching and jurisprudential inquiry rest mainly on the cognitive and constructivist perspectives of learning described in Chapter 2. Teaching from these perspectives, you remember, requires teachers to provide students with learning experiences that allow them to think, inquire, solve problems, and restructure their own knowledge. This perspective also draws from the theoretical base provided by Vygotsky (1978), which emphasized the importance of social interaction and **discourse skills** in all aspects of human learning.

The learning environment for case-based teaching and jurisprudential inquiry also rests on earlier comments we made in Chapters 10 and 11 in regard to context and discourse. These models accomplish their goals mainly through dialogue and discourse between teachers and their students and among students themselves. Because many of the issues being discussed are value laden, strong emotions are often evoked. This requires a classroom environment where students are free to express novel ideas without fear of negative judgments or recrimination. It also requires an environment where students have respect for each other and are tolerant of ambiguity and difference, a condition not always easy for teachers to create.

CASE-BASED TEACHING

Case-based teaching or method was developed initially in the late nineteenth and early twentieth centuries. According to McNergney et al. (1999), it was first used at Harvard Law School in the 1870s to prepare lawyers. These initial experiments were followed in the 1890s at Johns Hopkins Medical School as faculty used case-method as a new approach to medical education. In the early part of the twentieth century, Harvard Business School began using case-based approaches for the purpose of developing analytical and decision-making skills for students preparing for careers in business. Faculty and others associated with the Harvard Business School have written widely on how to write cases and how to teach using case methods (Barnes, Christensen, & Hansen, 1994; Christensen & Hansen, 1987). Since then, case-based teaching has been used quite widely in K-12 and higher education and across a variety of subject fields, including the sciences, social studies, history, literature, and the humanities. Perhaps some of you are familiar with case-based teaching because the professors in your teacher education program used cases and introduced you to various individuals (Campoy, 2004; Silverman & Welty, 1990) who have been advocates for this approach to teaching and learning. Case methods have been used at all levels of schooling, although, as we will see, modifications are required for use with younger students.

Instructional Outcomes for Case-based Teaching

In general, case-based teaching consists of providing students with a case that describes in some detail a real-world situation, preferably one that contains a dilemma that must be confronted and resolved by the individuals involved in the case. Students grapple with the dilemma through discourse and dialogue moderated by the teacher, who adopts a questioning stance and sometimes serves as provocateur. Good cases are complex, so students rarely can come up with a single, unqualified solution. Instead, multiple solutions are likely to be proposed, and students are encouraged to defend the ones they believe most appropriate. The primary outcomes for case-based teaching are fourfold and are highlighted in Figure 12.1.

Planning for Case-based Teaching

Two fundamental planning tasks are required when using the case method. One is finding or writing a case suitable for the developmental levels of students in the class and for the topic that is the focus of study. The second is deciding how to teach the case, particularly the type of discussion and discourse formats to follow. The first is discussed here; the second in a later section.

The developmental level of students is one of the most important factors in case selection. In our own experience, we have found that case-based teaching is suitable for students in the upper elementary grades through middle school, high school, and college. More simple cases (perhaps those with two clearly defined sides) are required for younger students, whereas more complex cases with multiple positions motivate older and more able students. Cases can be found in curriculum guides. Also, newspaper and television news contain stories every day that can be turned into a case. For instance, three different stories appeared in the newspaper the morning this section was being written that would make interesting cases:

- Story about a principal who ruled that a Hispanic student could not wear rosary beads in school because some believed they were a symbol of gang affiliation.
- Story about a college professor who was fired for refusing on religious grounds (she was a Quaker) to sign the state's loyalty oath.
- Story about the Ninth Circuit Court of Appeals claiming that it had over-extended

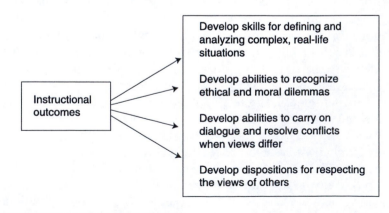

Figure 12.1 Instructional outcomes for case-based teaching

its authority when it overturned a public economic policy previously approved by the state legislature.

Many teachers like to use ideas found in news stories as a basis for writing their own case, because they are current and often reflect the value dilemmas and conflicts in their students' local communities. Obviously, teachers must choose cases with care and keep in mind that some will spark controversy in class that can spread to the larger community. In Table 12.1, we provide a list of topics/problems in various subjects that are suitable for case method in upper elementary, middle, and secondary schools.

Reynolds (1980) has written that there are several types of cases. We believe two types are most important for K-12 teaching: the dilemma case and the appraisal cases. The dilemma case normally has a story line with a beginning and an end and some type of central character (the protagonist in drama terms) who is confronted with a complex decision that involves a difficult dilemma. Writers of this type of case normally write an introductory paragraph to describe the situation plus any historical information required. These introductory statements are then followed by recent developments and the decision(s) the protagonist faces. Examples of this type of case might include:

- A governor trying to decide how to allocate scarce water resources among the various interest groups in her state.
- Authorities deciding whether to use "water boarding" against a known and dangerous enemy.

Table 12.1 Possible topics or problems for case-based teaching

	Upper elementary level	Middle level	Secondary level
Social Studies	Case about a school-board policy that requires public school students to wear uniforms.	Case about citizens' rights versus measures to provide for national security.	Case about NAFTA illustrating value issues in regard to free trade versus labor displacement.
Science	Case about scientific responsibility based on the movie *Jurassic Park*.	Case about private property versus environmental protection based on a current movie on this topic.	Case on evolution and its place in schools based on the movie *Inherit the Wind*.
Literature/ Humanities	Case drawn from Taylor's *Roll of Thunder, Hear My Cry*.	Case drawn from Orwell's *Animal Farm*.	Case drawn from Harper Lee's *To Kill A Mockingbird*.
History	Case drawn from the Salem village witchcraft trials.	Case about Thomas Jefferson owning slaves.	Race relations case drawn from Plessey versus Ferguson or Bakke versus University of California.
Geography/ Cultural Studies	Case about the use of motorized vehicles in National Parks	Case drawn from urban renewal policies versus displacement of homeless peoples.	Case drawn from situation in the West where citizens fight over use of scarce water resources.

- A doctor, a family, or a legislature deciding whether to keep an individual in a permanent coma on life support.

The appraisal case, on the other hand, lacks a central character and asks student to provide analyses rather than make decisions. Students in this type of case focus on the situation and attempt to analyze what is going on and possible consequences of various actions, both positive and negative. The analytical case is used most often in science and social studies classes. Examples of appraisal cases include: an oil spill on a beautiful Hawaiian beach or the positive and negative effects of using a particular drug for arthritis.

If teachers choose to write their own cases, as many do, several criteria should be considered regardless of the type of case being constructed:

- The case has to be an honest account of real or realistic events. This feature may outweigh all others.
- The case should have strong intrinsic appeal to the particular group of students who will be studying it. It must be engaging.
- A dilemma case needs to include some suspense and sufficient intriguing decision points to motivate students to inquire.
- An appraisal case should contain some ambiguity and discrepancies similar to the "discrepant event" described in Chapter 11 and the ambiguous problem statement required for a problem-based learning lesson.
- The best cases are those where multiple values exist.
- Cases need to be clearly written and appropriate for the age of students involved.

> **REFLECTION**
>
> Have you had experiences writing cases for your students? If so, what have you found to be the most important criteria? With a classmate or colleague, practice writing a case together using the guidelines we provide here.

Executing a Case-based Lesson

As with all approaches to teaching, case method has a syntax or series of phases that must be adhered to somewhat closely if the lesson is to be effective. In general, case method has five important phases. The phases listed in Figure 12.2 are adapted from those recommended by McNergney et al. (1999) and by Joyce, Weil, and Calhoun (2008).

During phase one, the teacher gives students the case and goes over it with them briefly. As with any lesson, care must be taken at the beginning to capture students' attention and spark their curiosity. The human dilemma in most cases will be of keen interest to students. Students are then asked to study the case. For older and/or more able students, this can be accomplished as a homework assignment. With younger and less motivated students, seat or small-group work are probably best.

Phase two has students identify the key issues and factual information in the case. Some teachers like to conduct this phase with the whole class. Others like to have the students first identify the issues and facts in the case in small groups and then share their views with the whole class. The Think–Pair–Share routine described in Chapters 10 and 13 works well for this purpose.

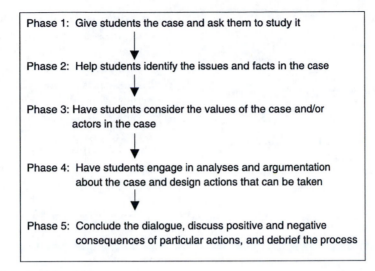

Figure 12.2 Phases of case-based lessons

Phases three and four are the heart of a case-based lesson. In phase three, teachers help students identify and consider the various value perspectives evident in the case and the competing values held by individuals involved in the case. Mostert and Sudzina (1996) have suggested that role-play can be used effectively during this phase to help students recognize multiple values and points of view represented in the case. In phase four, students engage in analysis and argumentation, and are asked to craft possible actions that may be taken. Again role-play or small groups can be used to facilitate this phase.

Many teachers prefer to conduct phases three and four with whole-group discussion. When the discussion format is used, a range of teacher behaviors may be observed. Some teachers adopt a directive, inquisitor questioning style normally associated with the Socratic method. Others prefer to assume the role of provocateur or devil's advocate. On the other side of the continuum are teachers who adopt a more nondirective style, staying quietly engaged while encouraging students to do their own analyses and to express their own ideas. Teachers using this approach see themselves as facilitators of student inquiry rather than questioners extracting ideas from their students. It has been our own experience that a directive approach can work with some older and more able students because it pushes them intellectually. On the other hand, this approach often frightens many students and causes them to withdraw from participation. We prefer the more indirect approach or one that assumes a middle ground. We will provide our rationale for this preference when we come back to discussion of appropriate discourse patterns later in the chapter.

The final phase of a case-based lesson consists of a wrapping up, summarizing main actions that have been proposed, considering the consequences of these actions, and an overall debriefing. The purposes of this phase are to get students to recognize that most actions have both positive and negative consequences and, because of value differences, to understand that one set of actions may be embraced by some while denounced by others. This final phase should also include getting students to debrief and analyze the lesson itself and their participation in it. This is accomplished by such questions as:

> **REFLECTION**
>
> Teachers can adopt various dialogue styles to encourage student thinking in case-based teaching. These can vary from very directive to nondirective. Which style do you prefer? Does your style vary with the nature of your class? Why? Compare your style with ones used by a classmate or colleague.

- How did the lesson go today? Did we cover the substantial points?
- Did we come up with plausible analyses and decisions? Why? Why not?
- How pleased were you with your participation? Would you have liked to have been more involved? Less involved?
- What new things ran through your head as the discussion proceeded? Did these surprise you?

Debriefing is a critical aspect of a case-based lesson and ample time must be provided for this activity.

Other Case-based Teaching Formats

There are several other formats that can be employed to study and analyze particular cases. Those most popular with teachers include trials, debates, and public hearings.

Trials A case can be studied by holding mock trials. Today, the public, including students, hold a fascination for real-life trials as demonstrated in the way they are followed on television and in the press. This fascination can be captured in the classroom as well. When teachers use the trial format, they must set up a case that has two rather clear opposing sides which can be represented by attorneys, witnesses, and so on. Obviously, a degree of role-playing is required when this format is used. Teachers (or students) must work out the scripts for the various roles that will be assumed as the trial proceeds. When using the trial format, ways must also be found to keep all students involved. Some teachers do this by having small groups of students meet periodically and react to what they are observing. Other teachers set up situations where the actual trial is conducted in a "Court TV" format, with television crews and reporters broadcasting and providing commentary on events as they unfold. Some students can also serve as consultants to the opposing attorneys or as coaches for the witnesses and members of the jury. The positive aspect of the trial format for studying a case is that it introduces a rather high level of drama and, if the roles are carefully crafted, they can illuminate the ambiguity of the opposing sides in the case. The downside of using the trial format is that sometimes it is difficult to keep the active participation of all students, and if the trial is not carefully orchestrated this learning activity can turn into mere entertainment rather that a rigorous analytical exercise. In Figure 12.3 we provide an example about how two creative teachers used and studied the trial format in a science class.

The Zebra Mussel Case

Judy Beck and Charlene Czerniak (2005) describe an interesting *mock trial activity* they created. The trial aimed at helping students learn important knowledge in the life sciences by bringing *unlawful disruption* charges against the zebra mussel.

The life science context. In the life sciences an *invasive species* is defined as an alien species that has been introduced into an ecosystem for which it is not a native. Often, invasive species can cause environmental damage and economic problems. Most states have science standards aimed at helping students understand concepts such as invasive species and other human-induced hazards, as well as concepts associated with the interdependence and diversity of organisms, and the behavior of populations within ecosystems.

The zebra mussel case. This case, according to Beck and Czerniak, is based on the introduction of zebra mussels in Lake Erie and their impact on Port Clinton, a beach community located on the lake's eastern shore that relies mainly on the tourist trade for its economic base. Zebra mussels, a native of the Baltic Sea, entered the lake through ballast tanks that crossed the ocean from the Baltic Sea. Concern is expressed regarding zebra mussels, who are bivalves (two shells held together by a ligament), having negative impact on native mussels. Zebra mussels also attach themselves to the bottom of boats and water intake cribs. This of course causes economic problems for the citizens of Port Clinton. On the other hand, zebra mussels filter water for feeding, and as a result, the water in Lake Erie around Fort Clinton has become clearer than it has been for many years. So, obviously, there are several views about what to do about the zebra mussel, making this situation a provocative case for students to tackle.

The classroom situation. This case is appropriate for use in middle or high school classrooms, and can be adapted to "invasive species" in other parts of the country. The overall strategy is to use the mock-trial format to put the zebra mussel on trial for unlawful disruption of the Great Lake's ecosystem. During the trial, students are asked to assume particular roles depending upon the size of the class:

- Six, nine or 12 members of the jury.
- Judge (teacher could play judge).
- At least two members of the defense team (could be more).
- At least two members of the prosecution team (could be more).
- Coaches for the defense and prosecution teams (as needed).
- One of several potential witness roles, listed in Figure 12.3.
- Roles to provide media and newspaper coverage (as needed).

Witnesses	Role description
Mr. or Ms. Beachcomber, resident	You are a local resident who spends many hours on the beach. You often bring your young children to the shore to search for shells.
Mr. or Ms. Fishbone, business owner	You are a third-generation commercial fisherman. Your grandfather has shown you special fishing spots that were productive in his day. The fish population has decreased in those specific areas, so you wonder if the area has been overfished.
Mr. or Ms. Waverunner, business owner	You own the largest personal watercraft rental facility on the lake. In recent years, your business has seen a steady decline that you attribute to the bad publicity surrounding the zebra mussel.
Mr. or Ms. Trekker, tourist	Your family has visited the Port Clinton community for generations. The lake is the clearest you ever remember seeing it. You are able to take your family snorkeling and swimming in clear water.

Mr. or Ms. Welcome, Convention and Visitor's Bureau Bureau director	This is your 25th year working for the Convention and you have seen a steady increase in the tourist trade for Port Clinton during that time. You partially attribute this to the apparent improvements in the lake water. New conventions have come to town, citing the beauty of the area, as well as the clarity of the lake water.
Mr. or Ms. Common, mayor	As mayor, you have seen the town go from a sleepy haven to a bustling, thriving tourist community. This activity has increased the tax base for the community and allowed you to make improvements to the infrastructure and landscaping of the community.

Prior to the trial students should be provided description cards of their role and assigned research to collect background information on both the science topic and on court procedures. This research will likely be only for a few days for younger students but longer for older ones.

The teacher should strive to make the trial as realistic as possible. For younger students, two hours is probably sufficient. The trial could go on for several days for high school students. As in real life, the trial should begin with opening arguments, followed by the prosecution and defense presenting their witnesses with opportunities for cross-examination. The trial should end with closing arguments.

After the trial, students should be asked to debrief the activity and can extend their thinking by discussing what they learned, differing points of view presented in the case, and the difficulties the jury faced in finding an acceptable resolution. In the final section of this chapter, we provide the oral presentation rubric that was designed by Beck and Czerniak to evaluate students' knowledge and participation in the zebra mussel case.

Figure 12.3 Description of trial content and role descriptions of witnesses
Source: These are just a few of the roles described by Beck and Czerniak. For a complete list, see Beck and Czerniak, (2005), p. 17. Reprinted with permission

Debate Debate is another format that can be used effectively if the case has two pretty clear points of view. Many debate formats exist, and older students will have seen some of these, particularly the formats used in televised political debates. In most instances, however, teachers must spend time teaching students about the purpose and structure of debates. A common format used by debate clubs is to have teams of students prepare to debate both sides of an issue and then flip a coin to decide on the actual side they will argue. Normally, two- or three-member teams do the actual "pro" and "con" presentations and subsequent rebuttals and summaries. Thus, as with the trial format, teachers must find ways to involve the other students. One way to do this is to have some students help the debaters prepare for the debate and serve as coaches as the debate proceeds. Another way is to use the format normally used in political or presidential debates, where reporters play a role in defining the issues and asking questions and where members of the audience are allowed to ask questions and provide critique and evaluation.

Public Hearings The public hearing is a final non-discussion format that can be used for studying a case. Most students can understand the rather straightforward purposes and procedures of public hearings, and many have viewed congressional or legislative hearings on television. In role-playing mode, this format allows students to prepare and present different points of view on an issue to a simulated hearing board or committee. The advantage of this format is that it can place large numbers of students in active roles. A disadvantage, like the trial format, is that the public hearing format requires students to take positions based on prescribed roles rather than taking positions based on their own values and beliefs.

> **REFLECTION**
>
> Think about the school and community where you teach. Would exploration of value differences be controversial? Why? Why not? Which issues would spark the most controversy? In the past, how have you dealt with controversial issues? It might be interesting to discuss this topic with your principal or a school board member.

JURISPRUDENTIAL INQUIRY

Jurisprudential inquiry is a particular class of case-based teaching. The model focuses on a specific type of issue, namely controversial issues related to public policy. The model is most often used in history and social studies classes, although it is appropriate for use in other subjects where public policy issues are addressed, such as a science class studying public environmental policies. Like case method, jurisprudential inquiry teaches students how to clarify issues, develop positions, and resolve complex and controversial policy questions. Also like case method, the model relies mainly on student discourse and dialogue.

Instructional Outcomes for Jurisprudential Inquiry

The overarching goal of jurisprudential inquiry, according to Newman and Oliver, two of its initial creators, is "to teach students to clarify and develop rational justifications for positions on public policy through oral dialogue" (1970, p. 237). More specific learning goals are listed in Figure 12.4.

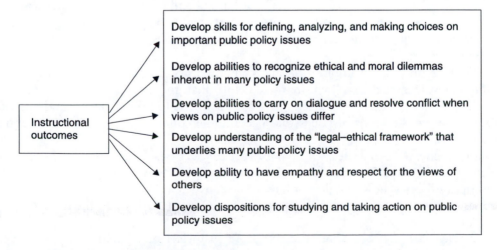

Figure 12.4 Instructional outcomes for jurisprudential inquiry

You will note that the set of outcomes in Figure 12.4 is very similar to those listed for case-based teaching. The major difference is the **public policy** focus in jurisprudential inquiry.

Planning for Jurisprudential Inquiry

Planning a jurisprudential lesson begins with identifying or writing a case. As contrasted with case method, jurisprudential cases are pretty much limited to those that, according to Oliver and Shaver (1968), fit into a particular "legal–ethical framework." What they mean by this is that there are a set of principles and values that frame the way we view government and public policy in the United States. These principles have been institutionalized in the Declaration of Independence, the Constitution, the Bill of Rights, and Supreme Court decisions that have been rendered over the past 200 years. Some of the basic principles include:

- rule of law
- equal protection under the law
- due process
- justice and equality
- preservation of peace and order
- personal liberty
- private property rights
- separation of powers
- state rights and local control

> **REFLECTION**
>
> Before going on with this chapter, think for a moment about these basic principles and values. Can you add to our list of those that make up our legal–ethical framework?

Many public policy issues stem from these principles and overall framework. These framing principles, however, are not always consistent nor have they been fully realized. In fact, they are often in conflict with one another. For example, free speech built on the principle of personal liberty is often in conflict with public policies aimed at preserving peace and order. Or, private property rights may conflict with policies to provide equal opportunities for ethnic and racial minorities or those meant to protect the environment.

Table 12.2 provides examples of some contemporary public policy issues and the conflicting values that exist within them. Note that the issues and value conflicts described in Table 12.2 are complex and pose dilemmas to policy makers and citizens alike. These are the kinds of issues that become the content for good jurisprudential inquiry lessons.

Many teachers like to write their own jurisprudential cases. If that route is chosen, use the information described in the previous section about how to write cases that pose dilemmas. All cases, however, do not have to be constructed from scratch because there are many sources for case materials. Newman and Oliver (1970) listed the following:

- *Stories and vignettes*: short excerpts from historical or contemporary novels or short stories.

Table 12.2 Contemporary public policy issues and questions that contain conflicting values

Policy issues	Conflicting values
Should police shut down a demonstration to protect demonstrators from harm?	Freedom of speech vs. public safety
Should a house owned by an individual be destroyed by the state to make way for a new freeway?	Property rights vs. public welfare
Should the government listen in on telephone conversations of known terrorists?	Personal privacy vs. national security
Should the government limit the logging operations of private companies on federal land?	Competition and property rights vs. conservation of natural resources for the public welfare
Should a school district prevent students from holding prayer meetings in a public-owned school building?	Separation of church and state vs. freedom of speech and assembly
Should the government pass laws that require people to wear seat belts or helmets?	Public good vs. Private rights
Should ethnic and racial minorities be admitted to college even though non-minorities have higher test scores?	Equal opportunities vs. affirmative action
Should the country use a pre-emptive strike to attack a sovereign state perceived to be a threat?	National sovereignty vs. national security
Should Muslim girls be permitted to cover their faces while in a public school?	Personal freedom vs. need for order and security

- *Journalistic historical narratives*: Careful descriptions or actual eyewitness accounts.
- *Research data*: Actual empirical studies, e.g., world hunger, gender differences, achievement gaps.
- *Documents*: court opinions, speeches, letters, diaries, laws.
- *Interpretative essays*: Essays written by journalists, bloggers, or others who have a point of view about an event.

In addition, cases for jurisprudential inquiry, as well as case method, do not always have to be in written form. They can be in video, film, or audio format. Many of the best cases, however, are drawn from real-life situations reported in the morning newspaper, the evening newscast, and on the Internet.

In writing or selecting cases, teachers must remain aware of the level of difficulty and complexity. Complex cases are more interesting for able and interpersonally strong students. Simpler cases are required for younger and less able students, or for those experiencing jurisprudential inquiry for the first time. Table 12.3 provides several examples of cases along a continuum from rather simple to more complex.

Executing Jurisprudential Lessons

The creators of jurisprudential inquiry (Oliver & Shaver, 1966; Newman & Oliver, 1970)

Table 12.3 Simple to complex cases

Simple to mildly complex cases	Conflicting values and principles	What to watch out for
Students should be required to wear uniforms in schools because most families don't have very much money and they don't want clothes to give some students status over others.	Community welfare vs. individual freedom	Works well in upper elementary grades; perhaps Social Studies class. Teachers, however, need to keep the focus on the principles involved rather than students' personal preferences.
Workers should have the right to strike even if the strike brings serious economic hardship to the community.	Fair collective bargaining vs. general welfare	Middle school students can deal with this issue quite well. However, this issue can engender strong emotions in communities where families have actually experienced controversy.
Employers should be able to hire anyone they want, independent of union demands or employee legal status.	Free markets and property rights vs. achieving economic equality	Again, teachers need to keep the discussion focused on the conflicting values of the case.
A school board or state agency should require each district or school to spend the same amount on each pupil.	Common welfare vs. local control	This issue pops up in many communities. This case works best if it is currently being considered in the students' local community.
More complex cases		
Students should have the right to bring pornographic and immoral materials to school.	Freedom of speech vs. local moral codes or public welfare	This can be a very touchy case. It can produce lots of emotion and student engagement. It can also boil over into controversy in the larger community.
Should children of a particular religion be forced to attend school regardless of the parents' wishes? Or, Should parents of a particular religion be allowed to withhold medical treatment from a very sick child?	Religious freedom vs. public welfare	Could be very controversial in some communities, particularly where the community has recently experienced one of these situations.
A killer should be set free because he was denied due process.	Due process vs. public safety	A pretty safe case and one where adult and student opinions will vary considerably.
Illegal immigrants should be denied access to public schools and health services	Rule of law vs. equal access to health and welfare	Makes an excellent case, although it must be handled with care in communities and schools that have a large number of immigrant students.
A person who has been declared brain dead should be kept on life support.	Moral codes vs. public welfare	Readers will recognize this is similar to the Terry Schiavo case. This type of case is highly complex and has religious as well as public policy implications. Proceed with care.
An individual who has deceived another person on the Internet and the deception led to the person's suicide should be charge with murder.	Freedom of speech vs. common welfare	This also is an actual case where a mother deceived a friend of her daughter. The deception led to the friend's suicide. This is a case that will engage students, but its discussion and resolution are very complex.

and those who have written about the model (Joyce, Weil, & Calhoun, 2008) identify a syntax with six phases. We have reduced this to five and list them in Figure 12.5.

In phase one, the teacher presents and orients students to the case. The case may be presented in written format or it may be in the form of a film, a story from the newspaper, or an incident that has been posted on the Internet. During this phase the teacher also describes the events pertaining to the case and goes over the facts. It is important that the value controversies in the case are clear to students prior to moving to the next phase.

During phase two, students are asked to identify the public policy issue(s) in the case and the ethical and value conflicts that are involved, such as freedom of speech, national security, local autonomy, and the like. Younger students, and often older students, will need help understanding these issues and require special instruction prior to engaging in the case. For instance, if the case involves a due process issue, students will need to know how "due process" was defined in the Constitution and how important amend-ments and court decisions have modified our views about due process over time. Obvi-ously, this gives teachers an excellent opportunity to delve deeply into the Constitution, the judicial process, and other important aspects of American history. Just as with case method, identifying the issues and values may be accomplished through dialogue with the whole class or it may be done in small groups or Think–Pair–Share teams. The former probably works best with students confident of their discourse abilities, whereas the latter provides more time for students to think and more opportunities for all students to participate. When small groups or pairs are used, the teacher should ask small groups to report the ethical and value problems they have identified to the whole class so these can be summarized and discussed.

In phase three, students are asked to state their own position on the issue and argue the basis for their decision. During this phase students should be asked to define the values they hold that lead them to their decision and how their position might be different if they held different values. Again, this can be done as a whole group or in small groups. Some teachers think it is best to have students write out their positions as part of a homework assignment. This approach affords more participation by students who may be reluctant or lack the confidence to speak out in class.

In phase four, various positions and arguments are explored. Observers differ on how

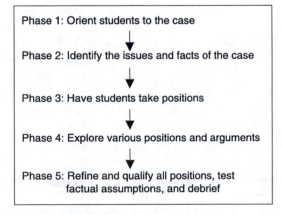

Phase 1: Orient students to the case

Phase 2: Identify the issues and facts of the case

Phase 3: Have students take positions

Phase 4: Explore various positions and arguments

Phase 5: Refine and qualify all positions, test factual assumptions, and debrief

Figure 12.5 Phases of jurisprudential inquiry lessons

this should be conducted. Joyce et al. (2008) say that, during this phase, the teacher should shift to a "confrontational" or argumentative style as they probe the students' positions. If the Socratic role is assumed, four patterns of argumentation may be used:

1. "Asking the students to identify the point at which a value is violated.
2. Clarifying the value conflict through analogies.
3. Asking students to prove desirable or undesirable consequences of a position.
4. Asking students to set value priorities: asserting priority of one value over another and demonstrating lack of gross violation of the second value" (p. 88).

Although challenging methods may hold some value, we caution against allowing the dialogue to become too confrontational. This style of argumentation can be very threatening to some students, particularly those who have not experienced friendly argument in their own families or cultures, or English language learners. Teacher questioning should be probing, but care must be taken to keep the focus on the case, not the student. It is also important to provide plenty of time to discuss the case thoroughly. Like in the previous phase, small groups may be employed. Students can be asked to formulate their positions and arguments in small groups and then argue together with other small groups. Particular individuals from each small group may also be identified to argue their group's position in front of the whole class.

> **REFLECTION**
>
> Finding a balance between challenging students' ideas while at the same time providing a safe environment so differing points of view can be expressed is difficult to achieve. In your classroom, what do you do to achieve this balance?

We provide these alternatives not because we believe students should be coddled or that teachers should not push them to think independently and critically. But, as a practical matter and based on our own experiences, we have found that, if students lack the confidence to speak out in class, no amount of confrontation will change this; they will simply "clam up." As teachers, we must find an appropriate balance between challenging students and their ideas while at the same time encouraging many different and competing opinions to be expressed.

In the final phase of a jurisprudential inquiry lesson, teachers ask students to think more about their positions and to refine and clarify them. They also ask students to consider the factual assumptions behind their positions and to explain how their arguments will hold up under other conditions. We have found that the boundaries between phases four and five are often blurry. Indeed, the discourse and argumentation are similar, and there is nothing wrong with moving back and forth between the two phases. Finally, as with earlier phases, phase five can be done in whole-group or small-group settings. Position refinement and clarification may also be done in writing as part of a homework or seatwork assignment.

Let's now look at an example of how the phases are played out in a classroom setting. You were introduced to Mr. Beaudet's classroom in the chapter's opening scenario and observed students discussing how much latitude the government should be given to monitor private telephone conversations. Let's return to Mr. Beaudet's classroom and observe a discussion on a different day. This time, students are exploring the question: "Which comes first, public law or private beliefs?" Below is an abbreviated look at how

Dialogue in the jurisprudential lesson

Teacher–student dialogue	What participants are doing
Mr. Beaudet: "OK, today I want us to explore the policy implications of the Cornelius Irving helmet case."	Teacher is orienting students to the case.
"You know from the reading I gave you yesterday, that this is a case about 15-year-old Cornelius Irving, a high school student who was arrested for failing to wear his bicycle helmet. His attorney father has taken his case to court, arguing that the law infringes on his son's private rights and beliefs."	
Mr. Beaudet: "So, what do you think? What are the major issues in this particular case?"	
Rouzan: "Well, it is apparent that Cornelius was breaking a law that is very clear. The law was passed by the legislature in 1992 through democratic processes."	Rouzan and William are identifying the issues in the case.
William: "Yes, the law was passed. However, it goes against a long-standing tradition that the 'protection of one's own person is a private matter'."	
Mr. Beaudet: "OK, let's move on and explore the various positions you hold in regard to this case."	Teacher is asking students to take a position in regard to the law and Cornelius's action.
Marshall: "I think that Cornelius should be forced to pay his fine. He broke the law. It is clear and simple."	Teacher is encouraging students to explore. their positions.
Mr. Beaudet: "But should a law be able to override an individual's private beliefs?"	Marshall is extending his position and arguing for it.
Marshall: "In this case, definitely yes. Individuals without helmets cause many injuries. This requires legislative remedy to protect the public good."	Students continue arguing their positions.
Edaya: "I see it a bit differently. I don't think the government has proven its case for the necessity of helmets. Has the law reduced injuries?"	
Joyce: "But more important, the helmet law also violates international standards of privacy."	
Brandon: "And, it has distracted attention from efforts to prevent accidents through public awareness and bicycle safety programs."	
Mr. Beaudet: "I wonder if anyone can describe the various values behind the various positions that you have been expressing."	Teacher asks students to consider values in the case and their positions.
Roy: "Well, it seems to me that Joyce and Edaya value above all else the importance of individual rights and beliefs. Marshall, on the other hand, values the welfare of the public over the rights of individuals."	Students identify values inherent in the case.
Mr. Beaudet: "What values do you hold on this issue?"	Teacher probes for Roy's position.
Roy: "I am not sure. I can see the point of view of both sides."	

Teacher–student dialogue	What participants are doing
Mr. Beaudet: "Class, what would you say if I told you that bicycle injuries have been reduced by 35 percent since the passage of the helmet law?"	Teacher introduces new factual information to encourage students to further explore and refine their positions.
Joyce: "That would not influence my opinion. The government should not interfere with private matters. And also, I have read that wearing helmets can increase brain injuries."	
Victoria: "I think this is a very important statistic. It shows that the law is effective and it is promoting the welfare of all of us by reducing public health costs."	Victoria is expressing her views about the consequences of particular actions.

that lesson was introduced and how it proceeded though the various phases of a jurisprudential inquiry.

Note that in this example the teacher is assuming a **non-directive discussion stance**. He allows the students to express their various positions and limits his contributions to asking questions and providing factual information. Different teachers would likely approach this case differently. The important thing, however, is that in a jurisprudential inquiry students should focus on the policy issues, understand the value conflicts inherent in the issue, be able to express and defend their own position, and see the consequences of one set of actions over another.

We conclude this section by considering the instructional effectiveness of case-based teaching and jurisprudential inquiry. Unfortunately, these models have not been studied as thoroughly as several of the models we described in previous chapters. In fact, there has been very little research in K-12 classrooms to test the instructional effectiveness of case-based teaching. We were, however, able to find two studies carried out on college-level introductory psychology course students and summarized in Research Box 12.1.

 **RESEARCH BOX 12.1**

Mayo, J. (2002). Case-based instruction: A technique for increasing conceptual application in introductory psychology. *Journal of Constructivist Psychology*, *15*, 65–74.
Mayo, J. (2004). Using case-based instruction to bridge the gap between theory and practice in psychology of adjustment. *Journal of Constructivist Psychology*, *17*, 137–146.

Study 1. Mayo randomly assigned two of his four sections (70 students) of introductory psychology to receive lecture-based instruction and two (66 students) to receive case-based instruction (CBI). Over the course of the study, all four sections were introduced to six psychological theories, with three hours of lectures on each. The CBI sections were then given specially prepared cases to examine and discuss in small groups. Students in the other sections were required to write a 150–250-word synopsis highlighting the main ideas of the theories. The final exam for all students tested conceptual analysis and application. Students were given several problem situations and asked to: (1) identify the theory that most closely fit the situation, and (2) provide a brief explanatory rationale for their selection.

Study 2. Essentially, study 2 is a replication of the first study, only this time with students in four sections of a psychology of adjustment course. The means scores and standard deviations from the test given to students are displayed in Table 12.4.

Table 12.4 Comparisons of case-based and lecture based teaching

	Case-based group		Lecture-based group	
Study 1	Mean	SD	Mean	SD
	83.23	10.29	76.76	12.43
Study 2	84.69	9.73	75.07	11.17

As can be observed in Table 12.4, the case-based groups out-performed their peers in the lecture-based groups, supporting the claim that case-based teaching increases student conceptual understanding and applied reasoning skills with problem situations that are complex and for which no single best solution exists. In addition, Mayo reported that case-based students reported being more interested in the class as measured by an attitude survey as compared to the lecture-based students.

The way Mayo conducted his study provided ample opportunity for error to creep in. He served as both the teacher and researcher, which could have introduced bias in the ways the problem situations were scored. Students in the sections assigned to the case- and lecture-based conditions could also have differed at the beginning of the instructional period. Regardless of these weaknesses, we believe Mayo's research points the way for further investigations that probe the effectiveness of case-based teaching.

THE DISCUSSION DISCOURSE ENVIRONMENT

The learning goals of case-based teaching and jurisprudential inquiry, like the models described in Chapter 11, are achieved mainly through dialogue and discourse. Teachers assume the role of question askers, discussion moderators, and sometimes provocateurs. As such, several aspects of the learning environment and the classroom discourse patterns are of critical importance. Previously, we described effective questioning strategies to use and how "slowing down" the pace of instruction can lead to more productive student thinking. Here, we expand this discussion by highlighting the importance of listening and responding appropriately to student ideas and of teaching them productive participation and communication skills.

Listening Actively

Teaching students thinking skills and helping them arrive at justifiable positions about complex issues requires teachers to listen carefully to their students and to respond in reflective and thoughtful ways. Sometimes called empathetic or **active**

listening, those who have written about this listening stance (Donoghue & Siegal, 2005; Rogers & Farson, 1987) emphasize that the key to listening is to grasp what the other person is saying from their point of view rather than our own point of view. Rogers and Farson have written that active listening requires several things. We summarize their list below:

- *Listen for total meaning.* This means listening not only to the content of the message but also the emotions behind it.
- *Respond to feelings.* Listeners must remain sensitive to the feelings being expressed and respond appropriately to messages, particularly those that express value preferences and that are loaded with feeling.
- *Pay attention to all cues.* Active listening requires paying attention to non-verbal as well as verbal cues, such as body posture and hand and eye movements.

Responding Empathetically

The way teachers listen is important, but equally important is the way we respond to students' ideas and opinions. Responses should be accepting and should aim at getting students to extend their thinking and to be more conscious of their judgments and their thinking processes. Statements and questions such as the following provide illustrations of **empathetic response:**

- *Reflect on student ideas:*
  "I heard you say. . . ."
  "What I think you're telling me is. . . ."
  "That's an interesting idea. I have never thought of it in quite that way. . . ."
- *Get students to consider alternatives:*
  "That's an interesting position to take. I wonder, though, if you have ever considered this as an alternative. . . ."
  "You have provided one point of view about the issue. How does it compare with the point of view expressed by . . .?"
  "Very insightful. On what values does this position rest?"
  "Evelyn has just expressed a unique position. I wonder if someone else would like to say why they agree or disagree with her position?"
  "Do you think that Charles would agree with your position? Why? Why not?"
- *Seek clarification:*
  "I think you have a good idea. But I'm a bit confused. Can you expand your thought a bit to help me understand it more fully? How does it back up the position you have expressed?"
- *Label thinking processes and statements, and ask for supportive evidence:*
  "It sounds to me like you have been performing a mental *experiment* with these data. How does that affect your position?"
  "You have made a very strong *inference* from the information you were given."
  "That's an interesting position. What *values* led you to it?"
  "If everyone held the *judgment* you just expressed, what would be the consequences?"
  (summarized from Arends, 2009).

Active listening and responding with thoughtfulness and empathy demonstrate to students that their ideas are being heard, and that they are not being negatively evaluated. In any discussion setting, but particularly when case method and jurisprudential inquiry are being used, these stances are required if we want students to express their views openly.

Teaching Students Interpersonal and Discourse Skills

Teachers are not only required to use active listening skills and accepting responses in case-based teaching and jurisprudential inquiry, they must also teach their students to be active listeners and to be accepting of each other's ideas. Several skills are important:

- *Paraphrasing*: The **paraphrase** is a communication skill used by listeners to make sure they understand the ideas being communicated by the sender. On the surface, this skill seems simple; however, many students (and adults for that matter) are not very effective in its use. It requires the listener to ask him or herself, what exactly does the sender's message mean to me and to inquire of the sender:
    "Do you mean?"
    "Is this what you are saying?"
    "This is what you said means to me. . . . Am I correct?"
- *Checking impressions*: A corollary to the paraphrase is **checking impressions**, a communication skill used to check the accuracy of another person's feelings or emotional state. Examples include:
    "I get the impression that my position on this issue is making you angry."
    "You took a position and no one paid any attention to it. Are you feeling put down?"
    "You look confused. Is that about something I said?"
- *Using "I" messages.* **I messages** are a communicative stance where an individual sends or responds in a clear, non-judgmental style. It helps communicate and take ownership for our reactions to what someone else did or said. "I" messages are sent in a straightforward way without making accusations.

Learning these skills is not difficult for most students. To teach them, however, requires allocating instructional time, just as it does for teaching any other skill. In our experience, we have found that modeling and using direct instruction described in Chapter 8 provides the most appropriate approach for teaching communication skills.

ASSESSING CASE-BASED TEACHING AND JURISPRUDENTIAL INQUIRY

A variety of approaches can be employed to assess case-based teaching and jurisprudential inquiry, many of which were described earlier in Chapter 6 on assessment. Essay questions and selected-response items work well for assessing instructional outcomes connected to the content of the case itself or to knowledge about the legal–ethical framework. However, assessing the instructional goals for identifying important issues, recognizing moral or ethical dilemmas, and/or taking a reasoned stand based on factual information will require other assessment processes. Many teachers find giving students a mini-case and having them identify the issues and values in the case and then taking

	Exceptional	Admirable	Acceptable	Amateur
Content	An abundance of material clearly related to argument; points are clearly made, and all evidence supports argument.	Sufficient information that relates to argument; many good points.	There is a great deal of information that is not clearly connected to the argument.	Thesis not clear; information included that does not support argument in any way.
Coherence and organization	Argument is clearly supported and developed; specific examples are appropriate and clearly develop argument; flows together well; succinct.	Most information presented in logical sequence; examples are appropriate and develop argument.	Concepts and ideas are loosely connected; examples are not related to argument.	Presentation is choppy and disjointed; does not flow; development of argument is vague; no apparent logical order of presentation.
Creativity	Very original presentation of material; uses the unexpected to full advantage; captures audience's attention.	Original presentation but not as creative; audience engaged.	Some originality apparent.	Material presented with little originality or interpretation.
Speaking skills	Poised, clear articulation; proper volume; steady rate; good posture and eye contact; enthusiasm; confidence.	Clear articulation but not as polished.	Some mumbling; little eye contact; uneven rate; little or no expression.	Inaudible or too loud; no eye contact; rate too slow or fast; speaker seems uninterested and uses monotone.

Figure 12.6 Rubric for assessing oral presentations and discussion
Source: Adapted from Beck and Czerniak (2005), p. 18. Reprinted with permission

and defending a position is the best test of students' understanding of case analysis, as well as the steps and processes of case method or jurisprudential inquiry. Others focus on student participation and discourse. In Figure 12.6, we provide a rubric developed by Beck and Czerniak (2005) for assessing oral presentation and discussion skills in the zebra mussel case.

SUMMARY AT A GLANCE

- Case-based teaching and jurisprudential inquiry are models that have been designed to help students think about social, ethical, and citizenship issues and about public policy issues that are value laden.
- The two models have much in common. Both require students to analyze complex, real-life situations. Unlike case method, however, jurisprudential inquiry cases are based on public policy issues, particularly policy issues that contain value conflicts stemming from basic principles of the American legal–ethical framework.
- An important aspect of case-based and jurisprudential inquiry is selection of the cases to study. An effective case is an honest account of real or realistic events and

it must be engaging to students. The best cases are those that contain human dilemmas, with complex and ambiguous decision points.

• The instructional outcomes of case-based teaching and jurisprudential inquiry are accomplished mainly through discussion and dialogue. This requires a classroom free of threat, norms of open communication and trust, and a discourse pattern that is challenging but non-evaluative.

• To develop this kind of classroom environment requires teachers to be active listeners and empathetic responders. It also requires teaching students to listen to each other and respect each other's ideas.

CONSTRUCTING YOUR OWN LEARNING

Some have argued that case-based teaching and jurisprudential inquiry are too difficult, except for the most able students. Others argue that these methods take too much time. Seek out a colleague in your school or a neighboring school and interview them about difficulty and time issues. You might also arrange to observe on a day when your colleague's students are studying an interesting case. Finally, you may find it useful to plan a case-based or jurisprudential inquiry lesson with a classmate or colleague and then make arrangements to observe and critique each other's lessons.

RESOURCES

American Jury: Bulwark of Democracy: www.crfc.org/americanjury/index.html.

Christensen, R., & Hansen, A. (1987). *Teaching and the case method*. Boston, MA: Harvard Business School.

CRFC Mock Trial Resources for Classrooms: www.crfc.org./mocktrial.html.

Joyce, B., Weil, M., & Calhoun, E. (2008). *Models of teaching* (8th ed.). Boston, MA: Allyn and Bacon.

McNergney, R., Ducharme, E., & Ducharme, M. (Eds.) (1999). *Educating for democracy: Case method teaching and learning*. Mahwah, NJ: Lawrence Erlbaum Associates.

Naunes, W., & Naunes, M. (2006). *Art and craft of case writing* (2nd ed.). Amonk, NY: Sharpe Reference.

13

COOPERATIVE LEARNING

Many students have chosen the Teaching Academy as their special learning community at Carter High School. They have made this choice because it is a setting that provides them with opportunities to work cooperatively with their classmates and to pursue both academic subjects and pedagogical practices. The teachers who teach in the Academy are known for the way they work with students, particularly for the way they use cooperative learning strategies in every aspect of their teaching. Take for instance:

- Ms. Collins, the English teacher, uses various versions of Jigsaw to engage students in reading, writing, and thinking activities.
- In history, Mr. Sanchez has his students participate in group investigation to examine and explore a number of historical topics.
- Mrs. Wong has organized cooperative learning study groups in her science classes and uses the Johnson and Johnson Learning Together approach. Her students meet every Friday in their learning groups to review the main ideas of the week's lessons. They prepare together for the weekly quiz, and after the quiz they help each other relearn if necessary.
- Mr. Jackson uses Student Teams Achievement Divisions (STAD) regularly in his math classes.
- All teachers use Kagan's cooperative learning structures to keep students engaged in core academic courses.
- Twice a month, Academy students go to nearby elementary schools and use cooperative learning strategies to teach younger children as part of their practicum on teaching.

Although cooperative learning is not embraced as fully in most schools as it is at the Teaching Academy, these strategies have nonetheless grown in popularity with teachers over the past three decades. They are used quite widely in schools today and are likely used by many of our experienced teacher readers. This chapter is about cooperative learning and is divided into several major sections. We begin with an overview of cooperative learning and

> **REFLECTION**
>
> Today, many teachers embrace and use cooperative learning. What about you? Do you use cooperative learning in your classroom? Which approaches have you used? With a classmate or colleague, compare your use of cooperative learning. What successes and/or failures have each of you experienced?

present the theoretical and empirical evidence that supports its use. For some of you, this may be simply a review of what you already know; however, we hope our presentation will include new ideas to consider. Next, we describe how to plan cooperative learning lessons and factors that need to be considered when preparing a cooperative learning environment. Five approaches for cooperative learning are then described in some detail. We conclude the chapter by highlighting the assessment and evaluation tasks associated with cooperative learning and some of the controversies that surround this topic.

OVERVIEW

Cooperative learning is a teaching model or strategy that is characterized by cooperative task, goal, and reward structures, and requires students to be actively engaged in discussion, debate, tutoring, and teamwork. As shown in Figure 13.1, the goals of cooperative learning are both cognitive and social. Students work in teams to acquire and master new information and to learn social and teamwork skills. They also learn to be more accepting of diversity and to be more tolerant of differences. Teams are made up of high-, average-, and low-achieving students, and, whenever possible, include a racial, cultural, and gender mix. The major instructional outcomes of cooperative learning are illustrated in Figure 13.1.

Cooperative learning theory asserts that students learn best when they work together, when they encourage and tutor each other, and when they are held individually accountable for their work. As opposed to models that are more teacher-centered and that require teachers to expend a great deal of time keeping students motivated and in their seats, teachers in cooperative learning encourage students to move about and interact with each other. As you read in Chapter 2, research from both the cognitive and neurosciences supports this type of active involvement.

Later in the chapter we discuss five different approaches to cooperative learning. You will find that each approach has its own features and specific procedures. However, there are some overall phases that are common to all cooperative learning approaches. We outline these phases in Figure 13.2, and then briefly discuss each below. More detailed descriptions are provided when we describe the different approaches to cooperative learning later in the chapter.

Cooperative learning begins with teachers clarifying the **cooperative goals** of the lesson and getting students ready to learn. This is an important phase of the lesson,

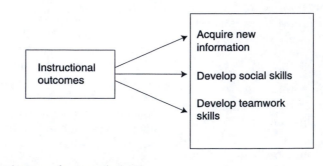

Figure 13.1 Instructional outcomes for cooperative learning

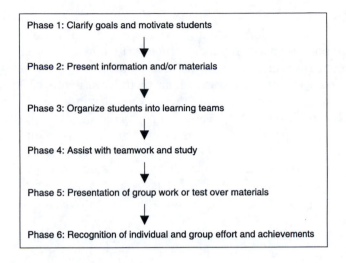

Phase 1: Clarify goals and motivate students

Phase 2: Present information and/or materials

Phase 3: Organize students into learning teams

Phase 4: Assist with teamwork and study

Phase 5: Presentation of group work or test over materials

Phase 6: Recognition of individual and group effort and achievements

Figure 13.2 Phases of cooperative learning lessons

particularly if students have had little experience with cooperative learning. Next, teachers provide students with information related to the lesson's topic. Sometimes this is accomplished with verbal presentation, but most often teachers provide students with printed learning materials. Students are then organized into learning teams and asked to study the learning materials provided for them. In some approaches these materials are be quite simple; in others, students are required to find materials in the library, on the Internet, or from community resources. Once students have completed their learning activities or investigations, they present what they have learned and the results of their work are recognized. In some approaches, they are tested on what they have learned. Finally, groups engage in reflection and debriefing.

The teacher's role in cooperative learning is one of facilitator, coach, and guide. Teachers prepare materials for students to use, intervene when groups need assistance, and ensure both individual and group accountability. A primary teaching responsibility is to build cooperative social environments and structures that will help students learn social and teamwork skills, as well as skills for problem solving and conflict resolution. Students are active participants in cooperative learning and are required to engage fully in group work. Group skills for listening, discussing, and compromising are required if cooperative learning groups are to be successful. Reading, research, writing, and presentation skills are also required to complete many of the assigned tasks.

CONNECTING COOPERATIVE LEARNING TO THE CONTEXT AND SCIENCE OF LEARNING

The roots of cooperative learning can be traced to the work of educational psychologists and pedagogical theorists at the beginning of the twentieth century, as well as to more recent cognitive and developmental theorists such as Jean Piaget and Lev Vygotsky. Three theoretical perspectives provide the intellectual support for cooperative learning: the concept of democratic classrooms, theories of intergroup relations, and experiential learning.

Democratic Classrooms

John Dewey has been the dominating figure in promoting democratic principles in education. In his book *Democracy and Education*, written in 1916, he recommended that schools be organized as miniature democracies. He believed that the best way to prepare students for a democratic society was to help them learn democratic practices in the classrooms they attend and by engaging them in inquiry in groups aimed to improve society. Later, Hebert Thelen (1954, 1960) also promoted the concept of the democratic classroom and developed particular processes and structures to accomplish group work. Thelen proposed that the classroom be organized so it would be similar to the larger society and have a social order and culture that allowed students to participate in setting standards and expectations. He saw life in classrooms as a series of "inquiries" and introduced the group investigation model described later in the chapter.

Acceptance and Tolerance of Differences

The need to reduce inter-racial prejudice and promote integration and better group acceptance led to the work on cooperative learning by Sharan (1980) and colleagues (Sharan, Kussell, Hertz-Lazarowitz, Bejarano, Raviv, & Sharan, 1984) in Israel, and by David and Roger Johnson (Johnson, Maruyama, Johnson, Nelson, & Skon, 1983) in the United States. The work in Israel was prompted by that country's need to find ways to promote better ethnic understanding between Jewish immigrants of European background and those of Middle Eastern background. Johnson and Johnson explored how cooperative learning environments might lead to better learning, more positive regard toward students with special needs who were included in regular classrooms, and more accepting and **cooperative behavior** by students of different racial and ethnic groups.

Experiential Learning

The third perspective that provides intellectual support for cooperative learning comes from educators (Kolb, 1984) and theorists in the **cognitive–constructivist perspectives**, such as Piaget (1954) and Vygotsky (1978), who were interested in the social aspects of learning; and by neuroscientists and cognitive psychologists who were interested in the effects of social environment on the brain and our memory systems. As described in Chapter 2, Vygotsky emphasized the importance of the social aspects of learning situations and believed that *social interaction* helped ignite the construction of new ideas and enhanced intellectual and social development. What better way to promote social interaction than to encourage students to work in cooperative learning groups?

Others (Kolb, 1984; Johnson & Johnson, 1975) have emphasized that people learn best when they are personally involved in a learning experience and when they turn learning into what Dewey (1938) called the "backward–forward connection." Often labeled **experiential learning**, this way of learning starts with direct experiences, continues with reflection upon these experiences, and concludes with the construction of personal knowledge ready to be tested in new situations. Experience thus provides insights, understandings, and skills that are difficult to describe to someone who has not had similar experiences.

Finally, as also described in Chapter 2, studies in the neurosciences provide intellectual support for the use of teaching models that are action-oriented, that stimulate multiple senses, and that help students personalize knowledge. Two important educational implications stem from this knowledge about how the brain works and processes information. First, information that has personal meaning (connected to **prior knowledge**) goes through the limbic system and is stored in long-term memory more quickly. Two, learning is more expeditious when more than the memory system is stimulated by multiple senses. All forms of experiential learning, including cooperative learning, stimulate multiple senses and help students personalize information.

Empirical Support for the Effects of Cooperative Learning

Cooperative learning is among the most widely researched teaching strategies. Much of the research has come from four groups of researchers who have worked for over 30 years studying the academic and social effects of this strategy. Three groups have worked in the United States; the fourth group worked in Israel. David and Roger Johnson of the University of Minnesota and their colleagues have investigated whether cooperative tasks and cooperative reward structures have positive effects on student achievement and behavior. They began their studies in the 1970s and have contributed over the past three decades to our understandings of cooperative learning. Robert Slavin (1980) and his colleagues (Slavin, Sharan, Kagan, Hertz-Lazarowitz, Webb, & Schmuck, 1985), working at Johns Hopkins University, studied the effects of cooperative learning strategies on group cohesion, cooperative behavior, intergroup relationships, and academic achievement. This work has generally confirmed that of Johnson and Johnson. Slavin has also looked at the effects of team composition on learning and attitudes toward self and others. Spencer Kagan and his colleagues (Kagan, 2001; Panitz, 2001) summarized the research on the use of Kagan's cooperative learning structures and strategies. Shlomo Sharan (Sharan & Sharan, 1990, 1992) and colleagues at Tel Aviv University studied the effect of a specific cooperative learning model called group investigation. They have investigated the model and its effects on cooperative behavior, intergroup relations, and lower- and higher-order achievement.

A number of literature reviews on cooperative learning have summarized the strategy's academic and social effects (Johnson & Johnson, 1989; Marzano et al., 2001; Panitz, 2001; Slavin, 1989, 1991, 1995; Stronge, 2007). Studies of cooperative learning have been conducted at all grade levels and in many subject areas, including: English as a second language, geography, language arts, math, reading, science, social studies, spelling, and writing. The evidence is largely positive. Consistently the studies have shown that students learn more, have more positive feelings towards tasks and others, and increase their social and cooperative skills. While it is not possible to review all the research on cooperative learning, we provide some brief summaries of this research in Research Box 13.1.

PLANNING FOR COOPERATIVE LEARNING LESSONS

Cooperative learning requires a different approach to planning as compared to other forms of instruction such as presentation teaching or direct instruction. The roles for both the teacher and students are also different. In cooperative learning, teachers spend considerable time in preparing and gathering learning materials and creating cooperative learning environments. Students are expected to play active rather than passive roles.

RESEARCH BOX 13.1

Cooperative Learning Effects

Effects on Academic Achievement

Cooperative learning strategies have positive effects on academic achievement for all students, but particularly for students with poor academic histories. Sharan and Hertz-Lazarowitz (1980) found that greater social complexity and interaction increased the learning of information and basic skills. Students of higher ability benefited more when working in cooperative groups as compared to individualistic or competitive classrooms (Johnson et al., 1983). Slavin et al. (1985) reported significantly higher levels of achievement in language arts and mathematics when they compared students in an elementary school that used cooperative learning with their peers in a traditional elementary school. Marzano et al. (2001) conducted a meta-analysis of cooperative learning studies and reported that effect sizes on academic achievement were modest but consistent.

Effects on Cooperative Behavior

Studies conducted by Sharan and his colleagues (1980, 1990) showed clearly that instructional methods (whole group teaching versus cooperative learning) influenced students' cooperative and competitive behaviors. Cooperative learning generated more collaborative behavior than did whole-class teaching. Students from cooperative learning classrooms displayed less competitive behavior and more cross-ethnic cooperation. Johnson and Johnson (1989) also reported considerable positive effects on social learning and personal esteem when comparisons were made between cooperative and individualistic classroom organizations. Dozens of studies (Slavin, 1995) have demonstrated that, when students are allowed to work together, they experience an increase in a variety of social skills, they become more capable of solving problems, better able to take the role of the other, and are generally more cooperative and willing to help and reward others.

Effects on Acceptance of and Tolerance for Diversity

The use of cooperative learning strategies has also been shown to result in better intergroup relations (Sharan & Hertz-Lazarowitz, 1980). Sharing responsibility and interaction produces more positive feelings towards tasks and others (Johnson & Johnson, 2005). Slavin (1995) also reported that heterogeneous groups learn more, form more positive attitudes toward the learning tasks, and become more positive toward individuals who are different.

Choosing an Approach to Cooperative Learning

As described Figure 13.2, all approaches to cooperative learning share some common characteristics; each, however, has different features that require specific preparation. A first planning step is to decide which of the several cooperative learning approaches to use. Kagan's structural approach can easily be incorporated into any lesson and used spontaneously once students have learned the different structures. Jigsaw and STAD require more planning and organization. Group investigation is the most complex approach and often requires coordination with other colleagues in the school and members of the larger community.

Choosing Lesson Goals and Content
Choosing an academic content focus and the social skills to be taught is the second planning task. Students' prior knowledge, their reading levels, and their interests influence the type of learning materials needed. Content of the lesson needs to be challenging but not too difficult. The type of social and teamwork skills to be taught need to be appropriate for the age and developmental levels of the students. Teaching social skills and group skills is an important aspect of all cooperative learning lessons. In fact, explicit teaching of these skills is one of the things that distinguish cooperative learning from other forms of small-group instruction. When a class initially begins using cooperative learning, considerable instructional time is required to teach social and teamwork skills, but this investment will pay dividends over time.

Grouping Students
In cooperative learning, students work in groups and group membership needs to be determined. While there are many ways of grouping students, including heterogeneously, homogeneously, randomly, or based on student interests, in general heterogeneous grouping has produced the most positive academic and cooperative results. If students are unaccustomed to cooperative work, it is best to start with simple groupings of two (dyads) or three (triads) to allow them to gain experience with working together. Later, a group with four to six members may be determined to be the ideal size. This group size allows for many variations: the group can be broken into dyads or triads, but can also work as a total group when needed. Most teachers report that groups larger than six are clumsy and allow some students to become disengaged. For some lessons, the teacher may wish to group students randomly and then disband the groups at the end of the lesson. For other cooperative learning lessons, groups may stay together for a period of time.

Gathering and Organizing Materials
All of the approaches to cooperative learning require careful planning in advance so that students can work in teams to study materials and accomplish the goals of the lesson. In contrast to whole-group teaching, where teachers present the information to students verbally, organizing for a cooperative learning lesson most often requires that teachers gather materials for students to read, discuss, and study. For some cooperative learning strategies, information needs to be carefully divided into portions so all students are accountable for the team's effort. For example, when using Jigsaw (explained later in the chapter) teachers select material that can be divided into four or five topics and each student assumes partial responsibility for learning their particular topic and then teaches others about it. For other cooperative learning lessons, the teacher needs to work closely with the school librarian and community resource people to ensure there is sufficient material for students to engage in required investigation, and in today's classrooms plans for helping students identify, access, and evaluate Internet materials are critical.

Organizing the Learning Environment
In cooperative learning, students work
together at tables or desks and these need
to be arranged to facilitate group work.
Places to store learning materials and the
group's products are also an important
element of the cooperative learning
environment. Group investigation requires
a strong school and community support
system. A high quality library that provides
a wide variety of materials, reliable Internet
access, and community resource people are
necessary to support all cooperative and
inquiry approaches to learning.

> **REFLECTION**
>
> Some educators believe that cooperative
> learning and having students work in
> small groups is a waste of time. What
> are your views on this topic? Do you
> agree or disagree? Has group work
> been a positive or a negative
> experience for you as a learner? As a
> teacher? Discuss these issues with a
> classmate or colleague who may have
> different views than you.

APPROACHES TO COOPERATIVE LEARNING

As described earlier, there are several approaches to cooperative learning that have been
developed over the past three decades. Five individuals or groups have normally been
given credit for these developments. In Table 13.1, we provide brief summaries of five
particular approaches: (1) David and Roger Johnson's *Learning Together*; (2) Spencer
Kagan's *Structural Approach*; (3) Elliott Aronson's *Jigsaw*; (4) Shlomo Sharan's *Group*

Table 13.1 Overview of five approaches to cooperative learning

Developer(s)	Name of approach and date(s) developed	Brief description
Roger and David Johnson	Learning Together (1975, 1998)	Provides five principles for organizing cooperative learning lessons. Promotes cooperative as contrasted to individualistic or competitive goals, structures, and rewards.
Spencer Kagan	Structural approach (1994, 2008)	Describes a variety of ways for structuring student interaction.
Elliott Aronson	Jigsaw (1978, 1997)	Divides up an overall topic into sub-topics so team members can become experts on a particular aspect of the topic and then teach their part to other group members.
Shlomo Sharan et al.	Group investigation (1990, 1992)	Outlines phases for leading student groups in somewhat large-scale investigations.
Robert Slavin	Student Teams Achievement Divisions (1994, 1995)	Teams study together and take weekly quizzes. They compete with other teams for points and recognition.

Investigation; and (5) Robert Slavin's Student Teams Achievement Divisions (STAD). We provide more detailed information about each approach below.

Johnson and Johnson's Learning Together

Roger and David Johnson, of the University of Minnesota, introduced the *Learning Together* approach to cooperative learning in the mid-1970s (Johnson & Johnson, 1975). They compared different task and reward structures and their impact on student learning. They also documented over a hundred studies spread over three decades that showed the positive benefits of cooperative versus individualistic or competitive approaches. Rather than providing steps or phases, as other cooperative learning models do, Johnson and Johnson have identified desired *patterns of interaction* and five basic *elements* necessary for structuring cooperative learning lessons. First, we explain **interaction patterns** and then we provide a brief overview of their basic elements.

Interaction Patterns Johnson and Johnson maintained that learning activities and assignments can be structured in three ways: competitive, individualistic, and cooperative. How learning activities and assignments are structured determines how students interact with one another, the teacher, and the learning materials. **Competitive activities** require students to compete with one another. Success depends on some people doing better than others. Grading on a curve or competing in a track meet are examples of competitive activities. **Individualistic activities** and assignments have students working mainly by themselves. Students learn to think and act alone. Achieving individualistic goals is unrelated to how well others do. Working toward predetermined standards is an example of an activity governed by individualistic task and goal structures. **Cooperative activities** and assignments require students to work together to learn. Success depends on the success of all group members.

While Johnson and Johnson strongly advocate cooperative task and goal structures, they also believe that there should be a balance of individualistic and competitive goals as well. They believe teachers should use all three patterns in an integrated way, and students should be taught the skills necessary to function in all three types of situation (Johnson & Johnson, 1998; Johnson, Johnson, & Holubec, 1990).

Basic Elements Johnson, Johnson, and Holubec (1990) outline five basic elements in their Learning Together model and contend lessons need to be designed with these elements in mind:

1. *Positive interdependence*: Create an environment where all members of a group feel connected to each other in accomplishing common goals. Individuals are supportive and caring. Individuals must succeed for the group to succeed, i.e., positive interdependence.
2. *Individual accountability*: Ensure each member of the group is responsible for and can demonstrate their own leaning.

> **REFLECTION**
>
> How would you describe the balance between individual, competitive, and cooperative task and goal structures in your classroom? How strongly do you feel about teamwork and cooperation? In your own teaching, do you lean more toward competition or cooperation?

3. *Face-to-face interaction*: Organize the environment to encourage interaction and dialogue among group members while working on common tasks.
4. *Collaborative skills*: Focus on social, communication, and critical thinking skills so students can work effectively in groups. Social skills include listening, understanding, clarifying, checking for understanding, taking turns, encouraging, and problem solving and conflict resolution skills.
5. *Processing*: Engage students in reflection on and assessment of group academic goals and collaborative interactions.

Kagan's Structural Approach

Spencer Kagan (1994, 1998, 2001) developed what he labeled the **structural approach** to cooperative learning. He articulated the differences between *cooperative activities* and *cooperative structures*. Cooperative activities, such as developing a team shield or engaging in a rope exercise, usually are intended to build effective teams or to teach specific social skills. Cooperative structures, on the other hand, are used to provide an organizational framework for student interaction. Kagan believes that cooperative structures can be used repeatedly in almost any subject area, at all grade levels, and at various points in a lesson. Activities, he says, get used up while structures can be used over and over. Kagan sees structures as the building blocks of a lesson and as tools to effectively engage students in learning. He contends that the art of good teaching is the ability to choose the best structure/content combinations to reach a given learning outcome. As with other approaches to cooperative learning, Kagan combines cognitive development with social development. He proposes four questions for teachers to consider when selecting a cooperative structure:

1. What kind of cognitive development does it foster?
2. What kind of social development does it foster?
3. Where in an overall lesson plan does it best fit?
4. With what kind of curriculum is it best used?

We provide a brief description of ten structures to help you understand the Kagan approach to cooperative learning:

- *Consultant line*: Students form two lines facing each other (groups of six to eight are best). Each student identifies a question they want advice on. Each pair consults on their respective questions. After a few minutes, one line moves and the other stays stationary. This creates a new consultant pair. Again, each new pair consults on their respective questions. One line progressively moves at intervals of approximately five minutes. Each student gets to consult (or share a great idea) with three or four other students.
- *Four corners*: The teacher labels each of the four corners of the classroom with statements or topics. Students move to the corner that represents their opinion or their area of interest. Once in the corner, students discuss and justify their choice. In a high school social studies class dealing with American involvement in a particular war, corners could be labeled "strongly agree," "agree," "disagree," and "strongly disagree." Alternatively, in a sixth-grade language class, corners could be labeled "biography," "novels," "poetry," and "short stories." Corners can be used

to assess prior knowledge, promote sharing of information, or serve as a review and summarizing activity for a unit of study.

- *Graffiti (Gibbs, 1997)*: The teacher posts flip charts or posters around the room. Each chart is labeled with a title. Students circulate in small groups of three or four with a felt marker. At each poster students discuss the topic and add comments to the chart. They can also draw pictures and symbols. Then they move (clockwise) on to the next chart. As students proceed around the room, they read what other groups have recorded and add additional thoughts. This is a great strategy to access prior knowledge or to review a topic.

- *Inside–outside circles*: Groups of students form two concentric circles, with half of the students on the inside circle and half on the outside circle. Inside students face out, outside students face in, and students pair up. Each pair engages in a discussion or a question and answer exchange using flash cards. After five minutes, the inside students rotate clockwise to create a new pair.

- *Numbered heads*: Tables are numbered 1, 2, 3, etc. Students in a group letter off A, B, C, etc. Therefore, each person has a specific and distinct number and letter. All students are responsible for individual learning and group members consult to be sure everyone is prepared. Then one student (such as 5B) is called on. Alternatively, all Bs can be asked to comment on the question: to agree, to disagree, to elaborate, or to offer an alternative perspective.

- *Pairs*: Half of the students in the class are given one set of materials to master and the other half are given a different set of materials. Students with the same material sit together and help each other learn. Students then find a partner who had different materials, and they teach each other what they have mastered.

- *Placemat (Bennett & Rolhesier, 2001)*: Each group is given a piece of chart paper. A space in the center is created (a square, a triangle, a rectangle, a circle, a heart) as group space. The rest of the placemat is divided so each individual has a section. A question is posed to the group and individuals record their answer in their individual section. Then individuals share their answers. Common responses or questions are recorded in the middle. For example, in a second-grade math class, students respond to a story problem using their part of the placemat as their workspace. All students share how they approached solving the problem. The correct answer and rationale are recorded in the group space. This allows for the teacher to ensure **individual accountability** as well as monitor group work.

- *Round table–round robin*: Organize students in triads. One person interviews, the second person is interviewed, and the third person is the recorder. Each triad completes three rounds so each person plays all roles. Alternatively, a set of questions can be circulated. Each student writes an answer to one question and passes it on to the next person. For high engagement, additional sets of questions can be circulated at the same time.

- *Teams consult*: All teammates put their pens in the pencil holder or the center of the table. A student reads the first question and then teams determine the answer by consulting resource materials and through discussion. The student on the left of the reader checks to see that teammates all understand and agree with the answer. When there is common agreement, all students pick up their pens and write the answer in their own words. Rotate roles and continue with question two, repeating the same steps: pens down, teams discuss, check for agreement, and individuals write.

- *Think–Pair–Share*: Described in Chapter 10, this was initially created by Frank Lyman (1986) to increase student engagement and facilitate more thoughtful responses. It has been widely distributed by Kagan. In **Think–Pair–Share**, the teacher poses a question, individual students *think* about (and record) their answer. Individuals then *pair* with another student to share their answer. The teacher calls on individuals or pairs to *share* with the large group.
- *Three-step interview*: Form groups of four and then two pairs. Students interview each other; first one way, then the other. Each student introduces the person they interviewed to the small group. A introduces B, B introduces A, C introduces D, and D introduces C. This can also be used as a review strategy, with each person being responsible for different questions.

Kagan's cooperative structures are quite easy to learn and easy for teachers to implement. They extend a teacher's repertoire of cooperative learning strategies and can help maximize student engagement. They are also compatible with strategies stemming from multiple and emotional intelligence theories. Stay tuned because Kagan and his colleagues (Kagan & Kagan, 2008) are continuously inventing new cooperative structures.

Jigsaw
Jigsaw was developed and first tested by Elliot Aronson and his colleagues (Aronson & Goode, 1978; Aronson & Patnoe, 1997). This approach to cooperative learning divides up the learning materials so group members can work on particular topics. Students start out in heterogeneous home or base teams comprised of four or five members. Members number off and then move to expert groups. Each expert group learns a different part or aspect of the assigned topic. They read and discuss learning materials provided by the teacher and help each other learn about their assigned topic. They also decide how best to present the material to others when their home teams reconvene. Each member of the team teaches their part to other home team members. Following home team meetings and discussions, students are tested independently on the material. Figure 13.3 illustrates the particular phases or steps in a Jigsaw lesson.

Over time, other versions of Jigsaw have been developed. Slavin and colleagues (Slavin, 1983) created Jigsaw II and Kagan and colleagues (Kagan, 1994) developed a number of variations on the original model. Regardless of the variation, Jigsaw is a powerful approach to cooperative learning. Like other approaches, it not only allows students to work together in groups, but has also been shown to be an effective way to cover a wide range of academic materials in a relatively brief period of time.

Group Investigation
The **group investigation** approach to cooperative learning blends the goals of academic inquiry and social-process learning. It can be used in all subject areas and at all age levels. In group investigation, students are actively engaged in planning and carrying out investigations and presenting their findings to peers and others. Group investigation begins with the teacher providing a stimulus or problem situation. Students then define more precisely the problem to be investigated, determine the roles required to conduct the investigation, organize themselves to collect information, analyze the data collected,

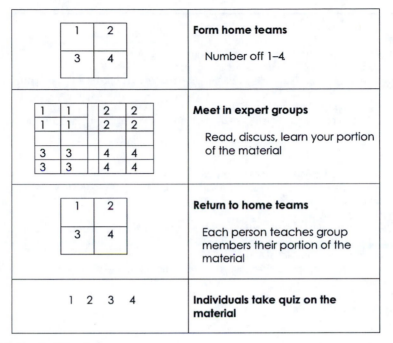

1 | **2** **3** | **4**	**Form home teams** Number off 1–4	
1 | 1 | 2 | 2 1 | 1 | 2 | 2 3 | 3 | 4 | 4 3 | 3 | 4 | 4	**Meet in expert groups** Read, discuss, learn your portion of the material	
1 | **2** **3** | **4**	**Return to home teams** Each person teaches group members their portion of the material	
1 2 3 4	**Individuals take quiz on the material**	

Figure 13.3 Illustration of a Jigsaw lesson

prepare and present a report, and evaluate the results of their work and the processes they used.

Thelen (1954, 1960) was the first to introduce group investigation. He believed that the classroom should be organized to reflect the larger social order and students should be required to work in democratic problem-solving groups to study academic and real-life problems using democratic processes and scientific methods of inquiry. Sharan and Hertz-Lararowitz (1980) and Sharan and Sharan (1990) used and studied the group investigation model over two decades and made refinements to Thelen's initial model. They outlined six steps or phases in the group investigation model. We summarize these in Figure 13.4.

You will note the similarities between the phases of group investigation and the problem-based learning model we describe in the next chapter.

Student Teams Achievement Divisions

Student Teams Achievement Divisions, or STAD, is another approach to cooperative learning. STAD was developed by Robert Slavin and his colleagues at Johns Hopkins University in the 1980s. It involves students working together in groups and groups that compete with each other. This approach has been quite thoroughly researched and been shown to be effective for helping students master declarative

> **REFLECTION**
>
> Which of the three models—Jigsaw, group investigation, or STAD—interests you most? With a classmate or colleague, arrange to experiment with one you haven't used before. Visit each other's classroom and meet to provide critique and feedback.

1. *Grouping*
   a. Present the topic
   b. Clarify the topic (compile a list of questions for group inquiry)
   c. Identify sub-topics (classify questions into categories)
   d. Form investigation groups (students select the sub-topic of their choice and form groups)
2. *Planning*
   a. Clarify the task—explore the sub-topic and formulate a research question
   b. Develop an action plan (what, when—deadlines, who—individually or in pairs, resources, responsibilities)
3. *Investigating*
   a. Prepare a daily plan
   b. Research—gather information from a variety of sources
   c. Analyze and evaluate the data—assess relevance of collected data related to the research topic
   d. Use the data to solve the group research problem
4. *Organizing the final product*
   a. Select the report format (learning center, guided tour, PowerPoint presentation, model, written report, drama, etc.)
   b. Plan the report (identify individual roles)
   c. Construct the report (group members complete individual assignments or responsibilities for the final presentation)
5. *Presenting*
   a. Groups present final reports
   b. Other groups react
6. *Evaluating*
   a. Establish criteria for the process (effective group investigation) and the product (presentation)
   b. Clarify components (roles, formative and summative assessment strategies, ratio of individual to group marks, weighting between evaluation of process and product)
   c. Check for understanding—do students understand how they will be evaluated in the group investigation activity?

Figure 13.4 Phases in group investigation
Source: Summarized from Sharan and Sharan (1992).

knowledge in the form of basic facts and conceptual information. Research (Slavin, 1994) on this approach has also revealed that it can lead to positive effects on the relationships among racial and ethnic groups. STAD involves organizing students into semi-permanent teams (usually together for about six weeks) and using an improvement point scoring system. STAD is made up of five interlocking elements, summarized in Figure 13.5

Summary of Cooperative Learning Approaches

Different approaches to cooperative learning are used for different reasons and to accomplish different learning goals. As described earlier, some approaches are quite easy to implement while other are more difficult. Using the Teaching Academy scenario we introduced at the beginning of the chapter as an illustration, in Table 13.2 we summarize the various approaches to cooperative learning and provide reasons why each might be used.

ASSESSMENT AND COOPERATIVE LEARNING

When using cooperative learning, it is important to assess both academic and social learning, an aspect of the model that has been somewhat controversial over the years.

1. *Class presentations*
   - teacher introduces STAD materials, most often with a lecture or reading materials followed by a discussion
   - presentation is clearly focused on information associated with the STAD unit
2. *Teams*
   - teams are composed of 4–5 students, who represent a cross-section of the class in academic levels, gender, and race or ethnicity
   - major function of the team is to prepare its members to do well on the quizzes
   - after the class presentation, the team meets to study worksheets or other materials
   - most often, the study takes the form of students quizzing one another back and forth
   - team members work to ensure that their teammates understand the content and work on correcting misconceptions and mistakes
   - teams are very important in STAD—emphasis is placed on team members doing their best for the team—the team provides peer support for academic performance and provides mutual concern and respect
   - only two worksheets and two answer sheets are given to each team
3. *Quizzes*
   - after one period of teacher presentation and one period of team practice, students take individual quizzes
   - quizzes are composed of course content-related questions
   - they are designed to test knowledge gained by students from class presentations and during team practice
   - students are not permitted to help one another during the quizzes—this makes sure that every student is individually responsible for knowing the material
4. *Individual improvement scoring*
   - students receive a quiz score and an improvement score each week
5. *Team recognition*
   - each week, teams receive recognition for the sum of the improvement scores of the team members
   - each week, the teacher prepares a newsletter to announce team scores and to recognize individuals who showed the greatest improvement or got perfect standings, and reports cumulative team standings
   - a newsletter is the primary means of rewarding teams and individual students for their performance; teachers can also use bulletin boards and special privileges

Figure 13.5 Critical elements of the STAD approach to cooperative learning
Source: Information taken and summarized from Slavin (1994).

Cooperative learning also allows for self-assessment, peer assessment, and teacher assessment, and there are many opportunities to provide students with ongoing feedback. Many of the assessment strategies described in Chapter 6—including paper-and-pencil tests, observations, checklists, rubrics, and group evaluations—can be used for assessing cooperative learning instructional outcomes.

STAD and Jigsaw require quizzes to be administered on a regular basis, normally at the end of a lesson or instructional segment. Group investigation requires assessing student projects, performances, and presentations. Rubrics can be used to assess products and presentations and also social skills. Checklists are useful for observing cooperative skill development. Kagan (1998) and Johnson and Johnson (1998) encourage the use of both self and group assessment. We comment on three issues related to assessment of cooperative learning activities and products: academic learning improvement scores, assessing cooperation, and individual versus team scores and rewards.

Academic Learning Improvement Scores
Slavin (1980) introduced the concept of the **improvement score** as a way to track individual and team progress. Each week, students receive points based on how much

Table 13.2 Summary of cooperative learning approaches and reasons for using each

Approach	Orientation	Reasons for using	Example
Aronson's Jigsaw	Cooperation	• to share the workload • to consider alternative perspectives	Ms. Collins used Jigsaw to look at different aspects of the novels she was teaching and to look at different kinds of texts/opinions on the same topic.
Johnson's Learning Together	Cooperative interdependence	• to promote support for learning • to develop social and teamwork skills	Mrs. Wong organized students into groups of four who could meet for peer tutoring the last 30 minutes of the science class on Fridays. They also met before and after quizzes.
Sharan's group investigation	Cooperative investigation	• to engage students in inquiry • to develop teamwork skills	Mr. Sanchez engaged students in several group investigations in his history course. This allowed him to cover diverse material while providing for student choice according to their interests.
Slavin's STAD	Cooperative competitive	• to structure support through competition • to focus on incremental improvement and teamwork	Mr. Jackson capitalized on students' inherent love of competition by using STAD in his Math class and weekly quizzes and improvement scoring.
Kagan's structures	Cooperation	• to actively engage students in learning • to develop social and teamwork skills	All of the teachers used Kagan's structures. Each year they decided on a range of structures they would emphasize in their different courses.

they improve as well as how well they do overall. A **baseline score** is established each week based on averages on past quizzes. Weekly quiz scores are compared to the base score. Students earn points based on the degree of improvement, as shown in Figure 13.6. Improvement scores are added together to create a team score. Teams are recognized weekly. In Slavin's model, the main method to provide team recognition is in a weekly class newsletter. Other rewards include class parties, privileges, and buttons of merit.

Kagan (1994) has adapted Slavin's improvement scoring system. He believes that students should receive two scores on quizzes and assignments: an individual score (in a square) and an improvement score (in a circle). Students are given 0, 1, 2, or 3 points each week, depending on how much they improve. Students who get 100 always get three points, and those who score between 95 and 99 get at least two points.

Assessing Cooperation
It is important to also assess teamwork and cooperation when using cooperative learning strategies. Students can complete self-assessments to assess their individual and collective success with using cooperation and teamwork skills. Table 13.3 provides an example of a rubric that can be used to assess cooperation.

```
                        Improvement scores

More than 10 points below base        _____   0 points
10 points below to 1 point below base _____   10 points
Base score to 10 points above base    _____   20 points
More than 10 points above base        _____   30 points
Perfect paper (regardless of base)    _____   30 points
```

Figure 13.6 Slavin's use of improvement scores
Source: Based on Slavin's scoring system (1995).

Individual versus Team Scores and Recognition

Assessing the work of individuals and of teams is important when using cooperative learning. While individuals are ultimately held accountable, group work must also be acknowledged and rewarded. **Team scores** or rewards are used to recognize the group's

Table 13.3 Rubric for assessing cooperation

Criteria	4	3	2	1
Works toward achievement of group goals	Actively helps identify group goals and works hard to meet them.	Communicates commitment to the group goals and effectively carries out assigned roles.	Communicates a commitment to group goals but does not carry out assigned roles.	Does not work toward group goals or actively works against them.
Demonstrates effective interpersonal skills	Actively promotes effective group interaction. Expresses ideas and opinions in a way that is sensitive to the feelings and knowledge base of others.	Participates in group interaction without prompting. Expresses ideas and opinions in a way that is sensitive to the feelings and knowledge base of others.	Participates in group interaction with prompting. Expresses ideas and opinions without considering the feelings and knowledge base of others.	Does not participate in group interaction, even with prompting. Expresses ideas in a way that is insensitive to the feelings and knowledge base of others.
Contributes to group maintenance	Actively helps the group identify changes or modifications necessary in the group process. Works toward making those changes.	Helps identify changes and modifications necessary in the group process. Works toward making those changes.	When prompted, helps identify changes or modifications necessary in the group process. Is only minimally involved in making those changes.	Does not attempt to identify changes or modifications necessary in group process, even when prompted. Refuses to work toward making changes.

Source: Developed based on information from Marzano, Pickering, and McTighe (1993).

effort. Improvement points and team scores, however, should never be used to report individual achievement or progress. Individual report card grades should always be a function of assessing what an individual can do, independent of their teammates (Kagan, 1994).

There has been controversy about cooperative learning approaches and assessment procedures. Students, teachers, and parents have raised questions and concerns about the appropriateness and fairness of assessing teams and assigning group scores. They worry about the negative effects of team scores on individual achievement. All the developers of cooperative learning approaches advocate team scores as a way to encourage and recognize teamwork and cooperation. All also agree that group or improvement scores should *not* be used in determining or reporting individual academic achievement. It is important for teachers to clearly explain both cooperative learning strategies and assessment procedures to students and parents. When used effectively, cooperative learning approaches acknowledge individual accountability while recognizing and rewarding the collective efforts of the team.

> **REFLECTION**
>
> **Cooperative grading** for effort remains controversial. Do you use this approach? If yes, how has it worked out? How do you do your calculations?

One fundamental problem with the recognition system in schools is that some students consistently get positive recognition and others do not. The traditional system (based on competition) works well for filtering and sorting, sending some, but not others, on to higher education and better jobs. The system works poorly for maximizing the learning potential and growth of particular students. Cooperative learning allows for all students to get feedback and some type of recognition related to what they have learned.

SUMMARY AT A GLANCE

- All approaches to cooperative learning are characterized by cooperative tasks, goals, and reward structures. Students learn in teams and are actively engaged in discussion, debate, tutoring, and teamwork. Teams are made up of high-, average-, and low-achieving students.
- The goals for cooperative learning are both cognitive and social. Students work together to master content and to learn social and teamwork skills.
- In general, there are six phases of a cooperative learning lesson: clarify goals and motivate students; present information; organize students into learning teams; assist with teamwork and study; presentation of group work or test on materials; and recognition of individual and group effort and achievement.
- Three theoretical perspectives provide intellectual support for cooperative learning: the concept of democratic classrooms, intergroup relations, and experiential learning.
- Cooperative learning is among the most widely researched teaching strategies and results demonstrate both academic and social effects. Studies have consistently shown that students learn more, have more positive feelings toward learning tasks, and increase their social and collaborative skills.
- Five primary approaches to cooperative learning have been developed. These include: Johnson and Johnson's learning together, Kagan's structural approach,

Aronson's Jigsaw, Sharan's group investigation, and Slavin's Student Teams Achievement Divisions (STAD).

- When using cooperative learning, it is important to assess both academic and social learning. Recognizing and acknowledging both individual and group efforts are important, but assessing group effort remains controversial.

CONSTRUCTING YOUR OWN LEARNING

With a colleague, develop a plan for introducing or increasing the use of cooperative learning strategies in your classrooms. Construct a table that indicates which approach you will use in what subject area during which week. Plan lessons together that incorporate cooperative learning strategies, implement them in your respective classrooms, and then meet to discuss how things worked out. Alternatively, one of you could conduct the lesson while the other observes, then revise the lesson together before the second round. Working with a plan and a partner in a systematic way over time will help you to integrate cooperative learning strategies into your repertoire.

RESOURCES

Bennett, B., & Rolheiser, C. (2001). *Beyond Monet: The art and science of the integration of instruction*. Durham, ON: Bookation.

Gibbs, J. (1997). *Tribes: A new way of learning together*. Sausalito, CA: Center Source Systems.

Johnson, D.W., & Johnson, R.T. (1998). *Learning together and alone: Cooperative, competitive, and individualistic learning* (5th ed.). Englewood, NJ: Prentice Hall.

Kagan, L., & Kagan, M. (2008). *Kagan cooperative learning*. San Juan Capistrano, CA: Kagan Publishing.

14

PROBLEM-BASED LEARNING

Why is there a waiting list for Mr. Singh's classes?
There is a waiting list of students who want to get into Mr. Singh's Physics classes and his course on Environmental Issues. Mr. Singh transferred to Taft High School three years ago after being recruited by the principal who was looking for teachers committed to student learning and teaching characterized by rigor, relevance, high engagement, and collaboration. Word spread quickly that Mr. Singh cared for his students and that he used problem-based learning in all his classes.

His approach turns teaching and learning topsy-turvy. Instead of listening to lectures and reading, students in Mr. Singh's classes work in small groups to develop plans for finding solutions to messy, ill-defined real-world problems. They are fully involved in all aspects of their learning, including deciding what and how to study. In addition to gaining broad knowledge and deep understanding, students leave Mr. Singh's courses with a commitment to self-directed learning and enriched skills in problem solving, teamwork, and project management.

Students report that they work hard but also have fun. They are motivated by the range of people they meet during their inquiries and the varied resources they get to use, such as the Internet, community experts, professional journals, and primary documents. They report that time just seems to fly. Other teachers in the school are starting to ask the question: What is Mr. Singh doing in his classroom that makes him so popular?

INTRODUCTION AND OVERVIEW

Mr. Singh centers much of his instruction around a teaching model called **problem-based learning (PBL)**, the model that is the focus of this chapter. We describe PBL by identifying its key characteristics, explaining the different roles for teachers and students, outlining the phases in the model, and describing strategies for organizing, monitoring, and assessing instructional outcomes. We present four ways that PBL can become part of a classroom teacher's repertoire: short problem-based activities, problem-based interdisciplinary learning days or units, PBL projects, and PBL units and courses. We also provide the rationale and the model's intellectual roots, and summarize evidence that supports the use of PBL. We end the chapter by describing challenges this model presents, and offer thoughts about how to get started. We begin with addressing four questions:

- What is PBL?
- What do teachers and students do in PBL?
- Where does PBL get its theoretical support?
- Why use PBL and is it effective?

What is Problem-based Learning?

Problem-based learning is a student-centered approach that organizes curriculum and instruction around carefully crafted "ill-structured" and real-world problem situations. Learning is active rather than passive, integrated rather than fragmented, and connected rather than disjointed. As in cooperative learning, students work in small groups, share responsibility for learning together, and in the process develop critical thinking and problem-solving skills and skills for collaboration and project management. Developers and theorists have identified a number of defining characteristics and features of PBL (Arends, 2009; Bridges & Hallinger, 1993; Levin, 2001). These are summarized below.

- *Problems or issues.* The starting point for PBL lessons and activities is a compelling problem or issue. The content of learning is organized around problems rather than academic disciplines.
- *Authentic.* Students seek realistic solutions to real-world and **authentic problem**s. Problems that focus student inquiries are socially important and ones students are likely to encounter later on in life.
- *Investigation and problem solving.* Rather than acquiring knowledge and skills by listening or reading, students in PBL are actively engaged in learning through inquiry, investigation, and problem solving.
- *Interdisciplinary perspectives.* Students explore a number of perspectives and draw on multiple disciplines while involved in PBL investigations.
- *Small-group collaboration.* Learning occurs within the context of small, five- or six-member, learning groups.
- *Products, artifacts, exhibitions, and presentations.* Students demonstrate their learning by creating products, **artifacts**, and exhibits. In many instances, they present the results of their work to peers and to invited guests from other classrooms or the community.

The learning environment for PBL is characterized by openness, active engagement, and an atmosphere of intellectual freedom. Independence and diversity are encouraged and recognized. Students work on multiple learning tasks in multiple locations (in the classroom, in the library, online, and in the community). Their investigations proceed at different rates and in different directions and require learning environments where they are free to express novel ideas without fear of negative judgment or recrimination. As with inquiry teaching and case-based and jurisprudential inquiry, PBL requires an environment where students have respect for each other and are tolerant of ambiguity and difference.

What Do Teachers and Students Do in Problem-based Learning?

In PBL, traditional teacher and student roles differ quite dramatically from those assumed when more teacher-centered practices are used. There is a clear shift from teacher-directed instruction to student-centered learning. Students work in small groups and assume responsibility for their own learning, both individually and together. They design and manage their own investigations. They explore and make decisions about what kinds of information to gather and which solutions to adopt. They also coach one another as they collaborate in learning teams. Finally, students are actively involved in the assessment of their own learning. They engage in reflection on and provide feedback to their peers about both their conceptual understandings and about the learning strategies they employ.

Teachers in PBL serve as models, coaches, questioners, guides, and mentors. As *models*, teachers think aloud with students; they model behaviors they want students to use. As *coaches*, teachers coax and prompt students; they provide feedback and encourage students to become independent and self-reliant learners. As *questioners*, they ask higher-order and meta-cognitive questions that help focus student inquiry. As *guides*, teachers provide instruction about local community resources, websites, and a variety of valuable textual materials. They also teach students about effective group processes and help groups that are stuck get back on track. In some cases, teachers serve as *mentors* to a select number of students. Mentoring happens most often when students are working on projects where the teacher has particular content expertise.

> **REFLECTION**
>
> Consider for a few minutes how you have used some form of PBL in your classroom. How has PBL worked for you? Highly successfully? Not so great? Discuss PBL with classmates or colleagues. What approaches have they used?

Connecting Problem-based Learning to the Context and Science of Learning

The strongest theoretical support for PBL rests on the constructivist perspectives about how people learn, particularly the work of two European psychologists, Jean Piaget and Lev Vygotsky, and the early work by the American philosopher, John Dewey. Piaget (1954, 1963) studied intellectual development for over 50 years. He confirmed that curiosity and the need to understand motivate children to investigate and to construct theories that will explain their environment and experiences. Vygotsky (1978) emphasized the social aspect of learning and believed that social interaction and inquiry are critical components for helping students construct new ideas and for developing their intellect. Dewey (1916, 1938), you remember from earlier discussions, envisioned schools as laboratories where students could engage in real-life inquiry and problem solving and learn about important social and intellectual issues.

Problem-based learning, like cooperative learning and inquiry-based teaching, also has theoretical underpinnings in cognitive psychology. These perspectives, you remember from Chapter 2 and elsewhere, emphasize the importance of providing learning experiences that allow students to construct meaning for themselves, and focus on cognition and what student are thinking in contrast to how they are behaving.

The modern history of PBL stems from work in the early 1970s when medical schools, particularly McMaster University in Canada (Barrow & Tamblyn, 1980), began using PBL as an alternative approach to medical education. However, the intellectual and historical roots are far older. Problem-based learning today embraces Socrates' question and answer dialectical approach, as well as the Hegelian thesis–antithesis–synthesis dialogue. During the twentieth century, several theorists and educators developed versions of PBL, such as the project method (Kilpatrick, 1918), experiential education

(Dewey, 1938), discovery learning (Bruner, 1966, 1973), and inquiry-based teaching (Suchman, 1962) that have strongly influenced the contemporary practices we describe here.

Why Use Problem-based Learning and Is It Effective?

There is a substantial knowledge base that has demonstrated the effectiveness of PBL in promoting student motivation and learning (David, 2008; Hmelo-Silver, 2004; Thomas, 2000). Several fields of inquiry have made contributions to this research.

Problem-based learning has been shown to *actively engage students in relevant learning experiences.* Active engagement in problems helps students' access prior knowledge and leads to deep understanding. It appears that new information is processed and understood better if students have an opportunity to elaborate on that information in problem-solving situations. Similarly, learning that occurs in the context of real-life situations is more likely to be retained and applied (Boaler, 1998; Bransford, Vye, Kinzer, & Risko, 1990).

Problem-based learning *capitalizes on students' natural curiosity, imagination, and search for understanding.* Real-world problems capture students' interest and are motivating. Students express substantially more positive attitudes toward learning when problem-based approaches are used as compared to reports that learning is irrelevant and anxiety producing in traditional programs (deVolder & deGrave, 1989; deVries, Schmidt, & deGraaff, 1989; Schmidt, Dauphinee, & Patel, 1987).

Problem-based learning *promotes achievement* and higher-order thinking. Learning activities that involve thinking, problem solving, and understanding often have more positive effects on student achievement than do more traditional teaching methods (Brown & Palincsar, 1989; Carpenter & Fennema, 1992; Knapp, Shields, & Turnball, 1992; Resnick, 1987). The inquiry focus of PBL requires critical thinking and the open-ended nature of student investigations provides opportunities for creative thinking. Creating artifacts and preparing presentations of their work allows students to move beyond using the cognitive processes of remembering and understanding and requires them to analyze, evaluate, and synthesize information from a variety of sources.

REFLECTION

How have you experienced PBL as a student in workshops or on courses you have taken? Has this been an effective or ineffective way for you to learn? Why?

Problem-based learning engages students in learning information in ways that are similar to how it will be learned and applied in future, out-of-school situations. PBL *assesses learning in ways that demonstrate understanding and not mere acquisition* (Glick & Holyoak, 1983). Further, **cross-disciplinary** studies on **experiential learning** show that exposure to concrete elements of real-world practice can increase a learner's ability to contemplate, analyze, and systematically plan strategies for action (Kolb, Boyatzis, & Mainemelis, 2001).

In Research Box 14.1 we summarize and highlight one study that illustrates the multi-effects of PBL on student motivation and achievement.

RESEARCH BOX 14.1

Boaler, J. (1998). Open and closed mathematics: Student experiences and understandings. *Journal for Research in Mathematics Education, 29,* 41–62.

In a very interesting study, Boaler used matched populations to compare two different approaches to mathematics instruction: project-based learning versus traditional approaches. She followed a cohort of students from two schools (300 students in total) as they moved from Year 9 (age 13) to Year 11 (age 16). The students in both schools were similar in socioeconomic status and had experienced the same approaches to mathematics instruction in prior years. Results from a national, standardized test of mathematics proficiency administered at the beginning of the study revealed no significant differences between the scores of students in the two schools.

In one school, "traditional" mathematics instruction followed a teacher-directed, didactic format. Mathematics was taught using whole-class instruction, textbooks, tracking, and the frequent use of tests. In the second school, "project-based learning" was used. Students worked on open-ended projects and in heterogeneous groups. Teachers taught using a variety of methods and students were allowed to work on their own or with others and to exercise a great deal of choice while completing mathematics lessons.

Data collection included observations of 90 one-hour lessons in each school, interviews with students in the second and third year of the study, annual student questionnaires, and interviews with teachers at the beginning and end of the research period. In addition, the researcher analyzed student responses to a standardized national assessment measure, the General Certificate of Secondary Education (GCSE).

Overall, students who learned mathematics from teachers using PBL outperformed and had more positive attitudes toward the subject than did their counterparts who learned using traditional, more didactic methods. In summary:

- *National examination.* Three times as many students in the project-based school as those in the traditional school attained the highest possible grade on the national examination. Overall, significantly more students at the project-based school passed the national examination administered in year three of the study as compared to students in the traditional school.
- *Rote knowledge of mathematical concepts.* Students in the project-based school performed as well or better than students in the traditional school on items that required rote knowledge of mathematics concepts.
- *Conceptual questions.* Students in the project-based school outperformed students at the traditional school on questions that could not be answered using verbatim information learned on the course or those that required thought and creative application of mathematical rules.
- *Knowledge application.* Students taught in a more traditional, didactic model developed an inert knowledge that they reported was of no use to them in the real world. In contrast, students taught using the open, project-based model reported acquiring useful forms of knowledge they could apply in a variety of settings.

> • *Attitudes toward mathematics.* At the traditional school, the majority of students reported that they "found the work boring and tedious. . . . They thought mathematical success rested on being able to remember and use rules." In contrast, students at the project-based school regarded mathematics as "a dynamic, flexible subject that involved exploration and thought."

PLANNING FOR PROBLEM-BASED LEARNING LESSONS

There are six major tasks to consider when planning for PBL: clarifying goals, selecting or designing problems, identifying resources, preparing assessments, organizing learning groups, and orienting students.

Clarifying Content and Process Goals

As with other strategies we have described, clarifying the goals for PBL projects and activities is the first planning step. As portrayed in Table 14.1, there are both content and process goals to consider.

Content goals focus on curriculum standards, concepts, and relationships stemming from the overall topic and problem situation. Process goals focus on inquiry, problem-solving and self-directed learning skills, as well as on collaborative and project management skills. Being clear about the specific goals for a PBL project or activity helps students understand what is expected and provides clarification on how they should proceed.

Table 14.1 Problem-based learning goals

Content goals	• curriculum standards • specific content concepts • relationships among ideas in the problem situation
Process goals Inquiry and problem-solving skills	• problem identification • problem investigation • analysis of alternative solutions • decision making with evidence
Self-directed learning skills	• identifying learning issues and questions • locating and evaluating information • organizing and synthesizing information • providing evidence of learning
Collaboration skills	• listening • problem solving • managing differences and conflict • encouraging, acknowledging, supporting
Project management skills	• setting goals • identifying learning strategies • dividing and assigning work • monitoring progress

Selecting or Designing Problems

Perhaps one of the most difficult and important tasks in PBL is identifying or designing good problem situations. Effective problems have several common characteristics:

- *Authentic*: The problem deals with a real-world situation or issue.
- *Ill-structured and messy*: The problem is complex, with many issues and sub-issues for which multiple solutions exist.
- *Relevant*: The problem or issue is meaningful and important to students' lives and to society.
- *Academically rigorous*: The problem provides opportunities for students to think critically and creatively and to practice research, writing, problem-solving, decision-making, and communication skills.
- *Interdisciplinary in nature*: The problem draws on knowledge and experiences from a range of disciplines and perspectives.

Sometimes PBL situations are linked to specific curriculum standards and benchmarks. Other times, they grow out of issues that emerge in local communities that are of interest to students. Table 14.2 provides examples of problem situations that can be used at various grade levels and subjects areas.

Table 14.2 Possible problem-based learning situations

	Upper elementary level	Middle level	Secondary level
Science	What is the cause and impact of over-population or endangered status of certain species?	What is the impact of wide-scale usage of chemicals on humans?	What are the pros and cons of stem cell research and therapy?
Environment	How do different weather patterns develop and affect how we live?	Who owns the water in North America and what would be a fair plan for its distribution and use?	Is global warming real and what has caused differences of opinion in regard to this question?
History	Where did local laws and rules come from? Do they still make sense, or do they need to be changed?	How has technology changed over time and influenced behavior and consumer patterns?	What does human slavery mean? How has it changed and stayed the same over time?
Geography/ Cultural Studies	What were the cultural traditions and rituals of our ancestors? How have they influenced life in America today?	How would life in the Pacific Northwest be affected if all the dams on the Columbia River were removed?	How accurate is the "world is flat hypothesis" and, if accurate, how will it affect where and how people live in the future?
Health	What is the meaning of "healthy" and what do we need to do to achieve a healthy society?	What diseases and conditions have affected humans over the past century?	What are the private and public issues related with "required" immunization policies?

Identifying Resources

Another key planning task is identifying and locating resources for students to use in their investigations. To facilitate different learning styles and different perspectives, a range of materials on the problem under investigation need to be secured. In addition to local libraries and media centers, today literally thousands of websites are a source of valuable information and documents. Knowledgeable persons from the local community, as well as organizations such as museums, businesses, and non-profit associations, can also provide important resources for PBL lessons and activities. Below is an example how one school used local museums as resources for PBL activities and projects:

> Normal Park Magnet Museum School (K-8) in Chattanooga, Tennessee established partnerships with seven local museums: the Creative Discovery Museum, the Hunter Museum of American Art, the Chattanooga African-American Museum, the Chattanooga Regional History Museum, the Chattanooga Nature Center, the Tennessee Aquarium, and the Chattanooga Zoo. School and museum educators worked together to plan quarterly curriculum projects, where students traveled to the museums on what they labeled "curriculum-based learning expeditions." Classrooms also hosted museum and community experts as guest instructors on a regular basis. Each quarter, students displayed what they had learned by building curriculum exhibits and presenting these to parents and community friends during school-sponsored "Exhibit Nights."
>
> (Adapted from www.normalparkmuseummagnet.com)

Preparing Assessments

Because problem-based learning is student-centered and has multiple and complex learning outcomes, preparing formative and summative assessment instruments and procedures in the planning phase is especially important. Identifying targets and establishing criteria for PBL provides direction and parameters for students as they pursue their investigations. Formative assessments create structured ways to monitor student progress and to provide feedback to students at regular intervals. Checklists and scoring rubrics provide criteria for evaluating final performances, products, and exhibits. We describe some specific assessment strategies for monitoring progress in a later section. The whole topic of using performance assessment for summative assessment was described in some detail in Chapter 6.

Organizing Learning Groups

Most PBL investigations are conducted in small **learning groups** comprised of five or six students. Teachers can assign groups or allow students to self-select. In most instances, it is best to provide criteria for group composition to ensure groups have balance and a range of students with a variety of skills. Sometimes, however, students' interests and preferences may determine group composition. The structure of learning groups can also vary. Some teachers prefer totally unstructured and student-centered groups. Others prefer more teacher-directed and organized groups.

Orienting Students to Problem-based Learning

It is important in the planning phase to decide how to orient students to PBL projects or activities. Students need to understand how PBL works and be clear about expectations when this instructional approach is being used. Students will benefit from an overview of the phases in the PBL process, as well as guidance about the specifics of the different phases. When PBL is introduced for the first time to a group of students, it is necessary to provide instruction on problem-solving, collaboration, and project management skills that facilitate small-group interaction. Sometimes, students resist PBL initially. In our own experiences, we have found that some students prefer to remain in more passive roles and to have information provided to them rather than figure things out on their own. Finding ways to reduce this type of resistance should be considered carefully as you plan for PBL.

> **REFLECTION**
>
> Which task of the PBL planning process would be easiest for you? Which would be most difficult? Which problem listed in Table 14.2 do you find intriguing? Consider getting together with a classmate or colleague and developing a problem situation appropriate for your respective classrooms.

EXECUTING PROBLEM-BASED LEARNING LESSONS

Later in the chapter we discuss four different approaches to problem-based learning. While each approach has its own guidelines and specific procedures, there are some overall phases that are common to all PBL strategies. We outline these in Figure 14.1 and then briefly discuss each below. More detailed descriptions will be provided as we explain the different variations of PBL.

Problem-based learning begins with the presentation of a problem situation and the organization of students into learning groups. Student groups are then asked to design and execute their investigations in pursuit of finding possible solutions. Students' progress is monitored by the teacher and by students themselves as the inquiries unfold. Finally, groups demonstrate their learning and engage in reflection and debriefing.

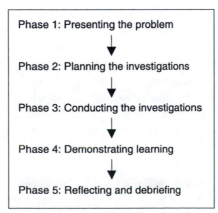

Figure 14.1 Phases of problem-based learning

Presenting the Problem

A PBL lesson or activity begins with the introduction of a somewhat ill-structured and complex problem situation. The introduction should be carefully executed so it inspires students and peaks their curiosity. During this phase of the lesson, teachers can also have students discuss what they already know about the problem, generate a list of questions, and record their initial thoughts and hypotheses about the problem. Discussion can be done either with the whole class or in small groups.

Planning the Investigation

Most forms of PBL require students to work in groups to plan their investigation and decide on the types of resources they will need to collect or consult. Sometimes teachers provide criteria, templates, and checklists to guide student planning and inquiry while the group members decide on the details and plan specific actions they need to take. Other times, student groups are given complete freedom to plan their investigations. Each learning group completes an overall plan at this phase that identifies tasks, resources, timelines, and responsibilities. Later in the chapter we provide additional guidance to help students plan investigations for problem-based projects.

Conducting the Investigation

Sometimes a problem situation can be solved in a single class period. More often, however, PBL investigations takes place over a series of days, or in some cases weeks, as students pursue answers to the questions outlined in their plans. In most instances, individual students will research information and then report back and share with other members of their learning group. Teachers and students monitor group progress as the investigations proceed. Usually, checkpoints or benchmarks are identified in the learning plan. Students are taught to monitor themselves, their understandings, and their learning strategies. Journals or problem logs are two ways to keep track of information, structure progress, and facilitate student self-assessment.

Demonstrating Learning

Problem-based learning culminates in some kind of group presentation or display of final products in exhibits. These activities provide opportunities for students to demonstrate what they have learned and to discuss and debate with each other. Sometimes, the final product or presentation is carefully defined at the beginning of a PBL project or unit and guides the investigation throughout. At other times, students are provided with choices about how they will demonstrate what they have learned. Sometimes, final presentations are made to small groups; at other times, each PBL group presents to the entire class. Experts and community resource people who have worked with the students during their investigations can also be invited to be part of the audience and to provide feedback to students on their work. Some teachers like to invite family members.

Reflecting and Debriefing

Reflecting and **debriefing** on the problem-solving process is an integral part of problem-based learning. It is important for students to reflect on the knowledge and skills they have acquired, the learning strategies they have employed, and the contributions they have made to their learning group. This allows them to summarize the concepts and understandings they have acquired. Learning groups should also participate in the reflection process and explore how well they worked together and how well they used their project management skills. Questions for PBL groups to consider might include: "What worked for us?", "What didn't work?", "What did we learn about working together?", and "What might we do differently next time?"

> **REFLECTION**
>
> How do you currently engage students in problem solving? How do you engage them in reflection? Discuss with a classmate or colleague how they provide opportunities for problem solving and reflection.

VARIATIONS OF PROBLEM-BASED LEARNING

We present four different ways teachers can incorporate PBL into their classrooms and schools. We place them on a difficulty of implementation continuum from simple to complex and from the amount of teacher versus student direction required. Each approach also varies in the amount of instructional time required. We encourage experimentation with PBL and hope our experienced teacher readers will consider moving along the continuum from the more teacher-directed activities to those that are more student-centered. We display the four PBL options in Figure 14.2, and illustrate how they vary along the "simple–complex" and "teacher–student directed" continuums.

Problem-based Activities

One way to get started with PBL is to introduce short problem-based activities that small groups of students can complete in 30- to 45-minute periods of time. These activities are well structured. They have a clear problem statement and a set of self-contained learning materials. Students work in pairs, triads, or quads to solve specific problems in two stages: (1) completion of the problem-solving activity, and (2) discussion and reflection on what has been learned. It is important to distinguish between puzzlers or brainteasers, and PBL activities. The former generally have one correct answer, while several solutions exist for the kinds of problem-based activities we recommend. Four examples of problem-based activities are displayed in Table 14.3. These types of problem-based learning activity are often included in programs for gifted and talented students, but we believe that with appropriate modifications they can work for all students.

Simple <---> Complex			
Problem-based activities	Problem-based interdisciplinary learning days and units	Problem-based learning projects	Problem-based learning units, courses, and programs
Teacher-directed <---> Student-centered			

Figure 14.2 Problem-based learning options

Table 14.3 Examples of problem-based activities

Plastic cup bridge	Newspaper fashion designs
Materials (per group) 24 plastic cups, one pair of scissors per person	*Materials* (per group) Used newspapers, masking tape, markers, scissors
Problem In 30 minutes, using only cutting and slotting methods, make a structure with a single, supporting cup at each end and the maximum span possible.	*Problem* In 45 minutes, design an outfit, create the outfit out of newspaper, dress a model, and prepare a commentary card to be read during the fashion show.
Issue collage	**Summer beach house design**
Materials (per group) A collection of magazines, one pair of scissors per person, glue stick, poster board	*Materials* (per group) Graphing paper, regular pencils, colored pencils, and an eraser
Problem In 45 minutes, choose a topic/issue and create a collage that illustrates a position on the topic.	*Problem* In 30 minutes, design a summer beach house that can accommodate six people. Some enjoy games, some enjoy sports, some like to read, and some like to write.

Problem-based activities can also be incorporated into classroom learning centers. Typically, **learning centers** are spaces in a classroom that are activity based and offer students some measure of choice in the type of learning experience to pursue. Some learning centers are organized around ideas associated with multiple intelligences or learning styles. Others are organized around particular subjects or specific kinds of problem situations. Learning centers are usually stocked with a variety of materials, such as books, manipulatives, artifacts, games, computers and software programs, and video and audio recordings. We have also seen learning centers organized into boxes of materials that students take to their desks rather than going to special locations in the classroom.

While learning centers are commonly associated with elementary classrooms, we know middle and high school teachers who use them as well. Here are examples of how two high school teachers incorporated PBL centers in their classrooms:

Tyler, a ninth-grade history teacher, uses learning centers to facilitate students' learning about world religions. He organizes teams of four to work in centers which represent different religions. At each center, students find a template to guide their work. They are asked first to identify what they know about a particular religion and to pose questions that need answering. Every ten minutes, teams rotate to the next center and pick up where the last group left off. Tyler's world religions unit lasts three weeks. During the first week, students work at all the learning centers for the purpose of acquiring basic knowledge about each religion. In the second week, teams select a center to study a particular religion in depth and to develop an exhibit or presentation that will demonstrate their understanding of this religion. During the third week, students participate in a learning fair, where they present the knowledge they have acquired about their religion and learn about other religions from their peers.

Lakesha has incorporated learning centers as the primary way she teaches her senior-level mathematics courses. She has divided her students into small learning groups of four or five and has developed a range and variety of learning center activities and problems for the concepts in her math courses. Each center has a different focus: an assessment center, a literacy center, a preview center, a practice center, a technology center, and a teaching center. All, however, are related to the same mathematical standard and/or concept. Students rotate from center to center and Lakesha, located in the teaching center, works regularly with small groups of students. Sometimes she groups and assigns students to centers based on their level of understanding and their need for different kinds of learning experiences. Lakesha has worked with up to 35 students using her learning center approach. As her classes expand or shrink, she makes adjustments by changing the number of centers. She started with small steps, and used learning centers occasionally. Now she can't imagine teaching without her learning center approach.

Problem-based Interdisciplinary Learning Days and Units
Traditionally, schools have compartmentalized subjects and taught each as disconnected disciplines in short segments of time. **Problem-based interdisciplinary learning days**, on the other hand, allow instruction to focus on a single topic in ways that reveal cross-disciplinary connections. This approach requires students to be immersed in a full day (sometimes more) of inquiry and discussion. Planning for a problem-based inter-disciplinary day begins with identifying an important or essential "big" question or problem situation. This problem may be related to particular curriculum standards or it may grow out of local issues relevant to students' lives. Teams of teachers, sometimes assisted by students, design a variety of problem-based and experiential activities for students to participate in during the interdisciplinary day. Sometimes, students are given a range of choices, and they follow their own agenda. At other times, activities are designed that require all students to participate. Regardless, students individually or in learning groups cycle through a variety of inquiry and problem-solving activities as the day unfolds. Below are examples of how three schools have organized for interdisciplinary learning days:

At Oceanside Elementary School teachers, students, and community members participate in problem-based interdisciplinary days four times a year. In the past, these days have focused on such diverse topics as: "What causes the changes in the weather?", "What are the ways we use mathematics in life?", and "What does culture mean and look like?" This format is also used during the last week of the school year, when each grade level picks a problem and students are engaged in mini-explorations that culminate in a school-wide learning walk-through to observe products and exhibits that have been created by the different classrooms. The fourth grade always investigates "What is the world like under the sea, and how is it changing?" Students research sea creatures and create papier mache replicas; they measure temperatures, explore waves, view excerpts from videos, engage in discussions about the power and mysteries of the ocean, and work on problems related to changes in the world's oceans.

At West Park Middle School each grade level participates in problem-based interdisciplinary days three times a year—in November, February, and May. Fridays of the designated month are devoted to the interdisciplinary inquiries. During the first Friday, students are exposed to the problem statement and participate in a variety of learning activities developed by grade level and subject area teams. These activities allow students to explore the problem from different perspectives. Students work in small groups and gather information and explore the topic over the next two Fridays. On the final Friday of the month, students display artifacts and exhibits in a school-wide "learning fair" demonstrating their new understandings. Some of the problems they have addressed include: "What are the rights and responsibilities of citizenship?", "How does one start and run a small business?", and "How do we protect and preserve the environment?"

At Best Practices High School in Chicago students participate in four, two-week interdisciplinary units (IDUs). This means that over the four years of a high school education, students will participate in 16 PBL experiences. Teachers organize the IDUs around student questions. Sometimes teachers team teach; other times, students rotate from teacher to teacher so they can get different perspectives on a particular problem. The key feature of IDUs is that students are engaged in inquiry and problem solving about issues relevant to their lives. Some of the topics that have been used include:

- Who am I? (a study of self and identity).
- The island nations (combining geography, English, and art).
- Careers (a chance to explore aspirations and choices).
- Isms (the nature, origins, and solutions to eliminate discrimination).
- Better pastures (a large-scale simulation of political, social, and economic conflict that highlights environmental concerns).

Problem-based Learning Projects

The PBL project is another form of problem-based learning. Typically, PBL projects begin with an end product or "artifact" in mind. Examples of culminating products can include: writing a report or proposal, designing a model, creating a multimedia production, making an oral presentation, participating in a panel discussion, designing a website, developing a blueprint, or creating a small business plan.

In this PBL variation, students are usually provided with rather detailed criteria for student projects and guidelines to structure some of the learning experiences. Students work in small groups and engage in decision making within the defined parameters. A template to guide planning for PBL projects is displayed in Table 14.4.

Anita Steinberg (1997), in her book *Real Learning, Real Work*, provides an alternative way of thinking about PBL projects and outlines six criteria for designing projects. She proposes that projects need to be *authentic*, require *academic rigor*, involve **applied learning**, engage students in *active exploration*, have *adult connections*, and have clear and varied *assessment* strategies. Questions related to each criteria are presented in Table 14.5. Below we provide four examples of PBL projects:

Table 14.4 Planning problem-based learning projects

Project theme	What is the driving question for the project?
Project outcomes	What are the project's content and process outcomes?
Project activities	What activities will students work through to learn about the topic?
Project products	What products will students produce during the project as evidence of learning? (poem, proposal, outline, log of interviews, PowerPoint presentation, model, website, scrapbook)
Project management	How will student progress be tracked? By the teacher? By students? How will feedback be provided? What are the timelines for different phases of the project?
Project assessment	How will the project's content and process learning outcomes be assessed? How will self-assessment and peer assessment be structured? How will the final grade be determined?

Source: Summarized and adapted from Markham et al. (2003).

Table 14.5 Six criteria for designing problem-based learning projects

Authentic	• Is it a "real-world" problem? • Is the problem or question meaningful to students? • What are appropriate audiences/locations for the students' work?
Academic rigor	• What is the central problem or question being addressed? • What are the learning standards, knowledge areas, and central concepts? • What "habits of mind" will students develop? (e.g., questioning and posing problems; precision of language and thought; persistence)
Applied learning	• How will students apply the knowledge they are learning? (e.g., designing a product, improving a system, organizing an event) • What workplace competencies does the project develop? (e.g., working in teams; using technology appropriately; communicating ideas; collecting, organizing, and analyzing information) • What self-management skills does the project require students to use? (e.g., developing a work plan, prioritizing pieces of work, meeting deadlines, conducting meetings, identifying and allocating resources)
Active exploration	• What field-based activities will students be involved in? (e.g., interviewing experts or job shadowing at a worksite) • Which methods and sources of information will students use in their investigations? (e.g., interviewing, observing, gathering and reviewing documents, model-building, using online services)
Adult connections	• Who are the adults with expertise and experience who can assist students? (answer questions, provide feedback, offer advice) • Will students be able to observe and participate with adults during a worksite visit? • Who can help students develop a sense of the real-world standards for this type of work?
Assessment practices	• What are the criteria for measuring desired student outcomes? • How are students involved in reviewing or establishing project criteria? • What methods of self- and peer-assessment will students use? • When and how will students receive timely feedback on their work? • What products will students complete during the life of the project? • What culminating exhibition or presentation will students complete?

Source: Summarized and adapted from Steinberg (1997).

Every Wednesday is "choice time" at Santa Fe Elementary School. This is a 90-minute period of time when students can choose what to study. Topics change every ten weeks, but a perennial favorite among fifth-grade students is robotics. Using a PBL approach, students learn the basics of electronics, mechanics, and software as they work in teams to build vehicles and other structures with Lego, participate in competitions, and arrange ways to demonstrate what they have learned.

At Loon Lake Middle School PBL is the approach for their related-arts program. Students work through a series of 30 projects at each grade level: ten in home arts, ten in technical arts, and ten in technology. Over a three-year period, students are engaged in 90 different projects. They rotate from one art form to another in ten-week cycles. The entire program is based on creating products that students have worked on individually, in pairs, or in triads. Table 14.6 provides examples of seventh-grade projects.

Jonathon, the art history teacher at Charleston High School, organizes PBL projects around an art exploration in the local community. The assignment is entitled "What is art?" Students work in triads for this project-based assignment. Each triad chooses an art form (sculpture, painting, installations, print making, carving). Then, individuals investigate local art works and eventually choose a particular piece of art from their community to learn about and profile. Students research their art piece, identifying what influenced it and the processes associated with its creation. They also research the artist, their background, and their other work. Students share the results of their investigations with each other. Finally, triads write a paper and prepare a presentation on their art form, their artist, and their selected piece of art.

Increasingly, many high schools and some states have introduced the "senior project" as a graduation requirement, and it is another example of a PBL project. The senior

Table 14.6 Seventh-grade related arts projects

Wk	Home arts	Technical arts	Technology
1	Compiling a calorie chart	Compiling a basic toolbox	Creating a word document
2	Developing a healthy snack list	Using duct tape to repair	Cutting and pasting
3	Making trail mix	Using a glue gun	Creating a table
4	Compiling a shopping list	Programming timers and machines	Tracking changes
5	Making French toast	Taking measurements	Formatting documents
6	Making a grilled cheese sandwich	Using different screwdrivers	Creating a graphic organizer
7	Preparing a veggie tray	Fixing a bicycle chain	Conducting a web search
8	Cooking eggs	Reading gauges	Creating an excel sheet
9	Making soup	Building a kite	Creating an invitation
10	Creating a daily menu	Constructing a mailbox	Creating a PPT

project combines student-centered and teacher-guided learning. While the entire process is generally guided by school-wide or district-wide policies and timelines, students are given considerable latitude in regard to the problem they choose to study. According to the Senior Project Center (www.seniorproject.net), senior projects are commonly organized around the four Ps: a paper, project, portfolio, and presentation. First, students conduct research and write a *paper* on their chosen topic. Then, they design a *project* that immerses them in some activity that furthers their learning about the topic. The project can involve a wide range of activities, including interviewing an expert, job shadowing, conducting a web search, designing a model, preparing a photo display, participating in community service, organizing an event, or going on a field trip. As the project proceeds, students collect artifacts for their *portfolio*, a product intended to demonstrate the knowledge and skills they have acquired. Finally, students *present* their senior project to a small board of judges that can include selected students, teachers, and members of the community. The formal presentation is followed by a question and answer session. Seniors are judged on their knowledge of their topic, effectiveness of their speaking skills, and ability to think on their feet.

Problem-based Units and Courses

Problem-based units and courses are the most complex variation of PBL. They are the most open-ended and student-centered form of PBL. In this variation, entire units or courses are organized around problem situations and students are actively involved in making decisions on all aspects of instruction: problem definition and planning, investigation and inquiry, presentation and demonstration, and reflection and debriefing.

Problem Definition and Planning A PBL unit or course begins by presenting students with an ill-structured, real-life problem situation. Several methods can be used to introduce the lesson: showing a video clip, reading an excerpt from an article, inviting a guest speaker, studying a short scenario, or sharing a letter from an outside organization or local newspaper that has expressed concern about the problem situation. The problem introduction can also identify roles and various perspectives for the students and situate the problem under investigation in a real-world context. For example, if the problem is about a medical issue, students may be asked to assume roles or consider the perspectives of doctors, patients, hospital administrators, or health insurers. If the problem is related to an environmental issue, students can assume or consider the roles of environmental activists, government regulators, corporate violators, or environmental agencies.

Students work to clarify the problem and identify their initial thoughts and questions. Teachers ask questions to guide student inquiry and map the unfolding of ideas and thinking on the board using a format similar to the one illustrated in Table 14.7.

The first question—"What do we know?"—allows students to share what they know about the problem and helps to activate prior knowledge. The second question—"What do we need to know?"—has students list questions and helps focus subsequent inquiries. As the class unfolds, the teacher asks, "What are you thinking?" and probes to surface ideas and hypotheses. In this initial stage, students define the problem and make plans for future work. Some have labeled this the "problem-finding" phase of PBL.

Table 14.7 Problem-based learning planning board

What do we know?	What do we need to know?	What are we thinking?	What is our action plan?

After the discussion, students work in small groups designing their investigations. They refine problem statements and generate additional questions. They identify possible sources of information and data collection methods. They develop an action plan detailing tasks to be accomplished and overall timelines.

Investigation and Inquiry After the planning phase, students begin their investigations by collecting information from a full range of print materials, the Internet, and interviews and observations. Time is divided between individual research and group problem solving. Group members check in regularly to share and combine their ideas and resources. Collectively, the group then discusses and revises initial ideas and hypotheses as new information becomes available. They conduct experiments and consider alternative solutions to the problem and weigh the pros and cons in efforts to arrive at a "best-fit" solution. The final task of the investigation is preparation of the group's final product and/or presentation. Depending on the breadth and complexity of the problem statement, investigations can last days, weeks, or a full quarter.

Presentation and Demonstration Toward the end of the unit or course members of learning groups present what they have learned and defend the decisions and choices they have made. Presenting groups also address questions about the way investigations were conducted and the decisions that were made along the way. Other students and community members participate in discussions and debates about each group's work. They also assess products and presentations using rubrics and checklists.

Reflection and Debriefing The final session in PBL unit and courses involves reflection. Individuals and groups reflect on their learning, thinking, choices, and mistakes, and the learning strategies and group processes they used. This activity helps develop metacognitive and self-directed learning skills. It is a key component of PBL and must not be short-changed.

Both teachers and students monitor progress and learning. Sometimes, teachers provide question prompts and exercises to check on student understanding and thinking at different stages of the overall lesson. Teachers can also provide feedback on the process, the progress, and the products being created. Consultation meetings are arranged with learning groups on a regular basis to discuss progress related to the students' learning plans. Questions posed to individuals and groups at all stages help guide and monitor the pace and direction of student investigations. Several questions are suggested in Figure 14.3. Below are examples of how two schools used PBL units or courses:

- During problem definition and planning
  1. What's going on here?
  2. What do we know about the problem?
  3. What do we need to know more about?
  4. What do we need to do to solve the problem?
- During investigation and inquiry
  5. What misconceptions do you have?
  6. What false starts did you follow?
  7. What data made you change your mind?
  8. What did you do that was effective?
- During presentations and demonstrations
  9. What is the best-fit solution you have at this time?
  10. What criteria did you use for deciding?
  11. What was your reasoning for your solution selection?
  12. Why did you rule out other solutions?
- During reflection and debriefing
  13. What new insights did you gain?
  14. What did you learn about your learning strategies?
  15. What successes and challenges did you have as a group?
  16. What would you do differently next time?

Figure 14.3 Questions to guide problem-based learning

At St. Elizabeth's Middle School students start each day with 45-minute "exploratories." This is a time set aside for enrichment and exploring a wide variety of topics. When needed, it can also be used for remediation. Jack has created a CSI-type module, where students work together to solve simulated crimes. Students who sign up for the nine-week module are presented with a problem statement on the first day of class and then they seek and evaluate evidence to solve particular crimes and problems presented to them. Investigations take several days. Typically, the students in the CSI module examine six crimes in a nine-week period.

At the Illinois Math and Science Academy (IMSA), all students experience PBL units and courses. Seniors can choose to take a semester-long elective course that focuses on unresolved science-related social issues. The course is interdisciplinary and taught by a team of teachers (one from science and one from social sciences). All sophomore students at IMSA take American History, where some sections use PBL methods. Over the years, more and more teachers and departments at IMSA have adopted a PBL approach.

REFLECTION

Which of the variations on PBL interest you? Which will you consider incorporating into your teaching repertoire? Explore with a colleague ways you might collaborate on an interdisciplinary PBL day or unit.

ASSESSING PROBLEM-BASED LEARNING

Assessing PBL involves four kinds of assessment: self, peer, teacher, and expert assessment. And, several learning outcomes must be assessed: content knowledge, inquiry skills, and **process skills** such as collaboration, problem solving, self-directed learning, and project management. Content knowledge can be assessed using paper-and-pencil tests, interviews, and performance assessments. Process skills can be assessed using surveys, observation checklists, and group feedback questionnaires.

Problem-based learning requires students to be actively involved in the assessment process. Individual students can assess their knowledge, skills, and group contributions. Journals can be used to help students keep track of their progress and their thinking processes, as can other forms of self-assessment such as reflective essays, surveys, and rating forms. Figure 14.4 provides an example of a rating form that allows students to assess their group skills and contributions.

Peer assessment is also important in PBL. This can be accomplished with the use of rating forms, surveys, and critical friends discussions that provide students with structured opportunities to provide feedback and critique their group's effectiveness. A rating form such as the one displayed in Figure 14.5 can facilitate peer assessment. As described in previous chapters, peer assessment should not be confused with peer evaluation; the latter is normally deemed inappropriate.

In addition, learning groups can be required to compile PBL portfolios that contain samples of the learning group's work, such as action plans, meeting notes, articles,

---

PBL self-assessment   Name: _____

Instructions: Evaluate your work using the criteria below. Rate each criterion from 1 (low) to 4 (high). The highest possible score is 24 points.

Criterion	Rating
Attended group meetings and was on time.	
Contributed to the overall group plan.	
Took responsibility for my share of the work.	
Completed assigned tasks on time.	
Was collaborative – supported and helped others.	
Worked to resolve differences and solve problems.	

What percentage of the work did you complete?

What was your most valuable contribution?

Figure 14.4 Problem-based learning self-assessment rating form
Source: Based on assessment example in Dean (2001).

PBL peer-assessment   **Peer name:** _____

Instructions: Evaluate your peer using the criteria below. Rate each criterion from 1 (low) to 4 (high). The highest possible score is 24 points.

Criterion	Rating
Attended group meetings and was on time.	
Contributed to the overall group plan.	
Took responsibility for their share of the work.	
Completed assigned tasks on time.	
Was collaborative – supported and helped others.	
Worked to address issues and solve problems.	

What percentage of the work did this person complete?

What was this person's most important contribution?

Figure 14.5 Problem-based learning peer assessment rating form
Source: Adapted from Dean (2001).

charts, and other artifacts the group has collected and that demonstrate what group members have learned.

In PBL it is important to meet regularly with learning groups to monitor and assess conceptual understanding, skill development, and project management skills. Checklists, such as the one displayed in Figure 14.6, are useful for tracking skill development.

Rating forms and rubrics can also be used to assess final presentations, products, and **exhibitions**. A sample rating form for evaluating a presentation is shown in Figure 14.7.

CHALLENGES WITH PROBLEM-BASED LEARNING

PBL has many benefits. It has been shown to be highly motivating and effective for promoting student learning. However, this strategy is not easy to implement and poses several challenges for students and teachers. Furthermore, the way most schools are structured presents difficulties for implementing PBL strategies.

Students can have difficulty conducting problem-based investigations for several reasons. We highlight a few that have been identified by Achilles and Hoover (1996), Edelson, Gordon, and Pea (1999), and Krajcik, Czerniak, and Berger (2003):

- *Finding meaningful questions.* Often, students can be found pursuing questions without examining their merits, and sometimes they pursue questions based on personal preference rather than those that warrant investigation.

1 = undeveloped	2 = basic skill level	3= good skill level	4 = excellent				
	1	2	3	4	Comments
Self-directed learning skills					
1. identifying learning issues/questions					
2. locating and evaluating information					
3. organizing and synthesizing information					
4. presenting evidence of learning					
Collaborative skills					
1. listening					
2. contributing					
3. managing conflict/tensions					
4. encouraging and supporting					
Problem-solving skills					
1. problem identification					
2. problem investigation					
3. analysis of alternative solutions					
4. decision-making					
Project management skills					
1. setting goals					
2. identifying learning strategies					
3. dividing and assigning work					
4. monitoring progress					

Figure 14.6 Problem-based learning skills checklist

- *Managing complexity and time.* Students can create plans that are incomplete or too elaborate to carry out.
- *Transforming data.* Students can present data and state conclusions without describing the link between the two. They don't necessarily use all their data in support of their final solutions and conclusions.
- *Using logical arguments.* Arguments to support claims can sometimes be weak or nonexistent.
- *Collaborating.* Some students lack the requisite group skills for working effectively with members of their learning group.

Teachers also face challenges and dilemmas as they strive to implement PBL. Marx, Blumenfeld, Krajcik, and Soloway (1997) identified the following:

- *Process versus content.* PBL engages students in self-directed study in pursuit of in-depth understanding of selected topics. Teachers are thus faced with the dilemma of pursuing problem-solving goals and processes against pressures to cover all the material identified in curriculum frameworks and standards.
- *Managing multiple groups and multiple topics.* Students in PBL groups work in different ways and at different speeds. This requires teachers to develop strategies and structures for monitoring and managing student work while at the same time promoting independent learning.
- *Common content versus differentiation.* As with most approaches to teaching, using PBL presents teachers with the dilemma of teaching to a common, prescribed curriculum as contrasted to allowing students to pursue problem situations tailored to their backgrounds and needs.

PBL group _____

Instructions: Please rate this presentation using the following criterion and scale:

1 = Group did not seem well prepared
2 = Group seemed prepared but not stimulating
3 = Group seemed well prepared, clear, and stimulating

Criterion	Rating
Problem/issue was presented clearly.	
Pertinent facts and data were presented.	
Presenters were knowledgeable about the issue.	
Presentation provided new and useful information.	
Presentation was interesting and creative.	
Solution presented was logical and sound.	
Pace and flow was good.	

Points I learned from this presentation:
1. _____
2. _____
3. _____

Questions I have:
1. _____
2. _____
3. _____

Suggestions for improvement:
1. _____
2. _____
3. _____

Figure 14.7 Problem-based learning group presentation assessment form
Source: Based on assessment example in Dean (2001).

- *Time.* PBL projects and activities generally require more instructional time than other approaches, and often more than anticipated. This presents teachers with difficult and painful decisions about how to allocate scarce time resources.
- *Empowerment versus control:* PBL requires finding a delicate balance between providing for students' autonomy and choice and for maintaining some degree of control and direction.
- *Assessing process skills.* As teachers, we are usually skilled at accessing content outcomes. Assessing process outcomes is more difficult and more subjective. It is challenging to develop good observational skills and to move beyond "generalizing" about student behavior and providing students with feedback about "specific" learning behaviors that lead to success in using PBL.

Finally, school policies and schedules can create challenges to the full implementation of PBL. For example, the traditional 50-minute class period found in many middle and high schools constrains student investigation efforts in serious ways. It simply does not allow sufficient time to work in groups effectively and to explore out-of-classroom resources. School policies related to students working in different areas of the school or in the community also inhibit access to resources. Schools that have adopted block schedules and more relaxed student movement and field trip policies afford more time for students to work in their learning groups and to access important resources. These policies promote PBL; however, they are often difficult to achieve.

GETTING STARTED: START SMALL, THINK BIG

Mr. Singh, the teacher we described at the beginning of the chapter, was always intrigued with problem situations. As a kid, he worked on puzzles, solved mysteries, and loved to figure things out on his own. As a student, he found himself drifting when teachers lectured and gave routine assignments. He was motivated, however, when teachers provided choice, assigned open-ended learning activities, and organized competitions. When he became a teacher, Mr. Singh was determined to have an engaging classroom, where students would be highly motivated and involved in taking responsibility for their own learning. Mr. Singh started PBL by first experimenting with rather straightforward PBL activities. Then he began conversations with other teachers, asking them to help him sponsor a problem-based interdisciplinary day. After a summer institute on PBL, he introduced group investigation projects into some of his classes. Today, he uses PBL approaches in all of his courses. His Environmental Issues course is organized completely around PBL and he uses PBL 50 percent of the time in his Physics courses. And, as we described at the beginning of the chapter, students love his classes.

SUMMARY AT A GLANCE

- PBL is a student-centered approach that engages learners in investigation into complex problem situations.
- PBL has six key features: ill-structured problems; authentic real-world issues; investigations and problem solving; interdisciplinary perspectives; collaborative small groups; and products, artifacts or presentations.
- Teachers serve as facilitators, guides, questioners, coaches, and mentors. Students are required to design their own learning, problem solve, and work together in small groups.
- Planning for PBL includes six tasks: clarifying content and process goals, selecting or designing problems, identifying resources, preparing assessments, organizing learning groups, and orienting students to PBL.
- PBL has five phases: presenting the problem, planning investigations, conducting investigations, demonstrating learning, and reflecting and debriefing.
- There are four primary variations of PBL: activities, interdisciplinary days or units, projects, and units or courses.
- PBL involves self, peer, teacher, and expert assessment. Both content and process learning outcomes are assessed with traditional and performance-oriented assessments.

- PBL can be challenging. Students need to be taught problem-solving skills and skills for working together. Teachers have to make choices between content versus process and between common content versus differentiation. They also have to make decisions about time and empowerment versus control. Scheduling, access to technology, and school policies can promote or inhibit PBL.

CONSTRUCTING YOUR OWN LEARNING

Working with a classmate or colleague, identify the range of PBL approaches you each use in your classroom. Discuss the successes you and your students have had and also the types of challenges you have faced.

Together, plan a problem-based activity, project, or unit that you can implement in your respective classrooms. Make arrangements to observe each other work at various stages of the activity or project and meet and provide critique and feedback. You may also want to brainstorm how you might approach other teachers in your school for the purpose of introducing a school-wide interdisciplinary day.

RESOURCES

Barell, J. (2006). *Problem-based learning: An inquiry approach* (2nd ed.). Thousand Oaks, CA: Corwin Press.

Lambros, A. (2002). *Problem-based learning in K-12 classrooms: A teacher's guide to implementation.* Thousand Oaks, CA: Corwin Press.

Markham, T., Larmer, J., & Ravitz, J. (2003). *Project-based learning: A guide to standards-focused project-based learning for middle and high school teachers* (2nd ed.). Oakland, CA: Buck Institute for Education.

Savin-Baden, M. (2003). *Facilitating problem-based learning.* Philadelphia: Open University Press.

Savin-Baden, M. (2008). *Problem-based online learning.* New York: Routledge.

Uden, L., & Beaumont, C. (2006). *Technology and problem-based learning.* New York: Information Science Publishing.

Part III
SCHOOL-WIDE CONDITIONS FOR STUDENT LEARNING

15

SCHOOL CHANGE AND TEACHER LEARNING

In previous chapters we focused our attention on foundational knowledge about teaching and learning and on instructional practices accomplished teachers use to effect student learning. In this chapter, we change our focus from what goes on in an individual teacher's classroom to what is required at the school level to help teachers and students learn. Providing teachers with the necessary support and feedback to learn and to implement effective instructional practices requires leadership and changes in the ways schools are traditionally organized. As our experienced teacher readers know, improving school-wide practices across classrooms is difficult and challenging.

Regardless of the difficulties, we believe that each of us can take some important first steps. Along with the principal, we can share responsibility for instructional improvement not only in our classrooms but also school-wide. We can create professional learning communities and make our schools organizations that provide structures and processes for continuous teacher learning similar to Brentwood Middle School where principal and teacher leadership have created and sustained a strong and vibrant professional learning community.

There have been many changes at Brentwood Middle School over the last few years. Teacher leadership, learning, and collaboration have been embedded in the culture of the school, and it has paid dividends in student achievement. This past year 90 percent of the students scored at proficient or advanced levels in literacy and numeracy and achievement in other subjects have outpaced other schools in the district.

When Jocelyn Martin first became principal of Brentwood, teachers worked mainly in isolation. Today, there is a vibrant professional learning community at Brentwood. Change came gradually, starting with monthly discussions and informal learning activities, but progressing as new structures and processes were created. Now, teachers participate in weekly grade-level meetings, monthly subject area critical friends groups, quarterly learning walks, school-based professional learning days, and an annual retreat. Teachers have learned to analyze data, design curriculum maps, and develop common assessments across grade levels and subject areas. Teachers are involved in observing and coaching each other, and many belong to external networks in the district and the profession. Understanding students and improving instruction are part of their everyday work.

Jocelyn Martin made early commitments for promoting and developing teacher leadership. Routinely, she recommended her teachers for the district's Leadership Fellows Program, where they learned about change processes, perspectives on leadership, the importance of teamwork, effective instructional practices, and the effects of school culture on student learning. As Leadership Fellows, teachers participated in monthly study groups, job shadowed principals known to be instructional leaders, and traveled to nationally recognized schools to learn what other teachers were doing. Teacher leaders have been a critical component of the development of the professional learning community at Brentwood. They act as mentors and coaches, facilitate monthly critical friends group meetings, and serve on the school's leadership team.

Turning a school into a learning organization that will help students meet high academic standards requires several important actions on the part of all members of the school community. Members must understand the complexities of improving schools and know how educational change can be managed. They must understand how to create structures, processes, and school environments that will support both teacher and student learning. In the sections that follow, we discuss three important aspects of this work and describe: (1) the difficulties and complexities of educational change; (2) how structures such as professional learning communities and critical friends groups can be used to support instructional improvement; and (3) specific processes and strategies known to support teacher learning.

MAKING CHANGES IN CLASSROOMS AND OUR SCHOOLS

"So much reform, so little change." The title of Charles Payne's (2008) recent book captures the dilemmas and realities of life in schools today, as did Seymour Sarason's (1971) observation 40 years ago, when he wrote, "the more things change in schools, the more they stay the same." For over a half century, people outside of schools have produced ideas and made plans they expect teachers inside schools to implement. Some of the ideas are research-based and practical; others are ill-conceived. Regardless of their merits, however, little has changed and effective innovative practices have been fully implemented in only a handful of schools. This situation is unfortunate because to get the schools we want will require changes in the ways we teach and learn and in the ways we provide leadership for improving our classrooms, our schools, and the profession. This work is complex and difficult; *change is hard*.

Why is School Change So Difficult?
Hundreds of studies and dozens of books have been written that address this question. Many explanations have been provided. We have more than 40 years of research that has documented the processes of educational change and detailed what works and what is problematic (Berman & McLaughlin, 1978; Elmore, 2004; Fullan, 2007, 2008a; Hall & Hord, 2005; Hargreaves, Lieberman, Fullan, & Hopkins, 2006; Lieberman & Miller 2008; Miles, 1992; Payne 2008). Regardless of how much we know about what works, too often our efforts flounder because we fail to use this knowledge in effective ways. As one observer wrote, "The question confronting . . . schools and districts is not, 'what do we need to know in order to improve?' but rather, 'Will we turn what we already know into action?' " (DuFour, DuFour, Eaker, & Karhanek, 2004, p. 1). Similarly, Pfeffer and

Sutton (2000) write about the "knowing–doing" gap, commenting on how we know much more about improvement and change than we put into action.

Below we describe eight reasons that make change so hard. These reasons are summarized from the school improvement and change literature and written in ways we think will be useful to teachers and teacher leaders as you consider actions you can take to create effective learning environments in your schools.

Insufficient Time for Teacher Learning Change takes learning and learning takes time. As teachers, we need time to learn new strategies and ideas, time to plan, time to figure out how to integrate "the new" into our existing practices, and time to reflect on what's working and what's not. Traditionally, there has been limited time allocated to teacher learning. Time during the school day is scarce, and most school districts have designated only a limited number of days for short-term and undifferentiated professional development activities.

Unrealistic Pace Often policy makers, as well as school administrators and all of us for that matter, want to change too much, too fast. We seem to be driven by a sense of urgency to tackle many problems and to install best practices immediately. Coupled with this are desires to expand innovative practices to other sites before experimental phases and pilot programs have been fully tested. Payne (2008) has observed that reformers typically under-conceptualize and over-promise on the ideas they propose. They want to move forward without taking time to learn from initial efforts and to determine adjustments that may be required.

Innovation Overload A number of years ago, Fullan and Miles (1992) identified "overload and fragmentation" as major impediments to change in education. Clutter, they wrote, often exists from multiple change agendas being pursued simultaneously. There are simply too many ideas coming from too many different places. One reform after another gets introduced before teachers have had time to fully understand the last one, resulting in **innovation overload**. Abrahamson (2004) has labeled it "**repetitive change syndrome.**"

Lack of Coherence Related to the problems of overload and pace is the fragmented nature of change. Generally, the strategies and initiatives are presented as independent solutions rather than a coherent and coordinated set of ideas to be implemented over time. Just as a school gets started on one path, another direction is taken. Teachers feel that **innovations** are "raining down on them" or, as they often report, "just one damned thing after another." This situation distracts in serious ways from efforts to address the long-term learning needs of students.

Lack of Ownership Many educational change efforts are introduced without sufficient ownership by teachers. Learning opportunities connected to school improvement efforts have been traditionally offered and organized around workshops, courses, and conferences where outsiders attempt to transmit ideas about an innovation rather than engage teachers through their day-to-day work. **Knowledge about practice** created by experts is valued over **knowledge of practice** generated by teachers through examination and reflection of their own work. Ownership in these situations belongs to staff developers, administrators, and consultants, not to teachers. Without ownership, teachers often ignore new ideas, return to their classrooms, and continue to use the practices that have worked for them in the past.

Traditional School Structures **Norms of autonomy**, privacy, egalitarianism, and seniority continue to persist in many schools (Lieberman & Miller, 2008; Little, 1990). These norms and ways of doing things prevent many innovative practices from being accepted and implemented. For instance, self-contained and age-graded classrooms keep teachers isolated and independent. Traditional scheduling arrangements prevent teachers from observing each other teach, stifle collaborative activity, and discourage reflective conversations about teaching and learning.

Lack of Support New ways of doing things require new resources. Brief awareness sessions that introduce a new program or approach are insufficient; more extended learning opportunities are required. Most reformers underestimate the time, cost, and level of support needed to implement new curricula, classroom practices, or cultural norms.

Inappropriate Leadership Traditionally, leadership for change has fallen mainly on the school's principal. However, as we described in Chapter 1, the expectations for principals are often unrealistic; they can't do it all. Further, some principals have capacities and styles that work against change. They may lack a deep understanding of teaching and learning, and, as a consequence, are ineffective in providing day-to-day assistance and guidance to teachers. Some may also lack understanding of educational change and change processes. They subsequently take actions that are counterproductive (Fullan, Cuttress, & Kilcher, 2005).

So what can teachers do? We believe they can take several actions to influence change in their schools. We summarize several of these actions in Table 15.1. You will note that all of these actions call for teachers to be proactive and to help create the conditions in their schools that will provide them with ongoing opportunities for learning and improvement.

What Works?

Those who study educational change have not only identified why it is so difficult, they have also documented cases and places where change has been successful (Barber & Mourshed, 2007; Chenoweth, 2007; Fullan, 2007). For instance, we know that only teachers can make change happen, a condition Lieberman and Miller (1999) observed several years ago when they wrote, "teachers are the ultimate decision makers. If they do not understand the change or think it is unreasonable, or if they do not have the time to learn and try out new ideas, the change will not happen" (p. 60). Today, we know how to support teachers in classrooms and we know how to change schools, and make whole system improvement. We also know a lot about the roles of principals and teacher leaders in schools where all students are learning at high levels (Leithwood, et al., 2007). A recent international study on high-performing school systems identified factors to guide improvement efforts, as described in Research Box 15.1.

Table 15.1 Ways teachers can influence change

Insufficient time for teaching learning	Become involved in planning ways to find time to support teacher learning. Use time provided to pursue learning opportunities and to work productively with colleagues.
Unrealistic pace	Remind school leaders and colleagues to be realistic about how long it takes to implement a new idea. Resist efforts to expand projects until initial efforts have been fully implemented and studied.
Innovation overload	Don't be afraid to work with administrators to set priorities and to remind them that only so many things can be changed at one time. Remind everyone that "less can be more."
Lack of coherence	Look for the connections between ideas and build on past efforts. Relate proposed changes to the overall vision and direction of the school.
Lack of ownership	Remind administrators and staff developers that ownership is important. Suggest ways, such as discussions using protocols, reflection activities, and opportunities for sharing to build ownership.
Lack of support	Ask for and make suggestions about the time, resources, and support required for implementing new ideas. Help secure these resources.
Inappropriate leadership	Step up and offer to provide leadership. Provide administrators with information about effective practices. Provide assistance to colleagues.

The Barber and Mourshed study described in Research Box 15.1, as well as most of the school improvement and change research, conclude consistently that good *school leaders* and opportunities for teacher learning are among the most important elements for getting instructional improvement and **high-performing schools**. These conclusions have led us to devote the remainder of this chapter to discussions about structures and strategies that we believe support continuous teacher learning and lead to instructional improvement.

> **REFLECTION**
>
> With a classmate or colleague, discuss your experiences with reform in your school. Has it been positive or negative? Which of the difficulties described above have you observed? What actions have you taken to help colleagues implement new practices?

CREATING STRUCTURES TO SUPPORT TEACHER LEARNING

For some time, reformers, such as Corcoran (1995), Loucks-Horsley (1998), and McLaughlin and Talbert (2006), have believed that bringing teachers together to learn from and with one another is the most effective way to provide the support necessary for making change happen in schools and classrooms. Professional learning communities and critical friends groups have been conceived as two important structures for doing this.

Professional Learning Communities

The idea of the professional learning community has been conceived over the past two decades as a forum for teachers to exchange ideas, share experiences, and reflect on professional practice. Lieberman and Miller (2008) define **professional learning communities** as "ongoing groups of teachers who meet regularly for the purpose of

---

(Inquiry) **RESEARCH BOX 15.1**

Barber, M., & Mourshed, M. (2007). *How the world's best-performing school systems come out on top.* London: McKinsey & Company.

Barber and Mourshed (2007) conducted a study of the best-performing school systems in the world based on results on an international test that compared achievement of 15 year olds in developed countries. Even though they focused on the system level, which was defined as a whole country, state or province, or school district, the findings are important to our discussion here. They found four consistent practices and strategies in place across three different continents (North America, Europe, and Asia); that produce high-performing systems:

1. *Recruit really good people* into teaching. They recruit people with good academic qualifications and the personal qualifications to be a good teacher (i.e., generosity, knowledge, liking children, inspiration).
2. Focus on teacher learning that is continuous, job-embedded, and close to the classroom.
3. Expect that every child will succeed. They *intervene early* when students fall behind by identifying learning barriers and developing a plan to address the issues.
4. Have *very strong school leaders*; people who are extremely well developed and who focus simultaneously on student and teacher learning.

   The researchers highlighted several key ways that these systems focused on improving instruction: teachers working together and learning from one another, coaching, and principals serving as instructional leaders. There was time in the school day and school year for teacher learning. There were teams of teachers working together, planning lessons, reviewing student work, comparing student work from different classes, and trying to understand why certain teaching strategies seemed to work more effectively than others. There were expert teachers—coaches—who modeled lessons, gave feedback, and helped teachers solve problems. Principals in these systems were instructional leaders. They had high learning expectations for all students and teachers, created cultures of professional learning, ensured there was time for teacher learning, and spent time every day in classrooms giving teachers feedback. All of these strategies and approaches were embedded in the practice of the school.

increasing their own and their students' learning" (p. 2). McLaughlin and Talbert (2006) describe a professional learning community as a place "where teachers work collaboratively to reflect on their practice, examine evidence about the relationship between practice and student outcomes, and make changes that improve teaching and learning for particular students in their classes" (p. 4), as well as school-wide. Notice some of the words and phrases used to describe a professional learning community— working collaboratively, discussing and reflecting, finding relationships between practice and learning, making changes. These words describe the essence of learning communities as settings for sharing experience and discourse.

Participating in joint work is the purpose of forming professional learning communities. These communities provide a structure for colleagues to come together to work on the everyday tensions of teaching and to collaborate on common issues. Teachers exchange ideas, share experiences, examine student work, deepen their understanding of content, and reflect on teaching practices. They also develop curriculum maps, create common assessments, and plan interdisciplinary units.

Several of the first learning communities were created outside of specific schools and instead brought teachers together from across schools and districts to share ideas and problem solve. We cite three examples. The National Writing Project, one of the oldest learning communities, began in 1973 and brought teachers together for summer institutes as learners and as writers (Lieberman & Wood, 2002). Over a period of 20 years, the Southern Maine Partnership convened educators from several districts to "dine and . . . have dialogue" about common educational issues (Miller, 2007). The League of Professional Schools (Allen, 1999) connected teams from different schools three times a year in conferences to learn from one another as they pursued school improvement using democratic governance structures and action research.

Collaboration among teachers in particular schools produces a synergy that cannot be achieved when teachers work alone, so more recently attention has been focused on how to create professional learning communities within particular schools. Well-conceived learning communities help advance this type of collaboration and sustain school norms and culture that support student learning. Below we summarize five key components of professional learning communities described by Louis, Kruse, and Marks (1996) and based on their national study of 24 restructured schools. Case studies were developed for each school. They found that in schools where the professional learning community were strong, pedagogy tended to be more authentic; and where the professional learning community were weak, pedagogy also tended to be weak. They established strong correlations between authentic pedagogy and student achievement:

- *Shared norms and values.* Teachers, through their actions and words, demonstrated common values about teaching, learning, assessment, and teachers' roles, and formed partnerships with administrators and parents in the service of student learning.
- *Collective focus on student learning.* Teachers expected that all students can learn at reasonably high levels despite obstacles and challenges they may face outside of school. Teachers worked together in learning communities to help students learn and be successful. They took responsibility for all students in the school and work collectively to challenged them and to support their learning.
- *Reflective dialogue.* Members of learning communities talked about their situations and the challenges they faced. They discussed teaching practices and student learning. They focused on subject content and how to instruct students and help them learn. They reflected on the social conditions of schooling and issues of equity and justice.
- *De-privatization of practice.* Teachers shared ideas and strategies, observed each other, and discussed their teaching philosophies and practices. They made their teaching public by talking about what they do and problem solving with colleagues.

- *Collaboration.* Teachers worked together to develop shared understandings of curriculum, instruction, and assessment. Jointly, they produce materials and develop activities to engage students in rigorous and challenging work. They shared and helped each other learn new strategies and approaches.

Making Professional Learning Communities Work Even though the use of professional learning communities is quite widespread, they are by no means part of most schools' cultures, and sustaining them has proven to be both challenging and time consuming. Sustainability requires support and encouragement by school leaders and environments that embrace norms of openness, risk taking, and experimentation. Below we highlight some of the necessary tasks for making professional learning communities work.

Organizing Learning Teams. As we illustrated in the scenarios about Southside High School in Chapter 1 and Brentwood Middle School at the beginning of this chapter, professional learning communities can be organized in a variety of ways: by grade level, by subject area, and as cross-disciplinary teams. Sometimes, the whole school is conceived as a professional learning community. Teachers may stay in the same learning community for the entire school year and sometimes for many years. In some schools, teachers may belong to two different learning communities: a grade-level community and a subject area community. In other schools, teachers belong to a grade-level learning team and a cross-disciplinary learning team.

Scheduling Time. School leaders support learning communities by ensuring meeting times during the school day. Professional learning communities meet for varying periods of time. Some schools are organized so learning teams can meet every week for an hour; others provide time so learning teams can meet twice a month; and still others organize time for teachers to meet monthly for a longer period. At Brentwood, teachers meet in grade-level professional learning communities every Thursday during a common planning time. They also participate in subject area team meetings once a month to coordinate lessons and assessments for the coming month. Schedules have been organized for students to be in related arts classes so teachers can be free to meet. Language Arts teachers meet the first Monday, science teachers meet the second, mathematics teachers meet the third, and social studies teachers meet the fourth. Other schools have been equally creative in finding time for teacher learning (see von Frank, 2007).

Selecting a Focus. In most instances, the focus of professional learning communities is on student learning needs. Teachers begin by analyzing student data or student work that lead to goals for study and collaboration. Some start by examining the school's curriculum content and develop curriculum maps and lesson plans together. Other teams focus on the teaching strategies they are using. Still others begin by examining assignments and formative assessment strategies. Teachers in professional learning communities examine their own practices, as well as read about research-based best practices.

Structuring Conversations. Traditional norms of autonomy and keeping silent about the practices of colleagues make talking about teaching difficult. Successful professional learning communities establish norms and structures to guide discussions and reflective conversations. Some learning communities develop rather formal rules and use protocols to structure participation and discourse; others proceed with more informal arrangements. Others decide to adopt and implement a particular approach, such as those we describe later in this chapter: critical friends groups, action research, and peer coaching. Each of these approaches has specific features and strategies. Success depends on open, focused, and disciplined discussions about teaching practices and student learning.

Providing Resources. Resources are required to facilitate teacher learning. These may include hiring substitutes to facilitate peer observation and coaching, buying books for a study group, or allocating funds for teams to visit other schools or attend professional conferences. Sometimes, learning communities require training in particular processes and strategies. Astute school administrators arrange for teacher leaders to attend training on how to facilitate professional learning community meetings.

Monitoring Progress and Celebrating Success. As with any initiative, it is important to track and monitor the growth and development of professional learning communities. McLaughlin and Talbert (2006) have observed that learning communities move through three stages—novice, intermediate, and advance—and at times they can get stuck and need assistance to get back on track or need fresh ideas to get redirected. It is also important to acknowledge and celebrate changes in teaching and learning.

> **REFLECTION**
>
> Has time been specifically scheduled for teacher learning at your school? Are you part of a professional learning community? If so, how successful has your community been? How did it get started? What problems has it faced?

Do Professional Learning Communities Make a Difference? Although professional learning communities are relatively new, several studies have examined their effects and the results have been consistent regarding how they can improve teaching (e.g., Hord & Sommers, 2008; Lieberman & Miller, 2008; Newmann, Secado, & Wehlage, 1995; Stoll & Louis, 2007; Vescio, Ross, & Adams, 2008). They have also provided evidence documenting the link between professional learning communities and student achievement. When teachers engage in joint work, they change their teaching practices, and students learn more. We have chosen to summarize one of the more prominent studies on professional learning communities in Research Box 15.2.

Sustaining Professional Learning Communities Before we leave this topic, we want to provide a caveat related to professional learning communities. McLaughlin and Talbert (2006) described the challenges and difficulties of establishing and sustaining school-based learning communities. They identified lack of trust, time, and talent as the usual culprits. They comment, "when teachers are unwilling to take the risks that go along with candid reflection, when they don't have many opportunities to come together over students' work, when they lack leadership or expertise at the school site, then

---

(Inquiry) **RESEARCH BOX 15.2**

McLaughlin, M., & Talbert, J. (2001). *Professional communities and the work of high school teaching.* Chicago, IL: University of Chicago Press.

In a large scale study of departments at 22 high schools in seven districts in Michigan and California, McLaughlin and Talbert found three different kinds of learning cultures: weak, strong traditional, and strong innovative cultures. They describe what they found in strong innovative teacher learning cultures:

- The greatest gains in student achievement.
- A focus on promoting teacher learning and connecting it to student learning.
- A common vision that all students are capable of increased achievement.
- Teachers seeking to achieve more equity in student outcomes and developing a shared language and knowledge base about how to accomplish this goal.
- Teachers working together to develop practices that serve all students well.
- Equity privileged over hierarchy.
- Class assignments more evenly distributed.
- Teachers see themselves as lifelong learners.
- Teachers shared their expertise with colleagues and collaborated to improve their practice.
- Teachers experienced collective—rather than individual—professional rewards and career progress.

In schools with strong professional learning communities, there was strong commitment to serving all students, innovation in subject matter instruction, and success in obtaining school and district resources to support their collaborative work. In addition, students surveyed and interviewed in one high school reported that they could feel the difference between the (collaborative) English department and the (isolated) History department. They gave significantly higher ratings to their English classes on teacher enthusiasm and support, challenging content, and the degree of effort that they (the students) put into learning in class. Students talked about liking English and being supported by teachers as contrasted to being bored in their Social Studies classes.

---

community-building initiatives are hamstrung and commitment erodes during faculty or leadership transitions" (p. 11).

Many attempts have been made over the past half century to get teachers to learn, talk to each other, and work together. Teacher inquiry and action research were introduced in the 1950s. Team teaching was promoted as far back as the 1960s. In the 1970s, cadres of teachers were trained to promote collaboration and school renewal in their schools and districts (Fullan, 2007; Miles, 1992; Schmuck & Runkel, 2002). Reform initiatives, such as the Coalition of Essential Schools (Sizer, 1985) and the Accelerated Schools Program (Levin, 1998), emphasized training of leadership teams and developing professional learning communities. However, these innovations have been fragile, and Joyce (2004) has reminded us that many of them have subsequently disappeared. He is not arguing against the school improvement and teacher transformation promoted by these reforms; he is simply reminding us that these are not easy things to achieve. Collaborative structures fight against the norms of isolation and teacher autonomy that have been with us for a very long time.

Critical Friends Groups

Critical friends groups (CFGs), developed initially by the Annenberg Institute for School Reform, is another structure to facilitate teacher and student learning. In some instances, this approach has been integrated into the work of professional learning communities and, in others, for "looking at student work." In other situations, critical friends groups operate independently of formal professional learning communities. The term "critical" as used by CFGs does not mean condemnatory, fault-finding, or judgmental. Instead, it implies something that is important or urgent, like the use of "critical patient care" in medical practice. Costa and Kallick (1993, p. 49) provided the following definition:

> A critical friend can be defined as a trusted person who asks provocative questions, provides data to be examined through another lens, and offers critiques of a person's work as a friend. A critical friend takes the time to fully understand the context of the work presented and the outcomes that the person or group is working toward. The friend is an advocate for the success of that work.

The idea of critical friends has been quite widely used in schools, and CFGs accept a variety of issues as legitimate topics for examination and discourse. Some critical friends groups consist of teachers from the same grade level or department; others are cross-curricula groups. In some schools, CFGs may be required and focus on larger school reform efforts, such as those associated with the Coalition of Essential Schools. In other schools, participation is voluntary. Instances can also be found where members make arrangements to visit each other's classes and provide feedback on the teaching they observe. As with other approaches for learning together, CFGs have been used to facilitate the functioning of already-formed professional learning communities, as well as to help create new ones. In all instances, however, CFGs' teachers are committed to improving teaching practices by working collectively with other teachers.

The basic mechanic for a critical friends group consists of teachers who meet regularly in small groups to present and talk about their and/or their students' work. In most instances, group meetings are facilitated by a consultant or coach who has been trained for this role; although this is not always the case. We also know of instances where facilitation is assumed and rotated among group members. Facilitators review and facilitate the group's progress by keeping time and encouraging equitable participation. Meetings begin by a designated teacher presenting an issue to the group. After the presentation, group members discuss the issue and provide feedback and suggestions. In some groups, the presenter does not participate in the discussion, but instead sits behind the group and takes notes until the end when they respond to the group's feedback by indicating what was helpful and what was not. At the end of the meeting the facilitator leads the group in a debriefing session. Here is an example drawn from the literature of one CFG's meeting in a Portland, Oregon, high school:

Fourth-year science teacher, Elisa Winger, was stumped. She couldn't figure out why some of her students were doing great lab work in class but not making sense of these same experiments in their laboratory books. So, she brought the books to her critical friends group.

Winger's six critical friend colleagues included a fellow science instructor, as well as English, art, Spanish, and family living teachers. Together, they examined the lab books and listened to Winger describe her quandary. And together, the group came up with a list of suggestions to help Winger improve her students' work, including:

- Lower the reading level in some areas.
- Use more pictures and visuals.
- Help students write a good, strong hypothesis and other aspects required in the laboratory book.

As Winger says, she realized then that she had to be "more of a writing and artwork teacher" to reach and teach her science students. She says, "critical friends provided me with another set of eyeballs to look at my and my student's work" (summarized from Having another set of eyeballs (2005)).

Requesting and providing feedback and having norms for collaborative inquiry are key components of a critical friends group. This has led some groups to formalize norms to help members inquire and analyze each other's work. Figure 15.1 contains group norms developed by the Bay Area Coalition of Essential Schools. Similarly, work in critical friends groups requires guidelines for providing feedback. The Bay Area Group's guidelines for feedback are summarized in Figure 15.2.

In way of summary, it is important to remember that professional learning communities and critical friends groups provide important structures to support teacher collaboration and learning, both conditions that in turn affect student learning.

STRATEGIES TO PROMOTE TEACHER LEARNING

Some of the teacher learning strategies we describe below are quite straightforward and can be initiated by teachers without much school-wide support. Others are more complex and usually require school-wide agreements and training. They also require

---

Describe only what you see. Do not try to describe what you don't see; express what you don't see in the form of questions.

Resist the urge to work on "solutions" until you are comfortable with what the data says and doesn't say.

Surface the perspectives and experiences you bring to the analysis. Effective teams use these as strengths.

Seek to understand differences of perception before trying to resolve them. Early consensus can inhibit depth and breadth of analysis. Hear from everybody.

Ask questions when you don't understand. Find the answers together.

Surface assumptions and use the data to challenge them. Look actively for both challenges to and support for what you believe is true.

Figure 15.1 CFG's norms for inquiry and analysis
Source: Summarized and adapted from Cushman (1998).

- Give honest feedback, both supportive and more distanced.
- Be specific; tie your feedback to the work.
- Presenter and participants may safely express their confusion, stress, or needs; be sensitive to them.
- Keep comments within the room. If you don't say it to the presenter, don't say it.
- Start with a question; check for understanding. Use probing questions, not leading questions; don't jump to solutions.
- Monitor your airtime so others have equal chance to speak. Take time to listen. Be flexible, balancing spontaneity with equal access to speak.
- Debrief what was helpful or not in the feedback process.

Figure 15.2 Guidelines for feedback in CFGs
Source: Summarized and adapted from Cushman (1998).

administrative support as well as structural arrangements in the school, such as professional learning communities or critical friends groups.

Book Study and Reflective Dialogue

As with several strategies to promote teacher learning, **book study** is not new. Some schools and teachers have used it for years. However, its use has become more widespread as we have come to believe that teacher learning is best accomplished when it is done within schools and among colleagues. Book study can vary in the time devoted to it, and can have varying degrees of structure. Sometimes, teachers themselves can take the lead and participate on a voluntary basis. Other times, as in our Southside example, principals or teacher-mentors provide the leadership and book study is a school-wide activity.

Most books we have observed used in book study groups have focused on various aspects of teaching, such as Ellin Keene and Susan Zimmermann's *Mosaic of Thought* (2007), Carol Tomlinson's *The Differentiated Classroom* (2004), or Peter Johnston's *Choice Words* (2004). Some teachers, however, choose to read other kinds of book that don't address teaching specifically but nonetheless have important implications for education in a more general sense. Thomas Friedman's *The World is Flat* (2005), Al Gore's *The Assault on Reason* (2007), or Jodi Picoult's *Nineteen Minutes* (2008) are examples of these types of book. Book study is an easy way to get started. It works best when teachers agree on the ways they are going to discuss the book and when they make commitments for becoming more reflective about their teaching practices.

Lesson Study

Lesson study, described by Danielson (2006) and Lewis (2002), is a strategy broadly used by teachers in Japan. It is a straightforward way for teachers to collaborate and to observe each other in their classrooms. Lesson study requires teachers who teach the same or a similar course to plan a lesson jointly. One member of the study group then teaches the lesson to students while the others observe. The group then analyzes the lesson, discusses how it might be improved, and revises the lesson. Another member of the group then teaches the revised lesson while team members again observe. The group then revises the lesson a third time and a different teacher teaches it while others observe. This process continues until the lesson is deemed "polished." Then the group tackles another lesson. An important feature and strength of lesson study is that the focus of the observation and discourse is definitely on the lesson, not the teacher.

Danielson (2006) has observed that this is an important distinction because making the discussion about the lesson "alters the tone of [the] professional conversation.... Teachers are engaged in a search for the best approach, not critiquing one another" (p. 102).

We tend to like lesson study because the mechanics associated with its use are quite simple and straightforward. Lesson study provides a good way for teachers to begin the process of learning together. All that is required is to find two or three other teachers who have similar interests and who are willing to find time to meet, plan, and visit.

Peer Observation and Coaching

As observed in Barber and Mourshed's (2007) international study (Research Box 15.1), **coaching** was found to be an important strategy employed by high-performing systems. The importance of coaching, however, has been known for some time. Berman and McLaughlin (1978) and Fullan and Pomfret (1977) noted how in-class assistance and teachers observing each other facilitated effective educational change. In the 1980s, Showers (1982a, 1982b, 1984a, 1984b, 1985) demonstrated the power of coaching in a set of studies she conducted. She found that implementation of new teaching strategies reached high levels of performance only when teachers benefited from coaching in the classroom. Understanding the theory, seeing a demonstration, and even practicing with feedback in a workshop setting increased teachers' knowledge and skills related to a new instructional model; however, that was not enough support for most teachers to use the new strategy effectively in the classroom. Coaching was required (Joyce & Showers, 2002).

Over the years, several models of coaching have been developed. Knight (2007, 2009), who studied coaching for over a decade, defined coaching as a partnership between teachers who engage in **peer observations** and conversations. He found that some coaching focuses on the individual teachers, while other coaching focuses on teams of teachers. Some coaching practices aim at implementing new content and new strategies; while others focus on examining and improving existing practices. All of the models share a common purpose: helping teachers to examine and think about their practices. We highlight several models to provide a glimpse of the range of perspectives and approaches.

Some coaching models have identified specific guidelines and questions for coaches to follow. Cognitive coaching, developed by Costa and Garmston (2002), is a very structured program that requires extensive training in skills, strategies, and steps to implement. Other coaching models promote group and whole-school development. Joyce and Showers (2002) believed that peer-coaching teams are more effective in implementing school-wide strategies to address identified student needs. They also discouraged the use of feedback and prefered conversations following observations. They contended that omitting feedback simplified the organization of peer coaching because learning to provide technical feedback effectively requires extensive training.

Some coaching models rest on beliefs that coaches need to have high levels of expertise both in a content area and in coaching skills (see Toll, 2005; West & Staub, 2003). The Boston Public Schools Collaborative Coaching Model (Guiney, 2001) focuses on expert coaches working with grade level teams at the elementary level or subject area teachers at the high school level. Initially trained Boston coaches focused on improving literacy instruction but later shifted to mathematics.

Other districts have implemented coaching models where teachers teach students for part of the day and coach colleagues for the other part. In elementary schools, the Lead Teacher Coaching Model consists of two teachers who share a classroom—one teacher has expertise in literacy and the other in mathematics. Each teacher spends half of the time with students and half of the time coaching other teachers in their respective areas. Some high schools have also used math and/or literacy coaches. As in elementary schools, high school coaches spend part of the day with students and spend the remainder of the time assisting colleagues.

All coaching models comprise similar components: a pre-conversation, an observation with data collection, and a follow-up conversation. The two teachers or the peer-coaching team decide on a focus and talk about the lesson to be observed. Most coaching sessions focus on what Knight (2007) has labeled "the big four" classroom issues: classroom management and the learning environment, curricular content, instructional strategies, and formative assessment practices. Sometimes coaches focus on a particular practice or a small group of students. The coach can observe either the students or the teacher and takes notes. Sometimes two colleagues have designed a template for collecting data. Other times the coach scripts the lesson or writes questions for the follow-up conversation.

A follow-up conversation is scheduled to debrief all observations. These sessions can be informal and unstructured or they can be quite formal and highly structured. Coaches describe what they observed during a visitation, ask questions, give feedback, and make suggestions. In most approaches to coaching, feedback following a visitation is a very important aspect of the process. It needs to be timely, accurate, and non-evaluative. Guidelines for providing feedback are provided in Figure 15.3.

As described earlier, however, some coaching experts (Joyce & Showers, 2002; Knight, 2007) believe that the follow-up meeting should be characterized by dialogue rather than feedback. What is important is that reflection and conversation takes place about teaching and learning. In another twist on the **reflective dialogue**, we know coaches who are convening a team of teachers to observe a colleague. Following the classroom visitation, the coach leads the teachers in a reflective dialogue about the teaching and learning they observed. The teacher who was observed "listens in" on the conversation but does not participate. These group sessions can result in powerful discussions about effective practices and encourage observers to try out some of the ideas considered. Figure 15.4 provides examples of questions coaches can use to guide teachers in reflective dialogue.

While individual teachers can decide to coach one another, more often coaching is adopted as a school-wide or district-wide initiative for teacher learning. Coaches benefit

---

- Start with a question inviting the teacher-peer to reflect on the lesson.
- Give honest feedback—both warm (positive) and cool (suggestive).
- Be specific in your comments—tie your feedback to specific notes you have taken.
- Ask probing questions and check for understanding—don't jump to solutions.
- Be sensitive to the teacher's confusion, stress, or needs.
- Be confidential—keep comments inside the classroom.
- Summarize learning and make plans for next steps.
- Debrief—inquire whether the feedback was helpful or not helpful.

Figure 15.3 Guidelines for giving feedback to peers

- What were your opening thoughts about the lesson?
- Overall, how did you feel the lesson went?
- What did you think was strong or particularly effective?
- What adaptations or "in-flight" decisions did you see?
- Was there a point where you thought the students were struggling?
- What would you change or suggest to strengthen the lesson?
- What are your final thoughts or comments about the lesson?

Figure 15.4 Questions to guide reflective dialogue
Source: Summarized and adapted from Paideia Consulting Group (2008).

REFLECTION

Who has been a coach for you? Who have you coached and assisted? Do you think a formal, structured approach is best or do you prefer informal, less-structured conversations about teaching and learning? Explore with a colleague or classmate how you might observe and coach each other's teaching.

from training for their roles and responsibilities and their knowledge of best teaching practices. Administrative and teacher support are crucial to the successful implementation of coaching programs.

Examining Student Work

Teachers have always looked at their students' work. They analyzed it for its conformity to expectations and for assigning a grade. Traditionally, this act was performed alone. Similarly, looking at student work together as a strategy for teacher learning has been around for some time. However, it obtained increased visibility in the 1980s and 1990s when groups such as the Annenberg Institute for School Reform, the Coalition of Essential Schools, and the National Education Association began using it as part of their school reform efforts. The popularity of this strategy stems from the fact that the information obtained from **examining student work**, perhaps more than any other piece of information, illustrates the connection between what teachers do and what their students learn.

But what does looking at student work mean? And, how do teachers perform this task collectively? In some instances, it has meant analyzing achievement data from standardized tests. In other instances, it has been inspecting the results of teacher-made assessments. Most often, however, looking at student work has consisted of examining writing samples, performance videos, and other artifacts that result from instruction and that represent student learning.

Prior to the looking-at-student-work movement, teachers came together mainly to examine their own work, such as sharing lesson plans or discussing a new curriculum unit. Looking at and discussing student work is a departure from these past experiences and often it has been a difficult process to implement. Little, Gearhart, Curry, and Kafka (2003) studied four schools where teachers were collectively looking at student work. One school was participating in the "Evidence Project" sponsored by Harvard's Project Zero, a second was a middle school associated with the Academy of Educational Development, and the final two were project high schools in the Coalition of Essential School's network. Although the procedures for looking at student work varied from school to school, researchers reported that they found three common elements:

1. Time had been secured for bringing teachers together to focus on the relationships between student learning and teaching practices.
2. Processes were established for getting and keeping student work, as contrasted to teacher work (lesson plans or videos of classroom activities), on the agenda and central to the conversation.
3. Tools and guidelines were created to structure the group's conversation.

Structuring the conversation for looking at student work is very important and guidelines and protocols have been developed to govern discourse patterns aimed at accomplishing several objectives: (1) slowing down the conversation so participants have time to consider what they want to say about a piece of student work; (2) structuring participation in ways that depart from ordinary conversations by prescribing timelines for individual and group participation; and (3) providing structured opportunities to ask questions, make comments, and give feedback. A variety of protocols[1] for guiding this process have been developed. Some provide few overall guidelines; others are much more detailed. In Figure 15.5, we summarize some of the primary guidelines recommended for structuring the conversation when teachers are discussing their students' work.

One of the reasons that rather detailed guidelines are required is that talking about student work requires teachers to ask tough questions of one another and, in many instances, to disagree openly about instructional practices. As we have explained before, these behaviors traditionally have not been allowed because of the strong **hands-off norms** found in

---

REFLECTION

Have you had opportunities to engage in discussion with colleagues about your students' work? Did you do this using the structure of a critical friends group? Did you use a protocol to structure the conversation? Was it useful?

Procedures and guidelines for looking at student work

Phase 1: Setting the agenda: Provide time for going over the agenda of the student work session, including goals, guidelines, and time requirements.

Phase 2: Presentation of student work: The identified teacher shares example(s) of their students' work. They include the context in which the work was done, goals for the assignment or performance, and assessment strategies used. Participants are provided time at the end of the presentation to ask clarifying questions and/or to seek additional information about the work.

Phase 3: Participant reflection: Working alone, participants take time to examine the student work that has been presented and to consider the type of feedback they would like to provide.

Phase 4: Providing feedback: Participants provide both positive and critical feedback to the presenting teacher using the guidelines for providing feedback similar to those listed in Figure 15.3. In most instances, the presenting teacher takes notes but is silent during the phase.

Phase 5: Reflection and reaction: Presenting teacher reacts to comments and feedback and reflects on the meaning these have to them. Teacher should take care not to be defensive.

Phase 6: Debrief: All teachers participate in an overall discussion about the session, including making recommendations about how the process might be improved next time.

Figure 15.5 Recommended procedures and guidelines for looking at student work

many schools, norms that deter colleagues from providing constructive criticism of each other's work or from seeking or offering feedback and advice. Protocols help provide a structured way to challenge traditional norms, and they provide a degree of comfort for teachers as they discuss their students' work.

Action Research

Action research, sometimes called classroom or teacher research, is another approach for helping teachers learn and examine relationships between teaching practices and student learning. Normally, action research processes are more formal than the other strategies we have described and projects require a longer timeframe to fully implement. There are several approaches to action research and specific methods vary from school to school. Overall, however, action research consists of using methods of scientific inquiry to collect and analyze data about professional practice and about students and their learning.

Action research has a history dating back almost a century. It was described in the work of John Dewey (1938) and Kurt Lewin (1946) as a means to extend scientific inquiry to social practice so individuals in all fields—education, race relations, and social policy—could test their ideas in practice. It was brought into education by Les Corey (1953) and his associates at Teachers College in the 1950s and has had a following since that time (see Schmuck, 2006). Today, the ideas of action research and teacher-as-researcher have gained rather widespread popularity throughout North America, Australia, and Great Britain and have been influenced by a wide array of researchers, such as Hopkins (1985), Cochran-Smith and Lytle (1993), and Zeichner and Noffke (2001). Both teacher associations, the American Federation of Teachers and the National Education Association, have embraced and advocated teacher research as a way to improve classroom teaching.

The goals and processes of action research as conceptualized today take on various purposes and use a variety of research methods. Some projects use more traditional qualitative and quantitative research methods, whereas others may consist of constructing narratives, writing reflective essays, creating inquiry-oriented journals, and/or focusing on the processes of oral inquiry. Space does not allow a thorough discussion of the various approaches. Instead, we will emphasize classroom studies (broadly defined) where teachers work in collaborative ways to study their own teaching and its effects on student behavior and learning. Often these studies incorporate most of the phases illustrated in Figure 15.6.

To see what action research might look like in a real situation, let's extend the example of Elisa Winger's critical friends group we observed earlier.

Plan An action research project begins with planning and selecting appropriate questions to ask. Questions are appropriate if they can be answered by inquiry and if means exist to collect valid and reliable information within a reasonable period of time and without significantly disrupting the class.

You remember that Elisa Winger brought to her critical friends group a problem that had her stumped. Students in her biology class did great lab work in class but their laboratory write-ups were poor. After a lengthy discussion, CFG members made several suggestions: find lower-level reading materials for students having trouble, be more

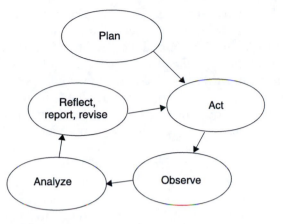

Figure 15.6 The action research process

explicit in explaining to students the importance of lab book write-ups, and help students improve their writing skills.

Elisa followed two of these suggestions immediately. She gathered a variety of textual materials with varying reading levels and she emphasized the importance of the lab write-ups. At the next meeting of the group, Elisa reported that the problem persisted. Lab book write-ups continued to be poor. Elisa's critical friends suggested that she experiment with their third recommendation—help students' improve their writing skills—and study the effects of this action more closely. Jason, the English teacher in the group, offered to help out and the group formulated the following question: *Will writing instructions for biology students result in better lab book write-ups?*

Act Elisa and Jason met to decide on the type of writing instruction to provide. The two of them decided that instruction should aim specifically at the type of technical writing required in the lab books, something that Elisa hadn't considered all that much before. They also agreed that students needed to hone their writing skills, particularly those required for describing laboratory experiments. Jason agreed to teach three, 30-minute lessons. The lessons would include a presentation on how to describe a scientific experiment, give students opportunities to practice, and provide them with feedback on their work.

Observe The third phase of a classroom study consists of gathering information that will help address the action research question. This phase requires teacher researchers to get clarity about how they are going to collect their information and methods they will use to ensure that the information is as valid and reliable as possible. Action researchers use a variety of tools to collect data: questionnaires, observations, focus groups, interviews, and student work samples. Space does not allow us to go into detail about these tools, but we have provided some valuable resources about this aspect of action research at the end of the chapter (Sagor, 2000; Schmuck, 2006).

For this inquiry, Elisa and members of her critical friends group decided that the best source of information would be the scores students received on their lab write-ups. Up to this point, Elisa had graded lab write-ups pretty much in a holistic fashion, paying attention, however, to both science content and writing clarity. To get a more precise measure of her students' work, it was decided that she needed to use a scoring rubric designed to assess student work in four very specific areas: accuracy of stating the hypothesis of the experiment, amount of detail used to describe the experiment, analysis of results, and overall clarity of the presentation.

To establish baseline data, it was decided that Alisa would use her new rubric to score student write-ups two times before introducing it to her students. After she introduced the rubric to students, she would then use it two more times prior to Jason's writing instruction. Finally, it would be used to score two experiments after the writing lessons.

Analyze An important phase in classroom research is to organize and analyze the information that has been collected. Often this means tabulating questionnaire data or assessment results in some type of table format. It may also mean summarizing information collected from interviews or observations and organizing it so it makes sense to the teacher researcher and to others who may be interested in the data.

Elisa and her colleagues decided to organize the data collected in their study in table format, as illustrated in Table 15.2.

When Elisa and members of her learning community met to analyze the results of their study, they were very surprised. It appeared that providing students with a scoring rubric had more effect on the quality of lab write-ups than did Jason's writing instruction. Total scores increased from 14 and 15 to 28 and 27 after the scoring rubric was introduced. It did appear, however, that writing instruction might have had some effect, particularly on "overall clarity." This was surprising because providing a scoring rubric was *not* one of the CFG's initial recommendations and was only included because they needed it to have a more precise measurement tool for the study.

Reflect, Report, and Revise A final phase in a classroom research project consists of reflecting on what the data mean, reporting it to relevant audiences (if appropriate) and perhaps revising and extending the study. The result of this study—that the rubric had more influence on student lab write-up than did writing instruction—provided grist for considerable discussion. It also motivated CFG members to pose a number of questions about the study and its results to consider at a later time.

We believe that action research is a valuable strategy for enhancing teacher and student learning. However, we are not naïve about its immediate, large-scale use. It will

Table 15.2 Mean scores on four variables and overall score for lab write-ups at six points in time

Data collection points	Accuracy of hypothesis (10 points)	Details of lab experiment (10 points)	Accuracy of results (10 points)	Overall clarity (10 points)	Overall score
1: prior to rubric	4	4	5	2	15
2: prior to rubric	4	3	4	3	14
3: after rubric	8	6	7	7	28
4: after rubric	8	7	6	6	27
5: after writing lessons	7	8	7	8	30
6: after writing lessons	8	7	7	8	30

remain hampered by lack of time and resources. As observed in our example, it takes time to plan and conduct a good study and results are not always all that clear, a condition characteristic of other research as well. Action research may also be hampered by differences among competing approaches and perceptions held by some that academic research conducted by professional researchers is more valuable for informing teaching and learning than research conducted by teachers. We do not agree with the latter assertion, and maintain that both classroom and academic research have a place in building a knowledge base on teaching and learning and for helping teachers become more reflective practitioners.

Networks

McLaughlin and Talbert (2006) and Lieberman and Miller (2008) highlight the importance of teachers' participation in professional development venues and learning opportunities beyond the school. They argue that courses, institutes, and networks contribute important and unique resources for teachers and their learning. McLaughlin and Talbert (2006, p. 64) write:

> Insulation from broader professional networks will stymie the improvement efforts of even the most engaged and collaborative teacher community. Without a flow of new knowledge and tools for effective instruction, a teacher community is dependent solely upon its members for solving problems of practice; such insular communities eventually use up their knowledge and energy resources.

Many reform initiatives have incorporated networks as part of their overall change strategy. These networks tend to bring individuals and teams together to focus on learning and sharing particular types of practice. Some well-known networks include:

- The National Writing Project brings together teachers of writing (Lieberman & Wood, 2002).
- The National Network of Partnership Schools at Johns Hopkins University brings together school teams to learn about and use research-based approaches to organize and sustain programs for family and community involvement (www.csos.jhu.edu/P2000).
- The Coalition of Essential Schools has brought school teams together for over 20 years to focus on high school reform and changes in teaching and learning (www.essentialschools.org).

District-wide, national, and international networks have also been formed to support teacher learning. High school science teachers in Atlanta public schools formed three specific science networks. Physics teachers, biology teachers, and chemistry teachers meet at different schools monthly in their respective networks to share lesson plans, discuss teaching strategies, and develop common assessments. These cross-district networks have become increasingly important and have led to the formation of several other collaborative groups in Atlanta.

Networking has become a major strategy for teacher and principal learning in Chattanooga, Tennessee. High school and middle school principals participate in monthly learning sessions. In addition, high school and middle school math coaches, high school college access coordinators, middle school instructional coaches, and literacy leaders all belong to learning networks. These teacher leaders meet monthly to learn about change, coaching, protocols, and best practices in teaching and learning. The intention of the **teacher networks** is to develop collective leadership capacity within the district and to facilitate sharing and problem solving across schools.

The largest example of using networks as a learning strategy for educators can be found in England. Networks have become a systematic part of that country's national reform agenda. Between 2001 and 2006, the National College for School Leadership's Networked Learning Communities Programme funded school networks that involved over 2,000 schools. Six forms of learning were promoted in the networks: pupil, adult, leadership, school-wide, school-to-school, and network-to-network learning. Each network selected a student learning goal, such as literacy, differentiated instruction, formative assessment, or multiple intelligences. Learning activities have included learning walks, action research, cross-school learning projects with students, study groups, and learning fairs. Networks are now embedded in many reform initiatives in England.[2]

Mace (2008) described how online multimedia resources and websites can be used to network teachers. Individual teachers can go to websites to access lesson plans, student assignments, references, video clips, and formative assessment strategies. The Carnegie Foundation sponsors one such website, where teachers can download teaching resources and engage in conversations with other teachers all around the world. The Teacher Leaders Network is another example of a virtual network and learning community created by the Center for Teaching (Barnett, Norton, & Byrd, 2007).

Fullan (2005) has described some of the benefits and potential shortcomings of "lateral capacity building" through networks. Lateral capacity is a powerful high-yield strategy because it mobilizes commitment and new ideas on the ground. He explains,

> People learn best from peers (fellow travelers who are further down the road) if there is sufficient opportunity for ongoing, purposeful exchange . . . and motivation and ownership at the local level are deepened, a key ingredient for sustainability of effort and engagement (pp. 18–19).

He also cautions that networks can have downsides: too many of them can add clutter instead of focus, and teachers may exchange unsubstantiated ideas and opinions rather than valid and reliable knowledge.

We have presented several approaches for facilitating teacher learning in schools: book study, lesson study, peer visitation and coaching, examining student work, action research, and networking. All of these strategies except networking are considered job-embedded learning. They happen at the school level, are conducted among colleagues, and involve dealing with practices that are part of the teacher's day-to-day work. We believe that learning together and "in context" is more powerful than learning alone and away from school.

REFLECTION

Have you used any of the strategies discussed in this section to enhance your own learning? If so, which ones? How did it work out? With a classmate or colleague, explore ways you might initiate particular learning strategies in your school.

SUMMARY AT A GLANCE

- Classroom and school improvements require change. Eight reasons explain why change is so hard: lack of time, unrealistic pace, innovation overload, lack of coherence, lack of ownership, traditional school structures, lack of support, and inappropriate leadership.
- Professional learning communities (PLCs) and critical friends groups (CFGs) provide structures, resources, and rewards for teachers' collaborative learning in schools.
- Five components of PLCs are: shared norms and values, collective focus on student learning, reflective dialogue, de-privatization of practice, and collaboration.
- Critical friends groups have become increasingly popular as a structure to support teacher learning and instructional improvement. CFGs have been used in a variety of ways. In some schools, they are a required aspect of larger school improvement initiatives; in other places, participation is voluntary.
- There are many approaches for teacher learning including: book study, lesson study, peer visitation and coaching, examining student work, action research, and networking.
- Book and lesson study are rather straightforward strategies and involve colleagues in reading or planning lessons together.
- Peer observation and coaching are important strategies, where teachers observe one another in the classroom, provide feedback, and discuss best teaching practices.
- Examining student work provides information showing the relationships between what teachers do and what their students learn.
- Action research involves teachers in classroom inquiries about their teaching practices and their impact on student learning.
- Professional networks connect teachers from other schools with peers to learn new knowledge and tools for effective instruction.

CONSTRUCTING YOUR OWN LEARNING

Working with a colleague or classmate, examine the structures and processes in the school where you teach that support teacher learning. Critique the effectiveness of each. Then, draw up a plan for extending learning opportunities for teachers. Be specific, including ways you might introduce your plan to your principal and/or the faculty.

RESOURCES

Blythe, T., Allen, D., & Powell, B. (2007). *Looking at student work* (2nd ed.). New York: Teachers College Press.

Easton, L.B. (2008). *Powerful designs for professional learning* (2nd ed.). Oxford, OH: National Staff Development Council.

Knight, J. (2007). *Instructional coaching: A partnership approach to improving instruction.* Thousand Oaks, CA: Corwin Press.

Lieberman, A., & Miller, L. (2008). *Teachers in professional communities: Improving teaching and learning.* New York: Teachers College Press.

Sagor, R. (2000). *Guiding school improvement with action research.* Alexandria, VA: Association for Supervision and Curriculum Development.

Schmuck, R. (2006). *Practical action research for change.* Thousand Oaks, CA: Corwin Press.

Teacher Learning websites: www.nsrfharmony.org; www.ncsl.uk.com.

NOTES

Chapter 1

1. This is the first example of a research box that you will find in each chapter. These are not intended to summarize research on a particular topic, but instead to give you a feel for some of the actual research in the field. They were chosen because we think you will find them interesting and because they help explain particular ideas we are trying to convey.

Chapter 2

1. Just as it is *not* necessary to have a complete technical understanding about how the heart works to know how to maintain a healthy heart, it is similarly not necessary to understand every aspect of brain anatomy and functioning for teachers to use instructional strategies that keep the "brain" in mind.
2. Definitions throughout these sections are taken mainly from information provided by Dana Alliance for Brain Initiatives (2003), Ashcraft (2006), and Willis (2006).

Chapter 3

1. We want to thank Dr. Tracy Coskie, a professor at Western Washington University, for bringing our attention to the idea of *agency* and introducing us to Peter Johnston's *Choice Words* (2004).

Chapter 5

1. While it is beyond the scope of this chapter to discuss multiple models for differentiation, teachers who are already differentiating and looking for additional ideas may want to consult Gregory and Chapman (2001) or explore the menu model for differentiation developed by Renzulli, Leppien, and Hays (2000).
2. Samples of a cubing activity, a learning center unit organizer, and a tiered assignment are provided in the *Fieldbook*.

Chapter 6

1. Popham (2008) reports that his definition has been adapted from one developed earlier by the Council of Chief State School Officers (CCSS).
2. See the following two references for dozens of summarizing strategies: Saphier and Haley (1993) and Wormeli (2005).

Chapter 7

1. To the best of our knowledge, the concept of "feeling tone" should be attributed to two sources: Jane Roberts and the late UCLA professor, Madeline Hunter. We will use this idea several times in subsequent chapters but will not reference it again.

Chapter 8

1. The directions for this demonstration are adapted from the Mayo Clinic's website (www.mayoclinic.com). It includes the breathing step, even though today some experts are recommending this step be eliminated. This topic has been chosen because it provides a good example of rather complex skills that are often taught in science, health, and physical education classes. The explanations here are not intended to teach CPR to our readers. To learn CPR properly, individuals should take an accredited first aid or CPR course.

Chapter 11

1. The initial idea for the Seymour lesson came from Concept Attainment (2008).
2. Ideas for the lesson came from the National Science Standards: www.nap.edu/readingroom.

Chapter 12

1. Some have noted that jurisprudential inquiry only works on issues that stem from principles held in the United States. This is true to some extent. The model could not be used to study and analyze issues that exist when competing "creeds" exist. The best contemporary example of this situation would be the rather wide differences that exist between the overarching value system of North America and Europe that has grown out of Judeo–Christian traditions and the value system of several countries in the Middle East based on Islamic traditions.

Chapter 15

1. A wide variety of protocols are described in *The Power of Protocols* (MacDonald, Mohr, Dichter, & McDonald, 2007) and online at the National School Reform Faculty website: www.nsrfharmony.org.
2. Many publications on networks and tools for facilitating networks are available on the National College for Schools website: www.ncsl.org.com.

GLOSSARY

academic preparation curriculum: School curriculum that is mainly aimed at preparing students for college.

academic readiness: The extent of student knowledge, understanding, and skills required for new learning to occur.

accomplished teacher: A teacher who is highly trained and skilled; a master teacher.

accountability: In education, pertains to holding teachers and educators responsible for using best practices and for what students learn.

achievement needs: Desires that prompt individuals to take actions for the purpose of feeling competent and experiencing success.

acronym: A word formed by the initial letter of a set of other words and used to help remember things.

ACT: A college entrance test that identifies the most academically able students for admission to colleges and universities (formally called the American College Test).

action research: Research conducted by teachers to improve teaching by examining relationships between teaching practices and student learning.

active listening: Listening for total meaning of both the content and the emotional aspects of a message.

active teaching: See *direct instruction*.

advance organizer: Statements made by teachers at the beginning of a presentation or explanation that provide structure and scaffolding for linking new information to the learners' prior knowledge.

affiliative needs: Desires that prompt individuals to take actions for the purpose of having close relations and friendship with others.

agency: Beliefs individuals hold that they can affect their environment and have the ability to accomplish desired goals.

alterable factors: Factors in students' lives and capabilities that teachers can help develop and change.

alternative assessment: Performance or authentic assessments that engage students in demonstrating or producing products of their learning.

amygdala: Area in the center of the brain that coordinates emotional reactions such as anger and fear and that influences eating reactions and sexual interests.

analogy: Statement or figure of speech that makes a comparison between two things.

analytical intelligence: Intelligence that allows individuals to deal well with problems that require reasoning and academic problem solving.

applied learning: Learning that can be used in real-life situations and/or to solve real-life problems.

art of teaching: Application of creativity, imagination, and experience to the practice of teaching.

Artful Thinking Program: Program that uses works from the visual arts and music to enhance student thinking.

artifact boxes: A collection of products students have produced that display their knowledge on a particular topic.

artifacts: Products such as reports, videos, and displays that students produce when engaged in problem-based learning.

assessment: The process of gathering information, both formally and informally, about students' understandings and skills.

assessment *as* learning: Situations in which students are engaged actively in self- and peer-assessment to facilitate self-direction, self-monitoring, and self-correction.

assessment *for* learning: Ongoing formative assessment that provides students with feedback on their learning at regular intervals and provides information for teachers to make instructional decisions.

assessment *of* learning: State, national, and international exams that provide summative assessments of student learning by comparing students to one another or to a predetermined set of standards.

attention: Process in which individuals choose to attend to some sensory stimuli while ignoring other stimuli.

attribution theory: Theory of motivation based on the premise that actions are influenced by the way individuals perceive the causes of their successes and failures.

auditory learners: Individuals who prefer, or learn more effectively from, auditory input.

authentic assessment: Assessments in which students demonstrate skills and abilities within a real-life context.

authentic problem: A problem that stems from real-world situations or issues.

authentic relationship: Refers to relationships that are accurate, reliable, and emotionally appropriate.

axons: Nerve fibers that transmit messages from dendrites to other neurons.

background knowledge: See *prior knowledge.*

backward curriculum design: A type of planning process where the planner begins with a statement about desired final outcomes and then proceeds to learning activities.

baseline score: A score based on past scores used in some approaches to cooperative learning to help determine student improvement.

basic thinking skills: Thinking that requires using lower-level cognitive processes such as remembering and understanding.

behavioral principles of learning: Principles of learning based on behaviorism.

behaviorism: Theories that posit that behavior (learning) can be explained in terms of external factors and conditioning.

benchmarks: Term used to link checkpoints of particular standards; they designate the degree of mastery of a particular standard at a particular point in time.

best practice: Teaching practices and processes that have been shown by research and experience to have positive effects on student learning.

Bloom's revised taxonomy: A system for classifying educational objectives and showing relationships among types of knowledge and cognitive processes.

book study: A teacher learning strategy in which teachers read common articles and books and then come together to discuss them on a regular basis.

brain filtering: Process used by the brain to attend to some information while ignoring other information.

brain growth: Refers to how the physical structure and internal functions of the brain change as a result of learning.

brain mapping: Techniques that allow neuroscientists to track (map) brain activity over time as it processes information.

caring relationship: Refers to relationship where individuals show care and respect for one another.

case-based teaching: An approach to teaching that provides students with opportunities to explore realistic situations that contain dilemmas that must be resolved.

cerebellum: The part of the brain that coordinates and regulates muscular activity and some aspects of reasoning and thinking.

cerebral cortex: Outer layer of the cerebrum that plays a role in consciousness.

cerebrum: The part of the brain consisting of two hemispheres and responsible for integrating sensory and neural functions and the coordination of some activity.

checking for understanding: Processes used by teachers to see if students have learned new material and content.

checking impressions: A communication skill in which a listener checks how accurately they have received the "feeling aspect" of a message.

choice boards: A board that displays options for learning activities and/or assessment strategies.

choice opportunities: A situation in which students are provided different reading selections, research topics, homework options, class activities, reporting formats, and assessment strategies.

chunking: Refers to dividing a larger assignment or topic into smaller sections or subtopics.

classroom discussion: An approach to teaching that relies on verbal exchange of ideas and opinions between teachers and students.

classroom environment: The overall physical and socio-emotional structure and processes of a classroom.

coaching: A teacher learning strategy in which a colleague observes a teacher and provides assistance and feedback.

cognitive monitoring: Refers to learners' abilities to select, use, and monitor the use of particular learning strategies.

cognitive principles of learning: Principles of learning based on cognitive psychology that learning is an active mental process of acquiring, storing, and retrieving knowledge for use.

cognitive processes: The type of thinking and processing involved as learners master particular kinds of new knowledge and skills; believed to lie along a continuum of complexity from more basic thinking to thinking that is more complex.

cognitive processing dimensions: Phrase used to refer to different levels of thinking, ranging from simple to more complex, in Bloom's revised taxonomy.

cognitive sciences: The scientific study of the mind, specifically of the human memory system and cognitive processes (Also cognitive psychology).

cognitive structure: The way knowledge and information is organized and stored in the mind.

cognitive theories of motivation: Theories of motivation that believe that motivation stems cognitive beliefs and interpretations.

cognitive–constructivist perspective: See *cognitive principles of learning*.

coherent curriculum: Content and learning experiences that have been organized in consistent ways and where the parts of different subjects or grade levels unite to form a whole.

collaborative skills: Social and communication skills required to work effectively in groups.

communities of learners: Refers to classrooms where students have developed a sense of community and where goals for learning together are valued.

competitive activities: Activities that require students to compete with one another.

concept attainment approach: An inductive approach to teaching concepts where students discover concepts and conceptual understanding by analyzing examples and non-examples of a concept.

concept attributes: Qualities and essential features regarded as characteristic of a particular concept.

concept teaching: Approach to teaching aimed at helping students develop conceptual understanding and showing them how to label ideas, objects, and experiences.

concepts: Mental abstractions that provide ways of organizing knowledge, experiences, objects, and events into categories for which items have common attributes.

conceptual map: A visual device that organizes and illustrates a set of ideas in a logical way so relationships among ideas can be observed visually.

conceptual web: See *conceptual map*.

conditional knowledge: Knowledge about when to apply particular declarative or procedural knowledge.

content standards: Standards specified for particular subject matter content, normally organized by grade level and subject area.

context of learning: The particular settings, situations, or backdrop where learning occurs.

convergent questions: Questions that require students to focus on coming up with a single or best answer.

convergent thinking: Thinking that involves moving toward a single answer or solution.

cooperative activities: Activities that require students to work together.

cooperative behaviors: Behaviors that help groups or teams accomplish group goals, such as: encouraging, supporting, listening, compromising, and recognizing the contributions of others.

cooperative goal: A goal requiring teamwork and collaboration to be accomplished.

cooperative grading: Situation in which a grade is assigned for cooperative behaviors and teamwork skills.

cooperative learning: A teaching model or strategy characterized by cooperative task, goal, and reward structures that requires students to work together, normally in mixed-ability groups.

cooperative reward: Group work situation where individuals can obtain their goals only if others in the group also obtain their goals.

creative intelligence: Intelligence where individuals can deal well with new and unusual situations and problems.

creative mind: A mind, according to Howard Gardner, that has a special temperament component and willingness to explore the unknown.

creative thinking: Thinking that involves creating novel solutions to problem situations.

criterion-referenced test: A type of assessment in which student performance scores are compared to a set of predetermined standards.

critical friends group (CFG): A group of teachers who meet regularly to study their teaching and to provide each other with constructive feedback and suggestions.

critical thinking: Thinking directed toward analyzing particular arguments, recognizing fallacies, and basing conclusions on sound evidence and judgment.

cross-disciplinary: Working on a problem that draws on knowledge from several disciplines.

cubing: A strategy in which students are exposed to different perspectives and ways of thinking about a particular topic.

curriculum alignment: Curriculum that is coherent and where what is taught is carefully connected to what is assessed.

curriculum compacting: A strategy that helps advanced learners maximize their learning time and allows them to engage in more rigorous and independent work.

curriculum control: Determines who should influence (design and implement) the curriculum.

curriculum frameworks: Term normally used to refer to formal documents that describe the content and skills students are expected to learn in particular subjects and at particular grade levels.

curriculum mapping: A tool that helps teachers analyze curriculum content and skills across subjects and grade levels.

curriculum standards: Precise descriptions of what students should know and able to do.

curriculum themes: The big and enduring ideas of a curriculum around which standards are organized.

curriculum: Set of purposes and body of knowledge about what students should learn.

debriefing: Term normally used to refer to the process that group members use to discuss the positive and negative aspects of their work together.

declarative knowledge: Knowledge about something or that something is the case.

deductive reasoning: Process of inferring particular instances from more general rules and principles.

dendrites: Short nerve fibers that extend from nerve cells (neurons) in the brain.

de-privatization of practice: A situation in which teachers invite colleagues into their classrooms to observe, coach, and share ideas and strategies about teaching.

diagnostic assessment: Information collected prior to instruction that is used to determine student prior knowledge and to identify misconceptions.

differentiated classroom: Classroom in which curriculum, learning activities, learning resources, and assessment strategies are adapted to meet the needs of particular learners.

differentiation: The practice of adjusting the curriculum, teaching strategies, assessment strategies, and the classroom environment to meet the needs of all students.

direct instruction: Approach to teaching procedural knowledge and sequential learning material that is goal directed and normally highly structured.

direct presentation approach: An approach to concept teaching that uses direct instruction.

disciplined mind: The kind of mind that has mastered a particular body of knowledge.

discourse patterns: The larger patterns of conversation and verbal exchange observed in classrooms between teachers and students and among students.

discourse skills: Skills individuals have for participating in verbal exchange in classrooms as well as other settings.

discovery learning: An approach to teaching that encourages students to learn through their own inquiries and explorations and to figure things out on their own.

discrepant event: A puzzling situation about cause and effect relationships used in inquiry-based teaching to spark curiosity and motivate inquiry.

discussion: See *classroom discussion*.

dispositions: See *thinking dispositions*.

distributed practice: Type of practice that is done for rather brief periods of time and spread over several practice sessions.

divergent questions: Questions that allow students to come up with multiple answers and to exhibit creative thinking.

divergent thinking: Thinking directed toward creating many different ideas and solutions.

diversity: Term used to describe the variety and range of student differences found in classrooms.

economy principle: Idea that the amount of information taught or included in a curriculum should be limited.

elaborative–interrogation question: Follow-up questions that require students to extend and support their answers or opinions.

emotional intelligence: The type of intelligence in which individuals have the capacity to recognize their own feelings and those of others and to mange emotions and relationships.

emotions: State of mind and feelings that result from circumstances and moods such as joy, anger, love, and hate.

empathetic response: Responses to student ideas and questions that are accepting and withholding of judgment.

enabling knowledge: Specific knowledge required before a more remote or complex standard or set of skills can be accomplished.

enacted curriculum: The curriculum planned, designed, and implemented by classroom teachers.

enduring understandings: The big ideas of a subject or topic that have enduring value and that constitute the heart of the subject or topic.

English language learners (ELLs): Learners who are learning English as a second language.

essential questions: See *enduring understandings*.

ethical mind: The kind of mind that knows how to focus on the rights, responsibilities, and ethical behavior associated with various roles individuals assume.

evaluation: The process of making judgments about the level of student achievement for the purpose of grading, accountability, promotion, and certification.

evidence-based practice: Teaching practices and processes that have been shown by research to have positive effects on student learning.

examining student work: A process in which teachers meet on a regular basis to examine the work their students have produced.

exhibition: A display or presentation that demonstrates the results of a problem-based learning investigation.

expectancy of failure: Beliefs held by individuals that future efforts will not result in successful outcomes.

expectancy of success: Beliefs held by individuals that future ambitions will likely be achieved and their efforts will be successful.

experiential learning: An approach to learning that relies on individuals learning from their direct experiences and subsequent reflections about these experiences.

explaining link: Statement used in a presentation to elaborate on an idea by explaining cause, meaning, or purpose of a set of ideas or events.

explicit memory: Information stored in the memory system which individuals are conscious of.

expository text: Written text composed to explain something.

expressed needs: Needs expressed by students themselves in regard to what they need or want to learn.

external attributions: Situations where individuals blame external causes or circumstances for what happens to them.

extrinsic motivations: Situations where individuals take actions to capture desired external rewards or to avoid punishments.

fairness: An assessment is fair if it offers all individuals the same chance of doing well and if it does not discriminate against any group because of race, gender, or ethnicity.

fear system: The emotional system that, when activated, causes individuals to run, fight, or hide.

feedback: Information provided to students about the accuracy of their knowledge or performance; same as knowledge of results.

field dependent: Term that refers to individuals who tend to perceive situations as a whole; they see the big picture.

field independent: Term that refers to individuals who tend to perceive the separate parts in a situation rather than the whole.

flat world: A label used by Thomas Friedman to describe the modern world that has been affected by geo-economics, instantaneous communication, and global access to information.

flexible grouping: Grouping students in different ways based on achievement, interest, and learning preferences.

flow experience: Experience or state where individuals feel total involvement and where they experience pure enjoyment from the experience.

formal curriculum: Curriculum planned and adopted by education agencies, normally state departments of education and school districts; grows out of the larger social purposes of education.

formative assessment: Information collected *during* learning that is used to make instructional decisions and in-flight decisions; also referred to as "assessment for learning."

frontal lobe: Location in the brain where some types of thinking, planning, and problem solving occur.

functional magnetic resonance imaging (MRI): A technology used to map and observe brain activity.

goal clarity: A situation where learning goals for students are clear and appropriately specific.

goal orientation: Orientations in regard to the types of goal (learning or performance) students are expected to pursue.

grade equivalent score: Measure of grade level by comparing a student's score to those established in a grade-level norming group.

grading on a curve: Norm-level grading that compares student scores to the average level in a class.

grading to criterion: Grading of students' achievement based on mastery of a predetermined set of standards or objectives.

grading: The process of assigning a mark (evaluation) to a piece of work or course.

graphic organizer: A visual representation or diagram of a set of ideas and the relationships they have to one another.

group investigation: An approach to cooperative learning in which students work in teams to investigate problem situations.

guided inquiry: Student inquiry that is focused and for which teachers provide appropriate guidance and scaffolding.

guided practice: Practice provided under the guidance and with the assistance of the teacher.

half-class strategy: Dividing the class into two halves—the teacher works with half of the class for 10–15 minutes while the other half works independently—then the teacher switches groups and teaches a mini-lesson at a different level.

hands-off norm: The expectation that teachers should not interfere with or criticize their colleagues' practices.

high expectations: Expectations that are set high and intended to be achieved by all students, not only the most capable.

higher-level thinking: Thinking that requires using higher-level cognitive processes such as analyzing, evaluating, and creating.

higher-order questions: Questions that require the more abstract cognitive processes such as analyzing, synthesizing, and evaluating.

higher-order thinking skills: Skills that facilitate higher-level thinking.

high-performing schools: Schools where the majority of students are achieving at high levels and high numbers of graduates are going onto further education.

high-stakes testing: Tests that are used to determine student achievement and to make decisions about placement, promotion, graduation, and certification.

high-stakes tests: Standardized tests administered by the state department of education or the federal government that measure what student know and can do.

hippocampus: Part of the brain involved with learning and memory.

homework: Independent practice and assigned work performed outside the classroom.

hypothalamus: Location in the brain where signals from the brain and the body's hormonal system interact.

I messages: Communication stance and skill in which senders or receivers of messages take ownership of what is said or for how one responds to what someone else said.

ill-structured problem: A problem that is complex and has many issues and sub-issues and for which multiple solutions exist.

implicit memory: Information stored in the memory system which individuals are unconscious of.

improvement score: A score used in certain approaches to cooperative learning that helps track individual and team progress.

in-context learning: Learning that takes place in the setting where it is needed or where it occurs naturally.

independent practice: Practice provided by teachers that requires students to work on their own and without the teacher's guidance.

individual accountability: A situation in which each member of a learning group is responsible for demonstrating their own learning.

individualistic activities: Activities where students work independently.

inductive reasoning: Process of inferring general rules and principles from more specific information and data.

inferred needs: Needs inferred by adults (teachers, parents, curriculum developers) about what they think students need to learn.

influence needs: Desires that prompt individuals to take actions for the purpose of having control over what is happening.

information processing: The process individuals use to take in, process, store, and retrieve information.

infusion strategies: Teaching strategies that infuse the teaching of thinking into regular curricula subjects.

initial learning: Learning that takes place the first time new information is introduced and taught.

initiation–response–evaluation pattern (IRE): The traditional discourse pattern found in most classrooms, consisting of the teacher asking a question, the students responding, and then the teacher evaluating the answer.

innovation: Term used to refer to new ideas, strategies, or programs.

innovation overload: A situation in which one reform after another is introduced, making it almost impossible for teachers to fully understand and implement anything.

inquiry-based teaching: Approach to teaching in which students are encouraged to inquire and solve problems on their own and to develop inquiry skills such as asking questions and reaching conclusions based on data.

in-school learning: Learning that occurs in school as contrasted to things individuals learn in out-of-school settings such as the home and the community.

instructional differentiation: See *differentiation*.

intelligence quotient (IQ): Standard score that compares an individuals' chronological and mental ages.

internal attributions: Situations where individuals attribute success and failure to themselves and their own abilities and efforts.

intrinsic motivation: Situations where individuals take actions to satisfy their own interests or for pure enjoyment.

inventories: Assessment tools for diagnosing students' prior knowledge, interests, and learning preferences.

Jigsaw: A cooperative learning model in which learning materials and work are divided up among group members.

jurisprudential inquiry: An approach to teaching that provides students opportunities to explore realistic situations in regard to public policy issues that contain dilemmas stemming from the American legal–ethical framework.

knowledge about practice: Knowledge about teaching created by experts through research.

knowledge dimensions: Refers to the four kinds of knowledge (factual, conceptual, procedural, and metacognitive) defined in Bloom's revised taxonomy.

knowledge of practice: Knowledge about teaching generated by teachers through examination of and reflection on their own practice.

knowledge of results: Feedback provided to students on their performance.

KWL strategy: A strategy that engages students in accessing prior knowledge and framing learning questions and goals prior to instruction, and then reflecting on what they learned following instruction.

language of thinking: Terms and language that describe various aspects of thinking and thinking processes.

lateral thinking: Thinking that is based on the use of the imagination and creativity.

learner profile: A record describing specific characteristics about an individual's academic readiness, intellectual strengths, interests, and learning preferences and styles.

learning centers: Places where students participate in different learning activities.

learning communities: See *professional learning communities*.

learning configurations: A situation where different learning arrangements (individually, in pairs, in small groups) are designed to allow students to work on particular learning tasks.

learning contract: A written agreement between the teacher and a student that guides independent work.

learning environment: See *classroom environment*.

learning goals: Goals that focus on improvement of particular content or skills independent of overall performance or in comparison to others.

learning log: A notebook where students record reflections about their learning.

learning preferences: Refers to the types of learning situation and environment learners prefer.

learning progression: A tool that illustrates and communicates a set of subskills and enabling knowledge for which mastery is required prior to mastering a more complex curriculum standard or set of skills.

learning styles: Refers to the different ways individuals perceive and process information.

lecture: See *presentation teaching*.

lesson study: A strategy, used initially in Japan, in which teachers jointly develop lessons and then engage in rounds of teaching and observation as they "polish" the lesson.

letter cards: A formative assessment strategy where students use cards to indicate their responses to verbal questions.

letter writing: A self-assessment strategy where students respond to prompts or sentence starters to identify their learning

long-term memory: Place in the memory system where information is stored permanently in the form of visual images and verbal codes.

massed practice: Type of practice performed during single and perhaps extended periods of time.

meta-analysis: A statistical procedure that combines the results from a number of studies to determine the average effect of a given instructional method.

metacognition: An individual's awareness and understanding of their own thinking and thought processes.

metacognitive knowledge: Knowledge about one's own thinking and thought processes.

metacognitive learning strategies: Strategies that assist students to diagnose a learning task, monitor progress toward accomplishing the task, and making adaptations if required.

metaphor: A figure of speech where one thing is applied to something else; a thing is regarded as symbolic of something else.

misconceptions: False or inaccurate ideas and interpretations held by learners.

mnemonics: A device or aid that uses patterns of letters, ideas, or associations to assist in remembering something.

models of teaching: Phrase used to describe a particular and systematic approach to teaching.

motivation: The reasons that prompt individuals to take actions or to behave in particular ways.

multiple intelligences: Theory that intelligence has more than a single dimension; normally associated with the work of Howard Gardner.

myelin: Substance that covers axons and protects the nerve fibers. Helps speed impulse transmission.

mystery spot: See *discrepant event.*

narrative text: Written text that includes elements such as theme, plot, character, and setting.

National Assessment of Educational Progress (NAEP): An assessment conducted periodically by the U.S. Department of Education to measure how students are doing nationwide in mathematics, reading, writing, science, and other subjects; sometimes referred to as the Nation's Report Card.

National Board for Professional Teaching Practices (NBPTP): Organization that provides national certification of highly-skilled and accomplished teachers.

needs disposition theory: Theory that individuals take actions to satisfy innate physical and psychological needs and intrinsic desires.

negative reinforcers: Actions in reinforcement theory that cause individuals to avoid certain behaviors.

neurons: The name of the nerve cells in the brain that store and transmit information.

neurosciences: The study of the structure and functions of the brain and of the nervous system.

neurotransmitters: A chemical between axons and dendrites that sends messages from one neuron to another.

No Child Left Behind (NCLB): A federal law implemented in 2002 designed to close the achievement gap between the races and to emphasize accountability, flexibility, and choice.

non-directive discussion stance: An approach to discussing case-based situations or cases in jurisprudential inquiry in which the teacher facilitates the discussion without taking sides or confronting students' ideas and opinions.

norming: A process for establishing normal achievement levels of students in different subject areas at different grade levels.

norm-referenced tests: Tests that compare student performance to a population of students who served as the "norming" group.

norms of autonomy: The expectation that teachers should work in their classroom on their own without interference from other teachers.

norms of privacy: See *norms of autonomy.*

occipital lobe: Location in the brain where visual processing occurs.

online text: Text found on the Internet as contrasted to text found in print media.

open communication: Communication among individuals that is honest and forthright.

origins: Individuals who believe they are in charge and have control over what happens in their lives.

out-of-context learning: Learning that takes place in settings, such as schools, that are not necessarily connected to the real and practical lives and needs of learners.

out-of-school learning: Learning that occurs in non-school settings, such as the home and the community.

paper-and-pencil tests: Teacher-made tests that require students to either *select* or *construct* a response.

paraphrase: A communication skill in which a listener checks with the sender of a message to make sure the message has been received accurately.

parietal lobe: Location in the brain that deals with sound and speech, some aspects of long-term memory, and language and emotion.

pawns: Individuals who believe that they have little influence or control over what happens in their lives.

PBL activities: Short problem-based activities that small groups of students can complete in 30–45-minute periods of time.

PBL interdisciplinary days: A day set aside for students, school-wide, to inquire and discuss particular problems and issues from a variety of perspectives.

PBL projects: Problem-based learning activities in which students complete projects that are guided by structured guidelines and processes.

PBL units and courses: The most open-ended and student-centered form of PBL, in which whole units or courses are organized around real-life problem situations.

peer assessment: Students giving each other feedback on work using a variety of strategies.

peer observation: A teacher learning strategy in which colleagues visit each other's classrooms and observe each other teaching.

peer tutoring: Pairing students to assist and support each other with their work.

percentile rank: A statistical device that shows the percentage of students in a group who scored at or below a particular individual's score.

perception: Process in which individuals become aware and interpret sensory stimuli.

performance assessments: Assessments in which students demonstrate with products or activities what they know and can do as contrasted to answering questions on paper-and-pencil tests.

performance goals: Goals that focus on comparing one's abilities with those of others or some predetermined standard.

performance indicator: Assessment items that measure student mastery of particular standards.

pleasure system: Emotional system that, when activated, causes us to come closer to get more.

portfolio: A collection of student work and their reflections on the work.

positive feeling tones: Classroom environments that are pleasant places to be and characterized by caring and supportive relationships.

positive interdependence: A learning situation in which individuals are required to work together to accomplish common goals.

positive reinforcers: Actions in reinforcement theory, normally in the form of rewards, that cause individuals to repeat desired behaviors.

positon emission technology (PET): A technology used to map and observe brain activity.

power principle: Idea that what is taught and included in a curriculum should represent the big ideas and structure of a subject or discipline.

practical intelligence: Intelligence that allows individuals to deal well with everyday and personal problems.

praise: Positive verbal and nonverbal reinforcers made by teachers to encourage and strengthen desirable student behaviors.

prediction reading strategies: Strategies students employ before commencing reading expository text in which they make predictions about what the text is going to be about.

pre-flight check list: A peer-assessment strategy where students trade papers and review each other's work using a pre-flight checklist provided by the teacher.

presentation teaching: An approach to teaching where the goal is to help students learn new declarative knowledge as a result of teacher lecturing and explaining new learning materials.

previewing text: Strategies students employ before commencing reading of expository text where they look for main ideas and topics that will be found in the text.

prior knowledge: Knowledge that learners have processed and stored in the brain's memory system prior to instruction.

problem-based learning (PBL): An approach to learning in which students work in teams to solve "ill-structured" and real-world problems.

procedural knowledge: Knowing about how to do something, ranging from rather basic behavioral skills to complex cognitive strategies.

process curriculum: How students come to know what is taught in contrast to the content itself.

process skills: Skills such as inquiry, problem solving, and project management that are required to participate effectively in PBL and other forms of learning.

process–product research: An approach to research where the relationships between teacher behavior (process) and student achievement (product) are studied.

product criteria cards: Cards that outline four or five criteria that will be used to assess student work and artifacts.

productions: Name given to basic units of procedural knowledge.

professional learning communities: A place where a group of professionals come together regularly to work collaboratively, to reflect on teaching practices, and to discuss strategies for improving teaching and learning.

propositions: Name given to basic units of declarative knowledge.

public policy: Policy that stems from actions taken by local, state, and federal governmental bodies, including regulations developed by legislatures and executive branches of government.

punishment: Something that inflicts or imposes a penalty on individuals for acts of undesirable or illegal behavior.

quantitative encephalography (qEEG): A technology used to map and observe brain activity.

questioning: Process used by teachers to check for student understanding and/or to help students extend and use their thinking and discourse skills.

RAN strategy: A strategy for reading and analyzing non-fiction.

reasoning: Process of forming judgments and/or justifying actions based on logic and evidence.

reciprocal teaching: An approach to teaching reading where students are taught to apply four or five comprehension learning strategies to the passage they are reading.

reconstituting standards: Process of taking a standard that consists of several outcomes or elements and rewriting it so single elements can be assessed accurately.

reflection: Careful and analytical thought about what one is doing or has done and its effect on desired outcomes.

reflective dialogue: Meaningful discussion among teachers about their situations and challenges, and about teaching practices and student learning.

reflective thought: See *reflection*.

reinforcement theory: Theory that posits that individuals are propelled to act by external events, primarily to capture desired rewards or to avoid punishment.

reliability: The degree to which an assessment will produce dependable results consistently and over time.

repertoire: The number and range of teaching practices and strategies which teachers have at their command and can use effectively to promote student learning.

repetitive change syndrome: See *innovation overload*.

respectful mind: The kind of mind that welcomes and respects diverse persons and groups and avoids prejudicial judgments.

restructured schools: Situation in which changes are made in the basic ways schools are organized and structured.

reward: Something given in recognition for effort, achievement, or desirable behavior.

rich learning environments: Environments that are rich in resources and have a variety of elements that stimulate the various senses, such as visual, auditory, taste, and smell.

rubric: A scoring guide that defines criteria and describes various levels of performance.

rule–example–rule device: A technique used when explaining a new idea—the rule is given first, followed by examples of the rule, and then summarized by stating the rule again.

SAT: A standardized test for college admissions in the United States (formerly called the Scholastic Aptitude Test and Scholastic Assessment Test).

scaffolding: Process of providing assistance (by a teacher or more advanced learner) to help a learner master new knowledge or skill that they could not master by themselves.

schema theory: Name used for an individual's knowledge structure and the way information is organized and stored in long-term memory.

school improvement imperative: Essential and urgent demands for schools to improve and become more effective in accomplishing student learning.

science of learning: The scientific study of learning through observation and experimentation, mainly in the fields of the neurosciences and cognitive psychology.

scientific basis of teaching: Application and decisions about teaching based on research and scientific evidence.

scientific thinking: Thinking associated with scientific inquiry that involves hypothesis testing through observation and experimentation.

scoring rubric: See *rubric.*

seatwork: Guided or independent practice and assigned work performed in the classroom.

selected-response item: A test item in which students select the correct answer from those provided, normally multiple-choice, true and false, and matching questions.

self-assessment: Assessments in which students monitor their own progress toward achieving learning goals, and make adjustments in learning strategies.

self-determination: Situations where individuals believe they control their own lives.

self-efficacy: Beliefs held by individuals that their efforts will be successful and caused by personal efforts rather than by external factors or luck.

self-guided independence: A situation in which students plan, execute, and assess their own learning tasks.

self-regulated learners: Learners who can employ metacognitive strategies effectively and thus control and be responsible for their own learning.

sensory memory: Component if the memory system that provides the first recognition and store very briefly stimuli from the environment.

shared independence: A situation where students generate problems to be solved, design learning tasks, and set timelines, and criteria for evaluation in cooperation with the teacher.

shared norms and values: Situation in which teachers reach common agreements about their teaching, student learning, assessment, and teachers' roles.

short-term working memory: Place in the memory system that first notes and provides temporary storage for new information; where mental work is first done.

simile: A figure of speech where one thing is compared to another.

Six Thinking Hats Program: Thinking program that emphasizes different ways of thinking, thinking styles, and the creative and emotional aspects of thinking.

social learning theory: Theory that emphasizes learning through observation and the importance of individuals' beliefs about their abilities and self-efficacy.

social purposes of education: The larger or overall goals and purposes a society holds for its educational system.

Socratic dialogue: Engages students in discussions to explore ideas, values, and issues and relies on questioning rather than telling.

stages of teacher development: Theories that describe how teachers develop over time and move from novice to expert status.

stand-alone thinking programs: Approaches to teaching students how to think that focus directly on thinking skills and dispositions and separate this instruction from subject matter instruction.

standardized tests: Summative exams and assessments designed and given under uniform conditions to provide information on the performance of students, schools, and districts.

standards-based curriculum: Curriculum designed around an agreed upon set of precise standards that attempt to define what students should know and be able to do.

standards-based education: Systems of education where agreed upon standards guide teaching, learning, and assessment; where high expectations are held for all students; and where educators are held accountable for student learning.

structural approach: An approach to cooperative learning that uses various structures and small-group activities to organize student interaction.

structured independence: A situation where students make choices from teacher-generated options, timelines, and criteria.

student diversity: See *diversity.*

student opinion journals: Notebooks where students record statements of belief and provide evidence to support their beliefs and opinions.

Student Teams Achievement Divisions (STAD): An approach to cooperative learning in which team members collaborate to master assigned learning materials then compete with members of other teams.

student-centered classrooms: Classrooms where teachers are responsive and proactive in meeting different student learning needs.

student-centered instruction: Instruction that starts where students are and that uses multiple approaches to help them progress as far as possible.

summarizing strategies: Strategies students can employ to extend their understanding after reading a particular piece of expository text or after some other type of learning experience.

summative assessment: Information collected *after* instruction that is used to summarize student performance, determine mastery, assign grades, and determine placements.

sustained silent reading (SSR): A strategy for providing students time on a regular basis to read independently whatever they want to read.

synapses: Junctions or small spaces between neurons where information is passed from neuron to neuron.

synthesizing mind: The kind of mind that can survey a wide range of information and information sources and decide what is important and worth paying attention to.

teacher clarity: Phrase used to describe aspects of teacher presentations that are clear and free from ambiguity.

teacher development: See *stages of development*.

teacher dispositions: Inherent attitudes and qualities of mind in regard to one's teaching, view of students, and how students learn.

teacher enthusiasm: Phrase used to describe aspects of teacher presentations, such as use of uplifting language or dramatic movement, aimed at capturing students' attention in regard to the learning material.

teacher expertise: The final progression in teacher development characterized by flexibility, ability to perform teaching tasks automatically, and to understand problems at a deeper level than novices.

teacher knowledge: The amount and type of knowledge teachers use to inform their practice.

teacher leadership: Actions taken by teachers and possession of skills that allow them to provide leadership to other teachers and educators.

teacher learning: Learning accomplished by teachers that expands their teaching repertoire and makes them more effective in affecting student learning.

teacher networking: Situation in which teachers come together physically or electronically to discuss and share ideas about teaching practices and student learning.

teacher-centered classrooms: Classrooms where teachers adopt mainly a standardized approach, curriculum, and instruction.

teacher-centered instruction: Teaching that is prescriptive and most often aimed at the whole class.

team scores: Scores that are calculated by averaging the individual scores of team members and then used to recognize team effort.

temporal lobe: Location in the brain that deals mainly with orientation, certain kinds of recognition, and processing of sensory information.

thalamus: Part of the brain that relays, sorts, and directs signals back and forth between the spinal cord and the cerebrum.

thinking dispositions: Inherent attitudes and qualities of mind and thinking, such as curiosity and open-mindedness.

thinking routines: Routines and structures that provide scaffolding to students' thinking processes and make their thinking visible to themselves and to their teachers.

Think–Pair–Share: A small group teaching technique to slow down the discourse pattern and provide opportunities for more students to participate.

tic-tac-toe organizer: A nine-box template for organizing student choice activities.

tier words: Refers to system in vocabulary instruction of dividing words into three categories (tiers) that help teachers decide which words are the most important to teach.

tiered lessons: Lessons that provide a series of tasks or learning activities at varying levels of complexity related to the same essential question or standard.

time-to-learn studies: Research conducted that provides information about what exactly is taught (the enacted curriculum) in classrooms and its effects on student learning.

tomographs: a three-dimensional computer image of the brain as it does its work and processes information.

traditional assessments: Teacher-made, paper-and-pencil tests, or homework assignments such as book reports and term papers.

traffic lights: A formative assessment technique where students show teachers their level of understanding of a particular idea or skill during a lesson using green, yellow, and red indicators.

transfer: The process of taking what is learnt in one setting (school) and using it in another setting (work or leisure).

transitions: Statements made by teachers during a presentation that help students move from one part of the presentation to the next.

triarchic instruction: Instruction and use of teaching materials that enable students to use their analytical, creative, and practical abilities.

triarchic theory of intelligence: Theory and description of mental abilities maintaining that intelligence consists primarily of three different cognitive processes or abilities.

two stars and a wish: A peer-assessment technique where students give each other feedback on their work by identifying two stars (positives) and one wish (suggestion for improvement).

unidimensionality: Having a single factor or element.

validity: The degree to which an assessment measures what it claims to measure.

verbal signposts: Statements made by teachers during a presentation that help students follow the lesson along and alert them to important points coming up.

vertical thinking: Linear thinking based mainly on logic and reasoning.

viewing skills: Skills individuals have for understanding media and visual messages and to evaluate their accuracy and worth.

visual learners: Individuals who prefer or learn more effectively from visual input.

visual literacy: Ability to understand visual messages and to communicate through visual means.

visual messages: Messages that are sent primarily by visual means and include such elements as font, typeface, and color.

Visual Thinking Program: Thinking program that teaches students skills and dispositions by creating classroom environments that focus on thinking and by using a set of thinking routines that help make thinking more transparent.

visual tools: Devices that assist in displaying information and knowledge in visual ways.

vocational preparation: School curriculum that is mainly vocational and aimed at preparing students for the world of work.

wagon wheel teaming strategy: A way to form heterogeneous groups of four with expert-, average-, and beginner-level learners.

wait-times: The time interval a teacher waits for students to respond to a question and the time a teacher waits to respond back.

whiteboards: A formative assessment technique where each student uses a whiteboard to respond to short answer-type questions.

zone of proximal development: Phase or the area between a learner's actual development and their level of potential development. Learning at this phase can be accomplished with appropriate help.

REFERENCES

Abrahamson, E. (2004). *Change without pain.* Cambridge, MA: Harvard Business School Press.

Achilles, C.M., & Hoover, S.P. (1996). Transforming administrative praxis: The potential of problem-based learning (PBL) as a school-improvement vehicle for middle and high schools. Paper presented at the annual meeting of the American Educational Research Association, New York.

Adams, M. (1990). *Beginning to read: Thinking and learning about print.* Cambridge, MA: MIT Press.

Ainsworth, L. (2003). *Unwrapping the standards: A simple process for making standards manageable.* Denver, CO: Advance Learning Press.

Ainsworth, L., & Viegut, D. (2006). *Common formative assessments.* Thousand Oaks, CA: Corwin Press.

Airasian, P.W. (2006). *Classroom assessment: Concepts and applications* (5th ed.). New York: McGraw-Hill.

Allen, L. (Ed.) (1999). *Lessons from the League of Professional Schools.* San Francisco, CA: Jossey-Bass.

Alschuler, A.S., Tabor, D., & McIntyre, J. (1970). *Teaching achievement motivation: Theory and practice in psychological education.* Middletown, CT: Education Ventures.

Amaile, T. (1996). *Creativity in context.* Boulder, CO: Westview Press.

American Jury: Bulwark of Democracy: www.crfc.org/americanjury/index.html

Amrein, A.L., & Berliner, D.C. (2003). The effects of high stakes testing on student motivation and learning. *Educational Leadership, 60*(5), 32–37.

Anderson, C., & Smith, E. (1997). Teaching science. In V. Richardson-Koehler (Ed.), *Educator's handbook: A research perspective.* New York: Longman.

Anderson, L., & Krathwohl, D. (Eds.). (2001). *A taxonomy for learning, teaching, and assessing: A revision of Bloom's taxonomy of education objectives.* New York: Longman.

Andrade, H.G. (2000). Using rubrics to promote thinking and learning. *Educational Leadership, 57*(7), 13–18.

Andrade, H.G., & Boulay, B.A. (2003). Role of rubric-referenced self-assessment in learning to write. *Journal of Educational Research, 97*(1), 21–34.

Andrade, H.G., & Du, Y. (2007). Student responses to criteria-referenced self-assessment. *Assessment and Evaluation in Higher Education, 32*(2), 159–181.

Ankeny Community School District (2008). Retrieved August 9, 2008, from www.ankeny.k12.ia.us/high-school/index.html.

Apple, M. (1990). *Ideology and the curriculum.* New York: Routledge.

Arends, R. (2009). *Learning to teach* (8th ed.). New York: McGraw-Hill.

Aronson, E., & Goode, E. (1978). *The jigsaw classroom.* Beverly Hills, CA: Sage Publications.

Aronson, E., & Patnoe, S. (1997). *The jigsaw classroom.* New York: Addison-Wesley Longman.

Ash, G. (2005). What did Abigail mean? *Educational Leadership, 63*(2), 36–41.

Ashcraft, M.H. (2006). *Cognition* (4th ed.). Upper Saddle River, NJ: Prentice Hall.

Association for Supervision and Curriculum Development (2008). Teaching students how to think. *Education Leadership, 65*(5).

Atkinson, J., & Feather, N. (1966). *A theory of achievement motivation.* New York: Wiley.

Audet, R., & Jordon, L. (2005). *Integrating inquiry across the curriculum.* Thousand Hills, CA: Corwin Press.

Ausubel, D. (1960). The use of advance organizers in the learning and retention of meaningful verbal learning. *Journal of Educational Psychology, 51*(5), 267–272.

Ball, D. & Cohen, D. (1999). Developing practice, developing practitioners: Toward a practice-based theory of professional education. In L. Darling-Hammond and G. Sykes (Eds.), *Teaching as the learning profession: Handbook of policy and Practice.* San Francisco, CA: Jossey-Bass.

Bandura, A. (1977). *Social learning theory.* Englewood Cliffs, NJ: Prentice Hall.

Bandura, A. (1986). *Social foundations of thought and action.* Englewood Cliffs, NJ: Prentice Hall.

Bandura, A. (1996). *Self-efficacy: The exercise of control.* New York: Freeman.

Bangert, R.L., Kulik, C.C., Kulik, J.A., & Morgan, M.T. (1991). The instructional effects of feedback on test-like events. *Review of Educational Research, 61*(2), 213–238.

Banks, J., Cochran-Smith, M., Moll, L., Richert, A., Zeichner, K., Lepage, P., Darling-Hammond, L., Duffy, H., & McDonald, M. (2005). Teaching diverse learners. In L. Darling-Hammond & J. Bransford (Eds.), *Preparing teachers for a changing world: What teachers should learn and be able to do* (pp. 235–236). San Francisco: Jossey-Bass.

Barber, M., & Mourshed, M. (2007). *How the world's best-performing school systems come out on top.* London: McKinsey & Company.

Barell, J. (2006). *Problem-based learning: An inquiry approach* (2nd ed.). Thousand Oaks, CA: Corwin Press.

Barnes, L., Christensen, R., & Hansen, A. (Eds.). (1994). *Teaching and the case method* (3rd ed.). Boston, MA: Harvard Business School Press.

Barnett, B., Norton, J., & Byrd, A. (2007). Lessons from networking. *Educational Leadership, 65*(1), 48–52.

Barrow, H.S., & Tamblyn, R.M. (1980). *Problem-based learning: An approach to medical education.* New York: Springer.

Beck, J., & Czerniak, C. (2005). Invasion of the zebra mussels: A mock trial activity. *Science Activities, Spring,* 18.

Beck, I., McKeown, M., & Kucan, L. (2002a). *Bringing words to life.* New York: Guilford Press.

Beck, I., McKeown, M., & Kucan, L. (2002b). *Creating robust vocabulary.* New York: Guilford Press.

Belgrad, S., Burke, K., & Fogarty, R. (2008). The portfolio connection: Student work linked to standards (3rd ed.). Thousand Oaks, CA: Corwin Press.

Benjamin, A. (2002). *Differentiated instruction: A guide for middle and high school teachers.* Larchmont, NY: Eye on Education.

Bennett, B., & Rolheiser, C. (2001). *Beyond Monet: The artful science of instructional integration.* Ajax, ON: Bookation.

Bennett, S., & Kalish, N. (2006). *The case against homework: How homework is hurting our children and what we can do about it.* New York: Crown.

Berliner, D. (1987). In pursuit of the expert pedagogue. *Educational Researcher, 15*(7), 5–13.

Berliner, D. (1994). Expertise: The wonder of exemplary performances. In J. Mangieri and C. Blocks (Eds.), *Creating powerful thinking in teachers and students: Diverse perspectives.* Fort Worth, TX: Harcourt Brace College Publishers.

Berliner, D. (2001). Learning about learning from expert teachers. *Journal of Educational Research, 35*(5), 463–483.

Berliner, D. (2009). *Poverty and potential: Out-of-school factors and school success.* Education and Policy Research Unit. Tempe, AZ: Arizona State University.

Berk, L. (2002). *Infants, children, and adolescents* (4th ed.). Boston, MA: Allyn & Bacon.

Berman, S. (2001). Thinking in context: Teaching for open-mindedness and critical understanding. In A. Costa (Ed.), *Developing minds: A resource book for teaching thinking* (3rd ed.). Alexandria, VA: Association for Supervision and Curriculum Development.

Berman, P., & McLaughlin, M. (1978). *Federal programs supporting educational change. Vol. IV: The findings in review.* Santa Monica, CA: Rand Corporation.

Beyer, B. (1979). *Teaching thinking in the social studies.* New York: Merrill.

Beyer, B. (1997). *Improving student thinking.* Boston: Allyn & Bacon.

Beyer, B. (2001a). A format for assessing thinking skills. In A. Costa (Ed.), *Developing minds: A resource book for teaching thinking* (3rd ed.). Alexandria, VA: Association for Supervision and Curriculum Development.

Beyer, B. (2001b). Developing a scope and sequence for thinking skills instruction. In A. Costa (Ed.), *Developing minds: A resource book for teaching thinking* (3rd ed.). Alexandria, VA: Association for Supervision and Curriculum Development.

Beyer, B. (2001c). Practical strategies for direct instruction in thinking skills. In A. Costa (Ed.), *Developing minds: A resource book for teaching thinking* (3rd ed.). Alexandria, VA: Association for Supervision and Curriculum Development.

Biancarosa, G. (2005). After third grade. *Educational Leadership, 63*(2), 16–22.

Black, P., & Wiliam, D. (1998). Inside the black box: Raising standards through classroom assessment. *Phi Delta Kappan, 80*(2), 139–148.

Black, P., Harrison, C., Lee, C., Marshall, B., & Wiliam, D. (2004). Working inside the black box: Assessment for learning in the classroom. *Phi Delta Kappan, 86*(1), 8–21.

Bloom, B. (1956). *Taxonomy of educational objectives: Handbook I: Cognitive Domain.* New York: David McKay.

Bloom, B. (1971). Mastery learning. In J. Block (Ed.), *Mastery learning: Theory and practice.* New York: Holt, Rinehart & Winston.

Blythe, T., Allen, D., & Powell, B. (2007). *Looking at student work* (2nd ed.). New York: Teachers College Press.

Boaler, J. (1998). Open and closed mathematics: Student experiences and understandings. *Journal for Research in Mathematics Education, 29*(1), 41–62.

Borg, W., & Gall, M. (1993). *Educational research* (4th ed.). New York: Longman.

Boud, D., & Falchikov, N. (1989). Quantitative studies of student self-assessment in higher education: A critical analysis of findings. *Higher Education, 18*(5), 529–549.

Bozeman, M. (1995). Signaling in the classroom. Unpublished data. Salisbury, MD: Salisbury State University.

Bransford, J., Brown, A., & Cocking, R. (2000). *How people learn: Brain, mind, experience, and school.* Washington, DC: National Academy Press.

Bransford, J.D., Vye, N., Kinser, C., & Risko, V. (1990). Teaching thinking and content knowledge: Toward an integrated model. In B.F. Jones & L. Idol (Eds.), *Dimensions of thinking and cognitive intelligence.* Hillsdale, NJ: Lawrence Erlbaum Associates.

Brewer, J., Zhao, A., Desmond, J., Glover, G., & Gabrieli, J. (1998). Making memories: Brain activity that predicts how well visual experience will be remembered. *Science, 281,* 1185–1187.

Bridges, E.M., & Hallinger, P. (1993). Problem-based learning in medical and managerial education. In P. Hallinger, K. Leithwood, & J. Murphy (Eds.), *Cognitive perspectives on educational leadership* (pp. 253–267). New York: Teachers College Press.

Brookhart, S.M. (1999). *The art and science of classroom assessment: The missing part of pedagogy.* San Francisco, CA: Jossey Bass.

Brookhart, S.M. (2004). *Grading.* Upper Saddle River, NJ: Pearson Education.

Brophy, J.E., & Good, T.L. (1986). Teacher behavior and student achievement. In M.C. Wittrock (Ed.), *Handbook of research on teaching* (3rd ed.). New York: Macmillan.

Brown, A. (1987). Metacognition, executive control, self-regulation, and other more mysterious mechanisms. In F. Weinert & R. Kluwe (Eds.), *Metacognition, motivation, and understanding.* Hillsdale, NJ: Lawrence Erlbaum Associates.

Brown, A., & Palinscar, A. (1989). Coherence and causality in science readings. Paper presented at the annual meeting of the American Educational Research Association, San Francisco.

Bruner, J. (1960). *The process of education.* Cambridge, MA: Harvard University Press.

Bruner, J. (1961). The act of discovery. *Harvard Educational Review, 31*(1), 21–32.

Bruner, J. (1966). *Toward a theory of instruction.* Cambridge, MA: Harvard University Press.

Bruner, J. (1973). *Beyond the information given.* New York: W. W. Norton.

Bruner, J. (1986). *Actual minds, possible worlds.* Cambridge, MA: Harvard University Press.

Bruner, J. (1999). In search of brain-based education. *Phi Delta Kappan, 80,* 648–657.

Bruner, J., Goodnow, J., & Austin, A. (1956). *A study of thinking.* New York: Wiley.

Bruning, R., Schraw, G., Norby, M., & Ronning, R. (2004). *Cognitive psychology and instruction* (4th ed.). Columbus, OH: Merrill.

BSCS Center (2009). *BSCS 5E Instructional Model.* Retrieved January 6, 2009, from www.BSCS.org.

Burbules, N.C., & Bruce, B.C. (2001). Theory and research on teaching as dialogue. In V. Richardson (Ed.), *Handbook of research on teaching* (4th ed.). Washington, DC: American Educational Research Association.

Burke, J. (2000). *Reading reminders: Tools, tips and techniques.* Portsmouth, NH: Boyton/Cook.

Burke, K. (1999). *How to assess authentic learning.* Arlington, IL: Skylight Training and Publishing Inc.

Burmark, L. (2002). *Visual literacy: Learn to see, see to learn.* Alexandria, VA: Association of Supervision and Curriculum Development.

Butler, R. (1989). Mastery versus ability appraisal: A developmental study of children's observation of peers' work. *Child Development, 60*(6), 1350–1361.

California State Department of Education (2008). Retrieved September 23, 2008, from www.cde.ca.gov.

Campoy, R. (2004). *Case study analysis in the classroom: Becoming a reflective teacher.* Thousand Oaks, CA: Sage Publications.

Carnine, D., Silbert, J., Kame'enui, E., & Tarver, S. (2004). *Direct instruction reading* (4th ed.). Upper Saddle River, NJ: Pearson.

Carpenter, T.P., & Fennema, E. (1992). Cognitively guided instruction: Building on the knowledge of students and teachers. In W. Secada (Ed.), *Curriculum reform: The case of Mathematics in the United States* (pp. 457–470). Elmsford, NY: Pergamon Press, Inc.

Carter, K., Cushing, K., Sabers, D., Stein, P., & Berliner, D. (1988). Expert–novice differences in perceiving and processing visual classroom information. *Journal of Teacher Education, 39*(3), 25–31.

Cavanagh, S. (2009). Depth matters in high school science studies. *Education Week, 28*(24), 1, 16–17.

Cazden, C.B. (1986). Classroom discourse. In M.C. Wittrock (Ed.), *Handbook of research on teaching* (3rd ed.). New York: Macmillan.

Cazden, C.B. (1988). *Classroom discourse.* Portsmouth, NH: Heinemann.

Center for Media Literacy (2007). Five key questions form foundation for media inquiry. Retrieved August 1, 2007, from www.medialit.org/reading.

Chapman, C. (2008). *Using graphic organizers to develop thinking skills, K-12.* Thousand Oaks, CA: Sage Publications.

Chenoweth, K. (2007). *It's being done: Academic success in unexpected schools.* Cambridge, MA: Harvard Education Press.

Chomsky, N. (2002). *Understanding power: The indispensable Chomsky.* New York: New Press.

Christensen, R., & Hansen, A. (Eds.) (1987). *Teaching and the case method.* Boston, MA: Harvard Business School Press.

Coalition of Essential Schools. Retrieved December 15, 2008, from www.essentialschools.org.

Cochran-Smith, M., & Lytle, S.L. (1993). *Inside/outside: Teacher research and teacher knowledge.* New York: Teachers College Press.

Coffield, F., Moseley, D., Hall, E., & Ecclestone, K. (2004). *Learning styles and pedagogy in post-16 learning: A systematic and critical review.* London: University of Newcastle upon Tyne.

Cohen, M. (2007). *Children, families, & media: A benchmark.* New York: Michael Cohen Group LLC.

Cohen, G.L., Garcia, J., Apfel, N., & Master, A. (2006). Reducing the racial achievement gap: A social-psychological intervention. *Science, 313*(5791), 1307–1310.

Coil, C. (2004). *Standards-based activities and assessments for the differentiated classroom.* Marion, IL: Pieces of Learning.

Coil, C. (2007). *Successful teaching in the differentiated classroom.* Marian, IL: Pieces of Learning.

Coiro, J. (2005). Making sense of online text. *Educational Leadership, 63*(2), 30–35.

Coiro, J., & Dobler, E. (2004). Investigating how less-skilled and skilled readers use cognitive reading strategies while reading on the Internet. Paper presented at the 54th annual meeting of the National Reading Conference, San Antonio, Texas.

Collins, M. (1978). Effects of enthusiasm training on preservice elementary teachers. *Journal of Teacher Education, 28*(1), 53–57.

Concept Attainment (2008). Retrieved February 18, 2008, from www.csus.edu/indiv/pofeiferj/EdTe22.

Connecticut State Department of Education (2008). Retrieved September, 2008, from www.sde.ct.gov/sde/site/default.asp.

Conway, P., & Clark, C. (2003). The journey inward and outward: A re-examination of Fuller's concerns-based model of teacher development. *Teaching and Teacher Education, 19*, 465–482.

Cooper, H. (1989). *Homework.* New York: Longman.

Cooper, H., & Valentine, J. (2001). Using research to answer practical questions about homework. *Educational Psychologist, 36*(3), 143–153.

Cooper, H., Jackson, K., Nye, B., & Lindsey, J. (2001). A model of homework's influence on the performance evaluation of elementary school students. *Journal of Experimental Education, 69*(2) 181–200.

Cooper, H., Robinson, J., & Patall, E. (2006). Does homework improve academic achievement? A synthesis of research, 1987–2003. *Review of Educational Research, 76*(1), 1–62.

Cooper, J. (1993). *Literacy: Helping children construct meaning* (2nd ed.). Boston, MA: Houghton Mifflin.

Corcoran, T. (1995). *Helping teachers teach well: Transforming professional development.* New York: Teachers College Press.

Corey, S.M. (1953). *Action research to improve school practices.* New York: Teachers College Press.

Corno, L. (2001). Homework is a complicated thing. *Educational Researcher, 25*(8), 27–30.

Costa, A. (Ed.) (2001a). *Developing minds: A resource book for teaching thinking* (3rd ed.). Alexandria, VA: Association for Supervision and Curriculum Development.

Costa, A. (2001b). Teacher behaviors that enable student thinking. In A. Costa (Ed.), *Developing minds: A resource book for teaching thinking* (3rd ed.). Alexandria, VA: Association for Supervision and Curriculum Development.

Costa, A. (2008). The thought-filled curriculum. *Education Leadership, 65*(5), 20–25.

Costa, A., & Garmston, R.J. (2002). *Cognitive coaching* (2nd ed.). Norwood, MA: Christopher-Gordon.

Costa, A., & Kallick, B. (1993). Through the lens of a critical friend. *Educational Leadership, 51*(2), 49–51.

Costa, A., & Kallick, B. (2000). *Discovering and exploring habits of mind.* Alexandria, VA: Association of Supervision and Curriculum Development.

Costa, A., & Kallick, B. (2004). *Assessment strategies for self-directed learning.* Thousand Oaks, CA: Corwin Press.

Costa, A., & Marzano, R. (2001). Teaching the language of thinking. In A. Costa (Ed.), *Developing minds: A resource book for teaching thinking* (3rd ed.). Alexandria, VA: Association for Supervision and Curriculum Development.

Cotton, K. (1995). *Effective school practices: A research synthesis.* Portland, OR: Northwest Regional Educational Laboratory.

Cowan, G., & Cowan, E. (1980). *Writing.* New York: Wiley.

CRFC Mock Trial Resources for Classrooms: www.crfc.org/mocktrial.html

Crooks, T. (1988). The impact of classroom evaluation on students. *Review of Educational Research, 58*(4), 438–481.

Cross, P.K. (1998). *What do we know about student learning and how do we know it?* Presented at the American Association for Higher Education National Conference, Atlanta, GA, March 24.

Csikszentmihalyi, M. (1990). *Flow: The psychology of optimal experience.* New York: Harper & Row.

Csikszentmihalyi, M. (1998). *Creativity: Flow and the psychology of discovery and invention.* New York: Harper & Row.

Cuban, L. (1993). *How teachers taught: Constancy and change in American classrooms 1890–1990* (2nd ed.). New York: Teachers College Press.

Cushman, K. (1998). How friends can be critical as schools made essential changes. *Horace, 14*(5), 3–4.

Dana Alliance for Brain Initiatives (2003). Washington, DC: Dana Center.

Danielson, C. (2006). *Teacher leadership that strengthens professional practice.* Alexandria, VA: Association for Supervision and Curriculum Development.

Darling-Hammond, L., & Bransford, J. (Eds.) (2005). *Preparing teachers for a changing world.* San Francisco, CA: Jossey-Bass.

Darling-Hammond, L., Wei, R., Andree, A., Richardson, N., & Orphanos, S. (2009). *Professional learning in the learning profession: A status report on teacher development in the United States and abroad.* Oxford, OH: National Staff Development Council.

David, J. (2008). What research says about project-based learning. *Educational Leadership, 65*(3), 80–82.

Davies, A. (2007). *Making classroom assessment work* (2nd ed.). Courtney, BC: Classroom Connections International Inc.

Dean, C.D. (2001). They expect teachers to do that: Helping teachers explore and take ownership of their profession. In B.B. Levin (Ed.), *Energizing teacher education and professional development with problem-based learning.* Alexandria, VA: Association for Supervision and Curriculum Development.

de Bono, E. (1983). The direct teaching of thinking as a skill. *Phi Delta Kappan, 64*(10), 703–708.

de Bono, E. (1986). *Six thinking hats.* London: Penguin Books.

deCharms, R. (1976). *Enhancing motivation.* New York: Irvington.

Deci, E., & Ryan, R. (1985). *Intrinsic motivation and self-determination in human behavior.* New York: Plenum Press.

deVolder, M.L., & deGrave, W.S. (1989). Schema training in problem-based learning. *Teaching and Learning in Medicine, 1,* 16–20.

deVries, M., Schmidt, H.G. & deGraaf, E. (1989). Dutch comparisons: Cognitive and motivational effects of problem-based learning on medical students. In H.G. Schmidt, M. Lipkin, M.W. de Vries, & J.M. Greep (Eds.), *New directions for medical education: Problem-based learning and community oriented medical education.* (pp. 230–240). New York: Springer-Verlag.

Dewey, J. (1916). *Democracy and education.* New York: Macmillan.

Dewey, J. (1938). *Experience and education.* New York: MacMillan.

Dewey, J. (1971). *How we think.* Chicago: Henry Regnery (original work published 1933).

Dodge, J. (2005). *Differentiation in action.* New York: Scholastic Inc.

Donoghue, P., & Siegal, M. (2005). *Are you really listening? Keys to successful communication.* Notre Dame, IN: Sorin Books.

Doyle, W. (1986). Classroom organization and management. In M.C. Wittrock (Ed.), *Handbook of research on teaching* (3rd ed.). New York: Macmillan.

Dreyfus, H.L., & Dreyfus, S.E. (1986). *Mind over machine.* New York: Free Press.

DuFour, R., DuFour, R., Eaker, R., & Karhanek, G. (2004). *Whatever it takes: How a professional learning community responds when kids don't learn.* Bloomington, IN: Solution Tree.

Dunlosky, J., & Metcalfe, J. (2008). *Metacognition.* London: Sage Publications.

Dunn, K., & Dunn, R, (1978). *Teaching students through their individual learning styles.* Reston, VA: National Council of Principals.

Dweck, C.S. (1986). Motivational processes affecting learning, *American Psychologist, 41*(10), 40–10.

Dweck, C.S. (2002). The development of ability conceptions. In A. Wigfield & J.S. Eccles (Eds.), *Development of achievement motivation* (pp. 57–91). San Diego, CA: Academic Press.

Eagleton, M., Dobler, E., & Leu, D.J. (2007). *Reading the web: Strategies for Internet inquiry.* New York: Guilford Press.

Earl, L. (2003). *Assessment as learning: Using classroom assessments to maximize student learning.* Thousand Oaks, CA: Corwin Press.

Easton, L.B. (2008). *Powerful designs for professional learning* (2nd ed.). Oxford, OH: National Staff Development Council.

Economic Policy Institute (2008). *A broader, bolder approach.* Retrieved September 15, 2008, from http://boldapproach.org.

Edelson, D.C., Gordon, D.N., & Pea, R.D. (1999). Addressing the challenge of inquiry based learning through technology and curriculum design. *Journal of the Learning Sciences, 8,* 391–450.

Edmonds, R. (1981). Making public schools effective. *Social Policy, 12*(2), 56–60.

Eisner, E.W. (1991). *The enlightened eye: Qualitative inquiry and the enhancement of educational practice.* New York: Macmillan.

Elmore, R. (2004). *School reform from the inside out: Policy, practice, and performance.* Cambridge, MA: Harvard University Press.

Epstein, R. (2007). Why high school must go: An interview with Leon Botstein. *Phi Delta Kappan, 88*(9), 659–663.

Erickson, H. (2002). *Concept-based curriculum and instruction: Teaching beyond the facts.* Thousand Hills, CA: Corwin Press.

Evaluating Web Pages: Techniques to apply and questions to ask. www.lib.berkeley.edu/Teaching Lib/Guides/Internet/Evaluate. Retrieved July 8, 2007.

Facione, P., Facione, N., & Sanchez, D. (1992). *The California critical thinking disposition inventory.* Millbrae, CA: California Academic Press.

Feather, N. (1969). Attribution of responsibility and valence of success and failure in relation to initial confidence and task performance. *Journal of Personal and Social Psychology, 13,* 129–144.

Feiman-Nemser, S. (1983). Learning to teach. In L.S. Shulman & G. Sykes (Eds.), *Handbook of teaching and policy.* New York: Longman.

Fenton, E. (1966). *Teaching the new social studies in secondary schools: An inductive approach.* Washington, DC: International Thomson Publishing.

Ferguson, D.L., Ralph, G., Meyer, G., Lester, J., Droege, C., Guojonsdottir, H., et al. (2001). *Designing personalized learning experiences for every student.* Alexandria, VA: Association for Supervision and Curriculum Development.

Fisher, C.W., Berliner, D., Filby, N., Marliave, R., Cahen, L., & Dishaw, M. (1980). Teacher behavior, academic learning time, and student achievement. In C. Denham & A. Lieberman (Eds.), *Time to learn.* Washington, DC: Department of Education.

Fisher, D., & Frey, N. (2007). *Checking for understanding: Formative assessment techniques for your classroom.* Alexandria, VA: Association for Supervision and Curriculum Development.

Fisher, D., & Frey, N. (2008). *Word wise and content rich: Five essential steps to teaching academic vocabulary.* Portsmouth, NH: Heinemann.

Flanders, N. (1970). *Analyzing teaching behavior.* Reading, MA: Addison-Wesley.

Flavell, L. (1985). *Cognitive development* (2nd ed.). Englewood Cliffs, NJ: Prentice Hall.

Flavell, J., Miller, P., & Miller, S. (2001). *Cognitive development* (4th ed.). Englewood Cliffs, NJ: Prentice Hall.

Fogarty, R. (2001). *Different learners: Different strokes for different folks.* Chicago, IL: Fogarty and Associates.

Forsten, C., Goodman, G., Grant, J., Hollas, B., & Whyte, D. (2006). *The more ways you TEACH, the more students you REACH: 86 strategies for differentiated instruction.* Peterborough, NH: Crystal Springs Books.

Friedman, T. (2005). *The world is flat: A brief history of the twenty-first century.* New York: Farrar, Straus, & Giroux.

Fuchs, L.S., & Fuchs, D. (1986). Effects of systematic formative evaluation: A meta analysis. *Exceptional Children, 53*(3), 199–208.

Fullan, M. (2001). *The new meaning of educational change* (3rd ed.). New York: Teachers College Press.

Fullan, M. (2005). *Leadership and sustainability.* Thousand Oaks, CA: Corwin Press.

Fullan, M. (2007). *The new meaning of educational change* (4th ed.). New York: Teachers College Record.

Fullan, M. (2008a). *Six secrets of change: What the best leaders do to help their organizations survive and thrive.* San Francisco, CA: Jossey-Bass.

Fullan, M. (2008b). *What's worth fighting for in the principalship?* New York: Teachers College Press.

Fullan, M., & Miles, M. (1992). Getting reform right: What works and what doesn't. *Phi Delta Kappan, 73*(10), 745–752.

Fullan, M., & Pomfret, A. (1977). Curriculum implementation and instruction improvement. *Review of Educational Research, 47*(2), 335–397.

Fullan, M., Cuttress, C., & Kilcher, A. (2005). Eight forces for leaders of change. *Journal of Staff Development, 26*(4), 54–64.

Fuller, F. (1969). Concerns of teachers: A developmental conceptualization. *American Education Research Journal, 6,* 207–226.

Gage, N. (1993). *An update of the scientific basis for the art of teaching.* Palo Alto, CA: Stanford University.

Gagné, E., Yekovich, C., & Yekovich, F. (1997). *The cognitive psychology of school learning* (2nd ed.). Boston: Allyn & Bacon.

Gagné, R.M. (1977). *The conditions of learning and theory of instruction* (3rd ed.). New York: Holt, Rinehart & Winston.

Gagné, R.M., & Briggs, L.J. (1980). *Principles of instructional design* (2nd ed.). New York: Holt, Rinehart & Winston.

Gall, J., & Gall, M. (1990). Outcomes of the discussion method. In W.W. Wilen (Ed.), *Teaching and learning through discussion.* Springfield, IL: Charles C. Thomas.

Gardner, H. (1983). *Frames of mind.* New York: Basic Books

Gardner, H. (1993). *Multiple intelligences: The theory in practice.* New York: Basic Books.

Gardner, H. (1999). Multiple intelligences: Myths and messages. In A. Woolfolk (Ed.), *Readings in educational psychology* (2nd ed.). Boston: Allyn & Bacon.

Gardner, H. (2007). *Five minds for the future.* Cambridge, MA: Harvard Business School Press.

Gardner, H. (2009). The five minds for the future.*School Administrator, 66*(2), 513–527.

Gay, G.D. (1997). Educational equality for students of color. In J.A. Banks & C.M. Banks (Eds.), *Multicultural education* (3rd ed.). Boston: Allyn & Bacon.

Gewertz, C. (2008). Consensus on learning time builds. *Education Week, 28*(5), 12.

Gibbs J. (1997). *Tribes: A new way of learning together.* Sausalito, CA: Center Source Systems.

Glaser, R. (1987). Thoughts on expertise. In C. Schooler & W. Schaie (Eds.), *Cognitive functioning and social structure over the life course.* Norwood, NJ: Ablex.

Glaser, R. (1990). Expertise. In M.W. Eysenk, A.N. Ellis, E. Hunt, & P. Johnson-Laird (Eds.), *The Blackwell dictionary of cognitive psychology.* Oxford: Blackwell Reference.

Glick, M. & Holyoak, K. (1983). Schema induction and analogical transfer. *Cognitive Psychology, 15,* 1–38.

Goleman, D. (1995). *Emotional intelligence.* New York: Bantam.

Good, T., & Brophy, J. (2008). *Looking in classrooms* (10th ed.). New York: Pearson Education.

Good, T.L., & Grouws, D.A. (1977). Teaching effect: A process–product study in fourth-grade mathematics classrooms. *Journal of Teacher Education, 28,* 49–54.

Good, T.L., & Grouws, D.A. (1979). The Missouri mathematics effectiveness project: An experimental study in fourth-grade classrooms. *Journal of Educational Psychology, 71,* 355–362.

Goodlad, S.J. (1984). *A placed called school: Prospects for the future.* New York: McGraw-Hill.

Goodlad, S.J. (2004). Democracy, schools, and the agenda. *Kappa Delta Pi Record, 41*(1), 17–20.

Gore, A. (2007). *The assault on reason.* New York: Penguin Press.

Goswami, U. (2008). *Cognitive development: The learning brain.* New York: Psychology Press.

Greenfield, P., & Yan, Z. (2006). Children, adolescents, and the Internet: A new field of inquiry in developmental psychology. *Developmental Psychology, 42*(3), 391–394.

Greenough, W. (1976). Enduring brain effects of differential experience and training. In M. Rosenzweig & E. Bennett (Eds.), *Neural mechanisms of learning and memory.* Cambridge, MA: MIT Press.

Greenough, W., Juraska, J., & Volkmar, F. (1979). Maze training effects on dendrite branching in occipital cortex of adult rats. *Behavioral and Neural Biology, 26,* 287–297.

Gregorc, A. (1982). *Inside styles: Beyond the basics.* Connecticut CT: Gregorc Associates.

Gregory, G., & Chapman, C. (2001). *Differentiated instructional strategies: One size doesn't fit all.* Thousand Oaks, CA: Corwin Press.

Gregory, K., Cameron, C., & Davies, A. (2000). *Self-assessment and goal*-setting. Merville, BC: Connections.

Grigororenko, E.L., Meier, E., Lipka, J., Mohatt, G., Yanez, E., & Sternbert, R.J. (2004). Academic and practical intelligence: A case study of the Yup'ik in Alaska. *Learning and Individual Differences, 14*(4), 183–207.

Gronlund, N.E., Linn, R.L., & Davis, K. (2000). *Measurement and assessment in teaching* (8th ed.). Englewood Cliffs, NY: Prentice Hall.

Grothe, M. (2008). *I never met a metaphor I didn't like: A comprehensive compilation of history's greatest analogies, metaphors, and similes.* New York: Harper-Collins.

Guild, P.B., & Garger, S. (1985). *What is differentiated instruction? Marching to different drummers.* Alexandria, VA: Association for Supervision and Curriculum Development.

Guilford, J. (1967). *The nature of human intelligence.* New York: McGraw-Hill.

Guiney, E. (2001). Coaching isn't just for athletes: The role of teacher leaders. *Phi Delta Kappan, 82,* 740–743.

Guskey, T.R. (Ed.) (1996). *Communicating student learning.* Alexandria, VA: Association for Supervision and Curriculum Development.

Guskey, T.R. (2000). Grading policies that work against standards . . . and how to fix them. *NASSP Bulletin, 84*(620), 20–29.

Guskey, T.R. (2004). Zero alternatives. *Principal Leadership, 5*(2), 49–53.

Guskey, T.R., & Bailey, J.M. (2001). *Developing grading and reporting systems for student learning.* Thousand Oaks, CA: Corwin Press.

Guzzetti, B. (2000). Learning counter-intuitive science concepts: What we have learned from over a decade of research. *Reading and Writing Quarterly, 16,* 89–98.

Hall, G.E., & Hord, S.M. (2005). *Implementing change: Patterns, principles, and potholes* (2nd ed.). Boston: Allyn & Bacon.

Hammerness, K., Darling-Hammond, L., Bransford, J., Berliner, D., Cochran-Smith, M., McDonald, M., et al. (2005). How teachers learn and develop. In L. Darling-Hammond and J. Bransford (Eds.), *Preparing teachers for a changing world.* San Francisco, CA: Jossey-Bass.

Hargreaves, A., Lieberman, A., Fullan, M., & Hopkins, D. (2006). *International handbook of educational change* (2nd ed.). New York: Springer Dordrecht.

Hatano, G., & Oura, Y. (2003). Commentary: Reconceptualizing school learning using insights from expertise research. *Educational Researcher, 32*(8), 26–29.

Hattie, J. (1992). Measuring the effects of schooling. *Australian Journal of Education, 36*(1), 5–13.

Hattie, J., & Timperley, H. (2007). The power of feedback. *Review of Educational Research, 77*(1), 81–112.

Having another set of eyeballs. (2005) *Northwest education.* Portland, OR: Northwest Regional Educational Laboratory, p. 1.

Haycock, K. (1998). Good teaching matters . . . a lot. *Thinking K-16, 3*(2), 1–16.

Hiller, J., Fisher, G.A., & Kaess, W. (1969). A computer investigation of verbal characteristics of effective classroom lecturing. *American Educational Research Journal, 6*(4), 661–675.

Hmelo-Silver, C.E. (2004). Problem-based learning: What and how do students learn? *Educational Psychology Review, 16,* 235–266.

Hopkins, D. (1985). *Classroom research.* Maidenhead: Open University Press.

Hord, S., & Sommers, W.A. (2008). *Leading professional learning communities: Voices from research and practice.* Thousand Oaks, CA: Corwin Press.

Hunt, D. (1974). *Matching models in education.* Toronto, ON: Ontario Institute for Studies in Education.

Hunter, M. (1982). *Mastery teaching.* El Segundo, CA: TIP Publication.

Hunter, M. (1994). *Mastery teaching.* Upper Saddle River, NJ: Prentice Hall.

Hunter, M. (1994). *Enhancing teaching.* New York: Macmillan.

Ivey, G., & Fisher, D. (2005). Learning from what doesn't work. *Educational Leadership, 63*(2), 8–15.

Jacobs, H.H. (1997). *Mapping the big picture.* Alexandria, VA: Association for Supervision and Curriculum Development.

Jacobs, H.H. (Ed.) (2003). *Getting results with curriculum mapping.* Alexandria, VA: Association for Supervision and Curriculum Development.

Johnson, D.W., & Johnson, R.T. (1975). Instructional goal structure: Cooperative, competitive, or individualistic. *Review of Educational Research, 44,* 213–240.

Johnson, D.W., & Johnson, R.T. (1989). *Cooperation and competition: Theory and research.* Edina, MI: Interaction Book Company.

Johnson, D.W., & Johnson, R.T. (1998). *Learning together and alone: Cooperative, competitive, and individualistic learning* (5th ed.). Englewood Cliffs, NJ: Prentice Hall.

Johnson, D.W., & Johnson, R.T. (2005). *Joining together: Group theory and group skills* (9th ed.). Englewood Cliffs, NJ: Prentice Hall.

Johnson, D.W., Johnson, R.T., & Holubec, E.J. (1990). *Cooperation in the classroom.* Edina, MN: Interaction Book Company.

Johnson, D.W., Maruyama, G., Johnson, R., Nelson, D., & Skon, L. (1983). Effects of cooperative, competitive, and individualistic goal structures on achievement: A meta-analysis. *Psychological Bulletin, 89,* 47–62.

Johnson, S.M., & Donaldson, M.L. (2007). Overcoming the obstacles to leadership. *Educational Leadership, 65*(1), 8–13.

Johnston, P. (2004). *Choice words: How our language affects children's learning.* Portland, ME: Stenhouse Publishing.

Joyce, B. (2004). How are professional learning communities created? History has a few messages. *Phi Delta Kappan, 86*(1), 76–83.

Joyce, B., & Showers, B. (2002). *Student achievement through staff development* (3rd ed.). Alexandria, VA: Association for Supervision and Curriculum Development.

Joyce, B., Hersh, R., & McKibbin, M. (1993). *The structure of school improvement.* New York: Longman.

Joyce, B., Weil, M., & Calhoun, E. (2000). *Models of teaching* (6th ed.). Boston, MA: Allyn & Bacon.

Joyce, B., Weil, M., & Calhoun, E. (2008). *Models of teaching* (8th ed.). Boston, MA: Allyn & Bacon.

Kagan, S. (1994). *Cooperative learning.* San Clement, CA: Resources for Teachers.

Kagan, S. (1998). *Cooperative learning resources for teachers.* San Juan Capistrano, CA: Resources for Teachers.

Kagan, S. (2001). *Kagan structures: Research and rationale.* Retrieved October 27, 2006, from http://kagan online.com/Catalog/index.html.

Kagan, S., & Kagan, M. (2008). *Kagan cooperative learning.* San Juan Capistrano, CA: Kagan Publishing.

Keene, E., & Zimmerman, S. (2007). *Mosaic of thought* (2nd ed.). Portsmouth, NJ: Heinemann.

Killion, J., & Harrison, C. (2006). *Taking the lead: New roles for teacher leaders and school-based staff developers.* Oxford, OH: National Staff Development Council.

Kilpatrick, T.H. (1918). The project method. *Teachers College Record, 19,* 319–334.

Kirschner, P., Sweller, J., & Clark, R. (2006). Why minimal guidance during instruction does not work: An analysis of the failure of constructivist, discovery, problem-based, experiential, and inquiry-based teaching. *Educational Psychologist, 41*(2), 75–86.

Klein, P. (2002). Multiplying the problem of intelligence by eight. In L. Abbeduto (Ed.), *Taking sides: Clashing on controversial issues in educational psychology.* Guilford, CT: McGraw-Hill/Duskin.

Kluger, A.N., & DeNisi, A. (1996). The effects of feedback interventions on performance: A historical review, a meta-analysis, and a preliminary intervention theory. *Psychological Bulletin, 119*(2), 254–284.

Knapp, M.S., Shields, P.M., & Turnball, B.J. (1992). *Academic challenge for the children of poverty: Summary report.* Washington, DC: U.S. Department of Education, Office of Policy and Planning.

Knight, J. (2007). *Instructional coaching: A partnership approach to improving instruction.* Thousand Oaks, CA: Corwin Press.

Knight, J. (Ed.) (2009). *Coaching: Approaches and perspectives.* Thousand Oaks, CA: Corwin Press.

Kohn, A. (1995). *Punishment by rewards: The trouble with gold stars, incentive plans, A's, praise, and other bribes.* Boston, MA: Houghton Mifflin.

Kohn, A. (1996). *Beyond discipline: From compliance to community.* Alexandria, VA: Association of Supervision and Curriculum Development.

Kohn, A. (2000). *The schools our children deserve: Moving beyond traditional classrooms and tougher standards.* New York: Mariner Books.

Kohn, A. (2004). *What does it mean to be well educated?* Boston, MA: Beacon Press.

Kohn, A. (2006). The truth about homework: Needless assignments persist because of widespread misconceptions about learning. *Education Week.* Retrieved September 8, 2006, from www.edweek.org/ew/section/tb/2006/09/06/954.html.

Kohn, A. (2007). *The homework myth: Why our kids get too much of a bad thing.* Cambridge, MA: Capo Lifelong Books.

Kolb, D. (1984). *Experiential learning: Experience as the source of learning and development.* Englewood Cliffs, NJ: Prentice Hall.

Kolb, D.A., Boyatzis, R.E., & Mainemelis, C. (2001). Experiential learning theory: Previous research and new directions. In R.J. Sternberg & L. Zhang (Eds.), *Perspectives on thinking, learning, and cognitive styles* (pp. 227–247). Mahwah, NJ: Lawrence Erlbaum Associates.

Kottler, J., Zehm, S., & Kottler, E. *On being a teacher: The human dimension* (3rd ed.). Thousand Oakes, CA: Corwin Press.

Krajcik, J., Czerniak, C.M., & Berger, C.F. (2003). *Teaching children science: A project-based approach.* New York: McGraw-Hill.

Kuhn, D. (2005). *Education for thinking.* Cambridge, MA: Harvard University Press.

Kuhn, D. (2007a). How to produce a high-achieving child. *Phi Delta Kappan, 88*(10), 757–763.

Kuhn, D. (2007b). Is direct instruction an answer to the right question? *Educational Psychologist, 42*(2), 109–113.

Ladson-Billings, G. (1994). *The dreamkeepers: Successful teachers of African American children.* San Francisco, CA: Jossey-Bass.

Lakoff, G., & Johnson, M. (1980). *Metaphors we live by.* Chicago, IL: University of Chicago Press.

Lakoff, G., & Johnson, M. (1999). *Philosophy in the flesh.* New York: Basic Books.

Lambros, A. (2002). *Problem-based learning in K-12 classrooms: A teacher's guide to implementation.* Thousand Oaks, CA: Corwin Press.

Landsberg, M. (2008, June 21). Graduation rates declining in L.A. Unified despite higher enrollment. *Los Angeles Times,* June 21, p. B1.

Leahy, S., Lyon, C., Thompson, M., & Wiliam, D. (2005). Classroom assessment: Minute-by-minute and day-by-day. *Educational Leadership, 63*(3), 18–24.

LeDoux, J. (1997). *The emotional brain.* New York: Putnam.

Lee, V., & Smith, J. (1996). Collective responsibility for learning and its effects on gains in achievement of early secondary school students. *American Journal of Education, 104,* 103–146.

Leinhardt, G. (2001). Instructional explanations: A commonplace for teaching and location for contrasts. In V. Richardson (Ed.), *Handbook of research on teaching* (4th ed.). Washington, DC: American Educational Research Association.

Leinhart, G., & Greeno, J. (1986). The cognitive skill of teaching. *Journal of Educational Psychology, 78*(2), 75–79.

Leithwood, K., Day, C., Sammons, P., Harris, A., & Hopkins, D. (2007). *Seven strong claims about school leadership.* Nottingham: National College for School Leadership.

Leithwood, K., Louis, K.S., Anderson, S., & Wahlstrom, K. (2004). *How leadership influences student learning.* New York: Wallace Foundation.

Leu, D., Leu, D., & Coiro, J. (2004). *Teaching with the Internet: New literacies for new times* (4th ed.). Norwood, MA: Christopher Gordon.

Levin, B.B. (Ed.) (2001). *Energizing teacher education and professional development with problem-based learning.* Alexandria, VA: Association for Supervision and Curriculum Development.

Levin, H. (1998). Accelerated schools: A decade of evolution. In A. Hargreaves, A., Lieberman, M. Fullan, & D. Hopkins (Eds.), *International handbook of educational change.* Norwell, MA: Kluwer Academic Publishers.

Levine, D., & Lezzote, L. (1990). *Unusually effective schools: A review and analysis of research and practice.* Madison, WI: National Center for Effective Schools Research and Development.

Lewbel, S.R., & Hibbard, K.M. (2001). Are standards and true learning compatible? *Principal Leadership, 1*(5), 16–20.

Lewin, K. (1946). Action research and minority problems. *Journal of Social Issues, 2*(4), 34–46.

Lewis, C.C. (2002). *Lesson study: A handbook of teacher-led instructional change.* Philadelphia, PA: Research for Better Schools.

Lieberman, A., & Miller, L. (1999). *Teachers: Transforming their world and their work.* New York: Teachers College Press.

Lieberman, A., & Miller, L. (2004). *Teacher leadership.* San Francisco, CA: Jossey-Bass.

Lieberman, A., & Miller, L. (2008). *Teachers in professional communities: Improving teaching and learning.* New York: Teachers College Press.

Lieberman, A., & Wood, D. (2002). *Inside the National Writing Project: Connecting network learning with classroom teaching.* New York: Teachers College Press.

Lionni, L. (1970). *Fish is fish.* New York: Scholastic Press.

Little, J.W. (1990). The persistence of privacy: Autonomy and initiative in teachers' professional relations. *Teachers College Record, 91*(4), 509–536.

Little, J., Gearhart, M., Curry, M., & Kafka, J. (2003). Looking at student work for teacher learning, teaching community, and school reform. *Phi Delta Kappan, 85*(3), 184–192.

Loucks-Horsley, S. (1998). JSD forum: I have changed my emphasis. *Journal of Staff Development, 19*(3), 7–8.

Louis, K.S., Kruse, K., & Marks, H. (1996). School-wide professional community. In F. Newman and Associates (Eds.), *Authentic achievement: Restructuring our schools for intellectual quality* (pp. 179–203). San Franciso, CA: Jossey-Bass.

Lou, Y., Abrami, P., Spence, J., Poulsen, C., Chambers, B., & d'Apollonia, S. (1996). Within-class grouping: A meta-analysis. *Review of Educational Research, 66*(4), 423–458.

Lozano, A. (2001). A survey of thinking and learning styles. In A. Costa (Ed.), *Developing minds: A resource book for teaching thinking* (3rd ed.). Alexandria, VA: Association for Supervision and Curriculum Development.

Luiten, J., Ames, W., & Aerson, G. (1980). A meta-analysis of advance organizers on learning and retention. *American Educational Research Journal, 17*(2), 211–218.

Lyman, F.T. (1981). The responsive classroom discussion: The inclusion of all students. In A. Anderson, (Ed.), *Mainstreaming Digest,* 109–113. College Park, MD: University of Maryland Press.

Lyman, F.T. (1986). Procedures for using the question–response cues. Unpublished data. College Park, MD: University of Maryland.

Mace, D.J.P. (2008). Learning from practice/learning in practice: Using multimedia to support teacher development. In A. Lieberman & L. Miller (Eds.), *Teachers in professional communities: Improving teaching and learning.* New York: Teachers College Press.

MacDonald, J.P., Mohr, N., Dichter, A., & McDonald, E.C. (2007). *The power of protocols: An educator's guide to better practice* (2nd ed.). New York: Teachers College Press.

Magnusson, S., & Palincsar. A. (1995). The learning environment as a site of science reform. *Theory into Practice, 34*(1), 43–50.

Mansilla, V., & Gardner, H. (2008). Disciplining the mind. *Educational Leadership, 65*(5), 14–19.

Marchand-Martella, N., Slocum, T., & Martella, R. (2004). *Introduction to direct instruction.* Boston, MA: Allyn & Bacon.

Markham, T., Larmer, J., & Ravitz, J. (2003). *Project based learning: A guide to standards-focused project based learning for middle and high school teachers* (2nd ed.). Oakland, CA: Buck Institute for Education.

Marx, R.W., Blumenfeld, P.C., Krajcik, J.S., & Soloway, E. (1997). Enacting project based science: Challenges for practice and policy. *Elementary School Journal, 97*(4), 341–358.

Marzano, R. (2003). *What works in schools: Translating research into action.* Alexandria, VA: Association of Supervision and Curriculum Development.

Marzano, R. (2004). *Building background knowledge for academic achievement.* Alexandria, VA: Association of Supervision and Curriculum Development.

Marzano, R. (2006). *Classroom assessment and grading that work.* Alexandria, VA: Association of Supervision and Curriculum Development.

Marzano, R. (2007). *The art and science of teaching.* Alexandria, VA: Association for Supervision and Curriculum Development.

Marzano, R., & Haystead, M. (2008). *Making standards useful in the classroom.* Alexandria, VA: Association of Supervision and Curriculum Development.

Marzano, R., & Pickering, D. (2007a). Errors and allegations about research on homework. *Phi Delta Kappan, 88*(7), 507–513

Marzano, R., & Pickering, D. (2007b). The case for and against homework. *Educational Leadership, 64*(6), 74–79.

Marzano, R.J., Pickering, D.J., & McTighe, J. (1993). *Assessing student outcomes: Performance assessment using the dimensions of learning.* Alexandria, VA: Association for Supervision and Curriculum Development.

Marzano, R., Pickering, D., & Pollock, J.E. (2001). *Classroom instruction that works: Research-based strategies for increasing student achievement.* Alexandria, VA: Association of Supervision and Curriculum Development.

Maslow, A. (1970). *Motivation and personality* (2nd ed.). New York: Harper & Row.

Mayer, R. (2003). *Learning and instruction.* Upper Saddle River, NJ: Prentice Hall.

Mayer, R. & Massa, L. (2003). Three facets of visual and verbal learners: Cognitive ability, cognitive style and learning preferences. *Journal of Educational Psychology, 95*(40), 833–846.

Mayo Clinic (2008). Retrieved April 3, 2008, from www.mayoclinic.com.

Mayo, J. (2002). Case-based instruction: A technique for increasing conceptual application in introductory psychology. *Journal of Constructivist Psychology, 15*, 65–74.

Mayo, J. (2004). Using case-based instruction to bridge the gap between theory and practice in psychology of adjustment. *Journal of Constructivist Psychology, 17*, 137–146.

McCarthy, B. (1996). *About learning.* Barrington, IL: Excel.

McClelland, D.C. (1958). *Human motivation.* New York: Scotts Foresman.

McCutcheon, G., & Milner, H. (2002). A contemporary study of teacher planning in a high school English class. *Teachers and Teaching: Theory and Practice, 8*(1), 81–94.

McLaughlin, M.W., & Talbert, J.E. (2001). *Professional communities and the work of high schools.* Chicago, IL: University of Chicago Press.

McLaughlin, M.W., & Talbert, J.E. (2006). *Building school-based teacher learning communities: Professional strategies to improve student achievement.* New York: Teachers College Press.

McNeil, L.M., Coppola, E., Radigan, J., & Vasquez Heilig, J. (2008). Avoidable losses: High-stakes accountability and the dropout crisis. *Education Policy Analysis Archives, 16*(3). Retrieved February 20, 2008, from http://epaa.asu.edu/epaa/v16n3.

McNergney, R., Ducharme, E., & Ducharme, M. (Eds.) (1999). *Educating for democracy: Case method teaching and learning.* Mahwah, NJ: Lawrence Erlbaum Associates.

McTighe, J., & O'Connor, K. (2005). Seven practices for effective learning. *Educational Leadership, 62*(3), 13–19.

McVee, M., Dunsmore, K., & Gavelek, J. (2005). Schema theory revisited. *Review of Educational Research, 75*(4), 531–566.

Meece, J.L. (2002). *Child and adolescent development for educators.* New York: McGraw-Hill.

Mertler, C.A. (2001). Designing and scoring rubrics for your classroom. *Practical Assessment, Research and Evaluation, 7*(25). Retrieved February 2, 2008, from http://PAREonline.net/getvn.asp?v=7&n=25.

Metros, S. (2008). The educator's role in preparing visually literate learners. *Theory Into Practice, 47*(2), 102–109.

Meyer, R. (2004). Should there be a three-strike rule against discovery learning? A case for guided methods of instruction. *American Psychologist, 59*(1), 14–19.

Miles, M. (1992). 40 years of change in schools: Some personal reflections. Paper presented at the annual meeting of the American Educational Research Association, San Francisco.

Miller, L. (2007). Reflections on professional community in the Southern Maine Partnership. Unpublished paper.

Monti, D. (2007). Personal correspondence with the authors.

Mostert, M., & Sudzina, M. (1996). Undergraduate case method teaching: Pedagogical assumptions vs. the real world. Paper presented at the annual meeting of the Association of Teacher Educators, St Louis, February.

Naftulin, D., Ware, J., & Donnelly, F. (1973). The doctor fox lecture: A paradigm of educational seduction. *Journal of Medical Education, 48*(7), 630–635.

Nagy, W., & Anderson, R. (1984). How many words are there in printed school English? *Reading Research Quarterly, 19*(3), 304–330.

National Center for Educational Statistics (2007). *The condition of education.* Washington, DC.

National Center for Teaching Thinking: www.nctt.net

National College for School Leadership. Retrieved December 20, 2008, from www.ncsl.uk.com.

National Commission on Excellence in Education (1983). *A nation at risk.* Washington, DC: National Commission on Excellence in Education.

National Education Commission on Time and Learning (1994). *Prisoners of time.* Washington DC: National Education Commission on Time and Learning.

National Network of Partnership Schools (2008). Retrieved December 20, 2008, from www.csos.jhu.edu/P2000.

National Reading Panel (2000). *Report of the National Reading Panel: Teaching children to read.* Bethesda, MD: National Institute of Child Health and Human Development.

National School Reform Faculty (2008). Retrieved December 15, 2008, from www.nsrfharmony.org.

National Science Standards (2008). Retrieved February 18, 2008, from www.nap.edu/readingroom.

Natriello, G. (1987). The impact of evaluation processes on students. *Educational Psychologist, 22*(2), 155.

Naunes, W., & Naunes, M. (2006). *Art and craft of case writing* (2nd ed.). Amonk, NY: Sharpe Reference.

Newman, F., & Oliver, D. (1970). *Clarifying public controversy.* Boston, MA: Little, Brown and Company.

Newman, F., Secado, N., & Wehlage, G. (1995). *Authentic achievement: Restructuring schools for intellectual quality.* San Francisco, CA: Jossey-Bass.

Nichols, S., & Berliner, D. (2007). *Collateral damage: How high stakes testing is corrupting American schools.* Boston, MA: Harvard Education Press.

Nickerson, R. (1987). Why teach thinking? In J. Baron & R. Sternberg (Eds.), *Teaching thinking skills: Theory and practice.* New York: Freeman.

Noddings, N. (2001). The caring teacher. In V. Richardson (Ed.), *Handbook of educational research* (4th ed.). Washington, DC: American Educational Research Association.

Noddings, N. (2005). Identifying and responding to needs in education. *Cambridge Journal of Education, 35*(2), 147–159.

Noddings, N. (2006). *Critical lessons: What our schools should teach.* Cambridge: Cambridge University Press.

Noddings, N. (2008). All our students' thinking. *Educational Leadership, 65*(5), 8–13.

Normal Park Magnet Museum School (2008). Retrieved September 10, 2008, from www.normalparkmuseummagnet.com.

Nyquist, J.B. (2003). The benefits of reconstructing feedback as a larger system of formative assessment: A meta-analysis. Unpublished Master's thesis, Vanderbilt University, Nashville, Tennessee.

Oakes, J., & Lipton, M. (2006). *Teaching to change the world* (3rd ed.). New York: McGraw-Hill.

O'Connor, K. (2002). *How to grade for learning.* Thousand Oaks, CA: Corwin Press.

O'Connor, K. (2007). *A repair kit for grading: 15 fixes for broken grades.* Portland, OR: Educational Testing Service.

Ogle, D.M. (1986). K–W–L: A teaching model that develops active reading of expository text. *Reading Teacher, 39*(6), 564–570.

Ohio Department of Education (2008). Retrieved October 21, 2008, from www.ode.state.oh.us/GD/Templates/Pages/ODE/ODEPrimary.aspx?

Oliver, D. & Shaver, J. (1968). *Cases and controversy: A guide to teaching the public issues series.* Middletown, CT: American Education Publishers.

Paideia Consulting Group, Inc. (2008). *Coaching workshop materials.* Halifax, NS: Paideia Consulting Group, Inc.

Palincsar, A.S., & Brown, A. (1984). Reciprocal teaching of comprehension-fostering and comprehension-monitoring activities. *Cognition and Instruction, 1*(2), 117–175.

Panitz, T. (2001). The case for student centered instruction via collaborative learning paradigms. Retrieved October 27, 2006, from http://home.capecod.net/~tpanitz/tedsarticles/coopbenefits.htm.

Paul, R. (1993). *Critical thinking: What every person needs to know to survive in a rapidly changing world.* Santa Rosa, CA: Foundation for Critical Thinking.

Payne, C. (2008). *So much reform, so little change.* Boston, MA: Harvard Education Press.

Pearson, P., Roehler, L., Dole, J., & Duffy, G. (1992). Developing expertise in reading comprehension. In S.J. Samuels & A.E. Farstrup (Eds.), *What research says about reading instruction* (2nd ed.). Newark, DE: International Reading Association.

Perkins, D.N. (2003). *Making thinking visible.* Retrieved September 15, 2008, from www.pz.harvard.edu/vt/VisibleThinking_html_files/VisibleThinking1.html.

Perkins, D.N., Jay, E., & Tishman, S. (1993a). Beyond abilities: A dispositional theory of thinking. *Merrill-Palmer Quarterly, 39*(1), 1–21.

Perkins, D.N., Jay, E., & Tishman, S. (1993b). New conceptions of thinking: From ontology to education. *Educational Psychologist, 28*(1), 67–85.

Pfeffer, J., & Sutton, R. (2000). *The knowing–doing gap: How smart businesses turn knowledge into action.* Cambridge, MA: Harvard Business School Press.

Piaget, J. (1954). *The construction of reality in the child.* New York: Basic Books.

Piaget, J. (1963). *The psychology of intelligence.* New York: Routledge.

Picoult, J. (2008). *Nineteen minutes.* New York: Simon and Schuster.

Pilgrim, J. (2000). *How to organize and manage a sustained silent reading program.* Portsmouth, NH: Heinemann Boynton/Cook Publishers.

Pintrich, P.R. (2003). A motivational science perspective on the role of student motivation in learning and teaching contexts. *Journal of Educational Psychology, 95*(4), 667–686.

Pintrich, P.R. & DeGroot, E.V. (1990). Motivational and self-regulated learning components of classroom academic performance. *Journal of Educational Psychology, 82*(1), 33–40.

Pintrich, P.R. & Schunk, D.H. (2002). *Motivation in education: Theory, research, and application* (2nd ed.). Englewood Cliffs, NJ: Prentice Hall.

Popham, W.J. (2006). Phony formative assessments: Buyer beware! *Educational Leadership, 64*(3), 86–87.

Popham, W.J. (2008). *Transformative assessment.* Alexandria, VA: Association for Supervision and Curriculum Development.

Postman, N. (1995). *The end of education: Redefining the value of education.* New York: Knopf.

Pressley, M., & Woloshyn, V. (1999). *Cognitive strategy instruction that really improves children's academic performance* (2nd ed.). Cambridge, MA: Brookline Books.

Pressley, M., Roehrig, A., Raphael, L., Dolezal, S., Bohn, K., Mohan, L., et al. (2003). Teaching processes in elementary and secondary education. In W.M. Reynolds & G.E. Miller (Eds.), *Comprehensive handbook of psychology: Vol. 7, Educational psychology.* New York: Wiley.

Pressley, M., Wood, E., Woloshyn, V. E., Martin, V., King, A., & Menke, D. (1992). Encouraging mindful use of prior knowledge: Attempting to construct explanatory answers that facilitate learning. *Educational Psychologist, 27*(1), 91–109.

Race, P. (2006). A lecturer's toolkit: *A practical guide to learning, teaching, and assessing* (3rd ed.). New York: Routledge.

Reeves, D.B. (2004). The case against zero. *Phi Delta Kappan, 86*(4), 324–325.

Reeves, D.B. (2008). Effective grading. *Educational Leadership, 65*(5), 85–87.

Reis, S., & Renzulli, J. (1992). Using curriculum compacting to challenge the above average. *Educational Leadership, 50*(2), 51–57.

Renzulli, J., Leppien, J.H., & Hays, T.S. (2000). *The multiple menu model: A practical guide for developing differentiated curriculum.* Mansfield Center, CT: Creative Learning Press.

Resnick. L. (1987). *Education and learning to think.* Washington, DC: National Academy Press.

Reynolds, J. (1980). *Case method in management development* (No. 17). Geneva, Switzerland: International Labour Office.

Richardson, V., & Placier, P. (2001) Teacher change. In V. Richardson (Ed.), *Handbook of research on teaching* (4th ed.). Washington, DC: American Educational Research Association.

Riddle, J. (2009). *Engaging the eye generation: Visual literacy strategies for K-5 classrooms.* Portland, ME: Stenhouse Publishers.

Riesland, E. (2007). Visual literacy and the classroom. Retrieved July 22, 2007, from www.newhorizons.org/strategies/literacy/riesland.

Rinne, C.H. (2007). Motivating students is a percentage game. *Phi Delta Kappan, 79*(8), 620–624, 626, 628.

Ritchhart, R. (2002). *Intellectual character: What it is, why it matters, and how to get it.* San Francisco, CA: Jossey-Bass.

Ritchhart, R. (2005). The seven cultural forces that define our classrooms. Unpublished data.

Ritchhart, R., & Perkins, D. (2008). Making thinking visible. *Educational Leadership, 65*(5), 57–61.

Ritchhart, R., Palmer, P., Church, M., & Tishman, S. (2006). Thinking routines: Establishing patterns of thinking in the classroom. Paper presented at the annual meeting of the American Educational Research Association, San Francisco, April.

Rogers, C., & Farson, R. (1987). Active listening. In R. Christensen & A. Hansen (Eds.), *Teaching and the case method.* Boston, MA: Harvard Business School Press.

Rosenshine, B. (1970). Enthusiastic teaching: A research review. *School Review, 78*(4), 499–514.

Rosenshine, B. (1979). Content, time, and direct instruction. In P. Peterson & H. Walberg (Eds.), *Research on teaching: Concepts, findings, and implications.* Berkeley, CA: McCutchan.

Rosenshine, B. (2002). Converging findings in classroom instruction. In A. Molnar (Ed.), *School reform proposals: The research evidence.* Tempe, AZ: Arizona State University Research Policy Unit.

Rosenshine, B., & Stevens, R. (1986). Teaching functions. In M.C. Wittrock (Ed.), *Handbook of research on teaching* (3rd ed.). New York: Macmillan.

Ross, J.A., Hogaboam-Gray, A., & Rolheiser, C. (2002). Student self-assessment in grade 5–6 mathematics: Effects on problem-solving achievement. *Educational Assessment, 8*(1), 43–59.

Ross, J.A., Rolheiser, C., & Hogaboam-Gray, A. (1999). Effects of self-evaluation training on narrative writing. *Assessing Writing, 6*(1), 107–132.

Rowe, M.B. (1974). Wait time and rewards as instructional variables, their influence in language, logic, and fate control: Part one—Wait-time. *Journal of Research in Science Teaching, 11*(2), 81–94.

Rowe, M.B. (1986). Wait time: Slowing down may be a way of speeding up. *Journal of Teacher Education, 37*(1), 43–50.

Sabers, D., Cushing, K., & Berliner, D.C. (1991). Differences among teachers in a task characterized by simultaneity, multidimensionality, and immediacy. *American Educational Research Journal, 28*(1), 63–88.

Sagor, R. (2000). *Guiding school improvement with action research.* Alexandria, VA: Association for Supervision and Curriculum Development.

Saphier, J., & Gower, R. (1997). *The skillful teacher: Building your teaching skills* (5th ed.). Acton, MA: Research for Better Teaching, Inc.

Saphier, J., & Haley, M.A. (1993). *Summarizers.* Acton, MA: Research for Better Teaching, Inc.

Saphier, J., Haley-Speca, M.A., & Gower, R. (2006). *The skillful teacher: Building your teaching skills* (6th ed.). Acton, MA: Research for Better Teaching, Inc.

Sarason, S. (1971). *The culture of schools and the problems of change.* Boston, MA: Allyn & Bacon.

Savin-Baden. M. (2003). *Facilitating problem-based learning.* Philadelphia, PA: Open University Press.

Savin-Baden, M. (2008). *Problem-based online learning.* New York: Routledge.

Schalock, D., Schalock, M., & Girod, M. (2007). Working in standards-based environments. Unpublished data. Monmouth, OR: Teaching Research.

Schmidt, H.G., Dauphinee, W.D., & Patel, V.L. (1987). Comparing the effects of problem-based and conventional curricula in an international sample. *Journal of Medical Education, 62*(4), 305–315.

Schmoker, M., & Marzano, R.J. (1999). Realizing the promise of standards-based education. *Educational Leadership, 56*(6), 17–21.

Schmuck, R. (2006). *Practical action research for change.* Thousand Oaks, CA: Corwin Press.

Schmuck, R., & Runkel, P. (2002). *The handbook of organization development in schools* (4th ed.). Long Grove, IL: Waveland Press.

Schmuck, R. & Schmuck, P. (2001). *Group processes in the classroom* (8th ed.). New York: McGraw-Hill.

Schwab, J. (1966). *Biological sciences curriculum study: Biology teacher's handbook.* New York: Wiley.

Schwartz, B. (2007). Money for nothing. *New York Times,* July 2. Retrieved July 3, 2007, from www.nytimes.com/2007/07/02/opinion/02schwartz.html.

Schwartz, D. Bransford, J., & Sears, D. (2005). Efficiency and innovation in transfer. In J. Mestre (Ed.), *Transfer of learning: Research and perspectives.* Greenwich, CT: Information Age Publishing.

Seed, A. (2008). Redirecting the teaching profession in the wake of A Nation at Risk and NCLB. *Phi Delta Kappan, 89*(8), 586–589.

Senge, P. (1990). *The fifth discipline: The art and practice of the learning organization.* New York: Doubleday.

Senior Project Center (2008). Retrieved September 15, 2008, from www.seniorproject.net.

Sfard, A. (1998). On two metaphors of learning and the dangers of choosing just one. *Educational Researcher, 27*(2), 4–13.

Sharan, S. (1980). Cooperative learning in small groups: Recent methods and effects on achievement, attitudes, and ethnic relations. *Review of Educational Research, 50*(2), 241–271.

Sharan, S., & Hertz-Lazarowitz, R. (1980). A group investigation method of cooperative learning in the classroom. In S. Sharan, P. Hare, C.D. Webb, & R. Hertz-Lazarowitz (Eds.), *Cooperation in education* (pp. 14–46). Provo, UT: Brigham Young University Press.

Sharan, S., Kussell, P., Hertz-Lazarowitz, R., Bejarano, Y., Raviv, S., & Sharan, Y. (1984). *Cooperative learning in the classroom: Research in desegregated schools.* Hillsdale, NJ: Lawrence Erlbaum Associates.

Sharan, Y., & Sharan, S. (1990). Group investigation expands cooperative learning. *Educational Leadership, 47*(4), 17–21.

Sharan, Y., & Sharan, S. (1992). *Expanding cooperative learning through group investigation.* New York: Teachers College Press.

Showers, B. (1982a). *A study of coaching in teacher training.* Eugene, OR: Center for Educational Policy and Management.

Showers, B. (1982b). *Transfer of training: The contribution of coaching.* Eugene, OR: Center for Educational Policy and Management.

Showers, B. (1984a). Peer coaching and its effect on transfer of training. Paper presented at the annual meeting of the American Educational Research Association, New Orleans, April.

Showers, B. (1984b). *Peer coaching: A strategy for facilitating transfer of training.* Eugene, OR: Center for Educational Policy and Management.

Showers, B. (1985). Teachers coaching teachers. *Educational Leadership, 42*(7), 43–49.

Shute, V. (2008). Focus on formative feedback. *Review of Educational Research, 78*(1), 153–189.

Silver, H.F., Strong, R.W., & Perini, M.J. (2000). *So each may learn: Integrating learning styles and multiple intelligences.* Alexandria, VA: Association of Supervision and Curriculum Development.

Silverman, R., & Welty, W. (1990). Teaching with cases. *Journal of Excellence in College Teaching, 1,* 88–97.

Simonton, D. (1999). Creativity from a historiometric perspective. In R. Sternberg (Ed.), *Handbook of creativity.* New York: Cambridge University Press.

Sizer, T. (1985). *Horace's compromise: The dilemma of the American high school.* Boston, MA: Houghton Mifflin.

Sizer, T. (1992). *Horace's school: Redesigning the American high school.* Boston, MA: Houghton Mifflin.

Slavin, R. (1980). Cooperative learning. *Review of Educational Research, 50*(2), 315–342.

Slavin, R. (1983). When does cooperative learning increase student achievement? *Psychological Bulletin, 94,* 429–445.

Slavin, R. (1989). *Cooperative learning: Theory, research, and practice.* Englewood Cliffs, NJ: Prentice Hall.

Slavin, R. (1991). *Synthesis of research on cooperative learning.* Educational Leadership, *48*(5), 71–82.

Slavin, R. (1994). *Using student team learning* (4th ed.). Baltimore, MD: Center for Social Organization of Schools, Johns Hopkins University Press.

Slavin, R. (1995). *Cooperative learning* (2nd ed.). New York: Longman.

Slavin, R., Sharan, S., Kagan, S., Hertz-Lazarowitz, R., Webb, C., & Schmuck, R. (Eds.) (1985). *Learning to cooperate, cooperating to learn.* New York: Plenum Press.

Spaulding, C.L. (1992). *Motivation in the classroom.* New York: McGraw-Hill.

Spillane, J.P. (2006). *Distributive leadership.* San Francisco, CA: Jossey-Bass.

Sprenger, M. (2005). *How to teach students to remember.* Alexandria, VA: Association for Supervision and Curriculum Development.

Stall, S. (2002). Different strokes for different folks? In L. Abbeduto (Ed.), *Taking sides: Clashing on controversial issues in educational psychology.* (pp. 98–107). Guilford, CT: McGraw Hill/Duskin.

Stead, A. (2005). *Reality checks: Teaching reading comprehension using non-fiction.* Portland, ME: Stenhouse.

Steinberg, A. (1997). *Real learning, real work.* Boston, MA: Jobs for the Future.

Sternberg, R. (1985). *Beyond IQ: A triarchic theory of human intelligence.* Cambridge, MA: Cambridge University Press.

Sternberg, R. (2002). *Cognitive psychology* (3rd ed.). Belmont, CA: Wadsworth.

Sternberg, R. (2009). Teaching for wisdom, intelligence, and creativity. *School Administrator, 66*(2), 2–4.

Sternberg, R., & Williams, W. (2002). *Educational psychology.* Boston, MA: Allyn & Bacon.

Sternberg, R., Jarvin, L., & Grigorenko, E.L. (2009). *Teaching for wisdom, intelligence, creativity and success.* Thousand Oaks, CA: Corwin Press.

Sternberg, R., Nokes, C., Geissler, P.W., Prince, R., Okatcha, F., Bundy, D.A., et al. (2001). The relationship between academic and practical intelligence: A case study in Kenya. *Intelligence, 29*(5), 401–418.

Sternberg, R., Torff, B., & Grigorenko, E. (1998). Teaching triarchically improves student achievement. *Journal of Educational Psychology, 90,* 374–384.

Stiggins, R. (2004). New assessment beliefs for a new school mission. *Phi Delta Kappan, 86*(1), 22–27.

Stiggins, R. (2005). *Student-involved classroom assessment* (4th ed.). Upper Saddle River, NJ: Merrill Prentice Hall.

Stiggins, R. (2006). Assessment for learning: A key to motivation. *Edge, 2*(2), 3–19. Retrieved February 22, 2008, from www.pdkintl.org.

Stiggins, R., & Chappuis, J. (2005). What a difference a word makes. *Journal of Staff Development, 27*(1), 10–14.

Stiggins, R., Arter, J.A., Chappius, J., & Chappuis, S. (2006). *Classroom assessments for student learning: Doing it right—using it well.* Portland, OR: Educational Testing Service.

Stoll, L., & Louis, K.S. (2007). *Professional learning communities: Divergence, depth, and dilemmas.* Maidenhead: Open University Press.

Stronge, J.H. (2002). *Qualities of effective teachers.* Alexandria, VA: Association for Supervision and Curriculum Development.

Stronge, J.H. (2007). *Qualities of effective teachers* (2nd ed.). Alexandria, VA: Association for Supervision and Curriculum Development.

Suchman, R. (1962). *The elementary school training program in scientific inquiry* (report to the U.S. Office of Education). Urbana, IL: University of Illinois.

Sullo, B. (2007). *Activating the desire to learn.* Alexandria, VA: Association for Supervision and Curriculum Development.

Sutton, R. (1997). *Assessment for learning.* Salford: RS Publications.

Taba, H. (1967). *Teacher's handbook for elementary school social studies.* Reading, MA: Addison-Wesley.

Taylor, M. (1976). *Roll of Thunder, Hear My Cry.* London: Penguin Books.

Tennyson, R., & Cocchiarella, M. (1986). An empirically-based instructional design theory for teaching concepts. *Review of Educational Research, 56*(1), 40–71.

Tennyson, R., & Park, O. (1980). The learning of concepts: A review of the instructional design research literature. *Review of Educational Research, 50*(1), 55–70.

Thelen, H.A. (1954). *Dynamics of groups at work.* Chicago, IL: University of Chicago Press.

Thelen, H.A. (1960). *Education and the human quest.* New York: Harper & Row.

Thomas, J.W. (2000). *A review of research on project-based learning.* San Rafael, CA: Autodesk Foundation.

Tishman, S., & Palmer, P. (2006). *Artful thinking: Stronger thinking and learning through the power of art.* Final report. Cambridge, MA: Harvard Graduate School of Education.

Tishman, S., Perkins, D., & Jay, E. (1995). *The thinking classroom: Creating a culture of thinking.* Boston, MA: Allyn & Bacon.

Thompson, F.T. (2007). *Television viewing and academic achievement revisited.* Retrieved July 22, 2007, from www.questia.com/googleScholar.qst;jsessionid.

Thompson, F.T., & Austin. W.P. (2003). Television viewing and academic achievement revisited. *Education, 124,* 194–202.

Toll, C.A. (2005). *The literacy coach's survival guide: Essential questions and practical answers.* Newark, DE: International Reading Association.

Tollefson, N. (2000). Classroom applications of cognitive theories of motivation. *Educational Psychology Review, 12*(1), 63–83.

Tomlinson, C. (1993). Independent study: A flexible tool for encouraging personal and academic growth in middle school learners. *Middle School Journal, 25*(1), 55–59.

Tomlinson, C. (1995). *How to differentiate instruction in mixed-ability classrooms.* Alexandria, VA: Association for Supervision and Curriculum Development.

Tomlinson, C. (1999). *The differentiated classroom: Responding to the needs of all learners.* Alexandria, VA: Association for Supervision and Curriculum Development.

Tomlinson, C. (2001). *How to differentiate instruction in mixed-ability classrooms* (2nd ed.). Alexandria, VA: Association for Supervision and Curriculum Development.

Tomlinson, C. (2004). *The differentiated classroom: Responding to the needs of all learners* (2nd ed.). Alexandria, VA: Association for Supervision and Curriculum Development.

Tomlinson, C., & Eidson, C.C. (2003a). *Differentiation in practice: A resource guide for differentiating curriculum, grade K-5.* Alexandria, VA: Association for Supervision and Curriculum Development.

Tomlinson, C., & Eidson, C.C. (2003b). *Differentiation in practice: A resource guide for differentiating curriculum, grades 5–9.* Alexandria, VA: Association for Supervision and Curriculum Development.

Tomlinson, C., & Strickland, C.A. (2005). *Differentiation in practice: A resource guide for differentiating curriculum, grades 9–12.* Alexandria, VA: Association for Supervision and Curriculum Development.

Tomlinson, C., & Germundson, A. (2007). Teaching as jazz. *Educational Leadership, 64*(8), 27–31.

Trotter, A. (2007). Getting up to speed. *Education Week, 26*(30), 10–16.

Turner, A., & Greenough, W. (1985). Differential rearing effects on rat visual cortex synapses. *Brain Research, 328,* 195–203.

Tyler, R. W. (1949). *Basic principles of curriculum and instruction.* Chicago, IL: University of Chicago Press.

Uden, L., & Beaumont, C. (2006). *Technology and problem-based learning.* New York: Information Science Publishing.

Vescio, V., Ross, D., & Adams, A. (2008). A review of the impact of professional development communities on teaching practices and student learning. *Teaching and Teacher Education, 24*(1), 80–91.

Viadero, D. (2008). Research yields clues on the effects of extra time for learning. *Education Week, 28*(5), 16–18.

Visible Thinking: www.pz.harvard.edu/vt/visiblethinking-htlm-files/VisibleThinking1.html

von Frank, V. (2007). *Finding time for professional learning.* Oxford, OH: National Staff Development Council.

Vygotsky, L.S. (1978). *Mind in society: The development of higher psychological processes.* Cambridge, MA: Harvard University Press.

Wagner, A., Schacter, D., Rotte, M., Koutstaal, W., Maril, A., & Dale, A.M. (1998). Building memories: Remembering and forgetting of verbal experiences as predicted brain activity. *Science, 281*(5830), 1185–1190.

Walberg, H. (1986). Synthesis of research on teaching. In M.C. Wittrock (Ed.), *Handbook of research on teaching* (3rd ed.). New York: Macmillan.

Walberg, H. (1999). Productive teaching. In H.C. Waxman & H. Walberg (Eds.), *New directions for teaching practice research.* Berkeley, CA: McCutchen.

Walsh, J., & Sattles, B. (2005). *Quality questioning: Research-based practice to engage every learner.* Thousand Oaks, CA: Corwin Press.

Watkins, C. (2005). *Classrooms as learning communities: What's in it for schools.* New York: Routledge.

Weiner, B. (1986). *On attributional theory and emotion.* New York: Springer.

Weiner, B. (1992). *Human motivation: Metaphors, theories, and research.* Newbury Park, CA: Sage Publications.

West, L., & Staub, F.C. (2003). *Content-focused coaching: Transforming mathematics lessons.* Portsmouth, NH: Heinemann.

White, B.Y., & Frederiksen, J.R. (1998). Inquiry, modeling, and metacognition: Making science accessible to all students. *Cognition and Instruction, 16*(1), 3–118.

Wigfield, A., & Eccles, J. (2002). *Development of achievement motivation.* San Diego, CA: Academic Press.

Wiggins, G. (1998). *Educative assessment: Designing assessment to inform and improve performance.* San Francisco, CA: Jossey-Bass.

Wiggins, G. (2005). *Educative assessment: Designing assessment to inform and improve performance* (2nd ed.). San Francisco, CA: Jossey-Bass.

Wiggins, G., & McTighe, J. (1998). *Understanding by design.* Alexandria, VA: Association for Supervision and Curriculum Development.

Wiggins, G., & McTighe, J. (2005). *Understanding by design* (2nd ed.). Alexandria, VA: Association for Supervision and Curriculum Development.

Wiliam, D. (2007). Content then process: Teacher learning communities in the service of formative assessment. In D.B. Reeves (Ed.), *Ahead of the curve: The power of assessment to transform teaching and learning* (pp. 183–204). Bloomington, IN: Solution Tree.

Williams, T. (2007). Reading the painting: Exploring visual literacy in primary grades. *Reading Teacher, 60*(7), 636–642.

Williams, W., & Ceci, S. (1997). How'm I doing? Problems with the use of student ratings of instructors and courses. *Change, 29*(5), 12–23.

Willis, J. (2006). *Research-based strategies that ignite student learning.* Alexandria, VA: Association for Supervision and Curriculum Development.

Willis, J. (2007). Which brain research can educators trust? *Phi Delta Kappan, 88*(9), 697–699.

Wolk, S. (2007). Why go to school? *Phi Delta Kappan, 88*(9), 648–654.

Woolfolk, A. (2005). *Educational psychology* (9th ed.). Boston, MA: Allyn & Bacon.

Woolfolk, A. (2007). *Educational psychology* (10th ed.). Boston, MA: Allyn & Bacon.

Wormeli, R. (2005). *Summarization in any subject: 50 strategies and techniques to improve student learning.* Alexandria, VA: Association for Supervision and Curriculum Development.

Wormeli, R. (2007). *Differentiation: From planning to practice, grades 6–12*. Portland, ME: Stenhouse Publishing.

York-Barr, J., & Duke, K. (2004). What do we know about teacher leadership? Findings from two decades of scholarship. *Review of Educational Research, 74*(3), 255–297.

Zeichner, K., & Noffke, S. (2001) Practitioner research. In V. Richardson (Ed.), *Handbook of research on teaching* (4th ed.). Washington, DC: American Educational Research Association.

Zull, J. (2002). *The art of changing the brain: Enriching teaching by exploring the biology of learning*. Sterling, VA: Stylus.

Zumwalt, K. (1989). The need for a curricular vision. In M.C. Reynolds (Ed.), *Knowledge base for the beginning teacher*. New York: Pergamon Press.

Author Index

Subject Index